Life-Span
Development

third edition
Life-Span
Development

John W. Santrock

University of Texas at Dallas

wcb

Wm. C. Brown Publishers
Dubuque, Iowa

Book Team

Editor *Michael Lange*
Developmental Editor *Sandra E. Schmidt*
Designer *Carol S. Joslin*
Production Editor *Diane S. Clemens*
Photo Editor *Marge Manders*
Permissions Editor *Mavis M. Oeth*
Visuals Processor *Joseph P. O'Connell*

wcb group

Chairman of the Board *Wm. C. Brown*
President and Chief Executive Officer *Mark C. Falb*

wcb

Wm. C. Brown Publishers, College Division

President *G. Franklin Lewis*
Vice President, Editor-in-Chief *George Wm. Bergquist*
Vice President, Director of Production *Beverly Kolz*
Vice President, National Sales Manager *Bob McLaughlin*
Director of Marketing *Thomas E. Doran*
Marketing Communications Manager *Edward Bartell*
Marketing Information Systems Manager *Craig S. Marty*
Marketing Manager *Kathy Law Laube*
Manager of Visuals and Design *Faye M. Schilling*
Production Editorial Manager *Colleen A. Yonda*
Production Editorial Manager *Julie A. Kennedy*
Publishing Services Manager *Karen J. Slaght*

To my parents, Ruth and John Santrock

B R I E F
C O N T E N T S

◼

Contents

C O N T E N T S

Preface xix

SECTION I

THE LIFE-SPAN DEVELOPMENTAL PERSPECTIVE 3

SECTION II

BEGINNINGS 69

SECTION III

INFANCY 125

■

SECTION IV

EARLY CHILDHOOD 215

SECTION V

MIDDLE AND LATE CHILDHOOD 283

SECTION VI

ADOLESCENCE 349

SECTION VII

EARLY ADULTHOOD 403

SECTION VIII

MIDDLE ADULTHOOD 459

■

SECTION IX

LATE ADULTHOOD 507

Contents　　xvii

SECTION X

DEATH AND DYING 557

■

PREFACE

■

*L*ife-Span Development, third edition, is about life's rhythm and meaning, and about weaving together a portrait of who we were, are, and will be. This text is about you and it is about me. It is about the life of every human being. It tells the story of human development from conception to death—from the point in time when life as we know it begins until the point in time when it ends. The complex and exciting story of how we develop, of how we become who we are, is written and presented in a manner that I believe you will find both informative *and* enjoyable.

You will see yourself as an infant, as a child, and as an adolescent, and will be asked to reflect on how those years have influenced who you are today. And what about your adult years? Isn't what has happened, or will happen, to you as an adult also important? You will see yourself as a young adult, as a middle-aged adult, and as an adult in old age, and will be asked to imagine how your experiences today will influence your development throughout the remainder of your adult years. You may think about how marriage, the birth of a child, divorce, the time when children leave, the change of a career, and the death of a spouse involve changes in our lives that require adaptation.

Balance, Integration, and Rhythm

Understanding the meaning of life's cycle involves balance and integration. Different strands of human development—biological,

cognitive, and social processes—are interwoven to make up an integrated human being. The third edition of *Life-Span Development* is similarly composed of interwoven elements, and provides a balanced approach to the study of human development. It involves science and research, writing, motivation, learning, and teaching. Each of these elements contributes a piece to more insightful understanding of life-span development. But as is true in understanding the human life cycle, so is the whole of *Life-Span Development* equal to more than the sum of its parts. Woven together, these elements combine to tell the odyssey of life's human cycle.

Science and Research

Beginning with the first edition and continuing with this, the third edition, *Life-Span Development* is above all else an extremely up-to-date presentation of research in the three primary domains of human development: biological processes, cognitive processes, and social processes. Research on biological, cognitive, and social processes continue to represent the core of *Life-Span Development*. This core includes both classic and leading edge research. *Life-Span Development* includes more than 350 references from 1986 to 1989 with more than 180 of these coming from 1988, 1989, and in-press sources. Life-span development's research is expanding on many frontiers, and, in each chapter, I have attempted to capture the excitement of these new discoveries as well as the classic studies that are the foundation of the discipline.

The third edition of *Life-Span Development* continues to provide balanced coverage of all periods in the human life cycle. This edition contains 20 chapters and 10 sections compared to 19 chapters and 9 sections in the second edition. The additional section is *Beginnings* and the additional chapter involves expanded coverage of prenatal development and the birth process.

Writing

In addition to the well-received strategy of providing extensive research updating and coverage of leading edge research, I asked myself what else I could do to improve the third edition of the book. Easily the most dramatic change in the third edition of *Life-Span Development* is the *improved writing style*. Those familiar with earlier editions of the book will notice this change after only a few minutes. To accomplish the goal of improving the writing style, I went over the book thoroughly, adding, subtracting, integrating, and simplifying. I examined alternative ways of presenting ideas and asked college students to give me feedback on which strategies were the most effective. Virtually every sentence, every paragraph, every section of the book were rewritten with these goals uppermost in my mind.

Most authors with successful editions of a book only make cosmetic changes in the third edition. Why spend so much time rewriting, adding, subtracting, integrating, and simplifying in the third edition? While the second edition was perceived as a solid scientific overview of life-span development, the book needed extensive fine-tuning. For example, when a concept is introduced, it is followed by a comprehensible definition and either research examples, personal examples, or both. Noticeable in the third edition is an increased use of examples taken from the lives of children and adults as they go through life's human cycle.

Motivation

In writing *Life-Span Development*, I have tried to convey the excitement of research and knowledge about each of the life cycle's periods. I have tried to communicate the discoveries of life-span development with enthusiasm, with energy, and with a constant awareness of their relevance to the reader. When a concept is introduced, lively examples and applications of the concept are provided. At the beginning of each chapter, an imaginative, high-interest piece focuses on a topic related to the chapter's content. For example, chapter 3, Biological Beginnings, begins with an interesting discussion of identical twins who were separated at four weeks of age and did not see each other again until they were 39 years old. Chapter 15, Social and Personality Development in Early Adulthood, begins with a description of Phil, a lovesick man, and Sherry, who is searching for Mr. Anybody. FOCUS ON LIFE-SPAN DEVELOPMENT boxes appear

several times in each chapter—a brief glimpse through any chapter reveals their special appeal. For example, chapter 4, Prenatal Development and Birth, includes a box on "kilogram kids," babies who weigh less than 2.3 pounds; chapter 8, Physical and Cognitive Development in Early Childhood, includes a box on pelicans kissing seals, cars floating on clouds, and humans being tadpoles, reflecting the symbolic, imaginative world of young children's thoughts and drawings; chapter 16, Physical and Cognitive Development in Middle Adulthood, includes a box on sexual behavior in the next generation of middle-aged women; and chapter 19, Social and Personality Development in Late Adulthood, includes a box on older adults' dating patterns.

Learning

Life-Span Development incorporates an effective and challenging learning system. Two special features of the learning system are CONCEPT TABLES and CRITICAL THINKING SKILLS. CONCEPT TABLES were introduced in the second edition of the book and were extremely well received by both students and instructors. The concept tables in the third edition have been refined by making them briefer and more focused. They are designed to activate the student's memory of and comprehension of major topics or key concepts that have been discussed to that point.

This allows the student to get a "handle" on complex concepts and ideas and to understand how key concepts are interrelated. Concept tables provide a visual picture, or cognitive framework, of the most important information in each section.

The second special feature of the learning system is the emphasis on CRITICAL THINKING SKILLS, which has been built into the book in a systematic fashion for the first time in the third edition. To encourage the student's critical thinking, this textbook asks the student many questions, questions that require the student to not only think about the material in the text in challenging ways, but also questions that go beyond the text and require the student to apply critical thinking skills to personal situations and applications in the real world. One way this was accomplished was to include three to five critical thinking questions in the margins of each chapter. Also, it is important for students to see things about the human life cycle from different points of view. Throughout this book, students are encouraged to think about both sides of issues and the multiple determination of development, challenging them to think critically.

In addition, CHAPTER OUTLINES at the beginning of each chapter show the overall organization of the material. At the end of the chapter, a detailed SUMMARY in outline form provides a helpful review. KEY

TERMS are boldfaced in the text, listed with page references at the end of each chapter, and defined in a page-referenced GLOSSARY at the end of the book. An annotated list of SUGGESTED READINGS also appears at the end of each chapter.

Teaching

Another important goal I have kept in mind while putting together the third edition of *Life-Span Development* is to construct a *teachable* text. The publisher and the ancillary team have worked together to produce an outstanding integrated teaching package to accompany *Life-Span Development*. The authors of the teaching supplements are all experienced teachers of the life-span development course. The supplements have been designed to make it as easy as possible to customize the entire package to meet the unique needs of individual professors and their students.

A very helpful Instructor's Manual has been prepared by Michael G. Walraven of Jackson Community College. The Instructor's Manual includes an essay on using the task group method in the classroom and a helpful essay on study skills. Each chapter includes a chapter overview, a page-referenced list of learning objectives, a list of key terms, lecture suggestions, classroom activities, and questions for review and discussion. Film suggestions are also provided for each chapter.

In addition, a comprehensive TEST ITEM FILE has been prepared by William J. Dibiase of Delaware County Community College. The Test Item File consists of two separate test banks of objective test questions. Each test item is referenced to both text page and learning objective, and is identified as factual, conceptual, or applied.

A TRANSPARENCY PACKAGE, with many illustrations in full color, includes graphics and tables from both the text and outside sources and can be used as lecture outlines. These acetate transparencies have been designed to help in classroom teaching and lecture organization.

A STUDENT STUDY GUIDE by Michael G. Walraven, Jackson Community College, includes the following for each chapter: a chapter preview, page-referenced learning objectives, page-referenced key terms exercise, guided review, student test questions, and an individual learning activity or student project.

wcb TestPak is a computerized system that enables you to make up customized exams quickly and easily. Test questions can be found in the Test Item File, which is printed in your instructor's manual or as a separate packet. For each exam you may select up to 250 questions from the file and either print the test yourself or have **wcb** print it.

Printing the exam yourself requires access to a personal computer—an IBM that uses 5.25- or 3.5-inch diskettes, an Apple IIe or IIc, or a Macintosh. TestPak requires two disk drives and will work with any printer. Diskettes are available through your local **wcb** sales representative or by phoning Educational Services at 319–588–1451. The package you receive will contain complete instructions for making up an exam.

If you don't have access to a suitable computer, you may use **wcb**'s call-in/mail-in service. First determine the chapter and question numbers and any specific heading you want on the exam. Then call Pat Powers at 800–351–7671 (in Iowa, 319–589–2953) or mail information to: Pat Powers, Wm. C. Brown Publishers, 2460 Kerper Blvd., Dubuque, IA 52001. Within two working days, **wcb** will send you via first-class mail a test master, student answer sheet, and an answer key.

wcb QuizPak, the interactive self-testing, self-scoring quiz program, will help your students review text material from any chapter by testing themselves on an Apple IIe, IIc, or Macintosh, or an IBM PC. Adopters will receive the QuizPak program, question disks, and an easy-to-follow user's guide. QuizPak may be used at a number of work stations simultaneously and requires only one disk drive.

Acknowledgments

A project of this magnitude requires the efforts of many people. I owe special thanks to my editor, James McNeil, and Senior Developmental Editor, Sandra Schmidt. They continue to have a marvelous sense of what is needed to make the very best college textbook in life-span development. Jim has provided key linkages between the editorial, production, and marketing phases of the book and Sandra has worked long hours shaping my words, sentences, paragraphs, and chapters. Diane Clemens, production editor, spent long hours copyediting and overseeing the production of the book. Carol Joslin, designer, provided creative touches that make the book extremely attractive. Marge Manders deserves special credit for tracking down elusive photographs. Mavis Oeth efficiently obtained permissions. Special thanks go to Michael G. Walraven, Jackson Community College, who prepared the helpful Instructor's Manual and Student Study Guide, and to William J. Dibiase, Delaware County Community College, who prepared the comprehensive Test Item File. I also continue to benefit from the contributions to the sections in second edition of *Life-Span Development* by James C. Bartlett, University of Texas at Dallas.

I have benefited extensively from the ideas and insights of many colleagues. I would like to thank the following individuals for their feedback on earlier editions of *Life-Span Development:* Linda E. Flickinger, St. Clair Community College; Joan B. Cannon, University of Lowell; Jon Snodgrass, California State University, Los Angeles; Peter

C. Gram, Pensacola Junior College; Helen E. Benedict, Baylor University; Ann M. Williams, Luzerne County Community College; James A. Blackburn, Montana State University; Donald Bowers, Community College of Philadelphia; Shirley Feldman, Stanford University; David Goldstein, Temple University; Martin D. Murphy, The University of Akron; and Lyn W. Wickelgren, Metropolitan State College.

I also express considerable gratitude to the following instructors who provided in-depth reviews of chapters from the current edition of *Life-Span Development:*

Joanne M. Alegre
Yavajai College

Belinda Blevin-Knabe
University of Arkansas–Little Rock

Joan B. Cannon
University of Lowell

Stephen Hoyer
Pittsburgh State University

Karen Kirkendall
Sangaman State University

Teri M. Miller-Schwartz
Milwaukee Area Technical College

Susan Nakayama Siaw
California State Polytechnical University

Vicki Simmons
University of Victoria

Donald Stanley
North Dallas County College

B. D. Whetstone
Birmingham Southern College

Sarah White
Reynolds Community College

A final note of thanks goes to my families—to my parents, Ruth and John Santrock, whose lives have reached late adulthood and who should feel a special pride in their contributions to the generations of younger people they have touched, and to my wife, Mary Jo, and my daughters, Tracy, 22, and Jennifer, 19, whose love and companionship I cherish.

About the Author

John W. Santrock received his Ph.D. from the University of Minnesota in 1973. He taught at the University of Georgia and currently is Professor of Psychology and Human Development at the University of Texas at Dallas. Professor Santrock is a member of the editorial board of *Developmental Psychology.* His research on father custody is widely cited and is used in expert witness testimony to promote flexibility and alternative considerations in custody disputes. The research involves videotaped observations in different contexts, extensive interviews, and standardized tests. He recently completed an NIMH grant to study family and peer relations in stepmother and stepfather families. He has authored or co-authored six other highly successful texts, including *Psychology,* 2nd ed., *Child Development,* 4th ed., and *Adolescence,* 3rd ed. Professor Santrock also is a professional tennis coach.

Life-Span Development

SECTION

I

◼

The Life-Span Developmental Perspective

All the world's a stage,
And all the men and women merely players;
They have their exits and their entrances,
And one man in his time plays many parts,
His acts being seven ages. At first the infant, . . .
Then the whining school-boy, . . .
creeping like a snail
Unwillingly to school. And then the lover,
Sighing like a furnace, . . .
Then a soldier,
Full of strange oaths and bearded like the pard,
Jealous in honor, sudden and quick in quarrel,
Seeking the bubble reputation
Even in the cannon's mouth. And then the justice, . . .
With eyes severe and beard of formal cut,
Full of wise saws and modern instances; . . .
The sixth age shifts
Into the lean and slippered pantaloon,
With spectacles on nose and pouch on side;
His youthful hose, well saved, a world too wide
For his shrunk shank, and his big manly voice,
Turning again toward childish treble, pipes
And whistles in his sound. Last scene of all,
That ends this strange eventful history,
Is second childishness and mere oblivion,
Sans teeth, sans eyes, sans taste, sans
everything. ◼

William Shakespeare

1

History, Issues, and Methods

Life-Span Development—Today and Yesterday
  Some Contemporary Concerns
  The Historical Perspective
Focus on Life-Span Development
1.1: *Adolescence,* **1904**
The Nature of Development
  Biological, Cognitive, and Social
  Processes
  Periods of Development

Focus on Life-Span Development
1.2: Are Many Age-related Themes
of Development Stereotypes?
  Maturation and Experience
  Continuity and Discontinuity
Concept Table 1.1: History and
Issues in Life-Span Development
The Science Base of Life-Span
Development
  Theory and the Scientific Method
  Collecting Information about Life-
  Span Development

Case Studies
  Strategies for Setting up Research
  Studies
  The Time Span of Inquiry
  Ethics in Research on Life-Span
  Development
Concept Table 1.2: The Science Base
of Life-Span Development
Summary
Key Terms
Suggested Readings

Why study life-span development? Perhaps you are or will be a parent or teacher. Responsibility for children is or will be a part of your everyday life. The more you learn about them, the better you can deal with them. Perhaps you hope to gain some insight into your own history—as an infant, a child, an adolescent, or a young adult. Perhaps you want to know more about what your life will be like as you grow through the adult years—as a middle-aged adult, as an adult in old age, for example. Or, perhaps you just stumbled onto this course thinking that it sounded intriguing and that the topic of the human life cycle would raise some provocative and intriguing issues about our lives as we grow and develop. Whatever your reasons, you will discover that the study of life-span development *is* provocative, *is* intriguing, and *is* filled with information about who we are, how we have come to be this way, and where our future will take us.

This book tells the story of human development from conception to death—from the point in time when life begins until the point in time when it ends, at least life as we know it. You will see yourself as an infant, as a child, and as an adolescent, and be stimulated to think about how those years influenced the kind of individual you are today. And you will see yourself as a young adult, a middle-aged adult, and as an adult in old age, and be stimulated to think about how your experiences today will influence your development through the remainder of your adult years.

In this chapter, you will be introduced to some contemporary concerns in life-span development and to an historical perspective on child, adolescent, and life-span development. You will learn what development is, what issues are raised by a life-span perspective on development, and what methods are used to study life-span development.

Life-Span Development—Today and Yesterday

Everywhere an individual turns in contemporary society, the development and well-being of children and adults capture public attention, the interest of scientists, and the concern of policy makers. Through history, though, interest in the development of children and adults has varied.

Some Contemporary Concerns

Consider some of the topics you read about in newspapers and magazines everyday—genetic research, child abuse, homosexuality, mental retardation, parenting, intelligence, career changes, divorce, retirement, and aging. What the experts are discovering in each of these areas has direct and significant consequences for understanding children and adults and our decisions as a society about how they are to be treated. Let's think about four of these areas in more detail—genetics, child abuse, divorce, and the aging population.

Genetics researchers are discovering new techniques to diagnose potential problems both prior to and after conception. They are learning to predict genetic disturbances in development, various forms of deformities and retardation, and the child's sex. Some remarkable breakthroughs also have occurred in the ability to fertilize a human egg outside of its natural mother. All of these techniques and capabilities have profound consequences on genetic counseling for parents, arguments about when life really begins, debates about the legal right of women to have abortions, and ethical dilemmas about tampering in the laboratory with the genetic makeup of unborn children.

Another contemporary social issue whose widespread occurrence has just become understood in the last decade is child abuse. Although there are no sure data on how many cases of abuse occur each year, we do know something about the profile of the individuals who abuse children, the emotional consequences of the children being abused, and short-term remedies for the abused and abusers. Medical professionals and social service practitioners have formed child abuse teams throughout the country to spot cases of abuse in their early stages and to offer help to the victims. Some progress is being made, but the hurdles are difficult to overcome. Chief among these is the complex historical and legal tradition in our country that places families in the driver's seat in any conflict over a child's welfare.

Divorce is another social issue in our culture for both new and old marriages. Those who divorce often remarry, resulting in a mixture of family structures. What effects do such family structures have on children's development? How do the family members cope with the stress involved? What effect does divorce have on an adult's self-esteem and relationships with the opposite sex? As you will see in later chapters, answers to such questions are beginning to be formulated.

Yet another major change in our culture is the increasing age of our population. Individuals are living longer, and, in addition, are breaking the close link to their families. Because of this, the elderly no longer maintain as strong a socializing role in the child's development as they once did. Who is to care for the elderly in our culture who do not live with or close to their own children and grandchildren? What kinds of social services are needed for the elderly, and how can they be implemented? Should we reconsider the retirement age for workers because of their increased longevity? Are there alternative work patterns in late adulthood that need to be explored? We address these and many other questions in our study of life-span development.

Genetic research, child abuse, homosexuality, mental retardation, parenting, intelligence, career changes, divorce, retirement, and aging are some contemporary concerns related to life-span development. What other contemporary concerns related to life-span development can you generate?

The Historical Perspective

The history of interest in children is long and rich. Interest in adolescents is more recent, and in adults has only seriously begun to develop in the latter half of the 20th century (Havighurst, 1973).

We reach backward to our parents and forward to our children, and through their children to a future we will never see, but about which we need to care.

Carl Jung

Child Development

Childhood has become such a distinct period it is hard to imagine that it was not always thought of in that way. But the analysis of Philip Aries (1962) suggested that childhood was not a distinctive period during much of history. Aries presented samples of art along with some available publications to conclude that development was divided into infancy—which lasted for many years—and adulthood—which extended somewhere from what we call middle childhood to post adolescence (figure 1.1 shows the artistic representation of children during the Middle Ages).

Figure 1.1
These artistic impressions show how children were viewed as miniature adults earlier in history. Artists' renditions of children as miniature adults may have been too stereotypical.
Maria Teresa de Borbon *by Francisco Goya.*
Don Manuel Osorio de Zuniga *by Francisco Goya. Courtesy Scala/Art Resource Inc., NY.*

A reawakening of interest in the study of children through history, though, casts doubt on Aries' conclusions, which seem to be overdrawn, reflecting artistic style, aristocratic subjects and artists, and an idealization of society at the time. In ancient Egypt, Greece, and Rome, rich conceptions of children's development were presented, for example (Borstelmann, 1983).

During the Renaissance, from the fourteenth to seventeenth centuries, philosophers speculated at length about the nature of children and how they should be reared. During the Middle Ages, the goal of child rearing was salvation—the purpose of parenting was to remove sin from the child's life. This perspective, called **original sin,** argued that children are born bad; only through the constraints of parenting or salvation would children become competent adults.

Two contrasting views about the nature of the child emerged during the Renaissance—the *tabula rasa* and **innate goodness** views. Near the end of the seventeenth century, John Locke argued that children are not innately bad, but instead they are like a "blank tablet," a *tabula rasa* as he called it. Locke believed that childhood experiences are important in determining adult characteristics; he advised parents to spend time with their children and to help them become contributing members of society. During the eighteenth century, Jean-Jacques Rousseau agreed with Locke that children are not basically bad, but he did not think they were a blank tablet either. Rousseau said children are inherently good and because of their innate goodness, they should be permitted to grow naturally with little parental monitoring or constraint.

The Life-Span Developmental Perspective

In the past century and a half, our view of children has changed dramatically. We now conceive of childhood as a highly eventful and unique period of life that lays an important foundation for the adult years and is highly differentiated from them. In most approaches to childhood, distinct periods are identified in which special skills are mastered and new life tasks are confronted. Childhood is no longer seen as a covenient "waiting" period during which adults must suffer the incompetencies of the young. We now value childhood as a special time of growth and change, and we invest great resources in caring for and educating our children. We protect them from the excesses of the adult work world through tough child labor laws; we treat their crimes against society under a special system of juvenile justice; and we have governmental provisions for helping children when ordinary family support systems fail or when families seriously interfere with the child's well-being.

Sociopolitical events and issues have spurred interest in children (Alexander, 1987; White, 1985; Zigler, 1987). Research on children flourishes when there is substantial national activity on behalf of children and families. The war on poverty in the 1960s led to the formation of Project Head Start, designed to give children from low-income families an opportunity to learn. In the 1980s, the changing nature of society has motivated research interest in the effects of divorce on children, working mothers and day care, and gender.

Adolescence

As in the concept of child development, the concept of adolescence was speculative before the nineteenth and twentieth centuries. In 1904, G. Stanley Hall, known as the father of the scientific study of adolescence, published his ideas in a two-volume set, *Adolescence*. According to Hall, adolescence is a time of storm and stress, full of contradictions and wide swings in mood. Thoughts, feelings, and actions oscillate between conceit and humility, good and temptation, happiness and sadness. The adolescent may be nasty to a peer one moment and kind the next moment. At one time the adolescent may want to be alone but seconds later want close companionship. Because he viewed adolescence as a turbulent time charged with conflict, Hall's perspective became known as the **storm and stress view.** To learn more about Hall's views on adolescence turn to Focus on Life-Span Development 1.1.

Today, we do not view adolescence as the jaundiced time Hall envisioned. The vast majority of adolescents make the transition from childhood to adulthood competently. As with any period of development, adolescence has its hills and valleys, issues to be negotiated, mistakes and adjustments, highs and lows, and ebbs and flows in life. Today we view adolescence in a much more balanced, positive way than earlier in this century.

Current interest in the history of adolescence raises the possibility that adolescence is an historical invention. As A. K. Cohen (1964) commented:

> Not quite children and certainly not adults, in many ways privileged, wielding unprecedented economic power as consumers of clothing, entertainment, and other amenities, the object of a peculiar blend of tenderness, indulgence, distrust, hostility, moving through a seemingly endless course of "preparation for life" . . . playing furiously at "adult" games but resolutely confined to a society of their own peers and excluded from serious and responsible participation in the world of their elders . . . a few years ago it occurred to me that when I was a teenager, in the early depression years, there were no teenagers! The teenager has sneaked up on us in our own lifetime, and yet it seems to us that he always has been with us. . . . The teenager had not yet been invented (though, and) there did not yet exist a special class of beings, bounded in a certain way . . . not quite children and certainly not adults (p. ix).

In youth, we clothe ourselves with rainbows, and go as brave as the zodiac.
Ralph Waldo Emerson,
The Conduct of Life, *1860*

G. Stanley Hall's two-volume set, published in 1904, included the following chapters:

Volume I
Chapter
1 Growth in Height and Weight
2 Growth of Parts and Organs During Adolescence
3 Growth of Motor Power and Function
4 Diseases of Body and Mind
5 Juvenile Faults, Immoralities, and Crimes
6 Sexual Development: Its Dangers and Hygiene in Boys
7 Periodicity
8 Adolescence in Literature, Biography, and History
Volume II
Chapter
9 Changes in the Sense and Voice
10 Evolution and the Feelings and Instincts Characteristic of Normal Adolescence
11 Adolescent Love
12 Adolescent Feelings Toward Nature and A New Education in Science
13 Savage Public Initiations, Classical Ideals and Customs, and Church Confirmations
14 The Adolescent Psychology of Conversion
15 Social Instincts and Institutions
16 Intellectual Development and Education
17 Adolescent Girls and Their Education
18 Ethnic Psychology and Pedagogy, or Adolescent Races and Their Treatment

G. Stanley Hall

Hall's strong emphasis on the biological basis of adolescence is present in the large number of chapters on physical growth, instincts, evolution, and periodicity. His concern for education also is evident, as is his interest in religion. Hall's preoccupation with the evils of adolescence are threaded throughout the volumes. Nowhere is this more clear than in his comments about masturbation:

One of the very saddest of all the aspects of human weakness and sin is masturbation. Tissot, in 1759, found every pupil guilty. Dr. G. Bachin (1895) argued that growth, especially in the moral and intellectual regions, is dwarfed and stunted by masturbation. Bachin also felt that masturbation caused gray hairs, and especially baldness, a stooping and enfeebled gait.

Perhaps masturbation is the most perfect type of individual vice and sin. It is the acme of selfishness.

Prominent among predisposing causes are often placed erotic reading, pictures, and theatrical presentations. Schiller protests against trousers pockets for boys, as do others against feather beds, while even horseback riding and the bicycle have been placed under the ban by a few extremest writers. The medical cures of masturbation that have been prescribed are almost without number: bromide, ergot, lupin, blistering, clitoridectomy, section of certain nerves, small mechanical appliances, of which the Patent Office at Washington has quite a collection. Regimen rather than special treatment must, however, be chiefly relied on. Work reduces temptation, and so does early rising. Good music is a moral tonic (Vol. I, pp. 411–471).

Our current beliefs about masturbation clearly differ from those of Hall's time.

As can be seen from his comments about masturbation, Hall's volumes are entertaining as well as informative. You might want to look up his original work in your library and compare his comments about other aspects of development with our current views.

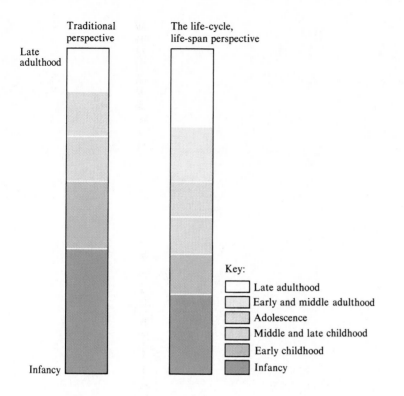

At a point not long ago, then, the "teenager" may not yet have been invented. While adolescence has a biological base, sociohistorical conditions also contributed to the emergence of the concept of adolescence. American society may have "inflicted" the status of adolescence on its youth through child-saving legislation (Elder, Caspi, & Burton, 1988; Lapsley, Enright, & Serlin, 1985). By developing laws for youth only, the adult power structure placed young people in a submissive position, one that restricted their options, encouraged dependency, and made their move into the world of adult work more manageable. From 1890–1920, virtually every state developed laws that excluded youth from work and required them to attend school. In this time frame, a 600% increase in the number of high school graduates occurred! (Tyack, 1976).

By 1950, the developmental period we refer to as adolescence had come of age. Not only did it possess physical and social identity, but received legal attention, too. By this time, every state had developed special laws for youth between the ages of sixteen and eighteen or twenty.

Life-Span Development
The *traditional approach* to development emphasizes extreme change from birth to adolescence, stability in adulthood, and decline in old age. By contrast, the **life-cycle perspective** emphasizes that changes occur during adulthood, while still recognizing the importance of infancy and childhood as building blocks for the adult years (Baltes, 1973, 1987; Baltes, Reese, & Lipsitt, 1980; Datan, Rodeheaver, & Hughes, 1987; Hetherington & Baltes, 1988). Figure 1.2 reveals how the traditional view of development contrasts with the life-span perspective. Note the powerful role alotted to infancy and early childhood and the absence of change in early and middle adulthood in the traditional view.

The first interest in the adult part of the life cycle was toward the end of the cycle—in aging (Riegel, 1977). Improvements in sanitation, nutrition, and medical knowledge led to dramatic increases in life expectancy. Until the

In what ways are today's adolescents the same as or different from the adolescents of ten years ago? twenty years ago?

Figure 1.3
*The aging of America: Millions of
Americans over age 65 from 1900 to the
present and projected to the year 2040.*
Source: U.S. Census Data: Social Security
Administration, The Statistical History of the
United States, 1976.

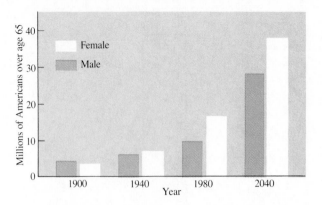

Figure 1.4
*Millions of Americans over age 85 in
1980 and projected in the year 2040.*
Source: Social Security Administration, The
Statistical History of the United States, 1976.

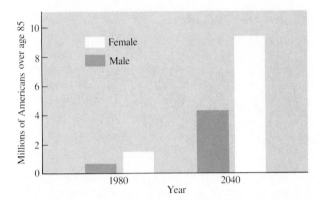

twentieth century, most individuals died before they reached the age of sixty-five. In 1900, only one American in twenty-five was over sixty-five; today, nine in twenty-five live to be this old. By the middle of the next century, one American in four will be sixty-five years of age or older. Figure 1.3 shows in millions the number of Americans over sixty-five in 1900, 1940, 1980, and the projected numbers for the year 2040. Not only will we experience a substantial increase in the number of people over the age of sixty-five, but the same trend will occur for individuals over the age of eighty-five (see figure 1.4).

An interest in old age has developed, and so has an interest in psychological changes between adolescence and old age. For too long we believed that development was something that only happened to children. To be sure, growth and development are dramatic in the first two decades of life, but a great deal of change goes on in the next five or six decades of life, too. In the words of Robert Sears and Shirley Feldman (1973):

> But the next five or six decades are every bit as important, not only to those adults who are passing through them but to their children, who must live with and understand parents and grandparents. The changes in body, personality, and abilities through these later decades is great. There are severe developmental tasks imposed by marriage and parenthood, by the waxing and waning of physical prowess and of some intellectual capacities, by the children's flight from the nest, by the achievement of an occupational plateau, and by the facing of retirement and the prospect of final extinction. Parents

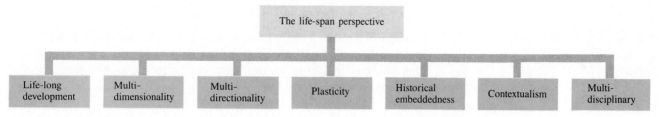

Figure 1.5
*The life-span perspective's
characteristics.*

have always been fascinated by their children's development, but it is high time adults began to look objectively at themselves, to examine the systematic changes in their own physical, mental, and emotional qualities, as they pass through the life cycle, and to get acquainted with the limitations and assets they share with so many others of their age (pp. v–vi).

Paul Baltes (1973, 1987) has summarized a number of characteristics of the life-span perspective:

Development is life-long; no age period dominates development.

Development is multidimensional. Development consists of biological, cognitive, and social dimensions. Even within a dimension, such as intelligence, there are many components, such as social intelligence, abstract intelligence, nonverbal intelligence, and so on.

Development is multidirectional. Some dimensions or components of a dimension may be increasing in growth, while others are decreasing. For example, an older adult may become wiser in being able to call on experience as a guide to intellectual decision making, but perform more poorly on tasks that require speed in processing information.

Development is plastic. Depending on the individual's life conditions, development may take many paths. A key developmental agenda is the search for plasticity and its constraints.

Development is embedded in history; it is influenced by historical conditions. The experiences of 40-year-olds in the Depression were very different than the experiences of 40-year-olds who lived in the optimistic aftermath of World War II.

Development is contextual. The individual is continually responding to and acting on contexts. Contexts include one's physical environment; one's biological context; and one's social, historical, and cultural context. In sum, the contextual view argues that individuals are changing beings in a changing world.

Development is studied by a number of disciplines. Psychological development needs to be considered in the interdisciplinary context provided by other disciplines—anthropology, sociology, and biology, for example—that also are concerned about human development.

A summary of the life-span perspective's characteristics is presented in figure 1.5.

When we truly comprehend and enter the rhythm of life, we shall be able to bring together the daring of youth with the discipline of age in a way that does justice to both.

J. S. Bixler, Two Blessings of Joseph

Each of you, individually, walkest with the tread of a fox, but collectively ye are geese.

Solon, Ancient Greece

The chess-board is the world. The pieces are the phenomena of the universe. The rules of the game are what we call laws of nature.

Thomas Henry Huxley, 1868

I think, therefore I am.

Rene Descartes

Man is by nature a social animal.

Aristotle

Figure 1.6
Biological, cognitive, and social processes in life-span development. Changes in life-span development are the result of biological, cognitive, and social processes. These processes are interwoven in the development of the individual through the human life cycle.

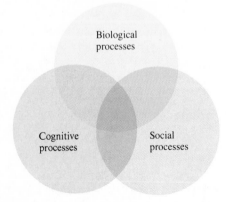

Each of us develops in certain ways like all other individuals, like some other individuals, and like no other individuals. Most of the time, our attention is directed to an individual's uniqueness. But psychologists who study life-span development are drawn to our shared as well as our unique characteristics. As humans, each of us has traveled some common paths. Each of us—Leonardo Da Vinci, Joan of Arc, George Washington, Martin Luther King, Jr., you, and me—walked at about the age of one, talked at about the age of two, engaged in fantasy play as a young child, and became more independent as a youth.

Just what do pyschologists mean when they speak of an individual's development? They use the term **development** to mean a pattern of movement or change that begins at conception and continues through the life cycle. Most development involves growth, although it can also consist of decay (as in the death process). The pattern of movement in development is complex because it is the product of several processes—biological, cognitive, and social.

Biological, Cognitive, and Social Processes

Biological processes involve changes in the individual's physical nature. Genes inherited from parents, the development of the brain, motor skills, the hormonal changes of puberty, menopause, the loss of brain cells in old age—all reflect the role of biological processes in development.

Cognitive processes involve changes in the individual's thought, perception, and language. Watching a colorful mobile swinging above the crib, putting together a two-word sentence, memorizing a poem, solving a math problem, imagining what it is like to be a movie star—all reflect the role of cognitive processes in development.

Social processes involve changes in an individual's relationships with other people, emotions, and personality. An infant's smile in response to her mother's touch, a young boy's aggressive attack on a playmate, an adolescent's joy at the senior prom, conflict between marital partners, and the life satisfaction of an elderly person—all reflect the role of social processes in development.

Remember as you read about biological, cognitive, and social processes that they are intricately interwoven. You will read about how social processes shape cognitive processes, how cognitive processes promote or restrict social processes, and how biological processes influence cognitive processes, for example. While it is helpful to study the different processes of life-span development in separate sections and chapters, keep in mind that you are studying the development of an integrated human being with only one mind and one body (see figure 1.6).

Periods of Development

For the purposes of organization and understanding, the life cycle is commonly divided into the following periods of development: the prenatal period, infancy, early childhood, middle and late childhood, adolescence, early adulthood, middle adulthood, and late adulthood. Approximate age bands are placed on the periods to provide a general idea of when a period first appears and when it ends.

The **prenatal period** is the time from conception to birth. It is a time of tremendous growth—from a single cell, an organism complete with a brain and behavioral capabilities is produced in approximately a nine-month period. You will read about the detailed biological timetable of the prenatal period in chapter 3 along with information about environmental hazards that can significantly alter the entire course of the life cycle.

Infancy extends from birth to eighteen- or twenty-four months. Infancy is a time of extreme dependence upon adults. Many psychological activities are just beginning—language, symbolic thought, sensorimotor coordination, and social learning, for example. You will read about physical, cognitive, and social development in infancy in chapters 4, 5, and 6 respectively.

Early childhood, which extends from the end of infancy to about five or six years, roughly corresponds to the period in which the child prepares for formal schooling. The early childhood years sometimes are referred to as the preschool years. During this time, the young child learns to become more self-sufficient and to care for herself, develops school readiness skills (following instructions, identifying letters), and spends many hours in play and with peers. First grade typically marks the end of this period. You will read about early childhood in chapters 7 and 8.

Middle and late childhood extends from about six to eleven years of age, approximately corresponding to the elementary school years; sometimes the period is called the elementary school years. The fundamental skills of reading, writing, and arithmetic are mastered. Formal exposure to the larger world and its culture takes place. Achievement becomes a more prominent theme of the child's world, and self-control increases. You will read about middle and late childhood in chapters 9 and 10.

Adolescence is the period of transition from childhood to early adulthood, entered approximately at ten to twelve years of age and ending at eighteen to twenty-two years of age. Adolescence begins with rapid physical change—dramatic gains in height, weight, change in body contour, and the development of sexual characteristics such as enlargement of breasts, development of pubic and facial hair, and deepening of voice. At this point in development, the individual pushes for independence and pursues an identity. Thought is more logical, abstract, and idealistic. More and more time is spent outside of the family during this period. You will read about adolescence in chapters 11 and 12.

Early adulthood begins in the late teens or early twenties and lasts through the thirties. It is a time of establishing personal and economic independence, a time of career development, and for many a time of selecting a mate, learning to live with someone in an intimate way, starting a family, and rearing children. You will read about early adulthood in chapters 13 and 14.

Middle adulthood is the period from approximately thirty-five to forty-five to forty-five to sixty-five years. It is a time of expanding personal and social involvement and responsibility; of assisting adolescents to become more responsible and happy adults; of adjusting to the physiological changes of middle age; and of reaching and maintaining satisfaction in one's career. You will read about middle adulthood in chapters 15 and 16.

Late adulthood lasts from approximately sixty to seventy years of age until death. It is a time of adjustment to decreasing strength and health and to retirement and reduced income. Reviewing one's life and adapting to social roles are prominent features of late adulthood, too. You will read about late adulthood in chapters 17 and 18.

The periods of development are shown in figure 1.6 along with the processes of development—biological, cognitive, and social. As can be seen in figure 1.7, the interplay of biological, cognitive, and social processes produces the periods of development in the life cycle.

In our description of the life cycle's periods, we placed approximate age bands on the periods. However, one expert on life-span development, Bernice Neugarten, argues that we rapidly are becoming an age-irrelevant society. To learn more about her views on age-related stereotypes, turn to Focus on Life-Span Development 1.2.

. . . One's children's children's children. Look back to us as we look to you; we are related by our imaginations. If we are able to touch, it is because we have imagined each other's existence, our dreams running back and forth along a cable from age to age.

Roger Rosenblatt, 1986

Figure 1.7
Processes and periods of life-span development. The unfolding of the life-cycle's periods of development is influenced by the interplay of biological, cognitive, and social processes.

Periods of development

Late adulthood

Middle adulthood

Early adulthood

Adolescence

Middle and late childhood

Early childhood

Infancy

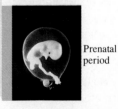
Prenatal period

Processes of development

Biological processes

Cognitive processes

Social processes

ARE MANY AGE-RELATED THEMES
OF DEVELOPMENT STEREOTYPES?

Bernice Neugarten (1980) says that we are already familiar with the twenty-eight-year-old mayor, the thirty-five-year-old grandmother, the fifty-year-old retiree, the sixty-five-year-old father of a preschooler, the fifty-five-year-old widow who starts a business, and the seventy-year-old student. She believes that "act your age" is an admonition that has little meaning in contemporary times. Yet an increasing number of popular books suggest common patterns for our complex lives. Gail Sheehy wrote about the "Trying Twenties" and "Passage to the Thirties" in her widely read *Passages,* for example. Neugarten says that individuals who read such books worry about their mid-life crises, apologize if they don't seem to be coping with them, and seem dismayed if they are not having one. Neugarten argues that such transformations, or crises, may not define what is normal or off-the-track. It is not that adults are changeless, but rather that adults change far more, and far less predictably, than oversimplified age approaches suggest. Neugarten points out that she has had trouble

Our social clocks have changed. New trends in work, health, and exercise are appearing. Older adults are healthier and exercise more than their counterparts in prior decades.

clustering people into age brackets that are characterized by particular conflicts; the conflicts won't stay put, and neither will the people. Choices and dilemmas do not sprout forth at ten-year intervals, and decisions are not made and then left behind as if they were merely beads on a chain.

Neugarten (1988) believes that it is no longer reasonable to describe the life cycle as a set of discrete stages. Our biological clocks have changed: puberty comes earlier than a generation ago; menopause comes later; and people are living longer. Our social clocks also have changed: new trends in work, family size, health, and education are appearing; people are starting new jobs and families at forty, fifty, and even sixty years of age.

Neugarten emphasizes that most adulthood themes appear and reappear throughout the life cycle. The issues of intimacy and freedom can haunt couples throughout their relationship, for example. Similarly, feeling the pressure of time, reformulating goals, and coping with success and failure are not the exclusive property of adults of any age.

Maturation and Experience

Not only can we think of development as produced by the interplay of biological, cognitive, and social processes, but also by the interplay of maturation and experience. **Maturation** is the orderly sequence of changes dictated by the genetic blueprint we each have. Just as a sunflower grows in an orderly way—unless flattened by an unfriendly environment—so does the human grow in an orderly way, according to the maturational view. The range of environments can be vast, but the maturational approach argues that the genetic blueprint produces communalities in our growth and development. We walk before we talk, speak one word before two words, grow rapidly in infancy and less so in early childhood, experience a rush of sexual hormones in puberty after a lull in childhood, reach the peak of our physical strength in late adolescence and early adulthood and then decline, and so on. The maturationists acknowledge that extreme environments—those that are psychologically barren or hostile—can depress development, but they believe basic growth tendencies are genetically wired into the human.

By contrast, other psychologists emphasize the importance of experiences in life-span development. Experiences run the gamut from the individual's biological environment—nutrition, medical care, drugs, and physical accidents—to the social environment—family, peers, schools, community, media, and culture.

The debate about whether development is influenced primarily by maturation or by experience is another version of the **nature-nurture controversy** that has been a part of psychology throughout its history. The "nature" proponents claim that biological and genetic factors are the most important determinants of development; the "nurture" proponents claim that environment and experience are more important.

The original sin, *tabula rasa,* and innate goodness view of the child's nature we discussed earlier initiated the nature-nurture debate. The original sin and innate goodness views place a premium on nature; the *tabula rasa* view emphasizes nurture.

As psychology developed as a science, the biological views of Charles Darwin influenced early theorizing on development. Darwin actually is credited with making the scientific study of development respectable when he developed a baby journal for recording systematic observations of an infant's behavior. Both G. Stanley Hall and Sigmund Freud believed the child went through developmental stages which were heavily controlled by biological maturation. In the spirit of the original sin view, Freud argued that children come into the world as a bundle of biological instincts. Arnold Gesell (1928) also stressed that a child's development unfolded according to a genetic blueprint. Gesell observed the characteristics of children at different ages in highly systematic ways. Figure 1.8 shows Gesell in the photographic dome he used to watch children without interrupting them.

The behaviorist John Watson (1928) proposed a view of development dramatically different from Darwin, Hall, Freud, and Gesell. Watson argued that children could be shaped into whatever society wanted, in line with the *tabula rasa* view. Watson stressed that parents were too soft on children; quit cuddling and smiling at babies so much, he told parents.

Ideas about the nature of child development have been like a pendulum, swinging between nature and nurture. Today we are witnessing a surge of interest in the biological underpinnings of development, probably because the

Give me a dozen healthy infants, well-formed, and my own specified world to bring them up in, and I'll guarantee to take any one at random and train him to become any type of specialist I might select—a doctor, lawyer, artist, merchant-chief and, yes, even into a beggar-man and thief, regardless of his talents, penchants, tendencies, abilities, vocations and race of his ancestors.

John B. Watson, 1926

The Life-Span Developmental Perspective

Figure 1.8
Gesell's photographic dome. Gesell is the man inside the dome with the infant. Cameras rode on metal tracks at the top of the dome and were moved as needed to record the child's activities. Others, such as the female scientist in this photo, could observe from outside the dome without being seen by the child.

pendulum had swung too far in the direction of thinking that development was due exclusively to environmental experiences (Hinde & Stevenson-Hinde, 1987). While nature has grown in popularity recently, all psychologists today believe that both nature *and* nurture are responsible for development; the key to development is the interaction of nature and nurture rather than either factor alone. For example, an individual's cognitive development is the result of heredity-environment interaction, not heredity or environment alone. Much more about the importance of heredity-environment interaction appears in chapter 3.

Continuity and Discontinuity

Think about your development for a moment. Did you gradually grow to become the person you are, not unlike the slow, cumulative growth of a seedling into a giant oak? Or did you experience sudden, distinct changes in your growth, not unlike the way a caterpillar changes into a butterfly? (See figure 1.9.) For the most part, developmentalists who emphasize experience have described development as a gradual, continuous process; those who emphasize maturation have described development as a series of distinct stages. In chapter 2, you will read about several prominent stage theories of development.

Some developmentalists emphasize the **continuity of development,** stressing a gradual, cumulative change from conception to death. A child's first word, while seemingly an abrupt, discontinuous event, is viewed as the result of weeks and months of growth and practice. Puberty, while also seemingly an abrupt, discontinuous occurrence, is viewed as a gradual process occurring over several years.

Figure 1.9
Continuity and discontinuity in development: Is development more like a seedling gradually growing into a giant oak or a caterpillar suddenly becoming a butterfly?

Other developmentalists emphasize the **discontinuity of development,** stressing distinct stages in the life span. Each of us is described as passing through a sequence of stages in which change is qualitatively rather than quantitatively different. As the oak moves from seedling to giant oak, it is *more* oak—its development is continuous. As the caterpillar changes to a butterfly, it is not just more caterpillar. It is a *different kind* of organism—its development is discontinuous. At some point, a child moves from not being able to think abstractly about the world to being able to. At some point, an adult moves from an individual capable of reproduction to one who is not. These are qualitative, discontinuous changes in development, not quantitative, continuous changes.

Another form of the continuity-discontinuity issue is whether development is best described by *stability* or *change.* Will the shy child who hides behind the sofa when visitors arrive be the wallflower at college dances, or will this child become a sociable, talkative individual? Will the fun-loving, care-free adolescent have difficulty holding down a nine-to-five job as an adult, or become a straight-laced, serious conformist? The **stability-change issue** basically addresses to what degree we become older renditions of our early existence or whether we can develop into someone different than we were at an earlier point in development. One of the reasons adult development was so late in being studied was the predominant belief for many years that nothing much changes in adulthood; the major changes were believed to take place in childhood, especially during the first five years of life. Today most psychologists believe that some change is possible throughout the life span, although scholars disagree, sometimes vehemently, about just how much change can take place, and how much stability there is. The important issue of stability-change in development will reappear on many occasions in our journey through the human life cycle.

At this point, you should be developing a sense of the life-span perspective on development. You have read about some contemporary interests, historical background, and the nature of development. To help you remember the main points of our discussion so far, turn to Concept Table 1.1.

The Science Base of Life-Span Development

Some individuals have difficulty thinking of life-span development as a science in the same way physics, chemistry, and biology are sciences. Can a discipline that studies how babies develop, parents nurture children, adolescents' thoughts change, and adults form intimate relationships be equated with disciplines that investigate how gravity works and the molecular structure of a compound? Science is not defined by *what* it investigates but by *how* it investigates. Whether you are studying photosynthesis, butterflies, Saturn's moons, or human development, it is the way you study that makes the approach scientific or not.

Theory and the Scientific Method

According to Henri Poincaré, "Science is built of facts the way a house is built of bricks, but an accumulation of facts is no more science than a pile of bricks a house." Science *does* depend upon the raw material of data or facts we have observed to make predictions, but science is more than just facts. The nature of theory and the scientific method illustrate Poincaré's point.

Science is not defined by what *it studies but by* how *it investigates it. Saturn's moons or relationships among people all can be studied in a scientific manner.*

History and Issues in Life-Span Development		
Concept	**Processes/Related Ideas**	**Characteristics/Description**
Life-Span Development—Today and Yesterday	Contemporary Concerns	Today, the well-being of children and adults is a prominent concern in our culture—four such concerns are genetic research, child abuse, divorce, and aging.
	The Historical Perspective	The history of interest in children is long and rich. In the Renaissance, philosophical views were prominent, including original sin, *tabula rasa,* and innate goodness. The scientific study of adolescence was promoted by G. Stanley Hall in the early 1900s. His storm and stress view contrasts with the inventionist view. The traditional approach emphasizes extensive change in childhood but stability in adulthood; the life-span perspective emphasizes that change is possible throughout the life span. Other characteristics of the life-span perspective are multidimensionality, multidirectionality, plasticity, historical embeddedness, contextualism, and multidisciplinary.
The Nature of Development	What Is Development?	Development is the pattern of movement or change that occurs throughout the life span.
	Biological, Cognitive, and Social Processes	Development is influenced by an interplay of biological, cognitive, and social processes.
	Periods of Development	The life cycle is commonly divided into the following periods of development: prenatal, infancy, early childhood, middle and late childhood, adolescence, early adulthood, middle adulthood, and late adulthood.
	Maturation and Experience	Development is influenced by the interaction of maturation and experience. The debate of whether development is due primarily to maturation or to environment is another version of the nature-nurture controversy.
	Continuity and Discontinuity	Some psychologists describe development as continuous (gradual, cumulative change); others describe it as discontinuous (abrupt, sequence of stages). Another form of the continuity-discontinuity issue is whether development is best described by stability or change.

Theories are general beliefs that help us to explain the data or facts we have observed and make predictions. A good theory has **hypotheses,** assumptions that can be tested to determine their accuracy. For example, a good theory about depression among the elderly would explain our observations of depressed elderly individuals and predict why elderly people get depressed. We might predict that elderly individuals get depressed because they fail to focus on their strengths and dwell excessively on their shortcomings. This prediction would help to direct our observations by telling us to look for overexaggerations of weaknesses and underestimations of strengths and skills.

Theories help us to make predictions about how we develop and how we behave. Do you believe that we can predict an individual's behavior and development? Explain your answer.

To obtain accurate information about life-span development, it is important to adopt the **scientific method.** To do this, we must follow a number of steps: identify and analyze the problem, collect data, draw conclusions, and revise theories. For example, you decide that you want to help elderly individuals overcome their depression. You have identified a problem, which does not seem like a very difficult task. But as part of this first step, you need to go beyond a general description of the problem by isolating, analyzing, narrowing, and focusing on what you hope to investigate. What specific strategies do you want to use to reduce depression among the elderly? Do you want to look at only one strategy, or several strategies? What aspect of depression do you want to study—its biological, cognitive, or social characteristics? One group of psychologists believe that the cognitive and social aspects of depression in the elderly can be improved through a course on coping with depression (Lewinsohn & others, 1984; Zeiss & Lewinsohn, 1986). One of the components of the course is to teach depressed elderly individuals to control their negative thoughts. In this first step in the scientific method, a problem has been identified and analyzed.

After we identify and analyze a problem, the next step is to collect information (data). Psychologists observe behavior and draw inferences about thoughts and emotions. For example, in the investigation of depression among the elderly, we might observe how effectively individuals who complete the course on coping with depression monitor their moods and engage in an active life style.

Once data have been collected, psychologists use statistical procedures to understand the meaning of quantitative data. They then try to draw conclusions. In the investigation of the elderly's depression, statistics would help the researchers determine whether or not their observations were due to chance. After data have been analyzed, psychologists compare their findings with what others have discovered about the same issue or problem.

The final step in the scientific method is revising theory. Psychologists have developed a number of theories about life-span development; they have also developed a number of theories about why individuals become depressed. Data such as those collected in our hypothetical study force us to study existing theories of depression to see if they are accurate. Over the years, some theories of life-span development have been discarded and others revised. Theories are so important in the study of life-span development that an entire chapter (2) has been set aside for their discussion.

Collecting Information about Life-Span Development

Systematic observations can be conducted in a variety of ways. For example, we can watch behavior in the laboratory or in a more natural setting such as a home or a street corner. We can question people using interviews and surveys, develop and administer standardized tests, conduct case studies, or carry out physiological research or research with animals. To help you understand how psychologists use these methods, we will apply each method to the study of aggression.

Observation

Sherlock Holmes chided Watson, "You see but you do not observe." We look at things all the time, but casually watching a mother and her infant is not scientific observation. Unless you are a trained observer and practice your skills regularly, you may not know what to look for, you may not remember what you saw, what you are looking for may change from one moment to the next, and you may not communicate your observations effectively.

Truth is arrived at by the painstaking process of eliminating the untrue.
Arthur Conan Doyle, Sherlock Holmes

For observations to be effective, we have to know what we are looking for, who we are observing, when and where we will observe, how the observations will be made, and in what form they will be recorded. That is, our observations have to be made in some *systematic* way. Consider aggression. Do we want to study verbal or physical aggression, or both? Do we want to study children or adults, or both? Do we want to evaluate them in a university laboratory, at work, at play, or at all of these locations? A common way to record our observations is to write them down, using shorthand or symbols; however, tape recorders, video cameras, special coding sheets, and one-way mirrors are used increasingly to make observations more efficient.

When we observe, frequently it is necessary to *control* certain factors that determine behavior but are not the focus of our inquiry. For this reason, much psychological research is conducted in a **laboratory,** that is, a controlled setting in which many of the complex factors of the "real world" are removed. For example, Albert Bandura (1965) brought children into a laboratory and had them observe an adult repeatedly hit a plastic, inflated Bobo doll about three feet tall. Bandura wondered to what extent the children would copy the adult's behavior. The children did copy the adult's behavior extensively.

Conducting laboratory research, however, can be costly. First, it is almost impossible to conduct without the participants knowing that they are being studied. Second, the laboratory setting may be *unnatural* and therefore cause *unnatural* behavior from the participants. Subjects often show less aggressive behavior in a laboratory than in a more familiar natural setting, such as in a park or at a home. They also show less aggression when they are aware of being observed. Third, some aspects of life-span development are difficult if not impossible to produce in the laboratory. Certain types of stress are difficult (and unethical) to investigate in the laboratory, for example, recreating the circumstances that stimulate marital conflict. In **naturalistic observation,** then, psychologists observe behavior in real-world settings and make no effort to manipulate or control the situation. Naturalistic observations have been conducted at hospitals, day care centers, schools, parks, homes, malls, dances, and other places where people live and frequent. Figure 1.10 shows a comparison of aggression in the laboratory and in a naturalistic situation.

Interviews and Questionnaires

Sometimes the best and quickest way to get information from people is to ask them for it. Psychologists use interviews and questionnaires to find out about the experiences and attitudes of people. Most **interviews** are conducted face-to-face, although they can take place over the telephone. An experienced interviewer knows how to put the subject at ease and encourage her to open up. A competent interviewer is sensitive to the way the individual responds to questions and often probes for more information.

Just as observations can take place in different settings, so can interviews. An interview might occur at a university, in an individual's home, or at an individual's place of work. For example, Brenda Bryant (1985) developed "The Neighborhood Walk," an interview conducted with a child while walking through the child's neighborhood. Bryant has found the interview especially helpful in generating information about the support systems available to children.

Interviews are not without their problems. Perhaps the most critical of these problems is the response set of "social desirability," in which an individual tells the interviewer what he thinks is most socially acceptable rather than what he truly thinks or feels. When asked about her marital conflict, Jane

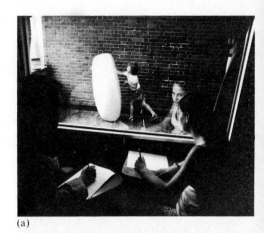
(a)

(b)

Figure 1.10
Observation of a child's aggressive behavior under controlled laboratory and naturalistic conditions. a. In this situation, the child's aggressive behavior is being observed through a one-way mirror. This allows the observer to exercise control over the observation of aggression. b. In this situation, the child's aggressive behavior is being observed in a naturalistic situation. This allows the observer to obtain information about the everyday occurrence of behavior.

may not want to disclose that arguments have been painfully tense in the last month. Another problem is that the individual simply may lie. Skilled interviewing techniques and questions to eliminate such defenses are critical in obtaining accurate information.

Psychologists also question individuals using questionnaires or surveys. A **questionnaire** is similar to a highly structured interview except that the respondent reads the question and marks her answer on the paper rather than verbally responding to the interviewer. One major advantage of surveys is that they can be given to a large number of individuals easily. Questions on surveys should be concrete, specific, and unambiguous, and an assessment of the authenticity of the replies should be made (Agnew & Pike, 1987).

Case Studies

A **case study** is an in-depth look at an individual. Case studies are used when the unique aspects of an individual's life cannot be duplicated, either for practical or ethical reasons, yet they have implications for understanding development. A case study provides information about an individual's hopes, fears, fantasies, traumatic experiences, family relationships, health, or anything that will help the psychologist understand life-span development.

Traumatic experiences have produced some truly fascinating case studies in life-span development. A 26-year-old school teacher shot his girlfriend while he was a passenger in the car she was driving. Soon after the act, he ran to the telephone booth to call his priest. He had met the woman only eight months before the shooting, yet it was an intense love affair with marriage planned. Several months after meeting the woman, the teacher became depressed, drank heavily, and talked about suicide. His actions became bizarre. On one occasion, he punctured the tires on her car. On another, he stood on the side of the road where she passed frequently in her car, extending his hand in his pocket so she would think he was holding a gun. His relationship with the woman vascillated between love and hate. He described the last several months before the murder as complete chaos. He informed another couple that he was going to kill his girl friend, but they interpreted it as mere talk due to his inebriated state (Revitch & Schlesinger, 1978).

This case reveals how depressive moods, bizarre thinking, and premonitions can precede violent acts, such as murder. Other case studies will appear throughout the text, among them a modern-day wild child named Genie, who lived in near isolation during her childhood (chapter 5).

Standardized Tests

Standardized tests require that individuals answer a series of written or oral questions. Two distinctive features of standardized tests are that the individual's answers usually are totaled to yield a single score, or a set of scores, that reflects something about the individual, and that the individual's score is compared to the scores of a large group of similar individuals to determine how the individual responded *relative* to the others. Scores often are decribed in percentiles. For example, perhaps you scored in the ninety-second percentile on the SAT. This method tells you how much higher or lower you scored than the large group of individuals who took the test previously. Among the most widely used standardized tests are the Stanford-Binet intelligence test and the Minnesota Multiphasic Personality Inventory (MMPI).

To continue our look at how different measures are used to evaluate aggression, consider the MMPI, which includes a scale to assess delinquency and antisocial tendencies. The items on this scale ask you to respond whether or not you are rebellious, impulsive, and have trouble with authority figures. The twenty-six-year-old teacher who murdered his girlfriend would have scored high on a number of MMPI scales, including the one designed to measure how strange and bizarre are our thoughts and ideas.

Physiological Research and Research with Animals
Two additional methods that psychologists use to gather data about life-span development are physiological research and research with animals. Increased research into the biological basis of life-span development have produced remarkable insights. For example, electrical stimulation of certain areas of the brain has turned docile, mild-mannered individuals into hostile, vicious attackers; and higher concentrations of some hormones have been associated with delinquent behavior in male adolescents (King, 1961; Susman & others, 1987).

Much physiological research cannot be carried out with humans, so psychologists use animals. With animals, we can control genetic background, diet, experiences during infancy, and countless other factors. In human studies, these factors have to be treated as random variation, or "noise," and they may interfere with accurate results. With animals, we can investigate the effects of treatments (brain implants, for example) that would be unethical to attempt with humans. Moreover, it is possible to track the entire life cycle of some animals over a relatively short period of time. Laboratory mice, for example, have a life span of approximately one year.

With regard to aggression, castration has turned ferocious bulls into docile oxen by acting on the male hormone system. After a number of breedings of aggressive mice, researchers have created mice who are absolutely ferocious, attacking virtually anything in sight (Lagerspetz, 1979). Do these findings with animals apply to humans? Hormones and genes do influence human aggression, but this influence is less than in animals. Because humans differ from animals in many ways, one disadvantage of research with animals is that the results may not apply to humans.

Strategies for Setting up Research Studies
How can we determine if responding nurturantly to an infant's cries increases attachment to the caregiver? How can we determine if listening to rock music lowers an adolescent's grades? How can we determine if an active life style in old age increases longevity? When designing research to answer such questions, a developmentalist must decide whether to use a correlational strategy or an experimental strategy.

Correlational Strategy
One goal of life-span developmental research is to describe how strongly two or more events or characteristics are related. When a psychologist has this goal, a **correlational strategy** is used. This is a useful strategy, because the more strongly events are correlated (related, or associated), the more we can predict one from the other. For example, consider one of our major national health problems in adulthood, high blood pressure. If we find that high blood pressure is strongly associated with the inability to manage stress, then we can use the inability to manage stress to predict high blood pressure.

Figure 1.11
Examining the correlation between the inability to manage stress and high blood pressure. This figure illustrates that an observed correlation between two events cannot be used to conclude that one event causes a second event. It could also be that the second event causes the first, or that a third event causes the correlation between the first two events.

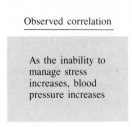

Observed correlation

As the inability to manage stress increases, blood pressure increases

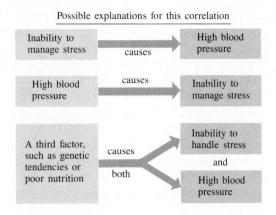

Possible explanations for this correlation

Inability to manage stress → causes → High blood pressure

High blood pressure → causes → Inability to manage stress

A third factor, such as genetic tendencies or poor nutrition → causes both → Inability to handle stress and High blood pressure

The next step, taken all too often, is to conclude from such evidence that one event *causes* the other. Following this line of reasoning, we would erroneously conclude that the inability to manage stress causes high blood pressure. Why is this reasoning *wrong?* Why doesn't a strong correlation between two events mean that one causes the other? A strong correlation could mean that the inability to manage stress causes high blood pressure, but it *also* could mean that high blood pressure causes an inability to handle stress. And, a third possibility exists: although strongly correlated, the inability to manage stress and high blood pressure do not cause each other at all. How could this be? Possibly a third factor underlies their association, such as a genetic tendency or poor nutrition (see figure 1.11). Throughout this text, you will read about studies based on a correlational strategy. Keep in mind that it is easy to think that because two events or characteristics are correlated, one causes the other; as we have just seen, this is not always the case.

Experimental Strategy

The **experimental strategy** allows us to determine the causes of behavior precisely. The psychologist accomplishes this task by performing an *experiment,* which is a carefully regulated setting in which one or more of the factors believed to influence the behavior being studied is manipulated and all others are held constant. If the behavior under study changes when a factor is manipulated, we say that the manipulated factor causes the behavior to change. Experiments are used to establish cause and effect between events, something correlational studies cannot do. *Cause* is the event being manipulated and *effect* is the behavior that changes because of the manipulation. Remember that in testing correlation, nothing is manipulated; in an experiment, the researcher actively changes an event to see the effect on behavior.

The following example illustrates the nature of an experiment. The problem to be studied is whether caffeine intake during pregnancy affects the development of the infant. We decide that to conduct our experiment we need one group of pregnant women who will ingest caffeine and another that will not. We randomly assign our subjects to these two groups. *Random assignment* reduces the likelihood that the experiment's results will be due to some preexisting differences in the two groups. For example, random assignment greatly reduces the probability that the two groups will differ on such factors as prior use of caffeine, health problems, intelligence, alertness, social class, age, and so forth.

The Life-Span Developmental Perspective

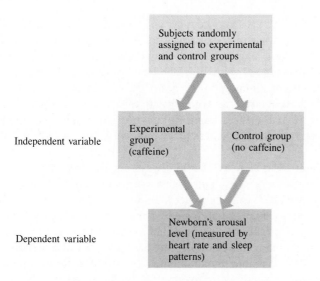

Subjects randomly
assigned to experimental
and control groups

Independent variable

Experimental
group
(caffeine)

Control group
(no caffeine)

Dependent variable

Newborn's arousal
level (measured by
heart rate and sleep
patterns)

Figure 1.12
Principles of the experimental strategy applied to a study of the effects of caffeine ingestion by pregnant women on arousal of their newborn children.

The subjects who take the caffeine are called the **experimental group,** that is, the group whose experience is manipulated. The subjects who do not take the caffeine are the **control group,** that is, a comparison group treated in every way like the experimental group except for the manipulated factor. The control group serves as a baseline against which the effects found in the manipulated condition can be compared.

After the subjects in the experimental group have taken caffeine during their pregnancy and their offspring are born, the infant behavior of the offspring of the two groups is compared. We choose to study the heart rate and sleeping patterns of the infants. When we analyze the results, we discover that the experimental group infants had a faster heart rate and more irregular sleep patterns. We conclude that ingestion of caffeine by pregnant women increases the arousal state of the newborn.

In an experiment, the manipulated, or influential, factor is called the **independent variable.** The label *independent* is used because this variable can be changed independently of other factors. In the caffeine experiment, the amount of caffeine taken was the independent variable. The experimenter manipulated how much caffeine the subjects experienced independently of all other factors. In an experiment, the researcher determines what effect the independent variable has on the **dependent variable.** The label *dependent* is used because this variable depends on what happens to the subjects in the experiment. In the caffeine experiment, the dependent variable was the heart rate and sleeping patterns of the infants. The infants' responses on these measures depended on the influence of the independent variable (whether or not caffeine was taken). An illustration of the nature of the experimental strategy, applied to the caffeine study, is shown in figure 1.12.

Remember that the correlational study of the relation between stress and blood pressure gave us little indication of whether stress influences blood pressure, or vice versa. A third factor may have caused the correlation. A research study that determined if stress management reduces high blood pressure serves to further understand the experimental strategy (Irvine & others, 1986). Thirty-two males and females from 34 to 65 years of age with high blood pressure were randomly assigned to either a group who were trained in relaxation and stress management (experimental group) or a group who received

What are the different strategies you could use to study the effects of caffeine on pregnant mothers and their offspring?

no training (control group). The independent variable consisted of ten weekly one-hour sessions that included educational information about the nature of stress and how to manage it, as well as extensive training in learning to relax and control stress in everyday life. The blood pressure of both groups was assessed before the training program and three months after it was completed. Nurses who were unaware of which group the subjects had been in measured blood pressure at the three-month follow-up. The results indicated that the relaxation and stress management program was effective in reducing high blood pressure.

It might seem as if we should always choose an experimental strategy over a correlational strategy, since the experimental strategy gives us a better sense of one variable's influence over another. Are there instances when a correlational strategy might be preferred? Three such instances are (1) when the focus of the investigation is so new that we have little knowledge of which factors to manipulate (for example, factors associated with AIDS); (2) when it is physically impossible to manipulate the variables (for example, suicide); and (3) when it is unethical to manipulate the variables (for example, determining the link between parenting strategies and children's competence).

The Time Span of Inquiry
A special concern of developmentalists is the time span of a research investigation. Studies that focus on the relation of age to some other variable are common in life-span development. We have several options: we can study different individuals of different ages and compare them; we can study the same individuals as they age over time; or we can use some combination of these two approaches. We consider each of these in turn.

Cross-Sectional Approach
In the **cross-sectional approach,** individuals of different ages are compared all at one time. A typical cross-sectional study might include a group of 5-year-olds, 8-year-olds, and 11-year-olds; another might include a group of 15-year-olds, 25-year-olds; and 45-year-olds. The different groups could be compared with respect to a variety of dependent variables—IQ, memory, peer relations, attachment to parents, hormonal changes, and so forth. All of this can be accomplished in a short time; in some studies the data are collected in a single day. Even large scale cross-sectional studies usually do not take longer than several months to complete data collection.

As an example of a cross-sectional study, Duane Buhrmester and Wyndol Furman (1987) investigated the development of companionship in 7-, 10-, and 13-year-olds. They found that family members were important providers of companionship for 7- and 10-year-old children, but significantly less so for 13-year-olds. Same-sex peers were important providers across all three age periods, becoming increasingly important with older children. Opposite-sex peers only were important as companions for the 13-year-olds.

The main advantage of the cross-sectional study is that the researcher does not have to wait for the individuals to grow up or become older. Buhrmester and Furman did not have to spend six years of time to wait until the 7-year-olds in their study became 10- then 13-years-old. They simply found children who were 7-, 10-, and 13-years old and compared their behavior.

Despite its time efficiency, the cross-sectional approach has its drawbacks. It gives no information about how individuals change or about the stability of their characteristics. The increases and decreases in development—the hills and valleys—of growth and development can become obscured in the cross-sectional approach. For example, in the cross-sectional approach to companionship, average increases and decreases in companionship were revealed. But the study did not show how the companionship of individual children waxed and waned over the years. It also did not tell us whether children who had stronger or weaker companionship as seven-year-olds maintained their relative degree of companionship as older children or adolescents. While cross-sectional studies cannot answer such questions, longitudinal studies can.

Longitudinal Approach
In the **longitudinal approach,** the developmentalist studies the same individuals over a period of time, usually several years or more. For example, in the study of companionship, if it were conducted longitudinally, the same children would be assessed over a six year time span—at the age of 7, 10, and 13.

As an example of a longitudinal study, Jacqueline Lerner and her colleagues (1988) studied 75 white, middle-class children from early in their infancy through the adolescent years. They wanted to know if negative emotional and behavioral characteristics (such as aggression, anxiety, undercompliance, and depressive mood) in the infancy and childhood years were related to adjustment in the adolescent years. They found that early negative emotional states in the years 1 through 6 were strongly related to adolescent adjustment problems with parents and peers. This pattern was specific to the type of emotional difficulty—aggression predicting poor family adjustment and anxiety predicting peer adjustment problems.

While longitudinal studies provide a wealth of information about such important issues as stability and change in development and the importance of early experience for later development, they are not without their problems. They are expensive and time-consuming. The longer the study lasts, the more subjects drop out—they move, get sick, lose interest, and so forth. Subject loss can bias the outcome of a study because those who remain may be dissimilar to those who drop out. Those individuals who remain in longitudinal study over a number of years may be more compulsive and conformity oriented, for example. Or they might have more stable lives.

Sequential Approach
Developmentalists also combine the cross-sectional and longitudinal designs in their effort to learn more about life-span development; the combined cross-sectional, longitudinal design is called the **sequential approach.** In most instances, this approach starts with a cross-sectional study that includes individuals of different ages. A number of months or years after the initial assessment, the same individuals are tested again—this is the longitudinal aspect of the design. At this later time, a new group of subjects is assessed at each age level. The new groups at each level are added at the later time to control for changes that might have taken place in the original group of subjects—some may have dropped out of the study or retesting might improve their performance, for example. The sequential approach is complex, it is expensive, and it is time-consuming, but it does provide information that is not possible to obtain from the cross-sectional or longitudinal approaches alone.

BY BILL HOEST

"That's my dad when he was 10...He was in some sort of cult."

You are faced with the task of designing an investigation of intergenerational relations. What problem do you want to study? What measure(s) would you use? What strategy would you follow—experimental or correlational? What would be the time span of your inquiry?

The mark of the historic is the nonchalance with which it picks up an individual and deposits him in a trend, like a house playfully moved in a tornado.
Mary McCarthy, On the Contrary, *1961*

The sequential approach has been especially helpful in calling attention to the importance of cohort effects in life-span development. **Cohort effects** are those due to a subject's time of birth or generation but not actually to age. For example, cohorts can differ in years of education, child-rearing practices, health, and attitudes toward sex and religion. Cohort effects are important because they can powerfully affect the dependent measures in a study ostensibly concerned with age. Researchers have shown that cohort effects are especially prominent in the assessment of adult intelligence, since individuals born at different points in time—such as 1920, 1940, and 1960—have had widely varying opportunities for education with the individuals born in earlier years having less access. Much more about the nature of cohort effects on adult intelligence appears in chapter 17.

We have covered a number of ideas about the science base of life-span development. To help you remember the main points of this discussion, turn to Concept Table 1.2.

Ethics in Research on Life-Span Development

When Anne and Pete, two nineteen-year-old college students, agreed to participate in an investigation of dating couples, they did not consider that the questionnaire they filled out would get them to think about issues that might lead to conflict in their relationship and possibly end it. One year after this investigation (Rubin & Mitchell, 1976), nine of ten participants said that they had discussed their answers with their dating partner. In most instances, the discussions helped to strengthen the relationships; but in some instances, the participants used the questionnaire as a springboard to discuss problems or concerns previously hidden. One participant said, "The study definitely played a role in ending my relationship with Larry." In this circumstance, the couple had different views about how long they expected to be together. She anticipated that the relationship would end much sooner than Larry thought. Discussion of their answers to the questions brought the long-term prospects of the relationship out in the open, and eventually Larry found someone who was more interested in marrying him.

CONCEPT TABLE

1.2

■

The Science Base of Life-Span Development		
Concept	**Processes/Related Ideas**	**Characteristics/Description**
Theory and the Scientific Method	Theory	General beliefs that help us to explain what we observe and make predictions. A good theory has hypotheses, which are assumptions that can be tested.
	Scientific Method	A series of procedures (identifying and analyzing a problem, collecting data, drawing conclusions, and revising theory) to obtain accurate information.
Ways of Collecting Information—Measures	Observation	A key ingredient in life-span development research that includes laboratory and naturalistic observation.
	Interviews and Questionnaires	Used to assess perceptions and attitudes. Social desirability and lying are problems with their use.
	Case Studies	Provides an in-depth look at an individual. Caution in generalizing is warranted.
	Standardized Tests	Designed to assess an individual's characteristics relative to those of a large group of similar individuals.
	Physiological Research and Research with Animals	Focus is on the biological dimensions of the organism. While greater control over conditions can be achieved with animals, generalization to humans may be problematic.
Strategies for Setting Up Research Studies	Correlational Strategy	Describes how strongly two or more events or characteristics are related. It does not allow causal statements.
	Experimental Strategy	Involves manipulation of influential factors, the independent variables, and measurement of their effect on the dependent variables. Subjects are randomly assigned to experimental and control groups in many studies. The experimental strategy can reveal the causes of behavior and tell us how one event influenced another.
Time Span of Inquiry	Cross-Sectional Approach	Individuals of different ages are compared all at one time.
	Longitudinal Approach	The same individuals are studied over a period of time, usually several years or more.
	Sequential Approach	A combined cross-sectional, longitudinal approach that highlights the importance of cohort effects in life-span development.

At first glance, you would not think that a questionnaire on dating relationships would have any substantial impact on the participants' behavior. But psychologists increasingly recognize that considerable caution must be taken to ensure the well-being of subjects in a study of life-span development. Today colleges and universities have review boards that evaluate the ethical nature of research conducted at their institutions. Proposed research plans must pass the scrutiny of an ethics research committee before the research can be initiated. In addition, the American Psychological Association (APA) has developed guidelines for its members' ethics.

The code of ethics adopted by APA instructs researchers to protect their subjects from mental and physical harm. The best interests of the subjects need to be kept foremost in the researcher's mind. All subjects must give their informed consent to participate in the research study, which requires that subjects know what their participation will involve and any risks that might develop. For example, dating research subjects should be told beforehand that a questionnaire might stimulate thought about issues they might not anticipate. The subjects also should be informed that in some instances a discussion of the issues raised can improve their dating relationships, while in other cases, it can worsen the relationship and even terminate it. After informed consent is given, the subject reserves the right to withdraw from the study at any time while it is being conducted.

Special ethical concerns govern the conduct of research with children. First, if children are to be studied, informed consent from parents or legal guardians must be obtained. Parents have the right to a complete and accurate description of what will be done with their children and may refuse to let them participate. Second, children have rights, too. The psychologist is obliged to explain precisely what the child will experience. The child may refuse to participate, even after parental permission has been given. If so, the researcher must not test the child. Also, if a child becomes upset during the research study, it is the psychologist's obligation to calm the child. Failing to do so, the activity must be discontinued. Third, the psychologist must always weigh the potential for harming children against the prospects of contributing some clear benefits to them. If there is the chance of harm—as when drugs are used, social deception takes place, or the child is treated aversively (that is, punished or reprimanded)—the psychologist must convince a group of peers that the benefits of the experience clearly outweigh any chance of harm. Fourth, since children are in a vulnerable position and lack power and control when facing an adult, the psychologist should always strive to make the professional encounter a positive and supportive experience.

Summary

I. **Life-Span Development—Today and Yesterday**
Today, the well-being of children and adults is a prominent concern in our culture—four such concerns are genetic research, child abuse, divorce, and aging. The history of interest in children is long and rich. In the Renaissance, philosophical views were prominent, including original sin, *tabula rasa,* and innate goodness. The scientific study of adolescence was promoted by G. Stanley Hall in the early 1900s. His storm and stress view contrasts with the inventionist view. The traditional approach emphasizes extensive change in childhood but stability in adulthood; the life-span perspective emphasizes that change is possible throughout the life span.

Other characteristics of the life-cycle perspective are multidimensionality, multidirectionality, plasticity, historical embeddedness, contextualism, and multidisciplinary.

II. **The Nature of Development**
Development is the pattern of movement or change that occurs throughout the life span. Development is influenced by an interplay of biological, cognitive, and social processes. The life cycle is commonly divided into the prenatal, infancy, early childhood, middle and late childhood, adolescence, early adulthood, middle adulthood, and late adulthood periods of development. Development is influenced by the interaction of maturation and experience. The debate of whether development is primarily due to maturation or to environment is another version of the nature-nurture controversy. Some psychologists describe development as continuous (gradual, cumulative change); others describe it as discontinuous (abrupt, sequence of stages). Another form of the continuity-discontinuity issue is whether development is best described by stability or change.

III. **Theory and the Scientific Method**
Theories are general beliefs that help us to explain what we observe and make predictions. A good theory has hypotheses, which are assumptions that can be tested. A series of procedures (identifying and analyzing a problem, collecting data, drawing conclusions, and revising theory) called the scientific method are followed to obtain accurate information about life-span development.

IV. Ways of Collecting Information—Measures

Observation is a key ingredient in life-span development research that includes laboratory and naturalistic observation. Interviews and questionnaires are used to assess perceptions and attitudes. Social desirability and lying are problems with their use. Case studies provide an in-depth look at an individual. Caution in generalizing is warranted. Standardized tests are designed to assess an individual's characteristics relative to those of a large group of similar individuals. Physiological research and research with animals focus on the biological dimensions of the organism. While greater control over conditions can be achieved with animals, generalization to humans may be problematic.

V. Strategies for Setting up Research Studies

The correlational strategy describes how strongly two or more events or characteristics are related. It does not allow causal statements. The experimental strategy involves manipulation of influential factors, the independent variables, and measurement of their effect on the dependent variables. Subjects are randomly assigned to experimental and control groups in many studies. The experimental strategy can reveal the causes of behavior and tell us how one event influenced another.

VI. Ethics in Research on Life-Span Development

Researchers must ensure the well-being of subjects in life-span development research. The risk of mental and physical harm must be reduced, and informed consent should occur. Special ethical considerations are involved when research with children is conducted.

Key Terms

original sin *8*
tabula rasa *8*
innate goodness *8*
storm and stress view *9*
life-cycle perspective *11*
development *14*
biological processes *14*
cognitive processes *14*
social processes *14*
prenatal period *14*
infancy *15*
early childhood *15*
middle and late childhood *15*
adolescence *15*

early adulthood *15*
middle adulthood *15*
late adulthood *15*
maturation *18*
nature-nurture controversy *18*
continuity of development *19*
discontinuity of development *19*
stability-change issue *19*
theories *21*
hypotheses *21*
scientific method *21*
laboratory *23*
naturalistic observation *23*
interviews *23*

questionnaire *24*
case study *24*
standardized tests *24*
correlational strategy *25*
experimental strategy *26*
experimental group *27*
control group *27*
independent variable *27*
dependent variable *27*
cross-sectional approach *28*
longitudinal approach *28*
sequential approach *28*
cohort effects *30*

Suggested Readings

Baltes, P. B. (1987). Theoretical propositions of life-span developmental psychology: On the dynamics between growth and decline. *Developmental Psychology, 23,* 611–626.
In this article, leading life-span development conceptualizer Paul Baltes describes the basic dimensions of the life-span perspective. Special attention is given to how these dimensions influence intelligence.
Borstelmann, L. J. (1983). Children before psychology: Ideas about children from antiquity to the late 1800s. In P. H. Mussen (Ed.), *Handbook of Child Psychology* (4th ed.), Vol. 1. New York: Wiley.
A comprehensive treatment of the historical conception of children from ancient times until the 18th century.
Brim, O. G., & Kagan, J. (Eds.) (1980). *Constancy and change in human development.* Cambridge, MA: Harvard U. Press.
A number of developmental experts contributed articles to this book focused on how stable or changeable our lives are as we go through the life span.
Child Development, Developmental Psychology, Journal of Gerontology. These are three of the leading journals in the field of life-span development. Go to your library and leaf through the issues of the last several years to get a feel for the research interests of developmentalists.
Hall, G. S. (1904). *Adolescence* (Vol. 1). Englewood Cliffs, NJ: Prentice-Hall.
An intriguing look into the mind of the father of the scientific study of adolescent development. Be sure to read about his views of sexuality in the early 20th century.
McClusky, K. A., & Reese, H. W. (Eds.) (1985). *Life-span developmental psychology: Historical and cohort effects.* New York: Academic Press.
This book gives insight into how historical events and year of birth influence life-span development.

CHAPTER

2

■

Theories

Sigmund Freud and Carl Rogers, whose theories we will address in this chapter, are giants in the field of psychological theorizing. The lives of theorists and their experiences have a major impact on the content of their theories. As with each of us, the search for understanding human behavior begins by examining our own.

Sigmund Freud's theory emphasizes the sexual basis of development. What were Freud's sexual interests like as he was growing up? History shows that Freud repressed most of his sexual desires while busily pursuing intellectual matters. In all of the writings about Freud's life, only one incident during his youth reveals something about his sexual desires:

> The story relates to his first love experience at the age of sixteen when—for the first time in his life—he revisited his birthplace. He stayed there with the Fluss family . . . with their daughter, Gisela, a year or two younger than himself, a companion of his early childhood, he fell in love with her on the spot. He was too shy to communicate his feelings or even to address a single word to her, and she went away to her school after a few days. The disconsolate youth had to content himself with the fantasy of how pleasant life would have been had his parents not left that happy spot where he could have grown up a stout country lad, like the girl's brothers, and married the maiden. So it was all his father's fault (Jones, 1953, pp. 25–26).

Carl Roger's theory stresses the importance of developing positive conceptions of ourselves and sensitivity to others' feelings. What was Roger's youth like? He had virtually no social life outside his family, although he does not remember that this bothered him (Rogers, 1967). At the age of twelve, his family moved to a farm; apparently his mother wanted to shield her children from the evils of city life. Even though he was saddled with extensive chores at home, such as milking the cows every morning at 5:00 A.M., Rogers managed to make straight A's in school. He had little time for friendship and dating, and never had what could be called a real date in high school. Once Carl had to take a girl to a class dinner as a matter of custom. He vividly remembers the anxiety of having to ask her to the dinner. She agreed to go, but Rogers said he does not know what he would have done if she had turned him down.

These experiences of Freud and Rogers are examples of how theorists' own experiences and behavior influence their thinking. Perhaps Freud's own sexual repression in adolescence contributed to his theory that behavior has a sexual basis. And perhaps Roger's anxieties about social contact as a youth fostered his theoretical emphasis on warmth in social relationships.

Freud's and Roger's theories are but two of many theories you will read about in this chapter. The diversity of theories make understanding life-span development a challenging undertaking. Just when you think one theory has the correct explanation of life-span development, another theory will crop up and make you rethink your earlier conclusion. To keep from getting frustrated, remember that life-span development is a complex, multi-faceted topic and no single theory has been able to account for all aspects of life-span development. Each theory has contributed an important piece to the life-span development puzzle. While the theories sometimes disagree about certain aspects of life-span development, much of their information is *complementary* rather than contradictory. Together they let us see the total landscape of life-span development in all its richness.

Psychoanalytic Theories

For psychoanalytic theorists, life-span development is primarily unconscious, beyond awareness, and made up of structures of thought heavily colored by emotion. Psychoanalytic theorists believe that behavior is merely a surface characteristic and that to truly understand someone's development, we have to look at the symbolic meanings of behavior and the deep inner workings of the mind. Psychoanalytic theorists also stress that early experiences with parents and underlying sexual tension shape our development. These characteristics are highlighted in the main psychoanalytic theory, that of Sigmund Freud.

Freud's Theory

Loved and hated, respected and despised, for some the master, for others misdirected—Sigmund Freud, whether right or wrong in his views, has been one of the most influential thinkers of the twentieth century. Freud was a medical doctor who specialized in neurology. He developed his ideas about psychoanalytic theory from his work with patients with mental problems. He was born in 1856 in Austria and he died in London at the age of eighty-three. Most of his years were spent in Vienna, though he left the city near the end of his career because of the Nazis' anti-Semitism.

Sigmund Freud.

The Structure of Personality

Freud (1917) believed that personality had three structures: the id, the ego, and the superego. One way to understand the three structures is to consider them as three rulers of a country (Singer, 1984). The id is king or queen, the ego is prime minister, and the superego is high priest. The id is an absolute monarch, owed complete obedience; it is spoiled, willful, and self-centered. The id wants what it wants right now, not later. The ego as prime minister has the job of getting things done right; it is tuned into reality and is responsive to society's demands. The superego as high priest is concerned with right and wrong; the id may be greedy and needs to be told that nobler purposes should be pursued.

The **id** is the reservoir of psychic energy and instincts that perpetually press us to satisfy our basic needs—food, sex, and avoidance of pain, for example. In Freud's view, the id is completely unconscious, beyond our awareness; it has no contact with reality. The id works according to the **pleasure principle,** that is, it *always* seeks pleasure and avoids pain. Freud believed the id is the only part of personality present at birth; even in adults, the id acts like a selfish infant, demanding immediate gratification.

It would be a dangerous and scary world if our personalities were all id. As the young child develops, he learns that he cannot eat twenty-six popsicles; sometimes he is not even allowed to eat one. He also learns that he has to use the toilet instead of his diaper. As the child experiences the demands and constraints of reality, a new structure of personality is being formed—the **ego.** The ego abides by the **reality principle;** it tries to bring the individual pleasure within the boundaries of reality. Few of us are cold-blooded killers or wild

What personal experiences in your own life might influence the kind of developmental theory you would construct?

They cannot scare me with their empty empty spaces
Between stars—on stars where no human race is.
I have it in me so much nearer home
To scare myself with my own desert places.

Robert Frost

If it were possible to talk to the unborn, one could never explain to them how it feels to be alive, for life is washed in the speechless real.

Jacques Barzun, The House of Intellect, *1959*

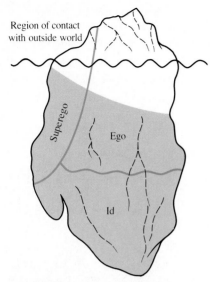

Region of contact
with outside world

Superego

Ego

Id

Figure 2.1
*This rather odd-looking diagram
illustrates Freud's belief that most of
personality's important thoughts occur
beneath the level of conscious awareness.
Whereas the ego and superego are partly
conscious and partly unconscious, the id
is completely unconscious, just like the
large, submerged part of an iceberg.*

wheeler-dealers; we take into account obstacles to our satisfaction that exist in our world. We recognize that our sexual and aggressive impulses cannot go unrestrained. The ego helps us to test reality—to see how far we can go without getting into trouble and hurting ourselves.

While the id is completely unconscious, the ego is partly conscious. It houses our higher mental functions—reasoning, problem solving, and decision making, for example. For this reason, the ego is referred to as the executive branch of personality; like an executive in a company, it makes the rational decisions that help the company succeed.

The id and the ego have no morality. They do not take into account whether something is right or wrong. This is left to the third structure of personality, the **superego,** which is referred to as the moral branch of personality. Think of the superego as what we often refer to as our "conscience." Like the id, the superego does not consider reality; it doesn't deal with what is realistic, only with whether the id's sexual and aggressive impulses can be satisfied in moral terms. You probably are beginning to sense that both the id and the superego make life rough for the ego. Your ego might say, "I will only have sex occasionally and be sure to take the proper precautions because I don't want the intrusion of a child in the development of my career." But your id is saying, "I want to be satisfied; sex is pleasurable." And your superego is at work, too, "I feel guilty about having sex."

Freud considered personality to be like an iceberg; most of personality exists below our level of awareness, just as the massive part of the iceberg is beneath the surface of the water. Figure 2.1 illustrates this analogy.

Defense Mechanisms
How does the ego resolve the conflict between its demands for reality, the wishes of the id, and the constraints of the superego? In Freud's view, the conflicting demands of the personality structures produce anxiety. For example, when the ego blocks the pleasurable pursuits of the id, an inner anxiety is felt. This diffuse, distressed state develops when the ego senses that the id is going to cause some harm for the individual. The anxiety alerts the ego to resolve the conflict by means of **defense mechanisms,** which protect the ego and reduce the anxiety produced by the conflict.

Freud thought that the most powerful and pervasive defense mechanism is **repression;** it works to push unacceptable id impulses out of our awareness and back into our unconscious mind. Repression is the foundation from which all other defense mechanisms work; the goal of every defense mechanism is to *repress* or push threatening impulses out of awareness. Freud said that our early childhood experiences, many of which he believed were sexually laden, are too threatening and conflictual for us to deal with consciously. We reduce the anxiety of this conflict through the defense mechanism of repression.

Among the other defense mechanisms we use to protect the ego and reduce anxiety are sublimation, reaction formation, and regression. **Sublimation** occurs when a socially useful course of action replaces a distasteful one. For example, an individual with strong sexual urges may turn them into socially approved behavior by becoming an artist who paints nudes. **Reaction formation** occurs when we express an unacceptable impulse by transforming it into its opposite. For example, an individual who is attracted to the brutality of war becomes a peace activist. Or an individual who fears his sexual urges becomes a religious zealot. **Regression** occurs when an individual behaves in a way that characterized a previous developmental level. When anxiety becomes too great for us, we revert to an early behavior that gave us pleasure. For example, a woman may run home to her mother every time she and her husband have a big argument.

Two final points about defense mechanisms need to be understood. First, they are unconscious; we are not aware we are using them to protect our ego. Second, when used in moderation or on a temporary basis, defense mechanisms are not necessarily unhealthy. For example, the defense mechanism of denial can help an individual cope with impending death. For the most part, though, we should not let defense mechanisms dominate our behavior and prevent us from facing reality's demands.

The Development of Personality

As Freud listened to, probed, and analyzed his patients, he became convinced that their problems were the result of experiences early in life. Freud believed that we go through five stages of psychosexual development and that at each stage of development we experience pleasure in one part of the body more than others. He called these body parts **erogenous zones** because of their pleasure-giving qualities.

Freud thought that our adult personality was determined by the way conflicts between these early sources of pleasure—the mouth, the anus, and then the genitals—and the demands of reality were resolved. When these conflicts are not resolved, the individual may become fixated at a particular stage of development. **Fixation** is closely linked with the defense mechanism of regression. Fixation occurs when an individual's needs are under- or overgratified. For example, a parent may wean a child too early, be too strict in toilet training the child, punish the child for masturbation, or smother the child with warmth. We will return to the idea of fixation and how it may show up in an adult's personality but first we need to learn more about the early stages of personality development.

During the first twelve to eighteen months of life, the activities that bring the greatest amount of pleasure center around the mouth; in the **oral stage** of development, chewing, sucking, and biting are chief pleasure sources. These actions reduce the infant's tension.

The period from about one and a half years to three years of life is called the **anal stage** because the child's greatest pleasure involves the anus, or the eliminative functions associated with it. In Freud's view, the exercise of the anal muscles reduces tension.

The **phallic stage** of development occurs approximately between the ages of three and six; its name comes from the word *phallus,* a label for penis. During the phallic stage, pleasure focuses on the genitals as the child discovers that self-manipulation is enjoyable.

In Freud's view, the phallic stage has special importance because it is during this period that the **Oedipus complex** appears. This name comes from Greek mythology, in which Oedipus, the son of the King of Thebes, unwittingly killed his father and married his mother. In the Oedipus complex, the young child develops an intense desire to replace the parent of the same sex and enjoy the affections of the opposite-sexed parent. How is the Oedipus complex resolved? At about five to six-years-of-age, children recognize that their same-sex parent might punish them for their incestuous wishes. To reduce this conflict, the child identifies with the same-sex parent, striving to be like him

(a)   (b)   (c)

(d)   (e)

Freud said we go through five stages of psychosexual development. In the oral stage (a), pleasure centers around the mouth. In the anal stage (b), pleasure focuses on the anus—the nature of toilet training is important here. In the phallic stage (c), pleasure involves the genitals—the opposite-sex parent becomes a love object here. In the latency stage (d), the child represses sexual urges—same-sex friendship is prominent. In the genital stage (e), sexual reawakening takes place—the source of pleasure now becomes someone outside of the family.

or her. If the conflict is not resolved, though, the individual may become fix-ated at the phallic stage. Table 2.1 reveals some possible links between adult personality characeristics and fixation, sublimation, and reaction formation involving the phallic stage, as well as the oral and anal stages.

In the **latency stage,** occurring between approximately six-years-of-age and puberty, the child represses all interest in sexual urges, showing more in-terest in developing intellectual and social skills. This activity channels much of the child's energy into emotionally safe areas and aids the child in forgetting the highly stressful conflicts of the phallic stage.

The **genital stage,** which occurs from puberty on, is a time of sexual reawakening; the source of sexual pleasure now becomes someone outside of the family. Freud believed that unresolved conflicts with parents reemerge during adolescence. When resolved, the individual is capable of developing a mature love relationship and functioning independently as an adult.

Because Freud explored so many new and uncharted regions of person-ality and development, it is not surprising that many individuals thought his views needed to be replaced or revised. One of these individuals, whose theory has become one of the most prominent perspectives on life-span development, was Erik Erikson.

TABLE 2.1
Possible Links Between Adult Personality Characteristics and Fixation at Oral, Anal, and Phallic Stages

Stage	Adult extensions	Sublimations	Reaction formations
Oral	Smoking, eating, kissing, oral hygiene, drinking, chewing gum	Seeking knowledge, humor, wit, sarcasm, being a food or wine expert	Speech purist, food faddist, prohibitionist, dislike of milk
Anal	Notable interest in one's bowel movements, love of bathroom humor, extreme messiness	Interest in painting or sculpture, being overly giving, great interest in statistics	Extreme disgust with feces, fear of dirt, prudishness, irritability
Phallic	Heavy reliance on masturbation, flirtatiousness, expressions of virility	Interest in poetry, love of love, interest in acting, striving for success	Puritanical attitude toward sex, excessive modesty

Phases of the life cycle	1	2	3	4	5	6	7	8
Late adulthood								Integrity vs. despair
Middle adulthood							Generativity vs. stagnation	
Young adulthood						Intimacy vs. isolation		
Adolescence					Identity vs. identity confusion			
Middle and late childhood				Industry vs. inferiority				
Early childhood			Initiative vs. guilt					
Infancy		Autonomy vs. shame, doubt						
	Trust vs. mistrust							

Figure 2.2
Erikson's eight stages of the life cycle.

Erik Erikson.

Erikson's Theory

Erik Erikson spent his childhood and adolescence in Europe. After working as a young adult under Freud's direction, Erikson came to the United States in 1933. He became a United States citizen and taught at Harvard University.

Erikson recognized Freud's contributions but he believed Freud misjudged some important dimensions of human development. For one, Erikson (1950, 1968) says that Freud placed too much emphasis on the sexual basis of development; Erikson thinks that psychosocial development holds the key to understanding life-span development. For another, Erikson says that Freud was wrong in thinking that developmental change does not occur in adulthood. And for yet another, Erikson says that humans have the potential to solve their conflicts and anxieties as they develop, painting a more optimistic picture of development than Freud's pessimistic view of the id's dominance.

For Erikson, the **epigenetic principle** guides our development through the life cycle. This principle states that anything that grows has a ground plan, out of which the parts arise, each having a special time of ascendency, until all of the parts have arisen to form a functioning whole.

In Erikson's theory, eight stages of development unfold as we go through the life cycle. He called these **psychosocial** stages (in contrast to Freud's **psychosexual** stages). The eight stages are shown in figure 2.2. Each stage consists of a unique developmental task that confronts the individual with a crisis that must be faced. For Erikson, the crisis is not a catastrophe, but a turning point of increased vulnerability and enhanced potential. The more the individual resolves the crises successfully, the healthier development will be.

The first stage, **trust versus mistrust,** corresponds to the oral stage in Freud's theory. An infant depends almost exclusively on parents, especially the mother, for food, sustenance, and comfort. Parents are the primary representative of society to the child. If parents discharge their infant-related

The Life-Span Developmental Perspective

duties with warmth, regularity, and affection, the infant will develop a feeling of trust toward the world, a trust that someone will always be around to care for one's needs. Alternatively, a sense of mistrust develops if parents fail to provide for the infant's needs in their role as caregivers.

The second stage, **autonomy versus shame and doubt,** corresponds to Freud's anal stage. The infant begins to gain control over eliminative functions and motor abilities. At this point, children show a strong push for exploring their world and asserting their will. Parents who are encouraging and patient allow the child to develop a sense of autonomy, but parents who are highly restrictive and impatient promote a sense of shame and doubt.

The third stage, **initiative versus guilt,** corresponds to Freud's phallic stage and the preschool years. The child's motor abilities continue to expand and mental abilities also become more expansive and imaginative. Parents who allow the child to continue to explore the world's unknowns and encourage symbolic thought and fantasy play promote initiative in their child; restrictive, punitive parents promote guilt and a passive recipience of whatever the environment brings.

The fourth stage, **industry versus inferiority,** corresponds to Freud's latency stage and the elementary school years. At this time, the child becomes interested in how things work and how they are made. Achievement becomes a more salient part of the child's life. If parents and teachers make work and achievement an exciting and rewarding effort, the child develops a sense of industry; if not, the child develops a sense of inferiority.

The fifth stage, **identity versus identity confusion,** corresponds to the adolescent years. At this time, indivdiuals are faced with finding out who they are, what they are all about, and where they are headed in life. Adolescents are confronted with many new roles and adult statuses—vocational and romantic, for example. Parents need to allow the adolescent to explore many different roles and different paths within a particular role. If the adolescent explores such roles in a healthy manner and arrives at a positive path to follow in life, then a positive identity will be achieved. If an identity is pushed on the adolescent by parents, if the adolescent does not adequately explore many roles, and if a positive future path is not defined, then identity confusion reigns. The stage of identity versus identity confusion is a key feature of Erikson's stages.

> Know thyself, for once we know ourselves, we may learn how to care for ourselves, otherwise we never shall.
>
> *Socrates*

The sixth stage, **intimacy versus isolation,** corresponds to the early adulthood years. Early adulthood brings a stronger commitment to an occupation and the opportunity to form intimate relationships with others. Erikson described intimacy as finding oneself yet losing oneself in another. If the young adult forms healthy friendships and an intimate close relationship with another individual, intimacy will be achieved; if not, then isolation will result.

The seventh stage, **generativity versus stagnation,** corresponds to the middle adulthood years. A chief concern of adults is to assist the younger generation in developing and leading useful lives—this is what Erikson meant by **generativity.** The feeling of having done nothing to help the next generation is **stagnation.**

> You come to a place in your life when what you've been is going to form what you will be. If you've wasted what you have in you, it's too late to do much about it. If you've invested yourself in life, you're pretty certain to get a return. If you are inwardly a serious person, in the middle years it will pay off.
>
> *Lillian Hellman*

The eighth and final stage, **integrity versus despair,** corresponds to late adulthood. In the later years of life, we look back and evaluate what we have done with our life. Through many different routes, the older individual may have developed a positive outlook in each of the previous stages of development. If so, the retrospective glances will reveal a picture of a life well spent, and the individual will feel a sense of satisfaction—integrity will be achieved.

Erikson's first psychosocial stage: trust vs. mistrust.

Second stage: autonomy vs. shame and doubt.

Third stage: initiative vs. guilt.

Fourth stage: industry vs. inferiority.

Fifth stage: identity vs. identity confusion.

Sixth stage: intimacy vs. isolation.

Seventh stage: generativity vs. stagnation.

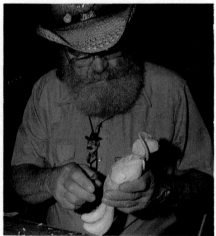

Eighth stage: integrity vs. despair.

If the older adult resolved one or more of the earlier stages negatively, the restrospective glances may yield doubt or gloom—the despair Erikson talks about.

Erikson does not believe the proper solution to a stage crisis is always completely positive in nature. Some exposure or commitment to the negative end of the individual's bipolar conflict is sometimes inevitable—you cannot trust all people under all circumstances and survive, for example. Nonetheless, in the healthy solution to a stage crisis, the positive resolution dominates.

Evaluating the Psychoanalytic Theories

While psychoanalytic theories have become heterogeneous, nonetheless, they share some core principles. Our development is determined not only by current experiences but by those from early in our life as well. The principles that early experiences are important determinants of personality and that we can better understand personality by examining it developmentally have withstood the test of time. The belief that environmental experiences are mentally transformed and represented in the mind likewise continues to receive considerable attention. Psychoanalytic theorists forced psychologists to recognize that the mind is not all consciousness; our minds have an unconscious portion that influences our behavior. Psychoanalytic theorists' emphasis on the importance of conflict and anxiety requires us to consider the dark side of our existence, not just its bright side. Adjustment is not always easy, and the individual's inner world often conflicts with the outer demands of reality.

However, the main concepts of psychoanalytic theories have been difficult to test. Inference and interpretation are required to determine whether psychoanalytic ideas are accurate. Researchers have not successfully investigated such key concepts as repression in the laboratory. Much of the data used to support psychoanalytic theories come from patients' reconstruction of the past, often the distant past, and are of doubtful accuracy. Other data come from clinicians' subjective evaluations of clients; in such cases, it is easy for the clinician to see what she expects because of the theory she holds. Some psychologists object that Freud overemphasized sexuality and the unconscious mind. The psychoanalytic theories also provide a model of the individual that is too negative and pessimistic. We are not born into the world with only a bundle of sexual and aggressive impulses; our compliance with the external demands of reality does not always conflict with our biological needs.

Cognitive Theories

Exploring the human mind has been regarded with a kind of mystical awe throughout most of human history. Now, ten thousand years after the dawn of civilization, a new understanding of the mind is flourishing. Mind is a complex term but primarily it is our cognitive activity—perception, attention, memory, language, reasoning, thinking, and the like. Whereas psychoanalytic theories emphasize unconscious thoughts, cognitive theories emphasize conscious thoughts. The developing individual is perceived as rational and logical, capable of using the mind to effectively interact with and control the environment. The cognitive theory that has dominated the study of development is the Swiss psychologist Jean Piaget's. A second important cognitive approach is information processing.

Jean Piaget.

What experiences in your own life provide examples of Piaget's concepts of assimilation and accommodation?

Piaget's Theory

Jean Piaget was born in 1896 in Switzerland. Piaget was a child genius. At the age of ten, he wrote an article about a rare albino sparrow, which was published in the *Journal of the Natural History of Neuchatel*. The article was so brilliant that the curators of the Geneva Museum of Natural History, who had no idea the article had been written by a ten-year-old, offered young Piaget the job of museum curator. The museum heads quickly rescinded their offer when they realized Piaget was only a child. Piaget continued to live in Switzerland as an adult and became one of the most influential forces in child development in the twentieth century. In a eulogy to Piaget following his death at the age of 84 in 1980, it was said that we owe him the present field of cognitive development. What was the theory of this giant in developmental psychology like?

Piaget's theory will be covered in greater detail as we discuss cognitive development in infancy, early childhood, middle and late childhood, and adolescence later in the book. Here we briefly present the main ideas in his theory. Piaget stressed that the child actively constructs his own cognitive world; information is not just poured into his mind from the environment. Two processes underlie the individual's construction of the world: organization and adaptation. To make sense of our world, we organize our experiences. For example, we separate important ideas from less important ideas. We connect one idea to another. But we not only organize our observations and experiences, we also *adapt* our thinking to include new ideas because additional information furthers understanding. Piaget (1954) believed that we adapt in two ways: assimilation and accommodation.

Assimilation occurs when we incorporate new information into our existing knowledge. **Accommodation** occurs when we adjust to new information. Consider a circumstance in which a five-year-old girl is given a hammer and nails to hang a picture on the wall. She has never used a hammer but from experience and observation she realizes that a hammer is an object to be held, that it is swung by the handle to hit the nail, and is usually swung a number of times. Recognizing each of these things, she fits her behavior into information she already has (assimilation). However, the hammer is too heavy, so she holds it near the top. She swings too hard and the nail bends, so she adjusts the pressure of her strikes. These adjustments reflect her ability to slightly alter her conception of the world (accommodation).

Piaget thought that assimilation and accommodation operate even in the young infant's life. Newborns reflexively suck everything that touches their lips (assimilation), but after several months of experience, they construct their understanding of the world differently. Some objects, such as fingers and the mother's breast, can be sucked, and others, such as fuzzy blankets, should not be sucked (accommodation).

Piaget also believed that we go through four stages in understanding the world. Each of the stages is age-related and consists of distinct ways of thinking. It is the *different* way of understanding the world that makes one stage more advanced than another; knowing *more* information does not make the child's thinking more advanced in the Piagetian view. This is what Piaget meant when he said that the child's cognition is *qualitatively* different in one stage compared to another. What are Piaget's four stages of cognitive development like?

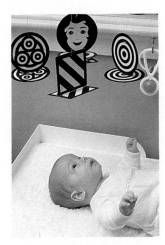

Piaget's first cognitive developmental stage: sensorimotor.

Second stage: preoperational.

Third stage: concrete operational.

Fourth stage: formal operational.

In the **sensorimotor stage,** which lasts from birth to about two years of age, the infant constructs an understanding of the world by coordinating sensory experiences (such as seeing and hearing) with physical, motoric actions—hence the term *sensorimotor.* At the beginning of this stage, the newborn has little more than reflexive patterns with which to work; at the end of the stage, the two-year-old has complex sensorimotor patterns and is beginning to operate with primitive symbols.

In the **preoperational stage,** which lasts from approximately two to seven year of age, the child begins to represent the world with words, images, and drawings; symbolic thought goes beyond simple connections of sensory information and physical action. But while the preschool child can symbolically represent the world, according to Piaget, she still cannot perform **operations,** that is mental operations that are reversible. This is why Piaget (1967) said children two to seven years of age were in the preoperational stage of thought.

In the **concrete operational stage,** which lasts from approximately seven to eleven years of age, the child can use operations—she can mentally reverse the liquid from one beaker to another and understand that the volume is the same even though the beakers are different in height and width. Logical reasoning replaces intuitive thought as long as the principles can be applied to specific or *concrete* examples. The concrete operational thinker needs objects and events present to reason about them. For example, she cannot imagine the steps necessary to complete an algebraic equation, which is far too abstract at this stage of development.

In the **formal operational stage,** which appears between the ages of eleven to fifteen, the adolescent moves beyond the world of actual, concrete experiences and thinks in abstract and more logical terms. As part of thinking more abstractly, the adolescent develops images of ideal circumstances. He may think about what an ideal parent is like and compare his parents with this ideal standard. He begins to entertain possibilities for the future and is fascinated with what he can be. In solving problems, the adolescent is more systematic, developing hypotheses about why something is happening the way it is; then he may test these hypotheses in a deductive fashion.

TABLE 2.2
Piaget's Stages of Cognitive Development

Stage	Description	Age Range
sensorimotor	The infant progresses from reflexive instinctual action at birth to the beginning of symbolic thought. The infant constructs an understanding of the world by coordinating sensory experiences with physical actions.	birth to 2
preoperational	The child begins to represent the world with words and images; these words and images reflect increased symbolic thinking and go beyond the connection of sensory information and physical action.	2 to 7
concrete operational	The child now can reason logically about concrete events and can mentally reverse information.	7 to 11
formal operational	The adolescent reasons in more abstract, idealistic, and logical ways.	11 to 15

The life cycle	Piaget's cognitive stages	Freud's psychosexual stages	Erikson's psychosocial stages	
Late adulthood			Ego integrity vs. despair	
Middle adulthood			Generativity vs. stagnation	Adolescent and adult stages
Early adulthood			Intimacy vs. isolation	
Adolescence	Formal operational	Genital	Identity vs. identity confusion (diffusion)	
Middle and late childhood	Concrete operational	Latency	Industry vs. inferiority	Middle and late childhood stages
Early childhood	Preoperational	Phallic	Initiative vs. guilt	Early childhood stages
Infancy	Sensorimotor	Anal / Oral	Autonomy vs. shame, doubt / Trust vs. mistrust	Infant stages

Figure 2.3
A comparison of Piaget's, Freud's, and Erikson's stages.

Man is a reed, the weakest in nature; but he is a thinking reed.

Pascal, 1670

Piaget's stages are summarized in Table 2.2. A comparison of Piaget's stages with Freud's and Erikson's stages is presented in figure 2.3. Notice that only Erikson's theory describes changes during the adult years. And remember that Piaget's theory stresses conscious thought while the psychoanalytic theories of Freud and Erikson stress unconscious thought. In particular, Freud was intrigued by the nature of our dreams and saw them as completely unconscious. Recently the possibility that dreams are much closer to conscious thinking than had been assumed has been explored. Focus on Life-Span Development 2.1 discusses Freud's view of dreaming and some recent Piaget-inspired research on children's dreams.

DREAMS, FREUD, AND PIAGET—

FROM BIRD-HEADED CREATURES TO BATHTUBS

Many of us dismiss the nightly excursion into the world of dreams as a second-rate mental activity not worthy of our rational selves. In focusing on the less mysterious waking world, we deny ourselves the opportunity of chance encounters with distant friends, remote places, dead relatives, gods and demons, and reworked childhood experiences. Aren't you curious about this remarkable ability of our minds and the minds of children to escape the limits of time and space?

Do you dream about pits, caves, bottles, apples, and airplanes? Do you dream about reptiles, serpents, umbrellas, and poles? If so, psychoanalytic theorists would argue that your dreams have a strong sexual symbolic content. They believe that dreams conceal but that they can be made to reveal the dreamer's conception of the world.

Freud viewed dreaming as completely unconscious and thought it reflected sexual and aggressive impulses that could not be expressed during waking hours. These impulses are always pressing for activation, he said, and dreams are an important way in which such tensions can be relieved. Freud argued that, in its final form, the dream is a distorted and symbolic version of the impulses that triggered it, and that the raw materials for dreams are traces of past perceptual experiences, including recent and distant

Figure 2.A *One of Freud's boyhood dreams. As a young boy, Freud dreamed that his mother was being carried off by two bird-headed creatures. The bird-headed creatures in the dream closely resembled illustrations from a* Bible *Freud had seen.*

encounters. He believed that dreams were highly unorganized with the pattern of elements often bizarre (see figure 2.A for a pictorial representation of one of Freud's own boyhood dreams).

Not all psychologists believe that dreams are a clash between sexual and aggressive instincts and the constraints of reality. Increasingly, psychologists describe both sleep and dreams as closer to conscious thought than had been believed in the past. For example, David Foulkes (1982) followed 42 children longitudinally from the time they were three years old until they were fifteen. Each child spent nine nights per year in

Foulke's sleep laboratory, where dream reports were obtained. Foulke's findings about dreams at different ages closely parallel Piaget's stages of conscious cognitive development. A sample of the simple dream of a preoperational child was, "I was asleep in the bathtub." There was no evidence of fantastic characters in the young children's dreams. The five- six-, and seven-year-olds began to tell more concrete stories when reporting their dreams, and the adolescents' dreams were much more abstract, reflecting the formal operational quality of their mental excursions during the night.

Figure 2.4
A model of cognition.

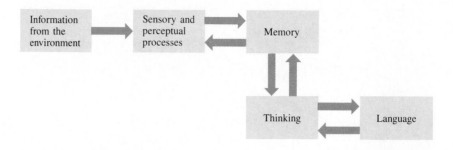

The Information Processing Approach

The **information processing approach** is concerned with how individuals process information about their world—how information enters our mind, how it is stored and transformed, and how it is retrieved to perform such complex activities as problem solving and reasoning. A simple model of cognition is shown in figure 2.4. Cognition begins when information from the world is detected through sensory and perceptual processes. Then information is stored, transformed, and retrieved through the processes of memory. Notice in our model that information can flow back and forth between memory and perceptual processes. For example, we are good at remembering the faces we see, yet at the same time, our memory of an individual's face may be different from how the individual actually looks. Keep in mind that our information processing model is a simple one, designed to illustrate the main cognitive processes and their interrelations. We could have drawn other arrows—between memory and language, between thinking and perception, and between language and perception, for example. Also, it is important to know that the boxes in the figure do not represent sharp, distinct stages in processing information. There is continuity and flow between the cognitive processes as well as overlap.

By the 1940s, serious challenges confronted the claim of behaviorists that organisms learn primarily through environment-behavior connections. The first successful computer suggested that machines could perform logical operations. This indicated that some mental operations might be modeled by computers, and possibly computers could tell us something about how cognition works. Cognitive psychologists often use the computer to help explain the relation between cognition and the brain. The physical brain is described as the computer's hardware and cognition as its software (see figure 2.5). The ability to process information has highlighted psychology's cognitive revolution since the 1950s.

What things can a computer do that a human mind cannot do? What things can a human mind do that a computer cannot?

The information processing approach raises important questions about changes in cognition across the life span. One of these questions is: Does processing speed increase as children grow older and decrease as adults grow older? The idea of speed of processing is an important aspect of the information processing approach. Many cognitive tasks are performed under real time pressure. For example, at school we have a limited amount of time to add and subtract and take tests; at work we have deadlines for completing a project. There is a good deal of evidence that processing speed is slower in younger

The Life-Span Developmental Perspective

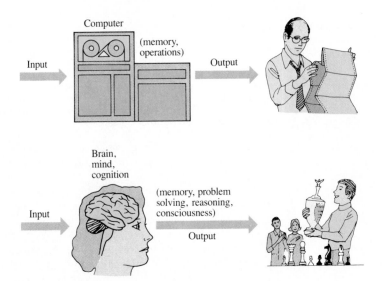

Figure 2.5
Computers and cognition: an analogy.

children than older children, and slower in elderly adults than in young adults. But the causes of these differences have not been determined. Although some might be biological in origin, they might reflect differences in knowledge about or practice on a task (Santrock & Bartlett, 1986).

Evaluating the Cognitive Theories

Both Piaget's cognitive-developmental theory and the information processing approach contribute in important ways to our knowledge about life-span development. Today, researchers enthusiastically evaluate the accuracy of Piaget's theory with the result that some of his ideas remain unscathed while others are requiring extensive modification. The information processing approach has opened up many avenues of research, offering detailed descriptions of cognitive processes and sophisticated methods for studying cognition. The cognitive theories provide an optimistic view of human development, ascribing to children and adults the ability and motivation to know their world and to cope with it in constructive ways.

Like all theories, the cognitive theories have their weaknesses. There is skepticism about the pureness of Piaget's stages and his concepts are somewhat loosely defined. The information processing approach has not yet produced an overall perspective on development. Both the Piagetian and information processing approaches may have underestimated the importance of the unconscious mind and environmental experiences, especially those involving families, in determining behavior.

So far we have discussed two main theories of life-span development— psychoanalytic and cognitive. A summary of the main ideas in these two theories is presented in Concept Table 2.1. The psychoanalytic and cognitive-developmental theories are stage theories, each highlighting the ascendence of certain characteristics at particular points in development. The remaining theories we will discuss do not specify stages in life-span development.

The Psychoanalytic and Cognitive Theories		
Concept	**Processes/Related Ideas**	**Characteristics/Description**
Psychoanalytic Theories	Freud's Theory	Freud said that our personality has three structures—id, ego, and superego—which conflict with each other. Most of our thoughts are unconscious in Freud's view and the id is completely unconscious. The conflicting demands of personality structures produce anxiety; defense mechanisms, especially repression, protect the ego and reduce anxiety. Freud was convinced that problems develop because of childhood experiences. He said we go through five psychosexual stages—oral, anal, phallic, latency, and genital. During the phallic stage, the Oedipus complex is a main source of conflict.
	Erikson's Theory	Erikson developed a theory that emphasizes eight psychosocial stages of development: trust vs. mistrust, autonomy vs. shame, doubt, initiative vs. guilt, industry vs. inferiority, identity vs. identity confusion, intimacy vs. isolation, generativity vs. stagnation, and integrity vs. despair.
	Evaluating the Psychoanalytic Theories	Strengths are an emphasis on the past, the developmental course of personality, mental representation of environment, unconscious mind, and emphasis on conflict. Weaknesses are the difficulty in testing main concepts, lack of an empirical data base and overreliance on past reports, too much emphasis on sexuality and the unconscious mind, and a negative view of human nature.

Behavioral and Social Learning Theories

Tom is engaged to marry Ann. Both have warm, friendly personalities and they enjoy being with each other. Psychoanalytic theorists would say that their warm, friendly personalities are derived from long-standing relationships with their parents, especially their early child experiences. They also would argue that the reason for their attraction is unconscious; they are unaware of how their biological heritage and early life experiences have been carried forward to influence their adult personality.

Psychologists from the behavioral and social learning perspectives would observe Tom and Ann and see something quite different. They would examine their experiences, especially their most recent ones, to understand the reason for their attraction. Tom would be described as rewarding Ann's behavior, and vice versa, for example. No reference would be made to unconscious thoughts, the Oedipus complex, defense mechanisms, and so on.

The Psychoanalytic and Cognitive Theories		
Concept	**Processes/Related Ideas**	**Characteristics/Description**
Cognitive Theories	Piaget's Theory	Piaget's theory is responsible for the field of cognitive development. He believes we are motivated to understand our world and use the processes of organization and adaptation (assimilation, accommodation) to do so. Piaget says we go through four cognitive stages: sensorimotor, preoperational, concrete operational, and formal operational.
	Information Processing Approach	Is concerned with how we process information about our world. Includes how information gets into our mind, how it is stored and transformed, and how it is retrieved to think and solve problems. The development of the computer promoted this approach, as the mind as an information processing system was compared to how a computer processes information. The information processing approach raises questions about life-span development, among them the rise and decline of speed of processing information.
	Evaluating the Cognitive Theories	Both the Piagetian and information processing approaches have made important contributions to life-span development. They have provided a positive, rational portrayal of humans as they develop, although they may have underestimated the importance of unconscious thought and environmental experiences. The purity of Piaget's stages have been questioned and the information processing approach has not yet produced an overall perspective on development.

Behaviorists believe we should examine only what can be directly observed and measured. At approximately the same time Freud was interpreting his patients' unconscious minds through early childhood experiences, behaviorists such as Ivan Pavlov and John B. Watson were conducting detailed observations of behavior under controlled laboratory conditions. Out of the behavioral tradition grew the belief that development is observable behavior, learned through experiences with the environment. The two versions of the behavioral approach that are prominent today are the behavioral view of B. F. Skinner and social learning theory.

You know more of a road by having travelled it than by all the conjectures and descriptions in the world.
William Hazlitt, Literary Remains, *1836*

Skinner's Behaviorism
During World War II, B. F. Skinner constructed a rather strange project—a pigeon-guided missile. A pigeon in the warhead of the missile operated the flaps on the missile and guided it home by pecking at an image of a target.

B. F. Skinner.

Consider your life during the last 24 hours. How did rewards and punishments influence the way you behaved during this time frame?

How could this possibly work? When the missile was in flight, the pigeon pecked the moving image on the screen. This produced corrective signals to keep the missile on its course. The pigeons did their job well in trial runs, but top Navy officials just could not accept pigeons piloting their missiles during a war. Skinner, however, congratulated himself on the degree of control he was able to exercise over the pigeons.

Following the pigeon experiment, Skinner (1948) wrote *Walden Two,* a novel in which he presented his ideas about building a scientifically managed society. Skinner envisioned a utopian society that could be engineered through behavioral control. Skinner viewed existing societies as poorly managed because individuals believe in myths such as free will. He pointed out that humans are no more free than pigeons; denying that our behavior is controlled by environmental forces is to ignore science and reality, he argued. In the long run, Skinner said we would be much happier when we recognized such truths, especially his concept that we could live a prosperous life under the control of positive reinforcement.

Skinner did not need the mind, conscious or unconscious, to explain development. For him, development was the individual's behavior. For example, observations of Sam reveal that his behavior is shy, achievement-oriented, and caring. Why is Sam's behavior this way? For Skinner, rewards and punishments in Sam's environment have shaped him into a shy, achievement-oriented, and caring individual. Because of interactions with family members, friends, teachers, and others, Sam has *learned* to behave in this fashion.

Since behaviorists believe that development is learned and often changes according to environmental experiences, it follows that rearranging experiences can change the individual's development. For the behaviorist, shy behavior can be changed into outgoing behavior; aggressive behavior can be shaped into docile behavior; lethargic, boring behavior can be turned into enthusiastic, interesting behavior.

Skinner describes the way in which behavior is controlled in the following way. The individual *operates* on the environment to produce a change that will lead to a reward (Skinner, 1938). Skinner chose the term *operants* to describe the responses that are actively emitted because of the consequences for the individual. The consequences—rewards and punishments—are *contingent,* or depend on the individual's behavior. For example, an operant might be pressing a lever on a machine that delivers a candy bar; the delivery of the candy bar is contingent on pressing the lever. In sum, **operant conditioning** is a form of learning in which the consequences of behavior lead to changes in the probability of that behavior's occurrence.

More needs to be said about reinforcement and punishment. **Reinforcement** (or reward) is a consequence that increases the probability a behavior will occur. By contrast, **punishment** is a consequence that decreases the probability a behavior will occur. For example, if someone smiles at you and the two of you continue talking for some time, the smile has reinforced your talking. However, if someone you meet frowns at you and you quickly leave the situation, the frown has punished your talking with the individual.

Social Learning Theory

Some psychologists believe the behaviorists basically are right when they say development is learned and is influenced strongly by environmental experiences. But they believe Skinner went too far in declaring that cognition is

The Life-Span Developmental Perspective

unimportant in understanding development. **Social learning theory** is the view of psychologists who emphasize behavior, environment, *and* cognition as the key factors in development.

The social learning theorists say we are not like mindless robots, responding mechanically to others in our environment. And we are not like weathervanes, behaving like a Communist in the presence of a Communist or like a John Bircher in the presence of a John Bircher. Rather, we think, reason, imagine, plan, expect, interpret, believe, value, and compare. When others try to control us, our values and beliefs allow us to restrict their control.

Albert Bandura (1977, 1986) and Walter Mischel (1973, 1984) are the main architects of the contemporary version of social learning theory, which was labeled **cognitive social learning theory** by Mischel. Bandura believes much of our learning occurs by observing what others do. Through observational learning (also called modeling or imitation), we cognitively represent the behavior of others and then possibly adopt this behavior ourselves. For example, a young boy may observe his father's aggressive outbursts and hostile interchanges with people; when observed with his peers, the young boy's style of interaction is highly aggressive, showing the same characteristics as his father's behavior. Or, a young female executive adopts the dominant and sarcastic style of her boss. When observed interacting with one of her subordinates, the young woman says, "I need this work immediately if not sooner; you are so far behind you think you are ahead!" Social learning theorists believe we acquire a wide range of such behaviors, thoughts, and feelings through observing others' behavior; these observations form an important part of our development.

Social learning theorists also differ from Skinner's behavioral view by emphasizing that we can regulate and control our own behavior. For example, another young female executive who observed her boss behave in a dominant and sarcastic manner toward employees found the behavior distasteful and went out of her way to be encouraging and supportive toward her subordinates. Someone tries to persuade you to join a particular social club on campus and makes you an enticing offer. You reflect about the offer, consider your interests and beliefs, and make the decision not to join. Your **cognition** (your thoughts) leads you to control your behavior and resist environmental influence in this instance.

Bandura's (1986) most recent model of learning and development involves behavior, the person, and the environment. As shown in figure 2.6, behavior, cognitive and other personal factors, and environmental influences operate interactively. Behavior can influence cognition and vice versa, the person's cognitive activities can influence the environment, environmental influences can change the person's thought processes, and so on.

Let's consider how Bandura's model might work in the case of a college student's achievement behavior. As the student diligently studies and gets good grades, her behavior produces positive thoughts about her abilities. As part of her effort to make good grades, she plans and develops a number of strategies to make her studying more efficient. In these ways, her behavior has influenced her thought and her thought influenced her behavior. At the beginning of the semester, her college made a special effort to involve students in a study skills program. She decided to join. Her success, along with that of other students who attended the program, has led the college to expand the program next semester. In these ways, environment influenced behavior, and behavior changed the environment. And the expectations of the college administrators that the study skills program would work made it possible in the first place.

Albert Bandura.

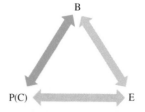

Figure 2.6
Bandura's model of the reciprocal influence of behavior, personal and cognitive factors, and environment. P(C) stands for personal and cognitive factors, B for behavior, and E for environment. The arrows reflect how relations between these factors are reciprocal rather than unidirectional. Examples of personal factors include intelligence, skills, and self-control. From Albert Bandura, Social Foundations of Thought and Action: A Social Cognitive Theory, *© 1986, p. 24. Reprinted by permission of Prentice-Hall, Inc., Englewood Cliffs, N.J.*

The program's success has spurred expectations that this type of program could work in other colleges. In these ways, cognition changed the environment, and the environment changed cognition. Expectations are an important variable in Bandura's model.

Like the behavioral approach of Skinner, the social learning approach emphasizes the importance of empirical research in studying development. This research focuses on the processes that explain development—the social and cognitive factors that influence what we are like as people.

Evaluating the Behavioral and Social Learning Theories

The behavioral and social learning theories emphasize that environmental experiences determine development. These approaches have fostered a scientific climate for understanding development that highlights the observation of behavior. Social learning theory emphasizes both environmental influences and cognitive processes in explaining development; this view also suggests individuals have the ability to control their environment.

The criticisms of the behavioral and social learning theories sometimes are directed at the behavioral view alone and at other times at both approaches. The behavioral view has been criticized for ignoring the importance of cognition in development and placing too much importance on environmental experiences. Both approaches have been described as being too concerned with change and situational influences on development, not paying adequate tribute to the enduring qualities of development. Both views are said to ignore the biological determinants of development. Both are labeled as reductionistic, which means they look at only one or two components of development rather than at how all of the pieces fit together. And critics have charged that the behavioral and social learning theories are too mechanical. By being overly concerned with several minute pieces of development, the most exciting and rich dimensions of development are missed, say the detractors. This latter criticism—that the creative, spontaneous, and human characteristics of development are missing from the behavioral and social learning theories—has been made on numerous occasions by adherents of the humanistic approach, which we consider next.

Phenomenological and Humanistic Theories

Remember our example of the engaged couple, Tom and Ann, who were described as having warm, friendly personalities. Phenomenological and humanistic psychologists would describe their warm, friendly personalities as reflecting their inner self; they would emphasize that a key to understanding their attraction is their positive perception of each other. Tom and Ann are not viewed as controlling each other's behavior; rather they have determined their own course of action and each freely chosen to marry. No recourse to biological instincts or unconscious thoughts as determinants of their attraction occurs in the phenomenological and humanistic theories.

The **phenomenological approach** stresses the importance of our perceptions of ourselves and our world in understanding development; the approach centers on the belief that for each individual, reality is what is *perceived*. The most widely known phenomenological approach is the **humanistic perspective,** which stresses the importance of self-perceptions, inner experiences, self-determination, and self-confidence. Humanistic psychologists emphasize the positive qualities of individuals, believing they have the ability to handle stress, control their lives, and achieve what they desire. Each of us has the ability to break through and understand ourselves and our world; we can burst the cocoon and become a butterfly, say the humanistic psychologists.

You may be able to sense that the phenomenological and humanistic approaches provide stark contrasts to the psychoanalytic approach to development, which is based on conflict and has little faith in the individual's ability to understand his development, and to the behavioral view, which emphasizes that an individual's behavior is determined by rewards and punishments from others. Two of the leading architects of the phenomenological and humanistic approaches are Carl Rogers and Abraham Maslow.

Roger's Theory

Like Freud, Rogers (1961) began his inquiry about human nature with troubled personalities. Rogers explored the human potential for change; in the knotted, anxious, defensive verbal stream of his clients, he concluded that individuals are prevented from becoming who they are.

Carl Rogers

Rogers believed that most individuals have considerable difficulty accepting their own true feelings, which are innately positive. As we grow up, significant others condition us to move away from these positive feelings. Our parents, siblings, teachers, and peers place constraints and contingencies on our behavior; too often we hear, "Don't do that," "You didn't do that right," "How could you be so stupid?" and "You didn't try hard enough." When we don't do something right, we often get punished. And parents may even threaten to take away their love. Thus, Rogers believed that each of us is a victim of **conditional positive regard,** meaning that love and praise are not given unless we conform to parental or social standards. The result is that our self-esteem is lowered.

These constraints and negative feedback continue during our adult lives. The result is that our relationships either carry the dark cloud of conflict or we conform to what others want; too infrequently are we allowed to express ourselves positively. As we struggle to live up to society's standards, we distort and devalue our true self. And we may even completely lose our sense of self by mirroring what others want (Rogers, 1961).

Through the individual's experiences with the world, a self emerges—this is the "I" or "me" of your existence. Rogers did not believe that all aspects of the self are conscious, but he did believe they are all accessible to consciousness. The self is construed as a whole; it consists of self-perceptions (how attractive I am, how well I get along with others, how good an athlete I am) and the values we attach to these perceptions (good-bad, worthy-unworthy, for example).

Rogers also considered the congruence between the real self, that is, the self as it really is as a result of our experiences, and the ideal self, which is the self we would like to be. (Figure 2.7 shows a portrait that reflects the real and ideal self.) The greater the discrepancy between the real self and the ideal self, the more maladjusted we will be, said Rogers. To improve our adjustment, we can develop more positive perceptions of our real self, not worry so much about what others want, and increase our positive experiences in the world. In such ways, our real self and ideal self will be closer.

Rogers thinks that each of us should be valued regardless of our behavior. Even when our behavior is obnoxious, below acceptable standards, or inappropriate, we need the respect, comfort, and love of others. When these

Figure 2.7
Half-naked, half-clothed, Picasso's 1932 portrayal of a Girl before a Mirror, *reflects the twin images of Carl Rogers' ideal and real self.*

positive behaviors are given without contingency, this is known as **unconditional positive regard.** Rogers believed strongly that unconditional positive regard elevates our self-worth and positive self-regard. Unconditional positive regard is directed to the individual as a person of worth and dignity, not to his behavior, which may not deserve positive regard (Rogers, 1974).

Rogers (1980) also stressed the importance of becoming a fully functioning person. What is a fully functioning person like? She is open to experience, is not very defensive, is aware of and sensitive to the self and the external world, and for the most part has a harmonious relationship with others. A discrepancy between our real self and our ideal self may occur; others may try to control us; and our world may have too little unconditional positive regard; but Rogers believed that we are highly resilient and capable of becoming a fully functioning person. He believed that our good side could not be kept down.

This self-actualizing tendency of ours is reflected in Rogers' comparison of a person with a plant he once observed on the coastline of northern California. Rogers was looking out at the waves beating furiously against the jagged rocks, shooting mountains of spray into the air. Rogers noticed a tiny palm tree on the rocks, no more than two or three feet high, taking the pounding of the breakers. The plant was fragile and top-heavy; it seemed clear that the waves would crush the tiny specimen. A wave would crunch the plant, bending its slender trunk almost flat and whipping its leaves in a torrent of spray. Yet the moment the wave passed, the plant was erect, tough, and resilient once again. It was incredible that the plant could take this incessant pounding hour after hour, week after week, possibly year after year, all the time nourishing itself, maintaining its position, and growing. In this tiny plant, Rogers saw the tenacity of life, the forward thrust of development, and the ability of a living thing to push into a hostile environment and not only hold its own, but adapt, develop, and become itself. So it is with each of us, in Rogers' view (Rogers, 1963).

Maslow's Theory

Abraham Maslow was one of the most powerful forces behind the humanistic movement in psychology. He called the humanistic approach the "third force" in psychology, that is, an important alternative to the psychoanalytic and behavioral forces. Maslow pointed out that psychoanalytic theories place too much emphasis on disturbed individuals and their conflicts. Behaviorists ignore the person altogether, he said.

Maslow (1971) set out to chart the human potential of creative, talented, and healthy individuals. These people, he believed, strive for self-actualization and try to become the best they can possibly be. Like Rogers, Maslow said each of us has a basic goodness, a drive to be something positive; each of us has the capacity for love, joy, and self-development.

Is getting an A in this class more important to you than eating? If the person of your dreams told you that you were marvelous would that motivate you to throw yourself in front of a car for her safety? According to Maslow (1954, 1971), our "basic" needs must be satisfied before we can satisfy our "higher" needs. Based on Maslow's **hierarchy of motives,** we would conclude that in most instances individuals need to eat before they can achieve and that they need to satisfy their safety needs before their love needs. Maslow believes that we have five basic needs, which unfold in the following sequence: physiological, safety, love and belongingness, self-esteem, and self-actualization (see figure 2.8).

We carry with us the wonders we seek without us.

Sir Thomas Browne, 1642

Abraham Maslow

TABLE 2.3
Maslow's Characteristics of a Self-Actualized Individual

Realistic orientation

Self-acceptance and acceptance of others and the natural world as they are

Spontaneity

Problem-centered rather than self-centered

Air of detachment and need for privacy

Autonomous and independent

Fresh rather than stereotyped appreciation of people and things

Generally have had profound mystical or spiritual, though not necessarily religious, experiences

Identification with humankind and a strong social interest

Tendency to have strong intimate relationships with a few special, loved people rather than superficial relationships with many people

Democratic values and attitudes

No confusion of means with ends

Philosophical rather than hostile sense of humor

High degree of creativity

Resistance to cultural conformity

Transcendence of environment rather than always coping with it

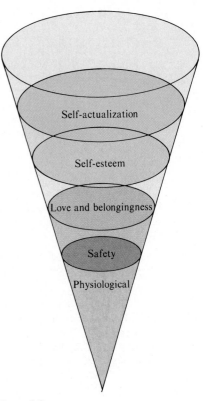

Figure 2.8
Maslow's hierarchy of needs. Only when the needs in the smaller circles are reasonably satisfied can self-actualization be accomplished.

It is the need for self-actualization that Maslow has described in the greatest detail. **Self-actualization** is becoming everything you are capable of becoming. According to Maslow, self-actualization is possible only after the other needs in the hierarchy are met. Obviously, you cannot be everything you are capable of being if you are hungry all of the time. Individuals who are self-actualized feel a sense of fulfillment and they are content with their philosophy and outlook on life. Their behavior reflects these feelings. Maslow cautions that most individuals stop maturing after they have developed a high level of self-esteem and thus they do not become self-actualized.

Many of Maslow's writings focus on how individuals can reach the elusive state of development he called self-actualization. Maslow developed psychological profiles of famous individuals and concluded that such individuals as Eleanor Roosevelt, Albert Einstein, Abraham Lincoln, Walt Whitman, William James, and Ludwig van Beethoven were self-actualized. On the basis of his interpretations of individuals' lives, he concluded that the characteristics listed in Table 2.3 reflect self-actualization.

Look carefully at the list of characteristics in table 2.3 that describe Maslow's self-actualized individual. Do you know any famous individuals or individuals in your everyday world who possess the package of characteristics described by Maslow?

Evaluating the Phenomenological and Humanistic Theories

The phenomenological and humanistic theories have sensitized us to the importance of phenomenological experience; our perceptions of ourselves and our world are key ingredients of development. The emphasis on consciousness likewise has had a significant impact on how we view development. The humanistic psychologists remind us that we need to consider the whole person and the individual's positive nature. The contribution of these approaches has been felt in human relations; many individuals believe the humanistic approach has helped them to understand both themselves and others. And the approaches have facilitated our ability to effectively communicate with others.

One weakness of these approaches is that they are very hard to test scientifically. Self-actualization, for instance, is not clearly defined. Psychologists are not certain how to study this concept empirically. Some humanistic psychologists even scorn the scientific approach, preferring clinical interpretation as a data base. Verification of humanistic concepts has come mainly from clinical experiences rather than controlled scientific efforts. Some critics also believe these approaches are *too* optimistic about human nature; they possibly overestimate the freedom and rationality of humans. And some critics say these approaches encourage self-love and narcissism.

Ethological Theories

Sensitivity to different kinds of experience varies over the individual's life cycle. The presence or absence of certain experiences at particular times in the life span influences the individual well beyond the time that they first occur. Ethologists believe that most psychologists underestimate the importance of these special time frames in development and the contribution biology makes to development.

Lorenz's Classical Ethological Theory

Ethology emerged as an important view because of the work of European zoologists, especially Konrad Lorenz. **Ethology** stresses that behavior is biologically determined. Ethologists believe that we can only fully appreciate a person's behavior if we recognize that the behavior is tied to evolution. Ethologists also remind us that early experience plays an important part in development and potentially is irreversible.

Working mostly with graylag geese, Lorenz (1965) studied a behavior pattern that was considered to be programmed within the genes of the animals. A newly hatched gosling seemed to be born with the instinct for following its mother. Observations showed that the gosling was capable of such behavior as soon as it was hatched from the egg. Lorenz proved that it was incorrect to assume that such behavior was programmed in the animal.

In a remarkable set of experiments, Lorenz separated the eggs laid by one female goose into two groups. One group he returned to the female goose to be hatched by her; the other group was hatched in an incubator. The goslings in the first group performed as predicted; they followed their mother as soon as they were hatched. But those in the second group, who saw Lorenz when they were first hatched, followed him everywhere, just as though he were their mother. Lorenz marked the goslings and then placed both groups under a box. Mother goose and "mother" Lorenz stood aside as the box lifted. Each group of goslings went directly to its "mother" (see figure 2.9). Lorenz called this process **imprinting**—rapid, innate learning within a limited critical period of time which involves attachment to the first moving object seen.

The ethological view of Lorenz and the European zoologists forced American developmental psychologists to recognize the importance of the biological basis of behavior. But the research and theorizing of ethology still seemed to lack some ingredients that would elevate it to the ranks of the other theories discussed so far in this chapter. In particular, there was little or nothing in the classical ethological view about the nature of social relationships across the human life cycle, something that any major theory of development must explain. And the concept of **critical period**—a fixed time period very early in

The tide of evolution carries everything before it, thoughts no less than bodies, and persons no less than nations.
George Santayana, Little Essays, *1920*

Figure 2.9
Konrad Lorenz, a pioneering student of animal behavior, is followed through the water by three imprinted graylag geese.

development during which certain behaviors optimally emerge—seemed to be overdrawn. Classical ethological theory had been weak in stimulating studies with humans. Recent expansion of the ethological view has improved its status as a viable developmental perspective.

Hinde's Neo-Ethological Theory

Ethologist Robert Hinde (1983) developed a view that goes beyond classical ethological theory by emphasizing the importance of social relationships, describing sensitive periods of development rather than critical periods, and presenting a framework that is beginning to stimulate research with human children and adults. Insight into Hinde's neo-ethological theory appears in the form of his discussion of selected issues of interest to ethologists.

Like behaviorists, ethologists are careful observers of behavior. Unlike behaviorists, ethologists believe that laboratories are not good settings for observing behavior; rather, they observe behavior in its natural surroundings. Behavior should be meticulously observed in homes, playgrounds, neighborhoods, schools, hospitals, and so on.

Robert Hinde, professor of psychology at Cambridge University, England.

Ethologists also point out that children's development is studied by adults, who see the end point of development being mature adulthood. However, ethologists believe that an infant's or child's behavior should not always be considered in terms of its importance for mature adulthood. Rather, a behavior may be adaptive at an early stage of development only. For example, caterpillars are excellent leaf eaters, but they do not pretend to be butterflies. Ethologists believe the word *development* too often diverts attention away from viewing each stage of development in its own right.

Ethologists emphasize sensitive periods. Hinde distinguishes between critical and sensitive periods. Classical ethologists, such as Lorenz, argued for the importance of critical periods in development. The more recently developed concept of **sensitive period** emphasizes a more flexible band of time for a behavior to optimally emerge; sensitive periods occur on the order of months and even years rather than days or weeks. With human children, there seem to be some flexible sensitive periods for processes such as language, vision, and attachment (Bornstein, 1987).

Behavioral and Social Learning, Humanistic and Phenomenological, and Ethological Theories		
Concept	Processes/Related Ideas	Characteristics/Description
The Behavioral and Social Learning Theories	Skinner's Behaviorism	Emphasizes that cognition is unimportant in development; development is observed behavior, which is influenced by the rewards and punishments in the environment.
	Social Learning Theory	The environment is an important determinant of development, but so are cognitive processes. We have the capability of controlling our own behavior through thoughts, beliefs, and values. Bandura's emphasis on observational learning exemplifies the social learning approach, as does his model of the reciprocal influences of behavior, person (cognition), and environment. The contemporary version of social learning theory is called cognitive social learning theory.
	Evaluating the Behavioral and Social Learning	The strengths of both theories include emphasis on environmental determinants and a scientific climate for investigating development, as well as the focus on cognitive processes and self-control in social learning theory. The behavioral view has been criticized for taking the person out of development and for ignoring cognition. These approaches have not given adequate attention to biological factors and to development as a whole.
The Phenomenological and Humanistic Theories	Their Nature	The phenomenological approach emphasizes our perceptions of ourselves and our world and centers on the belief that reality is what is perceived. The humanistic approach is the most widely known phenomenological approach.
	Roger's Theory	Each of us is a victim of conditional positive regard. The result is that our real self is not valued. The self is the core of development; it includes the real and ideal self. Rogers advocates unconditional positive regard to enhance our self-concept. Each of us has the innate, inner capacity of becoming a fully functioning person.

Ethologists also are becoming interested in social relationships and personality. Hinde argues that certain properties of relationships, such as synchrony and competitiveness, do not describe individuals in isolation. Relationships have properties that emerge from the frequency and patterning of interactions over time. For example, if the mother-infant relationship is studied at one point in development, researchers may not be able to describe it as rejecting, controlling, or permissive. But through detailed observations over a period of time, such categorization may be possible.

Behavioral and Social Learning, Humanistic and Phenomenological, and Ethological Theories		
Concept	**Processes/Related Ideas**	**Characteristics/Description**
	Maslow's Theory	Maslow called the humanistic approach the third force in psychology. He also proposed that we have a hierarchy of motives, with lower needs requiring satisfaction before the higher needs; self-actualization is the highest need.
	Evaluating the Phenomenological and Humanistic Approaches	These approaches sensitize us to the importance of subjective experience, consciousness, self-conception, the whole person, and our innate, positive nature. Their weaknesses focus on the absence of a scientific orientation, a tendency to be too optimistic, and an inclination to encourage self-love.
The Ethological Theories	Lorenz's Classical Ethological Theory	The biological and evolutionary basis of development needs to be emphasized. Critical periods, at which time a characteristic has an optimal time of emergence, occur in development.
	Hinde's Neo-ethological Theory	Emphasizes sensitive rather than critical periods. Places a premium on naturalistic observation and biological/evolutionary ties but also focuses on social relationships and personality.
	Evaluating the Ethological Theories	Strengths include the emphasis on the biological and evolutionary basis of behavior, naturalistic observation, and sensitive periods. Weaknesses include the rigidity of the critical period concept, an overemphasis on biology and evolution, a failure to generate studies of human development, and the inability to predict behavior prospectively.

Evaluating the Ethological Theories

Ethological theory emphasizes the biological and evolutionary basis of behavior, giving biology an appropriate, prominent role in development. Ethologists use careful observations in naturalistic surroundings to obtain information about development. And ethologists believe development involves sensitive periods.

However, like other theories we have discussed, ethology has its weaknesses. At times, even the emphasis on sensitive periods seems to be too rigid; the critical period concept is too rigid for human development. The emphasis still slants more toward biological-evolutionary explanations of behavior rather than a biological-environmental mix. The theory has been slow in generating research about human life-span development. The theory is better at explaining behavior retrospectively than prospectively. That is, ethology is better at explaining what happened to cause a child's behavior after it happens than predicting its occurrence in the future.

Since our overview of psychoanalytic and cognitive theories, we have discussed three additional theories—behavioral and social learning, phenomenological and humanistic, and ethological. A summary of the main ideas in these theories is presented in Concept Table 2.2.

An Eclectic Theoretical Orientation

No single indomitable theory is capable of explaining the rich complexity of life-span development. Each of the theories described in this chapter has made important contributions to our understanding of life-span development, but none provides a complete description and explanation. Psychoanalytic theory best explains the unconscious mind. Erikson's theory best describes the changes that occur in adult development. Piaget's theory is the most complete description of children's cognitive development. The behavioral and social learning theories have been the most adept at examining the environmental determinants of development. The phenomenological and humanistic theories have given us the most insight about self-conception. And the ethological theories have made us aware of biology's role and the importance of sensitive periods in development. It is important to recognize that, while theories are helpful guides in understanding life-span development, relying on a single theory to explain life-span development probably is a mistake.

An attempt was made in this chapter to present five theoretical perspectives objectively. The same eclectic orientation will be maintained throughout the book. In this way, you can view the study of life-span development as it actually exists—with different theorists making different assumptions about development, stressing different empirical problems, and using different strategies to discover information about life-span development.

These theoretical perspectives, along with the research issues and methods described in chapter 1, provide a sense of life-span development's scientific nature. Table 2.4 compares the five main theoretical perspectives in terms of how they view some of the issues we have discussed thus far. By studying Table 2.4, you should be able to integrate some of the most important ideas about issues and methods described in chapter 1 with the main theories described in chapter 2.

TABLE 2.4
Theoretical Comparisons and Issues and Methods in Life-Span Development

Issues and Methods	Theories				
	Psychoanalytic	Cognitive	Behavioral and Social Learning	Phenomenological and Humanistic	Ethological
Continuity and Discontinuity	Discontinuity between stages, but continuity between early experiences and later development; later changes in development emphasized in Erikson's theory.	Discontinuity between stages, but continuity between early experiences and later development in Piaget's theory; this has not been an important issue to information processing psychologists.	Continuity (No stages). Experience at all points of development important.	Continuity (No stages). Experience at all points in development important, especially immediate experience.	Discontinuity but no stages are given; critical or sensitive periods are emphasized.
Biological and Environmental Factors	Freud stressed biological determination interacting with early experiences in the family; Erikson provides a more balanced biological-cultural interaction perspective.	Piaget emphasizes biological adaptation. Environment provides the setting for cognitive structures to unfold. Information processing perspective has not addressed this issue extensively, but hardware-software metaphor emphasizes biological-environmental interaction.	Environment viewed as the cause of behavior in both the behavioral and social learning views.	Environmental influences emphasized, especially warmth and nurturance.	Strong biological view.
Importance of Cognition	Cognition is emphasized, but in the form of unconscious thought.	Cognition is the primary determinant of behavior.	Cognition is strongly deemphasized in the behavioral approach but plays an important mediating role in the social learning approach.	Cognition is important, especially in the form of self-perception.	Cognition is not emphasized.
Research Methods	Clinical interviews, unstructured personality tests, and psychohistorical analyses of lives.	Interviews and observations.	Observation, especially laboratory observation.	The scientific approach is deemphasized; self-report measures and interviews are used.	Observation in natural settings.

Summary

I. Freud's Theory

Freud said that our personality has three structures—id, ego, and superego—which conflict with each other. Most of our thoughts are unconscious in Freud's view, and the id is completely unconscious. The conflicting demands of personality structures produce anxiety; defense mechanisms, especially repression, protect the ego and reduce anxiety. Freud was convinced that problems develop because of childhood experiences. He said we go through five psychosexual stages—oral, anal, phallic, latency, and genital. During the phallic stage, the Oedipus complex is a main source of conflict.

II. Erikson's Theory and Evaluation of the Psychoanalytic Theories

Erikson developed a theory that emphasizes eight psychosocial stages of development: trust vs. mistrust, autonomy vs. shame and doubt, initiative vs. guilt, industry vs. inferiority, identity vs. identity confusion, intimacy vs. isolation, generativity vs. stagnation, and integrity vs. despair. Strengths of the psychoanalytic theories are an emphasis on the past, the developmental course of personality, mental representation of the environment, unconscious mind, and emphasis on conflict. Weaknesses are the difficulty in testing main concepts, lack of an empirical data base and overreliance on past reports, too much emphasis on sexuality and the unconscious mind, and a negative view of human nature.

III. Piaget's Theory

Piaget's theory is responsible for the field of cognitive development. He believed we are motivated to understand our world and use the processes of organization and adaptation (assimilation and accommodation) to do so. Piaget said that we go through four cognitive stages: sensorimotor, preoperational, concrete operational, and formal operational.

IV. Information Processing Approach and Evaluation of the Cognitive Theories

The information processing approach is concerned with how we process information about our world. It includes how information gets into the mind, how it is stored and transformed, and how it is retrieved to think and solve problems. The development of the computer promoted this approach; the mind as an information processing system was compared to the way a computer processes information. The information processing approach raises questions about life-span development, among them the rise and decline of speed of processing information. Both the Piagetian and information processing approaches have made important contributions to life-span development. They have provided a positive, rational portrayal of humans as they develop, although they may have underestimated the importance of unconscious thought and environmental experiences. The purity of Piaget's stages has been questioned, and the information processing approach has not yet produced an overall perspective on development.

V. The Behavioral and Social Learning Theories

Skinner's behaviorism emphasizes that cognition is unimportant in development; development is observed behavior, which is influenced by the rewards and punishments in the environment. In social learning theory, the environment is an important determinant of development, but so are cognitive processes. We have the ability to control our own behavior through thoughts, beliefs, and values. Bandura's emphasis on observational learning and his model of the reciprocal influences of behavior, person (cognition), and environment exemplify social learning theory. The contemporary version of social learning theory is called cognitive social learning theory.

VI. Evaluating the Behavioral and Social Learning Theories

The strengths of both theories include emphasis on environmental determinants and a scientific climate for investigating development, as well as a focus on cognitive processes and self-control in social learning theory. The behavioral view has been criticized for taking the person out of development and for ignoring cognition. These approaches have not adequately considered biological factors and development as a whole.

VII. The Phenomenological and Humanistic Theories

The phenomenological approach emphasizes our perceptions of ourselves and our world and centers on the belief that reality is what is perceived. The humanistic approach is the most widely known phenomenological approach. In Rogers' theory, each of us is a victim of conditional positive regard. The result is that our real self is not valued. The self is the core of development; it includes the real self and the ideal self. Rogers advocates unconditional positive regard to enhance our self-concept. Each of us has the innate, inner capacity to become a fully functioning person. Maslow called the humanistic approach the third force in psychology. He also proposed that we have a hierarchy of motives, with lower needs requiring satisfaction before higher needs; self-actualization is the highest need. These approaches have sensitized developmentalists to the importance of subjective experience, consciousness, self-conception, the whole person, and our innate, positive nature. Their weaknesses focus on the absence of a scientific orientation, a tendency to be too optimistic, and an inclination to encourage self-love.

VIII. The Ethological Theories

Ethological theories emphasize the biological and evolutionary basis of development. In Lorenz's classical ethological theory, critical periods—at which time a characteristic has an optimal time of emergence—are emphasized. In Hinde's neo-ethological theory, sensitive periods rather than critical periods are stressed, along with naturalistic observation, and social relationships and personality. Strengths include the emphasis on biological and evolutionary bases of behavior, naturalistic observation, and sensitive periods. Weaknesses include the rigidity of critical periods, an overemphasis on biology and evolution, a failure to generate studies of human development, and the inability to predict behavior prospectively.

IX. An Eclectic Theoretical Orientation

No single theory can explain the rich, awesome complexity of life-span development. Each of the theories has made a different contribution, and it probably is a wise strategy to adopt an eclectic theoretical perspective as we attempt to understand the nature of life-span development.

Key Terms

id *37*
pleasure principle *37*
ego *37*
reality principle *37*
superego *38*
defense mechanisms *38*
repression *38*
sublimation *38*
reaction formation *38*
regression *38*
erogenous zones *39*
fixation *39*
oral stage *39*
anal stage *39*
phallic stage *39*
Oedipus complex *39*
latency stage *40*

genital stage *40*
epigenetic principle *42*
psychosocial *42*
psychosexual *42*
trust versus mistrust *42*
autonomy versus shame and doubt *43*
initiative versus guilt *43*
industry versus inferiority *43*
identity versus identity confusion *43*
intimacy versus isolation *43*
generativity versus stagnation *43*
integrity versus despair *43*
assimilation *46*
accommodation *46*
sensorimotor stage *47*
preoperational stage *47*
operations *47*
concrete operational stage *47*

formal operational stage *47*
information processing approach *50*
operant conditioning *54*
reinforcement *54*
punishment *54*
social learning theory *55*
cognitive social learning theory *55*
cognition *55*
phenomenological approach *56*
humanistic perspective *56*
conditional positive regard *57*
unconditional positive regard *58*
hierarchy of motives *58*
self-actualization *59*
ethology *60*
imprinting *60*
critical period *60*
sensitive period *61*

Suggested Readings

Bandura, A. (1986). *Social foundations of thought and action.* Englewood Cliffs, NJ: Prentice-Hall.
This book presents Bandura's cognitive social learning view of development, including an emphasis on reciprocal connections between behavior, environment, and person.

Cowan, P. (1978). *Piaget with feeling.* New York: Holt, Rinehart, & Winston.
Provides a well-written overview of Piaget's theory and draws implications for understanding children's emotional development.

Erikson, E. H. (1968). *Identity: Youth and crisis.*
Must reading for anyone interested in developmental psychology. Erikson outlines his eight stages of the life cycle and talks extensively about identity.

Hinde, R. (1983). Ethology and child development. In P. H. Mussen (Ed.), *Handbook of child psychology* (4th ed.). Vol. 2. New York: Wiley.
Hinde's views are strongly influencing thinking about child development. Here he outlines the questions ethologists ask and the issues they research.

Shostrum, E. (1967). *Man, the manipulator.* New York: Bantam Books.
Shostrum presents an intriguing humanistic perspective on development, including many helpful ideas about adjustment and self-evaluation.

S E C T I O N
II

Beginnings

What endless questions
Vex the thought,
Of whence and whither,
When and how. ■

Sir Richard Burton, Kasidah

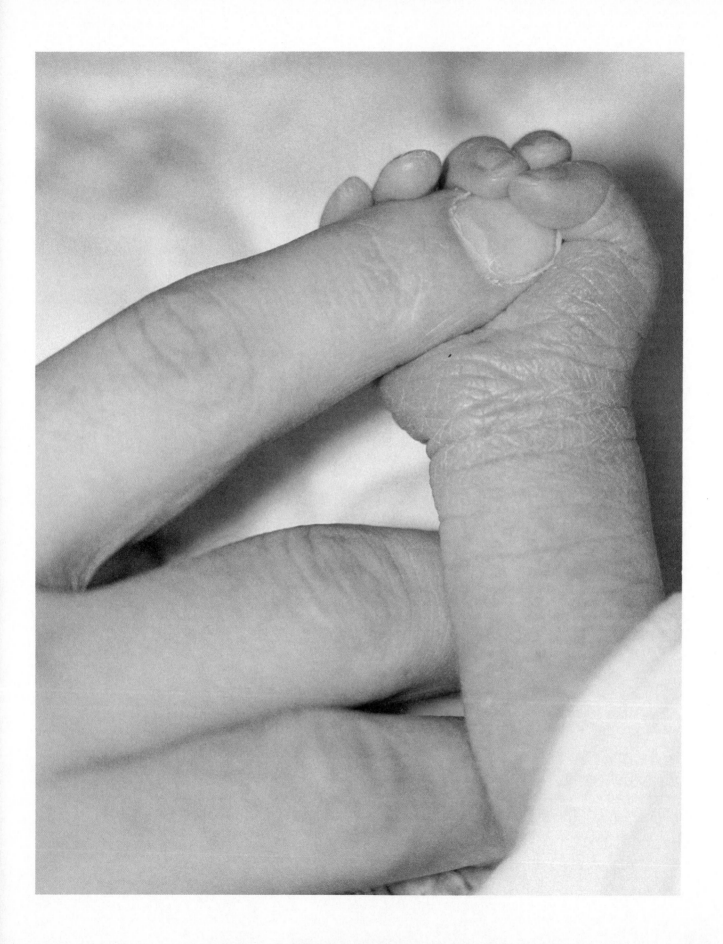

3

■

Biological Beginnings

1kw. 1/2

There is a grandeur in
this view of life . . .
whilst this planet has gone
cycling on
according to the fixed law of
gravity,
from so simple a beginning
endless
forms most beautiful and
wonderful
have been, and are being,
evolved. ■

Charles Darwin, On the Origin of
Species

How can identical twins be studied to evaluate heredity's influence on development?

Jim Springer and Jim Lewis are identical twins. They were separated at the age of four weeks and did not see each other again until they were thirty-nine-years-old. Both worked as part-time deputy sheriffs, both vacationed in Florida, both drove Chevrolets, both had dogs named Toy, and both married and divorced women named Betty. One twin named his son James Allan, and the other named his son James Alan. Both liked math but not spelling, enjoyed carpentry and mechanical drawing, chewed their fingernails down to the nubs, had almost identical drinking and smoking habits, had hemorrhoids, put on ten pounds at about the same point in development, first suffered headaches at the age of eighteen, and had similar sleep patterns.

But Jim and Jim had some differences. One wore his hair over his forehead, the other slicked back with sideburns. One expressed himself better orally, the other was more proficient in writing. But for the most part, their profiles were remarkably similar.

Another pair, Daphne and Barbara, were called the "giggle sisters" because they were always making each other laugh. A thorough search of their adoptive families' histories revealed no gigglers. The identical sisters handled stress by ignoring it, avoided conflict and controversy whenever possible, and showed no interest in politics.

Two other female identical twin sisters were separated at six weeks and reunited in their fifties. Both had nightmares, which they describe in hauntingly similar ways—both dreamed of doorknobs and fishhooks in their mouths as they smothered to death! The nightmares began during early adolescence and stopped in the last ten to twelve years. Both were bedwetters until about twelve to thirteen years of age, and they reported educational and marital histories that were remarkably similar.

These sets of twins are part of the Minnesota Study of Twins Reared Apart, directed by Thomas Bouchard and his colleagues. They bring identical (identical genetically because they come from the same egg) and fraternal (dissimilar genetically because they come from two eggs) twins from all over the world to Minneapolis to investigate their lives. For example, the twins are given a number of personality tests, and detailed medical histories are obtained, including information about diet, smoking, exercise habits, chest X rays, heart stress tests, and EEGs (brain wave tests). The twins are interviewed and asked more than 15,000 questions about their family and childhood environment, personal interests, vocational orientation, values, and aesthetic judgments. They also are given ability and intelligence tests (Bouchard & others, 1981; Lykken, 1982; Tellegen & others, in press).

The examples of Jim and Jim, the giggle sisters, and the identical twins who had the same nightmares stimulate us to think about our genetic heritage and the biological foundations of our existence. Organisms are not like billiard balls, moved by simple, external forces to predictable positions on life's pool table. Environmental experiences *and* biological foundations work together to make us who we are. Our coverage of biological beginnings starts by examining how the human species came to be. Then the question of how characteristics are transmitted from one generation to the next is tackled. These topics deal, respectively, with evolution and genetics.

The Evolutionary Perspective

In the H. G. Wells movie, *The Man Who Could Work Miracles,* the gods discuss Earth. The first god says, "They were apes only yesterday. Give them time." The second god responds, "Once an ape always an ape." The first god replies, "No, it will be different. Come back here in an age or so and you will see." The first god was right, evolution did not stop with apes. In evolutionary time, humans are relative newcomers to Earth, yet we have established ourselves as the most successful and dominant species. If we consider evolutionary time in terms of a calendar year, humans arrived late in December (Sagan, 1980). As our earliest ancestors left the forest to feed on the savannahs, and finally to form hunting societies on the open plains, their minds and behaviors changed. How did this evolution come about? The answer lies in the principle of natural selection.

Let's go back in time to the middle of the nineteenth century. Charles Darwin, a naturalist, is sitting in the study of his country home near London. He has just completed an around-the-world voyage on the H.M.S. Beagle, observing many different species of animals and their surrounding conditions. Darwin published his observations and thoughts in 1859 in *On the Origin of Species.* He believed that organisms reproduced at rates that would cause enormous increases in the populations of most species, yet populations remained nearly constant.

Darwin reasoned that an intense, constant struggle for food, water, and resources must occur among the many young born each generation. Because of this struggle, many of the young do not survive. Those that do pass their genes on to the next generation. And, as Darwin believed, those that do survive to reproduce probably are superior in a number of ways to those who do not. In other words, the survivors are better adapted to their world than the nonsurvivors. Over the course of many generations, organisms with the characteristics needed for survival would comprise a larger percentage of the population. Over many, many generations, this could produce a gradual modification of the whole population. If environmental conditions change, however, other characteristics might develop and this process could move in a different direction. For Darwin, and for most scientists today, this process of **natural selection** guides the evolutionary process (Campbell, 1985).

Over a million species have been classified, from bacteria to blue whales, with lots of beetles sandwiched in between. The work of natural selection resulted in the disappearing acts of moths and the quills of porcupines (see figure 3.1). And the effects of evolution are present in the technological advances, feeding behavior, intelligence, and longer parental care of human beings (see figure 3.2).

What seest thou else
in the dark backward and abysm of time.
William Shakespeare, The Tempest

I am a brother to dragons,
and a companion to owls.

Job 30:29

Figure 3.1
The black and white noctuid moth, easily spotted while flying, virtually vanishes against the bark of the birch tree.

Figure 3.2

The better an animal is adapted to its environment, the more successful it becomes. Humans, more than any other mammal, are able to adapt to and control most types of environments.
a. Technological advances give greater freedom of movement and independence.
b. Greater intelligence has led to the use of complex objects that enhance life.
c. Because of longer parental care, humans learn more complex behavior patterns, which contribute to adaptation.

(a)   (b)

(c)

There are one hundred and ninety-three living species of monkeys and apes. One-hundred and ninety-two of them are covered with hair. The exception is the naked ape self-named, homo-sapiens.

Desmond Morris, The Naked Ape, *1967*

Generally, evolution proceeds at a very slow pace. The lines that led to the emergence of human beings and the great apes began to diverge about fourteen million years ago! Modern humans, *Homo sapiens,* came into existence only about fifty thousand years ago. Figure 3.3 portrays the evolution of the human brain. No sweeping evolutionary changes in humans have occurred since then—for example, our brain is not ten times as big, we do not have a third eye in the back of our head, and we have not learned to fly.

Genetics

No matter what the species, there must be a mechanism for transmitting characteristics from one generation to the next. This mechanism is explained by the principle of genetics. Each of us carries a genetic code that we inherited from our parents. Physically, this code is located within every cell in our bodies. Our genetic codes are alike in one important way—they all contain the *human* genetic code. Because of the human genetic code, a fertilized human egg cannot grow into an eel, an egret, or an elephant.

Brain evolution

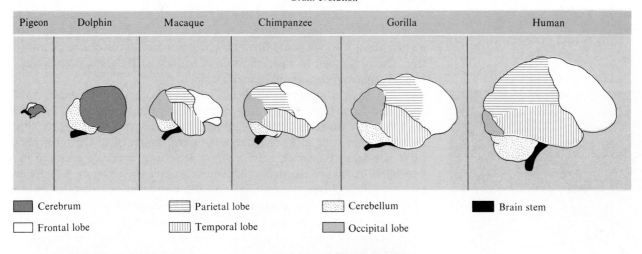

| Pigeon | Dolphin | Macaque | Chimpanzee | Gorilla | Human |

Cerebrum

Frontal lobe

Parietal lobe

Temporal lobe

Cerebellum

Occipital lobe

Brain stem

(a)

(b)

(c)

(d)

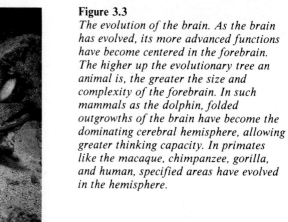

Figure 3.3
The evolution of the brain. As the brain has evolved, its more advanced functions have become centered in the forebrain. The higher up the evolutionary tree an animal is, the greater the size and complexity of the forebrain. In such mammals as the dolphin, folded outgrowths of the brain have become the dominating cerebral hemisphere, allowing greater thinking capacity. In primates like the macaque, chimpanzee, gorilla, and human, specified areas have evolved in the hemisphere.

Our genetic codes are alike in one important way—they all possess the human *genetic code. Because of the human genetic code, a fertilized human egg cannot grow into an elephant (a), an eel (b), or an egret (c).*

The seed of the cedar will become cedar,
The seed of the bramble can only become
bramble.
          Saint-Exupéry, Flight To Arras, *1942*

Figure 3.4
*A DNA molecule. The horizontal bars
are the important bases or "rungs" of the
DNA ladder. The sequence of these bases
plays a key role in scientists' efforts to
locate the identity of a gene.*

The turtle lives 'twixt plated decks
Which practically conceal its sex.
I think it clever of the turtle
In such a fix to be so fertile.
          Ogden Nash, Many Long Years Ago, *1945*

What Are Genes?

We each began life as a single cell weighing about one twenty-millionth of an ounce! This tiny piece of matter housed our entire genetic code—the information about who we would become. These instructions orchestrated growth from that single cell to a person made of trillions of cells, each containing a perfect replica of the original genetic code.

The nucleus of each human cell contains forty-six **chromosomes,** which are threadlike structures that come in structurally similar pairs. You inherited twenty-three chromosomes from your mother and another twenty-three chromosomes from your father. Chromosomes are composed of the remarkable substance deoxyribonucleic acid or *DNA.* **DNA** is a molecule arranged in a "double helix" shape that looks like a spiral staircase (see figure 3.4). **Genes,** the units of hereditary information, are short segments of the DNA "staircase." Genes act as blueprints for cells to reproduce themselves and manufacture the proteins that maintain life. Chromosomes, DNA, and genes can be mysterious. To help you turn mystery into understanding, see figure 3.5.

Reproduction

Genes are transmitted from parents to offspring by means of **gametes,** or sex cells, which are created in the testes of males and in the ovaries of females. Gametes are formed by the splitting of cells; this process is called **meiosis.** In meiosis, each pair of chromosomes in the cell separates, and one member of each pair goes into each gamete, or daughter cell. Thus, each human gamete has 23 unpaired chromosomes. **Reproduction** takes place when a female gamete (ovum) is fertilized by a male gamete (sperm) to create a single-celled **zygote** (see figure 3.6). In the zygote, two sets of unpaired chromosomes combine to form one set of paired chromosomes, one member of each pair being from the mother and the other member being from the father. In this manner, each parent contributes 50 percent of the offspring's heredity. At a point not too long ago, conception was straightforward; today's route to conception, however, has multiple paths, as discussed in Focus on Life-Span Development 3.1.

Abnormalities in Genes and Chromosomes

Geneticists and psychologists have identified a range of problems caused by some major gene or chromosome defect. In the **PKU syndrome** (phenylketonuria), the problem resides in a genetic code that fails to produce an enzyme necessary for metabolism. In the absence of this enzyme, the cells fail to break down an amino acid, phenylalanine, interfering with metabolic processes and generating a poisonous substance that enters the nervous system. Mental functioning rapidly deteriorates if the enzyme deficiency is not treated shortly after birth. Fortunately, the absence of this enzyme can be detected early and treated by diet to keep the phenylalanine at a very low level so that normal metabolism can proceed and the poisonous substance is not generated. A recessive gene is responsible for this disorder.

Perhaps the most common genetically transmitted form of retardation is **Down's syndrome.** The Down's child has a flattened skull, an extra fold of skin over the eyelid, and a protruding tongue. Among other characteristics are a short, thin body frame and retardation of motor abilities. The cause of Down's syndrome is an extra chromosome—Down's children have forty-seven chromosomes instead of the usual forty-six. It is not known why the extra chromosome occurs, but it may have to do with the health of the female ovum or the male sperm. This disorder occurs approximately in one of every 700 live births.

Figure 3.5
Facts about chromosomes, DNA, and genes.

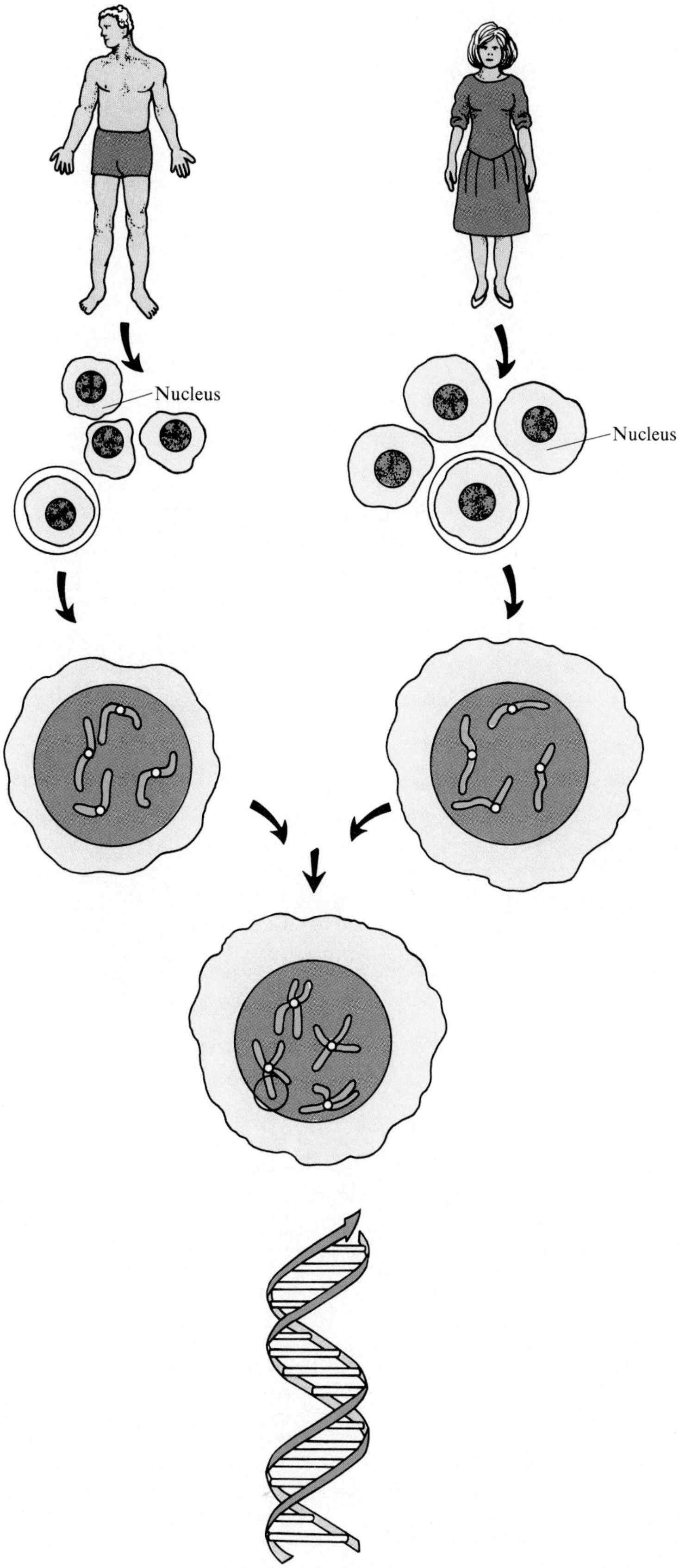

The body contains billions of cells that are organized into tissue and organs.

Nucleus

Nucleus

Each cell contains a central structure, the nucleus, which controls reproduction.

Chromosomes reside in the nucleus of each cell. The male's sperm and the female's egg are specialized reproductive cells that contain chromosomes.

At conception the offspring receives matching chromosomes from the mother's egg and the father's sperm.

The chromosomes contain DNA, a chemical substance. Genes are short segments of the DNA molecule. They are the units of hereditary information that act as a blueprint for cells to reproduce themselves and manufacture the proteins that sustain life. The rungs in the DNA ladder are an important location of genes.

LOUISE, LIFE IN A TEST TUBE

Figure 3.A Louise Brown, the first test-tube baby. Louise and other test-tube babies have not developed any problems associated with the in vitro *fertilization procedure.*

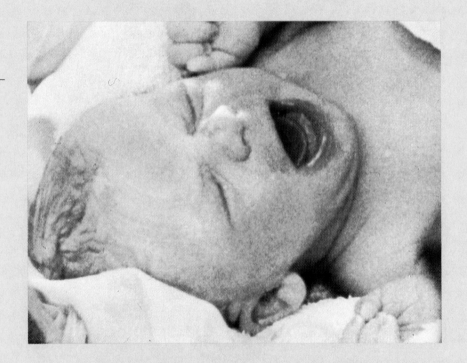

The year is 1978, and one of the most dazzling occurrences of the 1970s is about to unfold. Mrs. Brown is infertile, but her physician informs her of a new procedure that could enable her to have a baby. The procedure involves removing the mother's ovum surgically, fertilizing it in a laboratory medium with live sperm cells obtained from the father or a male donor, storing the fertilized egg in a laboratory solution that substitutes for the uterine environment, and finally implanting the egg in the mother's uterus. The procedure is called ***in vitro fertilization.*** In the case of Mrs.

Brown, the procedure was successful, and nine months later, her daughter Louise was born (see figure 3.A).

Since the first *in vitro* fertilization in the 1970s, variations of the procedure have brought hope to childless couples. A woman's egg can be fertilized with the husband's sperm, or the husband and wife may contribute their sperm and egg with the resulting embryo carried by a third party, who essentially is donating her womb. A summary of nature's way of reproduction and new ways of creating babies is presented in figure 3.B.

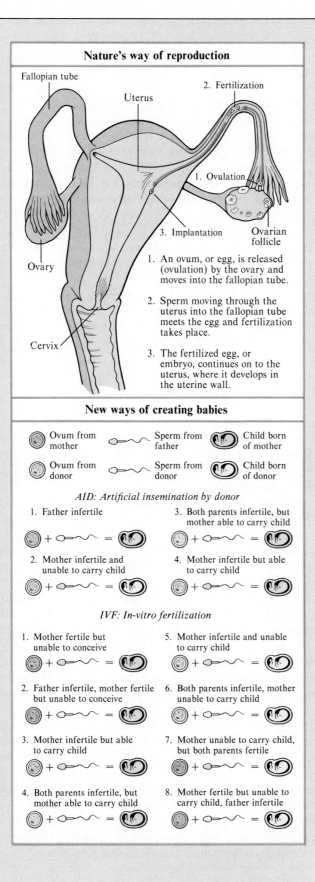

Nature's way of reproduction

Fallopian tube

Uterus

2. Fertilization

1. Ovulation

3. Implantation

Ovarian follicle

Ovary

Cervix

1. An ovum, or egg, is released (ovulation) by the ovary and moves into the fallopian tube.

2. Sperm moving through the uterus into the fallopian tube meets the egg and fertilization takes place.

3. The fertilized egg, or embryo, continues on to the uterus, where it develops in the uterine wall.

New ways of creating babies

Ovum from mother

Sperm from father

Child born of mother

Ovum from donor

Sperm from donor

Child born of donor

AID: Artificial insemination by donor

1. Father infertile

3. Both parents infertile, but mother able to carry child

2. Mother infertile and unable to carry child

4. Mother infertile but able to carry child

IVF: In-vitro fertilization

1. Mother fertile but unable to conceive

5. Mother infertile and unable to carry child

2. Father infertile, mother fertile but unable to conceive

6. Both parents infertile, mother unable to carry child

3. Mother infertile but able to carry child

7. Mother unable to carry child, but both parents fertile

4. Both parents infertile, but mother able to carry child

8. Mother fertile but unable to carry child, father infertile

***Figure 3.B** Reproduction variations.*

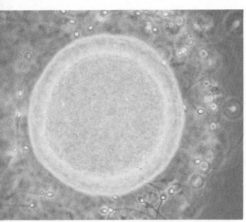

Figure 3.6
An ovum ready for release has been extracted and put into a nutritive solution together with a drop of specially treated seminal fluid. The sperm are eagerly striving toward the ovum. Notice the difference in size.

Imagine that you want to start a family. Probe your family background. What questions would you want to ask a genetic counselor?

Other disorders are associated with sex chromosome abnormalities. Remember that normal males have an X and a Y chromosome and that normal females have two X chromosomes. However, in **Klinefelter's syndrome,** males have an extra X chromosome (making them XXY instead of just XY); they have undeveloped testes and usually become tall and thin with enlarged breasts. This disorder occurs in approximately 1 in 800 live male births.

In **Turner's syndrome,** women are minus an X chromosome—they are XO instead of XX. These women are short in stature with a webbing of the neck. They may be mentally retarded and sexually underdeveloped. This disorder occurs in approximately one in every 3000 female live births.

Another sex chromosome abnormality has been given considerable attention in the last several decades—the **XYY syndrome.** Early interest in this syndrome suggested that the Y chromosome found in males contributed to male aggression and violence; the extra Y chromosome was said to be responsible for excessive aggression and violence. More recent research, however, indicates that XYY males are no more likely to commit crimes than XY males (Witkin & others, 1976).

Each year in the United States, approximately 100,000 to 150,000 infants with a genetic disorder or malformation are born. These infants make up about three to five percent of the three million births and account for at least 20 percent of infant deaths. Prospective parents increasingly are turning to genetic counseling for assistance, wanting to know their risk of having a child born with a genetic defect or malformation. To learn more about genetic counseling turn to Focus on Life-Span Development 3.2.

Some Genetic Principles

Genetic determination is a complex affair and much is unknown about the way genes work. But a number of genetic principles have been discovered, among them dominant-recessive genes, a sex-linked gene, polygenically inherited characteristics, reaction range, and canalization.

The important principle of **dominant-recessive genes** was worked out with such simple forms of life as peas by Gregor Mendel. Mendel found that when he combined round pea plants with wrinkled pea plants, the next generation consistently came out round. The gene for round pea plants was *dominant* and the one for wrinkled plants was *recessive* (tending to go back or recede).

What is the color of your parents' hair? If they both have brown hair, you probably have brown hair. If one of your parents has brown hair and the other has blond hair, you still probably have brown hair because brown hair is controlled by a dominant gene; blond hair is controlled by a recessive gene. But if both your parents have blond hair, then you probably have blond hair because there is no dominant gene to interfere with the appearance of blond hair. Examples of other dominant gene-linked characteristics are brown eyes, farsightedness, and dimples; examples of recessive gene-linked characteristics are blue eyes, normal vision, and freckles.

For thousands of years, individuals have wondered what determines whether an offspring will be a male or a female. Aristotle believed that the father's degree of arousal during intercourse determined the offspring's sex. The more excited the father was, the more likely the offspring would be a male, he reasoned. In the 1920s, researchers confirmed the existence of human sex chromosomes, 2 of the 46 chromosomes humans normally carry. Ordinarily, females have 2 X chromosomes, men have an X and a Y (figure 3.7 shows the chromosome makeup of a male and a female). However, it still was not clear whether the "switch" consisted of one gene or many.

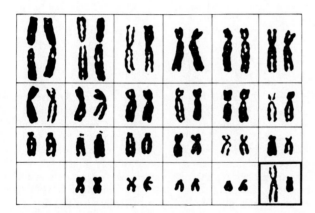

(a)

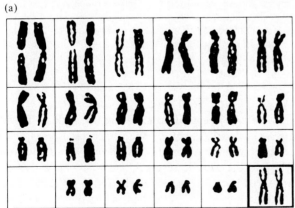

(b)

Figure 3.7
The genetic difference between males and females. At the top is the chromosome structure of a male (a), and at the bottom is the chromosome structure of a female (b). The twenty-third pair is shown in the bottom right box of each figure; notice that the Y chromosome of the male is smaller. To obtain this chromosomal picture, a cell is removed from the individual's body, usually from the inside of the mouth. The chromosomes are magnified extensively and then photographed.

GENETIC COUNSELING

Bob and Mary Sims have been married for several years. They would like to start a family, but they are frightened. The newspapers and popular magazines are full of stories about infants born prematurely who don't survive, infants with debilitating physical defects, and cases of congenital mental retardation. The Simses feel that to have such a child would create a social, economic, and psychological strain on them and on society.

Accordingly, the Simses turn to a genetic counselor for help. Genetic counselors are usually physicians or biologists who are well versed in the field of medical genetics. They are familiar with the kinds of problems that can be inherited, the odds for encountering them, and helpful measures for offsetting some effects.

The Simses tell their counselor that there has been a history of mental retardation in Bob's family. Bob's younger sister was born with Down's syndrome, a form of mental retardation. Mary's older brother has hemophilia, a condition in which bleeding is difficult to stop. They wonder what the chances are that a child of theirs might also be retarded or have hemophilia and what measures they can take to reduce their chances of having a mentally or physically defective child.

The counselor probes more deeply, because she understands that these facts in isolation do not give her a complete picture of the possibilities. She learns that no other relatives in Bob's family are retarded and that Bob's mother was in her late forties when his younger sister was born.

She concludes that the retardation was due to the age of Bob's mother and not to some general tendency for members of his family to inherit retardation. It is well known that women over forty have a much higher probability of giving birth to retarded children than younger women have. Apparently the ova (egg cells) are not as healthy in older women as in women under forty.

In Mary's case the counselor determines that there is a small but clear possibility that Mary may be a carrier of hemophilia and transmit that condition to a son. Otherwise, the counselor can find no evidence from the family history to indicate genetic problems.

The decision is then up to the Simses. In this case, the genetic problem will probably not occur, so

To discover how sexual differentiation takes place, David Page and his colleagues (1987) decided to study the sex chromosomes of individuals who are genetically abnormal: men with 2 X chromosomes and women with an X and a Y. Despite the genetic reversal, the XX men and XY women, while infertile, appeared normal. The researchers showed that 1 X chromosome in these men had a tiny bit of Y attached, while the women's Y chromosomes failed to have that tiny bit. They figured that a critical gene must be contained in that fragment, which sometimes breaks off from the Y.

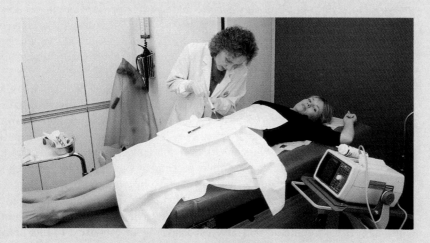

Figure 3.C *Amniocentesis being performed on a pregnant woman.*

the choice is fairly easy. But what should parents do if they face the strong probability of having a child with a major birth defect? Ultimately, the decision depends on the couple's ethical and religious beliefs. They must decide how to balance these against the quality of their child's life.

The moral dilemma is even more acute, of course, once a pregnancy has begun. **Amniocentesis** is a test that can detect more than 100 birth defects. It is performed in the fourteenth to sixteenth weeks of pregnancy. A long, thin needle is inserted into the abdomen to extract a sample of amniotic fluid, the liquid that cushions the fetus (see figure 3.C). Fetal cells in the fluid are grown in the laboratory for two to four weeks and then studied for the presence of defects. The later amniocentesis is performed, the better the diagnostic potential. But the earlier it is performed, the more useful it can be in deciding whether a pregnancy should be terminated.

Another type of prenatal assessment that is frequently used when a structural malformation is suspected is **ultrasound sonography**. High-frequency sound waves are directed into the pregnant woman's abdomen. The echo from the sounds is transformed into a visual representation of the fetus's inner structures. This technique has been beneficial in detecting such disorders as microencephaly, a form of mental retardation involving an abnormally small brain.

As scientists have searched for more accurate, safe assessments of high-risk prenatal circumstances, they have developed the **chorionic villus test.** Available since the mid-1980s, this test involves removing a small sample of the placenta nine to ten weeks into pregnancy. It takes two to three weeks to diagnose. The chorionic villus test allows a decision about abortion to be made near the end of the first trimester of pregnancy, a point when abortion is safer and less traumatic than after amniocentesis in the second trimester. These techniques provide valuable information about the presence of birth defects, but they also raise moral issues pertaining to whether an abortion should be obtained if birth defects are present.

Finding the suspect gene was a lengthy process involving several years of painstaking analysis. The researchers call the gene **testis determining factor,** or **TDF,** and it does appear to fix the infant's sex. To confirm their findings, Page and his coworkers plan to insert the TDF gene in a fertilized mouse egg to see if it will transform a female embryo into a male.

Another important genetic principle is **polygenic inheritance.** Genetic transmission is usually more complex than the simple examples we just examined. Few psychological characteristics are the result of the actions of single gene pairs. Most are determined by the interaction of many different genes.

There are as many as 50,000 or more genes, so you can imagine that possible combinations of these are staggering in number. Traits produced by this mixing of genes are said to be polygenically determined.

No one possesses all the characteristics that our genetic structure makes possible. The actual combination of genes produces what is known as the **genotype.** However, not all of this genetic material is apparent in our observed and measurable characteristics. These observed and measurable characteristics, called **phenotypes,** include physical traits—such as height, weight, eye color, and skin pigmentation—and psychological characteristics—such as intelligence, creativity, personality, and social tendencies.

For each genotype, a range of phenotypes can be expressed. Imagine that we could identify all the genes that would make a child introverted or extraverted. Would measured introversion-extraversion be predictable from knowledge of the specific genes? The answer is no, because even if our genetic model was adequate, introversion-extraversion is a characteristic shaped by experience throughout life. For example, parents may push an introverted child into social situations and encourage the child to become more gregarious.

To understand the cause of introversion in an individual think about a series of genetic codes that predispose the child to develop in a particular way and imagine environments that are responsive or unresponsive to this development. For example, the genotype of some individuals may predispose them to be introverted in an environment that promotes a turning inward of personality, yet in an environment that encourages social interaction and outgoingness, these individuals may become more extraverted. However, it would be unlikely for the individual with this introverted genotype to become a strong extravert. The term **reaction range** is used to describe the range of phenotypes for each genotype, suggesting the importance of an environment's restrictiveness or enrichment (see figure 3.8).

Sandra Scarr (1984) explains reaction range this way: Each of us has a range of potential. For example, an individual with "medium-tall" genes for height who grows up in a poor environment may be shorter than average. But in an excellent nutritional environment, the individual may grow up taller than average. However, no matter how well fed the individual is, an individual with "short" genes will never be taller than average. Scarr believes that characteristics such as intelligence and introversion work the same way. That is, there is a range within which the environment can modify intelligence, but intelligence is not completely malleable. Reaction range gives us an estimate of how modifiable intelligence is.

Genotypes, in addition to producing many phenotypes, may show the opposite track for some characteristics—those that are somewhat immune to extensive changes in the environment. These characteristics seem to stay on track—on a particular developmental course—regardless of the environmental assaults on them (Waddington, 1957). **Canalization** is the term chosen to describe the narrow path or developmental course that certain characteristics take. Apparently, preservative forces help to protect or buffer an individual from environmental extremes. For example, Jerome Kagan (1984) points to his research on Guatemalean infants who had experienced extreme malnutrition as infants, yet showed normal social and cognitive development later in childhood. And some abused children do not grow up to be abusers themselves.

That which comes of a cat will catch mice.

English Proverb

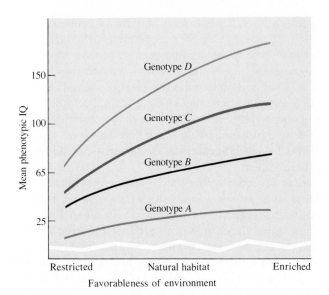

Figure 3.8
Hypothetical set of reaction ranges of intellectual development of several genotypes under environmental conditions that range from poor to good. Although each genotype responds favorably to improved environments, some are more responsive to environmental deprivation and enrichment than others.

The graph axes read: Mean phenotypic IQ (vertical, with values 25, 65, 100, 150); Favorableness of environment (horizontal, with Restricted, Natural habitat, Enriched). Curves labeled Genotype D, Genotype C, Genotype B, Genotype A.

Methods Used by Behavior Geneticists

Behavior genetics is concerned with the degree and nature of behavior's hereditary basis. Behavior geneticists assume that behaviors are jointly determined by the interaction of heredity and environment. To study heredity's influence on development, behavior geneticists often use either the adoption study or the twin study.

In the **adoption study,** researchers compare correlations between children's characteristics and those of their biological and adoptive parents. Adopted children share half their genes with each biological parent, but do not share an environment with them. In contrast, they share an environment with their adopted parents but not their genes.

In the **twin study,** identical (called **monozygotic**) twins and fraternal (called **dyzygotic**) twins are compared. Identical twins are born when a fertilized egg divides into two parts that then develop into two separate embryos. Since the twins come from the same fertilized egg, they share all of their genes. In contrast, fraternal twins develop when a woman's ovaries release two eggs instead of one and each egg is fertilized by different sperm. Fraternal twins share the same womb but they are no more alike genetically than any two siblings, and they may be of different sexes. By comparing groups of identical and fraternal twins, psychologists capitalize on the basic knowledge that identical twins are genetically more similar than fraternal twins. Several problems, though, crop up when the twin study method is used. Adults may stress the similarities of identical twins more than those of fraternal twins. And identical twins may perceive themselves as a "set" and play together more than fraternal twins. If so, observed similarities in identical twins could be environmentally influenced.

The concept of **heritability** is used in many adoption and twin studies. Heritability is a statistical estimate of the degree to which physical, cognitive, and social characteristics among individuals are due to their genetic differences. It is measured by the use of correlational statistical procedures. The highest degree of heritability is 1.00. A heritability quotient of .80 suggests a strong genetic influence, one of .50 a moderate genetic influence, and one of .20 a much weaker, but nontheless, perceptible genetic influence.

Although heritability values may vary considerably from one study to the next, it is possible to determine the average magnitude of a particular characteristic's quotient. For some kinds of mental retardation, the average heritability quotient approaches 1.00. That is, the environment makes almost no contribution to the characteristic's variation. This is not the same as saying the environment has no influence; the characteristic could not be expressed without the environment.

The heritability index is not a flawless measure of heredity's contribution to development. It is only as good as the information fed into it and the assumptions made about genetic-environmental interaction. First, it is important to consider how varied the environments are that are being sampled. The narrower the range of environments, the higher the heritability index; the broader the range of environments, the lower the heritability index. Another important consideration is the reliability and validity of the measures being used in the investigation. That is, what is the quality of the measures? The weaker the measure, the less confidence we have in the heritability index. A final consideration is that the heritability index assumes that heredity and environment can be separated; information can be quantitatively added together to arrive at a discrete influence for each. In reality, heredity and environment interact; their interaction is often lost when the heritability index is computed.

So far our coverage of the biological beginnings of the life cycle have taken us through the evolutionary perspective and some important aspects of heredity. A summary of the main ideas in these aspects of biological beginnings is presented in Concept Table 3.1. Now let's turn our attention to some aspects of development influenced by heredity.

Heredity's Influence on Development

What aspects of development are influenced by genetic factors? They all are. However, behavior geneticists are interested in more precise estimates of the variation in a characteristic accounted for by genetic factors. Intelligence and temperament are among the most widely investigated aspects of heredity's influence on development.

Intelligence

Arthur Jensen (1969) sparked a lively and at times hostile debate when he presented his thesis that intelligence is primarily inherited. Jensen believes that environment and culture play only a minimal role in intelligence. In one of his most provocative statements, Jensen claimed that clear-cut genetic differences are present in the average intelligence of races, nationalities, and social classes. When Jensen first stated in the *Harvard Educational Review* in 1969 that lower intelligence probably was the reason that blacks do not perform as well in school as whites, he was called naive and racist. He received hate mail by the bushel and police escorted him to his classes at the University of California at Berkeley.

Jensen examined a number of studies of intelligence, many of which involved comparisons of identical and fraternal twins. Remember that identical twins have identical genetic endowments, so their IQs should be similar. Fraternal twins and ordinary siblings are less similar genetically, so their IQs should

CONCEPT TABLE

3.1

The Evolutionary Perspective and Genetics		
Concept	**Processes/Related Ideas**	**Characteristics/Description**
The Evolutionary Perspective	Natural Selection	Proposed by Charles Darwin. Argues that genetic diversity occurs in each species. Some organisms have characteristics that help them adapt to their environment and these are likely to be perpetuated. Generally, evolution proceeds at a very slow pace.
Genetics	Chromosomes, DNA, Genes	The nucleus of each human cell contains forty-six chromosomes, which are composed of DNA. Genes are short segments of DNA and act as a blueprint for cells to reproduce and manufacture proteins that maintain life.
	Reproduction	Genes are transmitted from parents to offspring by gametes, or sex cells. Gametes are formed by the splitting of cells, a process called meiosis. Reproduction takes place when a female gamete (ovum) is fertilized by a male gamete (sperm) to create a single-celled zygote. In vitro fertilization has helped solve some infertility problems.
	Abnormalities in Genes and Chromosomes	A range of problems are caused by some major gene or chromosome defect, among them the PKU syndrome, Down's syndrome, Klinefelter's syndrome, Turner's syndrome, and the XYY syndrome. Genetic counseling has increased in popularity, as couples desire information about their risk of having a defective child. Amniocentesis, ultrasound sonography, and the chorionic villus test are used to determine the presence of defects once pregnancy has begun.
	Some Genetic Principles	Genetic transmission is complex but some principles have been worked out, among them dominant-recessive genes, testis determining factor, polygenic inheritance, genotype-phenotype distinction, reaction range, and canalization.
	Methods Used by Behavior Geneticists	Behavior genetics is the field concerned with the degree and nature of behavior's hereditary basis. Among the most important methods used by behavior geneticists are the twin study and the adoption study. The concept of heritability is used in many of the twin and adoption studies. The heritability index is not without its flaws.

be less similar. Jensen found support for his argument in these studies. Studies with identical twins produced an average correlation of .82; studies with ordinary siblings produced an average correlation of .50. Note the difference of .32. To show that genetic factors are more important than environmental factors, Jensen compared identical twins reared together with those reared apart; the correlation for those reared together was .89 and for those reared apart it was .78 (a difference of .11). Jensen argued that if environmental influences were more important than genetic influences, then siblings reared apart, who experienced different environments, should have IQs much further apart.

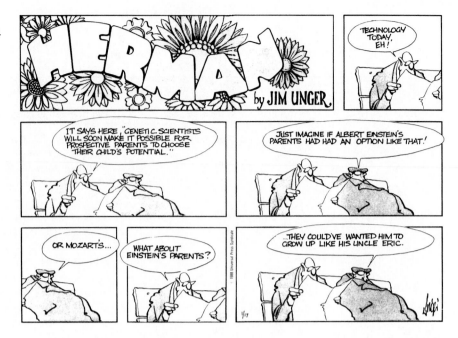

Many scholars have criticized Jensen's work. One criticism concerns the definition of intelligence itself. Jensen believes that IQ as measured by standardized intelligence tests is a good indicator of intelligence. Critics argue that IQ tests only tap a narrow range of intelligence. Everyday problem solving, work, and social adaptability, say the critics, are important aspects of intelligence not measured by the traditional intelligence tests used in Jensen's sources. A second criticism is that most investigations of heredity and environment do not include environments that differ radically. Thus, it is not surprising that many genetic studies show environment to be a fairly weak influence on intelligence.

Jensen and others place the importance of heredity's influence on intelligence at about 80 percent (e.g., Loehlin & Nichols, 1976). Intelligence *is* influenced by heredity, but most psychologists do not put the figure as high as this. In another review, the influence was placed at 50 percent (Hendersen, 1982).

Jensen believes that two genetically based levels of learning exist. At the first level, Level I, is **associative learning,** which involves short-term memory, rote learning, attention, and simple reasoning skills. At the second level, Level II, is **cognitive learning,** which involves abstract thinking, symbolic thought, conceptual learning, and the use of language in problem solving. Jensen argues that associative learning is equally distributed across racial and national lines, but that cognitive learning is concentrated more in middle-class Anglo-American populations than in lower-class black populations. Today, Jensen (1985) continues to argue that genetic differences among races, nationalities, and social classes exist. Indeed, Jensen is such a strong advocate of the influence of heredity on intelligence that he believes we could breed for intelligence. Just such an effort—the Repository for Germinal Choice—is being made today. To read more about the Nobel Prize sperm bank for breeding intelligence, see Focus on Life-Span Development 3.3.

DORAN, DR. GRAHAM, AND
THE REPOSITORY FOR GERMINAL CHOICE

Figure 3.D *Doran, one of the offspring born through the Repository for Germinal Choice.*

Figure 3.E *Robert Graham, the founder of the Repository for Germinal Choice, holding a container of frozen sperm.*

Doran (a name from the Greek word meaning "gift") learned all of the elements of speech by two years of age. An intelligence test showed that at the age of one, his mental age was four (see figure 3.D). Doran was the second child born through the Nobel Prize sperm bank, which came into existence in 1980. The sperm bank was founded by Robert Graham in Escondido, California, with the intent of producing geniuses (see figure 3.E). Graham collected the sperm of Nobel Prize-winning scientists and offered it free of charge to intelligent women of good stock whose husbands were infertile.

One of the contributers to the sperm bank is physicist William Shockley, who shared the Nobel Prize in 1956 for inventing the transistor. Shockley has received his share of criticism for preaching the genetic basis of intelligence. Two other Nobel Prize winners have donated their sperm to the bank, but Shockley is the only one who has been identified.

More than twenty children have been sired through the sperm bank. Are the progeny prodigies? It may be too early to tell. Except for Doran, little has been revealed about the children. Doran's genetic father was labeled "28 Red" in the sperm bank (the color apparently has no meaning). He is listed in the sperm bank's catalog as handsome, blond, and athletic, with a math SAT score of 800 and several prizes for his classical music performances. One of his few drawbacks is that he passed along to Doran an almost one-in-three chance of developing hemorrhoids. Doran's mother says that her genetic contribution goes back to the royal court of Norway and to the poet William Blake.

The odds are not high that a sperm bank will yield that special combination of factors required to produce a creative genius. George Bernard Shaw, who believed that heredity's influence on intelligence is strong, once told a story about a beautiful woman who wrote him saying that with her body and his brain they could produce marvelous offspring. Shaw responded by saying that unfortunately the offspring might get his body and her brain.

Not surprisingly, the Nobel Prize sperm bank is heavily criticized. Some say that brighter does not mean better. They also say that IQ is not a good indicator of social competence or human contribution to the world. Other critics say that intelligence is an elusive concept to measure and that it cannot reliably be reproduced like the sperm bank is trying to do. Visions of the German gene program of the 1930s and 1940s are created. The German Nazis believed that certain traits were superior. They tried to breed children with such traits and killed people without them.

While Graham's Repository for Germinal Choice (as the Nobel Prize sperm bank is formally called) is strongly criticized, consider its possible contributions. The repository does provide a social service for couples who cannot conceive a child, and individuals who go to the sperm bank probably provide an enriched environment for the offspring. To once-childless parents, the offspring produced by the sperm bank, or any of the new methods of conception available, are invariably described as a miracle (Garelik, 1985).

Figure 3.9
The means of intelligence for natural children from white families, interracial children adopted by middle-class white families, and black children reared by their own families.

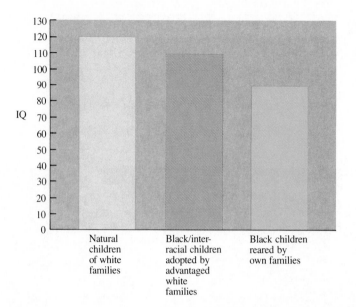

Critics such as Sandra Scarr and her colleague Richard Weinberg (1976, 1979; Weinberg, 1987) studied 130 black children who were adopted as infants by white, middle-class families. The IQs of a comparison group of children from the same area who lived with their natural black parents averaged 90. As shown in figure 3.9, after the black children were adopted by white, middle-class families, their average IQ was found to be 110. The IQs of the white children in the same families as the adopted black children also were assessed. Their IQs averaged 120. Thus, the IQs of the adopted black children were closer to their white step-siblings' IQs than to the national average for black children, which is an IQ of 85, or the comparison group.

But before we suggest that masses of black children be placed in white, middle-class homes, Scarr and Weinberg (1976) remind us that they do not endorse IQ as the ultimate human value. Their findings do support the belief, though, that social environment plays an important role in intelligence. Other recent research on adopted children provides support for the environment's role in intelligence (Plomin, 1987 a,b).

Temperament

Temperament is another widely studied aspect of human development, especially in infancy. Some infants are extremely active, moving their arms, legs, and mouths incessantly; others are tranquil. Some children explore their environment eagerly for great lengths of time; others do not. Some infants respond warmly to people; others fuss and fret. All of these behavioral styles represent an individual's temperament.

Alexander Chess and Stella Thomas (Chess & Thomas, 1977; Thomas & Chess, 1987; Thomas, Chess, & Birch, 1970) define temperament broadly in terms of an individual's behavioral style. They developed nine dimensions of temperament that fall into three clusters. The nine dimensions are: rhythmicity of biological functions, activity level, approach to or withdrawal from new stimuli, adaptability, sensory threshold, predominant quality of mood, intensity of mood expression, distractibility, and persistence/attention span. The

TABLE 3.1
Dimensions and Clusters of Temperament in Chess and Thomas's Research

Temperament dimension	Description	Temperament cluster		
		Easy child	Difficult child	Slow-to-warm-up child
rhythmicity	regularity of eating, sleeping, toileting	regular	irregular	
activity level	degree of energy movement		high	low
approach-withdrawal	ease of approaching new people and situations	positive	negative	negative
adaptability	ease of tolerating change in routine, plans	positive	negative	negative
sensory threshold	amount of stimulation required for responding			
predominant quality of mood	degree of positive or negative affect	positive	negative	
intensity of mood expression	degree of affect when pleased, displeased, happy, sad	low to moderate	high	low
distractibility	ease of being distracted			
attention span/ persistence				

three temperamental clusters are easy, difficult, and slow-to-warm-up. These clusters seemed to be moderately stable across the childhood years. Table 3.1 lists the nine different temperaments, their description, and the three temperamental clusters; the table also shows which of the nine dimensions were critical in spotting a cluster and what the level of responsiveness was for a critical feature. A blank space indicates that the dimension was not strongly related to cluster.

Other researchers suggest different basic dimensions of temperament. Arnold Buss and Robert Plomin (1984, 1987) believe that infants differ on three basic dimensions:

Emotionality is the tendency to be distressed. It reflects the arousal of the individual's sympathetic nervous system. Distress develops during infancy into two separate emotional responses—fear and anger. Fearful infants try to escape something that is unpleasant; angry ones protest it. Buss and Plomin argue that children are labeled "easy" or "difficult" on the basis of the emotionality.

Sociability is the tendency to prefer the company of others to being alone. It matches up with a tendency to respond warmly to others.

Activity involves tempo and vigor of movement. Some children walk fast, are attracted to high-energy games, and jump or bounce around a lot; others are more placid.

A number of scholars, including Chess and Thomas, conceive of temperament as a stable characteristic of newborns that comes to be shaped and modified by the child's later experiences (Thomas & Chess, 1987; Goldsmith & others, 1987). This raises the question of heredity's role in temperament. Twin and adoption studies have been conducted to answer this question (e.g., DeFries & others, 1981; Plomin, 1987; Matheny, Dolan, & Wilson, 1976). The researchers found a heritability index in the range of .50 to .60, suggesting a moderate influence of heredity on temperament. However, the strength of the association usually declines as infants become older (Goldsmith & Gottesman, 1981). This finding supports the belief that temperament becomes more malleable with experience. Alternatively, it may be that as the child becomes older, behavioral indicators of temperament may be more difficult to spot. The biological basis of the temperament of inhibition or shyness and its developmental course is currently the interest of Jerome Kagan (1986, 1987) and Stephen Suomi (1987). To learn about how stable our tendency to be shy is and how much it can be modified, turn to Focus on Life-Span Development 3.4.

The consistency of temperament depends in part on the "match" or "fit" between the child's nature and the parents' (Chess & Thomas, 1986; Rothbart, in press). Imagine a high-strung parent with a child who is difficult and sometimes slow to respond to the parent's affection. The parent may begin to feel angry or rejected. A father who does not need much face-to-face social interaction will find it easy to manage a similarly introverted baby, but he may not be able to provide an extraverted baby with sufficient stimulation. Parents influence infants, but infants also influence parents. Parents may withdraw from difficult children, or they may become critical and punish them; these responses may make the difficult child even more difficult. A more easygoing parent may have a calming effect on a difficult child, or may continue to show affection even when the child withdraws or is hostile, eventually encouraging more competent behavior.

In sum, heredity does seem to influence temperament. But the degree of influence depends on parents' responsiveness to the child and other environmental experiences of the child.

Consider your own temperament. Does it fit into one of the clusters described by Chess and Thomas? How stable has your temperament been in the course of your development? What factors contributed to this stability or lack of stability?

The frightening thing about heredity and environment is that we parents provide both.

Notebook of a printer

Beyond the fact that heredity and environment always interact to produce development, first argue for heredity's dominance in this interaction, and, second, argue for environment's dominance.

Heredity-Environmental Interaction and Development

Both genes and environment are necessary for an organism—from amoeba to human—to even exist. Heredity and environment operate—or cooperate—together to produce an individual's intelligence, temperament, height, weight, ability to pitch a baseball, career interests, and so on. No genes, no organism; no environment, no organism (Scarr & Weinberg, 1980). If an attractive, popular, intelligent girl is elected president of the student body, would we conclude that her success is due to enviroment or to heredity? Of course, it is both. Because the environment's influence depends on genetically endowed characteristics, we say that the two factors *interact*.

■

BORN TO BE SHY?

Each of you has seen a shy toddler—the one who clings to a parent and only reluctantly ventures into an unfamiliar place. Faced with a stranger, the shy toddler freezes, becomes silent, and stares fearfully. The shy toddler seems visibly tense in social situations; parents of such children often report they always seem to have been that way.

Despite parents' comments that shy children seem to have been shy virtually from birth, psychologists have resisted the notion that such characteristics are inborn, focusing instead on the importance of early experiences. Both the research of Jerome Kagan with extremely shy children and the research of Stephen Suomi with "uptight" monkeys supports the belief that shyness is a part of an individual's basic temperament.

Kagan (1987 a, b) collaborating with Steven Resnick and Nancy Snidman, followed the development of extremely inhibited and uninhibited two- to three-year-old children for six years. They evaluated the children's heart rates and other physiological measures as well as observing their behavior in novel circumstances. After six years, the very inhibited children no longer behave exactly as they did when they were two, but they still reveal the pattern of very inhibited behavior combined with intense physiological responsiveness to mild stress. Very uninhibited children typically speak within the first minute when they are observed in a social situation, but very inhibited children will

sometimes wait as long as 20 minutes before they say anything (see figure 3.F).

Suomi (1987) has discovered that uptight monkeys, like Kagan's inhibited children, do not easily outgrow their intense physiological response to stress and their frozen behavioral responses to social situations (see figure 3.G). Even as late as adolescence—which is four or five years of age in monkeys—those who were uptight at birth continued to respond in intense ways to stress, but at this point they became hyperactive. As adults, they seemed to regress in the face of stress, revealing the shy, inhibited behavior seen in infancy.

Kagan says that the proper environmental context can change the tendency to be shy. But if parents let their child remain fearful for a long time, it becomes harder to modify the shyness. Kagan discovered that 40 percent of the originally inhibited children—mainly boys—became much less inhibited by 5½ years, while less than 10 percent became more timid. Based on parent interviews, parents helped their children overcome their shyness by bringing other children into the home and by encouraging the child to cope with stressful circumstances.

Shyness's modification in some cases can be extreme. Some shy individuals even become performers. Celebrities such as Johnny Carson, Carol Burnett, Barbara Walters, and Michael Jackson have strong tendencies toward shyness but even with the biological underpinnings loaded against them turned the tables on heredity's influence (Asher, 1987).

Figure 3.F Extremely shy children at the age of 2 or 3 years old usually show similar inhibited behavior six years later, although environmental experiences can modify shyness to some degree.

Figure 3.G "Uptight" infant monkeys show some of the same shy, inhibited behaviors as their human counterparts.

But as we have seen, developmental psychologists probe further to determine more precisely heredity's and environment's influence on development. What do we know about heredity-environment interaction? According to Sandra Scarr and Kenneth Kidd (1983), we know that literally hundreds of disorders appear because of miscodings in DNA. We know that abnormalities in chromosomal number adversely influence the development of physical, intellectual, and behavioral features. We know that genotype and phenotype do not map onto each other in a one-to-one fashion. We know that it is very difficult to distinguish between genetic and cultural transmission. There usually is a familial concentration of a particular disorder, but familial patterns are considerably different than what would be precisely predicted from simple modes of inheritance. We know that when we consider the normal range of variation, the stronger the genetic resemblance, the stronger the behavioral resemblance. This holds more strongly for intelligence than personality or interests. The influence of genes on intelligence is present early in children's development and continues through the late adulthood years. And we also know that being raised in the same family accounts for some portion of intellectual differences among individuals, but common rearing accounts for little of the variation in personality or interests. One reason for this discrepancy may be that families place similar pressures on their children for intellectual development in the sense that the push is clearly toward the highest level, while they do not direct their children toward similar personalities or interests, in which extremes are not especially desirable. That is, virtually all parents would like their children to have above-average intellect, but there is much less agreement about whether a child should be highly extraverted.

What do we need to know about the role of heredity-environmental interaction in development? Scarr and Kidd (1983) commented that we need to know the pathways by which genetic abnormalities influence development. The PKU success story is but one such example. Scientists discovered the genetic linkage of the disorder and subsequently how the environment could be changed to reduce the damage to development. We need to know more about genetic-environmental interaction in the normal range of development. For example, what accounts for the difference in one individual's IQ of 95 and another individual's IQ of 125? The answer requires a polygenic perspective and information about cultural and genetic influences.

We also need to know about heredity's influence across the entire life cycle (Plomin & Thompson, 1987). For instance, puberty is not an environmentally produced accident; neither is menopause. While puberty and menopause can be influenced by such environmental factors as nutrition, weight, drugs, health, and the like, the basic evolutionary and genetic program is wired into the species. It cannot be eliminated, nor should it be ignored. This evolutionary and genetic perspective gives biology its appropriate role in our quest to better understand human development through the life cycle. A summary of the main ideas in our discussion of heredity's influence on development and heredity-environmental interaction is presented in Concept Table 3.2.

Heredity's Influence on Development and Heredity-Environmental Interaction		
Concept	**Processes/Related Ideas**	**Characteristics/Description**
Heredity's Influence on Development	Its Scope	All aspects of development are influenced by heredity.
	Intelligence	Jensen's argument that intelligence is primarily due to heredity sparked a lively and at times bitter debate. Intelligence is influenced by heredity but not as strongly as Jensen envisioned.
	Temperament	Temperament refers to behavioral style; it has been studied extensively in infancy. Chess and Thomas developed nine temperament dimensions and three temperament clusters. Temperament is influenced strongly by biological factors in early infancy but becomes more malleable with experience. An important consideration is the fit of the infant's temperament with the parents' temperament.
Heredity-Environmental Interaction and Development	Its Nature	No genes, no organism; no environment, no organism. Because the environment's influence depends on genetically endowed characteristics, we say that the two factors interact.

Summary

I. **The Evolutionary Perspective**
The theory of natural selection was proposed by Charles Darwin. It argues that genetic diversity occurs in each species. Some organisms have characteristics that help them adapt to their environment and these are likely to be perpetuated. Generally, evolution proceeds at a very slow pace.

II. **Chromosomes, DNA, and Genes**
The nucleus of each human cell contains forty-six chromosomes, which are composed of DNA. Genes are short segments of DNA and act as a blueprint for cells to reproduce and manufacture protein that maintains life.

III. **Reproduction**
Genes are transmitted from parents to offspring by gametes, or sex cells. Gametes are formed by the splitting of cells, a process called meiosis. Reproduction takes place when a female gamete (ovum) is fertilized by a male gamete (sperm) to create a single-celled zygote. *In vitro* fertilization has helped solve some infertility problems.

IV. **Abnormalities in Genes and Chromosomes**
A range of problems are caused by some major gene or chromosome defect, among them the PKU syndrome, Down's syndrome, Klinefelter's syndrome, Turner's syndrome, and the XYY syndrome. Genetic counseling has increased in popularity, as couples desire information about their risk of having a defective child. Amniocentesis, ultrasound sonography, and the chorionic villus test are used to determine the presence of defects once pregnancy has begun.

V. **Some Genetic Principles**
Genetic transmission is complex but some principles have been worked out, among them dominant-recessive genes, testis determining factor, polygenic inheritance, genotype-phenotype distinction, reaction range, and canalization.

VI. Methods Used by Behavior Geneticists

Behavior genetics is the field concerned with the degree and nature of behavior's heredity basis. Among the most important methods used by behavior geneticists are the twin study and the adoption study. The concept of heritability is used in many of the twin and adoption studies. The heritability index is not without its flaws.

VII. Heredity's Influence on Development

All aspects of development are influenced by heredity. Jensen's argument that intelligence is primarily influenced by heredity sparked a lively and at times bitter debate. Intelligence is influenced by heredity but not as strongly as Jensen envisioned. Temperament refers to behavioral style; it has been studied extensively in infancy. Chess and Thomas developed nine temperament dimensions and three temperament clusters.

Temperament is strongly influenced by biological factors in early infancy but becomes more malleable with experience. An important consideration is the fit of the infant's temperament with the parents' temperament.

VIII. Heredity-Environmental Interaction and Development

No genes, no organism; no environment, no organism. Because the environment's influence depends on genetically endowed characteristics, we say that the two factors interact.

Key Terms

Suggested Readings

Chess, S., & Thomas, A. (1986). *Temperament in clinical practice.* New York: Guilford.
Details of Chess and Thomas's classical longitudinal study of temperament are provided; applications to clinical problems are described.

Gould, S. (1983). *Hen's teeth and horse's toes: Reflections on natural history.* New York: Norton
This book is a collection of fascinating articles by a biologist interested in evolution. The essays originally were published in the magazine Natural History.

Lewontin, R. C., Rose, S., & Kamin, L. J. (1984). *Not in our genes.* New York: Pantheon.
Argues for an environmental view of development and provides many reasons as to why heredity's role is overestimated.

Plomin, R., DeFries, J. C., & McClearn, G. E. (1980). *Behavioral genetics: A primer.*

A good introduction to research on genes and behavior by leading behavior geneticists.

Watson, J. D. (1968). *The double helix.* New York: New American Library.
A personalized account of the research leading up to one of the most provocative discoveries of the twentieth century—the DNA molecules. Reading like a mystery novel, it illustrates the exciting discovery process in science.

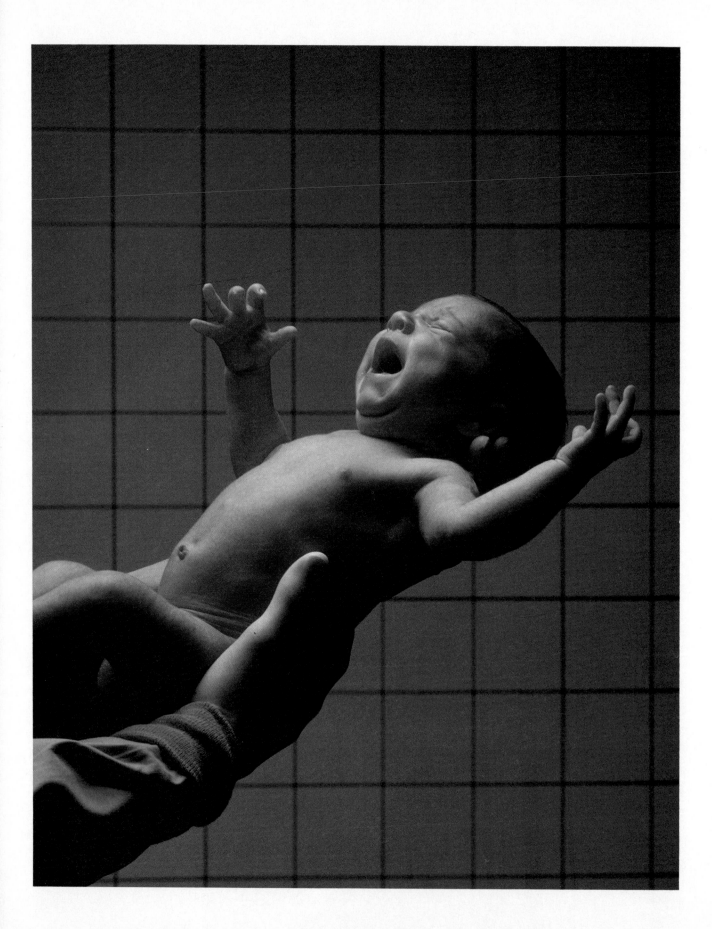

Prenatal Development and Birth

1 hr. 45 min

Teresa Block's second pregnancy was difficult—a rupture of the amniotic sac, an infection that sent her temperature skyrocketing, and an exhausting breech delivery. Robert weighed just less than two pounds at birth. His mother said she couldn't imagine a baby looking so tiny. The first time his mother saw him, he was lying on his back attached to a respirator and wires were connected all over his body. Robert stayed at the hospital until two weeks before his originally projected birthdate, at which time he weighed four pounds eight ounces. Teresa and her husband lived in a small town 60 miles from the hospital; they commuted each day to spend time with Robert and brought their other child along with them when it was practical.

A decade later, Robert is still at the bottom of the weight chart but he is about average in height and virtually the only physical residue of his early birth difficulties is a "lazy eye." He is 20/20 in his good eye but 20/200 in the other. He is doing special exercises for the weaker eye, and the doctor thinks he is not far from the day he can go without glasses. Robert is on the soccer team and the swim team (Fincher, 1982).

Considering his circumstances, Robert had a relatively uncomplicated stay at the hospital. Not all children born so frail survive, and those that do sometimes show the consequences many years in the future.

At one time, you were an organism floating in a sea of fluid inside your mother's womb. From the moment you were conceived until the moment you were born, some astonishing developments took place. This chapter chronicles the truly remarkable developments that occur from conception to birth and the nature of the birth process itself.

Prenatal Development

Imagine how you came to be. Out of thousands of eggs and millions of sperm, one egg and one sperm united to produce you. Had the union of sperm and egg come a day or even an hour earlier or later, you might have been very different—maybe even the opposite sex.

The Course of Prenatal Development

Remember from chapter 3 that conception occurs when a single sperm cell from the male unites with the ovum (egg) in the female's fallopian tube in a process called fertilization. The fertilized egg is called a **zygote.** By the time the zygote ends its three- to four-day journey through the fallopian tubes and reaches the uterus, it has divided into approximately 12 to 16 cells.

The period from conception until about 12 to 14 days later is called the **germinal period;** it includes the creation of the zygote, continued cell division, and attachment of the zygote to the uterine wall. Approximately one week after conception, when the zygote is composed of 100–150 cells, it is called the **blastula.** Differentiation of cells has already commenced in the blastula as inner and outer layers are formed. The inner layer of the blastula is called the

"My Mom says I come from Heaven. My Dad says he can't remember an' Mr. Wilson is positive I came from Mars!"

blastocyst, which later develops into the embryo. The outer layer is called the **trophoblast,** which later provides nutrition and support for the embryo. At about 10 days after conception, a major milestone in the germinal period takes place: **implantation.** This refers to the attachment of the zygote to the uterine wall.

During the **embryonic period,** the embryo differentiates into three layers, and support systems develop. As the zygote attaches to the uterine wall, its cells form two layers; it is at this time that the mass of cells changes names from zygote to embryo. The embryonic period lasts from about two weeks to eight weeks after conception. The inner layer of cells is called the **endoderm;** this will develop into the digestive and respiratory systems. The outer layer of cells is divided into two parts. The outermost layer, the **ectoderm,** will become the nervous system, sensory receptors (ear, nose, and eyes, for example), and skin parts (hair and nails, for example). The middle layer, the **mesoderm,** will become the circulatory system, bones, muscle, excretory system, and reproductive system. Every body part eventually develops from these three layers— the endoderm primarily produces internal body parts, the mesoderm primarily produces parts that surround the internal areas, and the ectoderm primarily produces surface parts.

As the embryo's three layers are formed, life support systems for the embryo mature and develop rapidly; these include the placenta, umbilical cord, and the amnion. The **placenta** is a disk-shaped group of tissues in which small blood vessels from the mother and the offspring intertwine but do not join. The **umbilical cord** contains two arteries and one vein, connecting the baby to

What web is this
Of will be, is, and was?

Jorge Luis Borges

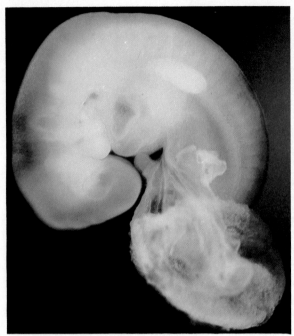

Figure 4.1
At 4 weeks, the embryo is about .2 inches long, and the head, eyes, and ears begin to show. The head and neck are half the body length; the shoulders will be located where the whitish arm buds are attached.

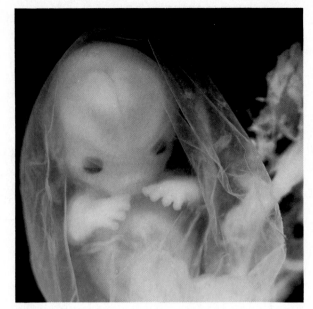

Figure 4.2
Fetus at 8 weeks, the beginning of the fetal period.

If I could have watched you grow
As a magical mother might,
If I could have seen through my magical
transparent belly,
There would have been such ripening
within . . .
—*Anne Sexton,* Little Girl, My String Bean,
My Lovely Woman

the placenta. Very small molecules—oxygen, water, salt, food from the mother's blood, and carbon dioxide and digestive wastes from the embryo's blood—pass back and forth between the mother and infant. Large molecules, such as red blood cells and harmful substances (most bacteria, maternal wastes, and hormones), cannot pass through the placental wall. The mechanisms that govern transfer of substances across the placental barrier are complex and still not entirely understood (Rosenblith & Sims-Knight, 1985). The **amnion,** an envelope or baglike membrane that contains a clear fluid in which the developing embryo floats, is another important life support system of the embryo.

Before most women even know they are pregnant, some other important embryonic developments take place. In the third week, the neural tube that eventually becomes the spinal cord forms. At about 21 days, eyes begin to appear, and by 24 days, the cells for the heart begin to differentiate. During the fourth week, the first appearance of the urogenital system is apparent, and arm and leg buds emerge. Four chambers of the heart take shape and blood vessels surface (figure 4.1 shows a four-week embryo). From the fifth to eighth weeks, arms and legs differentiate further; at this time, the face starts to form but still is not very recognizable. The intestinal tract develops and the facial structures fuse. At eight weeks, the developing organism weighs about one-thirtieth of an ounce and is just over 1 inch long.

The first eight weeks of development are a time when many body systems are being formed. When body systems are in the process of being formed, they are especially vulnerable to environmental changes. This process of organ formation is called **organogenesis;** it characterizes the first two months of development after conception. Later in the chapter, we detail the environmental hazards that are especially harmful during organogenesis.

The **fetal period** begins eight weeks after conception and lasts for seven months on the average. Growth and development continue their dramatic course during this time frame (figure 4.2 shows a fetus at eight weeks after conception). Three months after conception, the fetus is about 3 inches long and weighs

Figure 4.3
At 4½ months, the fetus has grown to a length of about 18 centimeters (just over 7 inches) when the thumb comes close to the mouth, the head may turn. The lips and tongue will begin their sucking motions—a survival reflex.

about 1 ounce. It has become active, moving its arms and legs, opening and closing its mouth, and moving its head. The face, forehead, eyelids, nose, and chin are distinguishable, as are the upper arms, lower arms, hands, and lower limbs. The genitals can be identified as male or female. By the end of the fourth month, the fetus has grown to 6 inches in length and weighs 4 to 7 ounces. At this time, a growth spurt occurs in the body's lower parts. Prenatal reflexes are stronger—arm and leg movements can be felt for the first time by the mother, for example. Figure 4.3 shows the fetus at 4½ months; notice the sucking reflex.

By the end of the fifth month, the fetus is about 12 inches long and weighs close to a pound. Structures of the skin have formed—toenails and fingernails, for example. The fetus is more active, showing a preference for a particular position in the womb. By the end of the sixth month, the fetus is about 14 inches long and already has gained another pound. The eyes and eyelids are completely formed. A fine layer of hair covers the head. A grasping reflex is present and irregular breathing occurs. By the end of the seventh month, the fetus is about 16 inches long and has gained another pound, now weighing about 3 pounds. During the eighth and ninth months, the fetus grows longer and gains substantial weight—about 4 pounds. At birth, the average American baby weighs 7 pounds and is 20 inches long. In these last two months, fatty tissues develop and the functioning of various organ systems—heart and kidneys, for example—is stepped up.

So the riders of the darkness pass on their circuits: the luminous island of the self trembles and waits, waits for us all, my friends, where the sea's big brush recolors the dying lives, and the unborn smiles.

Lawrence Durrell

Miscarriage and Abortion

A miscarriage, or spontaneous abortion, happens when pregnancy ends before the developing organism is mature enough to survive outside of the womb. This happens when the embryo separates from the uterine wall and is expelled by the uterus. Estimates indicate that about 30–50 percent of all pregnancies end in a spontaneous abortion, most in the first two to three months. Many spontaneous abortions occur without the mother's knowledge.

Early in history, it was believed that a woman could be frightened into a miscarriage by loud thunder or a jolt in a carriage. Today we recognize that this occurrence is highly unlikely; the developing organism is well protected. Abnormalities of the reproductive tract and viral or bacterial infections are more likely candidates for spontaneous abortion's causes. In some cases, severe traumas may be at fault.

Deliberate termination of pregnancy is a complex issue, medically, psychologically, and socially. Possibly carrying the baby to term will affect the mother's health, possibly her pregnancy resulted from rape or incest, possibly she is not married, is poor, and wants to continue her education. Abortion is again legal in the United States; in 1973, the Supreme Court ruled that any woman could obtain an abortion during the first six months of pregnancy. This decision continues to generate ethical objections from those opposed to induced abortion, especially advocates of the Right-to-Life movement.

An unwanted pregnancy is stressful for the woman regardless of how she resolves the problem—ending the pregnancy, giving the child up for adoption, or keeping the child and raising it. Depression and guilt are common reactions of the woman, both before and after an induced abortion. If an abortion is performed, it should not only involve competent medical care but the woman's psychological needs also should be considered. Yet another ethical issue related to abortion has appeared recently—medical use of tissues from aborted fetuses. To learn more about this ethical issue in abortion, turn to Focus on Life-Span Development 4.1.

Teratology and Hazards to Prenatal Development

Some expectant mothers tiptoe about in the belief that everything they do and feel has a direct effect on their unborn child. Others behave casually, assuming that their experiences have little impact on the unborn child. The truth lies somewhere between those two extremes. Although living in a protected, comfortable environment, the fetus is not totally immune to the larger environment surrounding the mother. The environment can affect the child in a number of well-documented ways. Thousands of babies are born deformed or mentally retarded every year as a result of events as early as one or two months prior to conception.

Teratology

The field of study that investigates the causes of congenital (birth) defects is called **teratology.** Any agent that causes birth defects is called a *teratogen* (from the Greek word *tera,* meaning "monster"). A specific teratogen (such as a drug) usually does not cause a specific birth defect (such as malformation of the legs). Virtually every fetus is exposed to at least some teratogens, so many exist. For this reason, it is difficult to determine which teratogen causes which birth defect. In addition, it may take a long time for the effects of a teratogen to show up—only about half are present at birth.

What are the arguments for and against abortion? Where do you stand on this sensitive ethical issue? Why?

ETHICS AND THE MEDICAL USE OF FETAL TISSUE

The increased interest in medical uses for tissue from aborted fetuses opens up a new debate about medical technology and the beginnings of life, adding a new dimension to the longstanding controversy over abortion. Evidence is increasing that the special properties of fetal tissue make it ideal for tissue transplants to treat Parkinson's disease, Alzheimer's disease, and other disorders. Most medical researchers believe it is only a matter of time until fetal tissue is routinely used. Scientists expect fetal tissue to be especially valuable in implant treatments because it grows faster than adult tissue, is more adaptable, and causes less immunological rejection. One of the most troubling possibilities is that some women will conceive children with the intent of aborting them, either to aid a family member or to sell them for their tissue.

The laws governing organ donations require the consent of the donor, or the donor's next of kin. In the case of fetuses, tissue may be donated with the consent of the pregnant woman. Many states have laws restricting experiments on fetuses, which may interfere with the new medical uses of fetal tissue. A recent panel on biomedical ethics at Case Western Reserve University in Cleveland made recommendations about the use of fetal tissue. First, the doctors involved in decisions regarding the abortion should conduct the procedures using fetal tissue. Second, anonymity should be maintained between the donor and recipient, and donors and recipients should not be related to each other. Almost everyone concerned with the use of fetal tissue agrees it is morally wrong, although not illegal, to become pregnant for the sole purpose of aborting a fetus to obtain certain tissue.

Biomedical ethicists say there is a big difference between taking advantage of a death to harvest tissue, and creating a life just to abort it. When an abortion is planned anyway, some ethicists say that donating the fetal tissue may help to relieve some of the sadness surrounding the decision. Donating tissue to help someone else can benefit the process of grieving or bereavement, say some ethicists. The National Right-to-Life Committee, however, says the idea is morally repulsive. They point out that people who kill tiny developing babies lose any moral right to use those tissues. They also believe that the medical use of fetal tissue offers an additional rationale to some individuals who defend abortion. As can be seen, the use of fetal tissue is a debate that probably will be with us for some time to come (Lewin, 1987).

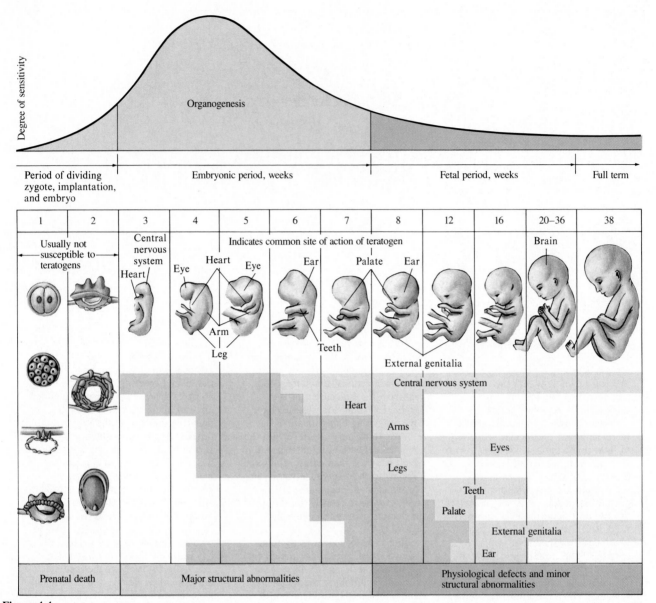

Figure 4.4

Teratogens and the timing of their effects on prenatal development. The danger of structural defects caused by teratogens is greatest early in embryonic development. This is the period of organogenesis and it lasts for several months. Damage caused by teratogens during this period is represented by the dark-colored bars. Later assaults by teratogens typically occur during the fetal period and, instead of structural damage, are more likely to stunt growth or cause problems of organ function.

Despite the many unknowns about teratogens, scientists have discovered the identity of some of these hazards to prenatal development and the particular point of fetal development at which they do their greatest damage (see figure 4.4). As figure 4.4 shows, sensitivity to teratogens occurs about three weeks after conception. Early in the embryonic period, the probability of a structural defect is greatest because this is when organs are being formed. After organogenesis is complete, teratogens are less likely to cause anatomical defects. Exposure later during the fetal period is more likely to stunt growth or to create problems in the way organs function. The preciseness of organogenesis is evident when teratologists point out that vulnerability of the brain is greatest at 15 to 25 days after conception, the eye at 24 to 40 days, the heart at 20 to 40 days, and the legs at 24 to 36 days (Tuchmann-Duplessis, 1975).

In the following sections, we explore how certain environmental agents influenced prenatal development. That is, we examine how maternal diseases and conditions as well as drugs influence the embryo or fetus.

Maternal Diseases and Conditions
Maternal diseases or infections can produce defects by crossing the placental barrier, or they can cause damage during the birth process itself.

Rubella (German measles) and syphilis (a venereal disease) are two maternal diseases that can damage prenatal development. A rubella outbreak in 1964–65 produced 30,000 prenatal and neonatal (newborn) deaths, and more than 20,000 infants were born with malformations, including mental retardation, blindness, deafness, and heart problems. The greatest damage occurs when mothers contract rubella in the third and fourth weeks of pregnancy, although infection during the second month is also damaging. Elaborate efforts ensure that rubella will never again have the same disastrous effects as it did in the mid-1960s. A vaccine that prevents German measles is routinely administered to children, and mothers who plan to have children should have a blood test before they become pregnant to determine if they are immune to the disease.

Syphilis is more damaging later in prenatal development—four months or more after conception. Rather than affecting organogenesis like rubella does, syphilis damages organs after they are already formed. Damage includes eye lesions, which can cause blindness, and skin lesions. When syphilis is present at birth, other problems involving the central nervous system and gastrointestinal tract can develop. Most states require a pregnant woman to be given a blood test to detect the presence of syphilis.

Another infection that has received widespread attention recently is genital herpes. Increased numbers of newborns contract this virus when they are delivered through the birth canal of a mother with genital herpes. About one-third of babies delivered through an infected birth canal will die; another one-fourth become brain damaged. If a pregnant woman detects an active case of genital herpes close to her delivery date, a cesarean section can be performed (in which the infant is delivered through the mother's abdomen) to keep the virus from infecting the newborn.

The Mother's Age
When the mother's age is considered in terms of possible harmful effects on the fetus and infant, two time periods are of special interest—adolescence and the 30s and beyond. Approximately one of every five births is to an adolescent; in some urban areas, the figure reaches as high as one in every two births. Infants born to adolescents are often premature. The mortality rate of infants born to adolescent mothers doubles that of infants born to mothers in their 20s (Graham, 1981). While such figures probably reflect the mother's immature reproductive system, they also may involve poor nutrition, lack of prenatal care, and low socioeconomic status. Prenatal care decreases the probability that a child born to an adolescent girl will have physical problems. However, adolescents are the least likely of all age groups to obtain prenatal assistance from clinics, pediatricians, and health services (Blum & Goldhagen, 1981; Timberlake & others, 1987; Worthington, 1988).

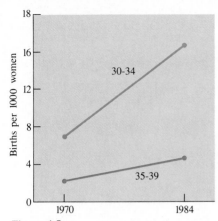

Figure 4.5
Birthrate by women 30 to 39 years old.
Source: National Center for Health Statistics.

Women increasingly seek to establish a career before beginning a family, delaying childbearing until their 30s (see figure 4.5). Down's syndrome, a form of mental retardation, is related to the mother's age. A baby with Down's syndrome rarely is born to a mother under the age of 30, but the risk increases after the mother reaches 30. By age 40, the probability is slightly over 1 in 100, and by age 50, it is almost 1 in 10.

Women also have more difficulty becoming pregnant after the age of 30. In one investigation (Schwartz & Mayaux, 1982), the clients of a French fertility clinic all had husbands who were sterile. To increase their chances of having a child, they were artificially inseminated once a month for one year. Each woman had 12 chances to become pregnant. Seventy-five percent of the women in their 20s became pregnant, 62 percent of the women 31 to 35 years old became pregnant, and only 54 percent in the over-35-year-old group became pregnant.

We still have much to learn about the role of the mother's age in pregnancy and childbirth. As women become more active, exercise regularly, and are careful about their nutrition, their reproductive systems may remain healthier at older ages than was thought possible in the past. Indeed, as we see next, the mother's nutrition influences prenatal development.

Nutrition
The developing fetus completely depends on the mother for its nutrition, which comes from the mother's blood. Nutritional state is not determined by any specific aspect of diet; among the important factors are the total number of calories and appropriate levels of protein, vitamins, and minerals. The mother's nutrition even influences her ability to reproduce. In extreme instances of malnutrition, women stop menstruating, thus precluding conception. And children born to malnourished mothers are more likely to be malformed (Hurley, 1980).

One investigation of Iowa mothers documents nutrition's important role in prenatal development and birth (Jeans, Smith, & Stearns, 1955). The diets of 400 pregnant women were studied and the status of the newborns was assessed. The mothers with the poorest diets were more likely to have offspring who weighed the least, had the least vitality, were born prematurely, and who died. In one investigation, diet supplements given to malnourished mothers during pregnancy improved the performance of offspring during the first three years of life (Werner, 1979).

Emotional State and Stress
Tales abound about the way the mother's emotional state affects the fetus. For centuries it was thought that frightening experiences—a severe thunderstorm or a family member's death—would leave birthmarks on the child or affect the child in more serious ways. Today, we believe that the mother's stress can be transmitted to the fetus, although we have gone beyond thinking that these happenings are somehow magically produced. We now know that, when a pregnant woman experiences intense fears, anxieties, and other emotions, physiological changes occur—heart rate, respiration, and glandular secretions among them. For example, the production of adrenaline in response to fear restricts blood flow to the uterine area and may deprive the fetus of adequate oxygen.

Nothing vivifies, and nothing kills, like the emotions.
Joseph Roux, Meditations of A Parish Priest, *1886*

Beginnings

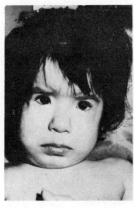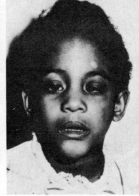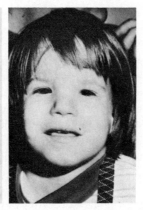

Children of different racial backgrounds, diagnosed with fetal alcohol syndrome.

The mother's emotional state during pregnancy can influence the birth process, too. An emotionally distraught mother might have irregular contractions and a more difficult labor. This may cause irregularities in the baby's oxygen supply, or it may lead to irregularities after birth. Babies born after extended labor may adjust more slowly to their world and be more irritable. One investigation revealed a connection between the mother's anxiety during pregnancy and the newborn's condition (Ottinger & Simmons, 1964). In this study, mothers answered a questionnaire about their anxiety every three months during pregnancy. When the babies were born, the babies' weights, activity levels, and crying were assessed. The babies of the more anxious mothers cried more before feedings and were more active than the babies born to the less anxious mothers.

Drugs

How might drugs affect prenatal development? Some pregnant women take drugs, smoke tobacco, and drink alcohol without thinking about the possible effects on the fetus. Occasionally, a rash of deformed babies are born, bringing to light the damage drugs can have on the developing fetus. This happened in 1961 when many pregnant women took a popular tranquilizer called thalidomide to reduce their morning sickness. In adults, the effects of thalidomide are mild; in embryos, they are devastating. Not all infants were affected in the same way. If the mother took thalidomide on day twenty-six (probably before she knew she was pregnant), an arm might not grow. If she took the drug two days later, the arm might not grow past the elbow. The thalidomide tragedy shocked the medical community and parents into the stark realization that the mother does not have to be a chronic drug user for the fetus to be harmed. Taking the wrong drug at the wrong time is enough to physically handicap the offspring for life.

Heavy drinking by pregnant women also can be devastating to an offspring. A cluster of characteristics called **fetal alcohol syndrome (FAS)** identifies children born to mothers who are heavy drinkers; it includes a small head (called microencephaly) as well as defective limbs, face, and heart. Most of these children are below average in intelligence. While no serious malformations such as those found in FAS are found in infants born to mothers who are moderate drinkers, infants whose mothers drank moderately during pregnancy (for example, one to two drinks a day) were less attentive and alert, with the effects present at four years of age (Streissguth & others, 1984).

Cigarette smoking by the pregnant woman also can adversely influence prenatal development, birth, and infant development. Fetal and neonatal deaths are higher among smoking mothers; also prevalent are higher preterm births and lower birth weights. In one investigation (Landesman-Dwyer & Sackett, 1983), 271 infant-mother pairs were studied during the infant's eighth, twelfth, and sixteenth weeks of life by having each mother keep a diary of her infant's activity patterns. Mothers who smoked during pregnancy had infants who were awake on a more consistent basis, a finding one might expect since the active chemical ingredient in cigarettes—nicotine—is a stimulant. Respiratory problems and sudden infant death syndrome (also known as crib death) are more common among the offspring of mothers who smoke. Recent evidence suggests that intervention programs designed to get pregnant women to stop smoking are successful in reducing some of the negative effects of cigarette smoking on offspring, being especially effective in raising their birth weights (Sexton & Hebel, 1984; Vorhees & Mollnow, 1987).

It is well documented that infants whose mothers are addicted to heroin show a number of behavioral difficulties (Hutchings & Fifer, 1986). The young infant shows withdrawal symptoms characteristic of opiate abstinence, such as tremors, irritability, abnormal crying, disturbed sleep, and impaired motor control. Behavioral problems are often still present at the first birthday and attention deficits may appear later in the child's development.

With the increased use of cocaine in the United States, there has been growing concern regarding its effects on the fetuses and neonates of pregnant cocaine abusers (Howard, 1988). In one recent investigation (Chasnoff, Burns & Burns, 1987), infants whose mothers were cocaine abusers during pregnancy showed less social interaction and more poorly organized responses to environmental stimuli than their counterparts whose mothers were not cocaine abusers.

At this point we have discussed a number of ideas about prenatal development. A summary of the main points in this discussion is presented in Concept Table 4.1. Next, we turn to the study of the birth process itself.

The Birth Process

Delivery can be as difficult for the baby as for the mother, lasting anywhere from four to twenty-four hours, from which the newborn emerges splattered with the mother's blood and a thick, greasy, white material called vernix, which improves movement through the birth canal. The newborn's head is not the most attractive in the world; it may be swollen at the top because of pressure against the pelvic outlet during the last hours of labor. The baby's face may be puffy and bluish; her ears may be pressed against her head in a bizarre position—matted forward on her cheeks, for example. Her nose may be flattened and skewed to one side by the squeeze through the pelvis. The baby may be bowlegged and her feet may be cocked pigeon-toed from being up beside her head for so long in the mother's womb. They can be flexed and put in a normal position at birth. How stunning it must be to be thrust suddenly into a new, bright, airy world so totally different from the dark, moist warmth of the womb. Despite the drama of human birth, newborns who have had a comfortable stay in the womb and are born when due are well-equipped by nature to withstand the birth process. Among the intriguing questions about the birth process are: What kinds of childbirth strategies are available? What are the stages of birth and what delivery complications can arise? What are preterm infants like? How can we measure the newborn's health and social responsiveness? How crucial is bonding? We consider each of these in turn.

How can we reduce the number of offspring born to drug dependent mothers? If you had $100 million dollars to spend to help remedy this problem, what would you do?

There was a star danced, and under that I was born.

William Shakespeare

Birth is not one act
It is a process.

Erich Fromm

CONCEPT TABLE

4.1

Prenatal Development		
Concept	**Processes/Related Ideas**	**Characteristics/Description**
The Course of Prenatal Development	Germinal Period	The period from conception to about 10–14 days later. The fertilized egg is called a zygote. The period ends when the zygote attaches to the uterine wall.
	Embryonic Period	The period that lasts from about two weeks to eight weeks after conception. The embryo differentiates into three layers, life support systems develop, and organ systems form (organogenesis).
	Fetal Period	The period that lasts from about two months after conception until nine months or when the infant is born. Growth and development continue their dramatic course and organ systems mature to the point where life can be sustained outside the womb.
Miscarriage and Abortion	Its Nature and Ethical Issues	A miscarriage, or spontaneous abortion, happens when pregnancy ends before the developing organism is mature enough to survive outside the womb. Estimates indicate that about 30–50% of all pregnancies end this way, many without the mother's knowledge. Induced abortion is a complex issue, medically, psychologically, and socially. An unwanted pregnancy is stressful for the woman regardless of how it is resolved. A recent ethical issue focuses on the use of fetal tissue in transplant operations.
Teratology and Hazards to Prenatal Development	Teratology	The field that investigates the causes of congenital (birth) defects. Any agent that causes birth defects is called a teratogen.
	Maternal Diseases and Conditions	Maternal diseases and infections can cause damage by crossing the placental barrier, or they can be destructive during the birth process itself. Among the maternal diseases and conditions believed to be involved in possible birth defects are rubella, syphilis, genital herpes, the mother's age, nutrition, and emotional state and stress.
	Drugs	Thalidomide was a tranquilizer given to pregnant mothers to reduce their morning sickness. In the early 1960s, thousands of babies were malformed as a consequence of their mothers taking this drug. Alcohol, cigarette smoking, heroin, and cocaine are other ways drugs can adversely affect prenatal and infant development.

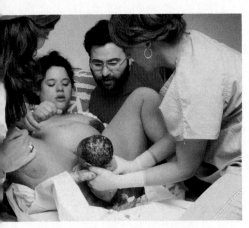

Birth marks a dramatic transition for the fetus. The baby is on a threshold between two worlds.

We must respect this instant of birth, this fragile moment. The baby is between two worlds, on a threshold, hesitating . . .

Frederick Leboyer,
Birth Without Violence

Childbirth Strategies

Controversy swirls over how childbirth should proceed. Some critics argue that the standard delivery practices of most hospitals and physicians need to be overhauled; others suggest that the entire family—especially the father—should be more involved in childbirth; and others argue that procedures that ensure mother-infant bonding should be followed.

In the standard childbirth procedure that was practiced for many years, the way you were probably delivered, the expectant mother was taken to a hospital, where a doctor was responsible for the baby's delivery. The pregnant woman was prepared for labor by having her pubic hair shaved and by having an enema. She was then placed in a labor room often filled with other pregnant women, some of whom were screaming. When she was ready to deliver, she was taken to the delivery room, which looked like an operating room. She was laid on the table with her legs in the air, and the physician, along with an anesthetist and a nurse, delivered the baby.

What could be wrong with this procedure? Critics list three things: 1) Important individuals related to the mother are excluded from the birth process. 2) The mother is separated from her infant in the first minutes and hours after birth. 3) Giving birth is treated like a disease and a woman is thought of as a sick patient (Rosenblith & Sims-Knight, 1985). As we see next, some alternative procedures differ radically from this standard procedure.

The **Leboyer method,** developed by French obstetrician Frederick Leboyer, intends to make the birth process less stressful for infants. Leboyer's procedure is referred to as "birth without violence." He describes standard childbirth as torture (Leboyer, 1975). He vehemently objects to holding newborns upside down and slapping or spanking them, putting silver nitrite into their eyes, separating them immediately from their mothers, and scaring them with bright lights and harsh noises in the delivery room. Leboyer also criticizes the traditional habit of cutting the umbilical cord as soon as the infant is born, a situation that forces the infant to immediately take in oxygen from the air in order to breathe. Leboyer believes that the umbilical cord should be left intact for several minutes to allow the newborn a chance to adjust to a world of breathing air. In the Leboyer method, the baby is placed on the mother's stomach immediately after birth so the mother can caress the infant. Then the infant is placed in a bath of warm water to relax.

While most hospitals do not use the soft lights and warm baths for the newborn suggested by Leboyer, they sometimes do place the newborn on the mother's stomach immediately after birth, believing that it will stimulate bonding between the mother and the infant.

Another well-known birth procedure that deviates markedly from the standard practice is the **Lamaze method,** a form of prepared or natural childbirth developed by Fernand Lamaze, a pioneering French obstetrician. It has become widely accepted in the medical profession and involves helping the pregnant mother to cope with the pain of childbirth in an active way to avoid or reduce medication. Lamaze classes are available on a widespread basis in the United States, usually consisting of six weekly classes. In these classes, the pregnant woman learns about the birth process and is trained in breathing and relaxation exercises.

As the Lamaze method grew in popularity, it became more common for the father to participate in the exercises and to assist in the birth process. To learn more about the father's role in the Lamaze method and his participation in the birth process, turn to Focus on Life-Span Development 4.2.

A FATHER IN THE DELIVERY ROOM:
"IT WAS OUT OF THIS WORLD!"

An interesting historical accident led to one of Lamaze training's major components as it is now practiced in the United States. In France, trained women assist the woman in labor. Since such assistants are not available in the United States, fathers assumed the assistant's function. Fathers attend childbirth classes with their wives, learn the strategies required, and assist in timing contractions, massaging the mother, and giving psychological support.

The father's participation in the birth process may help to strengthen his relationship with his wife and increase the probability that he will develop a stronger attachment bond with the infant. Data supporting the belief that the father's participation in Lamaze classes and in the birth process will benefit the infant's long-term development have not been generated. However, there is something intuitively positive about the father's involvement in the birth process, if he is motivated to participate. It may increase the family's sense as a cohesive, interdependent unit that works together. A survey indicated that the father's presence in the delivery room

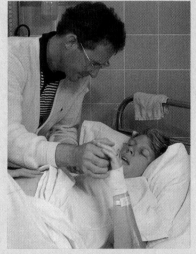

In recent years, what changes have taken place in the father's role in the baby's delivery?

is a positive experience (Pawson & Morris, 1972). Only 1 of the 544 fathers sampled said that he regretted participating in the birth process.

What are some reactions of fathers who have participated in the Lamaze-type natural childbirth classes and in the birth process in the delivery room? More than 20 years

ago, I was allowed in the delivery room by a progressive physician at a hospital that did not permit such practices. I still have a vivid image of those moments, moments that truly inspire a sense of awe and excitement in a father when he sees his child being born.

One father who participated in natural childbirth classes proudly described how he felt about his accomplishments and his sense of involvement in sharing the birth of the baby with his wife:

"It made me feel good to be able to help out. I know it was a painful experience, and I wanted to make it as easy as possible for her. She was willing to have the baby and go though nine months of carrying it around. The least I could do was go to the childbirth classes once a week and give her my support. There were times during her pregnancy when she did not feel well. I know she appreciated my willingness to assist her in the baby's birth. Then, in the delivery room itself—what a great, uplifting feeling. It was out of this world! I would not have missed that moment when the baby first came out for the world."

Medical doctors provide most maternity care in the United States. However, in many countries of the world, midwives are the primary caregivers for pregnant and laboring women. In the United States, midwives are not as well established, although all states have provisions for their practice. The emphasis of the midwife's training is that birth is a normal physiological event. Midwives support and promote the woman's physical and emotional well-being. Midwives do not care for women with complications of pregnancy. In the United States, certified nurse-midwives are the most numerous. They generally work in close cooperation with physicians in hospitals, in homes, or in birthing centers.

Most births in the United States take place in a hospital. In recent years, hospitals have offered more comfortable, home-like rooms for birth. Many hospitals now have birthing rooms—where the mother can labor, give birth, and spend time with her newborn afterward. Birthing centers have also emerged as an alternative setting to hospitals if the pregnant woman is healthy and no complications are foreseen. Birthing centers provide a sense of community and learning, with social gatherings and classes often being held there.

Stages of Birth and Delivery Complications

The birth process occurs in three stages. The first stage lasts an average of 12 to 24 hours for a woman having her first child—it is the longest of the three stages. In the first stage, uterine contractions are 15 to 20 minutes apart at the beginning and last up to a minute. These contractions cause the woman's cervix to stretch and open. As the first stage progresses, the contractions come closer together, appearing every 2 to 5 minutes. Their intensity increases, too. By the end of the first birth stage, contractions dilate the cervix to an opening of about four inches so that the baby can move from the uterus to the birth canal.

The second birth stage begins when the baby's head starts to move through the cervix and the birth canal. It terminates when the baby completely emerges from the mother's body. This stage lasts for approximately 1½ hours. With each contraction, the mother bears down hard to push the baby out of her body. By the time the baby's head is out of the mother's body, the contractions come almost every minute and last for about one minute.

The third birth stage, known as **afterbirth,** involves the detachment and expelling of the placenta, umbilical cord, and other membranes. This final stage is the shortest of the three birth stages, lasting only several minutes.

Complications can accompany the baby's delivery. When the baby moves through the birth canal too rapidly, the delivery is called **precipitate.** A precipitate delivery is one that takes the baby less than 10 minutes to be squeezed through the birth canal. This deviation in delivery can disturb the infant's normal flow of blood and the pressure on the infant's head can cause hemorrhaging. If the delivery takes very long, brain damage can occur because of **anoxia,** meaning that insufficient oxygen is available to the infant.

Another delivery complication involves the baby's position in the uterus. Normally, the crown of the baby's head comes through the vagina first. But in 1 of every 25 babies the head does not come through first. Some come with their buttocks first—called the **breech position.** A breech baby has difficulties because his head is still in the uterus when the rest of his body is out, which can cause respiratory problems. Some breech babies cannot be passed through the cervix and must be delivered by cesarean section.

The Use of Drugs during Childbirth

Drugs can be used to relieve pain and anxiety and to speed up delivery during the birth process. The widest use of drugs during delivery is to relieve the expectant mother's pain or anxiety. A wide variety of tranquilizers, sedatives, and analgesics are used for this purpose. Researchers are interested in the effects of these drugs because they can cross the placental barrier and because their use is so widespread. One survey of hospitals found that only 5 percent of deliveries involved no anesthesia, for example (Brackbill, 1979).

One drug that has been widely used to speed up delivery is **oxytocin,** a hormone that stimulates uterine contractions. Controversy surrounds the use of this drug. Some physicians argue that it can save the mother's life or keep the infant from being damaged. They also stress that using the drug allows the mother to be well-rested and prepared for the birth process. Critics argue that babies born to mothers who have taken oxytocin are more likely to have jaundice, that induced labor requires more pain-killing drugs, and that greater medical care is required after the birth, resulting in the separation of the infant and the mother.

What are some of the conclusions that can be reached based on research about the influence of drugs during delivery? Four such conclusions are (Rosenblith & Sims-Knight, 1985):

1. It is difficult to arrive at specific conclusions because the research studies are few in number and those that have been completed often have methodological problems. However, it can be said that all drugs do not have similar effects. Some drugs—tranquilizers, sedatives, and analgesics, for example—do not seem to have long-term effects. Other drugs—oxytocin, for example—are suspected of having long-term effects.
2. The degree to which a drug influences the infant is usually small. Birth weight and social class, for instance, are more powerful predictors of infant difficulties than drugs.
3. A specific drug may affect some infants but not others. In some cases, the drug may have a beneficial effect, while in others, it may have a harmful effect.
4. The overall amount of medication may be an important factor in understanding drug effects on delivery.

After reading the information on the use of drugs during childbirth, what considerations would be foremost in your mind if your offspring is about to be born? What questions about the use of drugs during delivery would you want to ask the individuals responsible for delivering the baby?

Preterm Infants and Age-Weight Considerations

A full-term infant is one who has grown in the womb for the full 38 to 42 weeks between conception and delivery. A **preterm infant** (also called a premature infant) is one who is born prior to 38 weeks after conception. Infants born after a regular gestation period (the term **gestation** refers to the length of time between conception and birth) of 38 to 42 weeks, but who weigh less than 5½ pounds, are called **low-birth-weight.** Both preterm and low-birth-weight infants are considered high risk infants. In one investigation (Milham & others, 1983), children were assessed at least once per year through the first four years of life. The most severe cognitive deficits appeared among those who were preterm or low-birth-weight babies and who came from an impoverished rather than a middle-class background.

A short-gestation period does not necessarily harm the infant; it is distinguished from retarded prenatal growth, in which the fetus has been damaged in some way (Kopp, 1983, 1987). The neurological development of the short-gestation infant continues after birth on approximately the same time-table as if the infant still were in the womb. For example, consider an infant

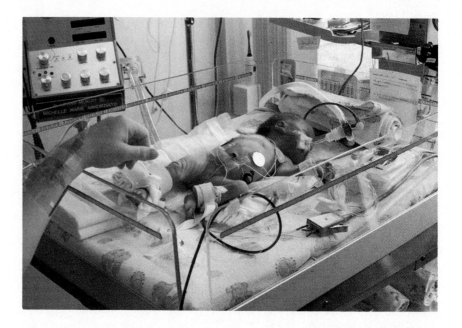

Preterm infants are often hooked up to electronic machines and computerized devices that constantly monitor, report, and sound warnings on vital signs—brain waves, heart beat, blood gases, and respiratory rate.

born after a gestation period of 30 weeks. At 38 weeks, approximately two months after birth, this infant shows the same level of brain development as a 38-week fetus who is yet to be born. Some infants are born precariously early and have a precariously low birth weight. To learn more about these so-called "Kilo babies," turn to Focus on Life-Span Development 4.3.

Without a doubt, preterm infants are perceived differently by the adults in their world. Consider the medical community—they know a great deal about the problems confronting preterm infants. The staff-patient ratio for preterm infants is often one of the most favorable in the hospital. And the preterm infant is immersed in an exotic environment of high-technology life-support equipment (Als, 1988). Parents undoubtedly also perceive their preterm infant differently than the parents of full-term infants. Parents know that their preterm infant is different and have reasonable fears about the infant's health and future. Preterm infants frequently remain in the hospital for a long time, making the parent's role as a competent caregiver difficult. Parents must cope with uncertainty for a lengthy period of time.

How do parents actually deal with their preterm infants? Before the newborn goes home from the hospital, mothers show less confidence in dealing with their preterm infant than the mothers of full-term infants. And they are less likely to hold the baby close, cuddle, and smile at the infant than the mothers of full-term infants. Possibly such mothers feel awkward or perceive the preterm baby as more fragile than a full-term baby. Anticipated interaction with the infant may be frustrated and a close attachment bond shut off (Campos & others, 1983).

Preterm infants do have a different profile than full-term infants. For instance, Tiffany Field (1979) found that four-month-old preterm infants vocalized less, fussed more, and avoided eye contact more than their full-term counterparts. Thus, because they have to deal with infants who are physically and behaviorally different from full-term infants, possibly the differences in the way mothers handle perterm infants are based on their sincere motivation to negotiate this infant difference.

KILOGRAM KIDS

"Kilogram kids" weigh less than 2.3 pounds (which is 1 kilogram or 1,000 grams) and are very premature. The task of saving one is not easy. At the Stanford University Medical Center in Palo Alto, California, 98 percent of the preterm babies survive; however, 32 percent of those between 750 and 1,000 grams do not and 76 percent of those below 750 grams do not. Approximately 250,000 preterm babies are born in the United States each year and 15 to 20,000 of these weigh less than 1,000 grams.

Neonatal intensive care units report not only increased survival rates but decreases in the severity of the handicap of those babies that suffer handicaps. In the neonatal intensive care units, banks of blipping lights, blinking numbers, and beeping alarms stand guard over the extremely preterm infant. He lies on a water bed that gently undulates; the water bed is in an incubator controlled for temperature and humidity by the baby's own body. So many electronic machines and computerized devices incessantly monitor, report, and sound warnings

A "kilogram" kid.

on such vital signs as brain waves, heartbeat, blood gases, and respiratory rate that a team of technicians is needed to service them

around the clock. All of this can be very expensive—five to six months can run as high as $200,000, although it usually is within five figures.

Kilogram babies are by definition not flawed but merely perilously ahead of schedule. After its size and sex, the question parents of a preterm infant ask is, "What is wrong with my baby?" The baby is normal. His form, his needs, how he is behaving—everything is precisely normal for his current stage of development. Preterm infants—even the kilogram kids—are no more sick than you are. But the kilogram kid is as close to death as you would be if you were quickly transported to the moon's surface or the ocean's bottom. Being on the moon or the ocean floor is not a disease, but it certainly is life-threatening. The kilogram kid has been taken from an environment to which he is beautifully adapted to one that can be deadly. Without an amniotic sac to protect him, without a placenta to feed him, breathe for him, oxygenate his blood, and eliminate his waste, he needs a space suit with all those tubes and wires and needles (Fincher, 1982).

Conclusions about Preterm Infants

What conclusions can we draw from the results of research about preterm infants? Four such conclusions seem appropriate at this time (Kopp, 1983, 1987):

1. As intensive care technology has improved, there have been fewer serious consequences of preterm births. For instance, from 1961 to 1965, the manner of feeding preterm infants changed and intravenous fluid therapy came into use. From 1966 to 1968, better control of hypoxemia (oxygen deficiency) resulted. In 1971, artificial ventilation was introduced. And in the mid-1970s, neonatal support systems became less intrusive and damaging to the infant.

2. Infants born with an identifiable problem are likely to have a poorer developmental future than infants born with no recognizable problem. For instance, extremely sick or extremely tiny babies are less likely to survive than healthy or normal-weight babies.

3. Social class differences are associated with the preterm infant's development. Put simply, the higher the socioeconomic status, the more favorable is the developmental outcome for a newborn. Social class differences are tied to a number of other differences. For example, quality of environment, cigarette and alcohol consumption, IQ and knowledge of competent parenting strategies are associated with social class; less positive characteristics are associated with lower-class families.

4. We do not have solid evidence that preterm infants, as a rule, have difficulty later in school. Nor is there good evidence that these preterm children perform poorly on IQ and information-processing tests. Such claims to the contrary were made just one or two decades ago.

Measures of Neonatal Health and Responsiveness

For many years, the **Apgar Scale,** shown in Table 4.1, has been used to assess the newborn's health. One minute and five minutes after birth, the obstetrician or nurse gives the newborn a reading of 0, 1, or 2 on each of five signs: heart rate, respiratory effort, muscle tone, body color, and reflex irritability. A high total score of 7 to 10 indicates that the newborn's condition is good, a score of 5 indicates that there may be developmental difficulties, and a score of 3 or below signals an emergency and indicates that survival may be in doubt.

While the Apgar scale is used immediately after birth to identify high risk infants who need resuscitation, another scale is used for long-term neurological assessment—the **Brazelton Neonatal Behavioral Assessment Scale** (Brazelton, 1973, 1984, 1988; Brazelton, Nugent & Lester, 1987). This scale includes an evaluation of the newborn's reactions to people. The Brazelton scale usually is given on the third day of life and then repeated several days later. Twenty reflexes are assessed along with reactions to circumstances, such as the neonate's reaction to a rattle. The examiner rates the newborn on each of 26 different categories (see Table 4.2). As an indication of how detailed the ratings are, consider item 14 in Table 4.2—"cuddliness."

TABLE 4.1
The Apgar Scale

	Score		
	0	**1**	**2**
Heart rate	Absent	Slow—less than 100 beats per minute	Fast—100–140 beats per minute
Respiratory effort	No breathing for more than one minute	Irregular and slow	Good breathing with normal crying
Muscle tone	Limp and flaccid	Weak, inactive, but some flexion of extremities	Strong, active motion
Body color	Blue and pale	Body pink, but extremities blue	Entire body pink
Reflex irritability	No response	Grimace	Coughing, sneezing and crying

From Virginia A. Apgar, "A Proposal for a new method of evaluation of a newborn infant" in Anesthesia and Analgesia, 32, 260–267, 1975. *Copyright © 1975 International Anesthesia Research Society. Reprinted by permission.*

TABLE 4.2
The 26 Categories on the Brazelton Neonatal Behavioral Assessment Scale (NBAS)

1. Response decrement to repeated visual stimuli
2. Response decrement to rattle
3. Response decrement to bell
4. Response decrement to pinprick
5. Orienting response to inanimate visual stimuli
6. Orienting response to inanimate auditory stimuli
7. Orienting response to animate visual stimuli—examiner's face
8. Orienting response to animate auditory stimuli—examiner's voice
9. Orienting responses to animate visual and auditory stimuli
10. Quality and duration of alert periods
11. General muscle tone—in resting and in response to being handled, passive, and active
12. Motor activity
13. Traction responses as he or she is pulled to sit
14. Cuddliness—responses to being cuddled by examiner
15. Defensive movements—reactions to a cloth over his or her face
16. Consolability with intervention by examiner
17. Peak of excitement and capacity to control self
18. Rapidity of buildup to crying state
19. Irritability during the examination
20. General assessment of kind and degree of activity
21. Tremulousness
22. Amount of startling
23. Lability of skin color—measuring autonomic lability
24. Lability of states during entire examination
25. Self-quieting activity—attempts to console self and control state
26. Hand-to-mouth activity

From B. M. Lester and T. B. Brazelton, "Cross-cultural assessment of neonatal behavior" in D. A. Wagner and H. W. Stevenson, Eds., Cultural Perspective on Child Development. *Copyright © 1982 W. H. Freeman and Company. Reprinted by permission.*

TABLE 4.3

The Assessment of Cuddliness on the Brazelton Neonatal Behavioral Assessment Scale

Score	Infant Behavior
1	The infant resists being held and continually pushes away, thrashes, and stiffens.
2	The infant resists being held most of the time.
3	The infant does not resist but does not participate either, acting like a rag doll.
4	The infant eventually molds into the examiner's arms after considerable nestling and cuddling efforts by the examiner.
5	The infant usually molds and relaxes when initially held, nestling into the examiner's neck or crook of the elbow. The infant leans forward when held on the examiner's shoulder.
6	The infant always molds at the beginning, as described above.
7	The infant always molds initially with nestling and turns toward body and leans forward.
8	The infant molds and relaxes, nestles and turns head, leans forward on the shoulder, fits feet into cavity of other arm, and all of the body participates.
9	All of the above take place, and in addition, the infant grasps the examiner and clings.

From In The Beginning: Development in the First Two Years, *by J. E. Rosenblith and J. E. Sims-Knight. Copyright © 1985 by Wadsworth, Inc. Reprinted by permission of Brooks/Cole Publishing Company, Pacific Grove, CA.*

As shown in Table 4.3, nine categories are involved in assessing this item, with infant behavior scored on a continuum that ranges from the infant being very resistant to being held to the infant being extremely cuddly and clinging. The Brazelton scale is used not only as a sensitive index of neurological integrity in the week after birth but it is also used widely as a measure in many research studies on infant development. In recent versions of scoring the Brazelton scale, Brazelton and his colleagues (1987) categorize the 26 items into four different categories—physiological, motoric, state, and interaction. They also classify the baby in global terms such as "worrisome," "normal," or "superior," based on these categories.

A very low Brazelton score can indicate brain damage. But if the infant merely seems sluggish in responding to social circumstances, parents are encouraged to give the infant attention and to undergo **Brazelton training,** which involves using the Brazelton scale to show parents how their newborn responds to people (Brazelton, 1979, 1987). As part of the training, parents are shown how the neonate can respond positively to people and how such responses can be stimulated. Brazelton training has improved the social interaction of high-risk infants and the social skills of healthy, responsive infants (Widmayer & Field, 1980; Worobey & Belsky, 1982). Considerable interest has been generated recently in increasing the caregiver's recognition and management of stress in the neonatal period (Gorski, 1988; Klauss, 1988).

Bonding

Perhaps the most controversial strategy focused on the mother's role in the newborn's life involves what is called **bonding.** Advocates of bonding argue that long-term consequences for the infant's development are set in motion during the first minutes, hours, or days of the newborn's interaction with the social world. Situations surrounding delivery may prevent or make difficult the occurrence of an emotional bond between the infant and mother. For example, preterm infants are isolated from their mothers to an even greater degree than full-term infants. In many hospitals, it is common to give the mother drugs to make the delivery less painful. The drugs may make the mother drowsy and may interfere with her ability to respond to and stimulate the newborn.

Many pediatricians have been adamant about bonding's importance during the initial hours and days of the newborn's life. In particular, Marshall Klaus and John Kennell (1976) influenced the introduction of bonding in many hospitals. They argue that the first few days of life are a critical period of development. During this period, close contact, especially physical contact, between the newborn and the mother is believed to create an important emotional attachment that provides a foundation for optimal development for years to come.

Is there evidence that such close contact between the mother and the newborn is absolutely critical for optimal development later in life? While some research supports the bonding hypothesis (Klaus & Kennell, 1976), a growing body of research challenges the significance of the first few days of life as a critical period (Bakeman & Brown, 1980; Rode & others, 1981). Indeed, the extreme form of the bonding hypothesis—that the newborn must have close contact with the mother in the first few days of life to develop optimally—simply is not true.

Nonetheless, the weakness of the maternal-infant bonding research should not be used as an excuse to keep motivated mothers from interacting with their infants in the postpartum period because such contact brings pleasure to many mothers. In the case of some mother-infant pairs—preterm infants, adolescent mothers, or mothers from disadvantaged circumstances—the practice of bonding may set in motion a climate for improved mother-infant interaction after the mother and infant leave the hospital (Maccoby & Martin, 1983).

We have discussed a number of dimensions of the birth process. To help you remember the main points of this discussion, see Concept Table 4.2.

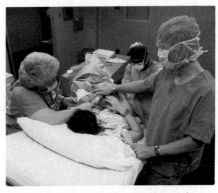

What is bonding? Is there evidence that bonding is critical for optimal development?

Summary

I. **The Course of Prenatal Development**

Prenatal development is divided into three periods. The germinal period lasts from conception to about 10–14 days later. The fertilized egg is called a zygote. The period ends when the zygote attaches to the uterine wall. The embryonic period lasts from two weeks to eight weeks after conception. The embryo differentiates into three layers, life support systems develop, and organ systems form (organogenesis). The fetal period lasts from two months after conception until nine months or when the infant is born. Growth and development continue their dramatic course and organ systems mature to the point where life can be sustained outside the womb.

II. **Miscarriage and Abortion**

A miscarriage, or spontaneous abortion, happens when pregnancy ends before the developing organism is mature enough to survive outside of the womb. Estimates indicate that about 30–50% of all pregnancies end this way, many without the mother's knowledge. Induced abortion is a complex issue—medically, psychologically, and socially. An unwanted pregnancy is stressful for the woman regardless of how it is resolved. A recent ethical issue focuses on the use of fetal tissue in transplant operations.

III. **Teratology and the Hazards to Prenatal Development**

Teratology is the field that investigates the causes of congenital (birth) defects. Any agent that causes birth defects is called a teratogen. Maternal diseases and infections can cause damage by crossing the placental barrier, or they can be destructive during the birth process itself. Among the maternal diseases and conditions believed to be involved in possible birth defects are rubella, syphilis, genital herpes, the mother's age, nutrition, and emotional state and stress. Thalidomide was a tranquilizer given to pregnant mothers to reduce their morning sickness. In the early 1960s, thousands of babies were born malformed as a

The Birth Process

Concept	Processes/Related Ideas	Characteristics/Description
Childbirth Strategies	Their Nature	A controversy currently exists over how childbirth should proceed. Standard childbirth has been criticized and the Leboyer and Lamaze methods have been developed as alternatives. Medical doctors deliver most babies in the United States, but midwives are sometimes used. Most babies in the United States are delivered in hospitals, but birthing centers also may be used.
Stages of Birth and Complications	Stages	Three stages of birth have been defined—the first lasts from 12 to 24 hours for a woman having her first child and the cervix dilates to about 4 inches; the second stage begins when the baby's head moves through the cervix and ends with the baby's complete emergence; the third stage is afterbirth.
	Complications	A baby can move through the birth canal too rapidly or too slowly. A delivery that is too fast is called precipitate; when delivery is too slow, anoxia may result.
Use of Drugs during Childbirth	Drugs Used to Relieve Pain and Anxiety and to Speed up Delivery	A wide variety of tranquilizers, sedatives, and analgesics are used to relieve the expectant mother's pain and anxiety, while oxytocin is used to speed up delivery. It is hard to come up with general statements about drug effects, but it is known that birth weight and social class are more powerful predictors of problems than drugs. A specific drug can have mixed effects and the overall amount of medication needs to be considered.
Preterm Infants and Age-Weight Considerations	Types	Preterm infants are those born after a briefer than normal time period in the womb. Infants who are born after a regular gestation period of 38 to 42 weeks but who weigh less than 5½ pounds are called low-birth-weight infants.
	Conclusions	As intensive care technology has improved, preterm babies have benefitted considerably. Infants born with an identifiable problem have a poorer developmental future than those born with no recognizable problem. Social class differences are associated with the preterm infant's development. There is no solid evidence that preterm infants perform more poorly than full-term infants when they are assessed years later in school.
Measures of Neonatal Health and Responsiveness	Types	For many years, the Apgar scale has been used to assess the newborn's health. A more recently developed test—the Brazelton Neonatal Behavioral Assessment Scale—is used for long-term neurological assessment. It not only assesses the newborn's neurological integrity but also social responsiveness. If the newborn is sluggish, Brazelton training is recommended.
Bonding	Its Nature	There is evidence that bonding—establishment of a close mother-infant bond in the first hours or days after birth—is not critical for optimal development, although for some mother-infant pairs, it may stimulate interaction after they leave the hospital.

consequence of their mother taking this drug. Alcohol, cigarette smoking, heroin, and cocaine are other ways drugs can adversely affect prenatal and infant development.

IV. **Childbirth Strategies**
A controversy exists over how childbirth should proceed. Standard childbirth has been criticized and the Leboyer and Lamaze methods have been developed as alternatives. Medical doctors deliver most babies in the United States, but midwives are sometimes used. Most babies in the United States are born in hospitals, but birthing centers may also be used.

V. **Stages of Birth and Complications**
Three stages of birth have been defined—the first lasts from 12 to 24 hours for a woman having her first child, and the cervix dilates to about 4 inches; the second stage begins when the baby's head moves through the cervix and ends with the baby's complete emergence; the third stage is afterbirth. A baby can move through the birth canal too quickly or too slowly. A delivery

that is too fast is called precipitate; when delivery is too slow, anoxia may result.

VI. **Use of Drugs during Childbirth**
A wide variety of tranquilizers, sedatives, and analgesics are used to relieve the expectant mother's pain and anxiety, while oxytocin is used to speed up delivery. It is hard to come up with general statements about drug effects, but it is known that birth weight and social class are more powerful predictors of problems than drugs. A specific drug can have mixed effects and the overall amount of medication needs to be considered.

VII. **Preterm Infants and Age-Weight Considerations**
Preterm infants are those born after a briefer than normal time period in the womb. Infants who are born after a regular gestation period of 38 to 42 weeks but who weigh less than 5½ pounds are called low-birth-weight infants. As intensive care technology has improved, preterm babies have benefitted considerably. Infants born with an identifiable problem have a poorer developmental

future than those born with no recognizable problem. Social class differences are associated with the preterm infant's development. There is no solid evidence that preterm infants perform more poorly than full-term infants when they are assessed years later in school.

VIII. **Measures of Neonatal Health and Responsiveness**
For many years, the Apgar Scale has been used to assess the newborn's health. A more recently developed test—the Brazelton Neonatal Behavioral Assessment Scale—is used for long-term neurological assessment. It not only assesses the newborn's neurological integrity but also social responsiveness. If the newborn is sluggish, Brazelton training is recommended.

IX. **Bonding**
There is evidence that bonding—establishment of a close mother-infant bond in the first hours or days after birth—is not critical for optimal development, although for some mother-infant pairs, it may stimulate interaction after they leave the hospital.

Key Terms

zygote *100*
germinal period *100*
blastula *100*
blastocyst *101*
trophoblast *101*
implantation *101*
embryonic period *101*
endoderm *101*
ectoderm *101*
mesoderm *101*
placenta *101*

umbilical cord *101*
amnion *102*
organogenesis *102*
fetal period *102*
teratology *104*
fetal alcohol syndrome (FAS) *109*
Leboyer method *112*
Lamaze method *112*
afterbirth *114*
precipitate *114*
anoxia *114*

breech position *114*
oxytocin *115*
preterm infant *115*
gestation *115*
low-birth-weight infants *115*
Apgar Scale *118*
Brazelton Neonatal Behavioral Assessment Scale *118*
Brazelton training *120*
bonding *120*

Suggested Readings

Brazelton, T. B., & Lester, B. M. (1982). *New approaches to developmental screenings of infants.* New York: Elsevier.
A group of experts on infant development relate new developments in the assessment of newborns.

Falkner, F., & Macy, C. (1980). *Pregnancy and birth.* New York: Harper & Row.
An easy-to-read description of experiences during pregnancy and the nature of childbearing.
Goldberg, S., & Devitto, B. A. (1983). *Born too soon: Preterm birth and early development.* San Francisco: W. H. Freeman.

Gives recent information about the nature of preterm infants and ways to socially interact with them.
Nilsson, L. (1966). *A child is born.* New York: Delacourt.
Contains an abundance of breathtaking photographs that take you inside the mother's womb to see the developmental unfolding of the zygote, embryo, and fetus.

S E C T I O N
III

Infancy

I n the end, the power behind
development is life. ∎

Erik Erikson, 1981, Harvard
Educational Review

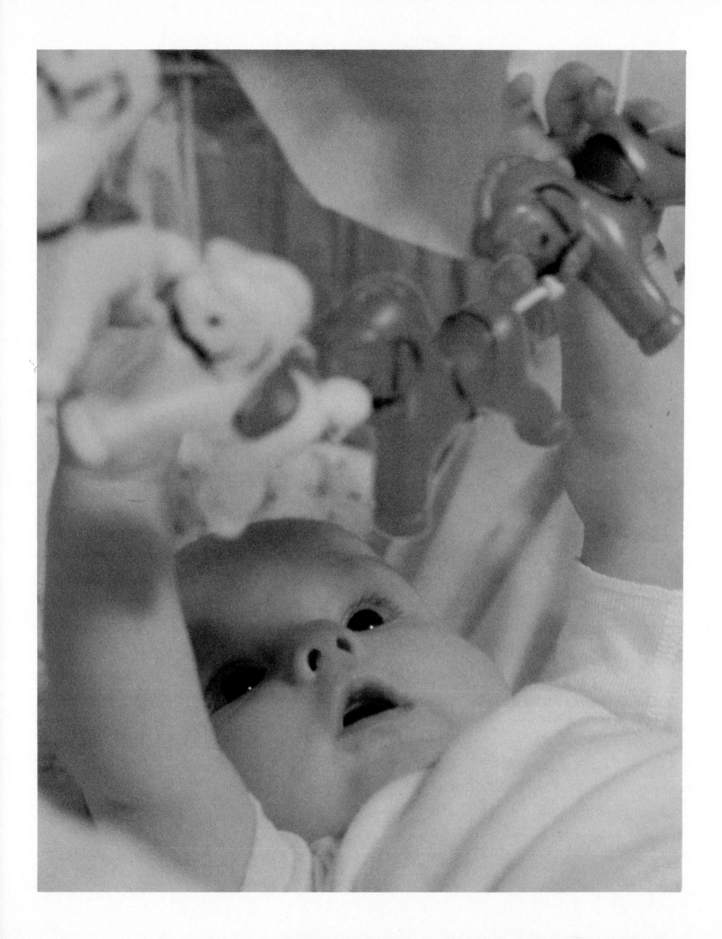

Physical and Perceptual Motor Development

Other than moving a large object toward a newborn's head to see if the newborn responds to it, can you think of other techniques that could be used to determine whether a newborn can see or not?

The creature has poor motor coordination and can move itself only with great difficulty. Its general behavior appears to be disorganized, and though it cries when uncomfortable, it has few other vocalizations. In fact, it sleeps most of the time, about 16 to 17 hours a day. You are curious about this creature and want to know more about what it can do. You think to yourself, "I wonder if it can see. How could I find out?"

You obviously have a communication problem with the creature. You must devise a way that will allow the creature to "tell" you that it can see. While examining the creature one day, you make an interesting discovery. When you move a large object toward it, it moves its head backward, as if to avoid a collision with the object. The creature's head movement suggests that it has at least some vision.

In case you haven't already guessed, the creature you have been reading about is the human infant and the role you played from outer space is that of a developmentalist interested in devising techniques to learn about the infant's visual perception. After years of work, scientists have developed research tools and methods sophisticated enough to examine the subtle abilities of infants and to interpret their complex actions. Videotape equipment makes it possible to investigate elusive behaviors, and high-speed computers make it possible to perform complex data analysis in minutes instead of months and years. Other sophisticated equipment is used to closely monitor respiration, heart rate, body movement, visual fixation, and sucking behavior, which provide clues to what is going on inside the infant.

Among the first things developmentalists were able to demonstrate was that infants have highly developed perceptual motor systems. Until recently, even nursery personnel in maternity hospitals often believed that newborns were blind at birth, and they told mothers this. Most parents were told that their newborns could not taste, smell, or feel pain. As you will discover later in this chapter, we now know that newborns can see, although their visual perception is fuzzy, that they can taste, that they can smell, and that they can feel pain. Before we turn to the fascinating world of the infant's perception, though, we discuss a number of ideas about physical development.

Physical Development

How do infants respond to their world? What kind of states do they experience? What kinds of activities do they perform? We consider each of these questions in turn.

Reflexes

The newborn is not an empty-headed organism. Among other things, it has some basic reflexes that are genetically carried survival mechanisms. For example, the newborn has no fear of water. It will naturally hold its breath and contract its throat to keep water out.

Infancy

Reflexes govern the newborn's movements, which are automatic and beyond the newborn's control. For example, if you stroke the newborn's hand or foot on the back or top, the whole arm or leg withdraws slightly and the hand or foot flexes and then returns so that fingers or toes may grasp your finger. This withdrawal reflex only exists until the baby begins to use his limbs in a different way—legs for standing and stepping, arms for reaching.

The newborn also has many other reflexes. If you hold the infant in a standing position and gently press the sole of one foot and then the other to the bed, the infant will draw up each leg successively as if walking. The newborn actually can "walk" across a bed. Almost a year after the newborn's walk reflex vanishes, it reappears as the voluntary, complex art of walking.

One of the most frequent and dramatic reflexes of the newborn is the **Moro reflex,** a vestige from our primate ancestory. If infants are handled roughly, hear a loud noise, see a bright light, or feel a sudden change of position, they startle, arch their back, and throw their head back. At the same time, they fling out their arms and legs, then rapidly close them to the center of their body, and then flex as if they were falling. As they cry, they startle, then cry because of the startle. This reflex—normal in all newborns—tends to disappear at three to four months of age. Steady pressure on any part of the infant's body calms the infant. If you hold the infant's arm flexed at her shoulder, she will quiet even though free of restraints. Table 5.1 presents additional information about the neonate's repertoire of reflexes.

Some reflexes are important in the baby's life—crying in response to pain, and sucking, for example. Although the usefulness of many neonatal reflexes is unclear, if some reflexes—such as the Moro reflex—are weak, brain damage may be indicated. Reflexes are tested in the neonate as a way of discovering whether the nervous system is working properly.

Some reflexes present in the newborn—such as coughing, blinking, and yawning—persist throughout our lives. They are important for the adult just as they are for the infant. Other reflexes, though, disappear in the several months following birth as the infant's brain functions mature and voluntary control over many behaviors develops. Let's look at three reflexes in greater detail—sucking, crying, and smiling.

TABLE 5.1
The Neonate's Reflex Repertoire

If You	Then the Baby's
Tap the bridge of the nose, shine a bright light suddenly into the eyes, clap hands about 18 inches from the infant's head, or touch the white of the eye with cotton	Eyes close tightly.
Make sudden contact or noise	Head drops backward, neck extends, arms and legs fling outward and back sharply (Moro reflex).
Extend forearms at elbow	Arms flex briskly.
Lightly prick soles of feet	Knee and foot flex.
Stand infant; press foot to bed	Feet step.
Pull baby to sit	Eyes snap open, shoulders tense. Baby tries unsuccessfully to right head (China doll reflex).
Pull baby on tummy on flat surface	Head turns to side and lifts. Baby crawls, lifts self with arms.
Support chest on water surface	Arms and legs "swim."
Place baby on back and turn head to side	Body arches away from face side; arm on face side extends, leg draws up, other arm flexes (tonic neck reflex).
Stroke foot or hand on top	Limb withdraws, arches, returns to grasp.
Stroke palm or sole at base of digits	Limb grasps.
Stroke outside of sole	Toes spread, large toe sticks up.
Tap upper lips sharply	Lips protrude.
Stroke cheek or mouth	Mouth roots; head turns, and tongue moves toward stroking object; mouth sucks.
Stroke cheek or palm	Mouth roots; arm flexes; hand goes to open mouth.
Place object over nose and mouth	Mouth works vigorously; head twists; arms fling across face.
Stroke leg, upper part of body	Opposite leg or hand crosses to push your hand away; withdraws.
Rotate baby to side	Head turns, eyes precede direction of rotation.
Suspend by legs	Body curls to upside-down ball, legs extend, arms drop into straight line; neck arches backward.

From The First Twelve Months of Life *by the Princeton Center for Infancy and Early Childhood, Frank Caplan, General Editor. Copyright © 1971, 1972, 1973 by Edcom Systems, Inc. Reprinted by permission of Bantam Books, Inc. All rights reserved.*

Sucking

Sucking is an important means of obtaining nutrition and it also is an enjoyable, soothing activity. An investigation by T. Berry Brazelton (1956) involved observations of infants for more than one year to determine the incidence of their sucking when they were not nursing and how their sucking changed as they grew older. More than 85 percent of the infants engaged in considerable sucking behavior unrelated to feeding, They sucked their fingers, their fists, and pacifiers. By one year old, most had stopped the sucking behavior.

Parents should not worry when infants suck their thumbs, fist, or even a pacifier. Many parents, though, do begin to worry when thumb sucking persists into the preschool and elementary school years. As many as 40 percent of children continue to suck their thumbs after they have started school (Kessen, Haith, & Salapatek, 1970). Most developmentalists do not attach a great deal of significance to this behavior and are not aware of parenting strategies that might have contributed to it. To some degree, individual differences in children's biological makeup may be involved in the late continuation of sucking behavior.

Infant researchers are interested in nonnutritive sucking for another reason. **Nonnutritive sucking** is used as a measure in a large number of research studies with young infants because young infants quit sucking when they attend to something, such as a picture or a vocalization. Nonnutritive sucking is one of the ingenius ways developmentalists, then, study the young infant's attention and learning.

Nutritive sucking is the infant's route to nourishment. Neonates' sucking capabilities vary considerably—some newborns are efficient at forceful sucking and getting milk while others are not so adept and also get tired before they are full. It takes most newborns several weeks to establish a sucking style that is coordinated with the way the mother is holding the infant, the way milk is coming out of the bottle or breast, and the infant's speed and temperament.

Crying and Smiling

Crying and smiling are emotional behaviors that are important in the infant's communication with the world. Crying is the infant's first emotional or affective behavior. Newborns spend 6 to 7 percent of their day crying, although some infants cry more, others less (Korner & others, 1981). Infants' earliest cries are reflexive reactions to discomfort. The cries may signify information about the infant's biological state and possibly indicate distress. They are highly differentiated and have different patterns of frequency, intensity, and pause.

Most adults can determine whether the infant's cries signify anger or pain. Even for brief segments of infant crying, adults distinguished between aversive and arousing cries (more distressful) and those indicating hunger (less distressful). Even shortly after birth, then, infants' cries communicate information (Zeskind, 1987; Zeskind & Marshall, 1988).

Should a crying infant be given attention and be soothed, or does such parental behavior spoil the infant? Many years ago, John Watson (1928) argued that parents spend too much time responding to the infant's crying and as a consequence reward the crying and increase its incidence. By contrast, recent arguments by ethologists such as Mary Ainsworth (e.g., 1979) stress that it is difficult to respond too much to the infant's crying. Ainsworth views caregivers' responsiveness to infant crying as contributing to the formation of a secure attachment between the infant and the caregiver. One investigation (Bell & Ainsworth, 1972) found that mothers who responded quickly to their infant's crying at three months of age had infants who cried less when assessed

He who binds himself to joy
Does the winged life destroy;
But he who kisses the joy as it
Flies lives in eternity's sun rise.

William Blake

Where do you stand on the controversial issue of how much parents should respond to the cries of their infants? Should parents respond more quickly and warmly to the cries of newborns and young infants than older infants? Explain your answer.

later in the first year of life. Other research by behaviorists (e.g, Gewirtz, 1977) suggests that a quick, soothing response by a caregiver to crying increases the infant's subsequent crying. Controversy, then, still swirls around the issue of when and how caregivers should respond to infant crying.

Smiling is another important communicative behavior of the infant. Two kinds of smiling can be distinguished in infants—one reflexive, the other social. At some point in the first month after birth, an expression appears on the infant's face that adults call a smile; this is a **reflexive smile** because it does not occur in response to external stimuli. The reflexive smile occurs most often during irregular patterns of sleep and does not appear when the infant is in an alert state. A **social smile,** which typically occurs in response to a face, usually does not occur until two to three months of age (Emde, Gaensbauer, & Harmon, 1976). Others, however, feel that social smiling appears earlier than two months of age, arguing that an infant grins in response to voices as early as three weeks of age (Stroufe & Waters, 1976).

States

To chart and understand the infant's development, developmentalists have constructed different classification schemes of the infant's states (Berg & Berg, 1987; Brown, 1964; Prechtl, 1965; Wolff, 1966). One classification scheme (Brown, 1964) describes seven infant states:

1. *Deep sleep.* The infant lies motionless with eyes closed, has regular breathing, shows no vocalization, and does not respond to outside stimulation.
2. *Regular sleep.* The infant moves very little, breathing might be raspy or involve wheezing, and respirations may be normal or move from normal to irregular.
3. *Disturbed sleep.* There is a variable amount of movement, the infant's eyelids are closed but might flutter, breathing is irregular, and there may be some squawks, sobs, and sighs.
4. *Drowsy.* The infant's eyes are open or partly open and appear glassy, there is little movement (although startles and free movement may occur), vocalizations are more regular than in disturbed sleep, and some transitional sounds may be heard.
5. *Alert activity.* This is the state most often viewed by parents as being awake. The infant's eyes are open and bright, a variety of free movements are shown, fretting may occur, skin may redden, and there may be irregular breathing when the infant feels tension.
6. *Alert and focused.* This kind of attention is often seen in older children but is unusual in the neonate. The child's eyes are open and bright. Some motor activity may occur, but it is integrated around a specific activity. This state may occur when focusing on some sound or visual stimulus.
7. *Inflexibly focused.* In this state, the infant is awake but does not react to external stimuli—two examples are sucking and wild crying. During wild crying the infant may thrash about, but the eyes are closed as screams pour out.

. . . He cooperates
With a universe of large and noisey feeling states
Without troubling to place
Them anywhere special, for, to his eyes, funnyface
Or elephant as yet
Mean nothing. His distinction between me and us
Is a matter of taste; his seasons are dry and wet;
He thinks as his mouth does.
            W. H. Auden, Mundus et Infans

Sleep that knits up the ravelled sleave of care . . .
Balm of hurt minds, nature's second course,
Chief nourisher in life's feast.
        William Shakespeare, Macbeth, *1605*

Using classification schemes such as the one just described, researchers have identified many different aspects of the infant's development. One such aspect is the sleeping-waking cycle. Each night, sleep lures us from our work, our play, our loved ones, claiming more of our time than any other pursuit. As an infant, sleep consumed even more of our time than it does now. Newborns sleep for 16 to 17 hours a day, although some sleep more, others less.

The range is from a low of about 10 hours to a high of about 21 hours (Parmalee, Wenner & Schulz, 1964). The longest period of sleep is not always between 11 P.M. and 7 A.M. While total sleep remains somewhat consistent for young infants, the patterns of sleep during the day do not always follow a rhythmic pattern—an infant might change from sleeping several long bouts of seven or eight hours to three or four shorter sessions only several hours in duration. By about one month of age, most infants have begun to sleep longer at night, and by about four months of age, they usually have moved closer to adultlike sleep patterns, spending their longest span of sleep at night and their longest span of waking during the day (Coons & Guilleminault, 1982, 1984).

Infant researchers also are intrigued by different forms of infant sleep. This intrigue focuses on how much is **REM sleep**— rapid eye movement sleep (Berg & Berg, 1987) (see figure 5.1). Children and adults who have been awakened in sleep laboratories after being in a state of REM sleep frequently report that they have been dreaming (Webb, 1975). Most adults spend about one-fifth of their night in REM sleep; their REM sleep usually appears about one hour after non-REM sleep. However, about half of an infant's sleep is REM sleep; infants often begin their sleep cycle with REM rather than non-REM sleep. By the time infants reach three months of age, the percentage of time spent in REM sleep falls to about 40 percent and no longer does REM sleep begin the sleep cycle. The large amount of time spent in REM sleep may provide young infants with added self-stimulation since they spend less time awake than older infants. REM sleep also may promote the brain's development.

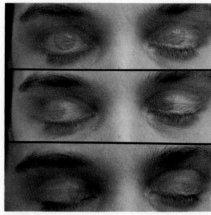

Figure 5.1
During REM sleep, our eyes move rapidly as if we were observing the images we see moving in our dreams.

Eating Behavior

Of course, infants not only sleep, they also eat. Because young infants are growing so rapidly, they must consume approximately 50 calories per day for each pound they weigh—more than twice an adult's requirement per pound. In the 1980s, we have become more nutrition conscious as adults. Does the same type of nutrition that makes us healthy as adults also make young infants healthy? For an answer to this question, turn to Focus on Life-Span Development 5.1.

Most experts agree that young infants should be fed several times a day, but controversy surrounds just how this should be accomplished. For years, developmentalists have debated whether breast-feeding of an infant has substantial benefits over bottle-feeding. The growing consensus is that it is generally better to breast-feed (Auerback, 1987; Corboy, 1987). Breast-feeding provides milk that is clean and digestible and helps to immunize the newborn from disease. Breast-fed babies also gain weight more rapidly than bottle-fed babies. However, only about one-half of mothers nurse newborns and even fewer continue to nurse their infants after several months. Mothers who work outside the home may find it impossible to breast-feed their young infant for many months, but even though breast-feeding provides more ideal nutrition for the infant, bottle-fed infants are not psychologically harmed.

Some years ago, controversy also surrounded the issue of whether a baby should be fed on demand or on a regular schedule. For example, John Watson (1928) argued that scheduled feeding was superior because it increased the child's orderliness. An example of a recommended schedule for newborns was four ounces of formula every six hours. In recent years, demand feeding—in which the timing and amount of feeding are determined by the infant—has become more popular.

If and when you become a parent, what considerations would you have about the nutrition your infant gets? How important do you believe breast feeding is for the infant's development? Explain.

■

WHAT'S GOOD FOOD FOR AN ADULT
CAN BE BAD FOOD FOR A BABY

S ome parents do not know the recipe for a healthy baby: whole milk and an occasional cookie, along with fruits, vegetables, and other foods. Some affluent, well-educated parents starve their babies by feeding them the lowfat, low-calorie diet they eat themselves. Diets designed for adult weight-loss and prevention of heart disease can retard growth and development in babies. Fat is very important. Nature's food—the mother's breast milk—is not low in fat or calories. No child below age two should be given skim milk.

In a recent investigation (Lifschitz and others, 1987), seven cases were documented in which babies aged seven-to-twenty-two months were unwittingly undernourished by their health-conscious parents. In some cases, the parents had been fat themselves and were determined that their child not go through what they went through. The well-meaning parents substituted vegetables, skim milk, and other lowfat foods for what they called junk food. Growing infants and young children need high-calorie, high-energy food for a well-balanced diet—in such cases, broccoli is not necessarily a good substitute for ice cream.

What hazards might the current trends in diet foods and health preoccupation on the part of parents have when it comes to choosing foods for their infants?

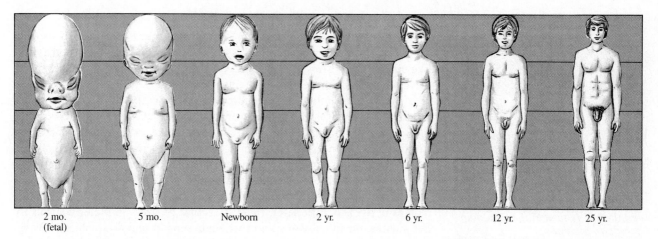

| 2 mo. (fetal) | 5 mo. | Newborn | 2 yr. | 6 yr. | 12 yr. | 25 yr. |

Figure 5.2
Changes in body form and proportion during prenatal and postnatal growth.
From Patten: Human Embryology. *Copyright © 1933 McGraw-Hill Book Company. Reprinted by permission.*

Physical Growth and Motor Development

Physically, newborns are admittedly limited. Tiny from head to heels, they are about 20 inches long and weigh seven pounds. They are bound by where they are put, and they are at the mercy of their bodily needs. Their heart beats twice as fast as an adult's—120 beats a minute—and they breathe twice as fast as an adult does—about 33 times a minute. They urinate as many as 18 times and move their bowels from 4 to 7 times in 24 hours. On the average, they are alert and comfortable for only about 30 minutes in a 4-hour period.

The infant's pattern of physical development in the first two years of life is exciting. At birth, the neonate has a gigantic head (relative to the rest of the body) that flops around in uncontrollable fashion; she possesses reflexes that are dominated by evolutionary movements. In the span of 12 months, the infant becomes capable of sitting anywhere, standing, stooping, climbing, and probably walking. During the second year, growth decelerates, but rapid increases in such activities as running and climbing take place.

Among the important changes in growth are those involving the cephalocaudal and proximodistal sequences, gross and fine motor skills, rhythmic motor behavior, and the brain. We examine each of these in turn.

Cephalocaudal and Proximodistal Sequences

The **cephalocaudal pattern** means that the greatest growth always occurs at the top of the individual—the head—with physical growth in size, weight, and feature differentiation gradually working its way down from top to bottom (for example, neck, shoulders, middle trunk, and so on). This same pattern occurs in the head area because the top parts of the head—the eyes and brain—grow faster than the lower parts—such as the jaw. This pattern is illustrated in figure 5.2. As shown in the figure, an extraordinary proportion of the total body is occupied by the head at birth, but by the time the individual reaches maturity, this proportion is almost cut in half.

A second pattern of development—the **proximodistal pattern**—means that growth starts at the center of the body and moves toward the extremities. An example of this is the early maturation of muscular control of the trunk and arms as compared with that of the hands and fingers.

> Growth is the only evidence of life.
> *John Henry, Cardinal Newman*
> Apologia pro Vita Sua, *1864*

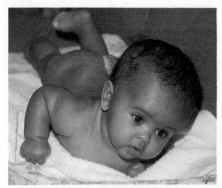

At about four months of age, infants develop the ability to hold their chest up in a facedown position.

A baby is an angel whose wings decrease as his legs increase.

French Proverb

At about eleven to twelve months of age, infants can walk with limited help from an adult.

Gross Motor and Fine Motor Skills

In addition to cephalocaudal and proximodistal growth patterns, we also can describe growth in **gross motor skills**—those involving large muscle activities like moving one's arms and walking—and **fine motor skills**—those involving more fine-grained movements like finger dexterity.

At birth, the infant has no appreciable coordination of the chest or arms. By about four months of age, however, two striking accomplishments occur in turn. The first is the infant's ability to hold the chest up in a facedown position (at about two months). The other is the ability to reach for objects placed within the infant's direct line of vision, without, of course, making any consistent contact with the objects (because the two hands don't work together and the coordination of vision and grasping is not yet possible at about 3 to 4 months of age). A little later, there is further progress in motor control: By five months, the infant can sit up with some support and grasp objects. By six months, the infant can roll over when lying down in a prone position.

At birth, the newborn is capable of supporting some weight with the legs. This is proven by formal tests of muscular strength. These tests use a specially constructed apparatus to measure the infant's leg resistance as the foot is pulled away by a calibrated spring device. This ability is also evidenced by the infant's partial support of its own weight when held upright by an adult. If the infant is given enough support by the adult, some forward movement is seen in a built-in stepping reflex, which disappears in a few months. Each leg is lifted, moved forward, and placed down, as if the infant were taking a series of steps. However, the sequence lasts only two to three steps, and, of course, the infant does not have sufficient balance or strength to execute the movement independently.

It is not until 11 months of age that the infant can walk with limited help from an adult. Sometime later (at about 12 to 14 months), the infant can pull up to a standing position, then stand alone, and finally walk (at about 15 months). The actual month at which some milestone occurs may vary by as much as 2 to 4 months, especially among older infants. What remains fairly uniform, however, is the sequence of accomplishments. The remarkable achievement of posture and locomotion in infants is summarized in figure 5.3. An important implication of these motor achievements of infants is the increasing degree of independence that children accomplish. They can explore their environment more extensively and initiate social interaction with caregivers and peers.

Rhythmic Motor Behavior

During the first year of life, repetitious movement of the limbs, torso, and head is common. Such **rhythmic motor behavior**—kicking, rocking, waving, bouncing, banging, rubbing, scratching, swaying—has intrigued developmentalists for many years. These infant motor behaviors stand out not only because they occur frequently, but also because of the pleasure infants seem to derive from performing the acts.

Explanations of rhythmic motor behavior are numerous. Arnold Gesell (1954) saw rocking as a specific stage of development, but warned that persistent rhythmic motor behavior was a sign of developmental delay or an impoverished environment. Jean Piaget (1967) referred to kicking and waving as a stage of sensorimotor development when infants try to repeat a behavior that has an interesting effect on the environment. Psychoanalytic theorists interpret rocking as the infant's attempt to establish relations with an aloof mother. And pediatricians suggest that head banging is due to a bad temper.

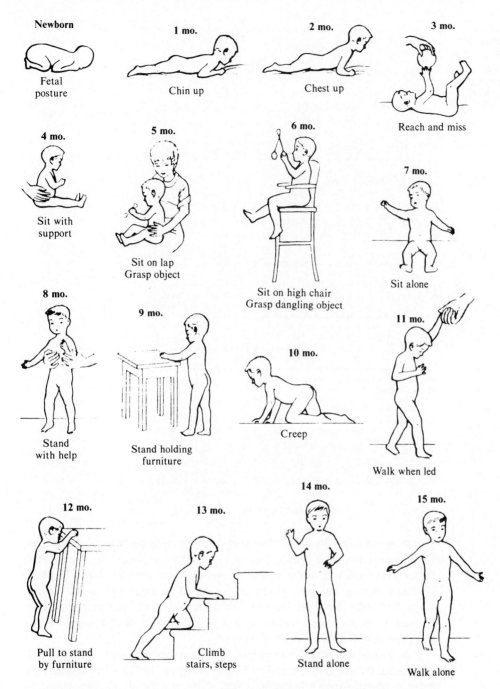

Figure 5.3
The development of posture and locomotion in infants.

Newborn — Fetal posture

1 mo. — Chin up

2 mo. — Chest up

3 mo. — Reach and miss

4 mo. — Sit with support

5 mo. — Sit on lap Grasp object

6 mo. — Sit on high chair Grasp dangling object

7 mo. — Sit alone

8 mo. — Stand with help

9 mo. — Stand holding furniture

10 mo. — Creep

11 mo. — Walk when led

12 mo. — Pull to stand by furniture

13 mo. — Climb stairs, steps

14 mo. — Stand alone

15 mo. — Walk alone

More recently, Esther Thelen (1981, 1987) argued that rhythmic motor behavior serves an important adaptive function for infants in the first year of life. She believes it is an important transition between uncoordinated activity and complex, coordinated motor behavior. She conducted extraordinarily detailed observations of 20 normal infants from the time they were four weeks old until they were one year old. More than 16,000 bouts of rhythmic behavior were observed. Infants spent about 5 percent of their time in rhythmic motor behavior, although some infants at some ages spent as much as 40 percent of the time they were observed in rhythmic motor behavior. The 47 distinct movements observed included variations of kicking, waving, bouncing,

Figure 5.4
Frequency of rhythmic motor behavior in the first year of life. Frequencies are expressed as a percentage of the total bouts of rhythmical behavior observed at each age. The bouts are grouped by body parts.

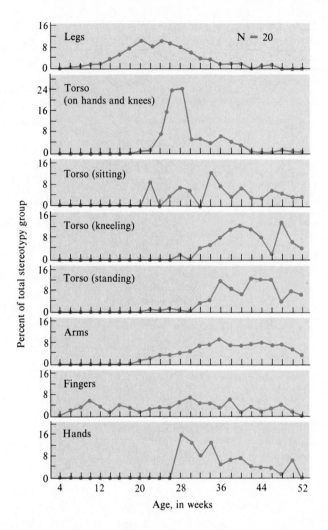

scratching, banging, rubbing, thrusting, swaying, and twisting. When stereotyped movements were grouped by body part and posture, their frequencies showed certain developmental profiles over the first year, as shown in figure 5.4. Rhythmic leg behavior gradually increased at about one month, peaked at 5 to 6 months, and then declined, for example. If all rhythmic cycles are summed, the age of peak frequency was 6 to 7 months, with a small decline in the last few months of the first year.

A dramatic confirmation of the developmental importance of rhythmic motor behavior was documented by Selma Fraiberg (1977) with blind infants. Motor development in blind infants was characteristically uneven. Blind infants attained postural milestones such as sitting alone, "bridging" on hands and knees, and standing at ages comparable to sighted infants. Their locomotor development was severely delayed, however, probably due to a lack of visual motivation to move forward. In normal infants, crawling follows soon after the infant assumes the hands and knees posture, for example. In blind infants, there may be 4 or more months delay between these events. Nonetheless, all the infants rocked vigorously in sitting, hands and knees, and standing postures; but unlike in normal infants, this rocking did not disappear. In Fraiberg's own words,

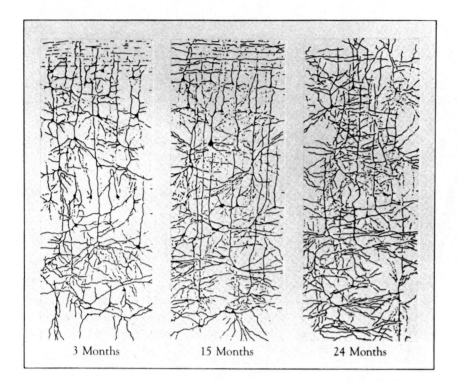

Figure 5.5
The development of dendritic spreading at birth, 3 months, 6 months, and 24 months in the cerebral cortex of the human infant. Note the increase in connectedness between neurons over the course of the first 2 years of life.
Source: Conel, J. L. (1939–1963) Postnatal development of the human cerebral cortex (Vols. I–VI). *Cambridge, MA: Harvard U. Press.*

3 Months   15 Months   24 Months

In the blind infant, rhythmic activity may be more prolonged because, at each point along the gross motor sequence, the self-initiated mobility that should follow upon the new posture is delayed. Thus, a child with good control of his trunk in a bridging posture, with "readiness" we would say for creeping, might be observed on all fours, rocking steadily, "ready to go" with "no place to go." The motor impetus, which normally leads mobility, was exercised in a vacuum. Again typically, when mobility was achieved, the stereotyped rocking was extinguished (pp. 217, 218).

The Brain

As the infant walks, talks, runs, shakes a rattle, smiles, and frowns, changes in the brain are occurring. Consider that the infant began life as a single cell and that in 9 months was born with a brain and nervous system that contained some 10 to 100 billion nerve cells. Indeed, at birth, the infant probably had all of the nerve cells—called neurons—it was going to have in its entire life. But at birth and in early infancy, the connectedness of all of these neurons was impoverished. As shown in figure 5.5, as the infant moves from birth to 2 years of age, the interconnections of neurons increase dramatically as the dendrites (the receiving part) of neurons branch out.

Undoubtedly, neurotransmitters are changing during prenatal and infant years, too—these are the tiny chemical substances that carry information across gaps from one neuron to the next. Little is known about neurotransmitter changes in infancy, although changes in one important neurotransmitter—dopamine—has been documented in monkeys (Goldman-Rakic and others, 1983). The concentration of dopamine in the prefrontal lobe—the area of the brain involved in higher cognitive functions such as problem solving—peaks at 5 months of age, declines until about 18 to 24 months, and then increases again at 2 to 3 years of age. These changes in dopamine concentration may reflect a switch from growth and nutritional functions to neurotransmitter function for this substance. Such speculation only begins to scratch the surface of the important role neurotransmitter substances might play in the brain's early development.

At this point we have discussed many ideas about physical development in infancy. A summary of the main points in this discussion is presented in Concept Table 5.1. Next, we explore the infant's fascinating sensory and perceptual development.

Sensory and Perceptual Development

At the beginning of this chapter, you read about how the newborn comes into the world equipped with sensory capacities. But what are sensation and perception? Can a newborn see, and if so, what can it perceive? What about the other senses—hearing, smell, taste, touch, and pain—what are they like in the newborn? These are among the intriguing questions we now explore.

What Are Sensation and Perception?
How does a newborn know that his mother's skin is soft rather than rough? How does a 5-year-old know what color her hair is? How does an 8-year-old know that summer is warmer than winter? How does a 10-year-old know that a firecracker is louder than a cat's meow? Infants and children "know" these things because of their senses. All information comes to the infant through the senses. Without vision, hearing, touch, taste, smell, and other senses, the infant's brain would be isolated from the world; the infant would live in dark silence—a tasteless, colorless, feelingless void.

Sensation occurs when information contacts sensory receptors—the eyes, ears, tongue, nostrils, and skin. The sensation of vision occurs as rays of light contact the two eyes and become focused on the retina. **Perception** is the interpretation of what is sensed. The sensation of hearing occurs when waves of pulsating air are collected by the outer ear and transmitted through the bones of the inner ear to the auditory nerve. The information about physical events that contacts the ears may be interpreted as musical sounds. The physical energy transmitted to the retina may be interpreted as a particular color, pattern, or shape, for example.

Developmental Theories of Perception
As with most aspects of development, theories have been proposed to explain perception's development. Two prominent theories of perceptual development are the **ecological view** of Eleanor and James Gibson and the **constructivist view** of Jean Piaget.

Physical Development		
Concept	**Processes/Related Ideas**	**Characteristics/Description**
Reflexes	Their Nature	The newborn is no longer viewed as a passive, empty-headed organism. Physically, though, newborns are limited, and reflexes—automatic movements—govern the newborn's behavior.
	Sucking	Sucking is an important means of obtaining nutrition, as well as a pleasurable, soothing activity, for infants. Nonnutritive sucking is of interest to researchers because it provides a means of evaluating attention.
	Crying and Smiling	Crying and smiling are affective behaviors that are important in the infant's communication with the world.
States	Classification	Researchers have put together different classification systems; one classification involves seven infant state categories, including deep sleep, drowsy, alert and focused, and inflexibly focused.
	The Sleeping-Waking Cycle	Newborns usually sleep 16 to 17 hours a day. By four months, they approach adultlike sleeping patterns. REM sleep, during which children and adults are most likely to dream, occurs much more in early infancy than in childhood and adulthood. The high percentage of REM sleep—about half of neonatal sleep—may be a self-stimulatory device, or it may promote brain development.
Eating Behavior	Its Nature	There are many health advantages to breast-feeding, but a large percentage of American mothers choose to bottle-feed their infants, mainly for convenience reasons. Debate also focuses on scheduled versus demand feeding; more recently, parents have been likely to adopt a demand feeding schedule.
Physical Growth and Motor Development	Cephalocaudal and Proximodistal Sequences	The cephalocaudal pattern is growth from the top down; the proximodistal pattern is growth from the center out.
	Gross Motor and Fine Motor Skills	Gross motor skills involve large muscle activity as in walking; fine motor skills involve more fine-grained activities like manual dexterity. Both gross and fine motor skills undergo extensive change in the first two years of development.
	Rhythmic Motor Behavior	During the first year, rhythmic motor behavior, involving rapid, repetitive movement of the limbs, torso, and head is common; it seems to represent an important adaptive transition in development.
	The Brain	There is a great deal of brain growth in infancy as well as in prenatal development. Dendritic spreading is dramatic in the first two years. Some important changes in neurotransmitters probably also take place, although these changes are just beginning to be charted.

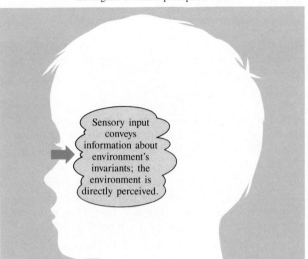

Ecological or direct perception view

Constructivist view

Figure 5.6
*Comparison of the ecological or direct
perception and constructivist views.*

Eleanor Gibson (1969, 1986, in press) and James J. Gibson (1979) argue
that the invariants—those aspects of the environment that do not change—in
stimulation in the infant's world provide rich information. These aspects of
the environment involve places (a room), objects (a face), and pictures (a picture of a face). Since these things are actually in the world, and since perceptual invariants specify their properties, the ecological theorists believe the
infant only has to attend to the appropriate information; she does not have to
build up internal representations to see them.

An important assumption of the ecological view is that even complex
things—like the spatial layout of a room—can be perceived "directly" by
picking up the invariants rather than engaging in any complex constructive
mental activity. This important dimension of the ecological view has led it to
also be labeled the *direct perception* view. If complex things can be perceived
directly, perhaps they can be perceived at young ages, maybe even by young
infants. This possibility has inspired investigators to search for the competencies of very young infants (Aslin, 1987; Bower, 1982; Kagan, 1987). The advocates of the ecological or direct perception view do not deny that perception
develops as infants and children grow. In fact, they assume that as perceptual
processes mature, a child becomes more efficient at discovering the environment's invariant properties that are available to the senses.

By contrast, the constructivist view advocated by Jean Piaget stresses
that perceiving the world is more than merely picking up information about
its invariant properties; says Piaget, perception is a mental construction based
on sensory input from the eyes or other sensory receptors plus information
retrieved from memory. It is a kind of *representation* of the world that builds
up in the mind. Figure 5.6 compares the ecological and constructivist views.

The constructivist view suggests that many changes in perception reflect
changes in how the infant or child constructs a representation of the world.
The constructivist view argues that, as the infant and child's memory develops,
changes in long-term memory knowledge play an important role in how the
infant or child perceives the world. In the next chapter, we explore the exciting
question of whether young infants have memory, and if so, when it emerges.
Much more about Piaget's theory of development also appears in the next
chapter.

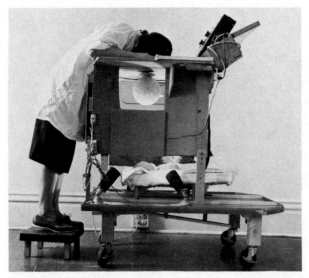

Figure 5.7
The "looking chamber" has been used to study visual preference in infants.

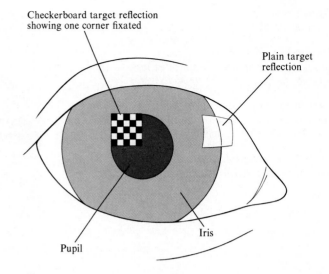

Checkerboard target reflection showing one corner fixated

Plain target reflection

Iris

Pupil

Figure 5.8
Drawing of an infant's eye as seen by the experimenter in the test chamber when the infant has been visually exposed to checked and plain squares. The more the target reflection overlays the pupil, the greater the degree of fixation.

Visual Perception

How do we see? Anyone who has ever taken photographs on a vacation appreciates the miracle of perception. The camera is no match for it. Consider a favorite scenic spot that you visited and photographed some time in the past. Compare your memory of this spot to your snapshot. Although your memory may be faulty, there is little doubt that the richness of your perceptual experience is not captured in the picture. The sense of depth that you felt at this spot probably is not conveyed by the snapshot. Nor is the sublety of the colors you perceived or the intricacies of textures and shapes. Human vision is complex and its development is complex, too.

Psychologist William James (1890) called the newborn's perceptual world a blooming, buzzing confusion. Was James right? A century later, we can safely say that he was wrong. To sum up the research on infant perception with one simple statement, infants' perception of visual information is *much* more advanced than previously thought.

Our tour of visual perception begins with the pioneering work of Robert Fantz (1958, 1961). Fantz placed infants in a "looking chamber," which has two visual displays on the ceiling of the chamber above the infant's head (see figure 5.7). An experimenter viewed the infant's eyes by looking through a peephole. If the infant was fixating on one of the displays, the experimenter could see the display's reflection in the infant's eyes (see figure 5.8). This allowed the experimenter to determine how long the infant looked at each display. The findings were simple: When presented with a pair of visual displays, an infant looked longer at one than the other. For instance, an infant looked longer at a display of stripes than a display of a solid gray patch. This demonstrates that newborns can see and also that they can tell the difference between two dissimilar objects. The newborn's visual world is not the blooming, buzzing confusion James envisioned.

Just how well can infants see? The newborn's vision is about 20/600 on the well-known Snellen chart that you are tested with when you have your eyes examined; this is about 30 times lower than normal adult vision (20/20). But by six months of age, vision is 20/100 or better (Banks & Salapatek, 1983).

A baby is the most complicated object made by unskilled labor.

Anonymous

Figure 5.9
A child's depth perception is tested on the visual cliff. The apparatus consists of a board laid across a sheet of heavy glass, with a patterned material directly beneath the glass on one side and several feet below it on the other. Placed on the center board, the child crawls to his mother across the "shallow" side. Called from the "deep" side, he pats the glass, but despite this tactual evidence that the "cliff" is in fact a solid surface, he refuses to cross over to the mother.

Young infants can see, but do they merely see a black-and-white world or do they see a world of color like normal adults can? Normal adults with full color vision have three types of cones in the retina of the eye that enable them to see colors—red, blue, and green. Infants as young as one week old appear to be able to see both greens and red, but not blues; by the third month, they appear to be able to see all three basic colors, just as normal adults do. Thus, infants are partially color-blind in the first few months of life, but by three months of age seem to be mature in their ability to see all the basic colors.

The human face is perhaps the most important visual pattern for the newborn to perceive. The infant masters a sequence of steps in progressing toward full perceptual appreciation of the face (Gibson, 1969). At about 3½ weeks, the infant is fascinated with the eyes, perhaps because the infant notices simple perceptual features such as dots, angles, and circles. At 1 to 2 months of age, the infant notices and perceives contour. At 2 months and older, the infant begins to differentiate facial features: The eyes are distinguished from other parts of the face, the mouth is noticed, and movements of the mouth draw attention to it. By 5 months, the infant has detected other facial features—its plasticity, its solid, three-dimensional surface, the oval shape of the head, the orientation of the eyes and the mouth. Beyond 6 months, the infant distinguishes familiar faces from unfamiliar faces—mother from stranger, masks from real faces, and so on.

How early can infants perceive depth? To investigate this question, Eleanor Gibson and Richard Walk (1960) conducted a classic experiment. They constructed a miniature cliff with a drop-off covered by glass. The motivation for this experiment happened when Gibson was eating a picnic lunch on the edge of the Grand Canyon. She wondered if an infant looking over the canyon's rim would perceive the dangerous drop-off and back up. In their laboratory, Gibson and Walk placed infants on the edge of a visual cliff (see figure 5.9) and had their mothers coax them to crawl out on the glass. Most infants would not crawl out on the glass, choosing instead to remain on the shallow

THE FETUS AND
THE CAT IN THE HAT

The fetus can hear sounds in the last few months of pregnancy—the mother's voice, music, loud sounds from television, the roar of an airplane, and so on. Given that the fetus can hear sounds, two psychologists wanted to find out if listening to Dr. Seuss's classic story, *The Cat in the Hat,* while they were still in the mother's womb would produce a preference for hearing the story after they were born (Spence & DeCasper, 1982). Sixteen pregnant women read *The Cat in the Hat* to their fetuses twice a day over the last 6 weeks of their pregnancies. When the babies were born, they were given a choice of sucking on either of two nipples. Sucking on one nipple produced a recording of their

What ingenious method did researchers develop to discover whether the fetus could hear its mother reading The Cat in the Hat?

mothers reading *The King, the Mice and the Cheese,* a story with a different rhyme and pace to it. Sucking on the other nipple produced a recording of their mothers reading *The Cat in the Hat.* The newborns preferred listening to *The Cat in the Hat,* which they had heard frequently as a fetus.

Two important conclusions can be drawn from this investigation. First, it reveals how ingenious scientists have become at assessing the development not only of infants but fetuses as well, in this case discovering a way to "interview" newborn babies who cannot yet talk. Second, it reveals the remarkable ability of the brain to learn even before the infant is born.

side, indicating that they could perceive depth. Because the 6- to 14-month-old infants had extensive visual experience, this research did not answer the question of whether depth perception is innate.

Exactly how early in life does depth perception develop? Since younger infants do not crawl, this question is difficult to answer. Research with 2- to 4-month-olds shows differences in heart rate when the infants are placed directly on the deep side of the visual cliff versus the shallow side of the cliff (Campos, Langer, & Krowitz, 1970). However, an alternative interpretation is that young infants respond to differences in some visual characteristic of the deep and shallow cliffs, with no actual knowledge of depth.

We have discussed a good deal of research on visual perception in infancy. Many fundamental aspects of vision are in working order by birth, and many others are present by several months of age. Yet, perception is not complete by 1 or 2 years of age. Many aspects of perception continue to grow more efficient and accurate during the childhood years (Bornstein, 1988).

Hearing

Immediately after birth, infants can hear, although their sensory thresholds are somewhat higher than those of adults. That is, a stimulus must be louder to be heard by a newborn than by an adult. Not only can a newborn hear, but the possibility has been raised that the fetus can hear, as it nestles within its mother's womb. To learn more about this possibility, read Focus on Life-Span Development 5.2.

Smell

Infants can smell soon after birth. In one investigation (Lipsitt, Engen, & Kaye, 1963), infants less than 24 hours old made body and leg movements and showed changes in breathing when they were exposed to asafetida, a bitter and offensive odor. Infants' sense of smell is not just for unpleasant odors. They apparently can recognize the smell of their mother's breasts, which presumably is pleasant. In one study (MacFarlane, 1975), 2- to 7-day-old infants were exposed to two breast pads, one to their right and one to their left. One of these breast pads had been used by the infant's mother, the other was clean. The infants were more likely to turn toward their mother's breast pad than toward the clean breast pad. Infants this young, though, may not respond to their mother's breast pad but to any mother's breast pad. To test this, MacFarlane (1975) replaced the clean breast pad with another mother's breast pad. Two-day-old infants showed no preference; it may not be until several weeks of age that infants recognize their own mother's smell.

Taste

Sensitivity to taste may be present prior to birth. When saccharin was added to the amniotic fluid of a near-term fetus, increased swallowing was observed (Windle, 1940). Sensitivity to sweetness is clearly present in the newborn. When sucks on a nipple are rewarded with a sweetened solution, the amount of sucking increases (Lipsitt & others, 1976). In another investigation (Steiner, 1979), newborns showed a smilelike expression after being stimulated with a sweetened solution but pursed their lips after being stimulated with a sour solution.

Touch

Just as newborns respond to taste, they also respond to touch. A touch to the cheek produces a turning of the head, while a touch to the lips produces sucking movements. An important ability that develops in infancy is to connect information about vision with information about touch. One-year-olds clearly can do this and it appears that six-month-olds also can (Acredelo & Hake, 1982). Whether still younger infants can coordinate vision and touch is yet to be determined.

Pain

If and when you have a son and need to consider whether he should be circumcised, the issue of an infant's pain perception probably will become important to you. Circumcision is usually performed on young boys about the third day after birth. Will your young son experience pain if he is circumcised when he is three-days-old? Increased crying and fussing occurs during the

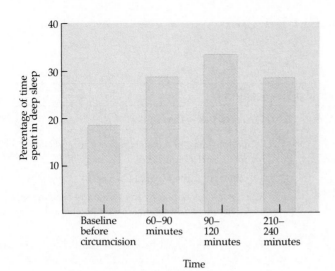

circumcision procedure, suggesting the three-day-old infant experiences pain (Anders & Chalemian, 1974; Gunnar, Malone, & Fisch, 1987; Porter, Porges, & Marshall, 1988).

In the recent investigation by Megan Gunnar and her colleagues (1987), the healthy newborn's ability to cope with stress was evaluated. The newborn infant males cried intensely during the circumcision, indicating that it was stressful. The researchers pointed out that it is rather remarkable the newborn infant does not suffer serious consequences from the surgery. Rather, the circumcised infant displays amazing resiliency and ability to cope. Within several minutes after the surgery, the infant can nurse and interact in a normal manner with his mother. And, if allowed, the newly circumcised newborn drifts into a deep sleep that seems to serve as a coping mechanism. As shown in figure 5.10, the percentage of time spent in deep sleep was greater in the 60 to 240 minutes after the circumcision than prior to it.

In our tour of the infant's perceptual world, we discussed a number of senses—vision, hearing, smell, taste, touch, and pain. A summary of the main ideas about these aspects of infant perception is presented in Concept Table 5.2. Next, we explore the fascinating idea that even the very young infant can relate information about the different senses.

Bimodal Perception

Is the young infant so competent that he can relate and integrate information from several sensory modalities? The ability to relate and integrate information about two sensory modalities—such as vision and audition (hearing)—is called **bimodal perception.** An increasing number of developmentalists believe the young infant experiences a related visual and auditory world (Bahrick, 1988; Gibson & Spelke, 1983; Kagan, 1987; Rose & Ruff, 1987). This remains a controversial view. For example, in one recent investigation of 6-month-old infants, the auditory sense dominated the visual sense, restricting bimodal perception (Lewkowicz, 1988). To learn more about bimodal perception, read Focus on Life-Span Development 5.3.

Perceptual Development		
Concept	**Processes/Related Ideas**	**Characteristics/Description**
What Are Sensation and Perception	Sensation	When information contacts sensory receptors—eyes, ears, tongue, nostrils, and skin.
	Perception	The interpretation of what is sensed.
Developmental Theories of Perception	Ecological or Direct Perception View	The view—developed by the Gibsons—that the infant perceives the world by picking up perceptual invariants in the environment.
	Constructivist View	The view—developed by Piaget—that what the infant perceives is a construction based on a combination of sensory input and information retrieved from memory.
Visual Perception	The Newborn's Visual World	William James said it was a blooming, buzzing confusion; he was wrong. The newborn's perception is more advanced than we previously thought.
	Visual Preferences	Fantz's research—by showing how infants prefer striped to solid patches—demonstrated that newborns can see.
	Quality of Vision	The newborn is about 20/600 on the Snellen chart; by 6 months vision has improved to at least 20/100.
	Color	Newborns seem to be partially color-blind, but by 3 months they appear to see all of the basic colors.
	The Human Face	Is an important visual pattern for the newborn; the infant gradually masters a sequence of steps in perceiving the human face.
	Depth Perception	A classic study by Gibson and Walk demonstrated through the use of the visual cliff that 6 month old infants can perceive depth.
Other Senses	Hearing	The fetus can hear several weeks before birth; immediately after birth newborns can hear, although their sensory threshold is higher than for adults.
	Smell, Taste, Touch, and Pain	Each of these senses is present in the newborn. Research on circumcision shows that 3-day-old males experience pain and have the ability to adapt to stress.

The claim that the young infant can relate information from one sensory dimension to another has important theoretical ties. The constructivist view of perception—reflected in Piaget's theory—argues that the main perceptual abilities—visual, auditory, and tactile, for example—are completely uncoordinated at birth, and further that young infants do not have bimodal perception. According to Piaget, it is only through months of sensorimotor interactions with the world that bimodal perception is possible. By contrast, the ecological or direct perception view—reflected in the Gibsons' theory—stresses that infants are born with some bimodal perceptual abilities or predispositions that enable them to develop these abilities early in infancy.

YELLOW KANGAROOS, GRAY DONKEYS, THUMPS, GONGS, AND FOUR-MONTH-OLD INFANTS

I magine yourself playing basketball or tennis. There are obviously many visual inputs: the ball coming and going, other players moving around, and so on. But there are also many auditory inputs: the sound of the ball bouncing or being hit and the grunts, groans, and curses emitted by yourself and others. There is also good correspondence between much of the visual and auditory information: When you see the ball bounce, you hear a bouncing sound; when a player leaps, you hear a groan.

We live in a world of objects and events that can be seen, heard, and felt. When mature perceivers look and listen to an event simultaneously, they experience a unitary episode. All of this is so commonplace that it

scarcely seems worth mentioning. But consider the task of the very young infant with little practice at perceiving. Can she put vision and sound together as precisely as adults?

To test bimodal perception, Elizabeth Spelke (1979) performed three experiments with the following structure: Two simple films were shown side-by-side in front of a four-month-old infant. One film showed a yellow kangaroo bouncing up and down, and the other showed a gray donkey bounding up and down. There also was an auditory sound track—a repeating thump or gong sound. A number of measures assessed the infant's tendency to look at one film versus the other.

In Experiment 1, the animal in one of the films bounced at a slower

rate than the animal in the other. And the sound track was synchronized either with the film of the slow-bouncing animal or with the film of the fast-bouncing animal. Infants' first looks were toward the film that was specified by the sound track. Experiments 2 and 3 explored two components of the relation between the sound track and the matching film: common tempo and simultaneity of sounds and bounces. The findings indicated that the infants were sensitive to both of these components.

Spelke's clever demonstration suggests that infants only four months old do not experience a world of unrelated visual and auditory dimensions; they can perceive these as unitary.

Pushing back the age barriers of when an infant can coordinate information from different senses has found support in recent research, such as that conducted by Elizabeth Spelke (1979) and others (Rose & Ruff, 1987). This research supports the ecological view of the Gibsons. Still, there are enough inconsistencies and methodological problems in this research to keep alive the debate on the degree to which such complex perceptual capabilities are inborn or are constructed over a longer period of time through interaction with the world. Nonetheless, if research in bimodal perception continues to be verified with young infants, the ecological interpretation will be difficult to refute. What we do know is that when newborns emerge into this world, they know a lot more than we used to think. They see more and hear more than we used to believe was possible.

Increasingly developmentalists have become surprised by the early competencies of newborns and young infants. Are we going too far in believing that newborns and young infants are competent in dealing with their world or are they really as sophisticated as the new wave of research seems to suggest?

Summary

I. **Reflexes**

The newborn is no longer viewed as a passive, empty-headed organism. Physically, newborns are limited, though, and reflexes—automatic movements—govern the newborn's behavior. Sucking is an important means of obtaining nutrition, as well as a pleasurable, soothing activity, for infants. Nonnutritive sucking is of interest to researchers because it provides a means of evaluating attention. Crying and smiling are affective behaviors that are important in the infant's communication with the world.

II. **States**

Researchers have put together different classification systems; one classification involves seven infant state categories, including deep sleep, drowsy, alert and focused, and inflexibly focused. Newborns usually sleep 16 to 17 hours a day. By four months, they approach adultlike sleeping patterns. REM sleep, during which children and adults are most likely to dream, occurs much more in early infancy than childhood or adulthood. The high percentage of REM sleep—about half of neonatal sleep—may be a self-stimulatory device, or it may promote brain development.

III. **Eating Behavior**

There are many health advantages to breast-feeding, but a large percentage of American mothers choose to bottle-feed their infants, mainly for convenience reasons. Debate also focuses on scheduled versus demand feeding; more recently, parents have been likely to adopt a demand feeding schedule.

IV. **Physical Growth and Motor Development**

The cephalocaudal pattern is growth from the top down; the proximodistal pattern is growth from the center out. Gross motor skills involve large muscle activity as in walking; fine motor skills involve more fine-grained activities, like manual dexterity. Both gross and fine motor skills undergo extensive change in the first two years of development. During the first year, rhythmic motor behavior—involving rapid, repetitive movement of the limbs, torso, and head—is common; it seems to represent an important adaptive transition in development. There is a great deal of brain growth in infancy as well as in prenatal development. Dendritic spreading is dramatic in the first 2 years. Some important changes in neurotransmitters probably also take place, although these changes are just beginning to be charted.

V. **What Are Sensation and Perception?**

Sensation is when information contacts sensory receptors—eyes, ears, tongue, nostrils, and skin. Perception is the interpretation of what is sensed.

VI. **Developmental Theories of Perception**

The ecological or direct perception view, developed by the Gibsons, says that the infant perceives the world by picking up perceptual invariants in the environment. The constructivist view, developed by Piaget, says that what the infant perceives is a construction based on a combination of sensory input and information retrieved from memory.

VII. **Visual Perception**

William James said that the newborn's perceptual world was like a blooming, buzzing confusion; he was wrong. The newborn's perception is more advanced than previously was thought. Fantz's research—by showing how infants prefer stripes to solids—demonstrated that newborns can see. Newborns seem to be partially color-blind, but by 3 months they appear to see all of the basic colors. The human face is an important visual pattern for the newborn; the infant gradually masters a sequence of steps in perceiving the human face. A classic study by Gibson and Walk demonstrated through the use of the visual cliff that 6-month-old infants can perceive depth.

VIII. **Other Senses**

The fetus can hear several weeks before birth; immediately after birth, newborns can hear, although their sensory threshold is higher than for adults. Smell, taste, touch, and pain are present in the newborn. Research on circumcision shows that 3-day-old males experience pain and have the ability to cope with stress.

IV. **Bimodal Perception**

Considerable interest focuses on the infant's ability to relate information across perceptual modalities; the coordination and integration of perceptual information across two modalities—such as the visual and auditory senses—is called bimodal perception. Research suggests that infants as young as 4 months of age have bimodal perception.

Key Terms

Suggested Readings

Banks, M. S., & Salapatek, P. (1983). Infant visual perception. In P. E. Mussen (Ed.), *Handbook of child psychology* (4th ed.), Vol. 2. New York: Wiley.
This authoritative version of research on infant perception covers in great detail the topics discussed in this chapter.

Bower, T. G. R. (1977). *The perceptual world of the child.* Cambridge, MA: Harvard University Press.
A scholarly introduction to the study of infant perception, including the topics of space perception, distance perception, and size constancy.

Caplan F. (1981). *The first twelve months of life.* New York: Bantam.
An easy-to-read, well-written account of each of the first twelve months of life.

Lamb, M. E., & Bornstein, M. C. (1987). *Development in infancy.* New York: Random House.
This portrayal of the infant by two leading researchers includes individual chapters on perceptual development as well as the ecology of the infant's development.

Osofosky, J. D. (1987). *Handbook of Infant Development,* 2nd ed. New York: Wiley.
Leading experts in the field of infant development have contributed chapters on a far ranging set of topics about infants.

C H A P T E R

6

∎

Cognitive and Language Development

Dra. 1/2

Matthew is 1 year old. He has already seen over 1,000 flash cards with pictures of shells, flowers, insects, flags, countries, words—you name it—on them. His mother, Billie, has made close to 10,000 such 11-inch square cards for Matthew and his 4-year-old brother, Mark. Billie has religiously followed the regimen recommended by Glenn Doman, the director of the Philadelphia Institute for the Achievement of Human Potential and the author of *How to Teach Your Baby to Read*. Using his methods, learned in a course called "How to Multiply Your Baby's Intelligence," Billie is teaching Matthew Japanese and even a little math. Mark is learning geography, natural science, engineering, and fine arts as well.

Parents using the card approach print one word on each card using a bright red felt-tipped pen. The parent repeatedly shows the card to the infant while saying the word. The first word usually is *mommy,* then comes *daddy,* the baby's name, parts of the body, and all the things the infant can touch. The infant is lavishly praised when he recognizes the word. The idea is to imprint the large red words in the infant's memory, so that in time, he accumulates an impressive vocabulary and begins to read. The parent continues to feed the infant with all manner of information in small, assimilable bits, just as Billie Rash has done with her two boys.

With this method, the child should be reading by 2 years of age, and by 4 or 5, should have begun mastering some math and be able to play the violin, not to mention the vast knowledge of the world he should be able to display because of a monumental vocabulary. Maybe the SAT or ACT test you labored through on your way to college might have been conquered at the age of 6 if your parents had only been enrolled in "How to Multiply Your Baby's Intelligence" course and made 10,000 flash cards for you.

Is this the best way for an infant to learn? A number of developmentalists believe Doman's "better baby institute" is a money-making scheme and is not based on sound scientific evidence. They believe that we should not be trying to accelerate the infant's learning so dramatically. Rather than have it poured into his mind, the infant should be permitted more time to spontaneously explore the environment and construct his knowledge. Jean Piaget called "What should we do to foster cognitive development?" the American question because it was asked of him so often when he lectured to American audiences. Developmentalists worry that children exposed to Doman's methods will become burned out on learning. What probably is more important is providing a rich and emotionally supportive atmosphere for learning.

The excitement and enthusiasm surrounding the infant's cognition has been fueled by an interest in what an infant knows at birth and soon after, by continued fascination about innate and learned factors in the infant's cognitive development, and by controversies over whether infants construct their knowledge—as Piaget believed—or whether they know their world through more direct connection with the environment. Primary topics include Piaget's theory

Infancy

of infant development, the nature of attention, memory, and imitation, measurement of infants' intelligence, and where the infant's language comes from and how it develops. We examine each of these topics in turn.

Piaget's Theory of Infant Development

Poet Nora Perry once asked, "Who knows the thoughts of the child?" As much as anyone, Piaget knew. Through careful, inquisitive interviews and observations of his own three children—Laurent, Lucienne, and Jacqueline—Piaget changed the way we think about infants' perception of their world. Remember that we studied an overview of Piaget's theory in chapter 2. It may be helpful for you to go over those basic features of his theory at this time.

Piaget believed that the child passed through a series of stages of thought from infancy to adolescence. Passage through the stages results from biological pressures to *adapt* to the environment (assimilation and accommodation) and to organize structures of thinking. The stages of thought are *qualitatively* different from one another—the way a child reasons at one stage is very different from the way she reasons at another stage. This contrasts with the quantitative assessments of intelligence made through the use of standardized intelligence tests, where the focus is on what the child knows, or how many questions the child can answer correctly. According to Piaget, the mind's development is divided into four such qualitatively different stages—sensorimotor, preoperational, concrete operational, and formal operational. Here our concern is with the stage that characterizes infant thought—the sensorimotor stage.

We are born capable of learning.
Jean Jacque Rousseau

The Stage of Sensorimotor Development

Piaget's sensorimotor stage lasts from birth to about 2 years of age—corresponding to the period of infancy. During this time, mental development is characterized by considerable progression in the infant's ability to organize and coordinate sensations with physical movements and actions—hence, the name *sensorimotor* (Piaget, 1952).

At the beginning of the sensorimotor stage, the infant has little more than reflexive patterns with which to work. By the end of the stage, the 2-year-old has complex sensorimotor patterns and is beginning to operate with a primitive symbol system. Unlike other stages, the sensorimotor stage is subdivided into six substages, which describe qualitative changes in sensorimotor organization. The term **scheme** (or schema) refers to the basic unit for an organized pattern of sensorimotor functioning. With a given substage, there may be different schemes—sucking, rooting, and blinking in Substage 1, for example. In Substage 1, they are basically reflexive in nature. From substage to substage, the schemes change in organization. This change is at the heart of Piaget's description of the stages. The six substages of sensorimotor development are (1) simple reflexes; (2) first habits and primary circular reactions; (3) secondary circular reactions; (4) coordination of secondary circular reactions; (5) tertiary circular reactions, novelty, and curiosity; and (6) internalization of schemes.

In Substage 1, **simple reflexes,** which corresponds to the first month after birth, the basic means of coordinating sensation and action is through reflexive behaviors—such as rooting and sucking—which the infant has at birth. In Substage 1, the infant exercises these reflexes. More importantly, the infant develops an ability to produce behaviors that resemble reflexes in the absence

(a) (b) (c)

(d) (e) (f)

Piaget's six substages of sensorimotor development. In substage 1 (a), the infant practices the reflexive behavior of sucking. In substage 2 (b), the infant will practice the sucking reflex when no bottle is present. In substage 3 (c), the infant becomes more object oriented. In substage 4 (d), the infant begins to coordinate action. In substage 5 (e), the infant becomes intrigued by an object's variety of properties. In substage 6 (f), the infant's functioning shifts to a symbolic plane.

of obvious reflexive stimuli. The newborn may suck when a bottle or nipple is only nearby, for example. The bottle or nipple would have produced the sucking pattern only when placed directly in the newborn's mouth or touched to the newborn's lips when the baby was just born. Reflexlike actions in the absence of a triggering stimulus is evidence that the infant is initiating action and is actively structuring experiences in life's first month.

In Substage 2, **first habits and primary circular reactions,** which develops between 1 to 4 months of age, the infant learns to coordinate sensation and types of schemes or structures, that is, habits and primary circular reactions. A *habit* is a scheme based upon a simple reflex, such as sucking, that has become completely divorced from its eliciting stimulus. For example, an infant in Substage 1 might suck when orally stimulated by a bottle or when visually shown the bottle, but an infant in Substage 2 might exercise the sucking scheme even when no bottle is present.

A **primary circular reaction** is a scheme based upon the infant's attempt to reproduce an interesting or pleasurable event that initially occurred by chance. In a popular Piagetian example, a child accidentally sucks his fingers when they are placed near his mouth; later, he searches for his fingers to suck them again, but the fingers do not cooperate in the search because the infant cannot coordinate visual and manual actions. Habits and circular reactions are stereotyped in that the infant repeats them the same way each time. The infant's own body remains the center of attention; there is no outward pull by environmental events.

In Substage 3, **secondary circular reactions,** which develops between 4 to 8 months of age, the infant becomes more object oriented or focused on the world, moving beyond preoccupation with the self in sensorimotor interactions. The chance shaking of a rattle, for example, may fascinate the infant, and the infant will repeat this action for the sake of experiencing fascination. The infant imitates some simple actions of others, such as the baby talk or burbling of adults, and some physical gestures. However, these imitations are limited to actions the infant is already able to produce. Although directed toward objects in the world, the infant's schemes lack an intentional, goal-directed quality.

In Substage 4, **coordination of secondary reactions,** which develops between 8 to 12 months of age, several significant changes take place. The infant readily combines and recombines previously learned schemes in a *coordinated* way. She may look at an object and grasp it simultaneously, or visually inspect a toy, such as a rattle, and finger it simultaneously in obvious tactile exploration. Actions are even more outwardly directed than before. Related to this coordination is the second achievement—the presence of **intentionality,** the separation of means and goals in accomplishing simple feats. For example, the infant might manipulate a stick (the means) to bring a desired toy within reach (the goal). She may knock over one block to reach and play with another one.

In Substage 5, **tertiary circular reactions, novelty, and curiosity,** which develops between 12 to 18 months of age, the infant becomes intrigued by the variety of properties that objects possess and by the multiplicity of things she can make happen to objects. A block can be made to fall, spin, hit another object, slide across the ground, and so on. **Tertiary circular reactions** are schemes in which the infant purposely explores new possibilities with objects, continually changing what is done to them and exploring the results. Piaget says that this stage marks the developmental starting point for human curiosity and interest in novelty. Previous circular reactions have been devoted exclusively to reproducing former events, with the exception of imitation of novel acts, which occurs as early as Substage 4. The tertiary circular act is the first to be concerned with novelty.

In Substage 6, **internalization of schemes,** which develops between 18 to 24 months, the infant's mental functioning shifts from a purely sensorimotor plane to a symbolic plane and the infant develops the ability to use primitive symbols. For Piaget, a *symbol* is an internalized sensory image or word that represents an event. Primitive symbols permit the infant to think about concrete events without directly acting them out or perceiving them. Moreover, symbols allow the infant to manipulate and transform the represented events in simple ways. In a favorite Piagetian example, Piaget's young daughter saw a matchbox being opened and closed; sometime later, she mimicked the event by opening and closing her mouth. This was an obvious expression of her image of the event. In another example, a child opened a door slowly to avoid disturbing a piece of paper lying on the floor on the other side. Clearly, the child had an image of the unseen paper and what would happen to it if the door opened quickly. Recently, however, developmentalists have debated whether 2-year-olds really have such representations of action sequences at their command (Corrigan, 1981; Escalona, 1988).

(a)

(b)

Object permanence is one of the infant's significant accomplishments. How do developmentalists study the infant's sense of object permanence?

Object Permanence

One of the infant's most significant accomplishments is the development of object permanence (Flavell, 1985). **Object permanence** is the development of the ability to understand that objects and events continue to exist even though the infant is not in direct contact with them. Imagine what thought would be like if you could not distinguish between yourself and your world. Your thought would be chaotic, disorderly, and unpredictable. This is what the mental life of the newborn is like; there is no self-world differentiation and no sense of object permanence (Piaget, 1952). By the end of the sensorimotor period, however, both are clearly present. The transition between these states is not abrupt; it is marked by qualitative changes that reflect movement through each of the substages of sensorimotor thought.

The principal way that object permanence is studied is by watching the infant's reaction when an attractive object or event disappears. If the infant shows no reaction, it is assumed that he believes it no longer exists. By contrast, if the infant is surprised at the disappearance and searches for the object, it is assumed that he believes it continues to exist. According to Piaget, six distinct substages characterize object permanence's development. Table 6.1 shows how these six substages reflect Piaget's substages of sensorimotor development.

Although Piaget's stage sequence is the best summary of what might happen as the infant fathoms the permanence of things in the world, some contradictory findings have emerged. Piaget's stages broadly describe the interesting changes reasonably well, but the infant's life is not so neatly packaged into distinct organizations as Piaget believed. Some of Piaget's explanations for the causes of change are debated.

Habituation, Memory, and Imitation

Other processes that developmentalists believe are involved in the infant's cognitive development are habituation, memory, and imitation each of which we consider in turn.

TABLE 6.1
The Six Substages of Object Permanence

Stage	Behavior
Sensorimotor Substage 1	There is no apparent object permanence. When a spot of light moves across the visual field, the infant follows it but quickly ignores its disappearance.
Sensorimotor Substage 2	A primitive form of object permanence develops. Given the same experience, the infant looks briefly at the spot where the light disappeared, with an expression of passive expectancy.
Sensorimotor Substage 3	The infant's sense of object permanence undergoes further development. With the newfound ability to coordinate simple schemes, the infant shows clear patterns of searching for a missing object, with sustained visual and manual examination of the spot where the object apparently disappeared.
Sensorimotor Substage 4	The infant actively searches for a missing object in the spot where it disappeared, with new actions to achieve the goal of searching effectively. For example, if an attractive toy has been hidden behind a screen, the child may look at the screen and try to push it away with a hand. If the screen is too heavy to move or is permanently fixed, the child readily substitutes a secondary scheme—for example, crawling around it or kicking it. These new actions signal that the infant's belief in the continued existence of the missing object is strengthening.
Sensorimotor Substage 5	The infant now is able to track an object that disappears and reappears in several locations in rapid succession. For example, a toy may be hidden under different boxes in succession in front of the infant, who succeeds in finding it. The infant is apparently able to hold an image of the missing object in mind longer than before.
Sensorimotor Substage 6	The infant can search for a missing object that disappeared and reappeared in several locations in succession, as before. In addition, the infant searches in the appropriate place even when the object has been hidden from view as it is being moved. This activity indicates that the infant is able to "imagine" the missing object and to follow the image from one location to the next.

Habituation

If a stimulus—a sight or sound—is presented to an infant several times in a row, the infant usually pays less attention to it each time, suggesting that he is bored with it. This is the process of **habituation**—repeated presentation of the same stimulus that causes reduced attention to the stimulus. If a different stimulus is then presented, the infant perks up and pays attention to it, suggesting he can discriminate between the two—this is the process of **dishabituation.** Among the measures infant researchers have used to study whether

Man is the only animal that can be bored.
Erich Fromm, The Sane Society, *1955*

(a)

(b)

Habituation is a common occurrence in the infant's perceptual world. How is this infant showing habituation?

habituation or dishabituation is occurring are heart and respiration rates, sucking behavior (sucking stops when the young infant attends to an object), and the length of time the infant looks at an object. Newborn infants can habituate to repetitive stimulation in virtually every sensory modality—vision, audition, touch, and so on (Rovee-Collier, 1987). However, habituation becomes more acute over the first three months of life. The extensive assessment of habituation in recent years has resulted in its use as a measure of an infant's maturity and well-being. Infants who have brain damage or have suffered birth traumas—such as lack of oxygen—do not habituate well, and may later have developmental and learning problems.

A knowledge of habituation and dishabituation can benefit parent-infant interaction. Infants respond to changes in stimulation. If stimulation is repeated often, the infant's response will decrease to the point that the infant no longer responds to the parent. In parent-infant interaction, it is important for parents to do novel things and to repeat them often until the infant stops responding. The wise parent senses that the infant shows an interest and that many repetitions of the stimulus may be necessary for the infant to process the information. The parent stops or changes behaviors when the infant redirects her attention (Rosenblith & Sims-Knight, 1985).

Memory

Researchers also have found that infants have surprisingly good memories. **Memory** is a central feature of cognitive development, pertaining to all situations in which an individual retains information over time. Sometimes, information is retained only for a few seconds or less, at other times for a lifetime. Memory is involved when we look up a telephone number and dial it, when we remember the name of our best friend from elementary school, and when an infant remembers who her mother is.

Carolyn Rovee-Collier and her colleagues (Rovee-Collier, 1987; Earley, Griesler, & Rovee-Collier, 1985; Borovsky, Hill, & Rovee-Collier, 1987), for example, hung a mobile over an infant's crib and attached a ribbon to one of the baby's limbs (see figure 6.1). Six-week-old infants quickly discovered which arm or leg would move the mobile. Two weeks later, the infants were placed in the same situation. They *remembered* which arm or leg to move, even though they were not attached to the mobile. These early signs of memory are the basis of the kinds of learning from experience that continue throughout our lifetime. Ongoing investigation of such abilities underscore just how surprisingly competent young infants are.

Life is all memory, except for the one present moment that goes by you so quick you hardly catch it going.
Tennessee Williams, The Milk Train Doesn't Stop Here Anymore, *1963*

Figure 6.1
The technique used in Rovee-Collier's investigation of infant memory. The mobile is connected to the infant's ankle by the ribbon and moves in direct proportion to the frequency and vigor of the infant's kicks.

Is the memory evidenced by the infant with the mobile conscious? As children and adults, our memory often involves conscious feelings, such as "I have seen that before," as well as additional retrieval abilities, such as "Where have I seen that before—was it at the zoo?" These conscious feelings probably are not present in the memory of young infants, who do not have the ability to consciously recall or reflect about objects when they are not present (Flavell, 1985).

Just when do infants acquire the ability to consciously remember the past? In one investigation, parents kept diaries of their 5 to 11-month-olds' memories (Ashmead & Perlmutter, 1979). An entry in one of the diaries describes the behavior of a 9-month-old girl who was looking for ribbons that had been removed from the drawer where they had been kept. She first looked in the "old" drawer. Failing to find the ribbons, she searched other drawers until she found them. The next day, the young girl went directly to the "new" drawer to find the ribbons. More formal experiments support the existence of such memory in infants over 6 months of age (Fox, Kagan, & Weiskopf, 1979). For example, when an object is shown to an infant and then subsequently removed, the 7-month-old infant will search for it, but younger infants will not. The memory of infants in the first six months of life is not like what we, as adults, commonly think of as memory; it is not conscious memory for specific past episodes but rather learning of adaptive skills.

Why does conscious memory develop later than other learning and memory skills? Possibly conscious memory must await the maturation of certain brain structures, such as the hippocampus (Schachter & Moscovitch, 1984). Possibly conscious memory depends on the development of cognitive structures, as Piaget's theory suggests (Mandler, 1983; Olson & Strauss, 1984).

What is meant by infantile amnesia?

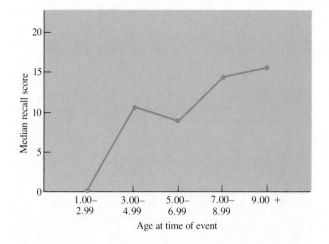

Median recall score

Age at time of event

Despite evidence of conscious memory in the first year of life, there is a sense that such recall is minimal until the child is about 3 years of age. Try to recall a specific episode in the first 3 years of your life—such as the birth of a sibling. Can you remember anything at all about the first 3 years of your life? As children and adults, we have little or no memory of events we experienced before 3 years of age. This phenomenon is called **infantile amnesia.** In one investigation (Sheingold & Tenney, 1982), college students who had at least one younger sibling were interviewed and asked such questions as, "Who told you that your mother was leaving to go to the hospital to have a baby?" "What time of day was it that she went to the hospital?" "Did you visit your mother in the hospital?" Recall for the college students is shown in figure 6.2. Recall was virtually zero unless their siblings were 3 years younger or more, supporting the concept of infantile amnesia.

Can you think of ways to measure infantile amnesia other than asking if you remember a sibling being born?

We are, in truth, more than half what we are by imitation.
Lord Chesterfield, Letters To His Son, *1750*

Imitation

In the next chapter, we describe how infants display a variety of their own emotions. But can they also imitate someone else's emotional expressions? If an adult smiles, will the baby follow with a smile? If an adult protrudes her lower lip, wrinkles her forehead, and frowns, will the baby show a saddened look? If an adult opens her mouth, widens her eyes, and raises her eyebrows, will the baby follow suit? Could infants only 1 day old do these things?

Tiffany Field and her colleagues (1982) explored these questions with newborns only 36 hours after their birth. The model held the newborn's head upright with the model's and the newborn's faces separated by 10 inches. The newborn's facial expressions were recorded by an observer who stood behind the model. The observer could not see which facial expressions the model was showing. The model expressed one of three emotions: Happiness, sadness, or surprise (see figure 6.3). As shown in figure 6.4, infants were most likely to imitate the model's display of surprise by widely opening their mouths. When the infants observed a happy mood, they frequently widened their lips. When the model expressed sadness, the infants followed with lips that reflected pouting. Other research supports the belief that young infants can imitate an adult's emotional expressions (Meltzoff, 1987; Meltzoff & Moore, 1977), but it is open to interpretation whether the imitation is learned or an innate ability (Wolff, 1987). And, one recent investigation found that newborns imitated an adult's tongue protrusion but not the adult's emotional expressions (Kaitz & others, 1988).

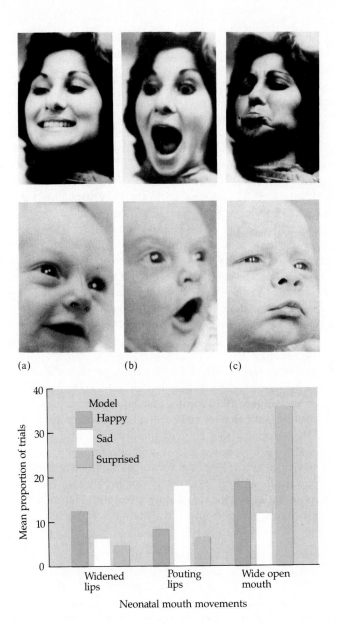

(a)   (b)   (c)

Figure 6.3
Sample photographs of a model's happy (a), surprised (b), and sad (c) expressions, and an infant's corresponding expressions.

Figure 6.4
Imitations of adult emotions by 36-hour-old newborns. The graph shows the mean proportion of trials during which newborn mouth movements followed a model's facial expression. Mouth movements included widened lips (happy), pouting lips (sad), and wide open mouth (surprised).

So far we have stressed general statements about how the cognitive development of infants progresses, emphasizing what is typical of the largest number of infants or the average infant. But the results obtained for most infants do not apply to all infants—the concept of individual differences. Individual differences in infant cognitive development have been studied primarily through the use of developmental scales or infant intelligence tests.

It is advantageous to know whether an infant is advancing at a slow, normal, or advanced pace of development. In chapter 4, we discussed the Brazelton Neonatal Behavioral Assessment Scale, which is widely used to evaluate newborns. Developmentalists also want to know how development proceeds during the course of infancy as well. If an infant advances at an especially slow rate, then some form of enrichment may be necessary. And if an infant progresses at an advanced pace of development, parents may be advised to provide toys that stimulate cognitive growth in slightly older infants.

The infant testing movement grew out of the tradition of IQ testing with older children. However, the measures that assess infants are necessarily less verbal than IQ tests that assess the intelligence of older children. The infant developmental scales contain far more items related to perceptual motor development. They also include measures of social interaction.

The most important early contributor to the developmental testing of infants was Arnold Gesell (1934). He developed a measure that was used as a clinical tool to help sort out potentially normal babies from abnormal ones. This was especially useful to adoption agencies who had large numbers of babies awaiting placement. Gesell's examination was used widely for many years and still is frequently used by pediatricians in their assessment of normal and abnormal infants. The version of the Gesell test now used has four categories of behavior: motor, language, adaptive, and personal-social. If the examiner wishes, the scores in these four domains can be combined into one overall score for the infant, called the **developmental quotient (DQ).** Gesell's intent was to give the infant an overall score, much like the IQ score given to older children. The scores on tests like the Gesell that obtain an overall DQ for the infant do not correlate highly with IQ scores obtained later in childhood. This is not surprising since the nature of the items on the developmental scales—as mentioned earlier—are considerably less verbal than the items on intelligence tests given to older children.

The **Bayley Scales of Infant Development,** developed by Nancy Bayley (1969), are widely used in the assessment of infant development. Unlike Gesell, whose scales were clinically motivated, Bayley wanted to develop scales that could document infant behavior and predict later development. The early version of the Bayley scales only covered the first year of development; in the 1950s, the scales were extended to assess older infants.

The version of the scales used today has three components—a Mental scale, a Motor scale, and an Infant Behavior Profile (which is based on the examiner's observations of the infant during testing). Our major interest here is the infant's cognitive development; the Mental scale includes assessment of the following:

> auditory and visual attention to stimuli
> manipulation, such as combining objects or shaking a rattle
> examiner interaction, such as babbling and imitation
> relation with toys, such as banging spoons together
> memory involved in object permanence, such as when the infant finds a hidden toy
> goal-directed behavior that involves persistence, such as putting pegs in a board
> ability to follow directions and knowledge of objects' names, such as understanding the concept of "one"

How well should a 6-month-old perform on the Bayley Mental scale? The 6-month-old infant should be able to vocalize pleasure and displeasure, persistently search for objects that are just out of immediate reach, and approach a mirror when the examiner places it in front of the infant. How well should a 12-month-old perform? By 12 months of age, the infant should be able to inhibit behavior when commanded to do so, imitate words the examiner says (such as "Mama"), and respond to simple requests (such as "Take a drink"). Figure 6.5 shows an infant being given the Bayley scales.

Is an older infant's intelligence just quantitatively different than a younger infant's intelligence or is it qualitatively different? What would Piaget have said about this question?

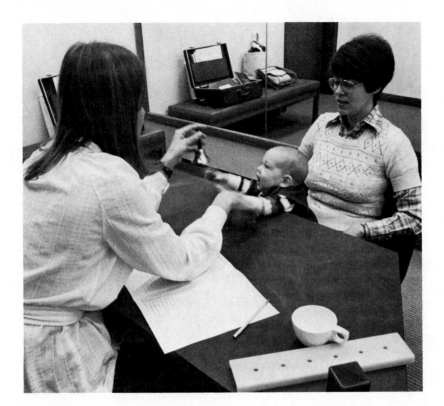

Figure 6.5
*An infant being administered the Bayley
Scales of Infant Development.*

Infant tests of intelligence have been more valuable in assessing the effects of malnutrition, drugs, maternal deprivation, and environmental stimulation than they have been in predicting later intelligence. While they predict reasonably well the intelligence of older children who have been badly damaged as infants, the infant tests have not been accurate in long-range forecasts of intelligence later in childhood and adolescence.

The explosion of interest in infant development has produced many new measures, especially tasks that evaluate the way the infant processes information. Evidence is accumulating that measures of habituation and dishabituation in infancy are better predictors of intelligence in childhood than developmental scales like the Bayley (Bornstein & Sigman, 1986). Quicker decays or less cumulative looking in the habituation situation and greater amounts of looking in the dishabituation situation reflect more efficient information processing. Both types of attention—decrement and recovery—when measured in the first 6 months of infancy, are related to higher IQ scores on standardized intelligence tests given at various times between the ages of 2 and 8. In sum, more precise assessment of the infant's cognition with information processing tasks involving attention have led to the conclusion that continuity between infant and childhood intelligence is greater than previously believed.

At this point, we have described a number of important ideas about the infant's cognitive development. To help you remember the main points of this discussion, turn to Concept Table 6.1. Next, we study another key dimension of the infant's development—language.

CONCEPT TABLE

6.1

∎

Infant Cognitive Development		
Concept	**Processes/Related Ideas**	**Characteristics/Description**
Piaget's Theory of Infant Development	Sensorimotor Stage	Lasts from birth to about 2 years of age; involves progression in the infant's ability to organize and coordinate sensations with physical movements. The sensorimotor stage has six substages: simple reflexes, first habits and primary circular reactions; secondary circular reactions; coordination of secondary circular reactions; tertiary circular reactions, novelty, and curiosity; and internalization of schemes.
	Object Permanence	Refers to the development of the ability to understand that objects and events continue to exist even though the infant no longer is in contact with them. Piaget believed that this ability developed over the course of the six substages.
Habituation, Memory, and Imitation	Habituation	Is the repeated presentation of the same stimulus causing reduced attention to the stimulus. If a different stimulus is presented and the infant pays attention to it, dishabituation is occurring. Newborn infants can habituate although habituation becomes more acute over the first 3 months of infancy.
	Memory	Memory is the retention of information over time. In the first 6 months, infants learn adaptive skills but conscious memory does not develop until later in the first year. Infantile amnesia is our inability to remember anything that happened in the first 3 years of our life.
	Imitation	Infants only 1 day old imitate facial expressions of emotion by adults; it is open to interpretation whether the imitation is learned or innate.
Individual Differences in Intelligence	History	Developmental scales for infants grew out of the tradition of IQ testing with older children. These scales are less verbal than IQ tests. Gesell was an early developer of an infant test. His scale is still widely used by pediatricians; it provides a DQ.
	Bayley Scales	The developmental scales most widely used today, developed by Nancy Bayley. Consist of a Motor scale, a Mental scale, and an Infant Behavior Profile.
	Conclusions about Infant Tests and Continuity in Mental Development	Infant intelligence tests have been better at assessing the influence of environmental events than at predicting later intelligence. However, recently, it has been found that assessment of habituation and dishabituation in infancy is related to IQ in childhood, suggesting greater continuity in intelligence between infancy and childhood than previously believed.

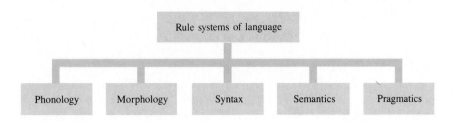

Figure 6.6
Language's rule systems.

Language Development

In the thirteenth century, the Holy Roman Emperor Frederick II had a cruel idea. He wanted to know what language children would speak if no one talked to them. He selected several newborns and threatened the adults who cared for them with their lives if they ever talked to the infants. Frederick never found out what language the children spoke because they all died.

About five centuries later, in 1799, a nude boy was observed running through the woods in France. The boy was captured when he was approximately 11 years old; it was believed that he had lived in the wild for at least 6 years. He was called the Wild Boy of Aveyron (Lane, 1976). When the boy was found, he made no attempt to communicate. Even after a number of years of care he never learned to communicate effectively.

Such circumstances bring up an important issue in language, namely, what are the biological and environmental contributions to language? The contributions of biology and environment figure prominently throughout our discussion of language.

What Is Language?

Every human society has language. Human languages number in the thousands, differing so much on the surface that many of us despair at learning more than even one. Yet all human languages have some things in common.

Language has been defined by one expert as a sequence of words (Miller, 1981). This definition describes language as having two different characteristics—the presence of words and sequencing. But language has other characteristics as well. The use of language is a highly creative process. For example, you can understand this sentence even though you have never seen or heard it. And you can create a unique sentence that you have not seen or heard before. This creative aspect of language is called **infinite generativity,** the individual's ability to generate an infinite number of meaningful sentences using a finite set of words and rules. Yet another characteristic of language is **displacement.** This means that we can use language to communicate information about another place and time, although we also use language to describe what is going on in our immediate environment. A final important characteristic of language is its different rule systems. These include phonology, morphology, syntax, semantics, and pragmatics, which we now discuss in turn (see figure 6.6).

Language's Rule Systems

Language is comprised of basic sounds or *phonemes*. In the English language there are approximately 36 phonemes. The study of language's sound system is called **phonology;** phonological rules ensure that certain sound sequences occur (e.g., *sp, ar, ba*) and others do not (e.g., *zx, qp*). A good example of a phoneme in the English language is /k/, the sound represented by the letter *k* in the work *ski* and by the letter *c* in the word *cat*. While the /k/ sound is slightly different in these two words, the variation is not distinguished and the /k/ sound is viewed as a single phoneme.

Language also is characterized by a string of sounds that give meaning to what we say and hear. The string of sounds is a *morpheme;* **morphology** refers to the rules of combining morphemes. Every word in the English language is made up of one or more morphemes. Not all morphemes are words, however (e.g., *pre-, -tion,* and *-ing*). Some words consist of a single morpheme (e.g., *help*). Other words are made up of more than one morpheme (e.g., *helper,* which has two morphemes, *help + er,* with the morpheme *er* meaning "one who," in this case, "one who helps"). Just as phonemes ensure that certain sound sequences occur, morphemes ensure that certain strings of sounds occur in particular sequences. For example, we would not reorder helper to *erhelp.* Morphemes have fixed positions in the English language, and these morphological rules ensure that some sequences appear in words (e.g., *combining, popular,* and *intelligent*) and others do not (e.g., *forpot, skiest*).

Syntax involves the way words are combined to form acceptable phrases and sentences. Because you and I share the same syntactic understanding of sentence structure, if I say to you, "Bob slugged Tom" and "Bob was slugged by Tom," you know who did the slugging and who was slugged in each case. You also understand that the sentence, "You didn't stay, did you?" is a grammatical sentence but that "You didn't stay, didn't you?" is unacceptable and ambiguous.

A concept closely related to syntax is **grammar,** the formal description of syntactical rules. In elementary school and high school, most of us learned rules about sentence structure. Linguists devise rules of grammar that are similar to those you learned in school but are much more complex and powerful. Many contemporary linguists distinguish between the "surface" and "deep" structure of a sentence. **Surface structure** is the actual order of words in a sentence; **deep structure** is the syntactic relation of the words in a sentence. By applying syntactic rules in different ways, one sentence (the surface structure) can have two very different deep structures. For example, consider this sentence: "Mrs. Smith found drunk on her lawn." Was Mrs. Smith drunk or did she find a drunk on the lawn? Either interpretation fits the sentence, depending on the deep structure applied.

Semantics refers to the meaning of words and sentences. Every word has a set of semantic features. Girl and woman, for example, share the same semantic features as the words female and human but differ in regard to age. Words have semantic restrictions on how they can be used in sentences. The sentence, "The bicycle talked the boy into buying a candy bar" is syntactically correct but semantically incorrect. The sentence violates our semantic knowledge—bicycles do not talk.

A final set of language rules involves **pragmatics**—the ability to engage in appropriate conversation. Certain pragmatic rules ensure that a particular sentence will be uttered in one context and not another. For example, you know that it is appropriate to say, "Your new haircut certainly looks good" to someone who just had their hair styled, but that it is inappropriate for you to say, "That new hairstyle makes you look awful." Through pragmatics we learn to convey intended meaning with words, phrases, and sentences. Pragmatics helps us to communicate more smoothly with others (Bates, O'Connell, & Shore, 1987; Hay, 1987; Nelson, 1978).

The adjective is the banana peel of the parts of speech.
Clifton Fadiman, Reader's Digest, *1956*

Is this ability to generate rule systems for language, and then use them to create an almost infinite number of words, learned or is it the product of biology and evolution?

Language's Biological Basis

In 1882, 2-year-old Helen Keller was left deaf, blind, and mute by a severe illness. By the time she was 7 years old, she feared the world she could not see or hear. Alexander Graham Bell suggested to her parents that they hire a tutor named Anne Sullivan to help Helen overcome her fears (see figure 6.7). By using sign language, Anne was able to teach Helen a great deal about language. Helen Keller became an honors graduate of Radcliffe College and had this to say, "Whatever the process, the result is wonderful. Gradually from naming an object, we advance step by step until we have traversed the vast distance between our first stammered syllable and the sweep of thought in a line of Shakespeare."

What is the process of learning language like? Helen Keller had the benefit of a marvelous teacher, which suggests that experience is important in learning language. But might there have been biological foundations responsible for Helen's ability to communicate? Did Helen, despite her condition, have some biological predisposition to learn language?

Figure 6.7
Helen Keller learning language from Anne Sullivan.
Source: UPI, Bettman Archive, Luis Lord.

The Biological Story

Newborn birds come into the world ready to sing the song of their species. They listen to their parents sing the song a few times and then they have learned it for the rest of their lives. Noam Chomsky (1957) believes that the language of humans works in much the same way. He says we are biologically predisposed to learn language at a certain time and in a certain way. Chomsky's ideas prompted David McNeil (1970) to propose that the child comes into the world with a **language acquisition device** (**LAD**) that is wired to detect certain language categories—phonology, syntax, and semantics, for example. McNeil also believes that we are able to detect deep and surface structures in language.

The contemporary view of language continues to stress that biology has a very strong role in language (Bates, O'Connell, & Shore, 1987; Miller, 1981; Pinker, 1984). For example, George Miller (1981) argues that biology is far more important than environment in determining language's nature. In his view, the fact that evolution shaped humans into linguistic creatures is inevitable.

Both physical and cultural evolution help to explain the development of language skills. The brain, nervous system, and vocal system changed over hundreds of thousands of years. Prior to *Homo sapiens,* the physical equipment to produce language was not present. Then social evolution occurred as humans, with their newly evolved language capacity, had to generate a way of communicating. *Homo sapiens* went beyond the groans and shrieks of their predecessors with the development of abstract speech. Estimates of how long ago humans acquired language vary from about 20,000 to 70,000 years. That means language is a very recent acquisition in evolutionary time. The role of language in human evolution has stimulated psychologists to think about the possibility that animals have language. Do chimpanzees and apes have language, for example? Is their language similar to human language? To discover the answer to this intriguing question and to learn about the way scientists teach apes and chimpanzees language, read Focus on Life-Span Development 6.1.

APE TALK—
FROM GUA TO NIM CHIMPSKY

It is the early 1930s. A seven-month-old chimpanzee named Gua has been adopted by humans (Kellogg & Kellogg, 1933). Gua's adopters want to rear her alongside their ten-month-old son, Donald. Gua was treated much the way we rear human infants today—her adopters dressed her, talked with her, and played with her. Nine months after she was adopted, the project was discontinued because the parents feared that Gua was slowing down Donald's progress.

About twenty years later, another chimpanzee was adopted by humans (Hayes & Hayes, 1951). Viki, as the chimp was called, was only a few days old at the time. The goal was straightforward: teach Viki to speak. Eventually she was taught to say "Mama," but only with painstaking effort. Day after day, week after week, the parents sat with Viki and shaped her mouth to make the desired sounds. She ultimately learned three other words—Papa, cup, and up—but she never learned the meanings of these words and her speech was not clear.

Approximately twenty years later, another chimpanzee named Washoe was adopted when she was about ten months old (Gardner & Gardner, 1971). Recognizing that the earlier

Figure 6.A *Washoe is learning to ask for objects by means of sign language.*

experiments with chimps had not demonstrated that apes have language, the trainers tried to teach Washoe the American sign language, which is the sign language of the deaf. Daily routine events, such as meals and washing, household chores, play with toys, and car rides to interesting places provided many opportunities for the use of sign language. In two years Washoe learned 38 different signs and by the age of five she had a vocabulary of 160 signs. Washoe learned how to put signs together in novel ways, such as "you drink" and "you me tickle" (see figure 6.A).

Yet another way to teach language to chimpanzees exists. The Premacks (Premack & Premack,

1972) constructed a set of plastic shapes that symbolized different objects and were able to teach the meanings of the shapes to a six-year-old chimpanzee, Sarah. Sarah was able to respond correctly using such abstract symbols as "same as" or "different from." For example, she could tell you that "banana is yellow" is the same as "yellow color of banana." Sarah eventually was able to "name" objects, respond "yes," "no," "same as," and "different from" and tell you about certain events by using symbols (such as putting a banana on a tray). Did Sarah learn a generative language capable of productivity? Did the signs Washoe learned have an underlying system of language rules?

Figure 6.B *Nim Chimpsky learning sign language.*

Herbert Terrace (1979) doubts that these apes have been taught language. Terrace was part of a research project designed to teach language to an ape by the name of Nim Chimpsky (named after famous linguist Noam Chomsky) (see figure 6.B). Initially, Terrace was optimistic about Nim's ability to use language as humans use it, but after further evaluation he concluded that Nim really did not have language in the sense that humans do. Terrace says that apes do not spontaneously expand on a trainer's statements like humans do; instead, the apes basically just imitate their trainer. Terrace also believes that apes do not understand what they are saying when they speak; rather they are responding to cues from the trainer that they are not aware of.

The Gardners take exception to Terrace's conclusions (Gardner & Gardner, 1986). They point out that chimpanzees use inflections in sign language to refer to various actions, people, and places. They also cite recent evidence that the infant chimp Loulis learned over fifty signs from his adopted mother Washoe and other chimpanzees who used sign language.

The ape language controversy goes on. It does seem that chimpanzees can learn to use signs to communicate meanings, which has been a boundary for language. Whether the language of chimpanzees possesses all of the characteristics of human language such as phonology, morphology, syntax, semantics, and pragmatics is still being argued (Maratsos, 1983).

Is There a Critical Period for Language Learning?

In addition to considering continuities in language between humans and animals and the role of evolution, another biological aspect of language involves the issue of whether there is a critical period for learning language. If you have listened to former secretary of state Henry Kissinger speak, you have some evidence for the belief that there exists a critical period for learning language. If an individual over 12 years of age emigrates to a new country and then starts to learn its language, the individual probably will speak the language with a foreign accent the rest of his life. Such was the case with Kissinger. But if an individual emigrates as a young child, the accent goes away as the new language is learned (Asher & Garcia, 1969; Oyama, 1973). Similarly, speaking like a native New Yorker is less related to how long you have lived in the city than to the age at which you moved there. Speaking with a New York "dialect" is more likely if you moved there before the age of 12. Apparently, puberty marks the close of a critical period for acquiring the phonological rules of different languages and dialects.

Eric Lenneberg (1962) speculated that lateralization of language in the brain also is subject to a similar critical period. He says that up until about twelve years of age, a child who has suffered damage to the brain's left hemisphere can shift language to the brain's right hemisphere; after this period, the shift is impossible. The idea of a critical period for shifting lateralization is controversial, and research on the issue is inconclusive (de Villiers & de Villiers, 1978).

The experiences of a modern day wild child named Genie raises further interest in the idea of whether a critical time period for acquiring language exists. To learn more about Genie, turn to Focus on Life-Span Development 6.2.

Such findings confirm the belief that language must be triggered to be learned and that the optimal time for that triggering is during the early years of childhood. Clearly, biology's role in language is powerful, but even the most heavily inherited aspects of human development require an environment for their expression.

The Behavioral View and Environmental Influences

Behaviorists view language as just another behavior, like sitting, walking, or running. They argue that language represents chains of responses (Skinner, 1957) or imitation (Bandura, 1977). But many of the sentences we produce are novel in the sense that we have not heard them or spoken them before. For example, a child hears the sentence, "The plate fell on the floor," and then says, "My mirror fell on the blanket," after she drops the mirror on the blanket. The behavioral mechanisms of reinforcement and imitation cannot completely explain this.

While spending long hours observing parents and their young children, Roger Brown (1973) searched for evidence that parents reinforce their children for speaking in grammatical ways. He found that parents did sometimes smile and praise their children for sentences they liked, but that they also reinforced sentences that were ungrammatical. Brown concluded that no evidence exists to document that reinforcement is responsible for language's rule systems.

GENIE, MODERN DAY WILD CHILD

Genie was found in 1970 in California (see figure 6.C). At the time, she was thirteen years old and had been reared by a partially blind mother and a violent father. She was discovered because her mother applied for assistance at a public welfare office. At the time, Genie could not speak and could not stand erect. She had lived in almost total isolation during her childhood years. Naked and restrained by a harness that her father had fashioned, she was left to sit on her potty seat day after day. She could only move her hands and feet and had virtually nothing to do every day of her life. At night, she was placed in a kind of straight jacket and caged in a crib with wire mesh sides and an overhead cover. She was fed, although sparingly. When she made a noise, her father beat her. He never spoke to her with words but growled and made barking sounds toward her.

Genie underwent extensive rehabilitation and training over a number of years (Curtiss, 1977).

Figure 6.C *Artist's drawing of the modern day wild child Genie after she was found.*

During her therapy, Genie learned to walk with a jerky motion and was toilet trained. She learned to recognize many words and to speak. At first she spoke in one-word utterances and eventually began to string together two-word utterances. She began to create some two-word sequences on her own, such as "big teeth," "little marble," and "two hand." Later she was able to put together three words—"small two cup," for example.

But unlike normal children, Genie never learned how to ask questions and she never understood grammar. Even four years later, after she began to put words together, her speech sounded like a garbled telegram. Genie never understood the differences between pronouns and between passive and active verbs. She continues as an adult to speak in short, mangled sentences, such as "father hit leg," "big wood," and "Genie hurt."

Most children are bathed in language from a very early age.

Another criticism of the behavioral view is that it fails to explain the extensive orderliness of language. The behavioral view predicts that vast individual differences should appear in children's speech development because of each child's unique learning history. But as we have seen, a compelling fact about language is its structure and ever-present rule systems. All infants coo before they babble. All toddlers produce one-word utterances before two-word utterances, and all state sentences in the active form before they state them in the passive form.

However, we do not learn language in a social vacuum. Most children are bathed in language from a very early age. We need this early exposure to language to acquire competent language skills. The Wild Boy of Aveyron did not learn to communicate effectively after being reared in social isolation for years. Genie's language was rudimentary even after a number of years of extensive training.

What are some of the ways the environment contributes to language development? Imitation is one important candidate. A child who is slow in developing her language ability can be helped if parents use carefully selected lists of words and grammatical constructions in their speech to the child (Whitehurst, 1985; Whitehurst & Valdez-Menchaca, 1988). Recent evidence also suggests that parents provide more corrective feedback for children's ungrammatical utterances than Brown originally thought (Penner, 1987). Nonetheless, a number of experts on language believe that imitation and reinforcement facilitate language but are not absolutely necessary for its acquisition (de Villiers & de Villiers, 1978).

One intriguing role of the environment in the young child's acquisition of language involves *motherese,* or the **baby-talk register,** a characteristic way of talking to young language learners. A *register* is a way of speaking to people (or pets) in a particular category, such as babies or foreigners. Motherese is somewhat of a misnomer because mothers, fathers, and people in general talk to babies this way. If you pay attention to your behavior when you talk to a baby, you will notice some interesting things. Your sentences will be short, you will use exaggerated intonation contours (speaking with great ups and downs in pitch), you will pause for long periods between sentences, and you will place great stress on important words. The baby-talk register is virtually universal. It was documented as early as the first century B.C. and is present in diverse languages (Brown, 1986; Grieser & Kuhl, 1988). When parents are asked why they use baby talk, they point out that it is designed to teach their baby to talk. Older peers also talk baby talk to infants, but observations of siblings indicate that the affectional features are dropped when sibling rivalry is sensed (Dunn & Kendrick, 1982).

Other than the baby talk register, are there other strategies adults use to enhance the child's acquisition of language? Four candidates are recasting, echoing, expanding, and labeling. **Recasting** is phrasing the same or a similar meaning of a sentence in a different way, perhaps turning it into a question. For example, if the child says, "The dog was barking," the adult can respond by asking, "When was the dog barking?" The effects of recasting fit with suggestions that "following in order to lead" helps a child to learn language (Schaffer, 1977). That is, letting a child initially indicate an interest and then proceeding to elaborate that interest—commenting, demonstrating, and explaining—may enhance communication and help language acquisition. In contrast, an overly active, directive approach to communicating with the child may be harmful.

Reprinted with special permission of NAS, Inc.

Echoing is repeating what the child says to you, especially if it is an incomplete phrase or sentence. **Expanding** is restating what the child has said in a linguistically sophisticated form. **Labeling** is identifying the names of objects. Young children are forever being asked to identify the names of objects. Roger Brown (1986) identified this as the great word game and claimed that much of the early vocabulary acquired by children is motivated by this adult pressure to identify the words associated with objects.

How Language Develops

In describing language, we have touched on language development a number of times. You just read about the baby talk register parents use with their infants. Earlier we discussed Frederick II's effort to learn which language children would speak, the Wild Boy of Aveyron, Genie, and Donald and Gua.

When does an infant utter her first word? The event usually occurs at about 10 to 13 months of age, though some infants take longer. Many parents view the onset of language development as coincident with this first word, but some significant accomplishments are attained earlier. Before babies say words, they babble, emitting such vocalizations as "goo-goo" and "ga-ga." Babbling starts at about 3 to 6 months of age; the start is determined by biological maturation, not reinforcement or the ability to hear. Even deaf babies babble for a time (Lenneberg, Rebelsky, & Nichols, 1965). Babbling exercises the baby's vocal apparatus and facilitates the development of articulation skills

In our discussion of language, we have emphasized the role of biological and environmental factors. How might cognitive factors be involved in language development?

Children pick up words as pigeons peas.
John Ray, English Proverbs, *1670*

that are useful in later speech (Clark & Clark, 1977). But the purpose of a baby's earliest communication is to attract attention from parents and others in the environment. Infants engage the attention of others by making or breaking eye contact, by vocalizing sounds, or by performing manual actions such as pointing. All of these behaviors involve pragmatics.

A child's first words include those that name important people (dada), familiar animals (kittie), vehicles (car), toys (ball), food (milk), body parts (eye), clothes (hat), household items (clock), or greeting terms (bye). These were the first words of babies fifty years ago; they are the first words of babies today (Clark, 1983). At times it is hard to tell what these one-word utterances mean. One possibility is that they stand for an entire sentence in the infant's mind. Because of limited cognitive or linguistic skills, possibly only one word comes out instead of the whole sentence. This is called the **holophrase hypothesis,** that is, a single word is used to imply a complete sentence.

For words that a child uses as nouns, the meanings can be overextended or underextended. Eve Clark (1983) has studied early words and described a number of **overextensions.** For instance, when a child learns to say the word "dada" for father, she often applies the term beyond the class of individuals it was intended to represent, using it for other men, strangers, or boys, for example. With time, such overextension decreases and eventually disappears. **Underextension** occurs when a child fails to use a noun to name a relevant event or object. For instance, the child may learn to use the word "boy" to describe a 5-year-old neighbor but not apply the word to a male infant or a 9-year-old male.

By the time children are 18 to 24 months of age, they usually utter two-word statements. During this two-word stage, they quickly grasp the importance of expressing concepts and the role that language plays in communicating with others. To convey meaning with two-word utterances, the child relies heavily on gesture, tone, and context. The wealth of meaning children can communicate with a two-word utterance includes (Slobin, 1972):

Identification: See doggie.
Location: Book there.
Repetition: More milk.
Nonexistence: Allgone thing.
Negation: Not wolf.
Possession: My candy.
Attribution: Big car.
Agent-action: Mama walk.
Action-direct-object: Give papa.
Action-instrument: Cut knife.
Question: Where ball?

One of the striking aspects of this list is that it is used by children all over the world. The examples are taken from utterances in English, German, Russian, Turkish, and Samoan, but the entire list could be derived from a 2-year-old's speech in any language.

A child's two-word utterance differs substantially from adult word combinations. Language usage at this time is called **telegraphic speech.** When we send telegrams to individuals we try to be short and precise, excluding any unnecessary words. As indicated in the examples of telegraphic speech from

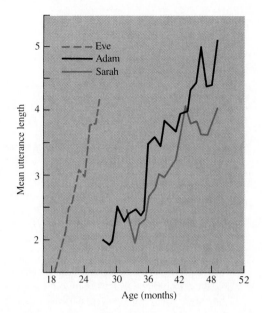

Figure 6.8
The average length of utterances generated by three children who ranged in age from 1½ to just over 4 years.

children around the world, articles, auxiliary verbs, and other connectives usually are omitted. Of course, telegraphic speech is not limited to two-word utterances. "Mommy give ice cream," or "Mommy give Tommy ice cream," also are examples of telegraphic speech.

One- and two-word utterances classify children's language development in terms of the number of utterances. Roger Brown (1973) expanded this concept by proposing that **mean length of utterance** (MLU) is a good index of a child's language maturity. Brown identified five stages based on an estimation of the number of words per sentence that a child produces in a sample of about 50 to 100 sentences. The mean length of utterance for each stage is:

Stage	MLU
1	1 + →2.0
2	2.5
3	3.0
4	3.5
5	4.0

The first stage begins when the child generates sentences consisting of more than one word, such as examples of two-word utterances we gave. The 1 + designation suggests that the average number of words in each utterance is greater than one but not yet two because some of the child's utterances are still holophrases. This stage continues until the child averages two words per utterance. Subsequent stages are marked by increments of 0.5 in mean length of utterance.

Brown's stages are important for several reasons. First, children who vary in chronological age as much as one-half to three-fourths of a year still have similar speech patterns. Second, children with similar mean lengths of utterance seem to have similar rule systems that characterize their language. In some ways, then, MLU is a better indicator of language development than chronological age. Figure 6.8 shows the individual variation in chronological age that characterizes children's MLU.

CONCEPT TABLE

6.2

◼

Language Development		
Concept	**Processes/Related Ideas**	**Characteristics/Description**
What Is Language?	Its Nature	A sequence of words that involves infinite generativity, displacement, and rules systems. Rule systems include phonology, morphology, syntax, semantics, and pragmatics.
The Biological Basis of Language	The Biological Story	Chomsky believes that we are biologically prewired to learn language. McNeil says that we have a language acquisition device that includes wiring for surface and deep structures. The fact that evolution shaped humans into linguistic creatures is undeniable.
	Critical Period	The experiences of Genie and other children suggest that the early childhood years are an optimal time for learning language. If exposure to language does not come before puberty, life-long deficits in grammar occur.
The Behavioral View and Environmental Influences	The Behavioral View	Language is just another behavior. Behaviorists believe language is learned primarily through reinforcement and imitation, although they probably play a facilitative rather than a necessary role.
	Environmental Influences	Most children are bathed in language early in their development. Among the ways adults teach language to infants are the baby talk register, recasting, echoing, expanding, and labeling.
How Language Develops	Its Nature	Vocalization begins with babbling at about 3 to 6 months of age. A baby's earliest communication skills are pragmatic. One-word utterances occur at about 10 to 13 months; the holophrase hypothesis has been applied to this. By 18 to 24 months, most infants use two-word utterances. Language at this point is referred to as telegraphic. Brown developed the idea of mean length of utterance (MLU). Five stages of MLU have been identified, providing a valuable indicator of language maturity.

As we have just seen, language unfolds in a sequence. At every point in development, the child's linguistic interaction with parents and others obeys certain principles. Not only is this development strongly influenced by the child's biological wiring, but the language environment the child is bathed in from an early age is far more intricate than was imagined in the past. A summary of the main ideas we have discussed about language development is presented in Concept Table 6.2.

Summary

I. **Piaget's Theory of Infant Development**

The stage of sensorimotor development lasts from birth to about 2 years of age. It involves progression in the infant's ability to organize and coordinate sensations with physical movements. The sensorimotor stage has six substages: simple reflexes, first habits and primary circular reactions; secondary circular reactions; tertiary circular reactions, novelty, and curiosity; and internalization of schemes. Object permanence is an important accomplishment in infant cognitive development; it refers to the development of the ability to understand that objects and events continue to exist even though the infant is no longer in contact with them. Piaget believed that this ability developed over the course of the six substages.

II. **Habituation**

Habituation is the repeated presentation of a stimulus causing reduced attention to the stimulus. If a different stimulus is presented and the infant pays attention to it, dishabituation is occurring. Newborn infants can habituate, although habituation becomes more acute over the first 3 months of infancy.

III. **Memory**

Memory is the retention of information over time. In the first 6 months, infants learn adaptive skills but conscious memory does not develop until later in the first year. Infantile amnesia is our inability to remember anything that happened in the first 3 years of our life.

IV. **Imitation**

Infants only 1 day old imitate facial expressions of emotion by adults; it is open to interpretation whether the imitation is learned or innate.

V. **Individual Differences in Intelligence**

Developmental scales for infants grew out of the tradition of IQ (intelligence quotient) testing with older children. These scales are less verbal than IQ tests. Gesell was an early pioneer in the development of infant scales. His scale is still widely used by pediatricians; it provides a DQ (developmental quotient). The Bayley scales are the most widely used today. They consist of a Motor scale, a Mental scale, and an Infant Behavior Profile. Infant intelligent tests have been better at assessing the influence of environmental events than at predicting later intelligence. However, recently, it has been found that assessment of habituation and dishabituation in infancy is related to IQ in childhood, suggesting greater continuity in intelligence between infancy and childhood than previously believed.

VI. **What Is Language?**

Language is a sequence of words that involves infinite generativity, displacement, and rule systems. Rule systems include phonology, morphology, syntax, semantics, and pragmatics.

VII. **The Biological Basis of Language**

Chompsky believes that we are biologically prewired to learn language. McNeil says that we have a language acquisition device that includes wiring for surface and deep structures. The fact that evolution shaped humans into linguistic creatures is undeniable.

The experiences of Genie and other children suggest that the early childhood years are an optimal time for learning language. If exposure to language does not come before puberty, life-long deficits in grammar occur.

VIII. **The Behavioral View and Environmental Influences**

Language is just another behavior in the behavioral view. Behaviorists believe language is learned primarily through reinforcement and imitation, although they probably play a facilitative rather than a necessary role. Most children are bathed in language early in their development. Among the ways adults teach language to infants are the baby talk register, recasting, echoing, expanding, and labeling.

IX. **How Language Develops**

Vocalization begins with babbling at about 3 to 6 months of age. A baby's earliest communication skills are pragmatic. One-word utterances occur at about 10 to 13 months; the holophrase hypothesis has been applied to this. By 18 to 24 months, most infants use two-word utterances. Language at this point is referred to as telegraphic. Brown developed the idea of mean length of utterance (MLU). Five stages of MLU have been identified, providing a valuable indicator of language maturity.

Key Terms

Suggested Readings

Bruner, J. (1983). *Child talk*. New York: Norton.
A fascinating view of the child's language development by one of the leading cognitive theorists.

Curtiss, S. (1977). *Genie*. New York: Academic Press.
Susan Curtiss tells the remarkable story of Genie, a modern day wild child and her ordeal of trying to acquire language.

Ginsburg, H., & Opper, S. (1979). *Piaget's theory of intellectual development* (2nd ed.). Englewood Cliffs, NJ: Prentice-Hall.
One of the best explanations and descriptions of Piaget's theory of infant development.

Maratsos, M. (1983). Some current issues in the study of the acquisition of grammar. In P. H. Mussen (Ed.), *Handbook of Child Psychology* (4th ed.), Vol. 2. New York: Wiley.
A thorough, informative review of what we know about language development.

Rovee-Collier, C. (1987). Learning and memory in infancy. In J. D. Osofsky (ed.), *Handbook of Infant Development*. New York: Wiley.
One of the leading researchers on infant memory describes how infants learn and remember; special attention is given to habituation.

Social And Personality Development

The newborns of some species function independently in the world; other species are not so independent. At birth, the opposum is still considered fetal and is capable of finding its way around only in its mother's pouch, where it attaches itself to her nipple and continues to develop. This protective environment is similar to the uterus. By contrast, the wildebeest must run with the herd moments after birth. The newborn wildebeest's behavior is far more adultlike than the opposum's, although the wildebeest does have to obtain food through suckling. The maturation of the human infant lies somewhere between these two extremes; much learning and development must take place before the infant can sustain itself (see figure 7.1) (Maccoby, 1980).

Because it cannot sustain itself, the human infant requires extensive care. What kind of care is needed and how does the infant begin the road to social maturity? Much of the interest in infant care focuses on attachment, although the infant's development of emotions, trust, a sense of self, and independence are important as well. Before we tackle these important dimensions of the infant's social development, some basic ideas about sociocultural and family processes need to be considered.

Sociocultural and Family Processes

In Brazil, almost every middle-class family can afford a nanny, and there is no such thing as a baby-sitting problem. However, because many of the nannies believe in black magic, it is not beyond the realm of possibility for Brazilian parents to return home from a movie and find their infant screaming, presumably, according to the nanny, from a voodoo curse. Contrast the world of the middle-class Brazilian family with the world of a typical family in Thailand, where farm families are large and can only afford to educate their most promising child—determined by which child is most capable of learning English. Such sociocultural and family experiences play important roles in the infant's development.

Sociocultural Influences

Sociocultural influences range from the broad-based, global inputs of culture to a mother or father's affectionate touch. A view that captures the complexity of this sociocultural world was developed by Urie Bronfenbrenner (1979, 1987). Figure 7.2 portrays Bronfenbrenner's ecological model for understanding sociocultural influences. Notice that the child is placed in the center of the model and that the child's most direct interactions are with the **microsystem,** the setting in which the child lives. These contexts include the child's family, school, peers, and neighborhood. The child is not viewed as a passive recipient of experiences in these settings, but as someone who helps to construct the environment. Most research on sociocultural influences focuses on the microsystem, emphasizing the infant's attachment to parents, parenting strategies, sibling relationships, peer relations and friendships, and school experiences.

(a)

Figure 7.1
The dependency of newborns in different species. Some species' newborns behave independently, others not so independently. The newborn opossum is fetal, capable of finding its way around only in its mother's pouch, where it attaches itself to her nipple and continues to develop (a). By contrast, the wildebeest runs with the herd moments after birth (b). The human newborn's maturation lies somewhere in between the opossum and the wildebeest.

(b)

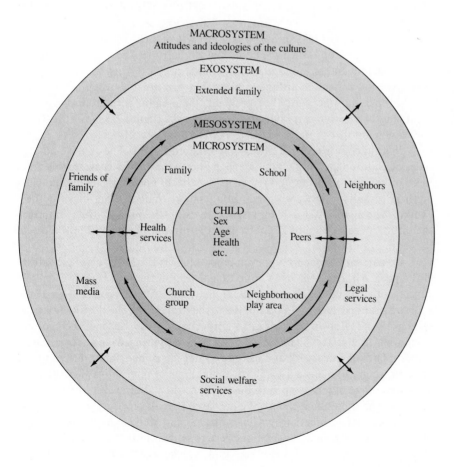

Figure 7.2
Bronfenbrenner's ecological model is one of the few comprehensive frameworks for understanding the environment's role in the child's development. Notice that the child is placed at the center and that four environmental systems are involved: microsystem, mesosystem, exosystem, and macrosystem.

(a)

(b)

Figure 7.3
a. *The peaceful !Kung of Southern Africa discourage any kind of aggression; the !Kung are called the "harmless people."*
b. *Hardly harmless, the violent Yanomamo Indians of South America are told that manhood cannot be achieved unless they are capable of killing, fighting, and pummelling others.*

The **mesosystem** involves relations between microsystems or connections between contexts. Examples include the relation of family experiences to school experiences, school experiences to church experiences, or family experiences to peer experiences. For example, a child's parents who have rejected him may have difficulty developing a positive relationship with his teachers. Developmentalists increasingly believe it is important to observe the child's behavior in multiple settings—such as family, peer, and school contexts—to provide a more complete picture of the child's social development.

Children also experience their environment in a more indirect way. The **exosystem** is involved when experiences in another social setting—in which the child does not have an active role—influences what the child experiences in an immediate context. For example, work experiences may affect a woman's relationship with her husband and children. She may receive a promotion that requires more travel. This might increase marital conflict and change caregiving—increased father care, increased day care, for instance. Another instance of an exosystem is the city government, which is responsible for the quality of parks and recreation facilities available to children.

The most abstract level in Bronfenbrenner's analysis of sociocultural influences is the **macrosystem**—the attitudes and ideologies of the culture. People in a particular culture share some broad-based beliefs. The people of Russia have certain beliefs; the people of China have certain beliefs; so do the people of a South Sea island culture. Consider the !Kung of southern Africa and the Yanomamo Indians of South America. The !Kung are peaceful people. They discourage any kind of aggression on the part of their children and resolve disputes calmly. The !Kung are described as "harmless people." By contrast, the Yanomamo Indians are called the "fierce people." They teach their sons that manhood cannot be attained unless they are capable of killing, fighting, and pummelling others. As they grow up, Yanomamo boys are instructed at great length in how to carry out these violent tasks (figure 7.3 shows the !Kung and Yanomamo).

Within countries, subcultures have shared beliefs. The values and attitudes of children growing up in an urban ghetto may differ considerably from those of children growing up in a wealthy suburb. For example, middle-class mothers verbally interact with their infants more than do lower-class mothers (Tulkin & Kagan, 1971). They respond more to the infant's frets, entertain the infant more, are more likely to give the infant objects, and talk more to the infant.

Of particular concern to developmentalists is the lower-class subculture of the poor. Although the most noticeable aspect of the poor is their economic poverty, other psychological and social characteristics are present. First, the poor are often powerless. In occupations, they rarely are the decision makers; rules are handed down to them in an authoritarian way. Second, the poor are vulnerable to disaster. They are not likely to be given advance notice when they are laid off from work and usually do not have financial resources to fall back on when problems arise. Third, their range of alternatives is restricted. A limited range of jobs is open to them. Even when alternatives are available, they may not know about them or be prepared to make a wise decision because of an inadequate education and inability to read well. Fourth, there is less prestige in being poor. This lack of prestige is transmitted to the child early in life; the poor child observes other children who wear nicer clothes and live in more attractive houses. Whether a child grows up in poverty or in a comfortable middle-class setting, experiences in the family constitute the most important sociocultural setting in the child's life.

cathy®
by Cathy Guisewite

Family Processes

Most of us began our lives in families and spent thousands of hours during our childhood interacting with our parents. What is the transition to parenthood like? What is the nature of family processes?

Transition To Parenthood

When individuals become parents through pregnancy, adoption, or stepparenting, they face a disequilibrium that requires adaptation. Parents want to develop a strong attachment with their infant, but they still want to maintain a strong attachment to their spouse and friends and possibly continue their careers. Parents ask themselves how this new being will change their lives. A baby places new restrictions on partners—no longer will they be able to rush off to a movie on a moment's notice, money will not be as readily available for vacations or other luxuries. The dual-career parents ask, "Will it harm the baby to place her in day care? Will we be able to find responsible baby-sitters?"

The excitement and joy that accompany the birth of a healthy baby are often followed by "postpartum blues" in mothers—a depressed state that lasts as long as nine months into the infant's first year (Culp & Osofsky, 1987; Osofsky & others, 1985). The early months of the baby's physical demands may bring not only the joy of intimacy but also the sorrow of exhaustion. Pregnancy and childbirth are demanding physical events that require recovery time for the mother. As one mother told it:

> When I was pregnant, I felt more tired than ever before in my life. Since my baby was born, I am 100 percent more tired. It's not just physical exhaustion from the stress of childbirth and subsequent days of interrupted sleep, but I'm slowed down emotionally and intellectually as well. I'm too tired to make calls to find a baby-sitter. I see a scrap of paper on the floor, and I'm too tired to pick it up. I want to be taken care of and have no demands made of me other than the baby's. (*Ourselves and Our Children*, 1978, pp. 42–43.)

Many fathers are not sensitive to these extreme demands placed on the mother. Busy trying to make enough money to pay the bills, he may not be at home much of the time. His ability to sense and adapt to the stress placed on his wife during the first year of the infant's life has important implications for

We never know the love of our parents until we have become parents.
Henry Ward Beecher, 1887

the success of the marriage and the family. Several research studies demonstrate that when fathers help mothers more and give them strong support, the mothers interact more competently with their infants by being more sensitive to their needs (Feiring & Lewis, 1978; Pedersen, Anderson, & Cain, 1980).

Becoming a father is both wonderful *and* stressful. For example, in a longitudinal investigation of couples from later pregnancy to three and a half years after the baby was born, Carolyn and Phillip Cowan (Cowan, 1988; Cowan & Cowan, 1987) found that the couples enjoyed more positive marital relations before the baby was born than after. Still, almost one third showed an increase in marital satisfaction. Some couples said that the baby had both brought them closer together *and* moved them farther apart. They commented that being parents enhanced their sense of themselves and gave them a new, more stable identity as a couple. Babies opened up men to a concern with intimate relationships, and the demands of juggling work and family roles stimulated women to manage family tasks more efficiently and pay attention to their personal growth.

At some point during the early years of the child's life, parents face the difficult task of juggling their roles as parents and self-actualizing adults. Until recently in our culture, nurturing our children and having a career were seen as incompatible. Fortunately, we have come to recognize that the balance between caring and achieving, nurturing and working—although difficult to manage—can be accomplished.

Reciprocal Socialization and Mutual Regulation

For many years, the socialization process between parents and children was viewed as a one-way affair. Children were considered to be the products of their parents' socialization techniques. By contrast, the socialization process between parents and their children is now viewed as reciprocal—children socialize their parents just as parents socialize children. This process is called **reciprocal socialization.** For example, the interaction of mothers and their infants is symbolized as a dance or a dialogue in which successive actions of the partners are closely coordinated. This coordinated dance or dialogue can assume the form of mutual synchrony (each person's behavior depends on the partner's previous behavior), or it can be reciprocal in a more precise sense—the actions of the partners can be matched, as when one partner imitates the other or there is mutual smiling (Cohn & Tronick, 1987, 1988; Fogel, 1988; Rutter & Durkin, 1987).

When reciprocal socialization has been investigated in infancy, mutual gaze or eye contact has been found to play an important role in early social interaction. In one investigation (Stern & others, 1977), the mother and infant engaged in a variety of behaviors while they looked at each other; by contrast, when they look away from each other, the rate of such behaviors dropped considerably. Quite clearly, the behaviors of mothers and infants are interconnected and synchronized.

The term **scaffolding** has been used to describe the mother's role in early parent-child interactions (Bruner & Sherwood, 1976; Ratner & Bruner, 1978). Through their attention and choice of behaviors, mothers are described as providing a framework around which they and their infants interact. For example, in the game of peekaboo, mothers initially cover their babies, then remove the covering, and finally register "surprise" at the reappearance. As infants become more skilled at peekaboo, the infants do the covering and uncovering. Recent research documents the importance of scaffolding in infant development (Hodapp, Goldfield, & Boyatzis, 1984; Vandell & Wilson, 1988). In the investigation by Deborah Vandell and Kathy Wilson, infants who had more extensive scaffolding experience with their parents, especially in the form of turn-taking, were more likely to engage in turn-taking interactions with peers.

The question arises as to which partner is driving the relationship—is the mother doing most of the work in the partnership, being sensitive to the infant's states and changing her behavior according to her perception of the infant's needs? When the infant is very young, the mother is performing more work in facilitating interaction than the infant. Through all of the first year and into the second year, the mother is more likely to join the infant's nonsocial behavior than vice versa. Over time, as the child becomes capable of regulating his behavior, the mother and child interact with each other on more equal terms; that is, both "drive" or initiate the relationship (Maccoby & Martin, 1983).

The Family as a System

As a social system, the family can be thought of as a constellation of subsystems defined in terms of generation, gender, and role. Divisions of labor among family members define particular subunits, and attachments define others. Each family member is a participant in several subsystems—some dyadic (involving two people), some polyadic (involving more than two people). The father and child represent one dyadic subsystem, the mother and father another; the mother-father-child represent one polyadic subsystem, the mother and two siblings another (Vuchinich, Emery, & Cassidy, in press).

An organizational scheme that highlights the reciprocal influences of family members and family subsystems is shown in figure 7.4 (Belsky, 1981). As can be seen by following the arrows in the figure, marital relations, parenting, and infant behavior can have both direct and indirect effects on each other. An example of a direct effect is the influence of the parent's behavior on the child; an example of an indirect effect is how the relationship between the spouses mediates the way a parent acts toward the child. For example, marital conflict might reduce the efficiency of parenting, in which case marital conflict would be an indirect effect on the child's behavior. In the family system, the infant's most important experiences involve the process of attachment.

Attachment

A small curly-haired girl named Danielle, age 11 months, is beginning to whimper. After a few seconds, she begins to wail. The psychologist observing Danielle is conducting a research study on the nature of attachment between infants and their mothers. The psychologist is watching Danielle's behavior in a university laboratory filled with dolls, teddy bears, and other toys. In Danielle's case, the observation session begins with Danielle seated on her mother's lap for several minutes. Then the mother places Danielle down and leaves the room. At this point, the whimpering described earlier begins, followed by a loud cry. Subsequently, the mother reenters the room, and Danielle's crying ceases. Quickly, Danielle crawls over to where her mother is seated and reaches out to be held. This scenario is one of the main ways that psychologists study the nature of attachment during infancy.

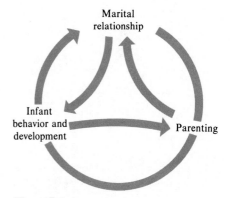

Figure 7.4
Direct and indirect effects of family interaction. Jay Belsky developed this model to describe the way that family interaction patterns can have both direct and indirect effects. For example, the parent's behavior can have a direct effect on the infant's development, or the marital relationship can have indirect effects on the infant's development by influencing parenting behavior.

Figure 7.5
In the classic Harlow and Zimmerman study, infant monkeys, even though fed from the wire "mother," clung to the cloth "mother." This study demonstrated that feeding is not the critical factor in attachment but that contact comfort is an important factor.

What Is Attachment?

In everyday language, attachment refers to a relationship between two individuals in which each individual feels strongly about the other and does a number of things to continue the relationship. Many pairs of people are attached: relatives, lovers, a teacher and a student. In the language of developmental psychology, though, **attachment** is often restricted to a relationship between particular social figures, and to a particular phenomenon thought to reflect unique characteristics of the relationship. The developmental period is infancy, the social figures are the infant and one or more adult caregivers, and the phenomenon in question is a bond.

There is no shortage of theories about infant attachment. Freud believed that the infant becomes attached to the person or object that provides oral satisfaction; for most infants, this is the mother, since she is most likely to feed the infant.

But is feeding as important as Freud thought? A classic study by Harry Harlow and Robert Zimmerman (1959) suggests the answer is no. They evaluated whether feeding or contact comfort was more important to infant attachment. Infant monkeys were removed from their mothers at birth and reared for six months by surrogate (substitute) "mothers." As shown in figure 7.5, one of the mothers was made of wire, the other of cloth. Half of the infant monkeys were fed by the wire mother, half by the cloth mother. Periodically the amount of time the infant monkeys spent with either the wire or the cloth monkey was computed. Figure 7.6 indicates that regardless of whether they were fed by the wire or the cloth mother, the infant monkeys spent far more

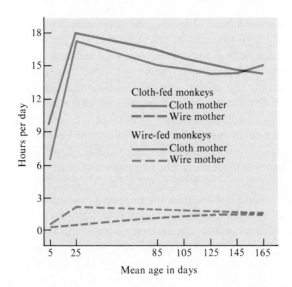

Figure 7.6
Harlow and Zimmerman's wire and cloth monkey study. The average amount of time infant monkeys spent in contact with their cloth and wire mothers is shown. The infant monkeys spent most of their time with the cloth monkey regardless of which mother fed them (Harlow & Zimmerman, 1959).

time with the cloth mother. This study clearly demonstrates that feeding is not the crucial element in the attachment process and that contact comfort is important.

Might familiarity breed attachment? The famous study by Konrad Lorenz (1965) suggests that the answer is yes. Remember from our description of this study in chapter 2 that newborn goslings became attached to "father" Lorenz rather than their mother because he was the first moving object seen. The time period during which familiarity is important for goslings is the first 36 hours after birth; for humans, it is more on the order of the first year of life.

Erik Erikson (1968) believes the first year of life is the key time frame for the development of attachment. Recall his proposal, also discussed in chapter 2, that the first year of life represents the stage of trust versus mistrust. A sense of trust requires a feeling of physical comfort and a minimal amount of fear and apprehension about the future. Trust in infancy sets the stage for a lifelong expectation that the world will be a good and pleasant place to be. Erikson also believes that responsive, sensitive parenting contributes to the infant's sense of trust.

The ethological perspective of British psychiatrist John Bowlby (1969, 1973, 1980, 1988) also stresses the importance of attachment in the first year of life and the responsiveness of the caregiver. Bowlby believes that the infant and the mother instinctively form an attachment. He believes the newborn is biologically equipped to elicit the mother's attachment behavior. The baby cries, clings, coos, and smiles. Later the infant crawls, walks, and follows the mother. The goal for the infant is to keep the mother nearby. Research on attachment supports Bowlby's view that, at about 6 to 7 months, attachment of the infant to the caregiver intensifies (Ainsworth, 1967; Schaffer & Emerson, 1964).

I am what I hope and give.

Erik Erikson

Individual Differences

Although attachment to the caregiver intensifies midway through the first year, isn't it likely that some babies have a more positive attachment experience than others? Mary Ainsworth (1979, 1988) thinks so and says this variation can be categorized as secure or insecure attachment. In **secure attachment,** the infant uses the caregiver, usually the mother, as a secure base from which to explore the environment. The securely attached infant moves freely away from the mother but processes her location through periodic glances. The securely attached infant also responds positively to being picked up by others, and when put back down, moves freely to play. An insecurely attached infant, by contrast, avoids the mother or is ambivalent toward her. The insecurely attached infant fears strangers and is upset by minor, everyday separations.

Ainsworth and her colleagues (1978) believe the insecurely attached infant can be classified as either anxious-avoidant or anxious-resistant, making three main attachment categories: secure (called **type B babies**), anxious-avoidant (called type A), and anxious-resistant (called type C). **Type A babies** exhibit insecurity by avoiding the mother, for example, ignoring her, averting her gaze, and failing to seek proximity. **Type C babies** exhibit insecurity by resisting the mother, for example, clinging to her but at the same time fighting against the closeness perhaps by kicking and pushing away.

Why are some infants securely attached and others insecurely attached? Following Bowlby's lead, Ainsworth believes attachment security depends on how sensitive and responsive the caregiver is to the infant's signals. For example, infants who are securely attached are more likely to have mothers who are more sensitive, accepting, and expressive of affection toward them than those who are insecurely attached.

If early attachment to the caregiver is important, it should relate to the child's social behavior later in development. Research by Alan Sroufe (1985, 1987) documents this connection. In one investigation, infants who were securely attached to their mothers early in infancy were less frustrated and happier at two years of age than their insecurely attached counterparts (see figure 7.7) (Matas, Arend, & Sroufe, 1978). And in another recent investigation, quality of attachment to the mother at age 6 was predicted from infancy attachment classification (Main & Cassidy, 1988).

Intergenerational relationships also play a role in the infant's attachment. Researchers are beginning to accumulate evidence about the transmission of relationships across generations from middle-aged grandparents through their young adult children and then to the offspring of the young adult parents. For example, in one investigation (Frommer & O'Shea, 1973) mothers who said they had poor relationships with their own parents more often reported problems with their 1-year-old infants than mothers who reported no such problems with their parents. In another investigation (Main, Kaplan, & Cassidy, 1985), the mothers and fathers of infants whose attachments had been classified according to Ainsworth's categories were interviewed. The infant's avoidance of the parent was related to parental reports of rejection in their own childhoods. Resistance of the infant toward the mother was associated with continuing anger and conflict between the mother and her own parents. Securely attached infants had parents whose own relationships with their parents were described as secure.

Attachment, Temperament, and the Wider Social World

Not all developmentalists believe that a secure attachment in infancy is the only path to competence in life. Indeed, some developmentalists believe that the power of the attachment bond in infancy is overdramatized. Jerome Kagan (1987), for example, believes that the infant is highly resilient and adaptive; he argues that the infant is evolutionarily equipped to stay on a positive developmental course even in the face of wide variations in parenting. Kagan and others stress that genetic and temperament characteristics play more important roles in the child's social competence than the attachment theorists

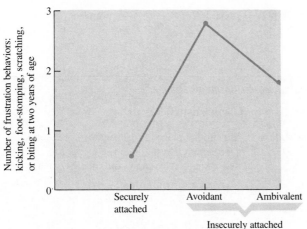

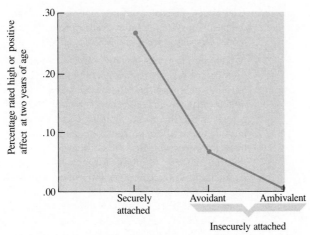

Figure 7.7
Research by Alan Sroufe and his colleagues demonstrates that secure attachment in infancy is related to the child's social competence. In this study (Matas, Arend, & Sroufe, 1978), infants who were securely attached to their mothers at 18 months of age showed less frustration behavior (top figure) and more positive affect (bottom figure) at 2 years of age.

like Bowlby, Ainsworth, and Sroufe are willing to acknowledge (Goldsmith, 1988; Goldsmith & others, 1987; Trudel & Jacques, 1987). For example, an infant may have inherited a low tolerance for stress; this, rather than an insecure attachment bond, may be responsible for his inability to get along with peers.

Another criticism of attachment theory is that it ignores the diversity of social agents and social contexts that exist in the infant's world. Experiences with both the mother *and* the father, changing gender roles, day care, and mother's employment, peer experiences, socioeconomic status, and cultural values are not considered adequately in the attachment concept (Lamb, 1988; Lamb & others, 1984). In all of these perspectives, the importance of social relationships with parents is recognized—their differences lie in the criticalness of the attachment bond. Keep in mind that currently there is a great deal of controversy surrounding the concept of secure attachment: some experts argue for its primacy in influencing the child's competent development; others argue that it is given too much weight.

At this point we have discussed a number of important ideas about sociocultural, family, and attachment processes. A summary of these ideas is presented in Concept Table 7.1. Now we turn our attention to other caregivers and settings in the infant's development, evaluating first the father's role, and second, day care.

Social and Personality Development

CONCEPT TABLE

7.1

Sociocultural, Family, and Attachment Processes		
Concept	**Processes/Related Ideas**	**Characteristics/Description**
Sociocultural Influences	Bronfenbrenner's Ecological Model	The child is placed at the center of the model; the four environmental systems in the model are: microsystem, mesosystem, exosystem, and macrosystem.
Family Processes	Transition to Parenthood	Produces a disequlibrium, requiring considerable adaptation. Becoming a parent is often both wonderful and stressful.
	Reciprocal Socialization and Mutual Regulation	Children socialize parents just as parents socialize children. Scaffolding, synchronization, and mutual regulation are important dimensions of reciprocal socialization.
	The Family as a System	The family is a system of interacting individuals with different subsystems, some dyadic, others polyadic. Belsky's model describes direct and indirect effects.
Attachment	What Is Attachment?	Attachment is a relationship between two people in which each person feels strong about the other and does a number of things to ensure the relationship's continuation. In infancy, attachment refers to the bond between the caregiver and the infant. Feeding is not the critical element in attachment although contact comfort, familiarity, and trust are important. Bowlby's ethological theory stresses that the mother and infant instinctively trigger attachment. Attachment to the caregiver intensifies at about 6–7 months.
	Individual Differences	Ainsworth believes individual differences in attachment can be classified into secure, avoidant, and resistant categories. Ainsworth believes that securely attached babies have sensitive and responsive caregivers. In some investigations, secure attachment is related to social competence later in childhood. Attachment is related to intergenerational relations.
	Attachment, Temperament, and the Wider Social World	Some developmentalists believe too much emphasis is placed on attachment's role; they believe that genetics and temperament, on the one hand, and the diversity of social agents and contexts on the other, deserve more credit.

The Father's Role

All men know their children mean more than life.

Euripides, 426 B.C.

A father gently cuddles his infant son, softly stroking his forehead. Another father dresses his infant daughter as he readies her for her daily trip to a day care center. How common are these circumstances in the lives of fathers and their infants? Has the father's role changed dramatically?

The father's role has undergone major changes (Bronstein, 1988; Lamb, 1986, 1987; Pleck, 1984). During the Colonial period of the Puritans, fathers were mainly responsible for moral teaching. Fathers provided moral guidance and values, especially through religion. As the Industrial Revolution progressed, the father's role changed—now he had the responsibility as the breadwinner, a role that continued through the Great Depression. By the end of

How involved are today's fathers in infant caregiving?

"Are you going to believe me, your own flesh and blood, or some stranger you married?"

World War II, another role for fathers emerged, that of a gender role model. While being a breadwinner and moral guardian continued to be important father roles, attention shifted to his role as a male, especially for sons. Then, in the 1970s, the current interest in the father as an active, nurturant, caregiving parent emerged. Rather than only being responsible for the discipline and control of older children and with providing the family's economic base, the father now is being evaluated in terms of his active, nurturant involvement with his children, even infants.

Are fathers more actively involved with their children than they were 10 to 20 years ago? Few data document changes in the father's involvement from one point in history to another. One recent study (Juster, in press), however, compared the father's involvement in 1975 and 1981. In 1981, fathers spent about one-fourth more time in direct interaction with the child than in 1975. Mothers increased their direct interaction about 7 percent over this time period, but fathers, while increasing their direct interaction, were still far below mothers in this regard. In this study, the father's involvement was about one-third of the mother's, both in 1975 and 1981. If the mother is employed, does the father increase his involvement with his children? Only slightly. In sum, the father's active involvement with the child has increased somewhat, although this involvement does not approach the mother's, even when she is employed. Although fathers are spending more time with their infants and children, more time does not necessarily mean more *quality* time. In one recent investigation, there was no relation between the amount of time fathers spent with their five-year-old children and the quality of fathering (Grossman, Pollack & Golding, 1988).

Can fathers do what mothers do? Observations of fathers and their infants suggest that fathers have the ability to act sensitively and responsively with their infants (Parke & Sawin, 1980). Probably the strongest evidence of

The father's role has changed considerably in the twentieth century. What do you think the father's role in the child's development will be like in the twenty-first century?

the plasticity of male caregiving abilities is derived from information about male primates who are notoriously low in their interest in offspring but are forced to live with infants whose female caregivers are absent. Under these circumstances, the adult male competently rears the infants (Parke & Suomi, 1981). But remember, while fathers can be active, nurturant, involved caregivers with their infants, it is apparent that in many instances they choose not to follow this pattern.

Do fathers behave differently toward infants than mothers do? While maternal interactions usually center around child care activities—feeding, changing diapers, bathing—paternal interactions are more likely to include playful activities. Fathers engage in more rough and tumble play, bouncing the infant, throwing him up in the air, tickling him, and so on (Lamb, 1986). Mothers do play with infants, but their play is less physical and arousing than that of fathers.

Do infants prefer their mother or their father in stressful circumstances? In one investigation (Lamb, 1977), twenty 12-month-olds were observed interacting with their parents. With both parents present, infants preferred neither their mother nor their father. The same was true when the infant was alone with the mother or the father. But, the entrance of a stranger, combined with boredom and fatigue, produced a shift in the infant's social behavior toward the mother. In stressful circumstances, then, infants show a stronger attachment to the mother.

Might the nature of parent-infant interaction be different in families who adopt nontraditional gender roles? This question was investigated by Michael Lamb and his colleages (1982). They studied Swedish families in which the fathers were the primary caregivers of their firstborn, 8-month old infants. The mothers were working full-time. In all observations, the mothers were more likely to discipline, vocalize to, hold, soothe, and kiss the infants than the fathers. These mothers and fathers dealt with their infants differently, along the lines of American fathers and mothers following traditional gender roles. Having fathers assume the primary caregiving role did not seem to substantially alter the way they interacted with the infant. These findings may be due to biological reasons or to deeply ingrained socialization patterns in cultures. To learn more about the father's role in different cultures, turn to Focus on Life-Span Development 7.1, where you will read about Swedish fathers, Chinese fathers, and Pygmy fathers.

Day Care

Each weekday at 8:00 A.M., Ellen Smith has taken her 1-year-old daughter to the day care center at Brookhaven College in Dallas. Then Mrs. Smith goes off to work and returns in the afternoon to take Tanya home. Now, after 3 years at the center, Mrs. Smith reports that her daughter is adventuresome and interacts confidently with peers and adults. Mrs. Smith believes that day care has been a wonderful way to raise Tanya.

In Los Angeles, however, day care has been a series of horror stories for Barbara Jones. After two years of unpleasant experiences with sitters, day care centers, and day care homes, Mrs. Jones quit her job as a successful real estate agent to stay home and take care of her two-and-a-half-year-old daughter, Gretchen. "I didn't want to sacrifice my baby for my job," said Mrs. Jones, who was unable to find good substitute care in day care homes. When she put Gretchen in a day care center, she said that she felt like her daughter was being treated like a piece of merchandise—dropped off and picked up.

Swedish Fathers,

Chinese Fathers,

and Pygmy Fathers

S weden has been a forerunner in promoting the father's involvement with infants. The Swedish government prominently displays posters of a large, muscular man holding a tiny baby, an effort to communicate that "real men" can be actively involved in infant care. This message is important because many men still feel that active, nurturant parenting and masculinity are incompatible (Lamb, 1987). In Sweden, fathers, like mothers, can take parental leave during the first 12 months of the infant's life, the first nine being fully paid leave. He can stay home and take care of the child and has the right to reduce his working time up to two hours per day until the child is 8 years old (Hwang, 1987).

The father's role in China has been slower to change than in Sweden, but it is changing. Traditionally, in China, the father has been expected to be strict, the mother kind (see figure 7.A). The father is characterized as a stern disciplinarian, concerned very little with the child's feelings; the child is expected to fear the father. The notion of the strict father has ancient roots. The Chinese character for father (*fu*) evolved from a primitive character representing the hand holding a cane, which symbolizes authority. However, the twentieth century has witnessed a decline in the father's absolute authority.

Figure 7.A *This Chinese father enjoys an outing with his toddler.*

Younger fathers are becoming more inclined to emphasize the child's expression of opinions and independence, and they also are becoming more involved in childcare, influenced to some degree by the increased employment of mothers. Intergenerational tension has resulted between fathers and sons, as younger generations behave in less traditional ways (Ho, 1987).

A culture markedly different from Sweden and China is the Aka pygmy culture of the south central region of Africa. Over the course of a year, the Aka spend about 56% of their time in hunting, 27% of their time in gathering food, and 17% of their time

Figure 7.B *Aka Pygmy fathers hold their infants extensively. This Aka father soothes his infant during the middle of the night. The father sings quietly as he dances and plays with the rattle.*

in village work. What is the Aka pygmy father's role in the infant's development? Aka fathers are intimate and affectionate with their infants. They are not the infant's vigorous playmate like the American father is, but Aka fathers hold their infants extensively, possibly because the infant mortality rate is very high (see figure 7.B) (Hewlitt, 1987).

North America harbors some rather unique cultures. We can better understand the father's role in our own culture when we compare it with the father's role in other cultures, such as Swedish, Chinese, and Aka pygmy.

Many parents worry whether day care will adversely affect their children. They fear that day care will lessen the infant's emotional attachment to them, retard the infant's cognitive development, fail to teach the child how to control anger, and allow the child to be unduly influenced by their peers. How extensive is day care? Are the worries of these mothers justified?

In the 1980s, far more young children are in day care than at any time in history—about 2 million children currently receive formal, licensed day care, and more than 5 million children attend kindergartens. Also, uncounted millions of children are cared for by unlicensed baby-sitters. Day care has become a basic need of the American family.

The type of day care that young children receive varies extensively. Many day care centers house large groups of children and have elaborate facilities. Some are commercial operations, others nonprofit centers run by churches, civic groups, and employers. Home care frequently is provided in private homes, at times by child care professionals, at others by mothers who want to earn extra money.

The quality of care children experience in day care also varies extensively. Some caregivers have no training, others extensive training; some day care has a low caregiver-child ratio, others have a high caregiver-child ratio. Some experts recently have argued that the quality of day care most children receive in the United States is of poor quality. Jay Belsky (1987, in press) not only believes the quality of day care children experience is generally poor, he also believes this translates into negative developmental outcomes for children. Belsky concludes that extensive day care experience during the first 12 months of life—at least as typically experienced in the United States—is associated with insecure attachment, as well as increased aggression, noncompliance, and possibly social withdrawal during the preschool and early elementary school years.

A recent longitudinal study by Deborah Vandell and Mary Anne Corasaniti (1988) supports Belsky's beliefs. They found that extensive day care in the first year of the infant's life was associated with long term negative outcomes. In contrast to children who began full time day care later, children who began full time day care (defined as more than 30 hours per week) as infants were rated by parents and teachers as being less compliant and as having poorer peer relations. In the first grade, they received lower grades and had poorer work habits.

Belsky's conclusions are controversial. Other respected scientists have arrived at a different conclusion—their review of day care research suggests no ill effects of day care (Clarke-Stewart, 1988; Clarke-Stewart & Fein, 1983; Scarr, 1984).

What can we conclude? Does day care have aversive effects on children's development? Trying to combine the results into an overall conclusion about day care effects is a problem because of the different types of day care children experience and the different measures used to assess the outcome. Belsky's analysis does suggest that parents should be very careful about the quality of day care they select for their infants, especially those 1 year of age or less. Even Belsky agrees, though, that day care itself is not the culprit, rather it is the quality of day care that is problematic in this country. Belsky acknowledges that no evidence exists to show that children in high-quality day care are at risk in any way (Doll, 1988).

What constitutes a quality day care program for infants? The demonstration program developed by Jerome Kagan and his colleagues at Harvard University (1978) is exemplary. The day care center included a pediatrician,

A major concern about quality day care is that the facilities should provide more than custodial care. While adequate food, warmth, and shelter are important, by themselves they do not constitute good day care. Experts recommend that parents seeking day care for their children concern themselves with the following:

1. *Nutrition, Health, and Safety.* A balanced, nutritionally sound diet should be provided; the child's health should be carefully monitored and provisions for a sick child should be available; the physical environment should be free of hazards, and the child's safety should be of utmost concern.
2. *Child-Caregiver Ratio.* The number of children for each caregiver is an important consideration. For children under the age of 2, no more than five children should be cared for by a single caregiver; an even lower ratio is better.
3. *Caregiver Training and Behavior.* A competent caregiver does not need a Ph.D. in child development, but the caregiver should have some training and extensive experience in working with children. The caregiver should smile at the child, talk with the child, ask the child questions, and provide many stimulating toys.
4. *Peers, Play, and Exploration.* Infants and children spend considerable time with peers in day care. Caregivers need to supervise peer relations carefully, providing a good balance of structured and unstructured play, handling aggression and a lack of self-control judiciously. Exploration should be encouraged; adequate, safe space in which to curiously and creatively investigate the world should be available.
5. *Language and Cognitive Development.* Language and cognitive development, as well as social development, should be emphasized. Conversation between the caregivers and children should be plentiful, and attention should be given to stimulating the child's cognitive abilities; reading books should be accessible. Long hours should not be spent watching television.
6. *Coordination of Home and Day Care.* What goes on in the child's home should be coordinated with what goes on in day care. Caregivers in quality day care maintain open communication with parents, being receptive to parent questions.

a nonteaching director, and an infant-teacher ratio of three to one. Teachers' aids assisted at the center. The teachers and aids were trained to smile frequently, to talk with the infants, and to provide them with a safe environment that included many stimulating toys. No adverse effects of day care were observed in this project. More information about what to look for in a quality day care center is presented in Focus on Life-Span Development 7.2. Using such criteria as those in Focus on Life-Span Development 7.2, Carollee Howes (1988) recently discovered that children who entered low quality child care

Of the criteria listed in Focus on Life-Span Development 7.2, which do you believe are the most important if your own children were going to day care? Are there other criteria not discussed in the box that you believe should be considered?

We have all the knowledge necessary to provide absolutely first-rate child care in the United States. What is missing is the commitment and the will.

Edward Zigler, 1987

Blossoms are scattered by the wind
And the wind cares nothing, but
The blossoms of the heart
No wind can touch.
Youshida Kenko, The Harvest of Leisure, *1330.*

as infants were least likely to be socially competent in early childhood (less compliant, less self-controlled, less task-oriented, more hostile, and more problems in peer interaction).

Edward Zigler (1987) recently proposed a solution to the day care needs of families. Zigler says that we should not think of school as an institution but rather as a building, one that is owned by taxpaying parents who need day care for their children. Part of the school building would be for teaching and part would be for child care and supervision. This system could provide parents with competent developmental child care services. Zigler believes it should be available to every child over the age of 3. He does not think children should start formal schooling at age 3—they would only be in the schools for day care. At the age of 5, children would start kindergarten, but only for half-days. If the child has a parent at home, the child would spend the remainder of the day at home. If the parents are working, the child would spend the second half of the day in the day care part of the school. For children aged 6 to 12, after-school and vacation care would be available to those who need it.

Zigler does not believe teachers should be the ones providing day care. They are trained as educators and are too expensive. What we need, he says, is a child development associate, someone who is trained to work with children, someone we can afford to pay. This is a large vision, one that involves a structural change in society and a new face for our school system. Zigler believes that in the early 1990s, a bill legislating such experimental schools will be introduced in congress. As Zigler remembers, between the fall of 1964 and the summer of 1965 we managed to put 560,000 children into Head Start programs, an educational program for impoverished children. He believes we can do the same thing with day care (Trotter, 1987).

Emotional and Personality Development

The sociocultural world, family processes, attachment, the father's role, and day care—all are important ingredients of the infant's social being. But there is more to understanding the nature of the infant. Emotions, trust, independence, and development of a sense of self all play key roles in the infant's development.

Emotional Development

If you cannot name an emotion, you cannot experience it. That was the dominant view of infant emotion for much of this century. But now a different picture has emerged, one that recognizes the infant's repertoire of emotions. Just as we found in chapters 5 and 6, that vision, hearing, and the ability to remember and learn are more highly developed in infancy than was originally believed, now we know that interest, distress, and disgust are present early in infancy and can be communicated to parents. Much earlier than the arrival of language, infants add other emotions like joy, anger, surprise, shyness, and fear to their capabilities.

What are the functions of emotions in infancy? Emotions are adaptive and promote survival, serve as a form of communication, and provide regulation (Barrett & Campos, 1987; Bretherton & others, 1986; Izard and Malatesta, 1987). For example, various fears—such as fear of the dark and fear of sudden changes in the environment—are adaptive because there are clear links between such events and possible danger. Infants also use emotions to inform others about their feelings and needs. The infant who smiles probably is telling others that she is feeling pleasant; the infant who cries probably is

communicating that something is unpleasant. And infants use emotions to increase or decrease the distance between themselves and others. The infant who smiles may be encouraging someone to come closer; the infant who displays anger may be suggesting that an intruder should go away. And emotions influence the information the infant selects from the perceptual world and the behaviors the infant displays.

How can we find out if the infant is displaying emotion? Psychologist Carol Izard and his colleagues (Izard, 1982; Izard & Malatesta, 1987; La Barbera & others, 1976) have developed a system for decoding the emotional expressions on infants' faces. Izard wanted to discover which emotions were inborn, which emerged later, and under which conditions they were displayed. The conditions included: being given an ice cube, having tape put on the backs of their hands, being handed a favorite toy and then having it taken away, being separated from and reunited with their mothers, being approached by a stranger, having their heads gently restrained, having a ticking clock held next to their ears, having a balloon popped in front of their faces, and being given camphor to sniff and lemon rind and orange juice to taste.

Izard's system for coding emotions has the imposing name, Maximally Discriminative Facial Movement Coding System—or MAX for short. The coder, using MAX, watches slow-motion and stop-action videotapes of the infant's facial reactions to the circumstances described earlier. Anger, for example, is indicated when the brows are sharply lowered and drawn together, the eyes are narrowed or squinted, and the mouth is open in an angular, square-like shape. The key elements of emotional facial codes in infants are shown in figure 7.8, and the developmental timetable of their emergence in infancy is shown in table 7.1.

Joy
Mouth forms smile, cheeks lifted, twinkle in eyes.

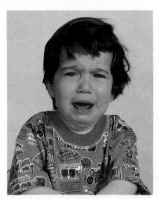

Anger
Brows drawn together and downward, eyes fixed, mouth squarish.

Interest
Brows raised or knit, mouth softly rounded, lips pursed.

Disgust
Nose wrinkled, upper lip raised, tongue pushed outward.

Surprise
Brows raised, eyes widened, mouth rounded in oval shape.

Distress
Eyes tightly closed, mouth, as in anger, squared and angular.

Sadness
Brows' inner corners raised, drawn out and down.

Fear
Brows level, drawn in and up, eyelids lifted, mouth retracted.

Figure 7.8
Facial expressions of emotion and their characteristics.

Personality Development

The individual characteristics of the infant that are often thought of as central to personality development are trust, the self, and independence.

Trust. According to Erik Erikson (1968), approximately the first year of life is characterized by the stage of development, trust versus mistrust. Following a life of regularity, warmth, and protection in the mother's womb, the infant faces a world that is less secure. Erikson believes that infants learn trust when they are cared for in a consistent, warm manner. If the infant is not well fed and kept warm on a consistent basis, a sense of mistrust is likely to develop.

We briefly described Erikson's ideas about the role of trust in attachment earlier. His thoughts have much in common with Mary Ainsworth's concept of secure attachment. The infant who has a sense of trust is likely to be securely attached and have confidence to explore new circumstances; the infant who has a sense of mistrust is likely to be insecurely attached and to not have such confidence and positive expectations.

Trust versus mistrust is not resolved once and for all in the first year of life; it arises again at each successive stage of development. There is both hope and danger in this. The child who enters school with a sense of mistrust may

TABLE 7.1
The Developmental Course of Infant Emotions

Emotional Expression	Approximate Time of Emergence
Interest	Present at birth
*Neonatal smile (a sort of half smile that appears spontaneously for no apparent reason)	
*Startled response	
*Distress	
Disgust	
Social smile	4–6 weeks
Anger	3–4 months
Surprise	
Sadness	
Fear	5–7 months
Shame/Shyness	6–8 months
Contempt	Second year of life
Guilt	

*The neonatal smile, the startled response, and distress in response to pain are precursors of the social smile and the emotions of surprise and sadness, which appear later. No evidence exists to suggest that they are related to inner feelings when they are observed in the first few weeks of life.

trust a particular teacher who has taken the time to make herself trustworthy—with this second chance, he overcomes his early mistrust. By contrast, a child who leaves infancy with a sense of trust can still have his sense of mistrust activated at a later stage if, perhaps, his parents are separated and divorced under conflicting circumstances. An example is instructive (Elkind, 1970). A 4-year-old boy was being seen by a clinical psychologist at a court clinic because his adoptive parents, who had had him for 6 months, now wanted to give him back to the agency. They said that he was cold and unloving, took things, and could not be trusted. He was indeed a cold and apathetic boy, but with good reason. About a year after his illegitimate birth, he was taken away from his mother, who had a drinking problem, and was shuttled back and forth among several foster homes. At first, he tried to relate to people in the foster homes, but the relationships never had an opportunity to develop because he was moved so frequently. In the end, he gave up trying to reach out to others because the inevitable separations hurt too much. Like the burned child who dreads the flame, this emotionally burned child shunned the pain of close relationships. He had trusted his mother, but now he trusted no one. Only years of devoted care and patience could now undo the damage to this child's sense of trust.

In addition to the description of the 4-year-old boy from an adopted family, can you think of other examples in which trust during infancy is an important aspect of development? Try to come up with at least two other specific cases.

Figure 7.9
The development of self-recognition in infancy. The graph gives the findings of two studies in which infants of different ages showed recognition of rouge by touching, wiping, or verbally referring to it. Notice that self-recognition did not occur extensively until the second half of the second year of life.

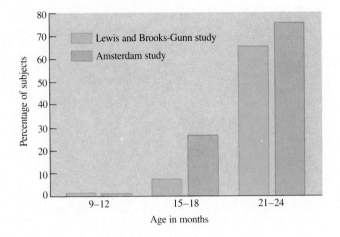

"One great splitting of the whole universe into two halves is made by each of us . . . we call the two halves "me" and "not me.""

William James, Principles of Psychology, *1890*

This 18-month-old shows a sense of self.

The Developing Sense of Self and Independence

Individuals carry with them a sense of who they are and what makes them different from everyone else. They cling to this identity and begin to feel secure in the knowledge that this identity is becoming more stable. Real or imagined, this sense of self is a strong motivating force in life. When does the individual begin to sense a separate existence from others?

Children begin to develop a sense of self by learning to distinguish themselves from others. To determine whether infants can recognize themselves, psychologists have used mirrors. In the animal kingdom, only the great apes learn to recognize their reflection in the mirror, but human infants accomplish this feat by about 18 months of age. How does the mirror technique work? The mother puts a dot of rouge on her infant's nose. The observer watches to see how often the infant touches his nose. Next, the infant is placed in front of a mirror and observers detect whether nose touching increases. Figure 7.9 reveals that in two separate investigations in the second half of the second year of life, infants recognized their own image and coordinated the image they saw with the actions of touching their own body (Amsterdam, 1968; Lewis, 1987; Lewis & Brooks-Gunn, 1979).

Not only does the infant develop a sense of self in the second year of life, but independence becomes a more central theme of the infant's life as well. The theories of Margaret Mahler and Erik Erikson have important implications for both self development and independence. Mahler (1979) believes that the child goes through a separation and then an individuation process—separation involves the infant's movement away from the mother and individuation involves the development of self.

Mother-child interaction can interfere with the development of individuation. For example, Anna's mother was emotionally unavailable. Never certain of her mother's availability, Anna was preoccupied with it; she found it difficult to explore her surroundings. After a brief spurt of practicing, she would return to her mother and try to interact with her in an intense way. Sometimes she would spill cookies on the floor, always with an eye to gaining her mother's attention. Anna's mother was absorbed with her own interests. During the preschool years, Anna threw temper tantrums and clung to her teacher. Then the clinging would turn to hitting and yelling. In Mahler's view, Anna wanted only one thing to happen—her mother to return through the door. As can be seen in Anna's case, an unsatisfactory mother-infant relationship led to problems in her development of independence.

The infant's development of a sense of self, then, is based on both the infant's relationship with caregivers (Bretherton, 1987; Mahler, 1979; Pines, 1987) and the infant's developing cognitive skills, especially the ability to represent an image (Harter, 1983; Piaget, 1952; Pipp, Fischer, & Jennings, 1987). Language may also be wrapped up in the self's representation early in life. In one recent investigation (Pipp, Fischer, & Jennings, 1987), at 18 to 23 months of age, girls detected more features of themselves than did boys. This is the age at which one type of representational ability, use of sophisticated language, is first emerging, and girls seem to be more advanced in this ability than boys (McCall, Eichorn, & Hogarty, 1977).

Erikson (1968), like Mahler, believes that independence is an important issue in the second year of life. Erikson describes the second stage of development as autonomy versus shame and doubt. Autonomy builds on the infant's developing mental and motor abilities. At this point in development, the infant can not only walk but can also climb, open and close, drop, push and pull, hold and let go. The infant feels pride in these new accomplishments and wants to do everything himself, whether it is flushing the toilet, pulling the wrapping off a package, or deciding what to eat. It is important for parents to recognize the toddler's need to do what he is capable of doing at his own pace and own time. Then, he can learn to control his muscles, his impulses, himself, and his environment. But when caregivers are impatient and do for him what he is capable of doing himself, shame and doubt are developed. Every parent has rushed a child from time to time. It is only when parents are consistently overprotective and critical of accidents (wetting, soiling, spilling, or breaking, for example) that the child develops an excessive sense of shame with respect to others and an excessive sense of doubt about his ability to control himself and his world.

Erikson also believes that the autonomy versus shame and doubt stage has important implications for the development of independence and identity during adolescence. The development of autonomy during the toddler years gives the adolescent the courage to be an independent individual who can choose and guide her own future.

Too much autonomy, though, can be as harmful as too little. A 7-year-old boy who had a heart condition learned quickly how afraid his parents were of any signs of his having cardiac problems. It was not long before he ruled the household. The family could not go shopping or for a drive if he did not approve. On the rare occasions his parents defied him, he would get angry and his purple hue and gagging would frighten them into submission. This boy actually was scared of his power and eager to relinquish it. When the parents and the boy realized this, and recognized that a little shame and doubt were a healthy opponent of an inflated sense of autonomy, the family began to function much more smoothly (Elkind, 1970).

At this point, we have discussed a number of ideas about the father's role, day care, and emotional and personality development. A summary of these ideas is presented in Concept Table 7.2. From time to time is this chapter, you have learned about the unhealthy outcomes when parent-child relationships go awry. Next, we describe other problems and disturbances in infant development.

We learn to curb our will and keep our overt actions within the bounds of humanity, long before we can subdue our sentiments and imaginations in the same mild tone.

William Hazlitt, 1826

I am what I can will freely.

Erik Erikson, 1968

The Father's Role, Day Care, and Emotional and Personality Development

Concept	Processes/Related Ideas	Characteristics/Description
The Father's Role	Its Nature	Over time, the father's role in the child's development has evolved from moral teacher to breadwinner to gender role model to active, nurturant caregiver.
	Father-Child Interaction and Attachment	Fathers have increased their interaction with their children, but they still lag far behind mothers, even when the mother is employed. Fathers can act sensitively to the infant's signals, but most of the time they do not. The mother's role in the infant's development is primarily caregiving, that of the father involves playful interaction. Infants generally prefer their mother under stressful circumstances. Even in nontraditional families, as when the father is the main caregiver, the behaviors of mothers and fathers follow traditional gender lines.
Day Care	Its Nature	Day care has become a basic need of the American family; more children are in day care today than at any time in history.
	Quality of Care and Effects on Development	The quality of day care is uneven. Belsky concludes most day care is inadequate and that extensive day care in the first twelve months of the infant's life has negative developmental outcomes. Other experts disagree with Belsky. Day care remains a controversial topic. Quality day care can be achieved and it seems to have little adverse effect on children.
Emotional and Personality Development	Emotional Development	Emotions in infancy are adaptive and promote survival, serve as a form of communication, and provide regulation. Izard developed the MAX system for coding infant facial expressions of emotion. Using this sytem, it was found that interest and disgust are present in the newborn, and that a social smile, anger, surprise, sadness, fear, and shame/shyness develop in the first year, while contempt and guilt develop in the second year.
	Trust	Erikson argues that the first year is characterized by the crisis of trust versus mistrust; his ideas about trust have much in common with Ainsworth's secure attachment concept.
	Developing a Sense of Self and Independence	At some point in the second half of the second year of life, the infant develops a sense of self. Independence becomes a central theme in the second year of life. Mahler argues that the infant separates herself from the mother and then develops individuation. Erikson stresses that the second year of life is characterized by the stage of autonomy versus shame and doubt.

Problems and disturbances in infancy can arise for a number of reasons. All development—normal and abnormal—is influenced by the interaction of heredity and environment. In a comprehensive study of children at risk, a variety of biological, social, and developmental characteristics were identified as predictors of problems and disturbances at age 18. They included: moderate to severe perinatal (or at near birth) stress and birth defects, low socioeconomic status at 2 and 10 years of age, level of maternal education below 8 years, low family stability between 2 and 8 years, very low or very high infant responsiveness at 1 year, a Cattell score below 80 at age 2 (the Cattell is one of the early measures of infant intelligence), and the need for long-term mental health services or placement in a learning disability class at age 10. When four or more of these factors were present, the stage was set for serious coping problems in the second decade of life (Werner & Smith, 1982). Among the problems in infancy that deserve special consideration are child abuse and autism.

Child Abuse

Unfortunately, parental hostility toward children in some families reaches the point where one or both parents abuse the child. Child abuse is an increasing problem in the United States. Estimates of its incidence vary, but some authorities say that as many as 500,000 children are physically abused in the United States every year. Laws in many states now require doctors and teachers to report suspected cases of child abuse. Yet, many cases go unreported, especially those of "battered" infants.

For some years, it was believed that parents who commited child abuse were severely disturbed, "sick" individuals. However, researchers find that parents who abuse their children rarely can be classified as having a severe mental illness (Blumberg, 1974). To better understand child abuse, it is helpful to shift the focus from parents' personality traits to three aspects of the social environment—culture, family, and community (Parke, 1976; Parke & Lewis, 1970).

The extensive violence in the American culture is reflected in the occurrence of violence in the family. A regular diet of violence appears on television screens and parents frequently resort to power assertion as a disciplinary technique. American television contains more violence than Japanese television. And, in China, where physical punishment rarely is used to discipline children, child abuse's incidence is very low (Geis & Monahan, 1976; Stevenson, 1974).

To understand child abuse in the family, the interaction of all family members should be considered, regardless of who actually performs the violent acts against the child. For example, even though the father may be the person who physically abuses the child, contributions of the mother, the child, siblings, *and* the father should be evaluated. Many parents who abuse their children come from families in which physical punishment was used. These parents may view physical punishment as a legitimate way of controlling the child's behavior, and physical abuse may be part of this sanctioning. The child himself may unwantingly contribute to child abuse—an unattractive child receives more physical punishment than an attractive child, and a child from an unwanted pregnancy may be especially vulnerable to abuse. The interaction of parents with each other may produce child abuse, too. Husband-wife violence and financial problems may result in displaced aggression toward a defenseless child. Displaced aggression is a common cause of child abuse.

Community support systems are especially important in alleviating stressful family situations and thereby preventing child abuse. An investigation of the support systems in 58 counties in New York State revealed a relation between the incidence of child abuse and the absence of support systems available to the family. Both family resources—relatives and friends, for example—and such formal community support systems as crisis centers and child abuse counseling were associated with a reduction in child abuse (Garbarino, 1976). One form of child abuse can be especially devastating to a young child—sexual abuse, which is described in Focus on Life-Span Development 7.3.

Autism

Autism is often diagnosed in infancy but may persist well into childhood. The most distinguishing characteristic of autistic children is their inability to relate to people (Wing, 1977). As babies, they require very little from their parents: They do not demand much attention and they do not reach out (literally or figuratively) for their parents. They rarely smile. When someone tries to hold them, they usually withdraw by arching their backs and pushing away from the person. In their cribs or playpens, they appear to be oblivious to what is going on around them, often sitting and staring into space for long periods of time. In addition to their attachment deficits, autistic children have speech problems. As many as one of every two autistic children never learns to speak. Those who do learn to speak may display a type of speech called *echolalia*— the child echos rather than responds to what he hears. If you ask, "How are you, Chuck?" Chuck responds with, "How are you, Chuck?" Autistic children also confuse pronouns, inappropriately substituting *you* for *I,* for example. A third major characteristic of autistic children is the degree to which they become upset over a change in their daily routine or their physical environment. Rearrangement of a sequence of events or even furniture in the course of a day may cause them to become extremely upset. This suggests that autistic children are not flexible in adapting to new routines and changes in their daily life.

What causes autism? Autism seems to involve some form of organic brain dysfunction and may also have genetic ties. There has been no satisfactory evidence developed to document that family socialization causes autism (Rutter & Schopler, 1987). To learn more about the everyday lives of autistic children, read Focus on Life-Span Development 7.4.

SHATTERED INNOCENCE—

THE SEXUAL ABUSE OF CHILDREN

Headlines about day-care center scandals and feminist protests against sexist exploitation have increased public awareness of what we now know is a widespread problem—children's sexual abuse. It has been estimated that as many as 40 million American children are sexually abused—about one in six. A 1984 Gallup poll of 2,000 men and women in 210 Canadian communities found that 22 percent of the respondents were sexually abused as children. Clearly, children's sexual abuse is more widespread than was thought in the past. One reason the problem of children's sexual abuse was a dark secret for so long is that people understandably kept this painful experience to themselves.

The sexual abuse of children occurs most often between the ages of 9 and 12, although the abuse of 2- and 3-year-olds is not unusual. The abuser is almost always a man and he typically is known to the child, often being a relative. In many instances, the abuse is not limited to a single episode. No race, ethnic group, or economic class is immune.

While children do not react uniformly to sexual abuse, certain behaviors and feelings occur with

some regularity. The immediate effects include sleeping and eating disturbances, anger, withdrawal, and guilt. The children often appear to be afraid or anxious. Two additional signs occur so often that professionals rely on them as indicators of abuse when they are present together. The first is sexual preoccupation— excessive or public masturbation and an unusually strong interest in sexual organs, play, and nudity. The second sign consists of a host of physical complaints or problems, such as rashes, headaches, and vomiting, all without medical explanation. When it is discovered that these children have been sexually abused, a check of their medical records usually produces years of such mysterious ailments. While there are patterns in the immediate effects of sexual abuse of children, it is far more difficult to connect such abuse with later psychological problems. It is impossible to say that every child who has been abused will develop this or that problem, and we still have not developed a profile of the child abuse victim that everyone can agree upon.

One of the most disturbing findings about childhood sexual abuse is its strong intergenerational pattern.

Boys who are sexually abused are far more likely to turn into offenders, molesting the next generation of children; girls who are sexually abused are more likely to produce children who are abused. And victimization can lead to revictimization. Individuals who have been sexually abused as children may later become victims of rape or attempted rape. Women, of course, are not to blame for being victims.

How can the intergenerational transmission of abuse be broken? In one recent investigation, the group of adults most likely to break the abuse cycle were more likely to receive emotional support from a nonabusive adult during childhood, participate in therapy, and have a less abusive and more stable, emotionally supportive and satisfying relationship with a mate (Egeland, Jacobvitz, & Papatola, in press; Egeland, Jacobvitz, & Sroufe, 1987). The prognosis also is better if an individual has not been abused by more than one person, when force is not used during the abuse, and when the abuser is not a close relative (Kohn, 1987).

A CHILD CALLED NOAH

The impact an autistic child can have on parents is described in the following excerpts from the popular book *A Child Called Noah,* written in 1972 by Josh Greenfield about his autistic son Noah.

4–16–67: We've decided to stop worrying about Noah. He isn't retarded, he's just pushing the clock hands about at his own slow speed. Yet . . .

8–16–67: We took Noah to a pediatrician in the next town, who specializes in neurology. He said that, since Noah is talking now, there was little cause to worry; that Noah seemed "hypertonic," a floppy baby, a slow developer, but that time would be the maturing agent. We came away relieved. But I also have to admit that lately I haven't worried that much.

6–6–69: Noah is two. He still doesn't walk, but I do think he's trying to teach himself how to stand up. We're still concerned. And I guess we'll remain concerned until he stands up and walks like a boy.

7–14–69: Our fears about Noah continue to undergo dramatic ups and downs. Because he doesn't respond when we call his name and fails to relate completely to his immediate environment we took him to a nearby hospital. . . . I guess we both fear that what we dread is so, that Noah is not a normal child, that he is a freak, and his condition is getting worse.

2–19–70: I'm a lousy father. I anger too easily. I get hot with Karl and take on a four-year-old kid. I shout at Noah and further upset an already disturbed one. Perhaps I am responsible for Noah's problems.

8–70: I also know how very few people can actually understand our situation as a family, how they assume we are aloof when we tend not to accept or extend the usual social invitations. Nor have I mentioned the extra expenses a child like Noah entails—those expenses I keep in another book.

8–71: Even more heartbreaking has

been the three-year period it has taken us to pierce the organized-medicine, institutionalized-mental-health gauze curtain. Most doctors, if they were unable to prescribe any form of curative aid, did their best to deter us from seeking it. Freudian-oriented psychiatrists and psychologists, if ill-equipped to deal with the problems of those not verbal, tried to inflict great feelings of guilt upon us as all-too-vulnerable parents. Neurologists and pediatricians, if not having the foggiest notions about the effects of diet and nutrition, vitamins and enzymes, and their biochemical workings, would always suggest such forms of therapy as practiced only by quacks. And county mental-health boards, we discovered, who have charge of the moneys that might be spent helping children like Noah, usually tossed their skimpy fundings away through existing channels that do not offer proper treatment for children like Noah. (pp. 91–92)

Summary

I. Sociocultural Influences
Bronfenbrenner developed a comprehensive ecological model that places the child at the center of the model; the four environmental systems in the model are: microsystem, mesosystem, exosystem, and macrosystem.

II. Family Processes
The transition to parenthood produces a disequilibrium, which requires considerable adaptation. It is not unusual for the postpartum blues to characterize mothers in the several months after the infant's birth. Infants socialize parents just as parents socialize infants—the process of reciprocal socialization. Parent-infant relationships are mutually regulated by the parent and the infant. In infancy, much of the relationship is driven by the parent, but as the infant gains self-control, the relationship is initiated more on an equal basis. The family is a system of interacting individuals with different subsystems, some dyadic, others polyadic. Belsky's model describes direct and indirect effects.

III. What Is Attachment?
Attachment is a relationship between two people in which each person feels strongly about the other and does a number of things to ensure the relationship's continuation. In infancy, attachment refers to the bond between the caregiver and the infant. Feeding is not the critical element in attachment, although contact comfort, familiarity, and trust are important. Bowlby's ethological theory stresses that the mother and infant instinctively trigger attachment. Attachment to the caregiver intensifies at about 6 to 7 months.

IV. Individual Differences in Attachment, Temperament, and the Wider Social World
Ainsworth believes individual differences in attachment can be classified into secure, avoidant, and resistant categories. Ainsworth believes that securely attached babies have sensitive and responsive caregivers. In some investigations, secure attachment is related to social competence later in childhood. Attachment is related to intergenerational relations. Some developmentalists believe too much emphasis is placed on attachment's role; they believe that genetics and temperament on the one hand, and the diversity of social agents and contexts on the other, deserve more credit.

V. The Father's Role
Over time, the father's role has evolved from moral teacher to breadwinner to gender role model to active, nurturant caregiver. Fathers have increased their interaction with their children, but they still lag far behind mothers, even when the mother is employed. Fathers can act sensitively to the infant's signals, but most of the time they do not. The mother's role in the infant's development is primarily caregiving, that of the father's involves playful interaction. Infants generally prefer their mother under stressful circumstances. Even in nontraditional families, as when the father is the primary caregiver, the behaviors of mothers and fathers follow traditional gender lines.

VI. Day Care
Day care has become a basic need of the American family. More children are in day care today than at any time in history. The quality of day care is uneven. Belsky contends that most day care is inadequate and that extensive day care in the first twelve months of the infants life has negative developmental outcomes. Other experts disagree with Belsky. Day care remains a controversial topic. Quality day care can be achieved, and it seems to have little adverse effect on children.

VII. Emotional Development
Emotions in infancy are adaptive and promote survival, serve as a form of communication, and provide regulation. Izard developed the MAX system for coding infant facial expressions of emotion. Using this system, it was found that interest and disgust are present in the newborn, and that a social smile, anger, surprise, sadness, fear, and shame/shyness develop in the first year while contempt and guilt develop in the second year.

VIII. Personality Development
Erikson argues that the first year is characterized by the crisis of trust versus mistrust; his ideas about trust have much in common with Ainsworth's concept of secure attachment. At some point in the second half of the second year of life, the infant develops a sense of self. Independence becomes a central theme in the second year of life. Mahler argues that the infant separates herself from the mother and then develops individuation. Erikson stresses that the second year of life is characterized by the stage of autonomy versus shame and doubt.

IX. Problems and Disturbances
Abnormal development—like normal development—is caused by the interaction of heredity and environment. An understanding of child abuse requires an analysis of cultural, familial, and community influences. Sexual abuse of children is now recognized as a more widespread problem than was believed in the past. Autism is a severe disorder involving an inability to relate to people, speech problems, and upset over change in routine or environment. Autism seems to involve some form of organic brain dysfunction and genetic disorder.

Key Terms

microsystem   184

mesosystem   186

exosystem   186

macrosystem   186

reciprocal socialization   188

scaffolding   188

attachment   190

secure attachment   191

Type A babies   192

Type B babies   192

Type C babies   192

autism   208

Suggested Readings

Birns, B., & Daye, D. (Eds.) (1988). *Motherhood and child care*. Boston: Auburn House.
A number of articles that describe the mother's role in the infant's development are provided; included is an excellent chapter on day care.

Izard, C. E. (1982). *Measuring emotion in infants and children*. New York: Cambridge U. Press.
Izard, one of the leading figures in the study of infant emotions, describes in fascinating detail how to assess the emotions of infants and young children.

Kohn, A. (1987). *No contest: The case against competition*. Boston: Houghton Mifflin.
The dark secrets of children's sexual abuse is told with extensive examples of case studies to illustrate its psychological damage.

Lamb, M. E. (1987). *The father's role: Cross-cultural perspectives*. Hillsdale, NJ: Erlbaum.
Intriguing descriptions of the father's role in different cultures are provided—includes information about English fathers, American fathers, Israeli fathers, Italian fathers, Chinese fathers, Swedish fathers, and Aka pygmy fathers.

Sroufe, L. A., & Fleeson, J. (1986). Attachment and the construction of relationships. In W. Hartup and Z. Rubin (Eds.), *Relationships and development*. Hillsdale, NJ: Erlbaum.
Insight into the importance of attachment in our development of relationships is given.

SECTION
IV

Early Childhood

T he childhood shows the man,
As morning shows the day. ■

Milton

Physical and Cognitive Development

The greatest poem ever known
Is one all poets have outgrown:
The poetry, innate, untold,
Of being only four years old. ∎

Christopher Morley

Amy began attending a Montessori school when she was three years old and has been attending the school for more than a year now. Her mother was interested in a preschool program for Amy that involved academic instruction rather than play. Amy's mother talked to a number of mothers in her neighborhood, read extensively about different approaches to early childhood education, and visited eight different preschool programs to observe a typical day and talk with teachers before making her decision about which school would be best for Amy.

Montessori schools are patterned after the educational philosophy of Maria Montessori, an Italian physician-turned-educator, who crafted a revolutionary approach to young children's education at the beginning of the twentieth century. Her work began with a group of mentally retarded children in Rome. She was successful in teaching them to read, write, and pass examinations designed for normal children. Some time later, she turned her attention to poor children from the slums of Rome and had similar success in teaching them. Her approach has since been adopted extensively in private nursery schools in the United States.

The **Montessori approach** is at once a philosophy of education, a psychology of the child, and a group of practical educational exercises that can be used to teach children. Children are given considerable freedom and spontaneity in choosing activities, and they can move from one activity to another when they desire. Each child is encouraged to work independently, to complete tasks in a prescribed manner once they have been undertaken, and to put materials away in assigned places. The teacher is a facilitator rather than a director or controller of learning. She shows the child how to perform intellectual activities, demonstrates interesting ways to explore curriculum materials, and offers help when the child requests.

While the Montessori approach is favored by some developmentalists, others believe that children's social development is neglected. For example, while Montessori fosters independence and the development of cognitive skills, verbal interaction between the teacher and child and peer interaction are deemphasized. Montessori's critics also argue that imaginative play is restricted. Later in this chapter, other preschool education programs will be described. Keep the Montessori approach in mind so that you can compare its focus with that of these other approaches.

The physical and cognitive worlds of the preschool child are creative, free, and fanciful. Striking, catching, throwing, kicking, balancing, rolling objects, rolling oneself, zipping, lacing, buttoning, fitting, pushing, pulling, dancing, and swimming—preschool children can do all of these things and more. A fascinating part of the "much more" is their drawing and symbolic thought. Suns sometimes show up as green, skies yellow. Cars float in the sky, pelicans kiss seals, and people are represented by tadpoles (Winner, 1986).

If the growth rate did not slow down in early childhood, we would become a species of giants.

Physical Development in Early Childhood

Remember from chapter 5 that the infant's growth in the first year is extremely rapid and follows cephalocaudal and proximodistal patterns. By 13 to 14 months of age, most infants have begun to walk. During the infant's second year, the growth rate begins to slow down, but both gross and fine motor skills progress rapidly. The infant develops a sense of mastery through increased proficiency in walking and running. Increased fine motor skills—such as being able to turn the pages of a book one page at a time—also contribute to the infant's sense of mastery during the second year.

Some Physical Changes

The growth rate continues to slow down in early childhood; otherwise we would be a species of giants. Continuing the theme of cephalocaudal development, the brain is closer to full growth than the rest of the child's body, attaining 75 percent of its adult weight by the age of three. The average child grows 2½ inches in height and gains 5 to 7 pounds a year during early childhood. As the preschool child grows older, the percentage of increase in height and weight decreases with each additional year of age. Table 8.1 shows the average height and weight of children as they age from three to six years. Girls are only slightly smaller and lighter than boys during this age period, a difference that continues until puberty. In early childhood, both boys and girls slim down as the trunk of their body becomes longer. Although their heads are still somewhat large for their bodies, by the end of early childhood, most children have lost their top-heavy look. Body fat also shows a slow, steady decline during early childhood—by the end of the period, the chubby baby looks thinner.

Growth patterns vary individually, though. Think back to your preschool years. This probably was the first time you noticed that some children were taller than you, some shorter; that some were fatter, some thinner; that some were stronger, some weaker. Much of the variation is due to heredity, but environmental experiences are involved to some degree. A review of the heights

Passing hence from infancy, I came to boyhood, or rather it came to me, displacing infancy, nor did that depart— and yet it was no more.

Confessions of St. Augustine

TABLE 8.1 Physical Growth, Ages Three to Six (50th Percentile)				
Height (Inches)			**Weight (Pounds)**	
Age	**Boys**	**Girls**	**Boys**	**Girls**
3	38	37¾	32¼	31¾
3½	39¼	39¼	34¼	34
4	40¼	40½	36½	36¼
4½	42	42	38½	38½
5	43¼	43	41½	41
5½	45	44½	45½	44
6	46	46	48	47

From George H. Lowrey, Growth and Development of Children, *7th ed. Copyright © 1978 Year Book Medical Publishers. Reprinted by permission.*

What gross motor skills are assessed by the Denver Development Screening Test?

of preschool children around the world concluded that the two most important contributors to height differences are ethnic origin and nutrition (Meredith, 1978). Urban, middle-class, and first born children were taller than rural, lower-class, and later-born children—probably because the former get better health care and nutrition. Children whose mothers smoked during pregnancy were one-half inch shorter than children whose mothers did not smoke during pregnancy. In the United States, black children are taller than white children.

Motor and Perceptual Development
Building towers with blocks . . . running as fast as you could, falling down, getting right back up, and running just as fast again . . . scribbling, scribbling, and then scribbling some more on lots of pieces of paper . . . cutting paper with scissors—during the preschool years you probably developed all of these motor activities. Table 8.2 summarizes how a number of gross and fine motor skills change during the preschool years.

The large muscles of preschool children develop extensively, especially those in the arms and legs. For this reason, daily exercise is recommended. Sedentary periods should be brief and few. Although fine motor skills also increase during the preschool years, they grow more rapidly during the elementary school years (Robinson, 1977).

How do developmentalists measure motor development? One widely used measure is the **Denver Developmental Screening Test.** It was devised to be a simple, inexpensive, and fast way to diagnose developmental delay in children from birth through 6 years of age. The test is individually administered and includes an evaluation of language and personal-social ability in addition to separate assessments of gross and fine motor skills. Among the gross motor skills that are measured are the child's ability to sit, walk, broad jump, pedal a tricycle, throw a ball overhand, catch a bounced ball, hop on one foot, and balance on one foot. Fine motor skills that are measured include the child's ability to stack cubes, reach for objects, and draw a person.

Another important development in early childhood is how children perceive the space in which they live. If you are sitting in the bedroom and the door is shut, can you identify what lies beyond each wall? Can you point toward the TV in the living area or the stove in the kitchen? Can you sketch a map showing the location of your house, your school, and the downtown area of the city where you live? Chances are that you can perform all of these tasks with some degree of accuracy. But some of us—those with a "good sense of direction"—are much better at such tasks than others. The rest of us—those with a mediocre or poor sense of direction—generally regard this as a significant failing. Studying the development of "mapping" in young children may help us to discover why individual differences in sense of direction occur. And mapping in children is important in its own right—how many cases of children getting lost are due to children's inability to map large-scale spaces (those too large to be seen all at once)? Research reveals that 3-year-old children have deficiencies in mapping large-scale spaces, but what is perhaps more surprising is that children as young as 3-years-old learn such layouts as well as they do. In one experiment (Hazen, Lochman, & Pick, 1978), 3-to-5-year-old children were led on a route through four rooms, each containing a toy. After training in identifying which doors to use and which toys would be present in successive rooms, the children were given a reversed route test. All of the children showed some ability to choose which doors to go through and to identify toys that would be present when they took the reverse route. However, younger children made more errors.

TABLE 8.2
Motor and Perceptual Development in Early Childhood

The following tasks are reasonable to expect in 75 to 80 percent of the children of the indicated ages. Children should be tested individually. The data upon which this is based have been collected from children in white middle-class neighborhoods.

A child failing to master four to six of the tasks for his or her age probably needs (a) a more thorough evaluation and (b) some kind of remedial help. Various sex differences are indicated.

Two to Three Years	Yes	No
1. Displays a variety of scribbling behavior	___	___
2. Can walk rhythmically at an even pace	___	___
3. Can step off low object, one foot ahead of the other	___	___
4. Can name hands, feet, head, and some face parts	___	___
5. Opposes thumb to fingers when grasping objects and releases objects smoothly from finger-thumb grasp	___	___
6. Can walk a 2-inch wide line placed on ground, for 10 feet	___	___

Four to Four-and-a-Half	Yes	No
1. Forward broad jump, both feet together and clear of ground at the same time	___	___
2. Can hop two or three times on one foot without precision or rhythm	___	___
3. Walks and runs with arm action coordinated with leg action	___	___
4. Can walk a circular line a short distance	___	___
5. Can draw a crude circle	___	___
6. Can imitate a simple line cross using a vertical and horizontal line	___	___

Five to Five-and-a-Half	Yes	No
1. Runs 30 yards in just over 8 seconds	___	___
2. Balances on one foot (girls 6 to 8 seconds) (boys 4 to 6 seconds)	___	___
3. Child catches large playground ball bounced to him or her chest-high from 15 feet away, four to five times out of five	___	___
4. Rectangle and square drawn differently (one side at a time)	___	___
5. Can high-jump 8 inches or higher over bar with simultaneous two-foot takeoff	___	___
6. Bounces playground ball, using one or two hands, a distance of 3 to 4 feet	___	___

Six to Six-and-a-Half	Yes	No
1. Can block-print first name in letters 1½ to 2 inches high	___	___
2. Can gallop, if it is demonstrated	___	___
3. Can exert 6 pounds or more of pressure in grip strength measure	___	___
4. Can walk balance beam 2 inches wide, 6 inches high, and 10 to 12 inches long	___	___
5. Can run 60 feet in about 5 seconds	___	___
6. Can arise from ground from back lying position, when asked to do so as fast as he or she can, in 2 seconds or under	___	___

From Cratty, B., *Psychomotor Behavior in Education and Sport.* © 1974 Charles C. Thomas, Publisher, Springfield, Illinois.

TABLE 8.3
Fat and Calorie Intake of Selected Fast-Food Meals

Selected Meal	Calories	Percent of Calories from Fat
Burger King Whopper, fries, vanilla shake	1,250	43
Big Mac, fries, chocolate shake	1,100	41
McDonald's Quarter-Pounder with cheese	418	52
Pizza Hut 10-inch pizza with sausage, mushrooms, pepperoni, and green pepper	1,035	35
Arby's roast beef plate (roast beef sandwich, two potato patties, and coleslaw), chocolate shake	1,200	30
Kentucky Fried Chicken dinner (three pieces chicken, mashed potatoes and gravy, coleslaw, roll)	830	50
Arthur Treacher's fish and chips (two pieces breaded, fried fish, french fries, cola drink)	900	42
Typical restaurant "diet plate" (hamburger patty, cottage cheese, etc.)	638	63

Reprinted by permission: Virginia DeMoss, "The Good, the Bad, and the Edible" in Runner's World, *June 1980.*

Nutrition, Health, and Exercise

We have become a health-conscious nation. In chapter 5, we learned that some weight-conscious parents may have gone too far in adopting adult nutritional guidelines for staying thin with their infants. What nutritional guidelines should we follow with preschool children? What is the health and illness of preschool children like? How much exercise do preschool children need? We consider each of these questions in turn.

Why have we simultaneously become such a health conscious nation and a nation with such poor health habits?

Nutrition

Feeding and eating habits are important aspects of development in early childhood. What we eat affects our skeletal growth, body shape, and susceptibility to disease. Recognizing that nutrition influences the child's growth, the federal government provides money for school lunch programs to be used for children from low-income families. On the average, the preschool child requires 1,400 to 1,800 calories a day. Children with unbalanced or malnourished diets show below-average physical development by the third year of life. When the appropriate nutrients are introduced into the diet of a malnourished child, physical development improves. For example, when provided milk supplements over a 20-month period, deprived children between the ages of 4 and 15 showed gains of 3.6 percent in height and 29 percent in weight.

A special concern in our culture is the amount of fat in our diet. In chapter 5, you learned that infants need a certain amount of fat—for example, we suggested that it might be better for a young child to have a Ding-Dong rather than broccoli. The nutritional needs of the infant and the preschool child are different—the preschool child's growth has slowed somewhat. Combined with the high fat and protein diet of many families, the preschool child's slowdown in growth (relative to infancy) has resulted in an increased number of obese young children.

Vast numbers of young children are being weaned on fast foods that are high in fat and protein. During the preschool years, many children get their first taste of fast foods, and unfortunately, eating habits may become ingrained early in life. Table 8.3 lists the number of calories and the percentage of fat in the offerings of different fast-food restaurants. The American Heart Association recommends that the daily limit for calories from fat should be approximately 35 percent. Compare this figure with the figures in Table 8.3.

Clearly, many fast-food meals contribute to excessive fat intake by young children. Not only is there concern about excessive fat in children's diet, but there also is concern about excessive sugar. To learn more about sugar's effect on young children's behavior turn to Focus on Life-Span Development 8.1. The jury is still out on how extensively sugar affects children's behavior. Some reviews conclude that we do not have good evidence for sugar's role in promoting hyperactive behavior (e.g., Pipes, 1988), although some well-controlled investigations such as the research described in Focus on Life-Span Development 8.1 argue for a closer look at sugar's contribution to children's behavior. In sum, parents need to monitor their young children's intake of fat, protein, and carbohydrates, ensuring that levels are neither too high nor too low on a regular basis. An occasional Ding-Dong does not hurt and can even be beneficial to a growing body, but a steady diet of Big Macs, milkshakes, and candy bars should be avoided.

Health and Illness

While there has been great national interest in the psychological aspects of health among adults, only recently has a developmental perspective on psychological aspects of health among children been proposed. The uniqueness of young children's health care needs is evident when we consider their motor, cognitive, and social development (Maddux & others, 1986). For example, think about infant's and preschool child's motor development—inadequate to ensure personal safety while riding in an automobile. Adults must take preventive measures to restrain infants and young children in car seats. Young children may lack the intellectual skills—including reading ability—to discriminate between safe and unsafe household substances. And they may lack the impulse control to keep them from running out in a busy street while going after a ball or a toy.

Health education programs for preschool children need to be cognitively simple. Three simple but important goals for health education programs for preschool children are (Parcel & others, 1979) (1) be able to identify feelings of wellness and illness and be able to express them to adults; (2) be able to identify appropriate sources of assistance for health-related problems; and (3) be able to independently initiate the use of sources of assistance for health problems.

Caregivers have an important health role for young children. For example, by controlling the speed of the vehicles they drive, by decreasing their drinking—especially before driving—and by not smoking around children, caregivers enhance children's health. In one recent investigation, it was found that, if the mother smokes, her children are twice as likely to have respiratory ailments (Etzel, 1988). Caregivers can actively affect young children's health and safety by training the child in appropriate dental hygiene, proper nutrition, recreational safety, and self-protection skills.

Illnesses, especially those that are not life threatening, provide an excellent opportunity for the young child to expand his development. The preschool period is a time when illnesses such as respiratory infections (colds, flu) and gastrointestinal upsets (nausea, diarrhea) peak. The illnesses usually are of short duration and are often handled outside of the medical community through the family, day care, or school. Such minor illnesses can increase the young child's knowledge of health and illness, sense of empathy, and realistic understanding of the sick role (Parmalee, 1986).

YOUNG CHILDREN'S SUGAR CONSUMPTION

AND INAPPROPRIATE BEHAVIOR

Robert, age 3, already loves chocolate. His mother lets him have a daily dose of a chocolate candy bar, a bag of M & M candy, and chocolate milk. Robert also drinks 3 to 4 soft drinks a day and eats sugar-coated cereal each morning for breakfast. It is estimated that the average American child in the United States consumes almost two pounds of sugar per week (Riddle & Prinz, 1984). How does sugar consumption influence young children's health and behavior?

The association of sugar consumption and children's health problems—dental cavities and obesity, for example—has been widely documented (e.g., Warren, 1975). In recent years, a growing

Is sugar consumption related to preschool children's aggression?

interest in sugar's influence on children's behavior has surfaced. In one recent investigation (Goldman & others, 1986), eight preschool children on separate mornings each received 6 ounces of juice, sweetened one morning with sucrose and on the other with an artificial sweetener. They were observed for 90 minutes following the drinks. After the sucrose drink, the children exhibited more inappropriate play—being less attentive and overly active, for example. Other findings support the belief that sugar consumption by young children increases their aggression, especially in unstructured circumstances and when the child is bored (Goldman & others, 1987).

Exercise

By the time they reach elementary school, many children are already out of shape. While we currently are in the midst of a trend toward greater exercise by adults, the exercise revolution has not been as extensive in children. The 1985 School Fitness Survey tested 18,857 children aged 6 to 17 on nine fitness tasks. The 1985 results—when compared with a similar survey in 1975— showed virtually no improvement. For example, 40 percent of boys between the ages of 6 and 12 could not do more than one pull-up, and 25 percent could not do any! Fifty percent of the girls between the ages of 6 and 17 and 30 percent of the boys between the ages of 6 and 12 could not run a mile in less than 10 minutes. One difference in the 1985 and 1975 comparisons suggested that, by adolescence, girls in 1985 were in worse shape. In a 50-yard-dash,

1985's adolescent girls were slower. There is likely a long history of exercise neglect on the part of our nation's children. The preschool years may be a good time to have children begin a regular exercise program.

Cognitive Development in Early Childhood

Dramatic cognitive progress is made during the preschool years. By the age of 5, a child can remember a long sentence and repeat the plot to a story; she can think symbolically on a regular basis, evidenced in such enjoyable activities as pretend play. Just as with infancy, Piaget's theory has changed the way we think about the preschool child's thought. Advances in the preschool child's information processing abilities also take place.

Preoperational Thought

Remember from chapter 5, that, during Piaget's sensorimotor stage of development, the infant progresses in the ability to organize and coordinate sensations and perceptions with physical movements and actions. What kind of changes take place in preoperational thought?

Since this stage of thought is called preoperational, it would seem that not much of importance is occurring until full-fledged operational thought appears. Not so. The preoperational stage stretches from approximately the age of 2 to the age of 7—it is a time when stable concepts are formed, mental reasoning emerges, egocentrism is stronger in the beginning and then weakens, and magical beliefs are constructed. Preoperational thought is anything but a convenient waiting period for concrete operational thought, although the label "preoperational" emphasizes that the child at this stage does not yet think in an operational way. What are **operations**? They are internalized sets of actions that allow the child to do mentally what before was done physically. They are highly organized and conform to certain rules and principles of logic. The operations appear in one form in concrete operational thought and in another form in formal operational thought. Thought in the preoperational stage is still flawed and not well organized. Preoperational thought is the beginning of the ability to reconstruct at the level of thought what has been established in behavior and as a transition from primitive to more sophisticated use of symbols (Ginsburg & Opper, 1988). Preoperational thought can be subdivided into two substages—the symbolic function substage and the intuitive thought substage.

One of the greatest pleasures of childhood is found in the mysteries which it hides from the skepticism of the elders, and works up into small mythologies of its own.
Oliver Wendall Holmes, The Poet At The Breakfast Table, *1872*

Symbolic Function Substage

The **symbolic function substage** of preoperational thought occurs roughly between the ages of 2 to 4 years. By 2 years of age, the child has the ability to mentally represent an object. At this point, the child has begun to use symbols to represent objects that are not present. The ability to engage in such symbolic thought is referred to as symbolic function, and it vastly expands the child's mental world during the 2 to 4 age period. Young children use shapes and scribbles to represent people, houses, cars, clouds, animals, and so on. More on young children's scribbles and art is presented in Focus on Life-Span Development 8.2. Other examples of symbolism in early childhood are the prevalence of pretend play, which will be discussed in chapter 9, and language, more about which appears later in this chapter. In sum, during this early substage of preoperational thought, the ability to think symbolically and represent the world mentally predominates. However, while the young child makes distinct progress during the symbolic function substage, her thought still has several important limitations, two of which are egocentrism and animism.

There are no days in life so memorable as those which vibrated to some stroke of imagination.
Ralph Waldo Emerson, The Conduct of Life, *1860*

WHERE PELICANS KISS SEALS, CARS FLOAT ON CLOUDS, AND HUMANS ARE TADPOLES

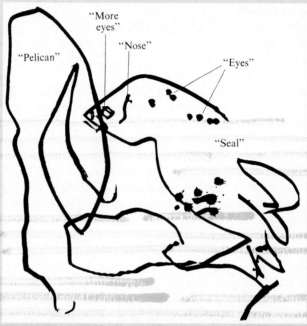

Figure 8.A *Halfway into this drawing, the 3½-year-old artist said it was "a pelican kissing a seal."* D. Wolf/J. Nove

At about 3 years of age and sometimes even at 2, children's spontaneous scribbles begin to resemble pictures. One 3½-year-old child looked at the scribble he had just drawn and said it was a pelican kissing a seal (see figure 8.A). At about 3 to 4 years of age, children begin to create symbols of humans. Invariably the first symbols look curiously like tadpoles; see the circle and two lines in figure 8.B—the circle represents a head and the two lines are legs.

These observations of children's drawings were made by Denise Wolf, Carol Fucigna, and Howard Gardner at Harvard University. They point out that many people think young children draw a human in this rather odd way because it is the best they can do. Piaget said children intend their drawings to be realistic; they draw what they know rather than what they see. So the tadpole with its strange exemptions of trunk and arms might reflect a child's lack of knowledge of the human body and how its parts fit together. However, children know more about the human body than they are capable of drawing. One 3-year-old child drew a tadpole but described it in complete detail, pointing out where the feet, chin, and neck were. When 3- and 4-year-old children are asked to draw

someone playing ball, they produce symbols of humans that include arms, since the task implicitly requires arms (see figure 8.C).

Possibly because preschool children are not very concerned about reality, their drawings are fanciful and inventive (see figure 8.D). Suns are blue, skies are yellow, and cars float on clouds in the preschool child's symbolic world. The symbolism is simple but strong, not unlike the abstractions found in some contemporary art. In the elementary school years, the child's symbols

become more realistic, neat, and precise. Suns are yellow, skies are blue, and cars are placed on roads (see figure 8.E).

A child's ability to symbolically represent the world on paper is related to the development of perceptual motor skills. But once such skills are developed, some artists revert to the style of young children's drawings. As Picasso once commented, "I used to draw like Raphael but it has taken me a whole lifetime to learn to draw like children" (Winner, 1986).

CHRYSTAL CHAITY KIRK

BALL PLAYING GIRL, 5.7

Figure 8.B *The 3-year-old's first drawing of a person: a "tadpole" consisting of a circle with two lines for legs.*

Figure 8.C *A young child, asked to draw people playing ball, includes only a single arm on the figures playing ball; the fourth figure, an observer, is armless.*

Figure 8.D *This 6-year-old's drawing is free, fanciful, and inventive.*

Figure 8.E *An 11-year-old's drawing is neater and more realistic than the 6-year-old's drawing, but is also less inventive.*

Physical and Cognitive Development

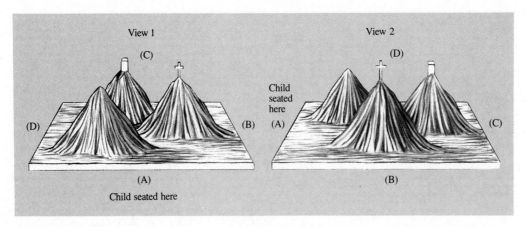

Figure 8.1
The three mountains task devised by Piaget and Inhelder (1967). View 1 shows the child's perspective from where he is sitting. View 2 is an example of the photograph the child would be shown mixed in with others from different perspectives. For the child to correctly identify this view, he has to take the perspective of a person sitting at spot (B). Invariably the preschool child who thinks in a preoperational way cannot perform this task. When asked what the perspective or view of the mountains will look like from position (B), the child selects a photograph taken from location (A), the view he has at the time.

Egocentrism is a salient feature of preoperational thought—it is the inability to distinguish between one's own perspective and someone else's perspective. The following telephone conversation between 4-year-old Mary, who is at home, and her father, who is at work, typifies Mary's egocentric thought:

Father: Mary, is Mommy there?
Mary: (Silently nods)
Father: Mary, may I speak to Mommy?
Mary: (Nods again silently)

Mary's response is egocentric in the sense that she fails to consider her father's perspective before replying. A nonegocentric thinker would have responded verbally.

Piaget and Barbara Inhelder (1969) initially studied young children's egocentrism by devising the three mountains task (see figure 8.1). The child walks around the mountains and becomes familiar with what the mountains look like from different perspectives. The child can see that there are different objects on the mountains as well. The child is then seated on one side of the table on which the mountains are placed. The experimenter takes a doll and moves it to different locations around the table, at each location asking the child to pick one photo from a series of photos that most accurately reflects the view the doll is seeing. Children in the preoperational stage often pick the view they have from where they are sitting rather than the view that the doll has. Perspective-taking does not seem to develop uniformly in the preschool child, who frequently shows perspective skills on some tasks but not others (Rubin, 1978; Shantz, 1983).

Animism is another facet of preoperational thought—the belief that inanimate objects have "life-like" qualities and are capable of action. The young child might say, "That tree pushed the leaf off, and it fell down," or "The sidewalk made me mad; it made me fall down," revealing animism. The young child who uses animism fails to distinguish the appropriate occasions for using human and nonhuman perspectives. Some developmentalists, though, believe that animism represents incomplete knowledge and understanding, not a general conception of the world (Dolgin & Behrend, 1984; Bullock, 1985). Other developmentalists believe that preschool children have a more elaborate and coherent knowledge of animals and inanimate knowledge than Piaget envisioned (Massey & Gelman, 1988).

Intuitive Thought Substage

As the preschool child becomes older, she moves from the symbolic thought substage to an inner world of thinking that is more intuitive, that is, knowing without the use of rational thinking. The preoperational stage of thought continues until about 7 years of age for most children—the **intuitive thought substage** stretches from approximately 4 to 7 years of age. During this time, the child begins to reason primitively and wants to know the answers to all sorts of questions. Children's thinking in this substage is prelogical. While reasoning and a search for many answers are present, the reasoning is highly imperfect compared to adult standards. Piaget referred to this period as *intuitive* because, on the one hand, young children seem so sure about their knowledge and understanding, yet on the other hand, they are so unaware of how they know what they know.

An example of the young child's reasoning ability is the difficulty she has putting things into their correct classes. Faced with a random collection of objects that can be grouped together on the basis of two or more properties, the preoperational child is seldom capable of using these properties consistently to sort the objects into appropriate categories. For example, look at the collection of objects in figure 8.2. You would respond to the direction, "Put the things together that you believe belong together" by sorting the characteristics of size and shape together. Your sorting might look something like that shown in figure 8.3. In the social realm, the 5-year-old girl might be given the task of dividing her peers into groups according to whether they are friends and whether they are boys or girls. She would be unlikely to arrive at the following classification: friendly boys, friendly girls, unfriendly boys, and unfriendly girls. Another example of classification shortcomings involves the preoperational child's understanding of religious concepts (Elkind, 1976). When asked, "Can you be a Protestant and an American at the same time?" 6- and 7-year-olds usually say no; 9-year-olds are likely to say yes, understanding that objects can be cross-classified simultaneously.

Many of these examples reveal a characteristic of preoperational thought called **centration**—the focusing, or *centering*, of attention on one characteristic to the exclusion of all others. Centration is most clearly evidenced in the young child's lack of **conservation**—the idea that amount stays the same or is conserved regardless of how shape changes. To adults, it is obvious that a certain amount of liquid stays the same regardless of a container's shape. But

Figure 8.2
A random array of objects.

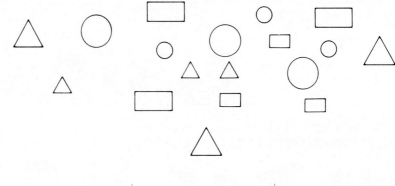

Figure 8.3
An ordered array of objects.

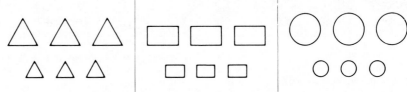

Figure 8.4
Piaget's beaker task. Piaget used the beaker task to determine whether children had conservation of liquid. In I, two identical beakers (A&B) are presented to the child; then the experimenter pours the liquid from B into beaker C, which is taller and thinner than A&B. The child is now asked if these beakers (A&C) have the same amount of liquid. The preoperational child says no, responding that the taller, thinner beaker (C) has more.

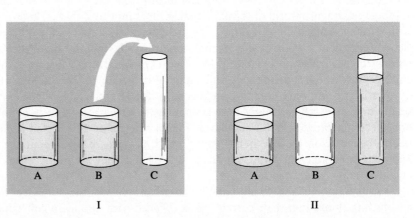

I   II

this is not obvious at all to young children; instead they are struck by the height of the liquid in the container. In this task—Piaget's most famous—the child is presented with two identical beakers, each filled to the same level with liquid (see figure 8.4). The child is asked if these beakers have the same amount of liquid, and she usually says yes. Then, the liquid from one beaker is poured into a third beaker, which is taller and thinner than the first two (see figure 8.4). The child is then asked if the amount of liquid in the tall, thin beaker is equal to that which remains in one of the original beakers. If the child is less than 7 or 8 years old, she usually says no and justifies her answer in terms of the differing height or width of the beakers. Older children usually answer yes and justify their answers appropriately ("If you poured the milk back, it would show that the amount is the same").

In Piaget's theory, failing the conservation of liquid task is a sign that a child is at the preoperational stage of cognitive development, while passing this test is a sign that he is at the concrete operational stage. In Piaget's view, the preoperational child not only fails to show conservation of liquid, but also number, matter, length, volume, and area (see figure 8.5). At this point we have discussed a number of Piaget's ideas about preoperational thought, among them egocentrism, animism, and conservation. To learn more about these fascinating aspects of the preschool child's thoughts, turn to Focus on Life-Span Development 8.3, where you will discover how these concepts were included in the story of *Winnie-the-Pooh*.

False would be a picture which insisted on the brutal egocentrism of the child, and ignored the physical beauty which softens it.

A. A. Milne

Type of conservation	Initial presentation	Manipulation	Preoperational child's answer	**Figure 8.5** *The domains of conservation.*
Number	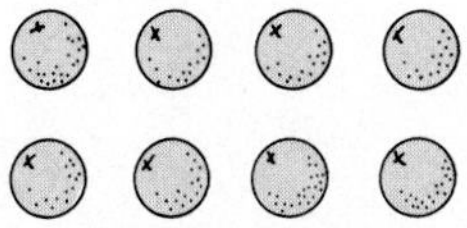 Two identical rows of objects are shown to the child, who agrees they have the same number.	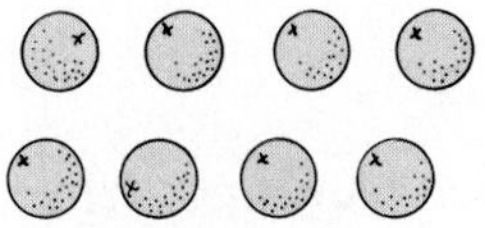 One row is lengthened and the child is asked whether one row now has more objects.	Yes, the longer row.	
Matter	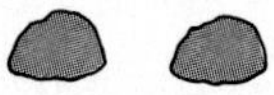 Two identical balls of clay are shown to the child. The child agrees they are equal.	 The experimenter changes the shape of one of the balls and asks the child whether they still contain equal amounts of clay.	No, the longer one has more.	
Length	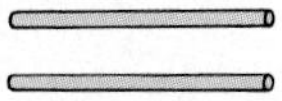 Two sticks are aligned in front of the child. The child agrees that they are the same length.	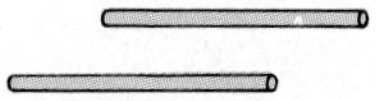 The experimenter moves one stick to the right, then asks the child if they still are equal in length.	No, the one on the top is longer.	
Volume	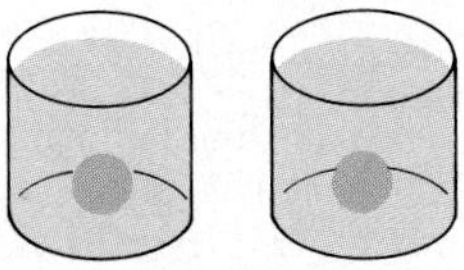 Two balls are placed in two identical glasses with an equal amount of water. The child sees the balls displace equal amounts of water.	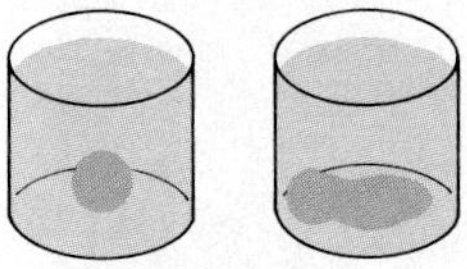 The experimenter changes the shape of one of the balls and asks the child if it still will displace the same amount of water.	No, the longer one on the right displaces more.	
Area	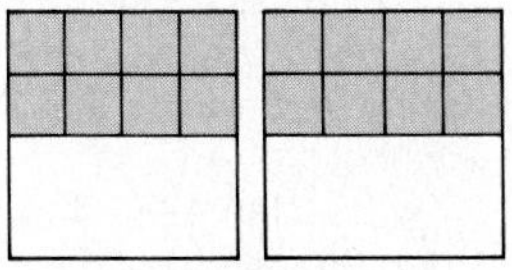 Two identical sheets of cardboard have wooden blocks placed on them in identical positions. The child agrees that the same amount of space is left on each piece of cardboard.	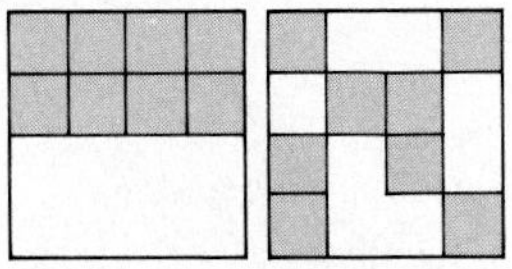 The experimenter scatters the blocks on one piece of cardboard and then asks the child if one of the cardboard pieces has more space covered up.	Yes, the one on the right has more space covered up.	

According to psychologist Dorothy Singer (1972), if Piaget had opened the pages of *Winnie-the-Pooh,* he would have discovered how A. A. Milne used some of the same concepts Piaget believed were so prominent in the preschool child's thought. Milne's psychological insight gives life and meaning to a little story about an imaginary forest, peopled with animals from the nursery (see figure 8.F).

We first meet Edward Bear as he is being dragged down the stairs on the back of his head. "It is, as far as he knows, the only way of coming down the stairs." This example of egocentrism sets the tone for the rest of the book. The narrator tells us that Edward's name is Winnie-the-Pooh. When asked if Winnie is not a girl's name, Christopher replies with a second example of egocentrism. "He's Winnie-ther-Pooh. Don't you know what *ther* means?" Again, an example of egocentrism. Christopher knows, so no further explanation is necessary, or forthcoming. Piglet, an egocentric friend of Pooh, is a weak and timid pig, and is certain that everyone knows when he is in distress. But Pooh is just as egocentric when he interprets a note. Pooh only recognizes the letter "P" and each "P" convinces him further that "P" means "Pooh" so "it's a very important Missage to me." In a later chapter, Pooh eats a jar of honey that he had intended to give to

Figure 8.F How were Piaget's ideas about cognitive development exemplified in A.A. Milne's classic book, Winnie the Pooh?

everyone else on his birthday. In egocentric form, though, Pooh rationalizes his gluttony and decides to give everyone the empty jar: "It's a very nice pot. Everyone could keep things in it."

Milne recognized the pervasiveness of animism in young children's thought. Each of the imaginary characters displays a talent for animism. In the first chapter, Pooh develops an elaborate plan to steal some honey from a bee's hive. He disguises himself as a cloud in a blue sky. He rolls over and over in the mud until he is as dark as a thundercloud. He borrows a sky-blue balloon from Christopher and floats off into the sky, singing as he goes. The singing cloud is an example of animism.

Milne's story of Eeyore's (the cynical and pessimistic donkey) birthday illustrates the principle of conservation. Piglet plans to give Eeyore a large red balloon. On the way, Piglet catches his foot in the rabbit's hole and falls down. When he recovers, he finds out to his dismay that the balloon has burst. All that he has left is a small piece of a damp rag. Nevertheless, Piglet is determined to give a present to Eeyore. When he finally reaches Eeyore, the conversation goes like this:

"Eeyore, I brought you a balloon."
"Balloon," said Eeyore, . . .
"one of those big colored things you blow up?" Gaiety, song-and-and-dance, here we are and there we are?"
"Yes . . . but I fell down . . . and I burst the balloon."
"My birthday balloon?"
"Yes, Eeyore," said Piglet, sniffing a little. "Here it is. With—many happy returns of the day."
"My present?"
Piglet nodded again.
"The balloon?"
"Yes."
"Thank you, Piglet," said Eeyore, "you don't mind my asking," he went on, "but what color was this balloon when it—when it *was* a balloon?"

Poor Eeyore cannot understand that red remains red even when the balloon is small and no longer round or full.

Some developmentalists do not believe Piaget was entirely correct in his estimate of when children's conservation skills emerge. For example, Rochel Gelman (1969, 1979; Gelman & Baillargeon, 1983) has shown that by improving the child's attention to relevant aspects of the conservation task, the child is more likely to conserve. And she has demonstrated that attentional training on one type of task, such as number, improves the preschool child's performance on another type of task, such as mass. Thus, Gelman believes that conservation appears earlier than Piaget thought and that the process of attention is especially important in explaining conservation.

Yet another characteristic of the preoperational child is the barrage of questions that are asked. The child's earliest questions appear around the age of 3, and by the age of 5, the child has just about exhausted the adults around him with "why" questions. The child's questions yield clues about mental development and reflect intellectual curiosity. These questions signal the emergence of the child's interest in reasoning and figuring out why things are the way they are. A sample of the questions children ask during the question-asking period of 4 to 6 years of age are (Elkind, 1976):

"What makes you grow up?"
"What makes you stop growing?"
"Why does a lady have to be married to have a baby?"
"Who was the mother when everybody was a baby?"
"Why do leaves fall?"
"Why does the sun shine?"

Earlier we mentioned that Gelman's research demonstrated that children may fail a Piagetian task because of their failure to attend to relevant dimensions of the task—length, shape, density, and so on. Gelman and other developmentalists also believe that many of the tasks used to assess cognitive development may not be sensitive to the child's cognitive abilities. Thus, rather than limitations on cognitive development, the limitations may be due to the tasks used to assess cognitive development. Gelman's research reflects the thinking of information processing psychologists who place considerable importance on the tasks and procedures involved in assessing children's cognition. At this point, we have discussed a number of ideas about the preschool child's physical and cognitive development. A summary of these ideas is presented in Concept Table 8.1. Next, we study some changes in the young child's information processing abilities.

Information Processing

Two limitations on the preschool child's thought are attention and memory. Yet considerable advances in these two important cognitive processes are made during the preschool years. What are the limitations and advances in attention and memory during the preschool years?

Attention

Remember from chapter 6 that attention was discussed in the context of habituation, which is something like being bored in the sense that the infant becomes disinterested in a stimulus and no longer attends to it. Habituation actually can be described as a decrement in attention while dishabituation is the recovery of attention. The importance of these aspects of attention in infancy for the preschool years was underscored by research showing that both decrement and recovery of attention—when measured in the first 6 months of infancy—were associated with higher intelligence in preschool years (Bornstein & Sigman, 1986).

CONCEPT TABLE

8.1

Physical Development and Preoperational Thought		
Concept	**Processes/Related Ideas**	**Characteristics/Description**
Physical Development	Some Changes	Growth is slower in early childhood than in infancy. The average child grows 2½ inches and gains between 5 and 7 pounds a year during early childhood. Both genetic and environmental circumstances contribute to growth. Ethnic origin and nutrition are important influences on height.
	Motor and Perceptual Development	Considerable progress in gross motor skills occurs in early childhood, especially in the arms and legs. Children's ability to map large-scale spaces markedly increases in the preschool years.
	Nutrition, Health, and Exercise	The average preschool child requires 1,400 to 1,800 calories per day. Poor nutrition influences not only physical development, but behavior as well—sugar may increase activity level and aggression. The effects of health and illness can be studied in terms of their relation to motor, cognitive, and social development. By the age of 6, many children already are in poor physical shape; the preschool years may be an important point to begin a physical fitness program.
Preoperational Thought	Its Nature	The beginning of the ability to reconstruct at the level of thought what has been established in behavior, and a transition from primitive to more sophisticated use of symbols. The child does not yet think in an operational way; operations are internalized sets of actions that allow the child to do mentally what was done before physically.
	Symbolic Function Substage	Occurs roughly between 2 to 4 years of age. The ability to think symbolically and represent the world mentally develops. Thought still has several important limitations, two of which are egocentrism and animism.
	Intuitive Thought Substage	Stretches from approximately 4 to 7 years of age. The substage is called intuitive because, on the one hand, children seem so sure about their knowledge, yet on the other hand, they are so unaware of how they know what they know. The preoperational child lacks conservation, the idea that amount stays the same or is conserved regardless of how shape changes. One of the main reasons young children cannot conserve is the process of centration, or focusing of attention on one characteristic to the exclusion of all others. Gelman believes conservation occurs earlier than Piaget thought and the process of attention is important in its appearance. The preoperational child also asks a barrage of questions, showing an interest in reasoning and finding out why things are the way they are.

How extensively does the child's attention develop during early childhood?

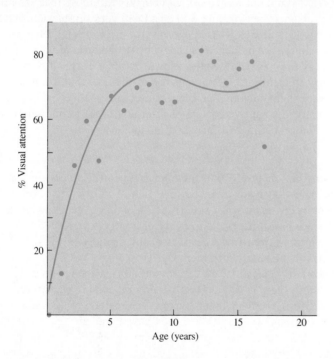

Figure 8.6
Increase in visual attention to TV during the preschool years. In this elaborate study, two video cameras and a time lapse recorder were used to observe young children's attention to television in their homes. Visual attention to television dramatically increased during the preschool years.

While the infant's attention has important implications for cognitive development in the preschool years, significant changes in the child's ability to pay attention take place in the preschool years. The toddler wanders around, shifting attention from one activity to another, generally seeming to spend little time focused on any one object or event. By comparison, the preschool child might be observed watching television for a half hour. In one investigation (Anderson & others, 1985), two video cameras and a time lapse recorder were used to observe the young child's attention to television in the natural setting of the home. Ninety-nine families that included 460 individuals were observed; the time samples included 4,672 hours of recordings. The results: Visual attention to television dramatically increased during the preschool years (see figure 8.6).

Physical and Cognitive Development

Figure 8.7
Memory span and age. Memory span increased from about two digits in 2- to 3-year-old children to about five digits in 7-year-old children. Between 7 and 13 years of age, memory span only increased by 1½ digits.

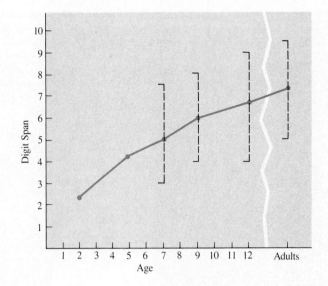

One deficit in attention during the preschool years concerns those dimensions that stand out or are *salient* compared to those that are relevant to solving a problem or performing well on a task. For example, a problem might have a flashy, attractive clown that presents the directions for solving a problem. Preschool children are influenced strongly by the features of the task that stand out—such as the flashy, attractive clown. After the age of 6 or 7, children attend more efficiently to the dimensions of the task that are relevant—such as the directions for solving a problem. Developmentalists believe this change reflects a shift to cognitive control of attention so that children act less precipitously and reflect more (Paris & Lindauer, 1982).

Memory
Remember from chapter 6 that memory is a central process in cognitive development and that it involves the retention of information over time. Conscious memory comes into play as early as 7 months of age, although as children and adults, we have little or no memory of events experienced before the age of 3. Among the interesting questions about memory in the preschool years are those involving short-term memory.

In **short-term memory,** we can retain information for up to 15 to 30 seconds, assuming there is no rehearsal. Using rehearsal, we can keep information in short-term memory much longer. One method of assessing short-term memory is the memory span task. If you have taken an IQ test, you probably were exposed to one of these tasks. You simply hear a short list of stimuli—usually digits—presented at a rapid pace (one per second, for example). Then you are asked to repeat the digits back. Research with the memory span task suggests that short-term memory increases during early childhood. For example, in one investigation, memory span increased from about two digits in 2-to-3-year-old children to about five digits in 7-year-old children; yet between 7 and 13 years of age, memory span only increased by 1½ digits (Dempster, 1981) (see figure 8.7). Keep in mind, though, memory span's individual differences, which is why IQ and various aptitude tests are used.

Why are there age differences in memory span? Rehearsal of information seems important—older children rehearse the digits more than younger children; so are the speed and efficiency of information processing, especially the speed with which memory items can be identified. For example, in one

Are there more *colored bars* or more bars?

Figure 8.8
Class inclusion reasoning. This requires the child to compare the relative number of objects in a subset with the number of objects in the larger set. The child is asked, "Are there more colored bars or more bars?" How do Piagetian and information processing psychologists attempt to understand this problem differently?

investigation (Case, Kurland, & Goldberg, 1982), children were tested on their speed at repeating auditorially presented words. Speed of repetition strongly predicted memory span using these same words. Indeed, when speed of repetition was controlled, the 6-year-olds' memory spans were equal to those of young adults!

The speed-of-processing explanation highlights an important point in the information processing perspective. That is, the speed with which a child processes information is an important aspect of the child's cognitive abilities. However, speed of processing is only one of several components we need to understand to discover how children process information about tasks and problems.

Task Dimensions and Analyses

Another major emphasis in the information processing perspective is to identify the components of the task the child is performing. Let's see how identifying task dimensions might work with a typical Piagetian problem involving **class inclusion reasoning,** which requires the child to compare the relative number of objects in a subset with the number of objects in the larger set. If, as in figure 8.8, there is a set of rectangular bars—some colored, some black—can the child compare the number of colored bars with the total number of bars in the total set? The question posed to the child in this classic experiment by Piaget is, "Are there more colored bars or more bars?" According to Piaget, concrete operational thinkers answer the question correctly; preoperational thinkers do not. Piaget believes that the problem involves some form of being able to deal with the whole-part comparison.

The information processing perspective takes a different view. The information processing psychologist suggests that we need to understand the component steps required to solve the task. For example, first the child must encode the key elements in the question. Roughly speaking, this means the child must attend to and store some key pieces of information. There are at least three concepts in the question about the bars: (1) which of the two sets has *more?* (2) the *colored* bars? or (3) all the *bars?* Next, the child must develop a *plan* to answer the question. One good plan is to take the first concept as a goal—that is, find the set with *more* items—and proceed with two *counting* steps: (1) count the colored bars, and (2) count all the bars. Finally, a *comparison* must be made between the outcome of counting steps (1), How many colored bars were there? and counting step (2), How many bars were there altogether?

Notice that in the information processing analysis, the child must do a number of things to solve the problem—he must encode the problem correctly, develop a goal, perform at least two counting steps, and compare the results of counting. Thus, the child's failure at a task can have many explanations, relating to different components of the task analysis. Piagetian theory often explains a young child's inability to offer a "grownup" response to a task by

How extensively do you think children's memory span can be improved through the use of strategies? Are there limits on how much improvement can be made? Explain your answer.

citing the child's early stage of cognitive development; the child does not yet have the cognitive skills and understanding to respond otherwise, in this view. By contrast, the information processing perspective focuses on the task requirements and considers the complexity of what the child is being asked to do. By understanding the components of the task, we may eventually be able to simplify them so that even young children can respond to a problem intelligently.

This strategy recently was followed to determine if a preschool child could reason about a syllogism—a type of reasoning problem, consisting of two premises, or statements, assumed to be true, plus a conclusion (Hawkins & others, 1984). To simplify problems, words like "some" and "all" were made implicit rather than explicit. The problems focused on fantasy creatures alien from practical knowledge. Imagine how wide a child's eyes become when stories about purple bangas who sneeze at people and merds who laugh and don't like mushrooms are told (see figure 8.9). Two such syllogisms read to children were:

> Every banga is purple.
> Purple animals always sneeze at people.
> Do bangas sneeze at people?
>
> Merds laugh when they're happy.
> Animals that laugh don't like mushrooms.
> Do merds like mushrooms?

By simplifying the problem and making its dimensions more appropriate, the researchers demonstrated that preschool children can reason about syllogisms.

Language Development

In chapter 6, we discussed the biological, cognitive, and social foundations of language development and the development of language in infancy. What kind of changes occur in language development during early childhood? Phonological, morphological, syntactic, semantic, and pragmatic changes take place.

Regarding phonology, some preschool children have difficulty speaking in consonant clusters (e.g., "*str*" as in "*string*"). Pronouncing some of the more difficult phonemes is still problematic—*r,* for example—and can continue to be a problem in the elementary school years. Also, some of the phonological rules for pronouncing word endings (in the past tense, for example) are not mastered until children are 6 to 8 years of age.

Regarding morphology, as children move beyond two-word utterances, there is clear evidence that they know morphological rules. Children begin using the plural and possessive forms of nouns (e.g., *dogs* and *dog's*), putting

How does language develop during early childhood?

Early Childhood

appropriate endings on verbs (e.g., *s* when the subject is third person singular, *ed* for the past tense, and *ing* for the present progressive tense), using prepositions (*in* and *on*), articles (e.g., *a* and *the*), and various forms of the verb *to be* (e.g., "I was going to the store"). Some of the best evidence for morphological rules appears in the form of **overgeneralizations** of these rules. Have you ever heard a preschool child say "foots" instead of "feet," or "goed" instead of "went?" If you do not remember having heard such things, talk to some parents who have young children—you will hear some interesting errors in the use of morphological rule-endings.

In a classic experiment, Jean Berko (1958) presented preschool and first grade children with cards such as the one shown in figure 8.10. Children were asked to look at the card while the experimenter read the words on the card aloud. Then the children were asked to supply the missing word. This might sound easy, but Berko was interested not just in the children's ability to recall the right word but their ability to say it "correctly" (with the ending that was dictated by morphological rules). "Wugs" would be the correct response for the card in figure 8.10. Although the children were not perfectly accurate, they were much better than chance. Moreover, they demonstrated their knowledge of morphological rules not only with the plural forms of nouns ("There are two wugs"), but also with possessive forms of nouns and with the third-person singular and past-tense forms of verbs. What makes the study by Berko impressive is that most of the "words" were fictional; they were created especially for the experiment. Thus, the children could not base their responses on remembering past instances of hearing the words. It seems, instead, that they were forced to rely on *rules*. Their performance suggested that they did so successfully.

Similar evidence that children learn and actively apply rules can be found at the level of syntax. After advancing beyond two-word utterances, the child speaks word sequences that show a growing mastery of complex rules for how words should be ordered. Consider the case of *wh-* questions—"Where is Daddy going?" and "What is that boy doing?", for example. To ask these questions properly, the child has to know two important differences between *wh-* questions and simple affirmative statements (e.g., "Daddy is going to work" and "That boy is waiting on the school bus"). First, a *wh-* word must be added at the beginning of the sentence. Second, the auxiliary verb must be "inverted," that is, exchanged with the subject of the sentence. Young children learn quite early where to put the *wh-* word, but they take much longer to learn the auxiliary-inversion rule. Thus, it is common to hear preschool children asking such questions as "Where daddy is going?" and "What that boy is doing?"

As children move into the elementary school years, they become skilled at using syntactical rules to construct lengthy and complex sentences. Sentences such as "The man who fixed the house went home," and "I don't want you to use my bike" are impressive demonstrations of how the child can use syntax to combine ideas into a single sentence. Just how a young child achieves the mastery of such complex rules—while at the same time she may be struggling with relatively simple arithmetic rules—is a mystery we have yet to solve.

Regarding semantics, as children move beyond the two-word stage, their knowledge of meanings also rapidly advances. The speaking vocabulary of a 6-year-old child ranges from 8,000 to 14,000 words (Carey, 1977). Assuming that word learning began when the child was 12 months old, this translates into a rate for new word meanings of five to eight words a day between the ages of 1 and 6. After 5 years of word learning, the 6-year-old child does not slow down. According to some estimates, the average child of this age is moving

Figure 8.10
In Jean Berko's (1958) study, young children were presented cards such as this one with a "wug" on it. Then the children were asked to supply the missing word; in supplying the missing word, they had to say it correctly, too. "Wugs" is the correct response here.

But whatever the process, the result is wonderful, gradually from naming an object we advanced step by step until we have traversed the vast distance between our first stammered syllable and the sweep of thought in a line of Shakespeare.
Helen Keller

Smithereens

along at the awe-inspiring rate of twenty-two words a day (Miller, 1981)! How would you fare if you were given the task of learning twenty-two new words every day? It is truly miraculous how quickly children learn language (Winner & Gardner, 1988).

Although there are many differences between a 2-year-old's language and a 6-year-old's language, none are more important than those pertaining to pragmatics, that is, rules of conversation. A 6-year-old is simply a much better conversationalist than a 2-year-old is. What are some of the improvements in pragmatics that are made in the preschool years? At about 3 years of age, children improve in their ability to talk about things that are not physically present—that is, they improve their command of the characteristic of language known as displacement. One way displacement is revealed is in games of pretend. Although a 2-year-old might know the word *table,* he is unlikely to use this word to refer to an imaginary table that he pretends is standing in front of him. But a child over 3 probably has this ability, even if he does not always use it—there are large individual differences in preschoolers' talk about imaginary people and things.

Somewhat later in the preschool years—at about 4 years of age—children develop a remarkable sensitivity to the needs of others in conversation (Gleason, 1988). One way in which they show such sensitivity is their use of the articles *the* and *an* (or *a*). When adults tell a story or describe an event, they generally use *an* (or *a*) when they first refer to an animal or an object, and then use *the* when referring to it later (e.g., "Two boys were walking through the jungle when *a* fierce lion appeared. *The* lion lunged at one boy while the other ran for cover"). Even 3-year-olds follow part of this rule (they consistently use the word *the* when referring to previously mentioned things). However, using the word *a* when something is initially mentioned develops more slowly—although 5-year-old children follow this rule on some occasions, they fail to follow it on others.

Another pragmatic ability that appears around 4 to 5 years of age involves speech style. As adults, we have the ability to change our speech style in accordance with the social situations and persons with whom we are speaking. An obvious example is that adults speak in a simpler way to a 2-year-old child than to an older child or to an adult. Interestingly, even 4-year-old children speak differently to a 2-year-old than a same-aged peer (they "talk down" to the 2-year-old using shorter utterance lengths). They also speak differently to an adult than to a same-aged peer, using more polite and formal language with the adult (Shatz & Gelman, 1973).

Early childhood education has become a pervasive experience of children in our society—even children from lower socioeconomic backgrounds have been widely exposed to education at the preschool level. The term **child-centered** is used to describe the most popular form of education before the first grade. Child-centered means an emphasis on the individual child, wide-ranging experiences, exploration, and enjoyment. But in reality, there are a diversity of goals and curricula in preschool education. Some nursery schools emphasize social development, others cognitive development. Some stress daily structured activities, others more flexible activities. Given the diversity of preschool education, can we reach an overall conclusion about its effect on children's development? Children who attend preschool (Clarke-Stewart and Fein, 1983):

> interact more with peers, both positively and negatively
> are less cooperative with and responsive to adults than home-reared children
> are more socially competent and mature in that they are more confident, extraverted, assertive, self-sufficient, independent, verbally expressive, knowledgeable about the social world, comfortable in social and stressful circumstances, and better adjusted when they go to school—exhibiting more task persistence, leadership, and goal direction, for example
> are less socially competent in that they are less polite, less compliant to teacher demands, louder, and more aggressive and bossy, especially if the school or family supports such behavior

In sum, early childhood education generally has a positive effect on children's development, since the behaviors just mentioned—while at times negative—seem to be in the direction of developmental maturity in the sense that they increase as the child ages through the preschool years.

For many years, children from low-income families did not receive any education before they entered the first grade. In the 1960s, an effort was made to try to break the poverty and poor education cycle for young children in the United States through compensatory education. As part of this effort, **Project Head Start** began in the summer of 1965, funded by the Economic Opportunity Act. The program was designed to provide children from low-income families with an opportunity to experience an enriched environment. It was hoped that early intervention might counteract the disadvantages these children had experienced and place them on an equal level with other children when they entered the first grade.

Project Head Start consisted of many different types of preschool programs in different parts of the country. Initially, little effort was made to find out whether some programs worked better than others, although it became apparent that this was the case. Consequently, **Project Follow-Through** was established in 1967. A significant aspect of this program was planned variation, in which different kinds of educational programs were devised to see whether specific programs were effective. In the Follow-Through programs, the enriched planned variation was carried through the first few years of elementary school.

Were some Follow-Through programs more effective than others? Many of the different variations were able to obtain their desired effects on children. For example, children in academically oriented, direct instruction approaches

Learning is an ornament in prosperity, a refuge in diversity.

Aristotle

What effects does preschool education have on children's development?

did better on achievement tests and were more persistent on tasks than children in the other approaches. Children in affective education approaches were absent from school less and showed more independence than children in other approaches. Thus, Project Follow-Through was important in demonstrating that variation in early childhood education does have significant effects in a wide range of social and cognitive areas (Stallings, 1975).

The efffects of compensatory education in early childhood continue to be studied and recent evaluations support the positive influence on both the cognitive and social worlds of disadvantaged young children (Lee, Brooks-Gunn, & Schnur, 1988). Of special interest is the long-term effect such intervention might have. Differences favor children who attended Head Start compared to those who did not by the time they reach early adulthood; the advantages also favor males more than females. These are the findings of an ongoing large study of improverished black children who participated in Head Start in Harlem during the 1960s (Deutch & others, 1981). More than 150 adults currently are involved in this study, half of whom entered Head Start when they were 4 years old. The others did not get this training and serve as the comparison group. All have been interviewed by psychologists every 2 to 3 years since the Head Start experience.

For the most part, the Head Start males have been successful in the school and the job market: 32 percent are attending college, only 20 percent of the non-Head Start group are; 57 percent are employed full- or part-time, compared with only 44 percent of the non-Head Start group. These positive benefits did not appear for the females, who seem to be no better off than those who started school at the usual age. The researchers are not sure why the young adult females are not doing as well as their male counterparts. The school system may absorb some of the blame. The preschool program stressed verbal skills, inquisitiveness, and self-confidence. In elementary school, boys were rewarded for these characteristics, but, in many instances, girls were punished for them. Some teachers even complained that the girls were too assertive and asked too many questions. But there are some indications that Head Start may indeed have left a positive impression on the females, too. Many females had to leave school because they became pregnant, but preliminary indications suggest that those who were in the Head Start program are more likely to return to school and continue their education.

Other studies also suggest that competent education programs with preschool children can have a lasting effect. Irving Lazar, Richard Darlington, and their colleagues (1982) established a number of different model programs for educating low-income preschool children in the 1960s and 1970s. They pooled their resources into what they called a consortium for longitudinal studies, developed to share information about the long-term effects of preschool programs so that better designs and methods could be created. At the time the data from the 11 different early education studies were analyzed together, the children ranged in age from 9 to 19 years. The early education models varied substantially, but all were carefully planned and carried out by experts in the field of early childhood education. Outcome measures included indicators of school competence (such as special education and grade retention), abilities (as measured by standarized intelligence and achievement tests), attitudes and values, and impact on the family. The results indicated substantial benefits of competent preschool education with low-income children on all four dimensions investigated.

In sum, there is ample evidence that well-designed and implemented preschool education programs with low-income children are successful. We have discussed a number of ideas about information processing, language development, and early childhood education. A summary of these ideas is presented in Concept Table 8.2.

Most of you went to a preschool or kindergarten. Can you remember what it was like? In what ways could the kindergarten you attended have been improved? How can we make our nation's preschool education programs better?

Information Processing, Language Development, and Early Childhood Education		
Concept	Processes/Related Ideas	Characteristics/Discussion
Information Processing	Attention	The child's attention dramatically improves during early childhood. One deficit in attention in early childhood is that the child attends to the salient rather than the relevant features of a task.
	Memory	Significant changes in short-term memory take place during early childhood. For example, memory span increases substantially. Improvement in short-term memory is influenced by increased rehearsal and speed of processing.
	Task Dimensions and Analyses	The information processing perspective emphasizes identification of the components of a task. By analyzing task components and making tasks more simple and relevant for young children, developmentalists have shown that some cognitive capabilities—such as syllogistic reasoning—appear earlier than once was thought.
Language Development	Its Nature	In early childhood, advances in phonology, morphology, syntax, semantics, and pragmatics continue.
Early Childhood Education	Its Nature	The predominant approach is child-centered. Children who attend preschool are usually more competent than those who do not attend, although they show more negative behaviors, too.
	Compensatory Education	Has tried to break through the poverty cycle with programs like Head Start and Follow-Through. Longitudinal studies indicate that Head Start's effect on development is positive.

Summary

I. **Physical Development**
Growth is slower in early childhood than in infancy. The average child grows 2½ inches and gains between 5 and 7 pounds a year during early childhood. Both genetic and environmental circumstances contribute to growth. Ethnic origin and nutrition are important influences on height.

II. **Motor and Perceptual Development**
Considerable progress in gross motor skills takes place in early childhood, especially in the arms and legs. Children's ability to map large scale spaces markedly improves in the early childhood years.

III. **Nutrition, Health, and Exercise**
The average child requires 1,400 to 1,800 calories per day. Poor nutrition influences not only physical development, but behavior as well—sugar may increase activity level and aggression. The effects of health and illness can be studied in terms of motor, cognitive, and social development. By the age of 6, many children are already in poor physical shape; the preschool years may be an important point to begin a physical fitness program.

IV. **Preoperational Thought**
Preoperational thought is the beginning of the ability to reconstruct at the level of thought

what has been established in behavior and a transition from primitive to more sophisticated use of symbols. The child does not yet think in an operational way; operations are internalized sets of actions that allow the child to do mentally what was done before physically.

V. **The Symbolic Function and Intuitive Thought Substages**
These are substages of preoperational thought. The symbolic function substage occurs roughly between 2 and 4 years of age. The ability to think symbolically and represent the world mentally develops. Thought still has several limitations, two of which are egocentrism and

animism. The intuitive thought substage occurs roughly between 4 and 7 years of age. The substage is called intuitive because, on the one hand, children are so sure about their knowledge, yet on the other hand, they are so unaware of how they know what they know. The preoperational child lacks conservation—the idea that amount stays the same or is conserved regardless of how shape changes. One of the main reasons young children cannot conserve is the process of centration, or focusing of attention on one characteristic to the exclusion of all others. Gelman believes that conservation occurs earlier than Piaget thought and that the process of attention is important in its appearance. The preoperational child also asks a barrage of questions, showing an interest in reasoning and finding out why things are the way they are.

VI. **Information Processing**
The child's attention dramatically improves in early childhood. One deficit in attention in early childhood is that the child attends to the salient rather than the relevant dimensions of a task. Significant changes in short-term memory take place in early childhood. For example, memory span increases substantially. Improvement in short-term memory is influenced by increased rehearsal and speed of processing. The information processing perspective emphasizes identification of a task's components. By analyzing task components and making tasks more simple and relevant, developmentalists have shown that some cognitive abilities—such as syllogistic reasoning—appear earlier than once was thought.

VII. **Language Development**
In early childhood, advances in phonology, morphology, syntax, semantics, and pragmatics continue.

VIII. **Early Childhood Education**
The predominant approach is child-centered. Children who attend preschool are usually more competent than those who do not attend, although they show more negative behaviors, too. Compensatory education has tried to break through the poverty cycle with programs like Head Start and Follow-Through. Longitudinal studies indicate that Head Start's effect on development is positive.

Key Terms

Suggested Readings

Clarke-Stewart, K. A., & Fein, G. G. (1983). Early childhood programs. In P. H. Mussen (Ed.), *Handbook of Child Psychology* (4th ed), Vol. 2. New York: Wiley.
A comprehensive review of what we know about early childhood education.

Daehler, M. W., & Bukatko, D. (1985). *Cognitive development.* New York: Random House.
A thorough review of children's cognitive development is provided. Topics include the development of attention, memory, and reasoning.

Kessel, F. (Ed.) (1988). *The development of language and language researchers,* Hillsdale, NJ: Erlbaum.
A number of chapters by experts on language development are presented; includes a chapter by Berko-Gleason on language and socialization and Winner and Gardner on creating a world with words.

Piaget, J. (1987) (Translated from the French by Helga Feider). *Possibility and necessity.* Minneapolis, MN: U. of Minnesota Press.
Children's understanding of possibility and how they learn to choose among alternatives was a major interest of Piaget late in his life. This book includes a description of a number of problems Piaget devised to assess these possibilities and choices.

Stevenson, H. W., & Siegel, A. E. (Eds.), (1987). *Child development research and social policy.* Chicago: U. of Chicago Press.
This book offers a number of important ideas about social policies pertaining to children. Included are chapters on nutrition and on child health.

C H A P T E R

9

■

Social and Personality Development

Imagine . . . two 4-year-olds are playing and one says to the other: "You stay here with the baby while I go fishing." Don't you immediately assume that one of the preschool children is a boy and the other is a girl? And don't you also infer that the sex of the child speaking is male? If you made these inferences, you are correct. These two preschool children—Shane and Barbara— were playing at their nursery school. As Shane walked away, Barbara called to him: "I want to go fishing, too." Shane replied, "No. Girls don't go fishing. But I will take you to a French restaurant when we get back."

Barbara returned to playing with her dolls after Shane left. The director of the nursery school talked to Shane's mother about his behavior. She wanted to know whether Shane was merely mimicking his father's behavior. Shane's mother said that he was not, because the entire family went fishing together. The gender roles children display, then, are not merely replications of parental actions.

Another play scene observed by the nursery school director focused on three boys sitting around a play table in a play kitchen. The boys began issuing orders: "I want a cup of coffee." "Some more jelly for the toast over here." Girls were running back and forth between the stove and the table as they cooked and served breakfast. In one situation, the boys got out of hand, demanding cups of coffee one after another as a 4-year-old girl, Ann, raced around in a dizzy state. Finally, Ann gained some control over the situation by announcing that the coffee was all gone. It didn't seem to occur to Ann to sit down at the table and demand coffee from the boys.

Sexist behavior from young children is nothing new, but viewing it as a problem is. Such behavior has become somewhat of an obsession with preschool teachers and directors, and it bothers many parents who are trying to rear their offspring free of sexist bias (Carper, 1978). More about the fascinating world of children's gender roles appears later in the chapter, along with information about self and moral development. We also spend time describing sibling and peer roles in early childhood, as well as television's influence on social development. But to begin, we continue to emphasize the powerful role played by parents in the young child's socialization. Carl Jung once captured the importance of this parenting by suggesting that we reach backward to our parents and forward to our children, and through their children to a future we never will see, but about which we need to care.

Families

In chapter 7, we learned that attachment is an important aspect of family relationships during infancy. Remember that some experts believe attachment to a caregiver during the first several years of life is the key ingredient in the child's social development, increasing the probability the child will be socially competent and well adjusted in the preschool years and beyond. We also learned that other experts believe secure attachment has been overemphasized and that the child's temperament, other social agents and contexts, and the complexity of the child's social world are also important in determining the child's social competence and well-being. Some developmentalists also emphasize that the infant years have been overdramatized as determinants of life-span development, arguing that social experiences in the early childhood years and later deserve more attention than they sometimes have been given.

In this chapter, we go beyond the attachment process as we explore the different types of parenting styles to which children are exposed, sibling relationships, and how—as we move toward the end of the twentieth century— more children are experiencing socialization in a greater variety of family structures than at any point in history. Keep in mind as we discuss these aspects of families the importance of viewing the family as a system of interacting individuals who reciprocally socialize and mutually regulate each other.

What are the ingredients of competent parenting in early childhood?

Parenting Styles

Parents want their children to grow into socially mature individuals, and they may feel frustrated in trying to discover the best way to accomplish this. Developmentalists have long searched for the ingredients of parenting that promote competent social development in children. For example, in the 1930s, John Watson argued that parents were too affectionate with their children. In the 1950s, a distinction was made between physical and psychological discipline, with psychological discipline, especially reasoning, emphasized as the best way to rear a child. In the 1970s and beyond, the dimensions of competent parenting have become more precise.

Especially widespread is the view of Diana Baumrind (1971), who believes parents should be neither punitive nor aloof from their children but rather should develop rules and be affectionate with their children. She emphasizes three types of parenting that are associated with different aspects of the child's social behavior: authoritarian, authoritative, and laissez-faire (permissive). More recently, developmentalists have argued that permissive parenting comes in two different forms—permissive indulgent and permissive indifferent. What are these forms of parenting like?

Authoritarian parents are restrictive, punitive, exhort the child to follow their directions, respect work and effort, place limits and controls on the child, and offer little verbal give-and-take between the child and parent. **Authoritarian parenting** is associated with these child behaviors: anxiety about social comparison, failure to initiate activity, and ineffective social interaction.

Authoritative parenting encourages that child to be independent but still places limits, demands, and controls on the child's actions. Verbal give-and-take is extensive and parents are warm and nurturant toward the child. Authoritative parenting is associated with the child's social competence, especially self-reliance and social responsibility.

Permissive indulgent parenting is undemanding but accepting and responsive. These parents are involved in their child's life but allow them extensive freedom and do not control their negative behavior. Their children grow up learning that they can get by with just about anything; they disregard and flaunt rules. In one family with permissive indulgent parents, the 14-year-old son moved his parents out of their master bedroom suite and claimed it—along with their expensive stereo system and color television—for himself. The boy is an excellent tennis player but behaves in the fashion of John McEnroe, raving and ranting around the tennis court. He has few friends, is self-indulgent, and never has learned to abide by rules and regulations. Why should he? His parents never made him follow any.

	Accepting, Responsive	Rejecting, Unresponsive
Demanding, Controlling	Authoritative	Authoritarian
Undemanding, Uncontrolling	Permissive Indulgent	Permissive Indifferent

Figure 9.1
Classification of parenting styles. The four types of parenting—authoritarian, authoritative, permissive indulgent, and permissive indifferent—involve the dimensions of acceptance, responsiveness, demand, and control (after Maccoby & Martin, 1983).

There's no vocabulary
For love within a family,
Love that's lived in
But not looked at,
Love within the light of which
All else is seen,
The love within which
All other love finds speech.
This love is silent.
　　　　　T. S. Eliot, The Elder Statesman

Permissive indifferent parenting refers to a style in which parents are highly uninvolved in their children's lives. These parents are neglecting and unresponsive. This type of parenting consistently is associated with a lack of self-control on the part of children. In our discussion of parenting styles, we have talked about parents who vary on the dimensions of acceptance, responsiveness, demand, and control. As shown in figure 9.1, the four parenting styles—authoritarian, authoritative, permissive indulgent, and permissive indifferent—can be described in terms of these dimensions. Further advice for parents that dovetails with the concept of authoritative parenting is presented in Focus on Life-Span Development 9.1.

Parents also need to adapt their behavior toward the child based on the child's developmental maturity. Parents should not treat the 5-year-old in the same way as the 2-year-old. The 2-year-old and the 5-year-old have different needs and abilities. In the first year, parent-child interaction moves from a heavy focus on routine caretaking—feeding, changing diapers, bathing, and soothing—to later include more noncaretaking activities like play and visual-vocal exchanges. During the child's second and third years, parents often handle disciplinary matters by physical manipulation: They carry the child away from a mischievous activity to the place they want the child to go; they put fragile and dangerous objects out of reach; they sometimes spank. But as the child grows older, parents turn increasingly to reasoning, moral exhortation, and giving or withholding special privileges. As children move toward the elementary school years, parents show them less physical affection, become less protective, and spend less time with them (Maccoby & Martin, 1983). Throughout childhood, socialization is reciprocal: Children socialize their parents, just as parents socialize their children. As we see next, in most families, there also are siblings to be socialized and socialized by.

Sibling Relationships and Birth Order
Sandra describes to her mother what happened in a conflict with her sister:

> We had just come home from the ball game. I sat down on the sofa next to the light so I could read. Sally (the sister) said, "Get up. I was sitting there first. I just got up for a second to get a drink." I told her I was not going to get up and that I didn't see her name on the chair. I got mad and started pushing her—her drink spilled all over her. Then she got really mad; she shoved me against the wall, hitting and clawing at me. I managed to grab a handful of hair.

At this point, Sally comes into the room and begins to tell her side of the story. Sandra interrupts, "Mother, you always take her side." Sound familiar? Any of you who have grown up with siblings probably have a rich memory of aggressive, hostile interchanges; but sibling relationships have many pleasant, caring moments as well. Children's sibling relations include helping, sharing, teaching, fighting, and playing. Children can act as emotional supports, rivals, and communication partners (Vandell, 1987). More than 80 percent of American children have one or more siblings—that is, brothers or sisters. Because there are so many possible sibling combinations, it is difficult to generalize about sibling influences. Among the factors to be considered are the number of siblings, age of siblings, birth order, age spacing, sex of siblings, and whether sibling relationships are different than parent-child relationships.

MAKING THE GRADE AS PARENTS

In the 1980s, the Missouri Department of Education has hired Michael Meyerhoff and Burton White to design a model parent-education program and help set it up in four school districts across the state: one urban, one suburban, one small town, and one rural town. The families cover a wide range of social and economic backgrounds. The services include get-togethers—at which 10 to 20 parents meet with a parent educator at the resource center—and individual home visits by a parent educator. Services begin during the final three months of pregnancy and continue until the child's third birthday, with increasing emphasis on private visits after the child is 6 months of age. The average amount of contact with the families is once a month for an hour and a half.

During group and private sessions, parents are given basic information about what kinds of parenting practices are likely to help or hinder their children's progress. Table 9.A shows the dos and don'ts told to parents, advice that makes sense and is likely to promote the child's competence (Meyerhoff & White, 1986; White, 1988).

TABLE 9.A
A Primer in Competent Parenting

The following recommendations are based on the lessons Michael Meyerhoff and Burton White learned from the parents of competent preschool children.

Things To Do:	Things Not To Do:
Provide children with the maximum opportunity for exploration and investigation.	Don't confine your children regularly for long periods of time.
Be available to act as your children's personal consultant as much as possible. You don't have to hover, just be around to provide attention and support as needed.	Don't allow them to concentrate their energies on you so much that independent exploration and investigation are excluded.
Respond to your children promptly and favorably as often as you can, providing appropriate enthusiasm and encouragement.	Don't ignore attention getting to the point where children have to throw a tantrum to gain your interest.
Set limits—do not give in to unreasonable requests or permit unacceptable behavior to continue.	Don't worry that your children won't love you if you say "no" on occasion.
Talk to your children often. Make an effort to understand what they are trying to do and concentrate on what they see as important.	Don't try to win all the arguments, especially during the second half of the second year when most children are passing through a normal period of negativism.
Use words they understand but also add new words and related ideas.	Don't be overprotective.
Provide new learning opportunities. Having children accompany you to the supermarket or allowing them to bake cookies with you is more enriching than sitting them down and conducting a flashcard session.	Don't bore your child if you can avoid it.
Give your children a chance to direct some of your shared activities from time to time.	Don't worry about when children learn to count or say the alphabet.
Try to help your children be as spontaneous emotionally as your own behavior patterns will allow.	Don't worry if they are slow to talk, as long as they seem to understand more and more language as time goes by.
Encourage your child's pretend activities, especially those in which they act out adult roles.	Don't try to force toilet training; it will be easier when they are two.
	Don't spoil your children, giving them the notion that the world was made just for them.

Source: Meyerhoff & White, 1986, p. 44

Is sibling interaction different than parent-child interaction? There is some evidence that it is. Observations indicate that children interact more positively and in more varied ways with their parents than with their siblings (Baskett & Johnson, 1982). Children also follow their parents' dictates more than those of their siblings, and they behave more negatively and punitively with their siblings than with their parents.

In some instances, siblings may be stronger socializing influences on the child than parents are (Cicirelli, 1977). Someone close in age to the child—such as a sibling—may be able to understand the child's problems and be able to communicate more effectively than parents can. In dealing with peers, coping with difficult teachers, and discussing taboo subjects—such as sex—siblings may be more influential in the socialization process than parents.

Birth order is a special interest of sibling researchers. When differences in birth order are found, they usually are explained by variations in interactions with parents and siblings associated with the unique experiences of being in a particular position in the family. This is especially true in the case of the firstborn child. The oldest child is the only one who does not have to share his parents' love and affection with other siblings—until another sibling comes along. An infant requires more attention than an older child; this means that the firstborn sibling now gets less attention than before the newborn arrived. Does this result in conflict between parents and the firstborn? In one research study, mothers became more negative, coercive, restraining, and played less with the firstborn following the birth of a second child (Dunn & Kendrick, 1982). Even though a new infant requires more attention from parents than does an older child, an especially intense relationship seems to be maintained between parents and firstborns throughout the life cycle. Parents have higher expectations for, put more pressure for achievement and responsibility on, and interfere more with the activities of firstborn than later-born children (Rothbart, 1971).

Birth order also is associated with variations in sibling relationships. The oldest sibling is expected to exercise self-control and show responsibility in interacting with younger siblings. When the oldest sibling is jealous or hostile, parents restrain her and protect the younger sibling. The oldest sibling is more dominant, competent, and powerful than the younger siblings; the oldest sibling also is expected to assist and teach younger siblings. Indeed, researchers have shown that older siblings are both more antagonistic—hitting, kicking, and biting—and more nurturant toward their younger siblings than vice versa (Abramovitch, & others, 1986). There also is something unique about same-sex sibling relationships. Aggression, dominance, and cheating occur more in same-sex than opposite-sex sibling relationships (Minnett, Vandell, & Santrock, 1983; Vandell, Minnett, & Santrock, in press).

Given the differences in family dynamics involved in birth order, it is not surprising that firstborns and later-borns have different characteristics. Firstborn children are more adult oriented, helpful, conforming, anxious, self-controlled, and less aggressive than their siblings. Parental demands and high standards established for first borns result in these children excelling in academic and professional endeavors. First borns are overrepresented in *Who's Who* and Rhodes scholars, for example. However, some of the same pressures placed on firstborns for high achievement may be the reason they also have more guilt, anxiety, difficulty in coping with stressful situations, and higher admission to child guidance clinics.

What is the working mother's role in child development?

What is the only child like? The popular conception of the only child is a "spoiled brat" with such undesirable characteristics as dependency, lack of self-control, and self-centered behavior. But research presents a more positive portrayal of the only child, who often is achievement-oriented and displays a desirable personality, especially in comparison to later-borns and children from large families (Falbo & Polit, 1986).

China has instituted a one-child family policy to reduce its population. How might parent-child relations be different after the one-child family policy takes hold?

The Changing Family in a Changing Society

Children are growing up in a greater variety of family structures than ever before in history. Many mothers spend the greatest part of their day away from their children, even their infants. More than one of every two mothers with a child under the age of five is in the labor force; more than two of every three with a child from 6 to 17 years of age is. And the increasing number of children growing up in single parent families is staggering. One estimate suggests that 25 percent of the children born between 1910 and 1960 lived in a single parent family sometime during their childhood. However, 40 to 50 percent of the individuals born in the 1970s will spend part of their childhood in a single-parent family (Bane, 1978). Further, about 11 percent of all American households now are made up of so-called blended families; that is, families with stepparents or cohabiting adults. And, as we saw in chapter 7, fathers perform more childrearing duties than in the past.

Working Mothers

Because household operations have become more efficient and family size has decreased in America, it is not certain that children with mothers working outside the home actually receive less attention than children in the past whose mothers were not employed. Outside employment—at least for mothers with school-aged children—may simply be filling time previously taken up by added household burdens and more children. It also cannot be assumed that, if the mother did not go to work, the child would benefit from the time freed by streamlined household operations and smaller families. Mothering does not always have a positive effect on the child. The educated, nonworking mother may overinvest her energies in her children, fostering an excess of worry and discouraging the child's independence. In such situations, the mother may inject more parenting than the child can profitably handle.

As Lois Hoffman (1979) comments, maternal employment is a part of modern life. It is not an aberrant aspect of it, but a response to other social changes that meets the needs the previous family ideal of a full-time mother and homemaker cannot. Not only does it meet the parent's needs, but in many ways, it may be a pattern better suited to socializing children for the adult roles they will occupy. This is especially true for daughters, but for sons, too. The broader range of emotions and skills that each parent presents is more consistent with this adult role. Just as his father shares the breadwinning role and the childrearing role with his mother, so the son, too, will be more likely to share these roles. The rigid gender role stereotyping perpetuated by the divisions of labor in the traditional family is not appropriate for the demands children of either sex will have made on them as adults. The needs of the growing child require the mother to loosen her hold on the child, and this task may be easier for the working woman whose job is an additional source of identity and self-esteem.

Effects of Divorce on Children

Early studies of the effects of divorce on children followed a **father absence tradition;** children from father absent and father present families were compared, and differences in their development were attributed to the absence of the father. But family structure (such as father present, divorced, and widowed) is only one of many factors that influence the child's adjustment. The contemporary approach advocates evaluating the strengths and weaknesses of the child prior to divorce, the nature of events surrounding the divorce itself, and post-divorce family functioning. Investigators are finding that the availability and use of support systems (baby-sitters, relatives, day care), an ongoing, positive relationship between the custodial parent and the ex-spouse, authoritative parenting, financial stability, and the child's competencies at the time of the divorce are related to the child's adjustment (Block, Block, & Gjerde, 1986; Chase-Landsdale & Hetherington, in press; Hetherington, in press; Hetherington, Cox, & Cox, 1982; Hetherington, Hagan, & Anderson, 1988; Kelly, 1987; Santrock & Warshak, 1986; Wallerstein & Kelly, 1980).

Many separations and divorces are highly emotional affairs that immerse the child in conflict. Conflict is a critical aspect of family functioning that seems to outweigh the influence of family structure on the child's development. Children in divorced families low in conflict function better than children in intact, never divorced families high in conflict, for example (Rutter, 1983; Wallerstein, Corbin, & Lewis, in press). Although escape from conflict may be a positive benefit for children, in the year immediately following the divorce, the conflict does not decline, but rather increases. At this time, children—especially boys—in divorced families show more adjustment problems than children in homes with both parents present. During the first year after the divorce, the quality of parenting the child experiences is often poor; parents seem to be preoccupied with their own needs and adjustment—experiencing anger, depression, confusion, and emotional instability—which inhibits their ability to respond sensitively to the child's needs. During the second year after the divorce, parents are more effective in their childrearing duties, especially with daughters (Hetherington, Cox, & Cox, 1982).

Recent evaluations of children six years after the divorce of their parents by Mavis Hetherington and her colleagues (Hetherington, in press; Hetherington, Hagan, & Anderson, 1988) found that living in a nonremarried mother custody home had long term negative effects on boys with deleterious outcomes appearing consistently from preschool to adolescence. In contrast, most girls from such families recovered from divorce occurring early in their lives. However, although preadolescent girls in divorced families adapted reasonably well, at the onset of adolescence these girls engaged in frequent conflict with their mothers, behaved in noncompliant ways, had lower self-esteem, and experienced more problems in heterosexual relations.

The sex of the child and the sex of the custodial parent are important considerations in evaluating the effects of divorce on children. One research study directly compared children living in father custody and mother custody families (Santrock & Warshak, 1979, 1986). On a number of measures, including videotaped observations of parent-child interaction, children living with the same-sex parent were more socially competent—happier, more independent, higher self-esteem, and more mature—than children living with the opposite-sex parent. Other research recently has supported these findings (Camara & Resnick, 1987; Furstenberg, in press).

Support systems are especially important for low-income divorced families (Coletta, 1978; Hetherington, in press). The extended family and community services may play a critical role in the functioning of low-income divorced families. These support systems may be crucial for low-income divorced families with infants and young children because the majority of these parents must work full-time but still may not be able to make ends meet.

The age of the child at the time of the divorce also needs to be considered. Young children's responses to divorce are mediated by their limited cognitive and social competencies, their dependency on parents, and their restriction to the home or inferior day care (Hetherington, Hagan, & Anderson, 1988). During the interval immediately following divorce, young children less accurately appraise the divorce situation. These young children may blame themselves for the divorce, may fear abandonment by both parents, and may misperceive and be confused by what is happening (Wallerstein, Corbin, & Lewis, in press).

The cognitive immaturity that creates extensive anxiety for children who are young at the time of their parents' divorce may benefit the children over time. Ten years after the divorce of their parents, adolescents have few memories of their own earlier fears and suffering or their parents' conflict (Wallerstein, Corbin, & Lewis, in press). Nonetheless, approximately one third of these children continue to express anger about not being able to grow up in an intact, never divorced family. Those who were adolescents at the time of their parents' divorce were more likely to remember the conflict and stress surrounding the divorce some ten years later in their early adult years. They too expressed disappointment at not being able to grow up in an intact family and wondered if their life wouldn't have been better if they had been able to do so.

In sum, large numbers of children are growing up in divorced families. Most children initially experience considerable stress when their parents divorce and they are placed at risk for developing problem behaviors. However, divorce also can remove children from conflicted marriages. Many children emerge from divorce as competent individuals. In recent years, researchers have moved away from the view that single-parent families are atypical or pathological, focusing more on the diversity of children's responses to divorce

Imagine that you are a judge in a custodial dispute. What are some of the key factors you will consider in awarding custody?

Families in Early Childhood		
Concept	**Processes/Related Ideas**	**Characteristics/Description**
Parenting Styles	The Four Major Categories	Authoritarian, authoritative, permissive indulgent, and permissive indifferent are four main categories of parenting. Authoritative parenting is associated with children's social competence more than the other styles.
	Maturation of the Child	Parents need to adapt their interaction strategies as the child grows older, using less physical manipulation and more reasoning in the process.
Sibling Relationships	Their Nature	More than 80 percent of American children have one or more siblings. Siblings interact with each other in more negative, less positive, and less varied ways than parents and children interact. In some cases, siblings are stronger socializing influences than parents.
	Birth Order	The relationship of the first born child and parents seems to be especially close and demanding, which may account for the greater achievement orientation and anxiety in first born children. Variations also are associated with those born later and only children.
The Changing Family	Working Mothers	A mother's working full-time outside the home can have both positive and negative effects on the child; there is no indication of long-term negative effects overall.
	Divorce	The early father absence tradition has been supplanted by an emphasis on the complexity of the divorced family, pre- and post-divorce family functioning, and varied response to divorce. Among the factors that influence the child's adjustment in divorced families are conflict, time since divorce, sex of the child and sex of the custodial parent, support systems, and age of the child.

From J. P. Galst, "Television food commercials and pronutritional public service announcements as determinants of young children's snack choices' in Child Development, 51, *935–938, 1980. © 1980 The Society for Research in Child Development, Inc.*

and the factors that facilitate or disrupt the development and adjustment of children in these family circumstances (Hetherington, Hagan, & Anderson, 1988).

We have discussed a number of ideas about family relationships in early childhood. A summary of these ideas is presented in Concept Table 9.1. Now we turn to the fascinating world of young children's peer relations and play.

Peers and Play

Peer relations take up an increasing amount of time during early childhood. Many of children's greatest frustrations and happiest moments come when they are with peers. And early childhood is a time when play becomes a central focus of the child's life.

Same-age peer interaction serves a unique role in our culture. Think of your own experiences with age-mates as you were growing up. Some of your most enjoyable and your most frustrating moments were spent in interaction with children similar to you in age, moments of sharing and caring and moments of anger. After all, one can only learn to become a good fighter among age-mates: the bigger ones will kill you, and the smaller ones offer no challenge.

Peer Relations

Peers are children who are about the same age or maturity level. Same-age peer interaction serves a unique role in our culture (Hartup, 1976). Age grading would occur even if schools were not age graded and children were left alone to determine the composition of their own societies. After all, one can only learn to be a good fighter among age-mates: The bigger guys will kill you, and the little ones are no challenge. One of the most important functions of the peer group is to provide a source of information and comparison about the world outside the family. From the peer group, children receive feedback about their abilities. Children evaluate what they do in terms of whether it is better than, as good as, or worse than what other children do. It is hard to do this at home because siblings are usually older or younger.

Are peers necessary for development? When peer monkeys who have been reared together are separated from one another, they become depressed and less advanced socially (Suomi, Harlow, & Domek, 1970). The human development literature contains a classic example of the importance of peers in social development. Anna Freud (Freud & Dann, 1951) studied six children from different families who banded together after their parents were killed in World War II. Intensive peer attachment was observed; the children were a tightly knit group, dependent on one another and aloof with outsiders. Even though deprived of parental care, they became neither delinquent nor psychotic.

The frequency of peer interaction, both positive and negative, continues to increase throughout early childhood (Hartup, 1983). Although aggressive interaction and rough-and-tumble play increase, the *proportion* of aggressive exchanges to friendly interchanges decreases, especially among middle-class boys. With age, children tend to abandon this immature and inefficient social interaction and acquire more mature methods of relating to peers. Nonetheless, some children show high rates of aggressive behavior. At times, their behavior can disrupt the preschool classroom. If you were a teacher and a boy in your classroom were highly aggressive, what would you do? And what if a girl rarely interacted with any other children during the course of virtually each day at school? What kind of procedures would you use to change her behavior? Focus on Life-Span Development 9.2 presents some possible solutions for improving preschool children's problem behavior.

■

NOSE PUNCHERS,
PINCHERS, AND ISOLATES

Put yourself in this situation. You are a preschool teacher and a boy in your classroom is extremely aggressive and disruptive. Yesterday he punched a classmate in the nose and today he beat up a younger boy on the playground. What can you do?

A lot depends on the situation. What is your relationship with the boy? What are the other children like—are many of them aggressive, or is he the only major aggression problem? Would it help to work with his parents, or has his home situation deteriorated to the point where the parents are out of touch with the boy or are uncooperative? How old is he? What is his history of aggressive behavior? Are there any clues to what might have helped reduce or eliminate his aggressive actions in similar situations? Is he getting rewarded with increased status or attention from peers and from you for his hostile actions? How much and in what ways does he reward himself for his aggression? Could he get more attention from peers and from you by engaging in more positive acts that may include assertive but nonhostile behavior? To what extent are painful and aversive frustrations present in his life? Can you identify these? Can some of them be removed or reduced? What kinds of aggressive cues are present in the child's environment? Can these

How might a preschool teacher control this aggression?

be removed or reduced? What is the subculture like in which he lives? What are his peers like? If there are sudden outbursts of aggression and violence with no apparent cause, a medical checkup or even a neurological examination might be considered in rare cases.

We could ask many other questions and speculate about the sources of the child's aggression. It is important, however, to recognize that controlling aggression is no easy task, that there are probably multiple causes of the aggression, and that as a teacher or parent, you alone probably will not be able to gain complete control over the aggression. But you can help, and you are one of the most important social agents in the child's life; you may be able to

make a difference in the child's social development by some combination of the answers to the questions asked here. The aggression should not be allowed to continue if it begins to disrupt the class.

As just mentioned, a possible contributor to aggression is the attention given to it. In one of the earliest behavior modification studies with children, behaviorists evaluated the extent the teacher's attention was the culprit in maintaining aggression in the preschool classroom (Harris, Wolf, & Baer, 1964). One boy repeatedly threw his glasses on the floor and broke them a number of times; another loved to pinch adults, including the teacher; one girl spent over 80 percent of her time on the floor; and another girl isolated herself from other children at least 85 percent of the school day. The teacher's reinforcement of desirable behaviors and the removal of her attention from undesirable ones had a powerful effect on increasing "isolate" children's behavior with peers. Researchers have found, however, that behavior modification is often more successful with withdrawn, isolated children than with children who display acting out, aggressive behavior. While the teacher's attention may be removed from the aggressive behavior, the behavior still can be rewarded through peer attention.

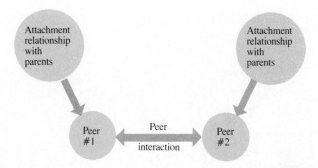

Figure 9.2
Peer interaction: the influence of the relationship histories of each peer. In the investigation by Olweus (1980), bullies had parents who were rejecting, had discord, used power assertive discipline, and were permissive toward aggression; by contrast, whipping boys' mothers were anxious and over involved with their sons and eschewed aggression.

What are some similarities and differences in peer and parent-child relationships? Children touch, smile, frown, and vocalize when they interact with both parents and other children. However, rough-and-tumble play occurs mainly with other children, not with adults. In times of stress, children usually move toward their parents rather than their peers.

The worlds of parent-child and peer relations are distinct but they are coordinated, too. Some developmentalists believe that secure attachment to parents promotes healthy peer relations (e.g., Ainsworth, 1979; Sroufe, in press). However, as we discussed in chapter 7, others believe the route to competency, including positive peer relations, is not always through secure attachment (e.g., Kagan, 1987). Nonetheless, the data are consistent with the theory that children's relationships with their parents serve as emotional bases for exploring and enjoying peer relations (Hartup, 1983; Pettit, Dodge, & Brown, 1988).

One investigation (Olweus, 1980) reveals how the relationship history of each peer helps to predict the nature of peer interaction (see figure 9.2). Some boys were typically aggressive and other boys were the recipients of aggression throughout the preschool years. The "bullies" as well as the "whipping boys" had distinctive relationship histories. The bullies' parents treated them with rejection and discord, power assertion, and permissiveness for aggression. By contrast, the whipping boys' mothers were anxious and over-involved with their children and eschewed aggression. The well-adjusted boys were not as involved in aggressive interchanges. Their parents did not sanction aggression; their responsive involvement with their children promoted the development of self-assertion as an adaptive pattern.

Play

An extensive amount of peer interaction during early childhood involves play. American children's freewheeling play once took place in rural fields and city streets, using equipment largely of their own making. Today, play is increasingly confined to backyards, basements, playrooms, and bedrooms, and derives much of its content from video games, television dramas, and Saturday morning cartoons (Sutton-Smith, 1985). Modern children spend an increasingly large part of their lives alone with their toys, which was inconceivable several centuries earlier. Childhood was once a part of collective village life. Children did not play separately but joined youth and adults in seasonal festivals that intruded upon the work world with regularity and boisterousness (see figure 9.3).

And that park grew up with me; That small world widened as I learned its secret boundaries, as I discovered new refuges in the woods and jungles: hidden homes and lairs for the multitudes of imagination, for cowboys and Indians, and the tall-terrible half-people who rode on nightmares through my bedroom. But it was not the only world—that world of rockery, gravel path, playbank, bowling green, bandstands, reservoir, dahlia garden, where an ancient keeper named Smoky, was the whiskered snake in the grass one must keep off. There was another world where with my friends I used to dawdle on half holidays along the bent and Devon-facing seashore, hoping for gold watches or the skull of a sheep or a message in a bottle to be washed up by the tide.

Dylan Thomas

Figure 9.3
Children's Games *by Pieter Breughel,*
1560. Is the play of today's children
different than the play of children in
collective village life?
The Kunthistorisches Museum, Vienna.

Play's Functions

Play increases affiliation with peers, releases tension, advances cognitive development, increases exploration, and provides a safe haven in which to engage in potentially dangerous behavior. Regarding affiliation, play increases the probability that children will converse and interact with each other. During this interaction, children practice the roles they will assume later in life.

For Freud and Erikson, play was an especially useful form of human adjustment, bringing the child mastery over anxieties and conflicts. Because these tensions are relieved in play, the child can cope with life's problems. Play permits the child to work off excess physical energy and to release pent up tensions. **Play therapy** allows the child to work off frustrations and is a medium through which the therapist can analyze the child's conflicts and ways of coping with them. The child may feel less threatened and be more likely to express his true feelings in the context of play.

Piaget (1962) saw play as a medium that advances the child's cognitive development. At the same time, he said that the child's cognitive development constrains the way she plays. Play permits children to practice their competencies and acquired skills in a relaxed, pleasurable way. Piaget believed that cognitive structures need to be exercised—play provides the perfect setting for this exercise. For example, a child who has just learned to add or multiply begins to play with numbers in different ways as she perfects these operations, laughing as she does so.

Daniel Berlyne (1960) sees play as exciting and pleasurable in itself because it satisfies the exploratory drive each of us possesses. This drive involves curiosity and a desire for information about something new or unusual. Play is a means whereby children can safely explore and seek out new information—something they might not otherwise do. Play encourages this exploratory behavior by offering children the possibilities of novelty, complexity, uncertainty, surprise, and incongruity (Görlitz & Wohlwill, 1987).

Play is an elusive concept. It ranges from an infant's simple exercise of a newfound sensorimotor talent to a preschool child's riding a tricycle to an older child's participation in organized games. One expert on play and games observed that there is no universally accepted definition of play because it encompasses so many different kinds of activities (Sutton-Smith, 1973).

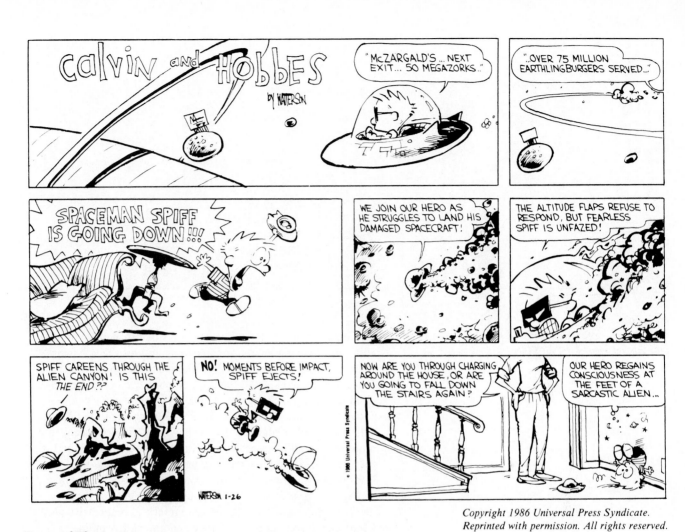

Types of Play

Many years ago Mildred Parten (1932) developed one of the most elaborate attempts to categorize children's play. Based on observations of children in free play at nursery school, Parten arrived at these play categories:

Unoccupied The child is not engaging in play as it is commonly understood. He may stand in one spot, look around the room, or perform random movements that do not seem to have a goal. In most nursery schools, **unoccupied play** is less frequent than other forms.

Solitary The child plays alone and independently of those around him. The child seems engrossed in what he is doing and does not care much about anything else that is happening. Two- and three-year-olds engage more frequently in **solitary play** than older preschoolers do.

Onlooker The child watches other children playing. He may talk with them and ask them questions but does not enter into their play behavior. The child's active interest in other children's play distinguishes **onlooker play** from unoccupied play.

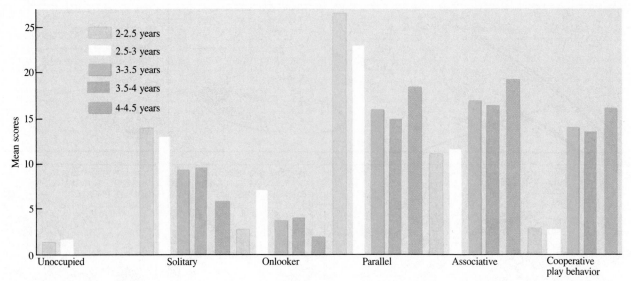

Figure 9.4
Mean scores in five categories of social play for 2-, 3-, and 4-year-olds.

Parallel The child plays alone, but with toys like those that other children are using or in a manner that mimics the behavior of other children who are playing. The older the child, the less frequently he engages in this type of play; even older preschool children, though, engage in **parallel play** quite often.

Associative Social interaction with little or no organization involved is called **associative play.** In this type of play, children seem to be more interested in associating with each other than in the tasks they are performing. Borrowing or lending toys and following or leading one another in line are examples of associative play.

Cooperative Social interaction in a group with a sense of group identity and organized activity characterizes **cooperative play.** Children's formal games, competition aimed at winning something, and groups formed by the teacher for doing things together are examples of cooperative play. Cooperative play is the prototype for the games of middle childhood; little of it is seen in the preschool years.

Parten's research on play was conducted more than half a century ago. To determine whether her findings were now out of date, Keith Barnes (1971) observed a group of preschoolers using Parten's categories of play. He found that children in the 1970s did not engage in as much associative and cooperative play as they did in the 1930s. These changes in play probably occurred because children have become more passive as a consequence of heavy television viewing and because toys are more abundant and attractive than they were 40 years ago. Today, solitary play may be more natural and parents may encourage children to play by themselves more than parents did years ago. The developmental changes that were observed by Parten also were observed by Barnes. That is, 3-year-old children engaged in solitary and parallel play more than 5-year-old children did, and 5-year-old children engaged in cooperative and associative play more than other kinds of play (see figure 9.4).

Another form of play that is pervasive in early childhood is **pretend play.** When children engage in pretend play, they transform the physical environment into a symbol (Fein, 1986). Make-believe play appears rather abruptly in the toddler's development, at about 18 months of age, continues to develop between 3 to 4 years of age, peaks between 5 to 6 years of age, and then declines. In the early elementary school years, children's interests shift to games.

In pretend play, children try out many different roles—they may be the mother, the father, the teacher, and next-door neighbor, and so on. Sometimes their pretend play reflects an adult role; at other times, it may make fun of it. Here is one example of pretend play:

> Harvey was playing with Karen, his twin sister. Karen began to push the carriage. Harvey said, "Let me be the baby, Karen," and started to talk like a baby. He got into the carriage. Karen pushed him around the room as he squinted his eyes and cried. She stopped the carriage, patted his shoulder, saying, "Don't cry, baby." He squirmed around, put his thumb in his mouth, and swayed his body.
>
> Josie came to the carriage and wanted to push Harvey. He jumped out and hit her in the face. She walked away almost crying. He went to her, put his arm around her, and said, in a sympathetic manner, "Come, you be the baby. I'll push you in the carriage." She climbed in. He ran and got the dog and gave it to her saying, "Here, baby." She smiled and began to play with the dog. He went to the housekeeping corner, got a cup, and held it to her mouth. He smacked his lips, looking at her, smiling. He pushed her around in the carriage. Karen ran to him and said, "Harvey, let me push the carriage. I'll be the mamma, you be the daddy." Harvey said, "O.K.," and reached his hand in his pocket and gave her money. He said, "Bye, baby," waving his hand (Hartley, Frank, & Goldenson, 1952, pp. 70–72).

You probably can remember many episodes of pretend play from your own childhood—playing doctor, teacher, and so on. As you think about your early childhood years, play probably is one of the predominant themes.

Television

Few developments in society over the past 25 years have had a greater impact on children than television has. Many children spend more time in front of the television set than they do with their parents. In chapter 8, we saw that children's attention to television increases dramatically during the preschool years. Although only one of mass media's vehicles that affects children's behavior—books, comics, movies, and newspapers being others—television is the most influential. The persuasion capabilities of television are staggering: the 20,000 hours of television watched by the time the average American adolescent graduates from high school is more than the number of hours spent in the classroom. Television's influence on children has been studied extensively, including its role in aggression, prosocial behavior, and eating behavior.

Television has been called a lot of things, not all of them good. Depending on one's point of view, it may be a "window on the world," "the one-eyed monster," or the "boob tube." Television has been attacked as one of the reasons that scores on national achievement tests in reading and mathematics are lower now than in the past. Television, it is claimed, attracts children away from books and schoolwork. In one recent study (Huston, Seigle, & Bremer, 1983), children who read books and the printed media watched television less than those who did not. Further, it is argued that television trains the child to become a passive learner; rarely, if ever, does television require active responses from the observer.

Television is a medium of entertainment which permits millions of people to listen to the same joke at the same time, and yet remain lonesome.

T. S. Eliot

"Mrs. Horton, could you stop by school today?"
Copyright © 1981 Martha Campbell.

Television also is said to deceive; that is, it teaches children that problems are easily resolved and that everything always comes out right in the end. For example, it usually takes only 30 to 60 minutes for detectives to sort through a complex array of clues and discover the killer—and they always find the killer. Violence is pictured as a way of life in many shows. It is all right for police to use violence and break moral codes in their fight against evildoers. And the lasting results of violence are rarely brought home to the viewer. An individual who is injured suffers only for a few seconds; in real life, the individual might take months or years to recover, or perhaps does not recover at all. Yet, one out of every two first-grade children says that the adults on television are like adults in real life (Lyle & Hoffman, 1972).

There are some positive aspects to television's influence on children. For one, television presents children with a world that is different than the one in which they live. This means that, through television, children are exposed to a wider variety of views and knowledge than may be the case when children only are informed by their parents, teachers, and peers.

Just how much television do young children watch? They watch a lot and they seem to be watching more all the time. In the 1950s, 3-year-old children watched television for less than one hour a day; 5-year-olds watched just over two hours a day. But in the 1970s, preschool children watched television for an average of four hours a day; elementary school children watched for as long as six hours a day (Friedrich & Stein, 1973). In 1980–81, children aged 2–5 years viewed 27.8 hours per week (Nielson Television Index, 1981). Of special concern is the extent children are exposed to violence and aggression on television. Up to 80 percent of the prime time shows include violent acts—beatings, shootings, and stabbings, for example. Violence's frequency even increases on the Saturday morning cartoon shows—they average more than 25 violent episodes per hour.

Some psychologists believe television violence has a profound influence on shaping children's aggressive thoughts and behaviors; others believe the effects are exaggerated (Liebert & Sprafkin, 1988; McQuire, 1986; Roberts & Maccoby, 1985). Does television violence merely stimulate a child to go out and buy a Darth Vadar ray gun? Or does it trigger an attack on a playmate and even increase the number of violent attacks and murders?

Violence on television is associated with aggression in individuals who watch it. For example, in one investigation the amount of television violence watched by children when they were in elementary school was associated with how aggressive they were at age 19 and at age 30 (Eron, 1987; Huesmann & others, in press; Lefkowitz & others, 1972). In another investigation, long-term exposure to television violence increased the likelihood of aggression in 1,565 boys aged 12 to 17 (Belson, 1978). Boys who watched the most aggression on television were the most likely to commit some violent action, swear, be aggressive in sports, threaten violence toward another boy, write slogans on walls, or break windows. The types of television violence most often associated with aggression were realistic, took place between individuals in close relationships rather than between strangers, and were committed by the "good guys" rather than the "bad guys."

But it is another step to conclude that television violence in itself causes aggressive behavior. Children who watch the most violence may be more aggressive in the first place; other factors such as poverty and unpleasant life experiences may be culprits, too. So far we have not been able to establish a causal link from television violence to aggression (Freedman, 1984). Like other behaviors, aggression is multiply determined.

TABLE 9.1
Average Proportion of Snacks with Added Sugar Selected during Four Weeks of Experimental Intervention

Intervention Week	Condition				
	S-NC	NS-NC	S-C	NS-C	CT
3	.86	.88	.80	.71	.90
4	.74	.80	.73	.58	.84
5	.77	.86	.76	.68	.87
6	.83	.81	.83	.71	.88

Note: S-NC Commercials for food products with added sugar viewed without adult commentary
NS-NC No sugar added and public service announcement without adult commentary
S-C Sugar added and adult commentary
NS-C No sugar added and pronutritional public service announcement with adult commentary
CT The control condition, in which children had no television exposure
Notice that the most effective treatment in reducing the child's selection of sugar snacks was exposure to commercial food products without added sugar and pronutritional public service announcements with accompanying positive comments by an adult (the NS-C condition with the lower proportions, .71 in week three, .58 in week four, .68 in week five, and .71 in week six).

Television can also teach children that it is better to behave in positive, prosocial ways rather than in negative, antisocial ways. Aimee Leifer (1973) demonstrated how television is associated with prosocial behavior in young children; she selected a number of episodes from the television show "Sesame Street" that reflected positive social interchanges. She was especially interested in situations that taught children how to use their social skills. For example, in one interchange, two men were fighting over the amount of space available to them; they gradually began to cooperate and to share the space. Children who watched these episodes copied these behaviors and, in later social situations, applied the prosocial lessons they had learned.

When we watch television, we are exposed to commercials as well as regular programming. For example, the average television-viewing child sees more than 20,000 commercials per year! A significant portion of the commercials that are shown during children's television shows involve food products that are high in sugar (Barcus, 1978). In one investigation, 3- to 6-year-old children were exposed to television cartoons over a four-week period; the advertising content of the shows consisted of either commercials for food products with added sugar, food products with no added sugar, or pronutritional public service announcements, with or without adult comments about the portrayed product (Galst, 1980). As shown in Table 9.1, the most effective treatment in reducing the child's selection of sugar snacks was exposure to commercial food products without added sugar combined with pronutritional public service announcements with accompanying positive comments by an adult.

How much do parents take an active role in discussing television with their children? For the most part, parents do not discuss the content of television shows with their children (Leiffer, Gordon, & Graves, 1974). Parents need to be especially sensitive to young children's viewing habits because the age period of 2½ to 6 is when long-term television-viewing habits begin to be established. Children from lower socioeconomic status families watch television more than children from higher socioeconomic status families (Huston, Seigle, & Bremer, 1983). And children who live in families involved in high conflict watch more television than children who live in families low in conflict (Price & Feshbach, 1982). In one recent investigation (Tangney, in press), parents who showed more empathy and were more sensitive to their children had children who preferred less fantasy fare on television. In dysfunctional families, children may use the lower developmental level of fantasy-oriented children's programs to escape from the taxing, stressful circumstances of the home environment.

Parents can make television a more positive influence in children's lives. The following guidelines developed by Dorothy and Jerome Singer (1987) can go a long way in reducing television's negative effects and improving its role as a positive influence in children's development.

1. Develop good viewing habits early in the child's life.
2. Encourage planned viewing of specific programs rather than random viewing. Be active with young children between planned programs.
3. Look for children's programs that feature children in the child's age group.
4. Make sure that television is not used as a substitute for participating in other activities.
5. Develop discussion about sensitive television themes with children. Give them the opportunity to ask questions about the programs.
6. Balance reading and television activities. Children can "follow up" interesting television programs by checking out the library book from which some programs are adapted and by pursuing additional stories by the authors of those books.
7. Help children to develop a balanced viewing schedule of education, action, comedy, fine arts, fantasy, sports, and so on.
8. Point out positive examples that show how various ethnic and cultural groups all contribute to making a better society.
9. Point out positive examples of females performing competently both in professions and at home.

At this point we have discussed a number of ideas about peers, play, and television. A summary of these ideas is presented in Concept Table 9.2. Next, we turn to some further developments during early childhood—those pertaining to the self, gender roles, and moral development.

Personality Development

During early childhood, children's sense of self develops, their sense of gender roles and being male or female emerges, and their sense of morality intensifies.

The Self
We saw in chapter 7 that, toward the end of the second year of life, children develop a sense of self. Early childhood is a time when Erikson believes the self develops further and comes to grips with the crisis of initiative versus guilt, when it is important to consider distinctions between the self as "I" and "me," and when the child begins to understand that the self has both inner and outer dimensions.

How does the child's sense of self develop in early childhood?

Peers, Play and Television		
Concept	**Processes/Related Ideas**	**Characteristics/Description**
Peers	The Nature of Peer Relations	Peers are powerful social agents. The term *peers* refers to children who are about the same age or maturity level. Peers provide a source of information and comparison about the world outside the family.
	The Development of Peer Relations	The frequency of peer interaction, both positive and negative, increases during the preschool years.
	The Distinct but Coordinated Worlds of Parent-Child and Peer Relations	Peer relations are both similar to and dissimilar from family relations. Children touch, smile, and vocalize when they interact with parents and peers. However, rough-and-tumble play occurs mainly with peers. In times of stress, children generally seek out their parents. Healthy family relations usually promote healthy peer relations.
Play	Functions	Includes affiliation with peers, tension release, advances in cognitive development, exploration, and provision of a safe haven in which to engage in potentially dangerous activities.
	Types	Unoccupied, solitary, onlooker, parallel, associative, and cooperative play are among the most characteristic play styles. One of the most enjoyable forms of play in early childhood is pretend play, in which the child transforms the physical environment into a symbol.
Television	Functions	Includes provision of information and entertainment. Television provides a portrayal of the world beyond the family, teachers, and peers. However, television may train children to become passive learners, is deceiving, and often takes children away from reading and studying.
	Children's Exposure	Children watch huge amounts of television, with preschool children watching an average of four hours a day. Up to 80 percent of prime-time shows have violent episodes.
	Aggressive Behavior, Prosocial Behavior, Eating Behavior, and Social Context	Television violence is associated with children's aggression, but no causal link has been established. Prosocial behavior on television also is associated with increased positive behavior on the part of young children. The average television viewing child sees more than 20,000 commercials per year! Commercials influence children's food preferences. Parents rarely discuss television's contents with their children. Television-viewing habits often are formed in the early childhood years.

Initiative Versus Guilt

According to Erikson (1968), the psychosocial stage that characterizes early childhood is **initiative versus guilt.** By now, the child has become convinced that she is a person on her own; during early childhood, she must discover what kind of person she will become. She is deeply identified with her parents, who most of the time appear to her to be powerful and beautiful, although often unreasonable, disagreeable, and sometimes even dangerous. During early childhood, children use their perceptual, motor, cognitive, and language skills to make things happen. They have a surplus of energy that permits them to forget failures quickly and to approach new areas that seem desirable—even if they seem dangerous—with undiminished zest and some increased sense of direction. On their own **initiative,** then, children at this stage exhuberantly move out into a wider social world.

The great governor of initiative is **conscience.** Children now not only feel afraid of being found out, but they also begin to hear the inner voice of self-observation, self-guidance, and self-punishment. Their initiative and enthusiasm not only may bring them rewards, but also punishments. Widespread disappointment at this stage leads to an unleashing of guilt that drastically lowers the child's self-concept.

Whether children leave this stage with a sense of initiative outbalancing their sense of guilt depends to a considerable degree on how parents respond to their self-initiated activities. Children who are given freedom and opportunity to initiate motor play such as running, bike riding, sliding, skating, tusseling, and wrestling have their sense of initiative supported. Initiative also is supported when parents answer their children's questions and do not deride or inhibit fantasy or play activity. In contrast, if children are made to feel that their motor activity is bad, that their questions are a nuisance, and that their play is silly and stupid, then they may develop a sense of guilt over self-initiated activities that will persist through life's later stages (Elkind, 1970).

The Self's "I" and "Me"

Early in psychology's history, William James (1890) distinguished between the "I" and the "me" of the self. "I" is the knower, "me" is the object of what is known. "I" is the active observer, "me" is the observed (the product of the observing process). "I" conveys the sense of independent existence, agency, and volition (that is, when my eyes close, it gets dark; when I cry, my mother comes; when I bump my hand, it hurts; and so on). This part of the self, "I," emerges first in development. Later, the child learns that not only do "I" exist, but "I" also know the categories that go into making "me." "I" know, for example, that I am a boy and not a girl. Some researchers refer to "I" as the **existential self** and to "me" as the **categorical self.** Development proceeds in a sequence from the existential to the categorical self—from a conception that I am, I exist, to what or who I am (Lapsley & Power, 1988; Lapsley & Quintana, 1985; Lewis & Brooks-Gunn, 1979; Ruble, 1987; Wylie, 1979). Most of our discussion of the self focuses on the categorical self, especially self-concept.

The greatest interest in the self, however, has focused on "me," represented by children's self-concept and self-esteem. Remember from chapter 2 that Carl Rogers's humanistic perspective emphasized the importance of self-concept in understanding the child's personality; indeed, Rogers believed that self-concept is the core, organizing force of personality. Children develop their picture of "me" through interactions with significant others, especially parents. Rogers believed that children are especially sensitive to the praise and

When I say "I," I mean a thing absolutely unique, not to be confused with any other.
Ugo Betti, The Inquiry, *1944*

blame emanating from adults. For example, the child's thoughts may add up to this conclusion: You are bad, your behavior is bad, and you are not loved or loveable when you behave in this way.

How can the child develop a healthy, positive self-concept? Rogers said that parents should unconditionally love the child. Through positive regard from parents, the child experiences the feeling of being accepted, loved, and special. Even when a child's behavior is obnoxious, below acceptable standards, or inappropriate, the child needs to be respected, comforted, and loved. Parents need to distinguish between the child as a person of worth and dignity and the child's behavior, which may not deserve positive regard (Rogers, 1974).

One recent investigation of parenting and children's self-esteem revealed the importance of consistent parenting and sensitivity of parents to the young child's signals (Burkett, 1985). In particular, parents' respect for their children as individuals separate from them and as having their own needs were the best predictors of the preschool child's self-esteem.

An increasing number of clinicians and developmentalists believe that the core of the self—its basic inner organization—is derived from regularities in experience (Kohut, 1977; Sroufe, 1988). The child carries forward into early childhood a history of experiences with caregivers that provide the child with expectations about whether the world is pleasant or unpleasant. And in early childhood, the child continues to experience the positive or negative affect of caregivers. Despite developmental changes and context changes (increased peer contact, a wider social world), an important feature of the self's healthy development is continuity in caregiving and support, especially in the face of environmental challenges and stresses. As the child moves through the early childhood years, this continuity and support in caregiving gives the child confidence to show initiative and to increasingly be the author of her own experiences, something that enhances self-pride and self-esteem. Many clinicians stress that difficulties in interpersonal relationships derive from low self-esteem, which in turn derives from a lack of nurturance and support (Erikson, 1968; Kohut, 1977; Rogers, 1974; Sullivan, 1953).

The Self's Emerging Inner and Outer Dimensions

Children as young as 3 years of age have a basic idea that they have a private self to which others do not have access (Flavell, Shipstead, & Croft, 1978). For example, consider this exchange between an experimenter and a 3-year-old:

> (Can I see you thinking?) "No." (Even if I look in your eyes, do I see you thinking?) "No." (Why not?) " 'Cause I don't have any big holes." (You mean there would have to be a hole there for me to see you thinking?) Child nods. (p. 16)

Another child said that the experimenter could not see his thinking processes because he had a skin over his head.

Once they have developed an awareness of an inner self, between the ages of 3 to 4, children distinguish between this inner self and their outer or bodily self. Indeed, when asked to describe themselves, preschool children present a self portrait of external characteristics. They describe themselves in terms of how they look ("I'm big"), where they live ("I live in Chicago"), and the activities in which they participate ("I play with dolls"). It is not until about 6 to 7 years of age that children begin to describe themselves more in terms of psychological traits—how they feel, their personality characteristics, and their relationships with others, for example.

When do children develop a distinction between the inner self and the outer self?

What are little boys made of?
Frogs and snails,
And puppy dogs' tails.
What are little girls made of?
Sugar and spice
And all that's nice.

J. O. Halliwell, Nursery Rhymes of England,
1844

Gender Roles

As the child develops during the preschool years, gender roles assume an increasingly important place in personality development. **Gender roles** are social expectations of how we should act and think as males and females. Developmentalists have described the biological, cognitive, and environmental contributions to gender roles, and they have charted the course of gender role development in early childhood.

Biological Influences

One of Freud's basic assumptions is that human behavior and history are directly related to reproductive processes. From this assumption arises the belief that sexuality is essentially unlearned and instinctual. Erikson (1968) extended this argument, claiming that the psychological differences between males and females stem from anatomical differences. Erikson argued that—because of genital structure—males are more intrusive and aggressive, females are more inclusive and passive. Erikson's belief has become known as "anatomy is destiny." Critics of the anatomy is destiny view believe that Erikson has not given experience an adequate audience. They argue that males and females are more free to choose their gender role than Erikson allows. In response to the critics, Erikson has modified his view, saying that females in today's world are transcending their biological heritage and correcting society's overemphasis on male intrusiveness.

Biology's influence on gender roles also involves sex hormones, among the most powerful and subtle chemicals in nature. These hormones are controlled by the master gland in the brain, the pituitary. In females, hormones from the pituitary carry messages to the ovaries to produce the hormone **estrogen.** In males, the pituitary messages travel to the testes where the sex hormone **androgen** is manufactured.

The secretion of androgen from the testes of the young male fetus (or the absence of androgen in the female) completely controls sexual development in the womb. If enough androgen is produced, as happens with a normal developing boy, male organs and genitals develop. In instances where the hormone level is imbalanced (as in a developing male with insufficient androgen, or a female exposed to excess androgen), the genitals are intermediate between male and female (Money, 1987; Money & Ehrhardt, 1972). Such individuals are referred to as **hermaphrodites.**

Although estrogen is the dominant sex hormone in females and androgen fills this role in males, each individual's body contains both hormones. The amount of each hormone varies from one individual to the next; for example, a preschool boy's bass voice has more androgen than a preschool tenor's voice (Durden-Smith & Desimone, 1983). As we move from animals to humans, hormonal control over sexual behavior is less dominant. For example, when the testes of the male rat are removed (castration), sexual behavior declines and eventually ceases. But in humans, castration produces much greater variation in sexual behavior.

No one argues about the presence of genetic, biochemical, and anatomical differences between the sexes. Even psychologists with a strong environmental orientation acknowledge that boys and girls will be treated differently because of their physical differences and their different roles in reproduction. The importance of biological factors is not at issue. What is at issue is the directness or indirectness of their effects on social behavior (Huston, 1983).

For example, if a high androgen level directly influences the central nervous system, which in turn produces a higher activity level, then the effect is more direct. By contrast, if a high level of androgen produces strong muscle development, which in turn causes others to expect the child to be a good athlete and in turn leads her to participate in sports, then the biological effect is more direct.

While virtually everyone is an interactionist in thinking that children's behavior as males and females is due to an interaction of biological and environmental factors, an interactionist position means different things to different people (Maccoby, 1987; Money, 1987). For some it suggests that certain environmental conditions are required to make preprogrammed dispositions appear. For others it suggests that the same environment will have different effects depending on the predispositions of the child. For yet others it means that children shape their environments, including their interpersonal environments, as well as vice versa. Circular processes of influence and counterinfluence unfold over time. Throughout childhood, boys and girls are involved in active construction of their own version of acceptable masculine and feminine behavior patterns. As we see next, cognitive factors play an important role in this active construction.

Cognitive Influences

Cognitive factors influence gender roles during early childhood through self-categorization and language. Lawrence Kohlberg (1966) argued that to have an idea of what is masculine or feminine, a child must be able to categorize objects into these two groups—masculine and feminine. According to Kohlberg, the categories become relatively stable by the age of six. That is, by the age of six, children have a fairly definite idea of which category is theirs. Further, they understand what is entailed in belonging to one category or the other and seldom fluctuate in their category judgments. From Kohlberg's perspective, this self-categorization is the impetus for gender role development. Kohlberg reasons that gender role development proceeds in the following sequence: I am a boy, I want to do boy things; therefore, the opportunity to do boy things is rewarding. Having acquired the ability to categorize, children strive toward consistency in the use of the categories and their actual behavior. The striving for consistency forms the basis for gender role development (Ruble, 1987).

An important theme in the cognitive approach to children's gender role development is that the child's mind is set up to perceive and organize information according to a network of associations called a schema. A **gender schema** organizes the world in terms of female and male (Bem, 1985). Gender is a powerful organizing category to which children connect many experiences and attitudes. The gender schema approach emphasizes children's active construction of their gender role but also accepts that societies determine which schemata are important and the associations that are involved.

Gender roles also are present in the language children use and are exposed to. The nature of the language children hear most of the time is sexist. That is, the English language contains sex bias, especially in the use of "he" and "man" to refer to everyone. For example, in one recent investigation, mothers and their 1- to 3-year-old children looked at popular children's books, such as *The Three Bears,* together (DeLoache, Cassidy, & Carpenter, 1987). The Three Bears almost always were boys: 95% of all characters of indeterminate gender were referred to by the mothers as males. To learn more about children's experiences with sexism in language, turn to Focus on Life-Span Development 9.3.

HOW GOOD ARE GIRLS

AT WUDGEMAKING

IF THE WUDGEMAKER IS A "HE"?

In one investigation, the following description of a fictitious, gender-neutral occupation, wudgemaker, was read to third- and fifth-grade children, with repeated reference to *he, she, he or she,* or *they* (Hyde, 1984):

Few people have heard of a job in factories, being a wudgemaker. Wudges are made of plastic, oddly shaped, and are an important part of video games. The wudgemaker works from a plan or pattern posted at eye level as *he or she* puts together the pieces at a table while *he or she* is sitting down. Eleven plastic pieces must be snapped together. Some of the pieces are tiny, so the *he or she* must have good coordination in *his or her* fingers. Once all eleven pieces are put together, *he or she* must test out the wudge to make sure that all of the moving pieces move properly. The wudgemaker is well paid, and must be a high school graduate, but *he or she* does not have to have gone to college to get the job (p. 702).

One fourth of the children were read the story with *he* as the pronoun, one fourth with *she,* one fourth with *he or she* (as shown

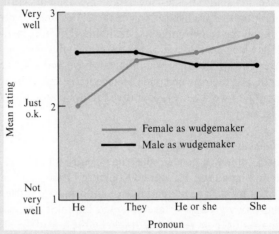

Figure 9.A *Mean ratings of how well women and men would do as wudgemakers, according to the pronoun used in the description. Notice that when she was used, children were more likely to say that women would perform well as wudgemakers than when other pronoun forms—he, he or she, and they—were used. From Janet Shibley Hyde, "Children's understanding of sexist language" in* Developmental Psychology, 20, *703, 1984. Copyright 1984 American Psychological Association. Reprinted by permission of the author.*

above), and one fourth with *they.* The children were asked to rate how well women could do the job of wudgemaking and also how well they thought men could perform the job. As shown in figure 9.A, ratings of how well women could make wudges was influenced by the pronoun used; ratings were lowest for *he,* intermediate for *they* and *he or she,* and highest for *she.* This suggests that the use of the gender-neutral *he*—compared to other pronouns—influences children's conception of how competent males and females are in our society.

Environmental Influences

In our culture, adults discriminate between the sexes shortly after the infant's birth. The "pink and blue" treatment may be applied to girls and boys before they leave the hospital. Soon afterward, differences in hairstyles, clothes, and toys become obvious. Adults and other children reward these differences throughout childhood, but girls and boys also learn appropriate gender role behavior by watching what other people say and do. For example, a 7-year-old boy who knows he is a boy and readily labels objects appropriately as male or female may have parents who support equality between the sexes; his behavior probably will be less stereotyped along masculine lines than that of boys reared in more traditional homes.

How is identification involved in psychoanalytic theory's portrayal of children's gender role development?

In recent years, the idea that parents are the critical socialization agents in gender role development has come under fire. Parents are only one of many sources—schools, peers, the media, and other family members are others—through which the child learns about gender roles. Yet it is important to guard against swinging too far in this direction, because—especially in the early years of development—parents do play important roles in children's gender roles.

Parents, by action and by example influence their children's gender role development. In the psychoanalytic view, this influence stems principally from the child's identification with the parent of the same sex. The child develops a sense of likeness to the parent of the same sex and strives to emulate that parent. But in reality, fathers and mothers are both psychologically important for children. Fathers seem to play an especially important part in gender role development. They are more likely to act differently toward sons and daughters than mothers are (Huston, 1983; Lamb, 1986). Parents provide the earliest discrimination of gender roles in the child's development, but before long, peers and teachers join the societal process of providing feedback about masculine and feminine roles.

Many parents encourage boys and girls to engage in different types of play and activities even during infancy (Lewis, 1987). Girls are more likely to be given dolls to play with, and when old enough, are more likely to be assigned baby-sitting duties. Girls are encouraged to be more nurturant and emotional than boys, and fathers are more likely to engage in rough-and-tumble play with sons than daughters. With increasing age, boys are permitted more freedom by parents who allow them to be away from home without supervision than are girls.

Without much doubt, parents do treat boys and girls differently in many instances. However, when parents treat boys and girls differently it is not always easy to sort through the direction of the effects (Maccoby, 1987). Do young boys like rough-and-tumble play because their fathers trained them to enjoy it, or because they, as well as their fathers, have a low threshold for initiation of this male-male pattern? The same types of questions crop up with regard to higher rates of punishment and other coercive treatment directed to boys by their parents. Is this a form of differential pressure initiated by parents that produces distinctively male behavior in boys or is it a consequence of something boys are doing in interacting with their parents that elicits this kind of parent behavior? Probably reciprocal and circular processes are at work as parents differentially socialize their sons and daughters and their sons and daughters socialize them.

Parents provide the earliest discrimination of gender roles in children's development, but before long, peers and teachers join the societal process of responding to and providing feedback about masculine and feminine behavior. Most children have already acquired a preference for masculine or feminine toys and activities before they are exposed to school. During the preschool and elementary school years, teachers and peers maintain these preferences through feedback to the boy or to the girl. Children who play in sex-appropriate activities tend to be rewarded for doing so by their peers. Those who play in cross-sexed activities tend to be criticized by their peers or left to play alone. Children show a clear preference for being with and liking same-sexed peers (Maccoby & Jacklin, in press), and this tendency often becomes stronger as children move from the preschool years through the middle elementary school years (Hayden-Thomson, Rubin, & Hymel, 1987). This increase probably reflects children's growing awareness of culturally prescribed expectancies for males and females. Even when a deliberately engineered program of reinforcing children for cross-sex play reduces segregation temporarily, playmate choices return quickly toward a segregated pattern once the behavior modification program is discontinued (Serbin, Tonick, & Sternberg, 1977).

After extensive observations of school playgrounds, two researchers characterized the play settings as "gender school," pointing out that boys teach others the required masculine behavior and enforce it strictly (Luria & Herzog, 1985). Girls also pass on the female culture (distinctively female games such as jump rope or jacks) and congregate mostly with each other. Individual "tomboy" girls can join boys' activities without losing their status in the girls' groups, but the reverse is not true for boys, reflecting our society's greater sex-typing pressure for boys.

Gender segregation is important because it provides the conditions under which two different childhood cultures are formed and maintained (Maccoby, 1987). Children's bias toward same sex play suggests that any society, or any set of parents, would have to exert extensive pressure if they wanted to get children to select playmates without regard to gender. Yet adults clearly do affect the extent that play is segregated by establishing the conditions under which play normally occurs.

In school, teachers react more negatively to boys than to girls in early schooling and are more likely to reward feminine behavior in boys and girls—being quiet, being conforming, and being unassertive, for example (Fagot, 1975). However, in one investigation in which the teachers were males, feminine and masculine behavior were equally rewarded (McCandless, 1973). This raises the intriguing—but untested—question of whether there would be more support for masculine behavior in children's early schooling if more of the teachers were males.

The Development of Gender Roles
During the 18-month to 3-year-old age period, children start expressing considerable interest in gender-typed activities and classify themselves according to gender. From 3 to 7 years of age, children begin to acquire an understanding of gender constancy and increasingly enjoy being with same-sex peers. During

early childhood, young children also tend to make grand generalizations about gender roles. For example, 3-year-old William accompanied his mother to the doctor's office. A man in a white coat walked by and William said, "Hi, Doc." Then a woman in a white coat walked by and William greeted her, "Hi, nurse." William's mother asked him how he knew which individual was a doctor and which was a nurse. William replied, "Because doctors are daddies and nurses are mommies." As Piaget warned, young children are so sure of their thoughts, yet so often inaccurately understand the world. William's "nurse" turned out to be his doctor, and vice versa (Carper, 1978).

Moral Development

In one sense, moral development has a longer history than virtually any topic we discuss in this book. In prescientific periods, philosophers and theologians heatedly debated the child's moral status at birth, which they felt had important implications for how the child should be reared. Recall from chapter 1 the original sin, *tabula rasa,* and innate goodness views of the child. Today, pepole are hardly neutral about moral development. Most have strong opinions about what is acceptable and unacceptable behavior, ethical and unethical conduct, and the ways that acceptable and ethical conduct should be fostered in children.

Moral development concerns rules and conventions about what people *should* do in their interactions with other people. In studying these rules, developmentalists examine three different domains. First, how do children *reason* or *think* about rules for ethical conduct? For example, consider cheating. The child can be presented with a story in which someone has a conflict about whether or not to cheat in a particular situation, such as taking a test in school. The child is asked to decide what is appropriate for the character to do and why. The focus is placed on children's reasoning that is used to justify their moral decisions.

Second, how do children actually *behave* in moral circumstances? In our example of cheating, emphasis is on observing the child's cheating and the environmental circumstances that produced and maintain the cheating. Children might be presented with some toys and asked to select which one they believed was the most attractive. Then, the experimenter tells the young child that the particular toy selected is someone else's and is not to be played with. Observations of different conditions under which the child deviates from the prohibition or resists temptation would be conducted.

Third, how does the child *feel* about moral matters? In the example of cheating, does the child feel enough guilt to resist temptation? If children do cheat, do feelings of guilt after the transgression keep them from cheating the next time they face temptation? In the remainder of this section, we focus on these three facets of moral development—thought, action, and feeling. Then, we will evaluate the positive side of children's moral development—altruism.

Piaget's View of Moral Reasoning

Interest in how the child thinks about moral issues has been stimulated by Piaget (1932), who extensively observed and interviewed children from the ages of 4 to 12. He watched them play marbles, wanting to learn how they used and thought about the game's rules. He also asked children questions about ethical rules—theft, lies, punishment, and justice, for example. Piaget concluded that children think in two distinctly different ways about morality depending on their developmental maturity. The more primitive way of thinking—**heteronomous morality**—is displayed by younger children (from 4 to 7 years of age); the more advanced way of thinking—**autonomous morality**—is displayed by older children (10 years of age and older). Children 7 to 10 years of age are in a transition between the two stages, evidencing some features of both stages.

What are some of the characteristics of heteronomous morality and autonomous morality? The heteronomous thinker judges the rightness or goodness of behavior by considering the consequences of the behavior, not the intentions of the actor. For example, the heteronomous thinker says that breaking twelve cups accidently is worse than breaking one cup intentionally while trying to steal a cookie. For the moral autonomist, the reverse is true; the actor's intention assumes paramount importance. The heteronomous thinker also believes that rules are unchangeable and are handed down by all-powerful authorities. When Piaget suggested that new rules be introduced into the game of marbles, the young children resisted. They insisted that the rules had always been the same and could not be changed. By contrast, older children—who were moral autonomists—accept change and recognize that rules are merely convenient, socially agreed-upon conventions, subject to change by consensus.

The heteronomous thinker also believes in **immanent justice**—if a rule is broken, punishment will be meted out immediately. He believes that the violation is connected in some automatic or mechanical way to the punishment. Thus, young children often look around worriedly after committing a transgression, expecting inevitable punishment. Research continues to verify that immanent justice declines toward the end of the elementary school years (e.g., Jose, 1985). Older children—who are moral autonomists—recognize that punishment is socially mediated and occurs only if a relevant person witnesses the wrongdoing and that, even then, punishment is not inevitable.

Piaget argued that, as children develop, they become more sophisticated in thinking about social matters, especially about the possibilities and conditions of cooperation. Piaget believed that this social understanding comes about through the mutual give-and-take of peer relations. In the peer group—where others have power and status similar to the individual—plans are negotiated and coordinated, disagreements are reasoned about and eventually settled. Parent-child relations—where parents have the power and the child does not—are less likely to advance moral reasoning because rules are often handed down in an authoritarian way, thought Piaget. Later, in chapter 11, we discuss another highly influential cognitive view of moral development, that of Lawrence Kohlberg.

Moral Behavior

The study of moral behavior has been influenced by social learning theory. The familiar processes of reinforcement, punishment, and imitation are invoked to explain how and why children morally behave. When children are rewarded for behavior that is consistent with laws and social conventions, they are likely to repeat that behavior. When models who behave morally are provided, children are likely to adopt their actions. And when children are punished for immoral behavior, those behaviors are likely to be reduced or eliminated. However, because punishment may have adverse side effects, it needs to be used judiciously and cautiously.

Another important point needs to be made about the social learning view of moral development: moral behavior is influenced extensively by the situation. What children do in one situation is often only weakly related to what

Every man takes care that his neighbor shall not cheat him. But a day comes when he begins to care that he does not cheat his neighbor. Then all goes well.
Ralph Waldo Emerson, The Conduct of Life, *1860*

Early Childhood

they do in other situations. A child may cheat in math class, but not in English class; a child may steal a piece of candy when others are not present, and not steal it when they are present; and so on. More than half a century ago, morality's situational nature was observed in a comprehensive study of thousands of children in many different situations—at home, at school, at church, for example. The totally honest child was virtually non-existent; so was the child who cheated in all situations (Hartshorne & May, 1928–30).

Social learning theorists also believe that the ability to resist temptation is closely tied to the development of self-control. Children must overcome their impulses for something they want but is prohibited. To accomplish this self-control, they must learn to be patient and to delay gratification. Today, social learning theorists believe cognitive factors are important in the child's development of self-control. For example, in one investigation (Mischel & Patterson, 1976), children's cognitive transformations of desired objects helped children to become more patient. Preschool children were asked to engage in a boring task. Close by was an enticing mechanical clown who tried to persuade the children to come play with him. The children who had been trained to say to themselves, "I'm not going to look at Mr. Clown when Mr. Clown says to look at him," controlled their behavior and continued working on the dull task much longer than those who did not instruct themselves.

Even young children respond with empathy.

What is moral is what you feel good after and what is immoral is what you feel bad after.
  Ernest Hemingway, Death in the Afternoon, *1932*

Moral Feelings and Guilt

In the psychoanalytic account of guilt, children avoid transgressing to avoid anxiety; by contrast, a child with little guilt has little reason to resist temptation. Guilt is responsible for harnessing the id's evil drives and for maintaining the world as a safe place to be. Early childhood is a special time for the development of guilt. It is during this time period, thought Freud, that through identification with parents and parents' use of love withdrawal for discipline, children turn their hostility inward and experience guilt. The guilt is primarily unconscious and reflects the structure of the personality known as the superego. Remember also that Erikson believes early childhood has special importance in the development of guilt; he even called the major conflict to be resolved in early childhood initiative versus *guilt*.

Moral feelings or affect have traditionally been thought of in terms of guilt, but recently there has been considerable interest in empathy's role in the child's moral development. **Empathy** is the ability to understand the feelings of another individual, and as we see next, it is believed to be an important aspect of the child's altruism.

Altruism

In studying guilt, cheating, lying, stealing, and resistance to temptation, we are investigating the antisocial, negative side of moral development. Today, we recognize that it is important not to dwell too much on the dark side of morality; perhaps we should spend more time evaluating and promoting the positive side of morality—prosocial behavior, altruism, and empathy, for example.

Altruism is an unselfish interest in helping someone. Human acts of altruism are plentiful—the hard-working laborer who places a $5 dollar bill in a Salvation Army kettle, rock concerts organized by Bob Geldof and Willie

Nelson to feed the hungry and help farmers, and a child who takes in a wounded cat and cares for it. How do psychologists account for such frequent accounts of altruism?

Reciprocity and exchange are important aspects of altruism (Brown, 1986). Reciprocity is found throughout the human world. It is not only the highest moral principle in Christianity but also is present in every widely practiced religion in the world—Judaism, Hinduism, Buddism, and Islam. Reciprocity encourages us to do unto others as we would have them do unto us. Certain human sentiments are wrapped up in this reciprocity: trust probably is the most important principle over the long run; guilt emerges if we do not reciprocate; and anger results if someone else does not reciprocate. Not all human altruism is motivated by reciprocity and social exchange, but this view alerts us to the importance of considering self-other interactions and relationships in understanding altruism. The circumstances most likely to involve altruism are empathetic or sympathetic emotion for an individual in need or a close relationship between the benefactor and the recipient (Batson, in press; Clark & others, 1987; Lerner, 1982).

Although altruism seems to increase as children become older, examples of caring for others and comforting someone in distress are abundant during the preschool years (Eisenberg, 1987). The following vivid episode suggests its presence even as early as the second year of life:

> Today, Jerry was kind of cranky; he just started completely bawling and he wouldn't stop. John kept coming over and handing Jerry toys, trying to cheer him up, so to speak. He'd say things like, "Here, Jerry," and I said to John: "Jerry's sad; he doesn't feel good; he had a shot today." John would look at me with his eyebrows kind of wrinkled together like he really understood that Jerry was crying because he was unhappy, not that he was just being a crybaby. He went over and rubbed Jerry's arm and said, "Nice Jerry" and continued to give him toys (Zahn-Waxler, Radke-Yarrow, & King, 1979, pp. 321–322).

One way to explain altruism's presence in young children is their motivation to understand the feelings of others and to experience those feelings themselves (Denham, 1986; Fogel & Melson, 1987). If we see people cry or become sad and we share their distress, we may become motivated to help them relieve the distress. The empathy we feel and share with others, then, may be altruism's engine. The early preschool years may have a special importance in understanding empathy and altruism because it is at this point in development when children begin to recognize that other people have their own feelings and needs. Are there ways parents can develop these positive feelings in their young children? Several suggestions include (Hoffman, 1984): Expose children to a wider range of feelings; it is hard for children to empathize with someone who is experiencing an emotion the children have never felt. Direct the child's attention to others' feelings—say to the child something like, "How do you think Sam felt when you socked him?" Ensure that children have models around them in their daily lives who not only show altruistic behavior but who verbalize the empathetic feelings that underlie it. Emerson once said, "The meaning of good and bad, better and worse, is simply helping or hurting." By developing the capacity for empathy and altruism young children possess, we can become a nation of *good* people who *help* rather than hurt.

Summary

I. **Parenting Styles**

Four major categories of parenting styles are: authoritarian, authoritative, permissive indulgent, and permissive indifferent. Authoritative parenting is associated with children's social competence more than the other styles. Parents need to adapt their interaction strategies as the child grows older, using less physical manipulation and more reasoning in the process.

II. **Sibling Relationships**

More than 80 percent of American children have one or more siblings. Siblings interact with each other in more negative, less positive, and less varied ways than parents and children interact. In some cases, siblings are stronger socializing influences than parents. The relationship of the first born child and parents seems to be especially close and demanding, which may account for the greater achievement and anxiety in first born children. Variations also are associated with those born later and only children.

III. **The Changing Family**

A mother's working full-time outside the home can have positive or negative effects on the child; there is no indication of long-term negative effects overall. Family conflict seems to outweigh family structure in its impact on the child; conflict is greatest in the first year after the divorce. A continuing ongoing positive relationship with the ex-spouse is important for the child's adjustment. Support systems are significant in the child's adaptation to divorce. Boys fare better in father custody families, girls in mother custody families.

IV. **Peers**

Peers are powerful social agents. The term *peers* refers to children who are about the same age or maturity level. Peers provide a source of information and comparison about the world outside the family. The frequency of peer interaction, both positive and negative, increases during the preschool years. Peer relations are both similar to and different from family relations.

V. **Play**

Play's functions include affiliation with peers, tension release, advances in cognitive development, exploration, and provision of a safe haven in which to engage in potentially dangerous activities. The types of play include unoccupied, solitary, onlooker, parallel, associative, and cooperative play, as well as pretend play.

VI. **Television**

Television's functions include entertainment and information. Television presents a more diverse view of the world than can be experienced in one's family, school, or peer group. However, television may train children to become passive learners, is deceiving, and often takes children away from studying and reading. Children watch huge amounts of television and this watching is associated with their aggression, altruism, eating behavior, and social contexts of viewing.

VII. **The Self**

Early childhood is a period when Erikson believes the self involves resolving the conflict between initiative versus guilt, when it is important to consider the distinction between "I" and "me," and when the child begins to understand that the self has both inner and outer dimensions. "I" is the existential self, the self as knower, "me" is the categorical self, the object of what is known, which usually is studied by investigating the child's self-concept. Rogers believes the child's self-concept can be improved by unconditionally loving the child.

VIII. **Gender Roles**

Gender roles are social expectations of how we should act and think as males and females. Gender roles are influenced by biological, cognitive, and environmental factors. Freud's and Erikson's theories promoted the idea that anatomy is destiny; hormones influence sexual development, although not as pervasively in humans as in animals. Today's psychologists are all interactionists in terms of biological and environmental influences on gender roles, but interaction means different things to different people. Cognitive factors that influence gender roles are self-categorization and language. An important theme in the cognitive approach is that children develop a gender schema. Environmental factors are parent-child relations, peer relations, and teacher-child relations. Considerable development in gender roles takes place during early childhood; at this time children often make grand generalizations about gender roles.

IX. **Moral Development**

Moral development concerns rules and regulations about what people should do in their interactions with others. Developmentalists study how children think, behave, and feel about such rules and regulations. Piaget distinguished between the heteronomous morality of younger children and the moral autonomy of older children. The study of moral behavior has been influenced by social learning theory; emphasis is placed on the importance of the situation and self-control. Psychoanalytic theory emphasizes the importance of moral feelings and guilt. Altruism is an unselfish interest in helping someone; reciprocity and exchange are important aspects of altruism. Empathy plays a key role in the development of altruism in young children.

Key Terms

authoritarian parenting   249
authoritative parenting   249
permissive indulgent parenting   249
permissive indifferent parenting   250
father absence tradition   254
peers   257
play therapy   260
unoccupied play   261
solitary play   261
onlooker play   261

parallel play   262
associative play   262
cooperative play   262
pretend play   262
initiative versus guilt   268
initiative   268
conscience   268
existential self   268
categorical self   268
gender roles   270

estrogen   270
androgen   270
hermaphrodites   270
gender schema   271
moral development   275
heteronomous morality   276
autonomous morality   276
immanent justice   276
empathy   278
altruism   278

Suggested Readings

Hetherington, E. M., Hagan, M. S., & Anderson, E. R. (1988). Family transitions: a child's perspective. *American Psychologist.*
Hetherington is a leading researcher in the investigation of the effects of divorce on children's development. In this article she and her colleagues review the recent literature on divorce, giving special attention to transitions in divorced and stepparent families.

Hartup, W. W. (1983). The peer system. In P. H. Mussen (Ed.), *Handbook of Child Psychology* (4th ed), Vol. 4. New York: Wiley.
A detailed look at the development of peer relations from one of the leading experts in the field, Willard Hartup.

Liebert, R. M., & Sprakin, J. N. (1988). *The early window: Effects of television on children and youth,* 3rd ed. Elmsford, NY: Pergamon.
An updated account of theory and research that addresses the effects of television on children's development.

Reinisch, J. M., Rosenblum, L. A., & Sanders, S. A. (Eds.) (1987). *Masculinity/femininity.* New York: Oxford U. Press.
An outstanding collection of articles by leading experts such as Eleanor Maccoby, John Money, and Jacqueline Eccles. Includes a special section of papers on the development of gender roles.

Rubin, K. H., Fein, G. G., & Vandenberg, B. (1983). Play: In P. H. Mussen (Ed.), *Handbook of Child Psychology* (4th ed.), Vol. 4. New York: Wiley.
A thorough, detailed analysis of what we know about children's play; describes directions in which developmentalists' interests in play are moving.

White, B. L. (1988). *Educating the infant and toddler.* Lexington, MA: Lexington Books.
Competent, extensive information about better ways for parents to interact with their children is provided by Burton White, a leader in the development of parent education programs.

S E C T I O N V

Middle and Late Childhood

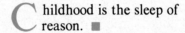

C hildhood is the sleep of
reason. ■

Rousseau

CHAPTER

10

■

Physical and Cognitive Development

Intelligence and intelligence tests frequently make the news. The following story appeared in the *Los Angeles Times:*

> IQ testing that leads to the placement of an unusually large number of black children in so-called mentally retarded classes has been ruled unconstitutional by a federal judge. On behalf of five black children, Chief District Court Judge Robert Peckham said the use of standardized IQ tests to place children in educable mentally retarded (EMR) classes violated recently enacted federal laws and the state and federal constitutions. . . . Peckham said the history of IQ testing and special education in California "revealed an unlawful discriminatory intent . . . not necessarily to hurt black children, but it was an intent to assign a grossly disproportionate number of black children to the special, inferior and dead-end EMR classes." (October 18, 1979).

As you might expect, this story sparked impassioned debate (Kail & Pellegrino, 1985). The use of IQ tests to selectively place children in special classes continues to be debated.

Robert Sternberg recalls being terrified of taking IQ tests as a child. He says that he literally froze when the time came to take such tests. When he was in the sixth grade, he was sent to take an IQ test with the fifth graders and still talks about how embarrassing and humiliating the experience was. Sternberg recalls that maybe he was dumb, but knows that he wasn't *that* dumb. He finally overcame his anxieties about IQ tests and performed much better on them. Sternberg became so fascinated with IQ tests that he devised his own at the age of 13 and began assessing the intellectual abilities of his classmates until the school psychologist scolded him. Later in the chapter you will see that Sternberg recently has developed a provocative theory of intelligence.

Intellectual performance and achievement are prized by our society and promoted by parents who enthusiastically encourage their charges to become brighter and more strongly motivated to achieve success. During middle and late childhood, the push for intellectual performance and achievment becomes more apparent to children than earlier in their development. Now, they usually are spending far more of their time in the achievement setting of school and are placed in circumstances that call on them to exhibit their intellectual skills in more pressurized ways than they were in early childhood. Before we consider these intellectual and achievement changes in middle and late childhood in greater depth, it is also important to evaluate the physical changes that are taking place at this time.

Physical Development

During the elementary school years, children grow an average of 2 to 3 inches per year until—at about the age of 11—the average girl is 4 feet, 10 inches tall and the average boy is 4 feet, 9½ inches tall. Weight increases range from 3 to 5 pounds per year until—at the age of 11—the average girl weighs 88½ pounds and the average boy weighs 85½ pounds (Krogman, 1970).

In middle and late childhood, children's legs become longer and their trunks slimmer, and they are steadier on their feet. Fat tissue develops more rapidly than muscle tissue (which increases substantially in adolescence). Children who had a rounded, somewhat "chubby" body build—referred to as **endomorphic**—have noticeably more fat tissue than muscle tissue; the reverse is true of children with athletic, muscular body builds—referred to as **mesomorphic.** Other children have a skinny, thin body build—they are referred to as **ectomorphic.**

During middle and late childhood, children's motor development becomes much smoother and more coordinated than in early childhood. For example, only one child in a thousand can hit a tennis ball over the net at the age of 4; most children, though, can learn to play this sport by the age of 11. In the early elementary school years, children become competent at running, throwing, climbing, catching, swimming, skipping a rope, bicycle riding, and skating, to name just a few of the physical skills, that when mastered, are sources of pleasure and accomplishment. There are usually marked sex differences in these gross motor skills, with boys outperforming girls handily. However, in fine motor skills—drawing and penmanship, for example—girls usually outperform boys.

During middle and late childhood, sensory mechanisms continue to mature. Early farsightedness is overcome, binocular vision becomes well developed, and hearing acuity increases. Children of this age have fewer illnesses than younger children, especially fewer respiratory and gastrointestinal problems. Widespread immunization has considerably reduced the incidence of disease, and many illnesses can be prevented by practicing good health, safety, and nutrition habits. By middle and late childhood, children seem to understand that good health is something they have to work at almost continually. They recognize that nutrition and physical fitness are important for maintaining good health. But while elementary school children *say* they have to work to have good health through nutrition and exercise, recall from chapter 8 that there is a gap between children's awareness and their *behavior;* recent surveys indicate that our nation's children are in poor physical shape by the time they enter the first grade and their poor physical fitness continues through the adolescent years.

Soccer, little league baseball, basketball, tennis, dance—as children's motor development becomes smoother and more coordinated, they are able to master these activities more competently in middle and late childhood than in early childhood.

Piaget's Theory and Cognitive Developmental Changes in Middle and Late Childhood

As discussed in chapter 8, according to Piaget (1967), the preschool child's thought is preoperational. Preoperational thought involves the formation of stable concepts, the emergence of mental reasoning, the prominence of egocentrism, and the construction of magical belief systems. Thought during the preschool years is still flawed and not well organized. Piaget believed that concrete operational thought does not appear until about the age of seven, but as we saw in chapter 8, he may have underestimated some of preschool children's cognitive skills. For example, by carefully and cleverly designing experiments on understanding the concept of number, Rochel Gelman (1972) demonstrated that some preschool children show conservation, a concrete operational skill. In chapter 8, we explored concrete operational thought by describing the preschool child's flaws in thinking about such concrete operational skills as conservation and classification; here we cover the characteristics of concrete operational thought again, this time emphasizing the elementary school child's competencies. Applications of Piaget's ideas to children's education and an evaluation of Piaget's theory are also considered.

Our life is what our thoughts make it.
Marcus Aurelius, Meditations,
2nd Century B.C.

Physical and Cognitive Development

Concrete Operational Thought

Remember that, according to Piaget, concrete operational thought is made up of operations—mental actions or representations that are reversible. In the well-known test of reversibility of thought involving conservation of matter, the child is presented with two identical balls of clay. The experimenter rolls one ball into a long, thin shape; the other remains in its original ball shape. The child is then asked if there is more clay in the ball or the long, thin piece of clay. By the time children reach the age of 7 or 8, most answer that the amount of clay is the same. To answer this problem correctly, children have to imagine that the clay ball is rolled out into a long, thin strip and then returned to its original round shape—imagination that involves a reversible mental action. Thus, a concrete operation is a reversible mental action on real, concrete objects. Concrete operations allow the child to coordinate several characteristics rather than focusing on a single property of an object. In the clay example, the preoperational child is likely to focus on height *or* width; the concrete operational child coordinates information about both dimensions.

Many of the concrete operations identified by Piaget focus on the way children reason about the properties of objects. One imporant skill that characterizes the concrete operational child is the ability to classify or divide things into different sets or subsets and to consider their interrelationships. An example of the concrete operational child's classification skills involves a family tree of four generations (see figure 10.1) (Furth & Wachs, 1975). This family tree suggests that the grandfather (A) has three children (B, C, & D), each of whom has two children (E through J), and that one of these children (J) has three children (K, L, & M). A child who comprehends the classification system can move up and down a level (vertically), across a level (horizontally), and up and down and across (obliquely) within the system. The concrete operational child understands that person J can at the same time be father, brother, and grandson, for example.

While concrete operational thought is more advanced than preoperational thought, it has its limitations. Concrete operational thought is limited in that the child needs to have clearly available perceptual physical supports. That is, the child needs to have objects and events present to reason about them. The concrete operational thinker is not capable of imagining the necessary steps to complete an algebraic equation, for example. More information about thought that is more advanced than concrete operational thought appears in chapter 12, where we discuss formal operational thought.

Piaget and Education

Americans—interested in improving children's intellect—moved swiftly to embrace Piaget and apply his ideas to children's education (Murray, 1978). Two social crises, the proliferation of behaviorism and the psychometric, IQ approach to intelligence, made the adoption of Piaget's theory inevitable. The first social crisis was the post-Sputnik concern of a country preoccupied with its deteriorating position as the world's leader in engineering and science, and the second was the need for compensatory education for minority groups and the poor. Curriculum projects that soon came into being after these social crises included the "new math," Science Curriculum Improvement Study, Project Physics, and Man: A Course of Study. All of these projects were based on Piaget's notion of cognitive developmental changes. Piaget's theory contains information about the child's reasoning in the areas of math, science, and logic—information not found anywhere else in developmental psychology.

Piaget was not an educator and never pretended to be. But he did provide a sound conceptual framework from which to view educational problems. What

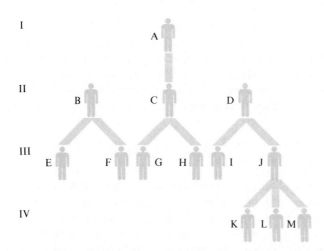

are some of the principles in Piaget's theory of cognitive development that can be applied to children's education? David Elkind (1976) described three. First, the foremost issue in education is *communication*. In Piaget's theory, the child's mind is not a blank slate; to the contrary, the child has a host of ideas about the physical and natural world, but these ideas differ from those of adults. We must learn to comprehend what children are saying and to respond in the same mode of discourse that children use. Second, the child is always unlearning and relearning in addition to acquiring knowledge. Children come to school with their own ideas about space, time, causality, quantity, and number. Third, the child is by nature a knowing creature, motivated to acquire knowledge. The best way to nurture this motivation for knowledge is to allow the child to spontaneously interact with the environment; education needs to ensure that it does not dull the child's eagerness to know by providing an overly rigid curricula that disrupts the child's own rhythm and pace of learning (Gallagher & Bidell, 1988; Liben, Downs, & Daggs, 1988).

Piagetian Contributions and Criticisms

Piaget was a genius when it came to observing children, and his insights are often surprisingly easy to verify. Piaget showed us some important things to look for in development, including the shift from preoperational to concrete operational thought. He also showed us how we must make experiences fit our cognitive framework, yet simultaneously adapt our cognitive orientation to experience. Piaget also revealed how cognitive change is likely to occur if the situation is structured to allow gradual movement to the next higher level.

But Piaget's view has not gone unquestioned. Four sorts of findings question the Piagetian approach to cognitive development (Gelman & Baillareon, 1983; Kuhn, 1984; Inhelder, De Caprona, & Cornu-Wells, in press). First, Piaget conceived of stages as unitary structures of thought, so his theory assumes that there is a synchrony in development. That is, various aspects of a stage should emerge at about the same time. However, several concrete operational concepts do not appear in synchrony—for example, children do not learn to conserve at the same time they learn to cross-classify. Second, small changes in the procedures involved in a Piagetian task sometimes have significant effects on a child's cognition. Third, in some cases, children who are at one cognitive stage—such as preoperational thought—can be trained to reason at a higher cognitive stage—such as concrete operational thought. This poses a problem for Piaget's theory, who argued that such training only works on a superficial level and is ineffective unless the child is at a transitional point

Figure 10.2
Use of the keyword method to improve children's memory. To help children remember the state capitals, the keyword method was used. A special component of the keyword method is the use of mental imagery, which was stimulated by the presentation to the children of a vivid visual image, such as the one shown here of two apples being married. The strategy is to help the children to associate apple *with Annapolis and* marry *with Maryland.*

from one stage to the next. Fourth, some cognitive abilities emerge earlier than Piaget believed and their subsequent development may be more prolonged than he thought. Conservation of number has been demonstrated in children as young as 3 years of age, although Piaget did not believe it came about until 7 years of age; some aspects of formal operational thought that involve abstract reasoning do not consistently appear as early in adolescence as Piaget believed.

Information Processing

Among the highlights of changes in information processing during middle and late childhood are improvements in memory, schemata, and scripts. Remember also, from chapter 8, that the attention of most children improves dramatically during middle and late childhood, and that at this time children attend more to the task-relevant than salient features of a problem.

Memory

In chapter 8, we concluded that tasks involving short-term memory—the memory span task, for example—reveal a considerable increase in short-term memory during early childhood, but after the age of 7 do not show as much increase. Is the same pattern found for **long-term memory,** information we retain indefinitely that can be used over and over again? Long-term memory shows a different pattern of development than short-term memory during childhood: Long-term memory increases with age during middle and late childhood. Two aspects of memory related to improvement in long-term memory are control processes and learner characteristics.

If we know anything at all about long-term memory, it is that long-term memory depends on the learning activities that individuals engage in when learning and remembering information. Most learning activities fit under the category of effortful **control processes.** These activities are under the learner's conscious control—they are also appropriately referred to as *strategies* (Weinert & Perlmutter, 1988; Wellman, 1988). Three important control processes involved in children's memory are rehearsal, organization, and imagery.

One control process or strategy for improving children's memory is **rehearsal,** which involves the repetition of information after it has been presented—as when a child is trying to remember a phone number, for example. Researchers have found that children's spontaneous use of rehearsal increases between the ages of 5 and 10 (Flavell, Beach, & Chimsky, 1966). The use of organization also improves memory—as with rehearsal, children in middle and late childhood are more likely to spontaneously organize information to be remembered than children in early childhood (Moely & others, 1969).

Another control process that develops as children move through middle and late childhood is imagery. A powerful imagery strategy is the *keyword method,* which has been used to practical advantage by teaching elementary school children how to rapidly master new information such as foreign vocabulary words, the states and capitals of the United States, and the names of United States Presidents. For example, in remembering that Annapolis is the capital of Maryland, children were taught the keywords for the states, such that when a state was given (*Maryland*) they could supply the keyword (*marry*) (Levin, 1980). Then, children were given the reverse type of keyword practice with the capitals. That is, they had to respond with the capital (*Annapolis*) when given a keyword (*apple*). Finally, an illustration was provided (see figure 10.2). The keyword strategy's use of vivid mental imagery, such as the image in figure 10.2, was effective in increasing children's memory of state capitals. Developmentalists today encourage the use of imagery in our nation's schools, believing it helps to increase the child's memory (McDaniel & Pressley, 1987).

In addition to these control processes, the characteristics of the child influence memory. Apart from the obvious variable of age, many characteristics of the child determine the effectiveness of memory. These characteristics include attitude, motivation, and health. However, the characteristic that has been examined the most thoroughly is the child's previously acquired knowledge. What the child's mind knows has a tremendous effect on what the child remembers. In one investigation, 10-year-old children who were chess experts remembered chess board positions much better than adults who did not play a lot of chess (Chi, 1978). However, the children did not do as well as the adults when both groups were asked to remember a group of random numbers; the children's expertise in chess gave them superior memories, but only in chess.

The two factors of knowledge and control factors are tightly intertwined. Indeed, one important type of memory knowledge actually concerns control processes; this knowledge is **metamemory**—knowledge about one's memory. Researchers have found that children's metamemory improves from the preschool years through adolescence (Brown & others, 1983; Flavell, 1985; Flavell & Wellman, 1977).

Schemata and Scripts

Many developmentalists believe that it is necessary to consider the concepts of schemata and scripts when we try to explain children's knowledge. When we reconstruct information, we often fit it into information already existing in our mind. The existing information we have about various concepts, events, and knowledge is called **schemata** (schema is the singular). Schemata come from prior encounters with the environment and influence the way children encode, make inferences about, and retrieve information. Children have schemata for stories, scenes, spatial layouts (a bathroom or a park), and common events (going to a restaurant, playing with toys, practicing soccer). Schemata for events are called **scripts** (Schank & Abelson, 1977). Children's first scripts appear very early in development, perhaps as early as the first year of life. Children clearly have scripts by the time they enter school; as they develop, their scripts become less crude and more sophisticated. For example, a 4-year-old's script for a restaurant might only include information about sitting down and eating food. By middle and late childhood, the child will have added information about the types of people who serve food, paying the cashier, and so on to the restaurant script.

So far, we have learned a great deal about how children process information about their world. Through a number of chapters, we have studied how they attend to information, perceive it, retain it over time, and draw inferences about it. Recently, ways the information processing approach can be applied to children's education have been considered (Gagne, 1985; White, in press). To learn more about this application, turn to Focus on Life-Span Development 10.1. A summary of our discussion of physical development, Piaget's theory and cognitive developmental changes, and information processing in middle and late childhood is presented in Concept Table 10.1.

Imagine you are a child standing on a beach feeding some seagulls. What characteristics might influence your ability to remember the details of feeding the seagulls?

The thirst to know and understand . . .
These are the goods in life's rich hand.
Sir William Watson, 1905

Imagine that you have been asked to develop an information processing curriculum for first grade students. What would be the curriculum's main themes?

INFORMATION PROCESSING,
THE INFORMATION AGE,
AND CHILDREN'S EDUCATION

When you were in elementary school, did any teacher at any time work with you on improving your memory strategies? Did any of your teachers work with you on your reading skills after the first and second grade? Did any of your teachers discuss with you ways in which imagery could be used to enhance your processing of information? If you are like most individuals, you spent little or no time in elementary school on improving these important processes involved in our everyday encounters with the world.

Why is it important to have an educational goal of improving the information processing skills of children? Think for a moment about yourself and the skills necessary for you to be successful in adapting to your environment and for improving your chances of getting a good job and having a successful career. To some extent, knowledge itself is important; more precisely, content knowledge in certain areas is important. For example, if you plan to become a chemical engineer, a knowledge of chemistry is required.

Our schools have done a much better job of imparting knowledge than in instructing students how to process information.

Another important situation in your life where instruction in information processing would have helped you tremendously was when you took the SAT or ACT test. SAT cram courses are popping up all over the United States, in part because schools have not done a good job of developing information processing skills. For example, is speed of processing information important on the SAT? Most of you probably felt that you did not have as much time as you would have liked to handle difficult questions. Are memory strategies important on the SAT? You had to read paragraphs and hold a considerable amount of information in your mind to answer some of the questions. And you certainly had to remember how to solve a number of math problems. Didn't you also have to remember the definitions of a large number of vocabulary words? And what about problem solving, inferencing, and understanding? Remember the difficult verbal problems you had to answer and the inferences you had to make when reasoning was required?

The story of information processing is one of attention, perception, memory (especially the control processes in memory), thinking, and the like. These information processing skills become even more crucial in education when we consider that we are now in the midst of a transition from an industrial to a post-industrial, information society, with approximately 65 to 70 percent of all workers involved in services. The information revolution in our society has placed strain on workers who are called on daily to process huge amounts of information in a rapid fashion, to have efficient memories, to attend to relevant details, to reason logically about difficult issues, and to make inferences about information that may be fuzzy or unclear. Students graduate from high school, college, or post-graduate work and move into jobs requiring information processing skills, yet they have had little or no instruction in improving these skills.

At this time, we do not have a specified curriculum of information processing that can be taught in a stepwise, developmental fashion to our nation's children. We also do not have the trained personnel for this

What are the effects of knowledge on memory?

instruction. Further, some information processing experts believe that processes such as attention and memory cannot be trained in a general way. Rather, they argue that information processing is domain- or content-specific. That is, we should work on improving information processing skills that are specific to math or specific to history. They do believe, though, that an infusion of the information processing approach into all parts of the curriculum would greatly benefit children (Lorden & Falkenberg, 1988).

Researchers are beginning to study the importance of information processing skills for school learning. Ellen Gagne (1985) provided a menu of information processing skills that need to be given attention when instructing children in specific content areas—reading, writing, math, and science, for example. Her review concludes that successful students—those who get better grades and higher achievement test scores—are better at information processing skills such as focusing attention, elaborating and organizing information, and monitoring their study strategies. As yet, though, we do not know to what extent these information processing skills can be taught. Nonetheless, in one investigation, Gagne and her colleagues (in press) demonstrated that children can be taught effective ways to elaborate information so that it can be remembered more efficiently. Elaboration refers to more extensive processing. Getting the child to think of examples of a concept is a good way to improve the child's memory of the concept; so is getting the child to think about how the concept relates to herself. Other experts in cognitive psychology also believe that information processing skills can be taught. For example, Joan Baron and R. J. Sternberg (1987) believe we need to teach children to think in less irrational ways; to be more critical of the first ideas that pop into their minds; to think longer about problems; and to search in more organized ways for evidence to support their views.

Physical Development, Piaget and Cognitive Developmental Changes, and Information Processing in Middle and Late Childhood		
Concept	**Processes/Related Ideas**	**Characteristics/Description**
Physical Development	Its Nature	Growth is slow and consistent—the calm before the rapid growth spurt of adolescence. With regard to body build, children can be classified as endomorphs, mesomorphs, and ectomorphs. Motor development becomes smoother and sensory mechanisms continue to mature. While elementary school-age children cognitively recognize the importance of nutrition and exercise, their behavior often does not reflect this recognition.
Piaget's Theory and Cognitive Developmental Changes	Concrete Operational Thought	Concrete operational thought is made up of operations, mental actions or representations that are reversible. The concrete operational child shows conservation and classification skills. The concrete operational child needs clearly available perceptual supports to reason; later in development, thought becomes more abstract.
	Piaget and Education	Piaget's ideas have been applied extensively to children's education. Emphasis is on communication and the belief that the child has many ideas about the world, that the child is always learning and unlearning, and that the child is by nature a knowing creature.
	Contributions and Criticisms	Piaget was a genius at observing children and developed fascinating insights about children's cognition. He showed us some important things to look for in development and mapped out some general cognitive changes in development. Criticisms of Piaget focus on the belief that the stages are not as unitary as he thought, that small changes in procedures affect the child's cognition, that children can sometimes be trained to think at higher stages, and that some cognitive skills appear earlier than Piaget thought while others are more protracted than he thought.
Information Processing	Memory	Children's long-term memory improves during middle and late childhood. Control processes or strategies such as rehearsal, organization, and imagery are among the important influences that are responsible for improved long-term memory. Children's knowledge also influences their memory. A special type of knowledge—metamemory—concerns control processes.
	Schemata and Scripts	Schemata refer to the existing information we have about concepts, events, and knowledge; scripts are schemata for events. Children's schemata and scripts become more complex and sophisticated in middle and late childhood.

Intelligence is an abstract concept that is difficult to define. While many psychologists and lay people equate intelligence with verbal ability and problem solving skills, others prefer to define it as the individual's ability to learn from and adapt to the experiences of everyday life. If we were to settle on a definition of intelligence based on these criteria, it would be that **intelligence** is verbal ability, problem solving skills, and the ability to learn from and adapt to the experiences of everyday life.

The components of intelligence are very close to the information processing and language skills that we have discussed at various points in children's development. The difference between how we discussed information processing skills and language and how we will discuss intelligence lies in the concepts of individual differences and assessment. Individual differences simply are the consistent, stable ways we are different from each other. The history of the study of intelligence has focused extensively on individual differences and their assessment. For example, an intelligence test will inform us whether a child can logically reason better than most other children who have taken the test. Our coverage of intelligence involves whether it has one or many faces, whether intelligence tests are culturally biased, knowledge versus process in intelligence, the use and misuse of intelligence tests, and the extremes of intelligence. Keep in mind as you think about intelligence our discussion of intelligence in chapter 3, where we concluded that intelligence is influenced by the interaction of heredity and environment, rather than either factor alone.

One Face or Many Faces?

Is it more appropriate to think of intelligence as an individual's general ability or a number of specific abilities? This question has been addressed on many occasions in intelligence's history. As we explore different approaches to what intelligence is and how it should be measured, you will discover that intelligence probably is *both* a general ability and a number of specific abilities.

Alfred Binet and the Binet Tests

In 1904, the French Ministry of Education asked psychologist Alfred Binet to devise a method that would determine which students did not profit from typical school instruction. School officials wanted to reduce overcrowding by placing those who did not benefit from regular classroom teaching in special schools. Binet and his student Theophile Simon developed an intelligence test to meet this request. The test is referred to as the 1905 Scale and consisted of thirty different items ranging from the ability to touch one's nose or ear when asked to the ability to draw designs from memory and define abstract concepts.

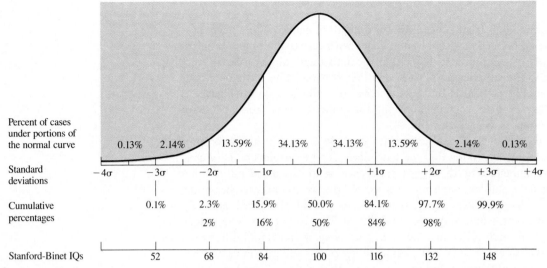

Percent of cases under portions of the normal curve	0.13%	2.14%	13.59%	34.13%	34.13%	13.59%	2.14%	0.13%
Standard deviations	-4σ	-3σ	-2σ	-1σ	0	$+1\sigma$	$+2\sigma$	$+3\sigma$	$+4\sigma$
Cumulative percentages		0.1%	2.3%	15.9%	50.0%	84.1%	97.7%	99.9%
			2%	16%	50%	84%	98%	
Stanford-Binet IQs		52	68	84	100	116	132	148

Figure 10.3

The normal distribution of intelligence test scores. Relationship of normal curve to scores on the Stanford-Binet Intelligence Test.

Binet developed the concept of **mental age (MA)**—an individual's level of mental development relative to others. Binet reasoned that mentally retarded children would perform like normal children of a younger age. He developed norms for intelligence by testing fifty nonretarded children from 3 to 11 years of age. Children suspected of mental retardation were given the test and their performance was compared with children of the same chronological age in the normal sample. Average mental-age scores (MA) correspond to chronological age (CA), which is age since birth. A bright child has an MA above CA, a dull child has an MA below CA.

The term **intelligence quotient (IQ)** was devised by William Stern. IQ is the child's mental age divided by chronological age multiplied by 100:

$$IQ = \frac{MA}{CA} \times 100$$

If mental age is the same as chronological age, then the child's IQ is 100; if mental age is above chronological age, the IQ is more than 100; if mental age is below chronological age, the IQ is less than 100.

Over the years, extensive effort has been expended to standardize the Binet test, which has been given to thousands of children and adults of different ages, selected at random from different parts of the United States. By administering the test to large numbers of individuals and recording the results, it has been found that intelligence approximates a **normal distribution** (see figure 10.3). This type of distribution is symmetrical, with a majority of cases falling in the middle of a possible range of scores and few scores appearing toward the ends of the range.

The current Stanford-Binet (named after Stanford University where revisions of the test were constructed) is given to individuals from the age of 2 through adulthood. It includes a wide variety of items, some requiring verbal responses, others nonverbal responses. For example, items that characterize a 6-year-old's performance on the test include the verbal ability to define at least six words such as "orange" and "envelope," and the nonverbal ability to trace a path through a maze. Items that reflect the average adult's intelligence include defining words such as "disproportionate" and "regard," explaining a proverb, and comparing idleness and laziness.

The fourth edition of the Stanford-Binet was published in 1985 (Thorndike, Hagan, & Sattler, 1985). One important addition to this version is the analysis of the individual's responses in four content areas: verbal reasoning, quantitative reasoning, abstract/visual reasoning, and short-term memory. A general composite score is also obtained to reflect overall intelligence. The Stanford-Binet continues to be one of the most widely used individual tests of intelligence.

The Wechsler Scales

Besides the Stanford-Binet, the other most widely used individual intelligence tests are the **Wechsler Scales,** developed by David Wechsler. They include the Wechsler Adult Intelligence Scale-Revised (WAIS-R); the Wechsler Intelligence Scale for Children-Revised (WISC-R), for use with children between the ages of 6 and 16; and the Wechsler Preschool and Primary Scale of Intelligence (WPPSI), for use with children from the ages of 4 to 6½ (Wechsler, 1949, 1955, 1967, 1974, 1981).

The Wechsler Scales not only provide an overall IQ but the items are grouped according to twelve subscales, six of which are verbal and six of which are nonverbal. This allows the examiner to obtain separate verbal and nonverbal IQ scores and to see quickly in which areas of mental performance the child is below average, average, or above average. The inclusion of a number of nonverbal subscales makes the Wechsler test more representative of verbal *and* nonverbal intelligence; the Binet test includes some nonverbal items but not as many as the Wechsler scales. Eleven of the twelve subscales on the Wechsler Intelligence Scale for Children-Revised are shown in figure 10.4, along with examples of each subscale.

Multiple Faces of Intelligence

Long before David Wechsler analyzed intelligence in terms of general and specific abilities (giving the child an overall IQ but also providing information about specific subcomponents of intelligence), Charles Spearman (1927) proposed that intelligence has two factors. Spearman's **two factor theory** argued that we have both a general intelligence, which he called *g,* and a number of specific intelligences, which he called *s.* Spearman believed that these two factors could account for an individual's performance on an intelligence test. One recent classification—developed by Howard Gardner (1983)—also describes intelligence as having many faces. By turning to Focus on Life-Span Development 10.2, you can read about Gardner's seven frames of mind.

What are some similarities and differences between the Stanford-Binet and the Wechsler Scales of Intelligence?

Are Intelligence Tests Culturally Biased?

Many of the early intelligence tests were culturally biased, favoring urban children over rural children, middle-class children over lower-class children, and white children over minority children. The norms for the early tests were based almost entirely on white, middle-class children. And some of the items themselves were culturally biased. For example, one item on an early test asked what should be done if you find a 3-year-old child in the street; the correct answer was "call the police." Children from impoverished inner-city families might not choose this answer if they have had bad experiences with the police; rural children might not choose it since they may not have police nearby. Such items clearly do not measure the knowledge necessary to adapt to one's environment or to be "intelligent" in an inner city minority neighborhood or in rural America (Scarr, 1984). The contemporary versions of intelligence tests attempt to reduce cultural bias.

Figure 10.4
The subtests of the WISC-R and examples of each subtest. Simulated items provided by and reproduced by permission of the Publisher of the Wechsler Intelligence Scale for Children-Revised. Copyright © 1974 by the Psychological Corporation. All rights reserved.

Verbal subtests

General information
The individual is asked a number of general information questions about experiences that are considered normal for individuals in our society.
    For example, "How many wings does a bird have?"

Similarities
The individual must think logically and abstractly to answer a number of questions about how things are similar.
    For example, "In what way are boats and trains the same?"

Arithmetic reasoning
Problems measure the individual's ability to do arithmetic mentally and include addition, subtraction, multiplication, and division.
    For example, "If two buttons cost 14¢, what will be the cost of a dozen buttons?"

Vocabulary
To evaluate word knowledge, the individual is asked to define a number of words. This subtest measures a number of cognitive functions, including concept formation, memory, and language.
    For example, "What does the word *biography* mean?"

Comprehension
This subtest is designed to measure the individual's judgment and common sense.
    For example, "What is the advantage of keeping money in the bank?"

Digit span
This subtest primarily measures attention and short-term memory. The individual is required to repeat numbers forward and backward.
    For example, "I am going to say some numbers and I want you to repeat them backward: 4   7   5   2   8."

Picture completion
A number of drawings are shown, each with a significant part missing. Within a period of several seconds, the individual must differentiate essential from nonessential parts of the picture and identify which part is missing. This subtest evaluates visual alertness and the ability to organize information visually.
    For example, "I am going to show you a picture with an important part missing. Tell me what is missing."

Picture arrangement
A series of pictures out of sequence are shown to the individual, who is asked to place them in their proper order to tell an appropriate story. This subtest evaluates how individuals integrate information to make it logical and meaningful.
    For example, "The pictures below need to be placed in an appropriate order to tell a meaningful story."

Object assembly

The individual is asked to assemble pieces into something. This subtest measures visual-motor coordination and perceptual organization.

For example, "When these pieces are put together correctly, they make something. Put them together as quickly as you can."

Block design

The individual must assemble a set of multi-colored blocks to match designs that the examiner shows. Visual-motor coordination, perceptual organization, and the ability to visualize spatially are measured.

For example, "Use the four blocks on the left to make the pattern on the right."

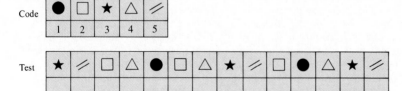

Coding

This subtest evaluates, how quickly and accurately an individual can link code symbols and digits. The subtest assesses visual-motor coordination and speed of thought.

For example, "As quickly as you can, transfer the appropriate code symbols to the blank spaces."

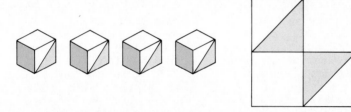

Note: A sixth nonverbal scale, Mazes, is not shown because it is rarely used by examiners. Digit Span also is considered to be an optional subtest, but examiners are more likely to administer it than the optional performance subtest, Mazes.

BIRD TO BEETHOVEN—SEVEN FRAMES OF MIND

Larry Bird, the six-foot-nine-inch superstar of the Boston Celtics, springs into motion. Grabbing a rebound off the defensive board, he quickly moves across two-thirds the length of the ninety-four-foot basketball court, all the while processing the whereabouts of his five opponents and four teammates. As the crowd screams, Bird calmly looks one way, finesses his way past a defender, and whirls a behind-the-back pass to a fast-breaking teammate, who dunks the ball for two points. Is there specific intelligence to Bird's movement and perception of the spatial layout of the basketball court?

Now we turn the clock back 200 years. A tiny boy just four years of age is standing on a footstool in front of a piano keyboard practicing. At the age of six, the young boy is given the honor of playing concertos and trios at a concert. The young boy is Ludwig von Beethoven, whose musical genius was evident at a young age. Did Beethoven have a specific type of intelligence, one we might call musical intelligence?

Bird and Beethoven are different types of individuals with different types of abilities. Howard Gardner

(1983), in his book, *Frames of Mind*, argues that Bird's and Beethoven's talents represent two of seven intelligences that we possess. Beyond the verbal and mathematical intelligences tapped by such tests as the SAT and most traditional intelligence tests, Gardner thinks that we have the ability to spatially analyze the world, movement skills, insightful skills for analyzing ourselves, insightful skills for analyzing others, and musical skills.

Gardner believes that each of the seven intelligences can be destroyed by brain damage, that each involves unique cognitive skills, and that each shows up in exaggerated fashion in both the gifted and *idiots savants* (individuals who are mentally retarded but who have unbelievable skill in a particular domain, such as drawing, music, or computing). I remember vividly an individual from my childhood who was mentally retarded but could instantaneously respond with the correct day of the week (say Tuesday or Saturday) when given any date in history (say June 4, 1926, or December 15, 1746).

Gardner is especially interested in musical intelligence, particularly

when it is exhibited at an early age. He points out that musically inclined preschool children not only have the remarkable ability to learn musical patterns easily, but that they rarely forget them. He recounts a story about Stravinsky, who as an adult could still remember the musical patterns of the tuba, drums, and piccolos of the fife-and-drum band that marched outside of his window when he was a young child.

To measure musical intelligence in young children, Gardner might ask a child to listen to a melody and then ask the child to recreate the tune on some bells he provides. He believes such evaluations can be used to develop a profile of a child's intelligence. He also believes that it is during this early time in life that parents can make an important difference in how a child's intelligence develops.

Critics of Gardner's approach point out that we have geniuses in many domains other than music. There are outstanding chess players, prize fighters, writers, politicians, physicians, lawyers, preachers, and poets, for example; yet we do not refer to chess intelligence, prize-fighter intelligence, and so on.

Larry Bird, NBA superstar of the Boston Celtics. Howard Gardner believes Bird's movement skills and spatial perception are forms of intelligence.

Ludwig van Beethoven. Gardner also argues that musical skills, such as those shown by Beethoven, are a form of intelligence.

1. A "gas head" is a person who has a:
   (a) fast-moving car
   (b) stable of "lace"
   (c) "process"
   (d) habit of stealing cars
   (e) long jail record for arson
2. "Bo Diddley" is a:
   (a) game for children
   (b) down-home cheap wine
   (c) down-home singer
   (d) new dance
   (e) Moejoe call
3. If a pimp is uptight with a woman who gets state aid, what does he mean when he talks about "Mother's day"?
   (a) second Sunday in May
   (b) third Sunday in June
   (c) first of every month
   (d) none of these
   (e) first and fifteenth of every month
4. A "handkerchief head" is:
   (a) a cool cat
   (b) a porter
   (c) an Uncle Tom
   (d) a hoddi
   (e) a preacher
5. If a man is called a "blood," then he is a:
   (a) fighter
   (b) Mexican-American
   (c) Negro
   (d) hungry hemophile
   (e) red man, or Indian
6. Cheap chitlings (not the kind you purchase at a frozen-food counter) will taste rubbery unless they are cooked long enough. How soon can you quit cooking them to eat and enjoy them?
   (a) forty-five minutes
   (b) two hours
   (c) twenty-four hours
   (d) one week (on a low flame)
   (e) one hour

Answers: 1. c 2. c 3. e 4. c 5. c 6. c

Even if the content of test items is made appropriate, another problem may exist with intelligence tests. Since many questions are verbal in nature, minority groups may encounter problems understanding the language of the questions. Minority groups often speak a language that is very different from standard English. Consequently, they may be at a disadvantage when they take intelligence tests oriented toward middle-class white individuals. Such cultural bias is dramatically underscored by tests like the one in figure 10.5. The items in this test were developed to reduce the cultural disadvantage black children might experience on traditional intelligence tests.

Culture fair tests were devised to reduce cultural bias. Two types of culture fair tests have been developed. The first includes items that are familiar to individuals from all socioeconomic and ethnic backgrounds, or items that are at least familiar to the individuals who are taking the test. For example, a child might be asked how a bird and a dog are different, on the assumption that virtually all children have been exposed to birds and dogs. The second type of culture fair test has all the verbal items removed. Figure 10.6 shows a sample item from the Raven Progressive Matrices Test, which exemplifies this approach. Even though tests like the Raven Test are designed to be culture fair, individuals with more education score higher on them than those with less education (Anastasi, 1988).

Culture fair tests remind us that traditional intelligence tests are probably culturally biased, yet culture fair tests do not provide a satisfactory alternative. Constructing a truly culture fair test, one that rules out the role of experience emanating from socioeconomic and ethnic background, has been difficult and may be impossible. Consider, for example, that the intelligence of the Iatmul people of Papua, New Guninea, involves the ability to remember the names of some 10,000 to 20,000 clans; by contrast, the intelligence of islanders in the widely dispersed Caroline Islands involves the talent of navigating by the stars.

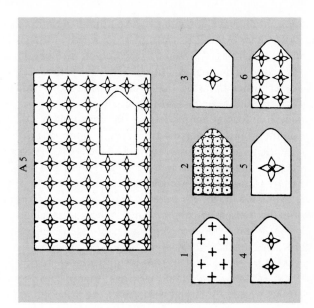

Figure 10.6
A sample item from the Raven Progressive Matrices Tests. The individual is presented with a matrix arrangement of symbols, such as the one at the top of this figure, and must then complete the matrix by selecting the appropriate missing symbol from a group of symbols. The Raven Progressive Matrices Test has no verbal items. Even though this and other nonverbal intelligence tests are designed to be culture fair, researchers find that individuals with more education score higher on them than those with less education.

Knowledge Versus Process in Intelligence

The information processing approach we have discussed at different points in development raises two interesting questions about intelligence: What are the fundamental information processing abilities? How do these develop?

Few of us would deny that changes in both processing and knowledge occur as we develop. However, a consensus does not exist on something more fundamental. We accumulate knowledge as we grow from an infant to an adult, but what may be growing is simply a reserve of processing capacity. That is, your greater processing capacity as an adult than as a child might be what allows you to learn more. By contrast, possibly your greater processing capacity as an adult is a consequence of your greater knowledge, which allows you to process information more effectively. It is not easy to choose between these two possibilities and the issue has been called the great **structure-process dilemma** of intelligence (Keil, 1984). That is, what are the mechanisms of intelligence and how do they develop? Does information processing ability change, or does knowledge and expertise change? Or do both change?

To make the structure-process dilemma more concrete, consider a simple computer metaphor. Suppose we have two computers, each of which is capable of solving multiplication problems (e.g., 13 × 24, 45 × 21), but one computer works faster than the other. What is the explanation? One possibility is that the faster computer has a greater capacity—that is, core memory—in which to do mental work. This greater core memory, which psychologists refer to as **working memory,** might allow the computer to work on two or more components of a problem at once. Another explanation is that the faster computer might have a greater store of relevant knowledge. Perhaps it has in its data bank (long-term memory) a complete multiplication table up to 99 × 99. The slower computer might have a table up to 12 × 12 (as do most humans). The faster computer need not be fundamentally faster—its subroutines may be relatively slow, but it is able to perform the multiplication task because of knowledge, not because of processing capacity.

Intelligence comes in many different forms. Developmentalists debate the nature of the forms and how many there are. For example, Sternberg argues that children's intelligence comes in three forms: componential, experiential, and contextual. Which of these forms would this young boy's behavior fit?

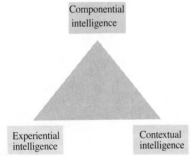

Figure 10.7
Sternberg's triarchic theory of intelligence.

Explaining intelligence is similar to explaining the difference between the fast and slow computers—is processing or knowledge responsible for how intelligence changes with age? Based on research on memory, it seems likely that the answer is both (Zembar & Naus, 1985). If so, the essential task becomes one of determining the ways that processing and knowledge interact in the course of intellectual development (Case, 1988).

The modern information processing approach does not argue that knowledge is unimportant. Rather, many information processing psychologists believe that attention should be given to the knowledge base generated by intellectual processes. One information processing approach to intelligence that recognizes the importance of both process and knowledge is R. J. Sternberg's model (1985, 1986, 1987a, b). He believes that each of us has three types of intelligence; for this reason he calls his approach the **triarchic theory of intelligence.** Consider Ann, who scores high on traditional intelligence tests such as the Stanford-Binet and is a star analytical thinker. Consider Todd, who does not have the best test results but has an insightful and creative mind. And consider Art, a street-smart individual who has learned how to deal in practical ways with his world, although his scores on traditional intelligence tests are low.

Sternberg calls Ann's analytical thinking and abstract reasoning *componential intelligence;* it is the closest to what we call intelligence in this chapter and what commonly is measured by intelligence tests. Todd's insightful and creative thinking is called *experiential intelligence* by Sternberg. And Art's street smarts and practical know-how is called *contextual intelligence* by Sternberg (see figure 10.7).

In Sternberg's view of componential intelligence, the basic unit of intelligence is a *component,* simply defined as a basic unit of information processing. Sternberg believes that such components include those used to acquire or store information, to retain or retrieve information, to transfer information, to plan, make decisions, and solve problems, and to carry out problem solving strategies or translate thoughts into performance.

The second part of Sternberg's model focuses on experience. An intelligent individual has the ability to solve new problems quickly, but also learns how to solve familiar problems in an automatic way so that her mind is free to handle problems that require insight and creativity (Sternberg & Lubart, 1988).

The third part of the model involves practical knowledge—such as how to get out of trouble, how to replace a fuse, and how to get along with people. Sternberg calls this practical knowledge *tacit knowledge.* It includes all of the information about getting along in the world that is not taught in school. Sternberg believes that tacit knowledge is more important for success in life than explicit, or "book," knowledge. Once again, we see—in Sternberg's model—the effort to determine the nature of intelligence's faces.

The Use and Misuse of Intelligence Tests
Psychological tests are tools. Like all tools, their effectiveness depends on the knowledge, skill, and integrity of the user. A hammer can be used to build a beautiful kitchen cabinet or it can be used as a weapon of assault. Like a hammer, intelligence tests can be used for positive purposes or they can be badly abused. It is important for both the test constructor and the test examiner to be familiar with the current state of scientific knowledge and intelligence tests (Anastasi, 1988).

Middle and Late Childhood

Even though they have limitations, intelligence tests are among psychology's most widely used tools. To be effective, though, intelligence tests must be viewed realistically. They should not be thought of as a fixed, unchanging indicator of an individual's intelligence. They also should be used in conjunction with other information about the individual and not relied upon as the sole indicator of intelligence. For example, an intelligence test should not be used as the sole indicator of whether a child should be placed in a special education or gifted class. The child's developmental history, medical background, performance in school, social competencies, and family experiences should be taken into account, too.

The single number provided by many IQ tests can easily lead to stereotypes and expectations about the individual. Many individuals do not know how to interpret the results of an intelligence test and sweeping generalizations about an individual too often are made on the basis of an IQ score. For example, imagine that you are a teacher in the teacher's lounge on the day after school has started in the fall. You mention a student—Johnny Jones—and a fellow teacher remarks that she had Johnny in class last year; she comments that he was a real dunce and points out that his IQ is 78. You cannot help but remember this information and it may lead to thoughts that Johnny Jones is not very bright so it is useless to spend much time teaching him. In this way, IQ scores are misused and stereotypes are formed (Rosenthal & Jacobsen, 1968).

We also have a tendency in our culture to consider intelligence or a high IQ as the ultimate human value. It is important to keep in mind that our value as humans includes other matters—consideration of others, positive close relationships, and competence in social situations, for example. The verbal and problem solving skills measured on traditional intelligence tests are only one part of human competence.

Despite their limitations, when used judiciously by a competent examiner, intelligence tests provide valuable information about individuals. There are not many alternatives to intelligence tests. Subjective judgments about individuals simply reintroduce the biases the tests were designed to eliminate.

How close are Piaget's view of intelligence and the psychometric view of intelligence described in this chapter? Explain your answer.

The Extremes of Intelligence

The atypical individual has always been of interest to developmentalists. Intellectual atypicality has intrigued many psychologists and drawn them to study both the mentally retarded and the gifted.

Mental Retardation

The most distinctive feature of mental retardation is inadequate intellectual functioning. Long before formal tests were introduced to assess intelligence, the mentally retarded were identified by a lack of age-appropriate skills in learning and caring for oneself. With the development of intelligence tests, more emphasis was placed on IQ as an indicator of mental retardation. But it is not unusual to find two retarded individuals with the same low IQ, one of whom is married, employed, and involved in the community and the other requiring constant supervision in an institution. These differences in social competence led developmentalists to include deficits in adaptive behavior in their definition of mental retardation. The currently accepted definition of **mental retardation** refers to an individual who has a low IQ, usually below 70 on a traditional intelligence test, and who has difficulty adapting to everyday life. About 5 million Americans fit this definition of mental retardation (Baumeiser, 1987; Robinson, 1987; Zigler, 1987).

Figure 10.8
A child with Down's Syndrome.

There are different classifications of mental retardation. About 80 percent of the mentally retarded fall into the mild category, with IQs of 50 to 70. About 12 percent are classified as moderately retarded, with IQs of 35 to 49; these individuals can attain a second-grade level of skills and may be able to support themselves as adults through some type of labor. About 7 percent of the mentally retarded fall into the severe category, with IQs of 20 to 34; these individual learn to talk and engage in very simple tasks, but they require extensive supervision. Only 1 percent of the mentally retarded are classified as profoundly retarded with IQs below 20; they are in constant need of supervision.

What causes retardation? The causes are divided into two categories: organic and cultural-familial. Individuals with **organic retardation** are retarded because of a genetic disorder or brain damage; **organic** refers to the tissues or organs of the body, so there is some physical damage that has taken place in organic retardation. Down's syndrome—a form of organic retardation (see figure 10.8)—occurs when an extra chromosome is present, possibly influenced by the health of the female ovum or the male sperm. Although those who suffer organic retardation are found across the spectrum of mental retardation IQ distribution, most have IQs between 0 and 50.

Individuals with **cultural-familial retardation** make up the majority of the mentally retarded population; they have no evidence of organic damage or brain dysfunction. Their IQs range from 50 to 70. Developmentalists seek to discover the cause of this type of retardation in the impoverished environments these individuals probably have experienced. Even with organic retardation, though, it is wise to think about the contributions of genetic-environment interaction. Parents with low IQs not only may be more likely to transmit genes for low intelligence to their offspring, but also tend to provide them with a less enriched environment.

Giftedness

Conventional wisdom has identified some individuals in all cultures and historical periods as gifted because they have talents not evident in the majority of people. Despite this widespread recognition of the gifted, developmentalists have difficulty reaching a consensus on the precise definition and measurement of giftedness. Some experts view the gifted as the top end of a continuum of intelligence (Humphreys, 1985; Zigler & Farber, 1985). Some of these advocates view this ability as a unitary characteristic that perhaps is hereditary. Others see the gifted as individuals who express specific talents that have been nurtured environmentally (Wallach, 1985). A comprehensive definition of **gifted** is an individual with well-above-average intelligence (an IQ of 120 or more) and/or a superior talent for something. Most school systems emphasize intellectual superiority and academic aptitude when selecting children for special instruction; however, they rarely consider competence in the visual and performing arts (art, drama, dance), psychomotor abilities (tennis, golf, basketball), or other special aptitudes.

A classic study of the gifted was begun by Lewis Terman (1925) more than 60 years ago. Terman studied approximately 1,500 children whose Stanford-Binet IQs averaged 150. His goal was to follow these children through their adult lives—the study will not be complete until the year 2010.

The accomplishments of the 1,500 children in Terman's study are remarkable. Of the 800 males, 78 have obtained PhDs (they include two past presidents of the American Psychological Association), 48 have earned MDs, and 85 have been granted law degrees. Nearly all of these figures are 10 to 30 times greater than found among 800 men of the same age chosen randomly from the overall population. These findings challenge the commonly held belief that the intellectually gifted are somehow emotionally or socially maladjusted. This belief is based on striking instances of mental disturbances among the gifted. Sir Issac Newton, Van Gogh, da Vinci, Socrates, and Poe all had emotional problems, but these are exceptions rather than the rule; no relationship between giftedness and mental disturbance in general has been found. Recent studies support Terman's conclusion that, if anything, the gifted tend to be more mature and have fewer emotional problems than others (Janos & Robinson, 1985).

In one investigation, individuals with exceptional talents as adults were interviewed about what they believe contributed to their giftedness (Bloom, 1983). The 120 individuals had excelled in one of six fields—concert pianists and sculptors (arts), Olympic swimmers and tennis champions (psychomotor), and research mathematicians and research neurologists (cognitive). They said the development of their exceptional accomplishments required special environmental support, excellent teaching, and motivational encouragement. Each experienced years of special attention under the tutelage and supervision of a remarkable set of teachers and coaches. They were also given extensive support and encouragement from parents. All of these stars devoted exceptional time to practice and training, easily outdistancing the amount of time spent in all other activities combined.

Creativity

Most of us would like to be gifted *and* creative. Why was Thomas Edison able to invent so many things? Was he simply more intelligent than most individuals? Did he spend long hours toiling away in private? Somewhat surprisingly, when Edison was a young boy, his teacher told him that he was too dumb to learn anything! Other examples of famous individuals whose creative genius

"I'm a gifted child."
Drawing by Drucker; © *1981 The New Yorker Magazine, Inc.*

Each of us would like to be talented. And if each of us has children we would like to be able to develop the talents of our children. Some children become extraordinarily gifted, reaching the status of "star." Becoming a "star" takes years of special tutelage with remarkable coaches, extensive support by parents, and day after day, week after week, month after month, and year after year of practice.

What should be the criteria for placing a child in a gifted program?

Figure 10.9
Creativity examples. Sample items from Guilford's (1967) Divergent Productions Tests.

1. *Sketches:* Add just enough detail to the circle below to make a recognizable object (two examples of acceptable responses are shown).

2. *Word fluency:* Write as many words as you can think of with the first and last letters R_____M ("rim" would be one).

3. *Name grouping:* Classify the following six names in as many different ways as you can (a person might group 1, 3, and 4 together because each has two syllables).

   1. GERTRUDE   2. BILL
   3. ALEX   4. CARRIE
   5. BELLE   6. DON

4. *Making objects:* Using two or more of the forms shown below, make a face. Now make a lamp (examples of good responses are shown).

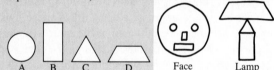

went unnoticed when they were young include Walt Disney, who was fired from a newspaper job because he did not have any good ideas; Enrico Caruso, whose music teacher told him that his voice was terrible; and Winston Churchill, who failed one year of secondary school. Among the reasons such individuals are underestimated is the difficulty of defining and measuring creativity.

The prevailing belief of experts who study intelligence and creativity is that the two are not the same thing (Monroe, 1988; Wallach, 1985). One distinction is between **convergent thinking,** which produces one correct answer, and **divergent thinking,** which produces many different answers to the same question (Guilford, 1967). For example, this problem solving task has one correct answer and requires convergent thinking: "How many quarters will you get for sixty dimes?" But this question has many possible answers and requires divergent thinking: "What are some unique things that can be done with a paper clip?" A degree of creativity is needed to answer this question. The following also detects whether an individual is oriented toward thinking creatively: Name words that belong to a particular class. For example, name as many objects as you can that weigh less than one pound. Even when you are not asked to, do you give divergent answers? For example, if you are asked what things can be done with a paper clip, do you spontaneously generate different categories of use for the paper clip? For more examples of items on tests of creativity, turn to figure 10.9.

Creativity is the ability to think about something in a novel way and to come up with unique solutions to problems. When individuals in the arts and sciences who fit this description are asked what enables them to produce their creative works, they say that they generate large amounts of associative content when solving problems and that they have the freedom to entertain a wide range of possible solutions in a playful manner (Wallach & Kogan, 1965).

How strongly is creativity related to intelligence? A certain level of intelligence seems to be required to be creative in most fields, but many highly intelligent individuals (as measured by IQ tests) are not very creative. We have discussed many different ideas about intelligence. A summary of these ideas is presented in Concept Table 10.2. Now we turn to another important aspect of the child's world in middle and late childhood—achievement.

Achievement

We are a species motivated to do well at what we attempt, to gain mastery over the world in which we live, to explore with enthusiasm and curiosity unknown environments, and to achieve the heights of success. When Vince Lombardi was coach of the Green Bay Packers, in his customary intense manner, he said, "Winning isn't everything, it is the only thing." A less intense promotion of achievement's importance in our lives was offered by Henry Wadsworth Longfellow, "Let us be up and doing with a heart for any fate; still achieving, still pursuing."

We live in an achievement-oriented world with standards that tell us success is important. The standards suggest that success requires a competitive spirit, a desire to win, a motivation to do well, and the wherewithal to cope with adversity and persist until objects are overcome. Some developmentalists, though, believe we are a nation of hurried, wired people who are raising our children to become the same way—too uptight about success and failure and far too worried about what we accomplish in comparison to others (Elkind, 1981). It was in the 1950s that an interest in achievement began to flourish. The interest initially focused on the need for achievement.

Need for Achievement

Think about yourself and your friends for a moment. Are you more achievement-oriented than they are or less so? If we asked you and your friends to tell stories about achievement-related themes, could we accurately determine which of you is more achievement-oriented?

David McClelland (1955) stressed that individuals vary in their motivation for achievement and that we can measure these differences. McClelland referred to achievement motivation as **n achievement** (need for achievement), meaning the individual's motivation to overcome obstacles, desire for success, and effort expended to seek out difficult tasks and do them well as quickly as possible. To measure achievement, children were shown ambiguous pictures that were likely to stimulate achievement-related responses. Then they were asked to tell a story about the picture, and their comments were scored according to how strongly they reflected achievement (McClelland & others, 1953).

A host of studies have correlated achievement-related responses with different aspects of the individual's experiences and behavior. The findings are diverse, but they do suggest that achievement-oriented individuals have a stronger hope for success than fear of failure, are moderate rather than high

Intelligence		
Concept	**Processes/Related Ideas**	**Characteristics/Description**
What Is Intelligence?	Its Nature	An abstract concept that is measured indirectly. Psychologists rely on intelligence tests to estimate intelligence. Verbal ability and problem solving skills are included in a definition of intelligence. Some developmentalists believe it includes an ability to learn from and adapt to everyday life. Extensive effort is made to assess individual differences in intelligence.
One Face or Many Faces?	Alfred Binet and the Binet Tests	Alfred Binet developed the first intelligence test, known as the 1905 Scale. He developed the concept of mental age and William Stern developed the concept of IQ. The Binet has been standardized and revised many times; the revisions are called the Stanford-Binet tests. The test approximates a normal distribution; the current edition is given to individuals from the age of 2 through childhood.
	The Wechsler Scales	Besides the Binet, the most widely used intelligence tests today. They include the WAIS-R, WISC-R, and WPPSI. These tests provide an overall IQ, verbal and performance IQ, and information about 11 subscales.
	Multiple Faces of Intelligence	Psychologists debate whether intelligence is a general ability or a number of specific abilities. Spearman's two-factor theory suggested that we possess both a general ability and a number of specific abilities.
Are Intelligence Tests Culturally Biased?	The Nature of the Bias	Early tests favored middle-class, white, urban children. Current tests attempt to reduce such bias. Culture fair tests are an alternative to traditional IQ tests; most developmentalists believe they cannot replace the traditional tests.
Knowledge versus Process	The Structure-Process Dilemma in Intelligence	The mechanisms of intelligence and its development are both those of changing information processing abilities and changing expertise and knowledge.
	Sternberg's Triarchic Model	Includes emphasis on both information processing and knowledge. He believes intelligence comes in three forms: Componential, experiential, and practical.
The Use and Misuse of Intelligence Tests	What Are Some of the Uses and Misuses?	Despite limitations, when used by a judicious examiner, tests can be valuable tools for determining individual differences in intelligence. The tests should be used with other information about the individual. IQ scores can produce unfortunate expectations and stereotypes. Intelligence or a high IQ is not necessarily the ultimate human value.
The Extremes of Intelligence	Mental Retardation	A mentally retarded individual has a low IQ, usually below 70 on a traditional IQ test, and has difficulty adapting to everyday life. Different classifications of retardation exist. The two main causes of retardation are organic and cultural-familial.
	Giftedness and Creativity	We defined giftedness as an individual with well-above-average intelligence (an IQ of 120 or more) and/or a superior talent for something. We defined creativity as the ability to think about something in a novel or unusual way and to come up with unique solutions to problems.

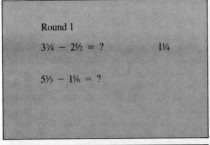

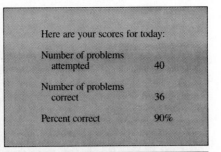

Figure 10.10
Examples of educational computer programs involving drill (top panel) versus game (lower panels) formats. The top panel shows a typical panel of a drill and practice program in which the child is praised after getting the problem right. The bottom panel is an example from the Fractions Basketball program developed by Sharon Dugdale and David Kibbey, 1973.

or low risk-takers, and persist for appropriate lengths of time in solving difficult problems (Atkinson & Raynor, 1974). Early research indicated that independence training by parents promoted children's achievement, but more recent research reveals that parents need to set high standards for achievement, model achievement-oriented behavior, and reward their children for their achievements to increase achievement (Huston-Stein & Higgens-Trenk, 1978).

Intrinsic and Extrinsic Motivation

As part of their interest in achievement motivation, psychologists have focused on the internal and external factors that contribute to such motivation. Considerable enthusiasm has greeted the issue of whether we should emphasize intrinsic or extrinsic motivation. Imagine that you must teach children about the addition and subtraction of fractions and help them practice these problems. One possibility would be to develop a simple "drill-and-practice" exercise that provides each child with a sequence of problems and praise after each correct answer. Such programs, indeed, are widespread. An alternative approach might be to present the same sequence of problems in the form of an instructional computer game specifically tailored to enhance the child's motivation. These programs are becoming available but they are less common than the drill-and-practice type. "Fractions Basketball" is one example developed by the PLATO PROJECT at the University of Illinois (Dugdale & Kibbey, 1980). Figure 10.10 shows how the drill-and-practice program and the computer game strategy vary (Lepper, 1985).

The interest in intrinsic motivation comes from ideas about motivation for challenge, competence, effectiveness, and mastery (Harter, 1981; White, 1959); curiosity, incongruity, complexity, and discrepancy (Berlyne, 1960); and perceived control and self-determination (Deci, 1975). **Intrinsic motivation** involves an underlying need for competence and self-determination. By contrast,

Figure 10.11
*Amount of time spent in art activity
following expected reward, no reward,
and unexpected reward for engaging in
same activity.*

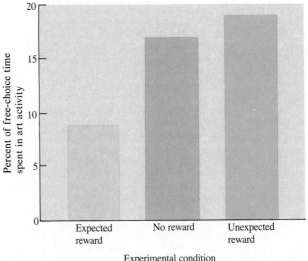

The reward of a thing well done
is to have done it.
  Ralph Waldo Emerson, Essays: Second Series,
                                    1844.

extrinsic motivation involves external factors in the environment, especially rewards. If you work hard in school because a personal standard of excellence is important to you, intrinsic motivation is involved. But if you work hard in school because you know it will bring you a higher paying job when you graduate, extrinsic motivation is at work.

An important consideration when motivating a child to do something is whether or not to offer an incentive (Pittman & Heller, 1987). If a child is not doing competent work, is bored, or has a negative attitude, it may be worthwhile to consider incentives to improve motivation. However, there are times when external rewards can get in the way of motivation. In one investigation, children with a strong interest in artistic work spent more time in a drawing activity when they expected no reward than their counterparts who knew that they would be rewarded (see figure 10.11) (Lepper, Greene, & Nisbett, 1973).

Intrinsic motivation implies that internal motivation should be promoted and external factors deemphasized. In this way, children learn to attribute the cause of their success and failure to themselves, especially how much effort they expend. But in reality, achievement is motivated by both internal and external factors. Children are never divorced from their external environment. Some of the most achievement-oriented children are those who have *both* a high personal standard for achievement and are also highly competitive. In one investigation, low-achieving boys and girls who engaged in individual goal setting *and* were given comparative information about peers worked more math problems and got more of them correct than their counterparts who experienced either condition alone (Schunk, 1983). Other research suggests that social comparison—by itself—is not a wise strategy (Nicholls, 1984). The argument is that social comparison puts the child in an ego-involved, threatening, self-focused state rather than a task-involved, effortful, strategy-focused state.

How can teachers work intrinsic motivation into their classroom activities?

Achievement in Minority Group Children

One of the primary limitations of existing research on minority group achievement is that there has been so little of it. The research literature on achievement has focused heavily on white males. And too often, research on minority groups has been interpreted as "deficits" by middle-class, white standards.

Rather than characterizing individuals as *culturally different,* many conclusions unfortunately characterize the cultural distinctiveness of blacks, Hispanics, and other minority groups as deficient in some way.

Much of the research on minority group children is plagued by a failure to consider socioeconomic status (determined by some combination of education, occupation, and income). In many instances, when race *and* socioeconomic status (also called social class) are investigated in the same study, social class is a far better predictor of achievement orientation than race (Graham, 1986). Middle-class individuals fare better than their lower-class counterparts in a variety of achievement-oriented circumstances—expectations for success, achievement aspirations, and recognition of the importance of effort, for example (McAdoo & McAdoo, 1985).

Sandra Graham has conducted a number of investigations that reveal not only stronger social class than racial differences but also the importance of studying minority group motivation in the context of general motivational theory (Graham, 1984, 1986, 1987). Her inquiries focus on the causes blacks give for their achievement orientation—why they succeed or fail, for example. She is struck by how consistently middle-class black children do not fit our stereotypes of either deviant or special populations. They—like their middle-class white counterparts—have high expectations and understand that failure is often due to lack of effort rather than to luck.

Not only can we compare the achievement orientation of children from different ethnic groups and social classes, but we can also compare the achievement orientation of children in different countries. Quite clearly, American children are more achievement-oriented than children in many countries. However, there has recently been concern about the achievement American children display in comparison to children in other countries that have developed strong educational orientations—Russia and Japan, for example. To learn more about the achievement orientation of American children compared to Japanese children, turn to Focus on Life-Span Development 10.3.

ACHIEVEMENT IN MATH
REQUIRES TIME AND PRACTICE—
COMPARISONS OF CHILDREN
IN THE UNITED STATES AND JAPAN

Harold Stevenson and his colleagues (1986) recently conducted a detailed investigation of math achievement in first and fifth grade children from the United States and Japan. The final sample included 240 first graders and 240 fifth graders from each country. Extensive time was spent developing the math test that was given to the children, the children were observed in their classrooms, and additional information was obtained from mothers, teachers, and the children themselves. As shown in table 10.A, the Japanese children clearly outscored the American children on the math test in both the first and fifth grades. And, by the fifth grade, the highest average score of any of the American classrooms fell *below* the worst performing score of the Japanese classrooms.

What are some reasons for these dramatic differences between American and Japanese children's math achievement? Curriculum did not seem to be a factor. Neither was the educational background of the children's parents. And neither was intelligence—the American children sampled actually scored slightly

TABLE 10.A
Average Mathematics Achievement by Japanese and American Children

Country	Boys	Girls
Grade 1		
Japan	20.7	19.5
United States	16.6	17.6
Grade 5		
Japan	53.0	53.5
United States	45.0	43.8

higher than the Japanese children on such components of intelligence as vocabulary, general information, verbal ability, and perceptual speed. Possibly the Japanese teachers had more experience? Apparently, this was not the case since both in terms of educational degrees and years of teaching experiences, no differences were found.

The amount of time spent in school and math classes probably was an important factor. The Japanese

school year consists of 240 days of instruction and each school week is 5½ days; the American school year consists of 178 days of instruction and each school week is 5 days. In the fifth grade, Japanese children were in school an average of 37.3 hours per week, American children only 30.4 hours. Observations in the children's classrooms revealed that Japanese teachers spent far more time teaching math than did American teachers; approximately one-fourth of total classroom time in the first grade was spent in math instruction in Japan, only approximately one-tenth in the United States. Observations also indicated that the Japanese children attended more efficiently to what the teacher was saying than American children did. And Japanese children spent far more time doing homework than American children—on weekends, 66 minutes versus 18 minutes, respectively.

The conclusion: Learning requires time and practice. When either is reduced, learning is impaired. Such seems to be the case in American children's poor math achievement in comparison to Japanese children's.

Summary

I. **Physical Development**
Growth is slow and consistent in middle and late childhood—the calm before the rapid growth spurt of adolescence. With regard to body build, children can be classified as endomorphs, mesomorphs, and ectomorphs. Motor development becomes smoother and sensory mechanisms continue to mature. While they cognitively recognize the importance of nutrition and exercise, their behavior often does not reflect this recognition.

II. **Piaget's Theory and Cognitive Developmental Changes**
Concrete operational thought is made up of operations, mental actions that are reversible. The concrete operational child shows conservation and classification skills. The concrete operational child needs clearly available perceptual supports to reason; later in development, thought becomes more abstract. Piaget's ideas have been applied extensively to education. Piaget was a genius at observing children; he showed us some important things to look for and mapped out some general cognitive changes. Criticisms of his theory focus on such matters as stages, which are not as unitary as he believed and do not always follow the time table he envisioned.

III. **Information Processing**
Children's long-term memory improves during middle and late childhood. Control processes or strategies such as rehearsal, organization, and imagery are among the important influences responsible for memory improvement. Children's knowledge also influences their memory. A special kind of knowledge—metamemory—concerns control processes. Schemata and scripts become more prominent in the cognitive world of the elementary school child.

IV. **What Is Intelligence?**
Intelligence is verbal and problem-solving ability, as well as the ability to learn from experience and adapt to everyday life. Extensive effort is made to assess individual differences in intelligence.

V. **Intelligence: One Face or Many Faces?**
Binet developed the first intelligence test in 1905. He developed the concept of mental age and Stern developed the concept of IQ. The Binet has been standardized and revised many times. The test approximates a normal distribution. Besides the Binet, the most widely used intelligence test today consists of the Wechsler scales. These scales provide an overall IQ, verbal and performance IQ, and information about 11 subscales. Psychologists debate whether intelligence is a general ability or a number of specific abilities. Spearman's two-factor theory suggested it is both.

VI. **Cultural Bias, Knowledge Versus Process, and the Use and Misuse of Intelligence Tests**
Early tests favored white, middle-class, urban children. Current tests try to reduce this bias. Culture fair tests are an alternative to traditional IQ tests; most developmentalists believe they cannot replace the traditional tests. The mechanism of intelligence and its development are both those of changing information processing abilities and changing expertise and knowledge. Sternberg's triarchic model emphasizes both information processing and knowledge. Despite limitations, when used by a judicious examiner, tests can be valuable tools for determining individual differences in intelligence.

VII. **The Extremes of Intelligence**
A mentally retarded individual has a low IQ, usually below 70, and has difficulty adapting to everyday life. Different classifications of retardation exist. The two main causes of retardation are organic and cultural-familial. We defined giftedness as an individual with well-above-average intelligence (an IQ of 120 or more), and/or a superior talent for something. We defined creativity as the ability to think about something in a novel or unusual way and to come up with unique solutions to problems.

VIII. **Achievement**
Early interest, stimulated by McClelland's ideas, focused on the need for achievement. Contemporary ideas on achievement include the distinction between intrinsic and extrinsic motivation, as well as a concern about achievement motivation in minority group children.

Key Terms

endomorphic 286

mesomorphic 286

ectomorphic 286

long-term memory 289

control processes 289

rehearsal 289

metamemory 290

schemata 290

scripts 290

intelligence 294

mental age (MA) 295

intelligence quotient (IQ) 295

normal distribution 295

Wechsler Scales 296

two factor theory 296

culture fair tests 302

structure-process dilemma 303

working memory 303

triarchic theory of intelligence 304

mental retardation 305

organic retardation 306

cultural-familial retardation 306

gifted 307

convergent thinking 308

divergent thinking 308

creativity 309

n achievement 309

intrinsic motivation 311

extrinsic motivation 312

Suggested Readings

Anastasi, A. (1988). *Psychological testing* (6th ed.). New York: Macmillan.
This widely used text on psychological testing provides extensive information about intelligence tests for children.

Horowitz, F. D., & O'Brien, M. (Eds.). (1985). *The gifted and the talented.* Washington, DC: The American Psychological Association.
This volume pulls together what we currently know about the gifted and the talented. Experts contributed chapters on the diverse nature of the gifted and the talented.

Kail, R. (1984). *The development of memory in children.* San Francisco: W. H. Freeman.
A readable review of developmental changes in children's memory. Includes information about many aspects of memory such as metamemory, control processes, and long-term memory.

McAdoo, H. P., & McAdoo, J. L. (1985). *Black children: Social, educational, and parental environments.* Beverly Hills, CA: Sage.
This book provides a contemporary look at the nature of achievement orientation in black children.

McDaniel, M. A., & Pressley, M. (1987). *Imagery and related mnemonic processes.* New York: Springer-Verlag.
This book provides a number of excellent strategies, especially those involving imagery, for improving children's memory.

C H A P T E R

11

■

Social and Personality Development

Can children in middle and late childhood understand concepts like discrimination, economic inequality, affirmative action, and comparable worth? Probably not if we used these terms, but might we be able to construct circumstances involving these terms that they might be able to understand? Phyllis Katz (1987) asked children to pretend that they had taken a long ride on a spaceship to a make-believe planet called Pax and to give opinions about different situations in which they found themselves. The situations involved conflict, socioeconomic inequality, and civil-political rights. For example, conflict items included asking what a teacher should do when two students were tied for a prize or when they have been fighting. The economic equality dilemmas included a proposed field trip that not all students could afford, a comparable worth situation where janitors were paid more than teachers, and an employment situation that discriminated against those with dots on their nose instead of stripes. The rights items dealt with minority rights and freedom of the press.

The elementary school children did indeed recognize injustice and often came up with interesting solutions to problems. For example, all but two children believed that teachers should earn as much as janitors—the holdouts said teachers should make less because they stay in one room or because toilet cleaning is more disgusting and therefore deserves higher wages. Children were especially responsive to the economic inequality items. All but one thought that not giving a job to a qualified applicant who had different physical characteristics (a striped rather than a dotted nose) was unfair. The majority recommended an affirmative action solution—giving the job to the one from the discriminated minority. None of the children verbalized the concept of freedom of the press or seemed to understand that a newspaper could have the right to criticize a mayor in print without being punished. What are our schools teaching children about democracy? Some of the courses of action suggested were intriguing. Several argued that the reporters should be jailed. One child said that if she were mayor she would worry, make speeches, and say I didn't do anything wrong, not unlike what American presidents have done in recent years. Another said that the mayor should not put the newspaper people out of work because that might make them print more bad things. "Make them write comics instead," he said.

Children believed that poverty existed on Earth but mainly in Africa, big cities, or Vietnam. War was mentioned as the biggest problem on Earth, although children were not certain where that is currently occurring. Other problems mentioned were crime, hatred, school, smog, meanness, and Delta Airlines. (The questions were asked soon after a Delta Airlines crash.) Overall, the types of rules the children believed a society should abide by were quite sensible—almost all included the need for equitable sharing of resources and work, and prohibitions against aggression.

Later in this chapter, we will discuss further children's thoughts about rules and regulations, as we continue our description of moral development. Additional aspects of the self and gender roles also are presented. To begin the chapter the social worlds of children's families, peers, and schools in middle and late childhood are examined.

Families

As children move into the middle and late childhood years, parents spend considerably less time with them. In one investigation, parents spent less than half as much time with their children aged 5 to 12 in caregiving, instruction, reading, talking, and playing than when the children were younger (Hill & Stafford, 1980). This drop in parent-child interaction may be even more extensive in families with little parental education. While parents spend less time with their children in middle and late childhood than in early childhood, parents continue to be extremely important socializing agents in their children's lives. What are some of the most important parent-child issues in middle and late childhood?

Parent-Child Issues

The focus of parent-child interaction during early childhood is on such matters as modesty, bedtime regularities, control of temper, fighting with siblings and peers, eating behavior and manners, autonomy in dressing, and attention seeking. While some of these issues—fighting and reaction to discipline, for example—are carried forward to the elementary school years, many new issues appear by the age of 7 (Maccoby, 1984). These include whether children should be made to perform chores, and, if so, whether they should be paid for them; how to help children learn to entertain themselves rather than relying on parents for everything; and how to monitor children's lives outside the family in school and peer settings.

Of all the animals, the boy is the most unmanageable, inasmuch as he has the fountain of reason in him not yet regulated; He is the most insidious, sharp-witted, and insubordinate of animals. Wherefore he must be bound with many bridles.

Plato, 350 B.C.

School-related matters are especially important for families during middle and late childhood. Later in this chapter, we will see that school-related difficulties are the number one reason that children in this age group are referred for clinical help. Children must learn to relate to adults outside the family on a regular basis—adults who interact with the child much differently than parents. During middle and late childhood, interactions with adults outside the family involve more formal control and achievement orientation.

Discipline during middle and late childhood is often easier for parents than was the case during early childhood, and may also be easier than during adolescence. In middle and late childhood, children's cognitive development has matured to the point where it is possible for parents to reason with them about resisting deviation and controlling their behavior. By adolescence, children's reasoning has become more sophisticated and they may be less likely to accept parental discipline. Adolescents also push more strongly for independence, which contributes to parenting difficulties. Parents of elementary school children use less physical discipline than the parents of preschool children. By contrast, parents of elementary school children are more likely to use deprivation of privileges, appeals directed at the child's esteem, comments designed to increase the child's sense of guilt, and statements indicating to the child that she is responsible for her actions.

During middle and late childhood, there is some transfer of control from parent to child, although the process is gradual and involves **coregulation** rather than control by the child or the parent alone (Maccoby, 1984). The major shift to autonomy does not occur until about the age of 12 or later. During middle and late childhood, parents continue to exert general supervision and control while children are allowed to engage in moment-to-moment self-regulation. This coregulation process is a transition period between the strong parental control of early childhood and the increased relinquishment of general supervision of adolescence.

During this coregulation, parents should:

monitor, guide, and support children at a distance
effectively use the times when they have direct contact with the child
strengthen in their children the ability to monitor their own behavior,
to adopt appropriate standards of conduct, to avoid hazardous
risks, and to sense when parental support and contact is
appropriate.

In the middle and late childhood years, parents and children increasingly label each other and make attributions about each others' motives. Parents and children do not react to each other only on the basis of each others' past behavior; rather, their reactions to each other are based on how they interpret behavior and their expectations for behavior. Parents and children broadly label each other. Parents label their children "smart" or "dumb," "introverted" or "extraverted," "mannerly" or "unruly," and "lazy" or "hard working." Children label their parents as "cold" or "warm," "understanding" or "not understanding," and so on. Even though there probably are specific circumstances when children and parents do not conform to these labels, the labels represent a distillation of many hours, days, months, and years of learning what each other is like as a person.

Life changes in parents also influence the nature of parent-child interaction in middle and late childhood. Parents are more experienced in child rearing than they were when their children were infants or preschoolers. As child-rearing demands are reduced in middle and late childhood, mothers are more likely to consider returning to a career or beginning a career. Marital relationships change as less time is spent in child rearing and more time is spent in career development, especially in the case of mothers.

Societal Changes in Families

As we discussed in chapter 9, increasing numbers of children are growing up in divorced and working-mother families. But there are several other major shifts in family life's composition that especially affect children in middle and late childhood. Parents are getting divorced in greater numbers than ever before, but many of them remarry. It takes time for parents to marry, have children, get divorced, and then remarry. Consequently there are far more elementary and secondary school children living in stepfamilies than infant or preschool children. In addition, an increasing number of elementary and secondary school children are latchkey children.

Stepfamilies

The number of remarriages involving children has steadily grown in recent years, although both the rate of increase in divorce and stepfamilies has slowed in the 1980s. Stepfather families, in which a woman has custody of children in a previous marriage, make up 70 percent of stepfamilies. Stepmother families make up almost 20 percent of stepfamilies, and a small minority are blended with both parents bringing children from a previous marriage. A substantial percentage of stepfamilies also produce children of their own.

Research on stepfamilies has lagged behind research on divorced families, but recently a number of investigators have turned their attention to this increasingly common family structure (e.g., Bray, in press; Brand, Clingempeel, & Bowen-Woodward, in press; Furstenberg, in press; Hetherington, Hagan, & Anderson, in press; Pasley & Ihinger-Tallman, 1987; Santrock & Sitterle, 1987; Zill, in press). Following remarriage, children of all ages show a resurgence of problem behaviors. Younger children seem to be able to eventually form an attachment to a stepparent and accept the stepparent in a parenting role. However, the developmental tasks facing adolescents make them especially vulnerable to the entrance of a stepparent. At the time they are searching for an identity and exploring sexual and close relationships outside the family, a nonbiological parent may increase the stress associated with the accomplishment of these important tasks.

Following the remarriage of the custodial parent, a reemergence of emotional upheaval in girls and intensification of problems in boys often take place. Over time, preadolescent boys seem to improve more than girls in stepfather families. Sons who frequently are involved in conflicted, coercive relations with their custodial mothers likely have much to gain from the introduction of a warm, supportive stepfather. In contrast, daughters who frequently have a close relationship with their custodial mothers and considerable independence may find a stepfather disruptive and constraining.

Children's relationships with biological parents are more positive than with stepparents regardless of whether a stepmother or a stepfather family is involved. Stepfathers often have a distant, disengaged relationship with their stepchildren. And, as a rule, the more complex the stepfamily, the more difficult the children's adjustment. Families in which both parents bring children from a previous marriage are associated with the highest level of behavioral problems, for example.

What might parents do to improve the adjustment of children in stepfamilies?

In sum, as with divorce, entrance into a stepfamily involves a disequilibrium in children's lives. Most children initially experience their parent's remarriage as stressful. Remarriage, though, can remove children from stressful single parent circumstances and provide additional resources for children. Many children emerge from their remarried family as competent individuals. As with divorced families, it is important to consider the complexity of stepfamilies, the diversity of child outcomes possible, and the factors that facilitate children's adjustment in stepfamilies (Hetherington, Hagan, & Anderson, 1988; Santrock, Sitterle, & Warshak, 1988).

Latchkey Children
While we concluded in chapter 9 that the mother's working is not associated with negative child outcomes, a certain set of children from working mother families bear further scrutiny: latchkey children. They typically do not see their parents from the time they leave for school in the morning until about 6:00 or 7:00 P.M. They are called latchkey children because they are given the key to their home, take the key to school, and then use it to let themselves into the home while their parents are still at work. Latchkey children are largely unsupervised for two to four hours a day during each school week. During the summer months, they may be unsupervised for entire days, five days a week.

Thomas and Lynette Long (1983) interviewed more than 1,500 latchkey children. They concluded that a slight majority of these children had negative latchkey experiences. Some latchkey children may grow up too fast, hurried by the responsibility placed on them (Elkind, 1981). How do latchkey children handle the lack of limits and structure during the latchkey hours? Without limits and parental supervision, it becomes easier for latchkey children to find their way into trouble—possibly abusing a sibling, stealing, or vandalizing. The Longs point out that 90 percent of the adjudicated juvenile delinquents in Montgomery County, Maryland, are latchkey children. Joan Lipsitz (1983), in testifying before the Select Committee on Children, Youth, and Families, called the lack of adult supervision of children in the after school hours one of the nation's major problems today. Lipsitz calls it the "three-six o'clock problem" because it is during this time frame that the Center for Early Adolescence in North Carolina, where she is director, experiences a peak of referrals for clinical help.

But while latchkey children may be vulnerable to problems, keep in mind that the experiences of latchkey children vary enormously, just as do the experiences of all children with working mothers. Parents need to give special attention to the ways their latchkey children's lives can be monitored effectively. Variations in latchkey experiences suggest that parental monitoring and authoritative parenting help the child cope more effectively with latchkey experiences, especially resisting peer pressure (Steinberg, 1986). The degree of latchkey children's developmental risk remains unsettled. A positive sign is that researchers are beginning to conduct more fine-grained analysis of children's latchkey experiences in an effort to determine which aspects of latchkey circumstances are the most detrimental (Rodman & others, 1988; Steinberg, 1988).

Children spend increasing amounts of time with peers as they grow older. What do children usually do when they are with their peers?

Peer Relations

Children spend an increasing amount of time in peer interaction during middle and late childhood. In one investigation, children interacted with peers 10 percent of their day at the age of 2, 20 percent at age 4, and more than 40 percent between the ages of 7 and 11. In a typical school day, episodes with peers totaled 299 times per day (Barker & Wright, 1955).

What do children do when they are with their peers? In one study, sixth graders were asked what they do when they are with their friends (Medrich & others, 1982). Team sports accounted for 45 percent of boys' nominations but only 26 percent of girls'. General play, going places, and socializing were common listings for both sexes. Most peer interactions occur outside the home (although close to home), occur more often in private than in public places, and occur more between children of the same sex than the opposite sex.

The little ones leaped, and shouted, and Laugh'd and all the hills echoed.
William Blake

Peer Popularity, Rejection, and Neglect

Children often think, "What can I do to get all of the kids at school to like me?" or "What's wrong with me? Something must be wrong with me or I would be more popular." What makes a child popular with peers? Children who give out the most reinforcements are often popular. So is a child who listens carefully to other children and maintains open lines of communication with peers. Being themselves, being happy, showing enthusiasm and concern for others, and being self-confident but not conceited are characteristics that serve children well in their quest to be popular with peers (Hartup, 1983).

Recently, developmentalists have distinguished between two types of children who are not popular with their peers—those who are neglected and those who are rejected (Asher & Dodge, 1986). **Neglected children,** while they may not have friends, are not especially disliked by their peers. However, **rejected children** are overtly disliked by their peers. Rejected children are more likely to be disruptive and aggressive than neglected children. And rejected children are more likely to continue to be unaccepted by peers even when they move into a new setting; neglected children seem to get a new social life in new groups. Rejected children say they are lonelier and less happy as well. And rejected children have more serious adjustment problems later in life. In sum, children who are rejected by their peers are more at risk for adjustment problems, while the risk status of children who are neglected by their peers is less certain (Coie & Kupersmidt, 1983; Dodge & others, 1986; East, Hess, & Lerner, 1987).

Social Cognition

Earlier we found that the mutual cognitions of children and parents become increasingly important in family relationships during middle and late childhood. Children's social cognitions about their peers also become increasingly important for understanding peer relationships in middle and late childhood. Of special interest are how children process information about peer relations and their social knowledge.

A peer accidentally trips and knocks a boy's soft drink out of his hand. The boy misinterprets the encounter as hostile, which leads him to retaliate aggressively against the peer. Through repeated encounters of this kind, peers come to perceive the boy as having a habit of acting inappropriately. Kenneth Dodge (1983) argues that children go through five steps in processing information about their social world: decoding of social cues, interpretation, response search, selecting an optimal response, and enactment. Dodge has found that aggressive boys are more likely to perceive another child's actions as hostile when the peer's intention is ambiguous. And when aggressive boys search for cues to determine a peer's intention, they respond more rapidly, less efficiently, and less reflectively than nonaggressive children. These are among the social cognitive factors believed to be involved in the nature of children's conflicts (Shantz, 1988).

Social knowledge also is involved in children's ability to get along with peers. An important part of children's social life involves what goals to pursue in poorly defined or ambiguous situations. Social relationship goals are also important, such as how to initiate and maintain a social bond. Children need to know what scripts to follow to get children to be their friends. For example, as part of the script for getting friends, it helps to know that saying nice things, regardless of what the peer does or says, will make the peer like the child more.

One investigation explored the possibility that children who are maladjusted do not have the social cognitive skills necessary for positive social interaction (Asarnow & Callan, 1985). Boys with and without peer adjustment difficulties were identified and their social cognitive skills were assessed. Boys without peer adjustment problems generated more alternative solutions to problems, proposed more assertive and mature solutions, gave less intense aggressive solutions, showed more adaptive planning, and evaluated physically aggressive responses less positively than boys with peer adjustment problems. Other researchers have successfully reduced maladaptive peer behavior through social skills training (Pepler, 1988).

The world of peers is one of varying acquaintances—children interact with some children they barely know and with others for hours every day. It is to the latter type—friends—that we now turn.

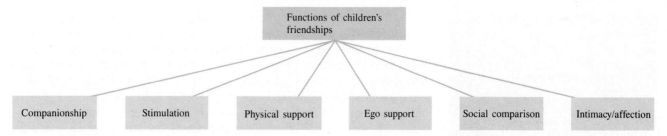

Figure 11.1
The functions of children's friendships.

Friends

"My best friend is nice. She is honest, and I can trust her. I can tell her my innermost secrets and know that nobody else will find out about them. I have other friends, but she is my best friend. We consider each other's feelings and don't want to hurt each other. We help each other out when we have problems. We make up funny names for people and laugh ourselves silly. We make lists of which boys we think are the ugliest, which are the biggest jerks, and so on. Some of these things we share with other friends, some we don't." This is a description of a friendship by a 10-year-old girl. It reflects the belief that children are interested in specific peers—in Barbara and Tommy—not just any peers. They want to share concerns, interests, information, and secrets with them.

Why are children's friendships important? They serve six functions: companionship, stimulation, physical support, ego support, social comparison, and intimacy/affection (Gottman & Parker, 1987). Concerning companionship, friendship provides children with a familiar partner and playmate, someone who is willing to spend time with them and join in collaborative activities. Concerning stimulation, friendship provides children with interesting information, excitement, and amusement. Concerning physical support, friendship provides time, resources, and assistance. Concerning ego support, friendship provides the expectation of support, encouragement, and feedback that helps the child maintain an impression of herself as a competent, attractive, and worthwhile individual. Concerning social comparison, friendship provides information about where the child stands vis-à-vis others and whether the child is doing OK. Concerning intimacy/affection, friendship provides children with a warm, close, trusting relationship with another individual in which self-disclosure takes place (see figure 11.1).

While friendships exist in early childhood, they become more predominant during middle and late childhood. Robert Selman (1980) proposed a developmental model that highlights friendship's changing faces. Friendship begins at 3 to 7 years of age with momentary friendship—friends are valued because they are nearby and have nice toys. At 4 to 9 years, friendship involves one-way assistance—a friend is a friend because he does what you want him to do. At 6 to 12 years of age, friendship consists of two-way fair-weather cooperation, followed at 9 to 15 years of age by intimate, mutually shared relationships. Finally, at 12 years of age and older, children gain enough perspective for autonomous interdependent friendships to become possible.

A man's growth is seen in the successive choirs of his friends.
Ralph Waldo Emerson, 1841

Hold a true friend with both hands.
Nigerian Proverb

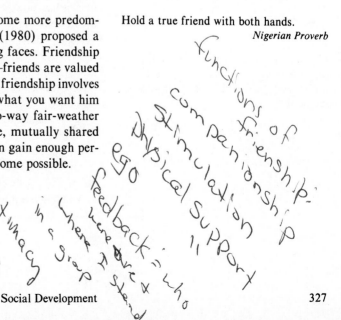

I remember my best friend from elementary school. He lived on the next street. We played football, basketball, tennis, Monopoly, and cards together. Most grades we were in the same room together at school. We came from a similar socioeconomic background and went to the same church. Occasionally we got into trouble together—our basketball kept landing in Mr. Philip's flower garden. Who was your best friend during elementary school? Think about your times together. What characteristics did you share? How private was the information you communicated?

Why does early elementary school involve so much feedback? What aspects of our culture and the nature of education are responsible?

Two of friendship's most common characteristics are intimacy and similarity. **Intimacy** in friendships is defined as self-disclosure and the sharing of private thoughts. Research reveals that intimate friendships may not appear until early adolescence (Berndt, 1982), and that intimacy characterizes girls' friendship more than boys (Bukowski, Newcomb, & Hoza, 1988). Also, throughout childhood, friends are more similar than dissimilar—in terms of age, sex, race, and many other factors. Friends often have similar attitudes toward school, similar educational aspirations, and closely aligned achievement orientations. Friends like the same music, the same kind of clothes, and the same kind of leisure activities.

Schools

It is justifiable to be concerned about the impact of schools on children—by the time individuals graduate from high school they have spent 10,000 hours in the classroom. Children spend many years in schools as members of a small society in which there are tasks to be accomplished, people to be socialized and socialized by, and rules that define and limit behavior, feelings, and attitudes. The experiences of children in this society probably are strong influences on their identity, sense of competence, images of life and career possibilities, social relationships, standards of right and wrong, and conceptions of how a social system beyond the family functions.

For most children, entering the first grade signals a change from being a "home-child" to being a "school-child" in which new roles and obligations are experienced. Children take up a new role (being a student), interact and develop relationships with new significant others, adopt new reference groups, and develop new standards by which to judge themselves. School provides children with a rich source of new ideas to shape their sense of self.

A special concern about children's early school experiences is emerging. While we know little about the transitional nature of teaching in the early grades, what research is available suggests that early schooling proceeds mainly on the basis of negative feedback. For example, children's self-esteem in the latter part of elementary school is lower than it is in the earlier part and older children rate themselves as less smart, less good, and less hard-working than do younger ones (Blumenfeld & others, 1981; Eschel & Klein, 1981; Morse, 1964). In one recent investigation (Entwisle & others, 1987), the emergence of children's academic self-image was different for boys and girls. The academic self-image of first grade girls strongly reflected stereotypic gender role notions. These first grade girls did not consider their ability in mathematics relevant to their academic self-image, even though they did as well in math as boys did and were exposed to the same kind of math instruction as boys. By contrast, first grade boys were more concerned with the achievement aspects of their student role.

Teachers and peers have a prominent influence on children in middle and late childhood. Teachers symbolize authority and establish the classroom's climate, conditions of interaction among students, and the nature of group functioning. The peer group is an important source of status, friendship, and belonging in the school setting; the peer group also is a learning community in which social roles and standards related to work and achievement are formed.

Virtually everyone's life is affected in one way or another by teachers: You were probably influenced by teachers as you grew up; you may become a teacher yourself or work with teachers through counseling or psychological services; and you may one day have children whose education will be guided by many different teachers through the years. You can probably remember several of your teachers vividly: Perhaps one never smiled, another required you to memorize everything in sight, and yet another always appeared happy and vibrant and encouraged verbal interaction. Psychologists and educators have tried to create a profile of a good teacher's personality traits, but the complexity of personality, education, learning, and individual differences make the task difficult. Nonetheless, some teacher traits are associated with positive student outcomes more than others—enthusiasm, ability to plan, poise, adaptability, warmth, flexibility, and awareness of individual differences, for example (Gage, 1965).

Erik Erikson (1968) believes that good teachers should be able to produce a sense of industry, rather than inferiority, in their students. Good teachers are trusted and respected by the community and know how to alternate work and play, study and games, says Erikson. They know how to recognize special efforts and to encourage special abilities. They also know how to create a setting in which children feel good about themselves and how to handle those children to whom school is not important. In Erickson's (1968) own words, children should be "mildly but firmly coerced into the adventure of finding out that one can learn to accomplish things which one would never have thought of by oneself" (p. 127).

Teacher characteristics and styles are important, but they need to be considered in concert with what children bring to the school situation. Some children may benefit more from structure than others, and some teachers may be able to handle a flexible curriculum better than others. The importance of both children's characteristics and the treatments or experiences they are given in classrooms is known as **aptitude-treatment interaction (ATI).** Aptitude refers to academic potential and personality dimensions on which students differ; treatment refers to educational techniques—structured versus flexible classrooms, for example (Cronbach & Snow, 1977). Research has shown that children's achievement level (aptitude) interacts with classroom structure (treatment) to produce the best learning and most enjoyable learning environment (Peterson, 1977). That is, high-achievement-oriented students usually do well in a flexible classroom and enjoy it; low-achievement-oriented students usually fare worse and dislike the flexibility. The reverse often appears in structured classrooms.

Sometimes it seems as though the major functions of schools in this country is to train children to contribute to a middle-class society. Politicians who vote on school funding are usually middle-class, school board members are usually middle-class, and principals and teachers usually are middle-class. Critics argue that schools have not done a good job in educating lower-class children to overcome the barriers blocking the enhancement of their position.

Teachers have lower expectations for children from low income families than for children from middle-income families. A teacher who knows that a child comes from a lower-class background may spend less time trying to help the child solve a problem and may anticipate that the child will get into trouble.

The world rests on the breath of the children in the schoolhouse.

The Talmud

The teacher may perceive that the parents in low-income families are not interested in helping the child so she may make fewer efforts to communicate with them. There is evidence that teachers with lower-class origins may have different attitudes toward lower-class students than teachers from middle-class origins (Gottlieb, 1966). Perhaps because they have experienced many inequities themselves, teachers with lower-class origins may be more empathetic to problems that lower-class children encounter. When asked to rate the most outstanding characteristics of their lower-class students, middle-class teachers checked lazy, rebellious, and fun-loving; lower-class teachers checked happy, cooperative, energetic, and ambitious. The teachers with lower-class backgrounds perceived the lower-class children's behaviors as adaptive; the middle-class teachers viewed the same behaviors as falling short of middle-class standards.

Martin Luther King once said, "I have a dream that my four little children will one day live in a nation where they will not be judged by the color of their skin but by the content of their character." Not only have children from lower-class backgrounds had difficulties in school, so have children from different ethnic backgrounds. In most American schools, blacks, Mexican Americans, Puerto Ricans, Native Americans, Japanese, and Asian Indians are minorities. The social and academic development of children from minority groups depends on teacher expectations, the teacher's experience in working with children from different backgrounds, the curriculum, the presence of role models in the schools for minority students, the quality of relations between school personnel and parents from different ethnic, economic, and educational backgrounds, and the relations between the school and the community (Minuchin & Shapiro, 1983).

When the schools of Austin, Texas, were desegregated through extensive busing, the outcome was increased racial tension among blacks, Mexican Americans, and Anglos, producing violence in the schools. The superintendent consulted with Eliot Aronson, a prominent social psychologist, who was at the University of Texas in Austin at the time. Aronson thought it was more important to prevent racial hostility than to control it. This led him to observe a number of elementary school classrooms in Austin. What he saw was fierce competition between individuals of unequal status. To learn how Aronson proposed to reduce the tension and fierce competition, turn to Focus on Life-Span Development 11.1.

At this point we have discussed a number of important ideas about families, peers, and schools, A summary of these ideas is presented in Concept Table 11.1. Next, we turn to children's personality development in middle and late childhood, exploring the self, gender roles, and moral development.

My country is the world;
My countrymen are mankind.
William Lloyd Garrison, 1803

Our most basic common link is that we all inhabit this planet. We all breathe the same air. We all cherish our children's future.
John F. Kennedy, address, The American University, *1963*

schools
- sense of identity
- " " competence self
- develop an academic self image

high-achieve need, self starters do well
DA open education
low-achievers don't like lack of structure

Aronson stressed that the reward structure of the elementary school classrooms needed to be changed from a setting of unequal competition to one of cooperation among equals, without making any curriculum changes. To accomplish this, he put together the **jigsaw classroom.** How might this work? Consider a class of thirty students, some Anglo, some black, some Hispanic. The lesson to be learned focuses on the life of Joseph Pulitzer. The class might be broken up into five groups of six students each, with the groups being as equal as possible in terms of ethnic composition and academic achievement level. The lesson about Pulitzer's life could be divided into six parts, with one part given to each member of the six-person group. The parts might be paragraphs from Pulitzer's biography, such as how the Pulitzer family came to the United States, his childhood, his early work, and so on. The components are like parts of a jigsaw puzzle. The have to be put together to form the complete puzzle.

Each student in the group is given an allotted time to study his part. Then the group meets and each member tries to teach a part to the group. After an hour or so, each member is tested on the entire life of Pulitzer with each member receiving an individual rather than a group score. Each student, therefore, must learn the entire lesson; learning depends on the cooperation and effort of the other members. Aronson (1986) believes this type of learning increases the students' interdependence through cooperatively reaching the same goal.

The strategy of emphasizing cooperation rather than competition and the jigsaw classroom have been widely used in classrooms in the United States. A number of research studies reveal that this type of cooperative learning is associated with increased self-esteem, better academic performance, friendships among classmates, and improved interethnic perceptions (Aronson, 1986; Slavin, 1983, 1987).

While the cooperative classroom strategy has many merits, it may have a built-in difficulty that restricts its effectiveness. Academic achievement is as much an individual as a team "sport" (Brown, 1986). It is individuals, not groups, who enter college, take jobs, and follow a career. A parent with an advantaged child in the jigsaw classroom might react with increased ethnic hostility when the child brings home a lower grade than he had been used to getting before the jigsaw classroom was introduced. The child tells the father, "The teacher is getting us to teach each other. In my group, we have a kid named Carlos who can barely speak English." While the jigsaw classroom can be an important strategy for reducing interracial hostility, caution needs to be exercised in its use because of the unequal status of the participants and the individual nature of achievement.

CONCEPT TABLE

11.1

Families, Peers, and Schools		
Concept	**Processes/Related Ideas**	**Characteristics/Description**
Families	Parent-child Interaction and Issues	Parents spend less time with children during middle and late childhood, including less time in caregiving, instruction, reading, talking, and playing. Nonetheless, parents still are powerful and important socializing agents in this period. New parent-child issues emerge and discipline changes. Control is more coregulatory, children and parents label each other more, and parents mature just as children do.
	Societal Changes in Families	Just as divorce produces disequilibrium and stress for children, so does the entrance of a stepparent. Over time, preadolescent boys seem to improve more than girls in stepfather families. Adolescence appears to be an especially difficult time for adjustment to the entrance of a stepparent. Children's relationships with biological parents are consistently better than with stepparents, and children's adjustment is adversely affected the more complex the stepfamily becomes.
Peer Relations	Peer Interaction	Children spend considerably more time with peers in middle and late childhood.
	Popularity, Rejection, and Neglect	Listening skills and effective communication, being yourself, being happy, showing enthusiasm and concern for others, and indicating self-confidence but not conceit are predictors of peer popularity. Rejected children are at risk for adjustment problems; the risk status of neglected children is less clear.
	Social Cognition	Social information processing skills and social knowledge are two important dimensions of social cognition in peer relations.
	Friends	Children's friendships serve six functions: companionship, stimulation, physical support, ego support, social comparison, and intimacy/affection. Intimacy and similarity are two common characteristics of friendships.
Schools	Their Nature	Children spend more than 10,000 hours in the classroom as members of a small society in which there are tasks to be accomplished, people to be socialized and socialized by, and rules that define and limit behavior, feelings, and attitudes. A special concern is that early schooling proceeds mainly on the basis of negative feedback to children. A profile of a good teacher's personality traits is difficult to establish, although some traits are clearly superior to others. Aptitude-treatment interaction is an important consideration. Schools have a stronger middle-class than lower-class orientation. Not only do many lower-class children have problems in schools, so do children from ethnic minorities. Efforts to reduce these biases are being made, among them the jigsaw classroom.

As children move through childhood's experiences and challenges, their feelings about themselves are an important dimension of their existence. Children need to feel good about themselves, to have confidence in their abilities, and to evaluate their thoughts and behaviors positively.

Personality Development

Children's expanding social worlds and increased cognitive sophistication in middle and late childhood contribute to how they perceive themselves, to their social competence, to their gender roles, and to their thoughts about standards of right and wrong.

The Self and Social Competence

What are some important changes in the self and self-concept in middle and late childhood? What makes a child socially competent in this period of development? What did Erikson believe was the most important consideration in middle and late childhood? We consider each of these questions in turn.

Self-Concept

An important dimension of children's self-concept is their increasing ability to understand how they are viewed by others. Young children have difficulty in understanding others' perspective of them, and they are often unaware of the impressions their behavior makes on others. But gradually, children come to understand that their behavior triggers reactions from others, and they begin to monitor their actions, acting differently depending on whom they are with and which aspect of their social self they wish to be seen. This represents a time when children are more cautious about revealing themselves to others (Maccoby, 1980).

Closely related to self-concept is the child's *self-esteem*—the value children place on themselves and their behavior. Children with high self-esteem feel good about themselves and evaluate their abilities highly. In one investigation, a measure of self-esteem was administered to elementary school boys, and the boys and their mothers were interviewed about their family relationships (Coopersmith, 1967). Based on these assessments, the following parenting attributes were associated with the boys' high self-esteem:

> expression of affection
> concern about the child's problems
> harmony in the home

When I was one,
I had just begun.
When I was two,
I was nearly new.
When I was three,
I was hardly me.
When I was four,
I was not much more.
When I was five,
I was just alive.
But now I am six, I'm as clever as ever.
So I think I'll be six now forever and ever.
A. A. Milne, Now We Are Six

Figure 11.2
The Harter Perceived Competence Scale for children.

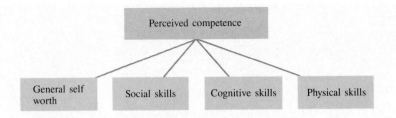

participation in joint family activities

availability to give competent, organized help to the boys when they need it

setting clear and fair rules

abiding by these rules

allowing the children freedom within well-prescribed limits

Efforts to measure self-concept and self-esteem have been numerous, but one measure deserves special attention. Susan Harter (1982) developed the **Perceived Competence Scale for Children.** This measure consists of four components. One set of questions measures general self-worth (sure of myself; happy the way I am). Self-perceptions of skills in three different areas represent other sets of questions: cognitive (good at schoolwork; remember things easily); social (have a lot of friends; most kids like me); and physical (do well at sports; first chosen for games). Harter's scale does an excellent job of separating the child's self-perceptions about abilities in different skill areas; and when general self-worth is measured, questions that focus on overall perceptions of the self are used rather than questions that are directed at specific skill domains (see figure 11.2). Notice that Harter calls her scale an assessment of perceived competence. Notice also that one of the important domains of perceived competence is social competence. Indeed, in recent years, developmentalists have shown an increased interest in mapping out what social competence is.

Social Competence

Socially competent children are able to use resources within themselves and in the environment to achieve positive developmental outcomes (Waters & Sroufe, 1983). Resources within the self include self-esteem, self-control, delay of gratification, resilience to stress, and a healthy orientation toward achievement and work. For example, socially competent children feel good about themselves and have confidence in their abilities; they can control their behavior in the face of temptation and threat; they are able to delay gratification when appropriate rather than seeking immediate satisfaction; they cope effectively with stress (often viewing stress as a challenge rather than a threat); and they persist with effort in achieving goals. Parents are important resources in children's environment throughout the childhood years; in early childhood and beyond, peers assume more importance.

The dimensions of social competence may be different at various points in development—dependency is a positive feature of social competence in the first year but later takes on more negative tones. We saw that Erikson believes the development of trust is the most salient component of social competence in the first year, that autonomy has this distinction in the second year, and that initiative is the key aspect of social competence to develop during early childhood. What does Erikson believe is the most important dimension of social competence during middle and late childhood?

What makes a child socially competent? Socially competent children draw upon resources within the self and in the environment to attain positive developmental outcomes. The dimensions of the social competence may vary according to the developmental status of the child. For example, for these elementary school children, peers have begun to assume greater prominence than early in the children's development.

Industry versus Inferiority

Erikson's fourth stage of the human life cycle is industry versus inferiority and it appears during middle and late childhood. The term *industry* captures a dominant theme of this period: children become interested in how things are made and how they work. It is the Robinson Crusoe age in the sense that the enthusiasm and minute detail Crusoe uses to describe his activities appeals to the child's own budding sense of industry. When children are encouraged in their efforts to make and build and work—whether building a model airplane, constructing a treehouse, fixing a bicycle, solving an addition problem, or cooking—their sense of industry is increased. However, parents who see their children's efforts at making things as "mischief" or "making a mess" encourage children's development of a sense of inferiority.

Children's social worlds beyond their families also contribute to a sense of industry. School becomes especially important in this regard. Consider a child who is slightly below average in intelligence. He is too bright to be in special classes but not bright enough to be in gifted classes. He experiences frequent failures in his academic efforts, developing a sense of inferiority. By contrast, consider a child who has his sense of industry derogated at home. A series of sensitive and committed teachers may revitalize his sense of industry (Elkind, 1970).

Gender Roles

Children's social competence and personality also involve gender roles. Nowhere in the social and personality development of children have more sweeping changes occurred in recent years than in the area of gender roles. At a point not too long ago, it was accepted that boys should grow up to be masculine and girls should grow up to be feminine. The feedback children received from parents, peers, teachers, and television was consistent with this thinking. Today, diversity characterizes the gender roles of children and the feedback they receive from their environment. A young girl's mother may promote femininity, but the girl may be close friends with a "tomboy" in the neighborhood and have teachers who encourage her assertiveness.

Figure 11.3
Categories used in androgyny scales.

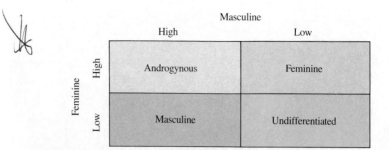

In the past, the well-adjusted male was expected to be independent, aggressive, and power-oriented; the well-adjusted female was expected to be dependent, nurturant, and uninterested in power and dominance. By the mid 1970s, though, the landscape of gender roles was changing. Many females were unhappy with the label "feminine" and felt stigmatized by its association with characteristics such as passive and unassertive. Many males were uncomfortable with being called "masculine" because of its association with such characteristics as insensitive and aggressive.

Many lay people as well as developmentalists believed that something more than "masculinity" and "femininity" was needed to describe the change in gender roles that was taking place. The byword became **androgyny,** meaning the combination of masculine and feminine characteristics in the same individual (Bem, 1977; Spence & Helmreich, 1978). The androgynous child might be a male who is assertive (masculine) and nurturant (feminine), or a female who is dominant (masculine) and sensitive to others' feelings (feminine).

The primary characteristics used to assess androgyny are self-assertiveness and integration (Ford, 1986). The self-assertive characteristics include: leadership, dominance, independence, competitiveness, and individualism. Integrative characteristics include: sympathy, affection, and understanding. The androgynous child is simply a female or male who has a high degree of both feminine and masculine characteristics—no new characteristics are used to describe the androgynous individual. An individual can be classified as masculine, feminine, or androgynous. A fourth category, **undifferentiated,** also is used to assess gender roles; this category describes an individual who has neither masculine nor feminine characteristics. The four classifications of gender roles are presented in figure 11.3.

Debate still flourishes on what the components ought to be that go into making up the masculine and feminine categories. Because these are combined to make up the androgyny category, the composition of masculinity and femininity is crucial to what it means to be androgynous. This raises an important issue in psychology. When a concept or construct is developed and evaluated, it is critical to pin down the dimensions of the concept. Specifying the dimensions of a concept in a logical, organized, and empirical way is one of psychology's great lessons. Unfortunately, in the case of androgyny, this lesson has sometimes been lost. In many cases, the concept of androgyny has been based on a hodgepodge of stereotypical ideas, especially those of college students, about personality differences between males and females (Downs & Langlois, 1988; Gill & others, 1987; Ford, 1986).

Adding to the complexity of determining whether a child is masculine, feminine, or androgynous is the child's developmental level (Maccoby, 1987). A 4-year-old boy would be labeled masculine if he enjoyed and frequently engaged in rough-and-tumble play, if he preferred to play with blocks and trucks, and if he tended to play outdoors in the company of other boys during free play periods at his preschool. A 4-year-old girl would be labeled feminine if she liked to wear dresses, played with dolls and art materials, and did not get into fights. At age 10, a masculine boy would be one who engaged in active sports, avoided girls, and was not especially diligent about his schoolwork. At age 10, a feminine girl would be one who had one or two close girlfriends, did not try to join boys' sports play groups, paid attention to the teacher in class, liked to baby-sit, and preferred romantic television fare. At age 15, a masculine boy would be one who excelled in spatial-visual tasks, liked and did well in math, was interested in cars and machinery, and knew how to repair mechanical gadgets. At age 15, a feminine girl would be more interested in English and history than math or science and would wear lipstick and makeup. These examples are not exhaustive but they give the flavor of how the characteristics of masculinity and femininity depend to some degree on the child's developmental status.

In a recent longitudinal investigation, both the developmental and multifaceted nature of gender roles was evident (Maccoby & Jacklin, in press). When the children were almost 4 years old, parents were asked whether their daughters were flirtatious, liked frilly clothes, cared how their hair looked, and liked to wear jewelry. These items formed a feminine scale. A second scale inquired about how rough and noisy their daughter was in playing with her agemates, whether she preferred to play with boys, girls, or both equally, whether she ever got into fights, and what her favorite pretend roles were. On the basis of these items, a "tomboy" scale was constructed, indicating the girls' motivation to play with boys, engage in rough and noisy play, fight occasionally, and engage in masculine fantasy roles. Somewhat surprising, the girls who were the most feminine on the first scale also were somewhat more likely to be tomboys. This finding raises several important points. Clearly, individuals may show some dimensions but not others among the set of stereotyped masculine or feminine attributes. Also, different aspects of the clusters may take on more or less importance at different ages. For example, two attributes—sexually attractive and gentle-kind-considerate-nurturant—are probably involved in the concept of femininity at all ages, but the sexual aspect probably is dominant in adolescence, while the second component may emerge most strongly in adulthood when many women are involved in the care of their children.

According to Martin Ford (1986), greater specification of gender roles is accomplished by describing masculinity in terms of self-assertion and femininity in terms of integration. **Self-assertion** includes such components as leadership, dominance, independence, competitiveness, and individualism. **Integration** includes such components as sympathy, affection, and understanding. An androgynous individual would be high on both self-assertion and integration. Sandra Gill and her colleagues (1987) believe greater specification in gender roles is accomplished by describing masculinity in terms of an instrumental orientation and femininity in terms of an expressive orientation. An **instrumental orientation** is concerned with the attainment of goals and an emphasis on the individual's accomplishments. An **expressive orientation** is concerned with facilitating social interaction, interdependence, and relationships. In both the descriptions by Ford and Gill and her colleagues, we find the same dual emphasis on the individual and social relations that also is proposed as the best way to describe social competence. Recall that earlier we described the most socially competent children as those who are both individually and socially oriented, who have both internal and external resources. So it is, too, with androgynous children. They are both self-assertive and integrative, instrumental and expressive.

Which children are the most competent? Children who are undifferentiated are the least competent; they are the least socially responsible, they have the least self-control, and they receive the poorest grades in school (Ford, 1986). This category is not well understood by psychologists and few children are classified in this way. But what about the majority of children, those who are either masculine, feminine, or androgynous—which group is the most competent?

This is not an easy question to answer because the dimensions of androgyny and the dimensions of competence are not clearly spelled out in research on the issue. In many instances, androgynous children are the most competent, but a key point involves the criteria for competence. If the criteria for competence involve self-assertion and integration or an instrumental and an expressive orientation, then androgynous children usually are more competent. However, if the criteria for competence primarily involve self-assertion or an instrumental orientation, then a masculine gender role is favored; if they primarily involve integration or an expressive orientation, then a feminine gender role is preferred. For example, masculine individuals might be more competent in school achievement and work while feminine individuals might be more competent in relationships and helping.

The self-assertive and instrumental dimensions of gender roles have been valued in our culture more than the integrative or expressive dimensions. When psychologists have assessed the relation of gender roles to competence, their criteria for competence have included twice as many self-assertive and instrumental as integrative and expressive items. A disturbing outcome of such cultural standards and research bias is that masculine dimensions are perceived to mean competence. We need to place a higher value on the integrative and expressive dimensions of our own and our children's lives and give these dimensions adequate weight in our assessment of competence.

How extensively are parents rearing their children to be androgonous today? Are there sex differences? Are there social class differences?

In addition to studying cultural expectations and attitudes about gender, we can also evaluate whether boys and girls actually differ on a number of dimensions. To sample some of the possible differences in gender, turn to table 11.1. According to a classic review of gender differences in 1974, Eleanor Maccoby and Carol Jacklin concluded that boys have better math skills, have superior visual-spatial ability (the kind of skills an architect would need to design a building's angles and dimensions), and are more aggressive, while girls are better at verbal abilities. Recently, Eleanor Maccoby (1987) revised her conclusion about several gender role dimensions. She commented that accumulation of research evidence suggests that boys now are more active than girls and she is less certain that girls have greater verbal ability than boys, mainly because boys score as high as girls on the verbal part of the Scholastic Aptitude Test (SAT).

Evidence is accumulating that some gender differences are vanishing, especially in the area of verbal abilities (Feingold, 1988; Hyde & Linn, 1986). In a recent analysis, Alan Feingold (1988) evaluated gender differences in cognitive abilities on two widely used tests—the Differential Aptitude Test and the SAT—from 1947 to 1983. Girls scored higher than boys on scales of grammar, spelling, and perceptual speed; boys scored higher on measures of spatial visualization, high school mathematics, and mechanical aptitude. No gender differences were found on verbal reasoning, arithmetic, and reasoning about figures. Gender differences declined precipitously over the years. One important exception to the rule of vanishing gender differences is the well-documented gender gap at the upper levels of performance on high school mathematics that has remained constant over three decades.

Middle and Late Childhood

TABLE 11.1
Adjectives that Describe Possible Gender Differences

What are the differences in the behavior and thoughts of boys and girls? For each of the adjectives below, indicate whether you think it *best* describes boys or girls—or neither—in our society. Be honest and follow your first impulse.

	Girls	Boys
Verbal skills	☐	☐
Sensitive	☐	☐
Active	☐	☐
Competitive	☐	☐
Compliant	☐	☐
Dominant	☐	☐
Math skills	☐	☐
Suggestible	☐	☐
Social	☐	☐
Aggressive	☐	☐
Visual-spatial skills	☐	☐

As can be seen, few data about gender differences seem to be cast in stone. As our culture has changed, so have some of our findings about gender differences and similarities. As our expectations and attitudes about gender roles have become more similar for boys and girls, in many areas, gender differences are vanishing.

But gender differences are not vanishing in all areas, as indicated by the differences that still persist in the area of math. One area of special concern about gender roles in today's society related to math and science focus on expectations and attitudes involving computer ability. In two recent novels, *Turing's Man* (Bolter, 1984) and *The Second Self* (Turkle, 1984), technology overwhelms humanity. In both stories, females are not portrayed as having integral roles in this technological, computer culture. One character notes, "There are few women hackers. This is a male world" (Turkle, 1984). Unfortunately, both boys and girls are socialized to associate computer programming with math skills and typically programming is taught in math departments by males. Male-female ratios in computer classes range from 2:1 to 5:1, although computers in offices tend to be used equally by females and males. Males also have more positive attitudes toward computers. It is hoped that Turkle's male computer hacker will not serve as the model for the future's computer users (Lockheed, 1985).

Moral Development

Remember from chapter 9 our description of Piaget's stage view of moral development. He believes that younger children are characterized by moral realism but that by 10 years of age have moved into a higher stage called moral autonomy. According to Piaget, older children consider the intentions of the individual, believe that rules are subject to change, and are aware that punishment does not always follow a deviation. A second major cognitive perspective on moral development has been proposed by Lawrence Kohlberg.

Kohlberg's provocative view stresses that moral development is based primarily on moral reasoning and unfolds in a series of stages (Colby & Kohlberg, 1987; Kohlberg, 1958, 1976, 1986; Kohlberg & Higgins, 1987). Kohlberg arrived at his view after some 20 years of using a unique interview with children. In the interview, children are presented with a series of stories in which characters face moral dilemmas. The following is the most popular of the Kohlberg dilemmas:

> In Europe a woman was near death from a special kind of cancer. There was one drug that the doctors thought might save her. It was a form of radium that a druggist in the same town had recently discovered. The drug was expensive to make, but the druggist was charging ten times what the drug cost him to make. He paid $200 for the radium and charged $2,000 for a small dose of the drug. The sick woman's husband, Heinz, went to everyone he knew to borrow the money, but he could only get together $1,000 which is half of what it cost. He told the druggist that his wife was dying and asked him to sell it cheaper or let him pay later. But the druggist said, "No, I discovered the drug, and I am going to make money from it." So Heinz got desperate and broke into the man's store to steal the drug for his wife. (Kohlberg, 1969, p. 379)

This story is one of eleven devised by Kohlberg to investigate the nature of moral thought. After reading the story, the interviewee answers a series of questions about the moral dilemma. Should Heinz have done that? Was it right or wrong? Why? Is it a husband's duty to steal the drug for his wife if he can get it in no other way? Would a good husband do it? Did the druggist have the right to charge that much when there was no law actually setting a limit on the price? Why?

Based on the reasons individuals gave to this and other moral dilemmas, Kohlberg believes three levels of moral development exist, each of which is characterized by two stages:

Level one: Preconventional Reasoning
At this low level the individual shows no internalization of moral values.
Stage 1. *Punishment and obedience orientation.* Moral thinking is based on punishments. Children obey because adults tell them to obey.
Stage 2. *Individualism and purpose.* Moral thinking is based on rewards and self-interest. Children obey when they want to obey and when it is in their best interest to obey. What is right is what feels good and what is rewarding.

Level two: Conventional Reasoning
At this level of morality, internalization is intermediate. The individual abides by certain standards (internal), but they are the standards of others (external).
Stage 3. *Interpersonal Norms.* The individual values trust, caring, and loyalty to others as the basis of moral judgments. At this stage, children often adopt their parents' moral standards, seeking to be thought of by their parents as a "good girl" or a "good boy."
Stage 4. *Social System Morality.* Moral judgments are based on understanding the social order, law, justice, and duty.

Level three: Postconventional Moral Reasoning
At this highest level, morality is completely internalized and not based on others' standards. The individual recognizes alternative moral courses, explores the options, and then decides on a personal moral code.

Stage description	Examples of moral reasoning that support Heinz's theft of the drug	Examples of moral reasoning that indicate Heinz should not steal the drug
Preconventional morality		
Stage 1: Avoid punishment	Heinz should not let his wife die; if he does, he will be in big trouble.	Heinz might get caught and sent to jail.
Stage 2: Seek rewards	If Heinz gets caught, he could give the drug back and maybe they would not give him a long jail sentence.	The druggist is a businessman and needs to make money.
Conventional morality		
Stage 3: Gain approval/ avoid disapproval especially with family	Heinz was only doing something that a good husband would do; it shows how much he loves his wife.	If his wife dies, he can't be blamed for it; it is the druggist's fault. He is the selfish one.
Stage 4: Conformity to society's rules	If you did nothing, you would be letting your wife die; it is your responsibility if she dies. You have to steal it with the idea of paying the druggist later.	It is always wrong to steal; Heinz will always feel guilty if he steals the drug.
Postconventional morality		
Stage 5: Principles accepted by the community *many reach this stage*	The law was not set up for these circumstances; taking the drug is not really right, but Heinz is justified in doing it.	You can't really blame someone for stealing, but extreme circumstances don't really justify taking the law in your own hands. You might lose respect for yourself if you let your emotions take over; you have to think about the long-term.
Stage 6: Individualized conscience *few reach this stage*	By stealing the drug, you would have lived up to society's rules, but you would have let down your conscience.	Heinz is faced with the decision of whether to consider other people who need the drug as badly as his wife. He needs to act by considering the value of all the lives involved.

Figure 11.4
Examples of moral reasoning at Kohlberg's six stages in response to the Heinz and the druggist story.

Stage 5. ***Community Rights Versus Individual Rights.*** The individual understands that values and laws are relative and that standards may vary from one individual to another. The individual recognizes that laws are important for society but also believes that laws can be changed. The individual believes that some values, such as liberty, are more important than the law.

Stage 6. ***Universal Ethical Principles.*** In rare instances, individuals have developed a moral standard based on universal human rights. When faced with a conflict between law and conscience, the individual will follow conscience, even though the decision might involve personal risk.

Some specific responses to the Heinz and the druggist dilemma are presented in figure 11.4, which should provide you with a better sense of moral reasoning at the six stages in Kohlberg's theory. Notice that whether Heinz steals the drug is not the important issue in Kohlberg's cognitive developmental theory. What is crucial is how the individual reasons about the moral dilemma.

Kohlberg believes these levels and stages occur in a sequence and are age-related: Before age 9, most children reason about moral dilemmas in a preconventional way; by early adolescence, they reason in more conventional ways; and by early adulthood, a small number of individuals reason in postconventional ways. In a 20-year longitudinal investigation, the uses of stages 1 and 2 decreased. Stage 4, which did not appear at all in the moral reasoning of the 10-year-olds, was reflected in 62 percent of the moral thinking of the

Figure 11.5
Mean percentage of each type (stage) of reasoning for each age group.

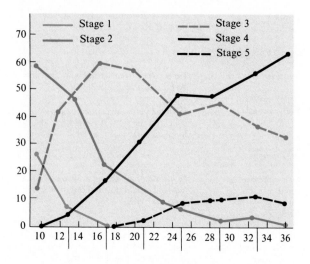

How are Gilligan's ideas about moral reasoning related to Ford's ideas about androgyny?

36-year-olds. Stage 5 did not appear until the age of 20 to 22 and never characterized more than 10 percent of the individuals. Thus, the moral stages appeared somewhat later than Kohlberg initially envisioned, and the higher stages, especially stage 6, were extremely elusive (see figure 11.5) (Colby & others, 1983). A recent review of data from 45 studies in 27 diverse world cultures provided striking support for the universality of Kohlberg's first four stages, although there was more cultural diversity at stages 5 and 6 (Snarey, 1987).

Kohlberg's provocative view has generated considerable research on moral development, and his theory has not gone unchallenged. One criticism of Kohlberg's view is that moral reasons can often be a shelter for immoral behavior—bank embezzlers and politicians address the loftiest of moral virtues when analyzing moral dilemmas but their own behavior may be immoral. No one wants a nation of cheaters and thieves who reason at the postconventional level; the cheaters and thieves may know what is right and what is wrong but still do what is wrong.

A second major criticism of Kohlberg's view is that it does not adequately reflect connectedness with and concern for others. Carol Gilligan (1982, 1985) argues that Kohlberg's theory emphasizes a **justice perspective,** that is, a focus on the rights of the individual. People are differentiated and seen as standing alone in making moral decisions. By contrast, the **care perspective** sees people in terms of their connectedness with others and the focus is on interpersonal communication. According to Gilligan, Kohlberg has vastly underplayed the care perspective in moral development. She believes this may be because most of his research was with males rather than females. More insight into Gilligan's belief in the importance of the care perspective in understanding children's moral development appears in Focus on Life-Span Development 11.2. Other experts on moral development also believe caring is a key aspect of morality (Damon, 1988).

Gilligan also thinks that moral development has three basic levels. She calls Level I preconventional morality, which reflects a concern for self and survival. Level II, conventional morality, shows a concern for being responsible and caring for others. Level III, postconventional morality, shows a concern for self and others as interdependent. Gilligan believes that Kohlberg has underemphasized the care perspective in the moral development of *both* males and females and that morality's highest level for both sexes involves a search for moral equality between one's self and others.

Middle and Late Childhood

The main character in Kohlberg's most widely used dilemma is a male—Heinz. Possibly females have a difficult time identifying with him. Some of the Kohlberg dilemmas are gender neutral, but one is about the captain of a company of marines. The subjects in Kohlberg's original research were all males. Going beyond her critique of Kohlberg's failure to consider females, Gilligan argues that an important voice is not present in his view. Following are two excerpts from children's responses to the story of Heinz and the druggist, one from 11-year-old Jake, the other from 11-year-old Amy. First, Jake's comments:

For one thing, human life is worth more than money, and if the druggist only makes $1,000, he is still going to live, but if Heinz doesn't steal the drug, his wife is going to die. *(Why is life worth more than money?)* Because the druggist can get $1,000 later from rich people with cancer, but Heinz can't get his wife again. (Gilligan, 1982, p. 26)

Now Amy's comments:

Well, I don't think so. I think there might be other ways besides stealing it, like if he could borrow the money or make a loan or something, but he really shouldn't steal the drug—but his wife shouldn't die either. *(Why shouldn't he steal the drug?)* If he stole the drug, he might save his wife then, but if he did, he might have to go to jail, and then his wife might get sicker again, and he couldn't get more of the drug, and it might not be good. So, they should really just talk it out and find some other way to make the money. (Gilligan, 1982, p. 28)

Jake's comments would be scored as a mixture of Kohlberg's stages 3 and 4, but also include some of the components of a mature level III moral thinker. Amy, by contrast, does not fit into Kohlberg's scoring system so well. Jake sees the problem as one of rules and balancing the rights of people. However, Amy views the problem as involving relationships—the druggist fails to live up to his relationship to the needy woman, the need to maintain the relationship between Heinz and his wife, and the hope that a bad relationship between Heinz and the druggist can be avoided. Amy concludes that the characters should talk it out and try to repair their relationships.

CONCEPT TABLE

11.2

The Self and Social Competence, Gender Roles, and Moral Development		
Concept	Processes/Related Ideas	Characteristics/Description
The Self and Social Competence	Self-Concept	An important dimension of children's self-concept is their increasing ability to understand how they are viewed by others. Closely related to self-concept is self-esteem; healthy relations with parents improve children's self-esteem. Harter's Perceived Competence Scale for Children investigates four domains: general self-worth, social skills, cognitive skills, and physical skills.
	Social Competence	The socially competent child can draw on effective resources from within and in the environment. The criteria for social competence may vary with the child's developmental status.
	Industry versus Inferiority	Erikson's fourth psychosocial stage; he believes social competence in middle and late childhood rests on the child's ability to resolve this conflict positively.
Gender Roles	Androgyny	Gender roles focus on society's expectations for males and for females. Recent interest emphasizes the concept of androgyny, the belief that competent individuals have both masculine and feminine characteristics. The four gender role classifications are: masculine, feminine, androgynous, and undifferentiated. Debate surrounds the criteria for masculine, feminine, and androgynous categories. The most widely used criteria for masculinity are self-assertion and instrumental orientation and for femininity are integration and expressive orientation.
	Androgyny and Competence	Controversy surrounds whether androgynous children are more competent. The criteria for competence need to be considered in evaluating this issue.
	Gender Differences	In the 1970s, it was concluded that boys have better math skills, have superior visual-spatial ability, and are more aggressive, while girls are better at verbal abilities. Today's conclusions suggest that boys are more active and the difference in verbal abilities has virtually vanished. The other differences—math, visual-spatial ability, and aggression—persist, although continued cultural change may chip away at these differences.
Moral Development	Kohlberg's Theory	Proposed three levels (each with two stages) that vary in the degree moral development is internalized—preconventional, conventional, and postconventional.
	Criticisms of Kohlberg's Theory	Moral reasons can always be a shelter for immoral behavior. Gilligan believes that Kohlberg vastly underplayed the role of the care perspective in moral development.

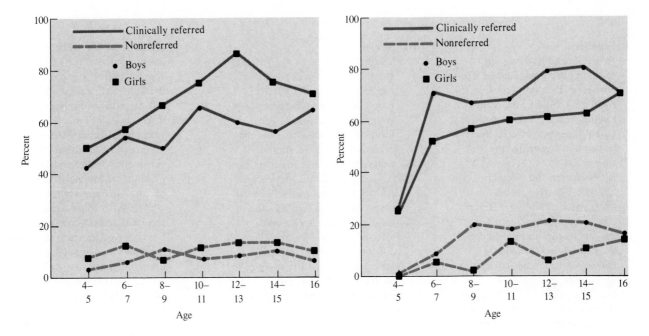

Figure 11.6
The two items most likely to differentiate between clinically referred children and nonreferred children.

At this point we have discussed a number of ideas about personality development including the self and social competence, gender roles, and moral development. A summary of these ideas is presented in Concept Table 11.2. Next, we turn to one final topic in middle and late childhood—problems and disturbances.

Problems and Disturbances

In a large scale investigation, it was found that children from a lower-class background have more problems and disturbances than children from a middle-class background (Achenbach & Edelbrock, 1981). Most of the problems reported for children from a lower-class background were undercontrolled, externalizing behaviors—destroys others' things, fighting, for example; these behaviors also were more characteristic of boys than girls. The problems and disturbances of middle-class children and girls were more likely to be overcontrolled and internalizing—anxiety or depression, for example.

The behavioral problems that most likely caused children to be referred to a clinic for mental health treatment were those in which the children felt unhappy, sad, or depressed, and were not doing well in school (see figure 11.6). Difficulties in school achievement, whether secondary to other kinds of disturbances or primary problems in themselves, seem to account for the most clinical referrals of children (Weiner, 1980). Investigations of underachieving children often reveal that they are more likely than their achieving counterparts to feel hostility that they cannot express directly. Parental demands for extraordinarily high achievement are likely to trigger poor school performance, which can be an indirect retaliation toward the achievement-demanding parents.

Sadness and depression are often reflected in children referred to psychological clinics.

Summary

I. Families

Parents spend less time with children during middle and late childhood, including less time in caregiving, instruction, reading, talking, and playing. Nonetheless, parents are still powerful and important socializing agents in this period. New parent-child issues emerge and discipline changes. Control is more coregulatory, children and parents label each other more, and parents mature just as children do. During middle and late childhood, two major changes in many children's lives are becoming latchkey children and moving into a stepfamily. Just as divorce produces disequilibrium and stress for children, so does the entrance of a stepparent. Over time, preadolescent boys seem to improve more than girls in stepfather families. Adolescence appears to be an especially difficult time for adjustment to the entrance of a stepparent. Children's relationships with biological parents are consistently better than with stepparents, and children's adjustment is adversely affected the more complex the stepfamily becomes.

II. Peer Relations

Children spend considerably more time with peers in middle and late childhood. Listening skills and effective communication, being yourself, being happy, showing enthusiasm and concern for others, and indicating self-confidence but not conceit are predictors of peer popularity. Rejected children are at risk for adjustment problems; the risk status of neglected children is less clear. Social information processing skills and social knowledge are two important dimensions of social cognition in peer relations. Children's friendships serve six functions: companionship, physical support, ego support, social comparison, and intimacy/affection. Intimacy and similarity are two common characteristics of friendships.

III. Schools

Children spend more than 10,000 hours in the classroom as members of a small society in which there are tasks to be accomplished, people to be socialized and socialized by, and rules that define and limit behavior, feelings, and attitudes. A special concern is that early schooling proceeds mainly on the basis of negative feedback to children. A profile of a good teacher's personality traits is difficult to establish, although some traits are clearly superior to others. Aptitude-treatment interaction is an important consideration. Schools have a stronger middle-class than lower-class orientation. Not only do many lower-class children have problems in school, so do children from ethnic minorities. Efforts to reduce these biases are being made, among them the jigsaw classroom.

IV. Self-Concept

An important dimension of children's self-concept is their increasing ability to understand how they are perceived by others. Closely related to self-concept is self-esteem; healthy relations with parents improve children's self-esteem. Harter's Perceived Competence Scale for Children investigates four domains: general self-worth, social skills, cognitive skills, and physical skills.

V. Social Competence

The socially competent child can draw on effective resources from within and in the environment. The criteria for social competence may vary with the child's developmental status.

VI. Gender Roles

Gender roles focus on society's expectations for males and for females. Recent interest emphasizes the concept of androgyny, the belief that competent individuals possess both masculine and feminine characteristics. The four gender role classifications are: masculine, feminine, androgynous, and undifferentiated. Debate surrounds the criteria for gender role categories. The most widely used criteria for masculinity are self-assertion and instrumental orientation, for femininity integration and expressive orientation. Controversy surrounds whether androgynous children are more competent; the criteria for competence need to be considered in this evaluation. In the 1970s, it was concluded that boys have better math skills, have superior visual-spatial ability, and are more aggressive, while girls are better at verbal abilities. Today's conclusions suggest that boys are more active and the difference in verbal abilities has virtually vanished. The other differences—math, visual-spatial ability, and aggression—still persist, although continued cultural change may chip away at these differences.

VII. Moral Development

Kohlberg proposed three levels (each with two stages) that vary in the degree moral development is internalized—preconventional, conventional, and postconventional. Kohlberg's theory has not gone uncriticized. For one, moral reasons can always be a shelter for immoral behavior. For another, Gilligan believes that Kohlberg vastly underplayed the role of the care perspective in moral development.

VIII. Problems and Disturbances

Children from lower-class backgrounds have more problems and disturbances than children from middle-class backgrounds. Boys and children from lower-class backgrounds have more externalized problems; girls and children from middle-class backgrounds have more internalized problems. Difficulties in school are the most common reason children are referred for clinical help.

Key Terms

coregulation *322*
neglected children *325*
rejected children *325*
intimacy *328*
aptitude-treatment interaction (ATI) *329*
jigsaw classroom *331*
Perceived Competence Scale for Children *334*

androgyny *336*
undifferentiated *336*
self-assertion *337*
integration *337*
instrumental orientation *337*
expressive orientation *337*
preconventional reasoning *340*
punishment and obedience orientation *340*
individualism and purpose *340*

conventional reasoning *340*
interpersonal norms *340*
social system morality *340*
postconventional moral reasoning *340*
community rights versus individual rights *341*
universal ethical principles *341*
justice perspective *342*
care perspective *342*

Suggested Readings

Development during middle childhood (1984). Washington, DC: National Academy Press.
An excellent collection of essays about what is currently known about the elementary school years. Includes chapters on families, peers, self, and problems and disturbances.

Gilligan, C. (1982). *In a different voice.* Cambridge, MA: Harvard U. Press.
Advances Gilligan's provocative view that a care perspective is a missing voice in Kohlberg's theory.

Gottman, J. M., & Parker, J. G. (Eds.), (1987). *Conversations of friends.* New York: Cambridge U. Press.
An excellent volume on how children become friends; explores the rich conversations of children.

Hyde, J. S. (1988). *Half the human experience* (4th ed.). Lexington, MA: D. C. Heath.
An excellent overview of gender roles, with special attention given to the female role.

Minuchin, P. P., & Shapiro, E. K. (1983). The school as a context for social development. In P. H. Mussen (Ed.), *Handbook of child psychology* (4th ed., Vol. 4). New York: Wiley.
An authoritative review of the school's role in children's development.

S E C T I O N
VI

■

Adolescence

I n no order of things is
adolescence the simple time of
life. ■

Janet Erskine Stewart

12

Physical and Cognitive Development

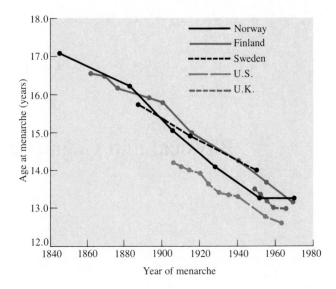

Figure 12.1
Age at menarche in selected northern European countries and the United States from 1845 to 1969.

As in the development of children, genetic, biological, environmental, and social factors interact in adolescent development. Also, continuity and discontinuity characterize adolescent development. The genes inherited from parents still influence thought and behavior during adolescence, but inheritance now interacts with the social conditions of the adolescent's world—with family, peers, friendships, dating, and school experiences. An adolescent has experienced thousands of hours of interaction with parents, peers, and teachers in the past 10 to 13 years of development. Still new experiences and developmental tasks appear during adolescence. Relationships with parents take a different form, moments with peers become more intimate, dating occurs for the first time as does sexual exploration and possibly intercourse. The adolescent's thoughts are more abstract and idealistic. Biological changes trigger a heightened interest in body image. Adolescence, then, has both continuity and discontinuity with childhood.

Imagine a toddler displaying all the features of puberty. Think about a 3-year-old girl with fully developed breasts or a boy just slightly older with a deep male voice. That is what we would see by the year 2250 if the age at which puberty arrives kept getting younger at its present pace (Petersen, 1979).

In Norway, **menarche**—the girl's first menstruation—occurs at just over 13 years of age, as opposed to 17 years of age in the 1840s. In the United States—where children mature up to a year earlier than children in European countries—the average age of menarche has declined from 14.2 in 1900 to about 12.45 today. The age of menarche has been declining at an average of about four months per decade for the past century (see figure 12.1).

Fortunately, however, we are unlikely to see pubescent toddlers, since what has happened in the past century is special. The best guess is that the something special is a higher level of nutrition and health. The available information suggests that menarche began to occur earlier at about the time of the Industrial Revolution, a period associated with increased standards of living and advances in medical science.

In this chapter, we consider further puberty's fascinating changes and other dimensions of the adolescent's physical development. The equally fascinating changes of cognitive development in adolescence are charted. The important contexts of school and work in adolescences are also evaluated.

Puberty involves a dramatic upheaval in bodily change. Young adolescents develop an acute concern about their bodies. Columnist Bob Greene (1988) recently dialed a party line in Chicago called Connections, to discover what young adolescents were saying to each other. The first thing the boys and girls asked—after first names—was physical descriptions. The idealism of the callers was apparent. Most of the girls described themselves as having long blond hair, five feet five inches tall, and weighing about 110 pounds. Most of the boys described themselves as having brown hair, said they lifted weights, were six feet tall, and weighed about 170 pounds.

Physical Development

Menarche is one event that characterizes puberty, but there are others as well. What are puberty's markers? What are the psychological accompaniments of physical changes in adolescence? What is the nature of sexuality in adolescence? We consider each of these questions in turn.

Pubertal Change

While **puberty** can be defined as rapid maturation, it is not a single sudden event. Puberty is part of a gradual process of development that begins at conception (about 10 to 15 percent of the variation in age at menarche is genetically determined, for example). We know when a young person is going through puberty, but pinpointing its beginning and its end is difficult. Except for menarche, which occurs rather late in puberty, no single marker heralds puberty. For boys, the first whisker or first wet dream are events that could mark its appearance, but both may go unnoticed.

Behind the first whisker in boys and widening of hips in girls is a flood of hormones, powerful chemical substances secreted by the endocrine glands and carried through the body by the bloodstream. The concentrations of certain hormones increase dramatically during adolescence. In boys, **testosterone** is associated with the development of external genitals, an increase in height,

I think that what is happening to me is so wonderful and not only what can be seen on my body, but all that is taking place inside. I never discuss myself with anybody; that is why I have to talk to myself about them.

Anne Frank

EXCUSE US, SIR...BUT WHAT--?

SSHH! I'M KEEPING AN EYE ON ONE OF MY BIGGEST ANXIETIES.

WHICH ONE IS THAT?

THAT ONE THERE... THE ONE LURKING IN THE SHADOWS... "IMPENDING PUBERTY."

NOT A SIGHT FOR THE FAINT OF HEART NOR THE HAIRLESS OF CHEST.

From Penguin Dreams and Stranger Things *by Berke Breathed. Copyright © 1985 by the Washington Post Company. Reprinted with permission.*

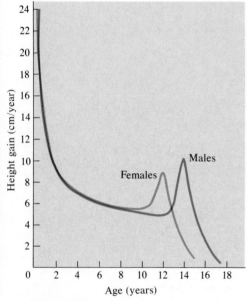

Figure 12.2
Growth curves for height in boys and girls. These curves represent the rate of growth of a typical boy and girl at a given age.

If we listen to boys and girls at the very moment when they seem most pimply, awkward and disagreeable, we can partly penetrate a mystery most of us once felt heavily within us, and have now forgotten. This mystery is the very process of creation of man and woman.
    Colin Macinnes, The World of Children.

and voice change. In girls, **estradiol** is associated with breast, uterine, and skeletal development (Dillon, 1980). In one investigation, testosterone levels increased eighteen-fold in boys but only two-fold in girls during puberty; estradiol increased eight-fold in girls but only two-fold in boys (Nottelmann & others, 1987). This same influx of hormones may be associated with psychological adjustment in adolescence. In the same investigation, a higher concentration of testosterone was present in boys who rated themselves more socially competent (Nottelmann & others, 1987).

These hormonal and body changes occur on the average about two years earlier in females (10½ years of age) than in males (12½ years of age) (see figure 12.2). Four of the most noticeable areas of body change in females are height spurt, menarche, breast growth, and pubic hair; four of the most noticeable areas of body change in males are height spurt, penile growth, testes growth, and pubic hair. The normal and average range of these characteristics is shown in figures 12.3 and 12.4. Among the most remarkable normal variations is that two boys (or two girls) may be the same chronological age, and yet one may complete the pubertal sequence before the other has begun it. For most girls, the first menstrual period may occur as early as the age of 10 or as late as the age of 15½ and still be considered normal, for example (Brooks-Gunn, 1988).

Psychological Accompaniments of Physical Changes
A host of psychological changes accompany an adolescent's physical development. Imagine yourself as you were beginning puberty. Not only did you probably think about yourself differently, but your parents and peers probably began acting differently toward you. Maybe you were proud of your changing body, even though you were perplexed about what was happening. Perhaps your parents no longer perceived you as someone they could sit in bed and watch television with or as someone who should be kissed goodnight.

One thing is certain about the psychological aspects of physical development—adolescents show a great deal of preoccupation with their bodies and develop individual images of what their bodies are like. Perhaps you looked in the mirror on a daily or sometimes even on an hourly basis to see if you could detect anything different about your changing body. Surveys of adolescents reveal that young adolescents are more dissatisfied with their bodies than late adolescents (Hamburg, 1974). Breast growth is associated with a more positive body image in young adolescent females (Brooks-Gunn & Warren, in press).

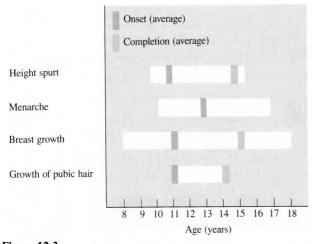

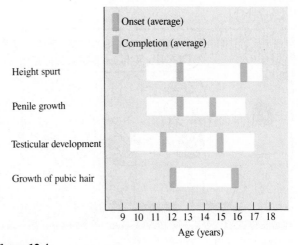

Figure 12.3
Normal range and average age of development of sexual characteristics in females.
From J. M. Tanner, "Growing Up," in Scientific American, *1973. Copyright © 1973 by Scientific American, Inc. All rights reserved.*

Figure 12.4
Normal range and average age of development of sexual characteristics in males.
From J. M. Tanner, "Growing Up," in Scientific American, *1973. Copyright © 1973 by Scientific American, Inc. All rights reserved.*

Some of you entered puberty early, others entered late. When adolescents mature earlier or later than their peers, might they perceive themselves differently? Some years ago, in the California Longitudinal Study, early maturing boys perceived themselves more positively and had more successful peer relations than their late maturing counterparts (Jones, 1965). The findings for early maturing girls were similar but not as strong as for boys. When the late maturing boys were studied in their thirties, however, they had developed a stronger sense of identity than the early maturing boys (Peskin, 1967). Possibly this occurred because the late maturing boys had more time to explore life's options or because the early maturing boys continued to focus on their advantageous physical status instead of career development and achievement.

More recent research confirms, though, that at least during adolescence, it is advantageous to be an early maturing rather than a late maturing boy (Blyth, Bulcroft, & Simmons, 1981; Pedersen, 1987; Simmons & Blyth, 1987). The more recent findings for girls suggest that early maturation is a mixed blessing: these girls experience more problems in school but also more independence and popularity with boys. When the time of maturation is assessed is also a factor. In the sixth grade, early maturing girls showed greater satisfaction with their figures than late maturing girls, but by the tenth grade, late maturing girls were more satisfied (see figure 12.5). The reason for this is that by late adolescence, early maturing girls are shorter and stockier while late maturing girls are taller and thinner. The late maturing girls in late adolescence have bodies that more closely approximate the current American ideal of feminine beauty—tall and thin.

Being on-time and off-time in terms of pubertal events is a complex affair (Brooks-Gunn, 1988). For example, the dimensions may involve not just biological status and pubertal age, but also chronological age, grade in school, cognitive functioning, and social maturity (Petersen, 1987). Adolescents may be at risk when the demands of a particular social context and the adolescents'

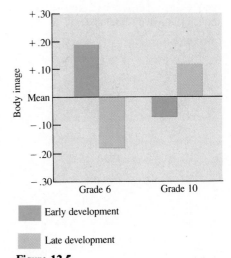

Figure 12.5
Early and late maturing adolescent girls perceptions of body image in early and late adolescence.

Physical and Cognitive Development   355

Reprinted with special permission of NAS, Inc.

Do you think puberty's effects are exaggerated? Has too much credit been given to early and late maturation? Do these changes possibly balance out over the long course of development?

Puberty: the time of life when the two sexes begin to first become acquainted.
Samuel Johnson

physical and behavioral characteristics are mismatched (Lerner, 1987). On-time dancers are one such example. In general peer comparisons, on-time dancers should not show adjustment problems. However, they do not have the ideal characteristics thought to be important in the world of dancers. That is, the ideal characteristics of dancers are generally those associated with late maturity—a thin, lithe body build. The dancers, then, are on-time in terms of their peer group in general, but there is an asynchrony to their development in terms of their more focused peer group—dancers (Brooks-Gunn, 1987). Clearly, understanding pubertal timing is a complex affair, and in many instances finding direct, consistent links between pubertal timing and social development or cognitive development has been elusive (Lerner, 1988).

Adolescent Sexuality

Many of the songs popular among adolescents have words such as "Tonight's the night," and "Good girls don't, but I do." The sexual themes of music and the sexual overtones that are rampant in magazines and on television often suggest a societal standard of sex as fun and harmless.

At age 16, slightly over 40 percent of males and between 30 to 40 percent of females have had sexual intercourse (Dreyer, 1982). The pressure on males to have sexual intercourse is evident in the greater percentage of males reporting that they have had intercourse (12 percent for males, only 5 percent for females) at the age of 13, even though male adolescents enter puberty on the average two years later than female adolescents. Recent data indicated that in some areas of the country, sexual experiences of young adolescents may even be greater. In an inner city, low income area of Baltimore, at age 14, 81 percent of the males said that they already had engaged in sexual intercourse; other surveys in inner city, low income areas also reveal a high incidence of early sexual intercourse (Clark, Zabin, & Hardy, 1984).

While premarital intercourse can be meaningful for older, mature adolescents, many are ill-equipped to handle sex (Petersen, Crouter, & Wilson, 1988). Adolescents may attempt sexual intercourse without really knowing what to do or how to satisfy their partner—leading to frustration and a sense of sexual inadequacy—and many are poorly informed about contraception or fail to use contraceptives; only about one-third use them (Zelnick & Kantner, 1980). Note in table 12.1 that while the pill and condom are the contraceptives most widely used by adolescents, the withdrawal method, especially as the first method used, is seeing increased use.

The sexual fantasies of adolescent boys focus specifically on sexual activity.

TABLE 12.1
Types of Contraceptives Used by Urban Adolescents

Method	Method first used		Method last used	
	1976	*1979*	*1976*	*1979*
Pill	33%	19%	48%	41%
IUD	2	1	3	2
Diaphragm	0	1	1	4
Condom	36	34	23	23
Douche	3	1	3	2
Withdrawal	18	36	15	19
Rhythm	5	5	4	6

From Melvin Zelnik and John F. Kantner, "Sexual activity, contraceptive use, and pregnancy among women aged fifteen to nineteen in 1976" in Family Planning Perspectives, *Vol. 12, No. 5, Sept/Oct 1980. Copyright © 1980 The Alan Guttmacher Institute. Reprinted by permission.*

Adolescents' knowledge of sex is not as advanced as we sometimes think it is. In one investigation, the majority of adolescents indicated that the greatest risk of pregnancy is during menstruation (Zelnick & Kantner, 1977).

The adolescent pregnancy rate is increasing even though the birth rate is declining. If current trends continue, four in ten females will become pregnant at least once while they are in adolescence (Alan Guttmacher Institute, 1981). As indicated in figure 12.6, adolescents in the United States have the highest pregnancy rate at all ages when compared with other countries. More than 1 million 15- to 19-year-old girls become pregnant every year in the United States (Hayes, 1987).

The consequences of our nation's high adolescent pregnancy rate are cause for great concern. Adolescent pregnancy increases the health risks of both the offspring and the mother. Infants born to adolescent mothers are more

You have been assigned to design a community program to reduce the rate of adolescent pregnancy in your community. What would the program be like?

Figure 12.6
Pregnancy rates per 1,000 women by women's age, 1981.

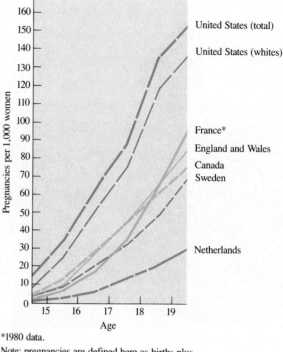

*1980 data.

Note: pregnancies are defined here as births plus abortions; age is the age at outcome.

likely to have low birth weights—a prominent cause of infant mortality, as well as neurological problems and childhood illnesses (Hamburg, 1986; Hayes, 1987; Schorr, in press). Approximately 90 percent of adolescent mothers presently keep their babies. They often drop out of school, fail to gain employment, and become dependent on welfare. Adolescent pregnancy rates have reached crisis proportions in our nation. Serious, extensive efforts need to be directed toward helping pregnant adolescents and young mothers stay in or return to school or work, helping them obtain competent day care, and helping them to plan for the future (Edleman, 1987; Furstenberg, Brooks-Gunn, & Morgan, 1987). According to leading adolescence authority, John Conger (1988), these efforts should include sex education and family planning, access to contraceptive methods, increased life options that allow adolescents to look to a future that encompasses self-sufficiency and success, and broad community involvement and support.

Peers are the most common source of sex information in adolescence. Little information about sex is obtained from parents, especially fathers, and less than 20 percent comes from schools (Thornburg, 1981). Sex education classes are more likely to teach the biological aspects of sex than the social aspects, although love, marriage, and gender roles sometimes are evaluated. The most likely place and time an adolescent will be exposed to sex education is in a biology class in the tenth grade. Discussion of a recently developed sex education program is presented in Focus on Life-Span Development 12.1.

At this point, we have discussed a number of ideas about physical development in adolescence. A summary of these ideas is presented in Concept Table 12.1. Now we turn to the intriguing cognitive changes that take place in adolescence.

The error of youth is to believe that intelligence is a substitute for experience, while the error of age is to believe that experience is a substitute for intelligence.

Slyman Bryson

Adolescence

Postponing Sexual Involvement is an approach designed for use with 13- through 15-year-old adolescents. It is aimed at reducing pregnancy by decreasing the number of adolescents who become sexually involved. It was developed in Atlanta, Georgia (Howard, 1983).

This program does not offer factual information about sexual reproduction and it does not discuss family planning. Rather the program concentrates on social and peer pressures that often lead an adolescent into early sexual behavior. Particular emphasis is placed on building social skills to help adolescents communicate better with each other when faced with sexual pressures.

One main difference between this curriculum and most sex education programs is that it starts with a given value—that is, you should not be having sex at such a young age. Everything in the curriculum is designed to support this argument. Traditional sex education programs invariably have the implicit goal of reducing teenage pregnancy, but they usually include information on birth control and reproduction so that if young adolescents choose to have sex,

they can behave in a responsible manner. This curriculum avoids the double message implied in such traditional programs.

The series is divided into four sessions, each one and a half hours long. The first three sessions occur fairly close together, while the fourth session is used as a reinforcement some three to six months later. The first session focuses on social pressure, with students given opportunities to explore why they feel adolescents engage in sex at an early age. The reasons they usually give involve various needs, such as to be popular, to hang onto a boyfriend, and so forth. The leaders then help the adolescents to understand that sexual intercourse will not necessarily fulfill these needs.

The second session presents further information about peer pressure, both in group sessions and in one-on-one sessions. Adolescents are provided with opportunities to become familiar with common pressure statements and after responses are modeled for them, they practice responding in their own words. Session three involves information and exercises about problem solving. It encourages an

understanding of limiting physical expression of affection and through developing and practicing skits, provides help in handling difficult sexual situations. As indicated earlier, the fourth session occurs a number of months later and is used to reinforce the ideas in the first three sessions by applying them to new situations.

This series on "how to say no" was designed to provide young adolescents with the ability to bridge the gap between their physical development and their cognitive ability to handle the implications for such development. It was not developed to replace the provision of actual factual information about sexuality and family planning.

It should be pointed out that as part of the Postponing Sexual Involvement Series, some adolescents' parents also are participating. The goal of the parental involvement is to determine the acceptance level both by the community (parents) and the young adolescents themselves, as well as to learn which delivery styles are most effective. For instance, some of the series are being delivered by peers several years older than the adolescents, while others have adult leaders.

Physical Development in Adolescence		
Concept	**Processes/Related Ideas**	**Characteristics/Description**
Pubertal Change	Its Nature	Puberty is a rapid change to maturation that does not involve a single event but rather is part of lengthy developmental process. Menarche is the girl's first menstruation and has been coming earlier in recent decades probably because of improved health and nutrition.
	Hormones	The endocrine glands secrete hormones. Testosterone is the sex hormone that increases the most in adolescent males; estradiol is the sex hormone that increases the most in adolescent females.
	Physical Changes	As adolescents undergo a growth spurt, they make rapid gains in height; the spurt occurs approximately two years earlier in girls (10½) than boys (12½).
Psychological Accompaniments of Physical Changes	Body Image	Adolescents show a considerable interest in their body image. Young adolescents are more preoccupied and dissatisfied with their bodies than late adolescents.
	Early and Late Maturation	Early maturation favors boys at least during adolescence; as adults, though, late maturing boys may achieve more successful identities. The results for girls are more mixed than for boys.
	On-time/Off-time	Being on-time or off-time in terms of pubertal development is complex. Adolescents may be at risk when the demands of a particular context and the adolescent's physical and behavioral characteristics are mismatched.
Sexuality	Sexual Behavior	At age 16, slightly over 40 percent of males and between 30–40 percent of females have had sexual intercourse; in some inner city areas the percentages are higher.
	Pregnancy Rate	Adolescents in the United States have an extremely high pregnancy rate. Adolescent pregnancy has become a national crisis.
	Sex Education and Knowledge	Peers are the most common source of sex education. Adolescent knowledge of sex is not as advanced as they sometimes try to make it appear.

Cognitive Development

Adolescents' developing power of thought opens up new cognitive and social horizons. The power of thought becomes more abstract, logical, and idealistic; more capable of examining one's own thoughts, others' thoughts, and what others are thinking about one's self; and more likely to interpret and monitor the social world. First, we evaluate Piaget's ideas about adolescent thought and, second, social cognition in adolescence.

Formal Operational Thought

Piaget believed that formal operational thought came into play between the ages of 11 and 15. Formal operational thought is more **abstract** than a child's thinking. The adolescent is no longer limited to actual concrete experience as the anchor of thought. Instead, she may conjure up make-believe situations, hypothetical possiblities, or purely abstract propositions and reason about them. The adolescent increasingly thinks about thought itself. One adolescent pondered, "I began thinking about why I was thinking what I was. Then I began thinking about why I was thinking about why I was thinking about what I was." If this sounds abstract, it is, and it characterizes the adolescent's increased interest in thought itself and the abstractness of thought.

Accompanying the abstract nature of adolescent thought is the quality of idealism. Adolescents begin to think about ideal characteristics for themselves and others and compare themselves and others to these ideal standards. In contrast, children think more in terms of what is real and what is limited. During adolescence, thoughts often take fantasy flights into the future. It is not unusual for the adolescent to become impatient with these newfound ideal standards and to be perplexed over which of many ideal standards to adopt.

At the same time, an adolescent thinks more abstractly and idealistically than a child, she also thinks more logically. The adolescent begins to think like a scientist in the sense of devising a plan to solve a problem and systematically testing solutions. This kind of problem solving has an imposing name: **hypothetical deductive reasoning.** The adolescent develops hypotheses, or best guesses, about ways to solve a problem, such as an algebraic equation. She then deduces, or concludes, which is the best path to follow in solving the equation. By contrast, a child is more likely to solve the problem in a trial-and-error fashion. See table 12.2 for one example of hypothetical deductive reasoning.

As the adolescent's thought becomes more abstract and logical, the use of language also changes. This development includes changes in the use of satire and metaphor, in writing skills, and in conversational skills.

A junior high school student is sitting in school making up satirical labels for his teachers. One he calls "the walking wilt Wilkie and his wilking waste." Another he describes as "the magnificent Manifred and his manifest morbidity." The use of nicknames increases during early adolescence as does their abstractness—"stilt," "spaz," "nerd," and "marshmallow mouth," for example. These examples reflect the aspect of language known as **satire,** which refers to irony, wit, or derision used to expose folly or wickedness. Adolescents use and understand satire more than children (Demorest & others, 1984). The satire of *Mad* magazine, which relies on double meaning, exaggeration, and parody to highlight absurd circumstances and contradictory happenings, finds a more receptive audience among 13- to 14-year-olds than 8- to 9-year-olds (see figure 12.7).

Another aspect of language that comes into use in adolescence is **metaphor.** A metaphor is an implied comparison between two ideas that is conveyed by the abstract meaning contained in the words used. For example, a person's faith and a piece of glass are alike in that both can be shattered. A runner's performance and a politician's speech are alike in that both are predictable. Children have a difficult time understanding metaphorical comparisons; adolescents are better able to understand their meaning.

Youth seeks to be, know, get, feel all that is highest, greatest, and best in man's estate . . . It is the glorious dawn of imagination, which supplements the individual limitations and expands the soul towards the dimensions of the race.

G. Stanley Hall, 1904

Figure 12.7
I was 12 years old the first time I read Mad *magazine. It was a time when my best friend and I were already starting to make up crazy nicknames for our teachers and peers. Think back to when you were a young adolescent—was your mind intrigued by absurdities and contradictory happenings?*

TABLE   12.2
An Example of Hypothetical Deductive Reasoning

A common task for all of us is to determine what can logically be inferred from a statement made by someone else. Young children are often told by teachers that, if they work hard, they will receive good grades. Regardless of the empirical truth of the claim, the children may believe that good grades are the result of hard work, and that if they do not get good grades, they did not work hard enough. (Establishing the direction of the relationship between variables is an important issue.)

Children in the late concrete operational stage, too, are concerned with understanding the relations between their behavior and their teachers' grading practices. However, they are beginning to question the "truths" of their childhood. First, they now know that there are four possible combinations if two variables are dichotomized (work hard—not work hard; good grades—not good grades):

Behavior	Consequences
1. Work hard	Good grades
2. Work hard	Not good grades
3. Not work hard	Good grades
4. Not work hard	Not good grades

Two combinations are consistent with the hypothesis that a student's hard work is necessarily related to good grades: (1) they work hard and get good grades, and (4) they do not work hard and do not get good grades. When the presumed "cause" is present, the effect is present; when the cause is absent, the effect is absent. There are also two combinations that do not fit the hypothesis of a direct relation between hard work and good grades: (2) they work hard and do not get good grades, and (3) they get good grades without working hard.

The adolescent's notion of possibility allows him or her to take this analysis of combinations one important step further. Each of the four basic combinations of binary variables may be true or it may not. If 1, 2, 3, or 4 are true alone or in combination, there are 16 possible patterns of truth values:

1 or 2 or 3 or 4 is true	4 patterns
1–2 or 1–3 or 1–4 or 2–3 or 2–4 or 3–4 are true	6 patterns
1–2–3 or 1–2–4 or 1–3–4 or 2–3–4 are true	4 patterns
All (1–2–3–4) are true	1 pattern
All are false	1 pattern
Total	16 patterns

The list is critically important because each pattern leads to a different conclusion about the possible relation between two variables.

Table, *"An Example of Hypothetical Deductive Reasoning" from* Piaget With Feeling, *Third Edition, copyright © 1978 by Holt, Rinehart and Winston, Inc., reprinted by permission of the publisher.*

The increased abstractness and logical reasoning of the adolescent's cognition can be witnessed in improved writing ability (Scardamalia, Bereiter, & Goelman, 1982). Organizing ideas is critical to good writing. Logical thinking helps the writer develop a hierarchical structure, which helps the reader understand which ideas are general, which are specific, and which are more important than others. Researchers have discovered that children are poor at organizing their ideas prior to writing and have difficulty detecting the salient points in prose passages (Brown & Smiley, 1977). While adolescents are not yet Pulitzer-Prize-winning novelists, they are better than children at recognizing the need for making both general and specific points in their writing.

The sentences adolescents string together make more sense than those constructed by children. And adolescents are more likely than children to include an introduction, several paragraphs that represent a body, and concluding remarks when writing an essay (Fischer & Lazerson, 1984).

Most adolescents are also better conversationalists than children are. Adolescents are better at letting individuals take turns in discussions instead of everyone talking at once; are better at using questions to convey commands ("Why is it so noisey in here?"); are better at using words like *the* and *a* in ways that enhance understanding ("He is *the* living end! He is not just *a* person); better at using polite language in appropriate situations (when a guest comes to the house, for example); and better at telling stories that are interesting, jokes that are funny, and lies that convince.

Are most adolescents formal operational thinkers as Piaget envisioned? There is more individual variation in formal operational thought than Piaget believed. Research indicates that some adolescents are formal operational thinkers but many are not (Neimark, 1982). And some adolescents may think in more formal operational ways in some domains but not others. For example, a 14-year-old boy may reason at the formal operational level when it comes to analyzing an algebraic equation, but not be able to do so in verbal problem solving or interpersonal relations.

How beautiful is youth! How bright it gleams
With its illusions, aspirations, dreams.
Henry Wadsworth Longfellow

Social Cognition

Impressive changes in social cognition characterize adolescent development. Adolescents develop a special type of egocentrism, begin to think about personality not unlike the way personality theorists do, and monitor their social world in sophisticated ways.

Adolescent thought is egocentric. David Elkind (1976) believes **adolescent egocentrism** has two parts: an imaginary audience and a personal fable. The **imaginary audience** is the adolescent's belief that others are as preoccupied with her as she herself is. Attention-getting behavior, so common in adolescence, reflects egocentrism and the desire to be on stage, noticed, and visible. Imagine the eighth-grade boy who thinks he is an actor and all others the audience as he stares at the small spot on his trousers. Imagine the seventh-grade girl who thinks that all eyes are riveted on her complexion because of the tiny blemish she has. Current controversy about egocentrism's nature focuses on whether it emerges because of formal operational thought (Elkind, 1986) or because of perspective-taking and interpersonal understanding (Lapsley & Murphy, 1985).

Jennifer converses with her best friend, Anne, about something she has just heard. "Anne, did you hear about Barbara? You know she fools around a lot. Well, the word is that she is pregnant. Can you believe it? That would never happen to me." Later in the conversation, Anne tells Jennifer, "I really like Bob, but sometimes he is a jerk. He just can't understand me. He has no clue about what my personal feelings are." The **personal fable** refers to the adolescent's sense of personal uniqueness and indestructibility, reflected respectively in Jennifer's and Anne's comments. In their efforts to maintain a sense of uniqueness and indestructibility, adolescents sometimes create a fictitious story, or a fable. Imagine a girl who is having difficulty getting a date. She may develop a fictitious account of a handsome young man living in another part of the country who is madly in love with her. More about the personal fable appears in Focus on Life-Span Development 12.2, where its application to understanding adolescent sexuality is examined.

Adolescents are good at making up stories. Sometimes they do this to protect their sense of uniqueness and indestructibility. This is called the personal fable. Can you think of times you or your friends made up personal fables as adolescents? What were they like?

PERSONAL FABLES AND PREGNANCIES

Our society has not handled adolescent sex very effectively. We tell adolescents that sex is fun, harmless, adult, and forbidden. Adolescents, 13 years old going on 21, want to try out new things and take risks. They see themselves as unique and indestructible—pregnancy couldn't happen to them, they think. Add to this the adolescent's increasing need for love and commitment, and the result all too often is social dynamite.

With their developing idealism and ability to think in more abstract and hypothetical ways, young adolescents often get caught up in a mental world far removed from reality, one that may involve a belief that things can't or won't happen to them and that they are omnipotent and indestructible. These cognitive changes, as well as others, have intriguing implications for the sex education of adolescents. Joan Lipsitz (1980) points out that having information about contraceptives is not enough—what seems to predict whether adolescents will use contraceptives or not depends on their acceptance of themselves and their sexuality. Such acceptance probably requires not only emotional maturity, but cognitive maturity as well.

Most discussions of adolescent pregnancy and its prevention assume that adolescents have the ability to anticipate consequences, to weigh the probable outcome of behavior, and to project into the future what will happen if they engage in certain acts, such as sexual intercourse. That is, prevention is based on the belief that adolescents have the cognitive ability to approach problem solving in a planned, organized, and analytical manner. However, many adolescents are just beginning to develop such capacities, and others have not developed them at all.

Lipsitz, in addressing the American Association of Sex Educators, Counselors, and Therapists, described the personal

fable and how it may be associated with adolescent pregnancy. The young adolescent may say, "Hey, it won't happen to me." If the adolescent is locked into this personal fable, she may not respond well to a course on sex education that preaches prevention. Lipsitz points out that the best of what we know about prevention is not appropriate for young adolescents. A developmental perspective on cognition may provide some insight into what can be taught in sex education courses for early adolescents.

Late adolescents (those 18 to 19 years of age) are at least to some degree realistic and future-oriented about sexual experiences, just as they are about careers and marriage.

Middle adolescents (those 15 to 17 years of age) often romanticize sexuality. However, young adolescents (those 10 to 15 years of age) appear to experience sex in a depersonalized way that is filled with anxiety and denial. This depersonalized orientation to sex is not likely to lead to preventive behavior.

Consider the outcome if the following are combined: the nature of early adolescent cognition, the personal fable, anxiety about sex, gender role definitions about what is masculine and what is feminine, the sexual themes of music in the adolescent culture, the sexual overtones that are rampant in magazines and on television, and a societal standard that says sex is appropriate for adults but promiscuous for adolescents. That is, our society tells adolescents: Sex is fun, harmless, adult, and forbidden. The combination of early physical maturation, risk-taking behavior, egocentrism, the inability to think futuristically, and our ambivalent contradictory culture make sex difficult for adolescents to handle. Add to this the growing need for adolescents to develop a commitment, especially in a career. Yet youth face a huge unemployment rate, which can turn them away from the future and intensively toward the present. Piece together early adolescent development, America's sexual ambivalence, and adolescents' vulnerability to economic forces and the result is social dynamite.

Adolescents also begin to interpret personality not unlike the way personality theorists do (Barenboim, 1981, 1985). First, when adolescents are given information about another person, they consider previously acquired information and current information, not relying solely on the concrete information at hand as children do. Second, adolescents are more likely to detect the contextual or situational variability in their and others' behavior, rather than thinking that they and others always behave consistently. Third, rather than merely accepting surface traits as a valid description of another individual or themselves, adolescents begin to look for deeper, more complex— even hidden—causes of personality.

As part of their increased awareness of others—including what others are doing and thinking—adolescents engage in social monitoring. For example, Bob, a 16-year-old, feels he does not know as much as he wants or needs to know about Sally, another 16-year-old. He also wants to know more about Sally's relationship with Brian, a 17-year-old. Bob decides that he wants to know more about the groups Sally belongs to—her student council friends, the clique she is in, and so on. There are a number of social monitoring methods that adolescents use on a daily basis. For example, an adolescent may check incoming information about an organization (school, club, or group of friends) to determine if it is consistent with the adolescent's impression of the group. Still another adolescent may question someone or paraphrase what that person has just said about her feelings to ensure that he has understood them correctly. Yet another adolescent may meet someone new and quickly think, "It's going to be hard to really get to know him" (Flavell, 1979).

Schools

The impressive changes in adolescents' cognition lead us to examine the nature of schools in adolescence. In chapter 10, we described different ideas about the effects of schools on children's development. Here we focus more exclusively on the nature of secondary schools. Among the questions we try to answer are: What should the function of secondary schools be? What are effective schools for young adolescents like? What is the nature of the transition from elementary to middle or junior high school?

The Controversy Surrounding the Function of Secondary Schools
Secondary schools seem to have always been wrapped in controversy. One of the controversies revolves around whether adolescents should be treated more like children or more like adults. In the United States, adolescents have been kept in school for as long as possible. This policy has practical implications because it has delayed the entry of youth into the labor force. Further, high schools have been perceived as the most competent environment for adolescents to gain the maturity and skills they need to function in the adult world. For more than 150 years, compulsory school attendance has been mandated.

However, in the 1960s, the distress over alienated and rebellious youth brought up the issue of whether secondary schools were actually beneficial to adolescents. During the 1970s, three independent panels agreed that high school contributes to adolescent alienation and actually restricts the transition to adulthood (Brown, 1973; Coleman & others, 1974; Martin 1976). These prestigious panels argued that adolescents should be given educational alternatives to the comprehensive high school—in the form of on-the-job community work, for example—to increase their exposure to adult roles and to decrease their sense of isolation from the adult world. In response to these reports, a number of states lowered the age at which adolescents could leave school from 16 to 14.

Now in the 1980s, the back-to-basics movement has gained momentum, arguing that the main function of schools should be rigorous training of intellectual skills through subjects like English, math, and science. Proponents of the back-to-basic movement emphasize that there is too much fluff in the secondary school curricula, with students being allowed to select from too many alternatives that will not give them a basic education in intellectual subjects. Critics of the fluff in secondary schools also argue that the school day should be longer and that the school year should be extended into the summer months. Some critics of schools believe that too much emphasis is placed on extracurricular activities. They argue that schools should be in the business of imparting knowledge to adolescents and should show little or no concern for their social and emotional development. Related to the issue of the function of secondary schools is the proverbial dilemma of whether schools should include a vocational curriculum in addition to training in such basic subjects as English, math, science, and history.

Should the main and perhaps only goal of schooling for adolescents be the development of an intellectually mature individual? Or should schools also show a strong concern for emotional and social maturity? Should schools be comprehensive and provide a multifaceted curriculum that includes many elective and alternative subjects in addition to a basic set of core subjects? These provocative questions continue to be debated in educational and community circles (Cross, 1984; Goodlad, 1983; Sizer, 1984).

What Are Effective Schools for Young Adolescents Like?

Analyze your own middle school or junior high school. How does it measure up to Lipsitz's criteria for effective schools for adolescents?

Joan Lipsitz (1984) extensively evaluated what makes an effective school for young adolescents. She and her colleagues searched the nation for the best middle schools. Extensive contacts and observations were conducted. Eventually, based on the recommendations of education experts and observations in schools in different parts of the United States, four middle schools were chosen for their outstanding ability to educate young adolescents. What were these middle schools like? The most striking feature of the four best middle schools was their willingness and ability to adapt all school practices to the individual differences in physical, cognitive, and social development of their students. The schools took information about early adolescent development seriously. This seriousness was reflected in decisions about different aspects of school life. For example, one middle school fought to keep its schedule of minicourses on Friday so that every student could be with friends and pursue personal interests. Two other middle schools expended considerable energy on a complex school organization so that small groups of students worked with small groups of teachers who could vary the tone and pace of the school day, depending on the students' needs. Another middle school developed an advisory scheme so that each student had daily contact with an adult who was willing to listen, explain, comfort, and prod the adolescent. Such school policies reflect thoughtfulness and personal concern about individuals whose developmental needs are compelling.

Another aspect of the effective middle schools observed was that, early in their existence—the first year in three of the schools and the second year in the fourth school—they emphasized the importance of creating an environment that was positive for the adolescent's social and emotional development. This goal was established not only because such environments contribute to academic excellence but also because social and emotional development are intrinsically valued as important in themselves in the schooling of adolescents. Focus on Life-Span Development 12.3 presents more information about effective middle schools, as well as information about some that are not so effective.

When teachers complain about young adolescents, animal imagery is pervasive: "This school is a zoo," "Those students are like animals," "It is a jungle in the classroom." In schools that seem like "zoos," students usually do not learn effectively and often are not very happy. Consider these vignettes about four ineffective middle schools:

A teacher sits in the back of the room, her legs up on her desk, asking students questions from a textbook. The students, bored and listless, sit in straight rows facing no one in the front of the room, answering laconically to a blank blackboard. When the principal enters the room, the teacher lowers her legs to the floor. Nothing else changes.

A teacher drills students for a seemingly endless amount of time on prime numbers. After the lesson, not one of them can say why it is important to learn prime numbers.

A visitor asks a teacher if hers is an eighth-grade class. "It's called eighth grade," she answers archly, "but we know it's really kindergarten—right, class?"

In a predominantly Hispanic school, only the one adult hired as a bilingual teacher speaks Spanish.

In a biracial school, the principal and the guidance counselor cite test scores with pride. They are asked if the difference between the test scores of black and white students is narrowing. "Oh, that's an interesting question!" the guidance counselor says in surprise. The principal agrees. It has never been asked by or of them before.

A teacher in a social studies class squelches several imaginative questions, exclaiming, "You're always asking 'what if' questions. Stop asking 'what if'!" When a visitor asks who will become president if the president-elect dies before the electoral college meets, the teacher explodes: "You're as bad as they are! That's another 'what if' question!" (Lipsitz, 1984, pp. 169–170)

By contrast, consider the following circumstances in effective middle schools:

Everything is peaceful. There are open cubbies instead of locked lockers. There is no theft. Students walk quietly in the corridor. "Why?" they are asked. "So as not to disturb the media center," they answer, which is self-evident to them but not the visitor who is left wondering. . . .When asked, "Do you like this school?" (They) answer: "No, we don't like it. We love it!" (Lipsitz, 1984, p. 27)

When asked how the school feels, one student answered, "It feels smart. We're smart. Look at our test scores." Comments from one of the parents of a student at the school are revealing: "My child would have been a dropout. In elementary school, his teacher said to me: 'That child isn't going to give you anything but heartaches.' He had perfect attendance here. He didn't want to miss a day. Summer vacation was too long and boring. Now he's majoring in communications at the University of Texas. He got here and all of a sudden someone cared for him. I had been getting notes about Roger every other day, with threats about expulsion. Here, the first note said: 'It's just a joy to have him in the classroom.' " (Lipsitz, 1984, p. 84)

The humane environment that encourages teachers' growth . . . is translated by the teachers . . . into a humane environment that encourages students' growth. The school feels cold when one first enters. It has the institutional feeling of any large school building with metal lockers and impersonal halls. Then one opens the door to a team area, and it is filled with energy, movement, productivity, doing. There is a lot of informal relating among students and between students and teachers. Visible from one vantage point are students working on written projects, putting the last touches on posters, watching a film, and working independently from reading kits. . . .Most know what they are doing, can say why it is important, and go back to work immediately after being interrupted. (Lipsitz, 1984, p. 109)

Authors' Week is yet another special activity built into the school's curriculum that entices students to consider themselves in relation to the rich variety of making and doing in people's lives. Based on student interest, availability, and diversity, authors are invited . . . to discuss their craft. Students sign up to meet with individual authors. They must have read one individual book by the author. . . .Students prepare questions for their sessions with the authors. . . .Sometimes, an author stays several days to work with a group of students on his or her manuscript. (Lipsitz, 1984, p. 141)

These excerpts about a variety of schools in different areas of the United States reveal the great diversity among schools for adolescents. They also tell us that—despite the ineffectiveness of many schools for adolescents—others are very effective. Secondary schools can be breeding grounds for competent academic *and* social development.

Any transition from one school to the next presents challenges and requires adaptation. The transition from elementary school to middle or junior high school is especially stressful because it coincides with so many physical, cognitive, and social changes in development. What are these changes? How might parents and school officials make the change less stressful?

The Transition to Middle or Junior High School

The organization of junior high schools—and more recently middle schools—has been justified on the basis of early adolescence's physical, cognitive, and social changes. The growth spurt and the onset of puberty were the basis for removing seventh- and eighth-grade students from elementary schools (Hill, 1980). Because puberty has been coming earlier, the same kind of thinking has been applied to the formation of middle schools that house sixth- and sometimes fifth-graders in separate buildings along with seventh- and eighth-graders.

The transition to middle or junior high school from an elementary school is of interest to developmentalists because, even though it is a normative experience for virtually all children in our society, this transition can be stressful because of the point in development at which the transition takes place (Hawkins & Berndt, 1985; Simmons & others, 1987). Transition to middle or junior high school occurs at a time in development when a number of simultaneous changes are occurring:

> puberty and related concerns about body image
> emergence of at least some aspects of formal operational thought and social cognition
> increased responsibility and independence and decreased dependency on parents
> change from a small, contained classroom structure to a larger, more impersonal school structure
> change from one teacher to many teachers and from a small, homogenous set of peers to a larger, more heterogeneous set of peers
> increased focus on achievement and performance, and their assessment

Moving from the top position (in elementary school, as the oldest, biggest, and most powerful students in the school) to the bottom position (in middle or junior high school, as the youngest, smallest, and least powerful group of students) may create a number of problems for students. This has been referred to as the **top-dog phenomenon.**

The transition to middle or junior high school does have some positive possibilities, too. Students are more likely to feel grown up, to have more subjects from which to select, to have more opportunities to spend time with peers and more chances to locate compatible friends, to enjoy increased indepen-

CONCEPT TABLE
12.2

Cognitive Development and Schools		
Concept	**Processes/Related Ideas**	**Characteristics/Description**
Cognitive Development	Formal Operational Thought	Piaget believed that formal operational thought came into play between 11 and 15 years of age. Formal operational thought is more abstract, idealistic, and logical than concrete operational thought. Piaget believed that adolescents become capable of using hypothetical deductive reasoning. Language changes that accompany formal operational thought involve an increased understanding of satire and metaphor, improved writing ability, and superior conversational skills. There is more individual variation in formal operational thought than Piaget believed; many adolescents do not think in formal operational ways.
	Social Cognition	Impressive changes in social cognition characterize adolescent development. Adolescents develop a special type of egocentrism that involves an imaginary audience and a personal fable about being unique and indestructible, begin to think about personality not unlike the way personality theorists do, and monitor their social world in more sophisticated ways.
Schools	The Functions of Secondary Schools	Are wrapped in controversy. Some maintain that the function should be the intellectual development of the adolescent. Others argue that secondary schools should have more comprehensive functions—in addition to intellectual development, secondary schools should foster social and emotional development, and they should prepare the adolescent for adult work and existence as a life-long learner.
	Effective Schools for Young Adolescents	They take individual differences in development seriously and show a deep concern for what is known about early adolescence. These successful schools emphasize social and emotional development as much as intellectual development.
	Transition to Middle or Junior High School	The organization of junior high schools—and more recently middle schools—has been justified on the basis of physical, cognitive, and social changes in adolescents. The earlier onset of puberty has led to the formation of middle schools. The transition coincides with a number of individual, familial, and social changes; one problem involves going from the top-dog position to the bottom-dog position.

dence from direct parental and teacher monitoring, and to be more challenged intellectually by academic work. Researchers have found that schools providing more supportiveness, less anonymity, more stability, and less complexity have a salutary effect on student adustment in the transition to middle and junior high school (Hawkins & Berndt, 1985).

At this point, we have discussed a number of ideas about both the adolescent's cognitive development and schools for adolescents. A summary of these ideas is presented in Concept Table 12.2. Now we turn to another increasingly important setting in the adolescent's life—work.

Work

In 1974, the government Panel on Youth, headed by James Coleman, concluded that work has a positive influence on adolescents. Coleman and his colleagues argued that a job during adolescence creates a positive attitude toward work, allows students to learn from adults other than teachers or parents, and may help keep them out of trouble. The Panel on Youth recommended that more youth be included in the work force of our nation. To accomplish this goal, the panel suggested that more work/study programs be developed, that the minimum wage be lowered, and that more flexible school/work schedules be allowed.

Over the last century, the percentage of youth who work full time as opposed to those who are in school has decreased dramatically. During the last half of the 1800s, fewer than 1 out of every 20 high school-aged adolescents were in school, whereas more than 9 out of every 10 adolescents receive high school diplomas today. In the nineteenth century, many adolescents learned a trade from their father or some other adult member of the community. Now a much more prolonged period of educational training keeps most adolescents out of the full-time work force. The part-time work force, however, is another story. Huge numbers of adolescents combine part-time work with school today.

Most high school seniors already have had some experience in the world of work. In a national survey of 17,000 high school seniors, three out of every four reported that they had some job income during the average school week (Bachman, 1982). For 41 percent of the males and 30 percent of the females, this income exceeded $50 a week. The typical part-time job for high school seniors involves 16 to 20 hours a week, although 10 percent work 30 or more hours a week. In 1940, only 1 out of 25 tenth-grade males attended school and simultaneously worked part-time; in 1970, the number had increased to more than 1 out of 4. More recent estimates suggest that 1 out of 3 ninth- and tenth-graders combine school and work (Cole, 1981). Adolescents today also work longer hours than in the past. For example, the number of 14- and 15-year-olds who work more than 14 hours per week has increased substantially in the last two decades. A similar picture emerges for 16-year-olds. In 1960, 44 percent of the 16-year-olds who attended school worked more than 14 hours a week; by 1970, the figure had increased to 56 percent.

Does this increase in work have a positive influence on the adolescent's development? In some cases yes, in others no. Ellen Greenberger and Laurence Steinberg (1981) examined the work experiences of students in four California high schools. Their findings disproved some common myths. For example, generally it is assumed that adolescents get extensive on-the-job training when they are hired for work—the reality is that they get little training at all. Also, it is assumed that youths—through work experiences—learn to get along better with adults. However, adolescents reported that they rarely felt close to the adults with whom they worked. The work experiences of the adolescents did help them to understand how the business world works, how to get and keep a job, and how to manage money. Working also helped the youths to learn to budget their time, to take pride in their accomplishments, and to evaluate their goals. But working adolescents often have to give up sports, social affairs with peers, and sometimes sleep. And they have to balance the demands of work, school, family, and friends.

Greenberger and Steinberg asked students about their grade point averages, school attendance, satisfaction from school, and the number of hours spent studying and participating in extracurricular activities since they began working. They found that working adolescents had lower grade point averages

TABLE 12.3
Percentages of Unemployed Youths and Adults

	Whites	Blacks and Other Minorities
Men 20 years and older	5.1	8.3
Women 20 years and older	3.5	10.2
Men 16 to 19 years old	14.1	34.8
Women 16 to 19 years old	13.9	35.9

U.S. Department of Labor, Special Labor Force Report No. 218. *(Washington, D.C.: U.S. Government Printing Office, 1979) p. 9.*

than nonworking adolescents. More than one out of four students reported that their grades dropped when they began working; only one out of nine said that their grades improved. But it was not just working that affected adolescents' grades—more importantly, it was *how long* they worked. Tenth-graders who worked more than 14 hours a week suffered a drop in grades; 11th graders worked up to 20 hours a week before their grades suffered. When adolescents spend more than 20 hours a week working, there is little time to study for tests and to do homework assignments.

In addition to the effects of work on grades, working adolescents also feel less involved in school, are absent more, and say they don't enjoy school as much (compared to their nonworking peers). Adolescents who work also spend less time with their families—but just as much time with their peers—as their nonworking counterparts. Adolescents who work long hours also are more frequent users of alcohol and marijuana.

Some states have responded to these findings by limiting the number of hours adolescents can work while they are attending secondary school. In 1986, in Pinellas County, Florida, a state law was enacted that placed a cap on the previously unregulated hours that children 16 years of age and over could work while school was in session. The allowable limit was set at 30 hours, which—based on research evidence—is still too high (Greenberger, 1987).

The media also have focused heavily on unemployment among adolescents. Overall, it appears that unemployment among adolescents is not as widespread as the media reports suggest. For example, based on data collected by the U.S. Department of Labor, 9 of 10 adolescent boys were either in school, working at a job, or both; only 5 percent were out of school, without a job, looking for full-time employment (Feldstein & Ellwood, 1982). Most of the adolescents who did not have a job were not unemployed for long periods of time. For example, almost half of the adolescents who did not have a job were not unemployed for a lengthy time period; only 10 percent had been without a job for six months or more. The major portion of adolescents who are unemployed are individuals who have dropped out of school.

While the media have overexaggerated the degree of unemployment among adolescents, certain segments of the youth population merit special consideration. A disproportionate percentage of unemployed adolescents are black, for example. As indicated in table 12.3, the unemployment situation is especially acute for blacks and other minorities between the ages of 16 and 19. One survey revealed that, in 1979, only 50 percent of Hispanic adolescents held jobs (Rosenbaum, 1983). Since 1969, though, the job situation has improved for black adolescents, especially black males. For example, in 1969, 44 percent of black male adolescents were unemployed; by 1979, the figure had been reduced to 30 percent (Rosenbaum, 1983).

How might high unemployment rates among certain segments of the adolescent population be involved in high rates of adolescent pregnancy?

Summary

I. Pubertal Change

Puberty is a rapid change to maturation that does not involve a single event but rather is part of a lengthy developmental process. Menarche is the girl's first menstruation and has been coming earlier in recent decades probably because of improved health and nutrition. The endocrine glands are heavily involved in pubertal change; they secret hormones. Testosterone is the sex hormone that increases the most in adolescent males; estradiol is the sex hormone that increases the most in adolescent females. As adolescents undergo a growth spurt, they make rapid gains in height; the spurt occurs approximately two years earlier in girls (10½) than boys (12½).

II. Psychological Accompaniments of Physical Change

Adolescents show a considerable interest in their body image. Young adolescents are more preoccupied and dissatisfied with their bodies than late adolescents. Early maturation favors boys at least during adolescence; as adults, though, late maturing boys may achieve more successful identities. The results for girls are more mixed than for boys. Being on-time or off-time in terms of pubertal development is complex. Adolescents may be at risk when the demands of a particular context and the adolescent's physical and behavioral characteristics are mismatched.

III. Sexuality

At age 16, slightly over 40 percent of males and between 30 to 40 percent of females have had sexual intercourse; in some inner city areas, the percentages are higher. Adolescents in the United States have an extremely high pregnancy rate. Adolescent pregnancy has become a national crisis. Peers are the most common source of sex education.

Adolescents' knowledge of sex is not as advanced as they sometimes try to make it appear.

IV. Formal Operational Thought

Piaget believed that formal operational thought came into play between 11 and 15 years of age. Formal operational thought is more abstract, idealistic, and logical than concrete operational thought. Piaget believed that adolescents become capable of using hypothetical deductive reasoning. Language changes that accompany formal operational thought involve an increased understanding of satire and metaphor, improved writing ability, and superior conversational skills. There is more individual variation in formal operational thought than Piaget believed. Many adolescents do not think in formal operational ways.

V. Social Cognition

Impressive changes in social cognition characterize adolescent development. Adolescents develop a special type of egocentrism that involves an imaginary audience and a personal fable about being unique and indestructible, begin to think about personality not unlike the way personality theorists do, and monitor their social world in more sophisticated ways.

VI. Functions of Secondary Schools

The functions of secondary schools have always been wrapped in controversy. Some maintain that the function should be the intellectual development of the adolescent. Others argue that secondary schools should have more comprehensive functions—in addition to intellectual development, they should foster social and emotional development, and they should prepare the adolescent for adult work and existence as a life-long learner.

VII. Effective Schools for Young Adolescents

They take individual differences in development seriously and show a deep concern for what is known about early adolescence. These successful schools emphasize social and emotional development as much as intellectual development.

VIII. Transition to Middle or Junior High School

The organization of junior high schools—and more recently middle schools—has been justified on the basis of physical, cognitive, and social changes in adolescents. The earlier onset of puberty has led to the formation of middle schools. The transition coincides with a number of individual, familial, and social changes; one problem involves going from a top-dog position to a bottom-dog position.

IX. Work

There has been a tremendous increase in the number of adolescents who have part-time jobs and continue to go to school. The jobs adolescents have are both advantageous and disadvantageous to their development. With regard to school, working more than 14 hours a week lowers the grades of 10th graders; working more than 20 hours a week lowers the grades of 11th graders. While there has been widespread media attention directed at youth unemployment, youth unemployment is not as pervasive as the media stereotype. The major portion of unemployed youth are high school dropouts. The most acute unemployment problems reside with black and other minority group adolescents, as well as youth who have grown up in low-income families.

Key Terms

menarche   *352*

puberty   *353*

testosterone   *353*

estradiol   *354*

abstract   *361*

hypothetical deductive reasoning   *361*

satire   *361*

metaphor   *361*

adolescent egocentrism   *363*

imaginary audience   *363*

personal fable   *363*

top-dog phenomenon   *368*

Suggested Readings

Early Adolescent Sexuality: Resources for parents, professionals, and young people. (1983). Chapel Hill, NC: Center for Early Adolescence, U. of North Carolina.
This compendium of resources provides an excellent annotated bibliography of a wide variety of topics related to sexuality in early adolescence.

Journal of Early Adolescence
This journal focuses primarily on the 10- to 15-year age range and includes research articles on a wide variety of topics. Leaf through the issues of the last several years to discover the nature of research conducted with adolescents.

Lerner, R. M., & Foch, T. T. (Eds.). (1987). *Biological-psychological interactions in early adolescence.* Hilllsdale, NJ: Erlbaum.

Includes articles on a wide range of topics related to pubertal changes and their effects on development.

Lipsitz, J. (1984). *Successful Schools for Young Adolescents.* New Brunswick, NJ: Transaction Books.
Must reading for anyone interested in better schools for young adolescents. Filled with rich examples of successful schools and the factors that contribute to the effective education of young adolescents.

13

Social and Personality Development

You have lived through adolescence. I once was an adolescent. No one else experienced adolescence in quite the same way you or I did—your thoughts, feelings, and actions during your adolescent years, like mine, were unique. But we also encountered and handled some experiences in the same ways during adolescence. In high school, we learned many of the same skills that other students learned and grew to care about the same things others cared about. Peers were important to us. And, at one time or another, we probably felt that our parents had no idea what we were all about.

Not only did we feel that our parents misunderstood us, but our parents felt that we misunderstood them. Parents want to know why adolescents have mercurial moods—happy one moment, sad the next. They want to know why their teenagers talk back to them and challenge their rules and values. They want to know what parenting strategies will help them rear a psychologically healthy, competent adolescent who will become a mature adult. What should they do when their adolescents increasingly rely on peers to influence their decisions—in some cases, peers whose backgrounds the parents detest? Parents worry that their adolescent will have a drinking problem, a smoking problem, a drug problem, a sex problem, a school problem, and so on. They want to know if the situations they are experiencing with their adolescents are unique, or if other parents are experiencing the same difficulties and frustrations with their youth.

The social worlds of adolescence are many and fascinating—through experiences with parents, siblings, peers, friends, clique members, teachers, and other adults, adolescents make the transition from being a child to being an adult. There are many hills and valleys in this transition, and there are times when parent-adolescent relationships become exacerbated, as reflected in the comments of Mark Twain that opened this chapter. But a large majority of adolescents make the transition from childhood to adulthood competently, continuing to be attached to their parents while exploring an ever-widening social world as they move toward more autonomous behavior and decision making. As they make the transition from child to adult, a major concern of adolescents is the development of an identity—who am I, what am I all about, and where am I headed in life? In this chapter, we explore the social worlds of adolescence and the adolescent's concern with identity. And we study the problems and disturbances that confront adolescents.

Families and Adolescent Development

In chapter 11, we discussed how—during middle and late childhood—parents spend less time with their children than in early childhood, how discipline involves an increased use of reasoning and deprivation of privileges, how there is a gradual transfer of control from parents to children but still within the boundary of coregulation, and how parents and children increasingly respond to each other on the basis of labels. What are some of the most important issues and questions that need to be raised about family relationships in adolescence? They include: What is the nature of autonomy and attachment in adolescence? How extensive is parent-adolescent conflict and how does it influence the adolescent's development? Do maturation of the adolescent and maturation of parents contribute to understanding parent-adolescent relationships? What are the effects of divorce on adolescents?

Autonomy and Attachment

The adolescent's push for autonomy and a sense of responsibility puzzles and angers many parents. Parents see their teenager slipping away from their grasp. The urge may be to take stronger control as the adolescent seeks autonomy and responsibility. Heated emotional exchanges may ensue, with either side calling names, making threats, and doing whatever seems necessary to gain control. Parents may seem frustrated because they *expected* their teenager to heed their advice, to want to spend time with the family, and to grow up to do what is right. To be sure, they anticipated that their teenager would have some difficulty adjusting to the changes that adolescence brings, but few parents imagine and predict just how strong adolescents' desires will be to spend time with peers and how adolescents want to show that it is they—not their parents—who are responsible for their successes and failures.

The ability to attain autonomy and gain control over one's behavior in adolescence is acquired through appropriate adult reactions to the adolescent's desire for control. At the onset of adolescence, the average individual does not have the knowledge to make appropriate or mature decisions in all areas of life. As the adolescent pushes for autonomy, the wise adult relinquishes control in those areas in which the adolescent can make reasonable decisions and continues to guide the adolescent to make reasonable decisions in areas in which the adolescent's knowledge is more limited. Gradually, adolescents acquire the ability to make mature decisions on their own.

But adolescents do not simply move away from parental influence into a decision-making process all their own. There is continued connectedness to parents as adolescents move toward autonomy and gain autonomy. Attachment to parents increases the probability the adolescent will be a competent adolescent and become a competent adult. Just as in childhood, parents provide an important support system that helps the adolescent to explore in a healthy way a wider, more complex social world full of uncertainties, challenges, and stresses (Cooper & Ayers-Lopez, 1985; Hill & Holmbeck, in press; Kobak & Sceery, 1988; Santrock, 1987). Although adolescents show a strong desire to spend more time with peers, they do not move into a world isolated from parents. For example, in one investigation, adolescent girls who had the best relationships with their girl friends showed a strong identification with their mothers, indicating that they would like to be like their mothers (Gold & Yanof, 1985). Of course, there are times when adolescents reject this closeness as they try to assert their own ability to make decisions and develop an identity. But, for the most part, the worlds of parent-adolescent and adolescent-peer relationships are coordinated and connected, not uncoordinated and disconnected.

Parent-Adolescent Conflict

While attachment and connectedness to parents remains strong during adolescence, the attachment and connectedness is not always smooth. Early adolescence is a time when conflict with parents escalates beyond childhood levels (Montemayor & Hanson, 1985; Steinberg, 1987). This increase may be due

Adolescents push for autonomy. They want to make their own decisions, select their own clothes, stay out later, have their own phone, drive their own car, have their own room, fix their hair the way they want it to look, and choose their own friends. During the elementary school years, they were more likely to adhere to their parents' choices about such matters. Now they want more freedom. Parents sometimes become frustrated because the adolescent's push for autonomy violates their expectations for the adolescent's behavior. The wise parent relinquishes control in areas where the adolescent shows mature behavior but monitors more closely and retains more control in those areas where the adolescent behaves immaturely. And the wise parent remembers that it takes 10 to 15 years to become an adult, not 10 to 15 minutes, or 10 to 15 days.

Youth is the time to go flashing from one end of the world to the other, both in mind and body.

Robert L. Stevenson

We cannot build the future for our youth, but we can build our youth for the future.
Franklin D. Roosevelt, 1940

to a number of factors: the biological changes of puberty, cognitive changes involving increased idealism and logical reasoning, social changes focused on independence and identity, maturational changes in parents, and violated expectations on the part of parents and adolescents. The adolescent compares her parents to an ideal standard and then criticizes the flaws. A 13-year-old girl tells her mother, "That is the tackiest-looking dress I have ever seen. Nobody would be caught dead wearing that." The adolescent demands logical explanations for comments and discipline. A 14-year-old boy tells his mother, "What do you mean I have to be home at 10 P.M. because it's the way we do things around here? Why do we do things around here that way? It doesn't make sense to me."

Many parents see their adolescent changing from a compliant child to someone who is noncompliant, oppositional, and resistant to parental standards. The tendency on the part of parents is to clamp down and put more pressure on the adolescent to conform to parental standards (Collins, 1985, 1987). Parents often expect their adolescents to become mature adults overnight instead of understanding that the journey takes ten to fifteen years. Parents who recognize that this transition takes time handle their youth more competently and calmly than those who demand immediate conformity to adult standards. The opposite tactic—letting adolescents do as they please without supervision—also is unwise.

While conflict with parents does increase in early adolescence, it does not reach the tumultuous proportions envisioned by G. Stanley Hall, at the beginning of the twentieth century. Rather, much of the conflict involves the everyday events of family life such as keeping a bedroom clean, dressing neatly, getting home by a certain time, not talking forever on the phone, and so on. The conflicts rarely involve major dilemmas like drugs and delinquency.

It is not unusual to talk to parents of young adolescents and hear them say, "Is it ever going to get better?" Things usually do get better as adolescents move from the early part of adolescence toward the end. Conflict between parents usually escalates during early adolescence, remains somewhat stable during the high school years, and then lessens as the adolescent reaches 17 to 20 years of age. Parent-adolescent relationships become more positive if adolescents go away to college than if they stay at home and go to college (Sullivan & Sullivan, 1980).

The everyday conflicts that characterize parent-adolescent relationships may serve a positive developmental function (Blos, 1982; Hill, 1987). These minor disputes and negotiations facilitate the adolescent's transition from being dependent on parents to becoming an autonomous individual. For example, in one investigation adolescents who expressed disagreement with parents more actively explored identity development than adolescents who did not express disagreement with their parents (Cooper & others, 1982).

As suggested earlier, one way for parents to cope with the adolescent's push for independence and identity is to recognize that adolescence is a 10 to 15 year transition period rather than an overnight accomplishment. Recognizing that conflict and negotiation can serve a positive developmental function can tone down parental hostility too. Understanding parent-adolescent conflict, though, is not simple. As we observe next, both the maturation of the adolescent and the maturation of parents probably are wrapped up in this conflict.

The Maturation of the Adolescent and Parents

Physical, cognitive, and social changes in the adolescent's development influence the nature of parent-adolescent relationships. Parental changes also influence the nature of these relationships. Among the changes in the adolescent are puberty, expanded logical reasoning and increased idealistic and egocentric thought, violated expectations, changes in schooling, peers, friendship, and dating, and movement toward independence. Several recent investigations have shown that conflict between parents and adolescents, especially between mothers and sons, is the most stressful during the apex of pubertal growth (Hill & others, 1985; Steinberg, 1981, 1988).

Parental changes include those involving marital dissatisfaction, economic burdens, career reevaluation and time perspective, and health and body concerns. Marital dissatisfaction is greater when the offspring is an adolescent than a child or an adult. A greater economic burden is placed on parents during the rearing of their adolescents. Parents may reevaluate their occupational achievement, deciding whether they have met their youthful aspirations for success. Parents may look to the future and think about how much time they have remaining to accomplish what they want. Adolescents, however, look to the future with unbounded optimism, sensing that they have an unlimited amount of time to accomplish what they desire. Health concerns and an interest in body integrity and sexual attractiveness become prominent themes of adolescents' parents. Even when their body and sexual attractiveness are not deteriorating, many parents of adolescents perceive that they are. By contrast, adolescents are at or are beginning to reach the peak of their physical attractiveness, strength, and health. While both adolescents and their parents show a heightened preoccupation with their bodies, the adolescent's outcome probably is more positive.

The changes in adolescents' parents are those that characterize our development in middle adulthood. The majority of adolescents' parents either are in middle adulthood or are rapidly approaching middle adulthood. And, if current trends continue, adolescents' parents will be even older in the future since adults are waiting longer to get married and once married waiting longer to have children as they pursue career goals. More about these adult developmental changes appears later in the sections of the book on early and middle adulthood.

The Effects of Divorce on Adolescents

In chapter 9, we saw that divorce is a highly stressful experience for children. Here we will discover that divorce is a highly stressful experience for adolescents as well. The research of Judith Wallerstein and Joan Kelly (1980) included 21 individuals who were 13 years or older at the time of the divorce decision. Almost without exception, these adolescents perceived the divorce as painful. The adolescents who distanced themselves from marital conflict seemed to cope more effectively than those who did not. Especially helpful were strong ties with peers and friends during the divorce transition. In a 10-year follow-up of these adolescents as they moved into their adult years (Wallerstein, 1982), they continued to report that the divorce of their parents a decade earlier had been carried forward and had a lasting impact on their lives. Many of the young adults sensed that their parents' divorce had burdened their efforts at growing up and becoming mature adults. As young adults, they looked backward with emotions filled with sadness and with wishes that they had grown up in an intact, never-divorced family. They also evidenced considerable concern about repeating the divorce in their own marriages and were anxious to avoid having their own children grow up in divorced circumstances.

It is not enough for parents to understand children. They must accord children the privilege of understanding them.
Milton Sapirstein, Paradoxes of Everyday Life, *1955*

As the parents of adolescents will be increasingly older in the future because of delays in marriage and childbearing, how do you think this will influence the nature of parent-adolescent relationships?

TABLE 13.1

The Behavior of Young Adolescent Girls from Divorced, Widowed, and Intact Families at a Recreation Center

Observational Variable	Father Absent		Group Father Present
	Divorce	Death	
Subject-initiated physical contact and nearness with male peers	3.08	1.71	1.79
Male areas	7.75	2.25	4.71
Female areas	11.67	17.42	14.42

The numbers shown are means. Notice that the daughters of divorcees were more likely to initiate contact with males and spend time in male areas. Notice also that the daughters of the widows were more likely to spend time in female areas of the recreation center.

From E. Mavis Hetherington, "Effects of father absence on personality development in adolescent daughters" in Developmental Psychology, 7, 313–326, 1972. *Copyright © 1972 by the American Psychological Association. Reprinted by permission of the author.*

Divorce also influences the adolescent's heterosexual behavior. In an investigation by Mavis Hetherington (1972), adolescent girls with absent fathers acted in one of two extreme ways: They either were very withdrawn, passive, and subdued around males or were overly active, aggressive, and flirtatious. The girls who were inhibited, rigid, and restrained around males were more likely to be from widowed homes; those who sought the attention of males, who showed early heterosexual behavior, and who seemed more open and uninhibited around males were more likely to come from divorced homes.

Several examples of the girls' behavior provide further insight. The girls were interviewed by either a male or a female interviewer. Four chairs were placed in the room, including one for the interviewer. Daughters of the widows more often chose the farthest from the male interviewer; daughters of the divorcees more often chose the chair closest to him. There were no differences when the interviewer was female. The girls also were observed at a dance and during activities at a recreation center. At the dance, the daughters of the widows often refused to dance when asked. One widow's daughter spent the entire evening in the restroom. The daughters of the divorcees were more likely to accept the boys' invitations to dance. At the recreation center, the daughters of the divorcees were more frequently observed outside the gym where boys were playing; the daughters of the widows were more frequently observed in traditional female activities, like sewing and cooking (see table 13.1).

Hetherington (1977) continued to study these girls, following them in late adolescence and early adulthood to determine their sexual behavior, marital choices, and marital behavior. The daughters of the divorcees tended to marry younger and select marital partners who were more likely to have poor work histories and drug problems. In contrast, daughters of widows tended to marry males with a more puritanical makeup. In addition, both the daughters of the divorcees and the daughters of the widows reported more sexual adjustment problems than the daughters from the intact homes; for example, the daughters from the homes in which the father was absent had fewer orgasms than daughters from intact homes. The daughters from the intact homes seem to have worked through their relationships with their fathers and were more psychologically free to deal successfully in their relationships with other males.

In contrast, the daughters of the divorcees and the daughters of the widows appeared to be marrying images of their fathers.

It should be recognized that findings such as Hetherington's (1972, 1977) may not hold as the woman's role in society continues to change. Also, the findings are from a restricted sample of middle class families living in one city—the results might not be the same in other subcultures. Nonetheless, Hetherington's results do point to some likely vulnerabilities of adolescent girls growing up in divorced and widowed families.

Peers and Adolescent Development

In chapter 11, we discussed how, in middle and late childhood, children spend more time with their peers than in early childhood. We also found that friendships become more important in middle and late childhood and that popularity with peers is a strong motivation for most children. Advances in cognitive development during middle and late childhood also allow children to take the perspective of their peers and friends more readily, and their social knowledge of how to make and maintain friends increases.

Imagine you are back in junior and senior high school, especially during one of your good times. Peers, friends, cliques, dates, parties, and clubs probably come to mind. Adolescents spend huge chunks of time with peers, more even than in middle and late childhood. Among the important issues and questions to be asked about peer relations in adolescents are: What is the nature of peer pressure and conformity? How important are cliques in adolescence? How do children and adolescent groups differ? What is the nature of dating in adolescence?

Peer Pressure and Conformity

Consider the following statement made by an adolescent girl:

> Peer pressure is extremely influential in my life. I have never had very many friends, and I spend quite a bit of time alone. The friends I have are older. . . .The closest friend I have had is a lot like me in that we are both sad and depressed a lot. I began to act even more depressed than before when I was with her. I would call her up and try to act even more depressed than I was because that is what I thought she liked. In that relationship, I felt pressure to be like her. . . .

During adolescence, especially early adolescence, we conformed more to peer standards than in childhood. Investigators have found that around the eighth and ninth grades, conformity to peers—especially to their antisocial standards—peaks (Berndt, 1979; Douvan & Adelson, 1966). For example, at this point in adolescence, an individual is most likely to go along with a peer to steal hubcaps off a car, draw grafitti on a wall, or steal cosmetics from a store counter.

Cliques and Crowds

Most peer group relationships in adolescence can be categorized in one of three ways: The crowd, the clique, or individual friendships. The largest and least personal of these is the **crowd.** Members of the crowd meet because of their mutual interest in activities, not because they are mutually attracted to each other. By contrast, the members of cliques and friendships are attracted to each other on the basis of similar interests and social ideals. **Cliques** are smaller, involve greater intimacy among members, and have more group cohesion than crowds.

Young adolescents express an extremely strong desire to be like their peers, to be accepted, to conform to their ideas, their dress, their language, and their behavior. This conformity is especially strong around the eighth and ninth grades. Think back to your own life when you were in the eighth or ninth grade. In what ways did you conform to your peers?

Each of you, individually, walkest with the tread of a fox, but collectively ye are geese.

Solon, Ancient Greece

Go to virtually any secondary school in the country and you will find three to six well-defined cliques. What was the nature of the cliques in the schools you attended? What were the benefits of clique membership? The drawbacks?

Allegiance to cliques, clubs, organizations, and teams exerts powerful control over the lives of many adolescents. Group identity often overrides personal identity. The leader of a group may place a member in a position of considerable moral conflict by asking, in effect, "What's more important, our code or your parents'?" or "Are you looking out for yourself, or the members of the group?" Labels like "brother" and "sister" sometimes are adopted and used in the members' conversations with each other. These labels symbolize the bond between the members and suggest the high status of group membership.

One of the most widely cited studies of adolescent cliques and crowds is that of James Coleman (1961). Students from 10 different high schools were asked to identify the leading crowds in their schools. They also were asked to identify the students who were the most outstanding in athletics, popularity, and different school activities. Regardless of the school sampled, the leading crowds were composed of athletes and popular girls. Much less power in the leading crowd was attributed to the bright student. Coleman's finding that being an athlete contributes to popularity for adolescent boys was reconfirmed in a more recent investigation (Eitzen, 1975).

In virtually any junior or senior high school, we would find three to six well-defined cliques. If you were a member of a clique, weren't you proud of your identity? A recent investigation revealed that clique membership is associated with the adolescent's self-esteem (Brown & Lohr, in press). Cliques included: jocks ((athletically oriented), populars (well-known students who lead social activities), normals (middle-of-the-road students who make up the masses), druggies/toughs (known for illicit drug use or other delinquent activities), and nobodies (low in social skills or intellectual abilities). The self-esteem of the jocks and the populars was highest while that of the nobodies was the lowest. But one group of adolescents not in a clique had self-esteem equivalent to the jocks and the populars—this group was the independents, who indicated that clique membership was not important to them. Keep in mind that these data are correlational—self-esteem could increase an adolescent's probability of becoming a clique member just as clique membership could increase the adolescent's self-esteem.

Children and Adolescent Groups

Children groups differ from adolescent groups in several important ways. The members of children groups often are friends or neighborhood acquaintances. Their groups usually are not as formalized as many adolescent groups. During the adolescent years, groups tend to include a broader array of members—in other words, adolescents other than friends or neighborhood acquaintances often are members of adolescent groups. Try to recall the student council, honor society, or football team at your junior high school. If you were a member of any of these organizations, you probably remember that they were made up of many individuals you had not met before and that they were a more heterogeneous group than your childhood peer groups. Rules and regulations were probably well defined, and captains or leaders were formally elected or appointed in the adolescent groups.

A well-known observational study by Dexter Dunphy (1963) supports the notion that opposite-sex participation in groups increases during adolescence. In late childhood, boys and girls participate in small, same-sex cliques. As they move into the early adolescent years, the same-sex cliques begin to interact with each other. Gradually, the leaders and high-status members form further cliques based on heterosexual relationships. Eventually, the newly

He who would learn to fly one day must first learn to stand and walk and climb and dance: one cannot fly into flying.
Friedrich Nietzche, Thus Spoke Zarathustra, *1883*

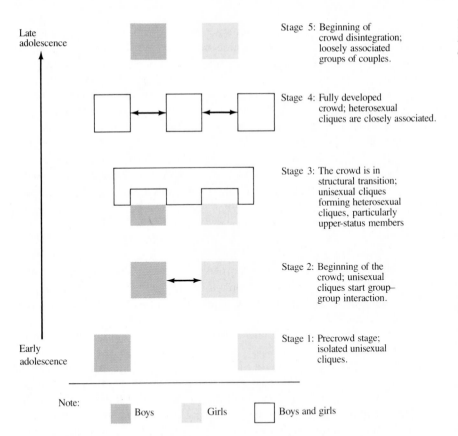

Stage 5: Beginning of crowd disintegration; loosely associated groups of couples.

Stage 4: Fully developed crowd; heterosexual cliques are closely associated.

Stage 3: The crowd is in structural transition; unisexual cliques forming heterosexual cliques, particularly upper-status members

Stage 2: Beginning of the crowd; unisexual cliques start group–group interaction.

Stage 1: Precrowd stage; isolated unisexual cliques.

Late adolescence

Early adolescence

Note: ▢ Boys ▢ Girls ▢ Boys and girls

Figure 13.1
Dunphy's stages of group development in adolescence.

created heterosexual cliques replace the same-sex cliques. The heterosexual cliques interact with each other in large crowd activities, too—at dances and athletic events, for example. In late adolescence, the crowd begins to dissolve as couples develop more serious relationships and make long-range plans that may include engagement and marriage. A summary of Dunphy's ideas is presented in figure 13.1.

Dating
Dating takes on added importance during adolescence. As Dick Cavett (1974) remembers, the thought of an upcoming dance or sock hop was absolute agony, "I knew I'd never get a date. There seemed to be only this limited set of girls I could and should be seen with, and they were all taken by the jocks." Adolescents spend considerable time either dating or thinking about dating, which has gone far beyond its original courtship function to a form of recreation, a source of status and achievement, and a setting for learning about close relationships.

Most girls in the United States begin dating at the age of 14, while most boys begin sometime between the ages of 14 and 15 (Douvan & Adelson, 1966; Sorenson, 1973). The majority of adolescents have their first date between the ages of 12 and 16. Fewer than 10 percent have a first date before the age of 10, and by the age of 16, more than 90 percent have had at least one date. More than 50 percent of high school students average one or more dates per week (Dickinson, 1975). About 15 percent date less than once per month, and about three of every four students have gone steady at least once by the end of high school.

Adolescents either spend a lot of time dating, or as is more often the case, spend a lot of time thinking about dating. Remember the anxieties of your first date and the excitement of exploring new territory in your life. Dating serves many functions for us, especially providing us with an opportunity to learn about the nature of close relationships.

How do you think variations in adolescents' observations of their parents' marital lives and relationships with their parents influence dating relationships in adolescence?

During adolescence, we enter a psychological moratorium during which we seek answers to who we are and what we are going to do with our lives.

The thoughts of youth are long, long thoughts.

Henry Wadsworth Longfellow, 1858

Female adolescents bring a stronger desire for intimacy and personality exploration to dating than male adolescents (Duck, 1975). Adolescent dating is a context in which gender-related role expectations intensify. Males feel pressured to perform in "masculine" ways and females feel pressured to perform in "feminine" ways. Especially in early adolescence when pubertal changes are occurring, the adolescent male wants to show that he is the very best male possible and the adolescent female wants to show that she is the very best female possible.

At this point, we have discussed a number of ideas about families and peers during adolescence. A summary of these ideas is presented in Concept Table 13.1. Next, we turn to the powerful motivation of the adolescent to develop an identity.

Identity

By far the most comprehensive and provocative story of identity development has been told by Erik Erikson. As you may remember from chapter 2, identity versus identity confusion (diffusion) is the fifth stage in Erikson's eight stages of the life cycle, occurring at about the same time as adolescence. It is a time of interest in finding out who one is, what one is all about, and where one is headed in life.

During adolescence, world views become important to the individual, who enters what Erikson (1968) calls a "psychological moratorium"—a gap between the security of childhood and the autonomy of adulthood. Numerous identities can be drawn from the surrounding culture, and adolescents experiment with different roles. The youth who successfully copes with these conflicting identities during adolescence emerges with a new sense of self that is both refreshing and acceptable. The adolescent who does not successfully resolve this identity crisis is confused, suffering what Erikson calls identity confusion. This confusion takes one of two courses: The individual withdraws, isolating himself from peers and family, or he may lose his identity in the crowd.

Because Erikson's ideas about identity represent one of the most important statements about adolescent development and because they reveal rich insight into the thoughts and feelings of adolescents, you are strongly encouraged to read one or more of his original writings. A good starting point is *Childhood and Society* (1950) or *Identity: Youth and Crisis* (1968). Other works that portray identity crises successfully resolved include *Young Man Luther* (1962) and *Gandhi's Truth* (1969)—the latter won a Pulitzer Prize. A sampling of Erikson's writings from these books is presented in Focus on Life-Span Development 13.1.

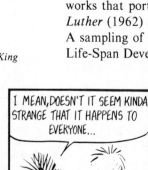

Families and Peers		
Concept	**Processes/Related Ideas**	**Characteristics/Description**
Families	Autonomy and Attachment	Many parents have a difficult time handling the adolescent's push for autonomy, even though this push is one of the hallmarks of adolescent development. Adolescents do not simply move into a world isolated from parents; attachment to parents increases the probability the adolescent will be socially competent and explore a widening social world in healthy ways.
	Parent-Adolescent Conflict	Conflict with parents does seem to increase in early adolescence. Such conflict usually is of the moderate variety. The increase in conflict probably serves the positive developmental function of promoting autonomy and identity.
	The Maturation of the Adolescent and Parents	Physical, cognitive, and social changes in the adolescent's development influence parent-adolescent relationships. Parental changes—marital dissatisfaction, economic burdens, career reevaluation and time perspective, and health and body concerns—also influence parent-adolescent relationships.
	The Effects of Divorce on Adolescents	Divorce is a stressful experience for adolescents, just as it is for children. Adolescents carry forward the experience of their parents' divorce into their adult years. Divorce influences the heterosexual behavior of girls, increasing their approach behavior toward males.
Peers	Peer Pressure and Conformity	The pressure to conform to peers is strong during adolescence, especially during the eighth and ninth grades.
	Cliques and Crowds	There usually are three to six well-defined cliques in every secondary school. Membership in certain cliques—especially jocks and populars—is associated with increased self-esteem. Independents also show high self-esteem.
	Children and Adolescent Groups	Children groups are less formal, less heterogeneous, and less heterosexual than adolescent groups. Dunphy found that the development of adolescent groups moves through five stages.
	Dating	Dating can be a form of recreation, a source of status and achievement, a setting for learning about close relationships, and a means of mate sorting or selection. Most adolescents are involved in dating. It appears that adolescent females are more interested in intimacy and personality exploration than adolescent males are.

E rik Erikson is a master at using the psychoanalytic method to uncover historical clues about identity formation. Erikson has used the psychoanalytic method both with the youths he treats in psychotherapy sessions and in the analysis of the lives of famous individuals. Erikson (1950) believes that the psychoanalytic technique sheds light on human psychological evolution. He also believes that the history of the world is a composite of individual life cycles.

In the excerpts that follow from Erikson's writings, the psychoanlytic method is used to analyze the youths of Tom Sawyer, Adolf Hitler, Martin Luther, and Mahatma Gandhi.

The occasion, while not pathological, is nevertheless a tragic one: a boy named Tom Sawyer, by verdict of his aunt, must whitewash a fence on an otherwise faultless spring morning. His predicament is intensified by the appearance of an age-mate named Ben Rogers, who indulges in a game. It is Ben, the man of leisure, whom we want to observe with the eyes of Tom, the working man.

"He took up his brush and went tranquilly to work. Ben Rogers hove in sight presently—the very boy, of all boys, whose ridicule he had been dreading. Ben was impersonating the *Big Missouri,* and considered himself to be drawing nine feet of water. He was boat and captain and engine-bells combined. Tom went on whitewashing—paid no attention to the steamboat. Ben stared a

moment, and then said: 'Hiyi! You're a stump, ain't you! You got to work, hey?' "(Erikson, quoting Twain, 1950, pp. 209–210)

Erikson presented this conversation between Tom and Ben to a class of psychiatric social work students and asked them to interpret Ben's behavior. They indicated that Ben must have been a frustrated boy to take so much trouble to play so strenuously. They went on to say that the frustrations likely emerged as a consequence of having a tyrannical father. But Erikson provided them with a more positive analysis— namely, that Ben was a growing boy, and growing means that he has to gradually master his gangling body and divided mind. Flexible and happy might be better labels to place on Tom's friend Ben.

In other passages, Erikson (1962) describes the youth of Adolf Hitler:

I will not go into the symbolism of Hitler's urge to build except to say that his shiftless and brutal father had consistently denied the mother a steady residence: one must read how Adolf took care of his mother when she wasted away from breast cancer to get an inkling of this young man's desperate urge to cure. But it would take a very extensive analysis, indeed, to indicate in what way a single boy can daydream his way into history and emerge a sinister genius, and how a whole nation becomes ready to accept the emotive power of that genius as a hope of fulfillment for its national aspirations and as a warrant for national criminality. . . .

The memoirs of young Hitler's friend indicate an almost pitiful fear on the part of the future dictator that he might be nothing. He had to challenge this possibility by being deliberately and totally anonymous; and only out of this self-chosen nothingness could he become everything. (Erikson, 1962, pp. 108–109)

But while the identity crisis of Adolf Hitler led him to turn toward politics in a pathological effort to create a world order, the identity crisis of Martin Luther in a different era led him to turn toward theology in an attempt to deal systematically with human nothingness or lack of identity.

In confession, for example, he was so meticulous in the attempt to be truthful that he spelled out every intention as well as every deed; he splintered relatively acceptable purities into smaller and smaller impurities; he reported temptations in historical sequence, starting back in childhood; and after having confessed for hours, would ask for special appointments in order to correct previous statements. In doing this, he was obviously both exceedingly compulsive and, at least unconsciously, rebellious. . . .

At this point, we must note a characteristic of great young rebels: their inner split between the temptation to surrender and the need to dominate. A great young rebel is torn between, on the other hand, tendencies to give in and fantasies of defeat (Luther used to resign himself to an early death at

Hitler in elementary school. He is in the center of the top row.

What did Erikson believe were some of the key ingredients in Mahatma Gandhi's development of identity?

times of impending success), and the absolute need, on the other hand, to take the lead, not only over himself but over all the forces and people who impinge on him. (Erikson, 1968, pp. 155–157)

And in his Pulitzer Prize-winning novel on Mahatma Gandhi's life, Erikson (1969) describes the personality formation of Gandhi during his youth:

Straight and yet not stiff; shy and yet not withdrawn; intelligent and yet not bookish; willful and yet not stubborn, sensual and yet not soft. . . .We must try to reflect on the relation of such a youth to his father, because the Mahatma places service to the father and the crushing guilt of failing in such service in the center of his adolescent turbulence. Some historians and political scientists seem to find it easy to interpret this account in psychoanalytic terms; I do not. For the question is not how a particular version of the Oedipal complex "causes" a man to be both great and neurotic in a particular way, but rather how such a young person . . . manages the complexes which constrict other men. (Erikson, 1969, p. 113)

In these passages, the workings of an insightful, sensitive mind is shown looking for a historical perspective on personality development. Through analysis of the lives of such famous individuals as Hitler, Luther, and Gandhi, and through the thousands of youth he has talked with in person, Erikson has pieced together a descriptive picture of identity development.

The Four Statuses of Identity

James Marcia (1966, 1980) analyzed Erikson's theory of identity development and concluded that four identity statuses, or modes of resolution, appear in the theory—identity diffusion, identity foreclosure, identity moratorium, and identity achievement. The extent of an adolescent's commitment and crisis is used to classify the individual according to one of the four identity statuses. **Crisis** is defined as a period during which the adolescent is choosing among meaningful alternatives. Most researchers now use the term *exploration* rather than *crisis,* although in the spirit of Marcia's original formulation, we will refer to crisis. **Commitment** is defined as the extent to which the adolescent shows a personal investment in what she is going to do.

In **identity diffusion,** adolescents have not yet experienced a crisis (that is, they have not explored meaningful alternatives) or made any commitments. Not only are they undecided upon occupational or ideological choices, they also are likely to show little interest in such matters. In **identity foreclosure,** adolescents have made a commitment but have not experienced a crisis. This occurs most often when parents simply hand down commitments to their adolescents, more often than not in an authoritarian way. In these circumstances, adolescents have not had adequate opportunities to explore different approaches, ideologies, and vocations on their own. In **identity moratorium,** adolescents are in the midst of a crisis but their commitments either are absent or are only vaguely defined. These adolescents are searching for commitments by actively questioning alternatives. In **identity achievement,** adolescents have undergone a crisis and have made a commitment. A summary of Marcia's four statuses of identity is presented in table 13.2.

The identity status approach has come under sharp criticism by some researchers and theoreticians (Blasi, 1988; Lapsley & Power, 1988). They believe the identity status approach distorts and trivializes Erikson's notions of crisis and commitment. For example, concerning crisis, Erikson emphasized the youth's questioning of the perceptions and expectations of one's culture and developing an autonomous position with regard to one's society. In the identity status approach, these complex questions and development are dealt with by simply evaluating whether a youth has thought about certain issues and considered alternatives. Erikson's idea of commitment loses the meaning of investing one's own self in certain lifelong projects in the identity status approach, simply being interpreted as having made a firm decision or not.

Contemporary views of identity development suggest several important considerations. First, identity development is a lengthy process, in many instances a more gradual, less cataclysmic transition than Erikson's term *crisis* implies. Second, identity development is extraordinarily complex (Marcia, 1980, 1987). Identity formation neither begins nor ends with adolescence. It begins with the appearance of attachment, the development of a sense of self, and the emergence of independence in infancy and reaches its final phase with a life review and integration in old age. What is important about identity in adolescence, especially late adolescence, is that for the first time physical development, cognitive development, and social development advance to the point at which the individual can sort through and synthesize childhood identities and identifications to construct a viable pathway toward adult maturity. Resolution of the identity issue at adolescence does not mean identity will be stable through the remainder of one's life. An individual who develops a healthy identity is flexible and adaptive, open to changes in society, in relationships, and in careers. This openness assures numerous reorganizations of identity contents throughout the identity-achieved individual's life.

In the beginning was alpha and the end is omega, but somewhere in between occurred delta, which is nothing less than the arrival of man himself into the daylight of . . . being himself and not being himself, of being at home and being a stranger.

Walker Percy, Message in the Bottle

Adolescence

TABLE 13.2 The Four Statuses of Identity				
	Identity Status			
Position on Occupation and Ideology	Identity Moratorium	Identity Foreclosure	Identity Diffusion	Identity Achievement
Crisis	Present	Absent	Absent	Present
Commitment	Absent	Present	Absent	Present

Identity formation does not happen neatly and it usually does not happen cataclysmically. At the bare minimum, it involves commitment to a vocational direction, an ideological stance, and a sexual orientation. Synthesizing the identity components can be a long and drawn out process with many negations and affirmations of various roles and faces. Identity development gets done in bits and pieces. Decisions are not made once and for all, but have to be made again and again. And the decisions may seem trivial at the time: whom to date, whether or not to break up, whether or not to have intercourse, whether or not to take drugs, whether to go to college or finish high school and get a job, which major, whether to study or whether to play, whether or not to be politically active, and so on. Over the years of adolescence, the decisions begin to form a core of what the individual is all about as a person, what is called identity.

Family Influences on Identity

Parents are important figures in the adolescent's development of identity. Harold Grotevant and Catherine Cooper (Grotevant, 1984; Grotevant & Cooper, 1985) highlight the power of both connectedness to parents and the presence of a family atmosphere that promotes individuation in the adolescent's identity development. **Connectedness** is reflected in mutuality and permeability. Mutuality refers to the adolescent's sensitivity to and respect for others' views. Permeability refers to openness and responsiveness to others' views. Mutuality provides adolescents with support, acknowledgement, and respect for their own beliefs; permeability lets the adolescent sense how to manage the boundaries between the self and others. **Individuation** has two main components—separateness and self-assertion. Separateness is seen in the expressions of how distinctive the self is from others. Self-assertion is involved in the adolescent's expression of her personal point of view and in taking responsibility for communicating this clearly. Parents who have both a connectedness with their adolescents and who promote individuation encourage the adolescent's development of identity.

Problems and Disturbances in Adolescence

The problems and disturbances encountered by adolescents are different than those encountered by children. Two of the most pervasive problems experienced by adolescents are drug abuse and delinquency. Suicide and eating disorders also are major concerns, and depression increases in adolescence, especially among girls. School-related problems continue to be a major concern, just as in middle and late childhood.

Drugs

Extensive monitoring of drug use by adolescents has been conducted by Lloyd Johnston, Patrick O'Malley, and Gerald Bachman (1987, 1988) for a number of years. Each year since 1975, they have surveyed the drug use of high school seniors in a wide range of public and private high schools across the United States. From time to time, they also sample the drug use of younger adolescents and young adults as well.

An encouraging finding from the most recent survey (conducted in 1987) of 16,300 high school seniors is that the continued gradual downturn in the overall use of illicit drugs is just that—a stall. The downward trend resumed again in 1986. Only 3.3 percent of the high school seniors used marijuana on a daily basis, down from mid 1980s levels and substantially down from the peak level of 10.7 percent observed in 1978. Also encouraging is that in 1987, for the first time in 8 years, cocaine showed a significant drop in use. Slightly more than 10 percent of high school seniors used cocaine at least once a year, down from 12.7 percent annual prevalence in 1986. Cocaine use by college students also declined from 17.1 percent annual prevalence in 1986 to 13.7 percent in 1987. A growing proportion of high school seniors and college students are reaching the conclusion that cocaine use entails considerable, unpredictable risk for the user. Still, the percentage of adolescents and young adults using cocaine is precariously high. About 1 of every 6 high school seniors has tried cocaine at least once, and 1 in 18 has tried crack cocaine specifically, for example.

Another troublesome part of the cocaine story appears in a dangerous shift in the mode of administration being used, due in large part to the advent of crack cocaine—an inexpensive, purified, smokeable form of the drug. The proportion of seniors who said they smoked cocaine more than doubled between 1983 and 1986, from 2.5 percent to 6 percent. For the first time, in 1986, seniors were asked specifically about crack use. In 1986 and 1987, 4 percent of the seniors said they had used crack in the prior 12 months. Crack use was especially heavy in noncollege-bound youth and in urban settings.

Another widely-used class of illicit drugs showed an important shift in 1986 and 1987—stimulants, more specifically amphetamines. There were sizeable declines in use among high school seniors, college students, and young adults. Since 1982, annual use of amphetamines fell from 20 percent to 13 percent among seniors and from 21 percent to 10 percent among college students. However, there has been a sharp increase in the use of over-the-counter stay-awake pills, which usually contain caffeine as their active ingredient. Their annual prevalence has risen from 12 percent in 1982 to more than 20 percent in 1986 and 1987. Two other classes of stimulants—"look alikes" and over-the-counter diet pills—actually declined in use in recent years. Still, 40 percent of females have tried diet pills by the end of their senior year, and 10 percent have used them within the last month. Another drug with stimulant, as well as mildly hallucinogenic qualities, is **MDMA.** Only recently has the public become aware of MDMA as a street drug. To learn more about this intriguing drug and the controversy surrounding designer drugs, turn to Focus on Life-Span Development 13.2.

ocaine usually gives me an up-and-down jagged feeling that lasts only for a short time. I alternately like it and hate it, though for some reason it has very seductive qualities. Ecstasy, on the other hand, is just as its name implies. It's 'state of the art.' It puts me in a place of total bliss for three or four hours. Whereas coke makes me feel jittery, MDMA is very smooth. I know it has amphetamine in it, but I feel so relaxed" (Murphy, 1986).

MDMA, also known by a variety of street names—Ecstasy, Adam, and XTC—is one of the **designer drugs,** drugs made by chemically reengineering an existing controlled substance to create a drug that is currently legal (Beck & Morgan, 1986). One reason for its popularity in Texas undoubtedly is its sale in student and gay bars. The blatancy of sales presented a very public and thus potentially problematic drug-use pattern to authorities. Major stories in *Newsweek, Time, Life,* and many other popular magazines in the mid-1980s often sensationalized the euphoric and therapeutic qualities of MDMA.

With the publicity has come increased street use of MDMA, which escalated from an estimated 10,000 doses in 1976 to 30,000 doses *per month* in 1985 (Siegel, 1985). MDMA has effects similar to amphetamines but seems to produce a longer, smoother euphoria than cocaine. This type of euphoria means the drug has a high potential for abuse. Heavy use of MDMA may impair the body's immune system and deplete the brain's supply of an important neurotransmitter-serotonin (Frith, 1986; Schuster, 1986).

MDMA also is used by some therapists as an adjunct to therapy. Some of the therapeutic claims are wildly positive, indicating that MDMA lets the client put on a therapist's cap for a few hours and see oneself with a new vision (Leverant, 1986). While MDMA has been heralded by some as a cure for everything from personal depression to cocaine addiction, research on its effects are still in their infancy and support for its therapeutic success has yet to occur.

There are many controversies surrounding MDMA. The advent of designer drugs led to the passage of a federal law permitting emergency control for 12 to 18 months of substances that pose imminent hazards to public safety. Do liberal pharmaceutical adventurists have the right to engineer these substances and challenge the government regulatory agencies' effort to prohibit the private ingestion of drugs for psychic exploration? Drug engineers argue that the government allows other dangerous activities to take place. On the other side are those who argue that drugs like MDMA should be prohibited because they pose hazards to the users. They stress that these psychoactive substances should undergo a series of animal toxicity studies before being declared safe.

The issue of MDMA's medical potential is another topic of passionate debate with strongly held convictions and little convincing data. Complex issues such as the potential therapeutic benefit versus actual toxicity continue to be the focus of considerable debate. The drug is both a threat and a promise, and the debate is both intense and vocal. Little scientific data have been collected, so support for either side is not available (Seymour, Wesson, & Smith, 1986).

A number of important findings have emerged from the study of adolescent patterns of cigarette smoking, in which the active drug is nicotine, a stimulant. By late adolescence, sizeable portions of youth are still establishing regular cigarette habits, despite the demonstrated health risks associated with smoking. Since the national surveys by Johnston, O'Malley, and Bachman began in 1975, cigarettes have been the substance most frequently used by high school students on a daily basis. While their daily smoking rate did drop considerably between 1977 and 1981 (from 29 percent to 20 percent), it has dropped little in the last five years (by another 1.6 percent). A full one-third of high school seniors still do not feel that there is a great risk associated with smoking. Initiation of daily smoking is most likely to occur in grades 7 through 9.

But one of the most alarming drug-use patterns has yet to be discussed—alcohol. During the period of recent decline in the use of marijuana and other drugs, there appears not to have been a displacement effect in terms of any increase in alcohol use by high school seniors. The opposite actually seems to have occurred. Since 1980, the monthly prevalence of alcohol use by seniors has gradually declined, from 72 percent in 1980 to 66 percent in 1987. Daily use declined from a peak of 6.9 percent in 1979 to 4.8 percent in 1984, with no further decline through 1987. And the prevalence of drinking five or more drinks in a row during the prior two-week interval fell from 41 percent in 1983 to 37 percent in 1987. There remains a substantial sex difference among high school seniors in the prevalence of heavy drinking (28 percent for females versus 46 percent for males in 1986), but this difference has been diminishing gradually over the last decade. However, data from college students show little drop in alcohol use and an increase in the prevalence of heavy drinking actually has occurred—45 percent in 1986, up 2 percent from the previous year. Heavy party drinking among college males is common and becoming more common.

What factors are associated with drug abuse by adolescents? In one recent longitudinal investigation (Block & Block, 1988), undercontrol by boys at age 4 was related to their drug use in adolescence, and permissive parenting in the families of girls at age 4 was related to their drug use in adolescence. And in another study (Newcomb & Bentler, 1988), social support during adolescence substantially reduced drug use. In this investigation, social support included good relationships with parents, family, adults, and peers. Multiple drug use in adolescence was related to drug and alcohol, health, and family problems in early adulthood. More about factors involved in a specific type of drug abuse—alcohol—will be discussed shortly.

Alcohol

Some mornings, Annie, a 15-year-old cheerleader, was too drunk to go to school. Other days, she'd stop for a couple of beers or a screwdriver on the way to school. She was tall and blonde and good-looking, and no one who sold her liquor, even at 8:00 in the morning questioned her age. Where did she get her money? From baby-sitting and what her mother gave her to buy lunch. Annie is no longer a cheerleader—she was kicked off the squad for missing practice so often. Soon, she and several of her peers were drinking almost every morning. Sometimes, they skipped school and went to the woods to drink. Annie's whole life began to revolve around her drinking. It went on for two years, and during

Why do you think alcohol use has remained so high?

the last summer, anytime she saw anybody she was drunk. After awhile, her parents began to detect Annie's problem. But even when they punished her, it did not stop her drinking. Finally, this year, Annie started dating a boy she really likes and who would not put up with her drinking. She agreed to go to Alcoholics Anonymous and has just successfully completed treatment. She has stopped drinking for four consecutive months now, and it is hoped that her abstinence will continue.

Unfortunately, there are hundreds of thousands of adolescents just like Annie. They live in both wealthy suburbs and inner-city housing projects. Annie grew up in a Chicago suburb and said she started drinking when she was 10 because her older brothers always looked like they were having fun when they were doing it. Researchers have found that young adolescents who take drugs are more likely to have older friends than their counterparts who do not take drugs (e.g., Blyth, Durant, & Moosbrugger, 1985). Adolescents also have strong expectancies that alcohol will produce personal effects, such as tension reduction, even moreso than adults expect (McLaughlin & Chassin, 1985). The use of alcohol to reduce stress and tension in their lives seems to be very common among adolescents. For adolescent males, a strong motive for power also is evident. Adolescent alcohol use also is related to parent and peer relations. Adolescents who drink heavily often come from unhappy homes in which there is a great deal of tension and also from homes in which parents sanction alcohol use (Barnes, 1984). And the peer group provides the social context for drinking and reinforces adolescent behavior that is learned as part of the family socialization process. The ability of the family to function as a support system for the adolescent seems to be an especially important factor in preventing heavy drinking by adolescents.

A strong family support system is clearly an important preventive strategy in reducing alcohol abuse by adolescents. Are there others? Would raising the minimum drinking age have an effect? In one investigation, raising the minimum drinking age did lower the frequency of automobile crashes involving adolescents, but raising the drinking age alone did not seem to reduce alcohol abuse (Wagennar, 1983). Another effort to reduce alcohol abuse involved a school-based program in which adolescents discussed alcohol-related issues with peers (Wodarski & Hoffman, 1984). At a one-year follow-up, students in the intervention schools reported less alcohol abuse and had discouraged each other's drinking more often than had students in schools who had not been involved in the peer discussion of alcohol-related issues. Efforts to help the adolescent with a drinking problem vary enormously. Therapy may include working with other family members, peer group discussion sessions, and specific behavioral techniques. Unfortunately, there has been little in the way of interest in identifying different types of adolescent alcohol abusers and then attempting to match treatment programs to the particular problems of the adolescent drinker. Most efforts simply assume that adolescents with drinking problems are a homogeneous group and do not take into account the varying developmental patterns and social histories of different adolescents. Some adolescents with drinking problems may be helped more through family therapy, others through peer counseling, and yet others through intensive behavioral strategies, depending on the type of drinking problem and the social agents who have the most influence on the adolescent (Finney & Moos, 1979; Schwartzberg, 1988).

What is the pattern of alcohol consumption among adolescents?

Delinquency

The label **juvenile delinquent** is applied to an adolescent who breaks the law or engages in behavior that is considered illegal. Like other categories of disturbance, juvenile deliquency is a broad concept; legal infractions range from littering to murder. Because the adolescent technically only becomes a juvenile delinquent after being judged guilty of a crime by a court of law, official records do not accurately reflect the number of illegal acts committed. Nevertheless, there is every indication that in the last 10 to 15 years, juvenile delinquency has increased in relation to the number of crimes committed by adults. Estimates regarding the number of juvenile delinquents in the United States are sketchy, although FBI statistics indicate that at least 2 percent of all youths are involved in juvenile court cases. The number of girls found guilty of juvenile delinquency has increased substantially in recent years. Delinquency rates among blacks, other minority groups, and the lower class are especially high in comparison to the overall population of these groups. However, such groups have less influence over the judicial decision-making process in the United States and therefore may be judged delinquent more readily than their white, middle-class counterparts (Binder, 1987; Gold, 1987).

What causes delinquency? Many causes have been proposed, including heredity, identity problems, community influences, and family experiences. Erik Erikson (1968), for example, believes that adolescents whose development has restricted them from acceptable social roles or made them feel that they cannot measure up to the demands placed on them may choose a negative identity. The adolescent with a negative identity may find support for his delinquent image among peers, reinforcing the negative identity. For Erikson, delinquency is an attempt to establish an identity, although it is a negative identity.

Although delinquency is less exclusively a lower-class phenomena than it was in the past, some characteristics of the lower-class culture may promote delinquency. The norms of many lower-class peer groups and gangs are antisocial, or counterproductive, to the goals and norms of society at large. Getting into and staying out of trouble become prominent features of some adolescents in low-income neighborhoods. Adolescents from low-income backgrounds may sense that they can gain attention and status by performing antisocial actions. Being "tough" and "masculine" are high status traits for lower-class boys, and these traits often are measured by the adolescent's success in performing delinquent acts and getting away with them. A community with a high crime rate also lets the adolescent observe many models who engage in criminal activities. These communities may be characterized by poverty, unemployment, and feelings of alienation toward the middle class. Quality schooling, educational funding, and organized neighborhood activities may be lacking in these communities (Offord & Boyle, 1988).

Family support systems are also associated with delinquency (Snyder & Patterson, 1987). The parents of delinquents are less skilled in discouraging antisocial behavior and in encouraging skilled behavior than the parents of nondelinquents. Parental monitoring of adolescents is especially important in whether an adolescent becomes a delinquent. In one investigation, parental monitoring of the adolescent's whereabouts was the most important family factor in predicting delinquency (Patterson & Stouthamer-Loeber, 1984). "It's 10 P.M., do you know where your children are?" seems to be an important question for parents to answer affirmatively. Family discord and inconsistent and inappropriate discipline are also associated with delinquency.

A special concern in delinquency has surfaced in recent years—escalating gang violence. Gang violence is being waged on a more lethal level than ever before. Knives and clubs have been replaced with grenades and automatic

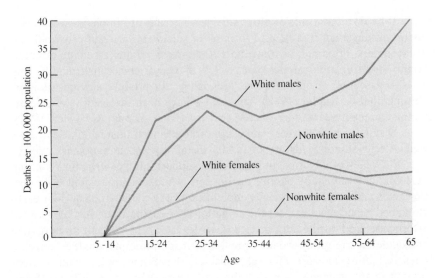

Figure 13.2
Suicide rates by sex, age, and race in the United States.
Source: After data presented by the United States Bureau of Census, 1980. U.S. Government Printing Office.

weapons, frequently purchased with money made from selling drugs. The lure of gang membership is powerful, especially for children who are disconnected from family, school, work, and the community. Children as young as 9 to 10 years of age cling to the fringes of neighborhood gangs, eager to prove themselves worthy of membership by age 12. Once children are members of a gang, it is difficult to get them to leave. Recommendations for prevention of gang violence involve attempts to identify disconnected children in elementary schools and initiate counseling of the children and their families (Calhoun, 1988).

Suicide
In Shakespeare's words,

> To be or not to be—that is the question.
> Whether 'tis nobler in the mind to suffer
> The slings and arrows of outrageous fortune,
> Or to take arms against a sea of troubles
> And by opposing end them. To die, to sleep—
> No more, and by a sleep to say we end
> The heartache and the thousand natural shocks
> That flesh is heir to. "This a consummation
> Devoutly to be wished."

Suicide is a common problem in our society. Its rate has quadrupled during the last thirty years in the United States; each year about 25,000 individuals take their own lives. Beginning at about the age of 15, the rate of suicide begins to rise rapidly (see figure 13.2). Males are about three times as likely to commit suicide as females; this may be due to their more active methods for attempting suicide—shooting, for example. By contrast, females are more likely to use passive methods such as sleeping pills, which are less likely to produce death. While males commit suicide more frequently, females attempt it more frequently (Masten, 1988).

Estimates indicate that six to ten suicide attempts occur for every suicide in the general population; for adolescents, the figure is as high as fifty attempts for every life taken. As many as two in every three college students has thought about suicide on at least one occasion; their methods range from drugs to crashing into the White House in an airplane.

How might cognitive changes during adolescence be linked to the increase in suicide attempts in adolescence?

Social Development

Why do adolescents attempt suicide? There is no simple answer to this important question. It is helpful to think of suicide in terms of proximal and distal factors. Proximal, or immediate, factors can trigger a suicide attempt. Highly stressful circumstances such as loss of a boyfriend or girlfriend, failing a class at school, or an unwanted pregnancy can produce suicide attempts (Blumenthal & Kupfer, 1988). Drugs also have been involved in suicide attempts in recent years more than in the past (Rich, Young, & Fowler, 1986).

Distal, or earlier, experiences are often involved in suicide attempts as well. A long-standing history of family instability and unhappiness may be present. A lack of affection and emotional support, high control, and a strong push for achievement by parents during early childhood are related to depression among adolescents, especially adolescent girls; a combination of these early childhood experiences can set the stage for poor coping when further stresses are encountered during adolescence (Gjerde, 1985). In a recent investigation of suicide among gifted women, previous suicide attempts, anxiety, conspicuous instability in work and relationships, depression, or alcoholism were present in the women's lives (Tomlinson-Keasey, Warren, & Elliott, 1986). These factors are similar to those found to predict suicide among gifted women (Shneidman, 1971).

Just as genetic factors are an issue in depression, they appear in suicide, too; the closer the genetic relation to someone who has committed suicide, the more likely the individual will commit suicide (Wender & others, 1986). We do not have the complete answers for detecting when an individual is considering suicide or how to prevent it, but the advice offered in table 13.3 provides some valuable suggestions about effective ways to communicate with someone you think may be contemplating suicide.

Anorexia Nervosa and Bulimia

Fifteen-year-old Jane gradually eliminated foods from her diet to the point where she subsisted by eating *only* applesauce and eggnog. She spent hours observing her own body, wrapping her fingers around her waist to see if it was getting any thinner. She fantasized about becoming a beautiful fashion model who would wear designer bathing suits. But even when she reached 85 pounds, Jane still felt fat. She continued to lose weight, eventually emaciating herself. She was hospitalized and treated for **anorexia nervosa,** an eating disorder that involves the relentless pursuit of thinness through starvation. Eventually anorexia nervosa can lead to death, as it did for popular singer Karen Carpenter.

Anorexia nervosa afflicts primarily females during adolescence and early adulthood (only about 5 percent of anorexics are male). Most individuals with this disorder are white and from well-educated middle and upper income families. Although anorexics avoid eating, they have an intense interest in food, they cook for others, they talk about food, and they insist on watching others eat. Anorexics have a distorted body image, perceiving themselves as beautiful even when they have become skeletal in appearance. As self-starvation continues and the fat content of the body drops to a bare minimum, menstruation usually stops. Behavior is often hyperactive (Polivy & Thomsen, 1987).

Numerous causes of anorexia nervosa have been proposed: they include societal, psychological, and physiological factors. The societal factor most often held responsible is the current fashion of thinness. Psychological factors include motivation for attention, desire for individuality, denial of sexuality, and a way of coping with overcontrolling parents. Anorexics sometimes have families that place high demands for achievement on them. Unable to meet their parents' high standards, anorexics feel an inability to control their own lives.

Anorexia nervosa has become an increasingly frequent problem among adolescent females.

Adolescence

TABLE 13.3
What to Do and What Not to Do When You Suspect Someone Is Likely to Commit Suicide

What to do

1. Ask direct, straightforward questions in a calm manner. "Are you thinking about hurting yourself?"
2. Assess the seriousness of the suicidal intent by asking questions about feelings, important relationships, who else the person has talked with, and the amount of thought given to the means to be used. If a gun, pills, rope, or other means has been obtained and a precise plan developed, clearly the situation is dangerous. Stay with the person until some type of help arrives.
3. Be a good listener and be very supportive without being falsely reassuring.
4. Try to persuade the person to obtain professional help and assist him or her in getting this help.

What not to do

1. Do not ignore the warning signs.
2. Don't refuse to talk about suicide if a person approaches you about the topic.
3. Do not react with horror, disapproval, or repulsion.
4. Don't give false reassurances by saying things like, "Everything is going to be o.k." Also don't give out simple answers or platitudes like "You have everything to be thankful for."
5. Do not abandon the adolescent after the crisis has gone by or after professional help has commenced.

From Living With 10- to 15-Year-Olds: A Parent Education Curriculum *by Gayle Dorman, et al. Copyright 1982 by the Center for Early Adolescence, University of North Carolina, Carrboro, NC.*

By limiting their food intake, anorexics gain some sense of self-control. Physiological causes focus on the hypothalamus, which becomes abnormal in a number of ways when the individual is anorexic (Garfinkel & Garner, 1982). But the bottom line is that at this time, we are uncertain of exactly what causes anorexia nervosa.

An eating disorder related to anorexia nervosa is **bulimia.** Anorexics occasionally follow a binge-and-purge pattern, but bulimics do this on a regular basis. The bulimic binges on large amounts of food and then purges by self-induced vomiting or using a laxative. The binges sometimes alternate with fasting or at other times with normal eating behavior. Like anorexia nervosa, bulimia is primarily a female disorder. Bulimia has become prevalent among college women. Some estimates suggest that one in two college women binge and purge at least some of the time. However, recent estimates suggest that true bulimics—those who binge and purge on a regular basis—make up less than 2 percent of the college female population (Stunkard, in press). While anorexics can control their eating, bulimics cannot. Depression is a common characteristic of bulimics. Bulimia can lead to gastric irritation and chemical imbalance in the body. Many of the same causes proposed for anorexia nervosa are offered for bulimia.

At this point, we have discussed a number of ideas about identity and problems and disturbances in adolescence. A summary of these ideas is presented in Concept Table 13.2.

Identity and Problems and Disturbances

Concept	Processes/Related Ideas	Characteristics/Description
Identity	Erikson's Theory	The most comprehensive and provocative view of identity development. Identity versus identity diffusion is the fifth stage in Erikson's life cycle theory. During adolescence, world views become important and the aolescent enters a psychological moratorium, a gap between childhood's security and adulthood's autonomy.
	The Four Statuses of Identity	Marcia proposed that four statuses of identity exist, based on a combination of conflict and commitment: identity diffusion, identity foreclosure, identity moratorium, and identity achievement.
	Family Influences	Both connectedness to parents and the presence of a family atmosphere that promotes individuation are related to the adolescent's successful pursuit of identity.
Problems and Disturbances	Drugs	A downward trend in overall illicit drug use by adolescents has been observed. Cocaine use by high school seniors declined in 1987, the first significant downturn in 8 years, but still remains precariously high. Amphetamines are used less now than in the past, although a sharp increase in over-the-counter stay-awake pills has occurred. Current concern also focuses on MDMA and the designer drugs. Cigarette smoking has decreased, but in light of demonstrated health risks, remains alarmingly high. One of the most pervasive drug problems in adolescence is alcohol abuse—use of alcohol has slightly decreased among high school seniors, but its use is still extremely high.
	Alcohol	Adolescent drinkers have a strong expectancy that alcohol will produce personal effects, such as tension reduction. The ability of the family to function as a support system for the adolescent seems to be an especially important factor in preventing heavy drinking by adolescents.
	Delinquency	A juvenile delinquent is an adolescent who breaks the law or engages in conduct that is considered illegal. Heredity, identity problems, community influences, and family experiences have been proposed as delinquency's causes. Parents' failure to discourage antisocial behavior and encourage skilled behavior, as well as parents' lack of monitoring of the adolescent's whereabouts, are related to delinquency.
	Suicide	Suicide's rate has increased; suicide increases dramatically at about the age of 15. Both proximal and distal factors are involved in suicide's causes.
	Anorexia Nervosa and Bulimia	Anorexia nervosa and bulimia have become increasing problems for adolescent and college-aged females. Societal, psychological, and physiological causes of these disorders have been proposed.

Summary

I. **Autonomy-Attachment and Parent-Adolescent Conflict**
Many parents have a difficult time handling the adolescent's push for autonomy, even though this push is one of the hallmarks of adolescent development. Adolescents do not simply move into a world isolated from parents; attachment to parents increases the probability the adolescent will be socially competent and explore a widening social world in healthy ways. Conflict with parents does seem to increase in early adolescence. Such conflict usually is of the moderate variety. The increase in conflict probably serves the positive developmental function of promoting autonomy and identity.

II. **The Maturation of the Adolescent and Parents**
Physical, cognitive, and social changes in the adolescent's development influence parent-adolescent relationships. Parental changes—marital dissatisfaction, economic burdens, career reevaluation and time perspective, and health and body concerns—also influence parent-adolescent relationships.

III. **The Effects of Divorce on Adolescents**
Divorce is a stressful experience for adolescents, just as it is for children. Adolescents carry forward the experience of their parents' divorce into their adult years. Divorce influences the heterosexual behavior of girls, increasing their approach behavior toward males.

IV. **Peers**
The pressure to conform to peers is strong during adolescence, especially during the eighth and ninth grades. There usually are three to six well-defined cliques in every secondary school. Membership in certain cliques—especially jocks and populars—is associated with increased self-esteem. Independents also have high self-esteem. Children's groups are less formal, less heterogeneous, and less heterosexual than adolescent groups. Dunphy found that the development of adolescent groups moves through five stages.

V. **Dating**
Dating can be a form of recreation, a source of status and achievement, a setting for learning about close relationships, and a means of mate sorting or selection. Most adolescents are involved in dating. It appears that adolescent females are more interested in intimacy and personality exploration than adolescent males are.

VI. **Identity**
The most comprehensive and provocative theory of identity development was proposed by Erikson. Identity versus identity diffusion is the fifth stage in his eight-stage life-cycle view, corresponding approximately to the adolescent years. World views become important and the adolescent enters a psychological moratorium between childhood's security and adulthood's autonomy. Marcia proposed that four statuses of identity exist. Both connectedness to parents and individuation are related to the adolescent's successful achievement of identity.

VII. **Drugs**
A downward trend in overall illicit drug use by adolescents has been observed. Cocaine use by high school seniors declined in 1987, the first significant downturn in 8 years, but still remains precariously high. Amphetamines are used less now than in the past, although a sharp increase in over-the-counter stay-awake pills has occurred. Current concern also focuses on MDMA and the designer drugs. Cigarette smoking has decreased, but in light of demonstrated health risks, remains alarmingly high. One of the most pervasive drug problems in adolescence is alcohol abuse—use of alcohol has decreased slightly among high school seniors, but its use is still extremely high.

VIII. **Alcohol**
Adolescent drinkers have a strong expectancy that alcohol will produce personal effects, such as tension reduction. The ability of the family to function as a support system for the adolescent seems to be an especially important factor in preventing heavy drinking by adolescents.

IX. **Delinquency**
A juvenile delinquent is an adolescent who breaks the law or engages in conduct that is considered illegal. Heredity, identity problems, community influences, and family experiences have been proposed as delinquency's causes. Parents' failure to discourage antisocial behavior and encourage skilled behavior, as well as parents' lack of monitoring of the adolescent's whereabouts, are related to delinquency.

X. **Suicide**
Suicide's rate has increased; suicide increases dramatically at about the age of 15. Both proximal and distal factors are involved in suicide's causes.

XI. **Anorexia Nervosa and Bulimia**
Anorexia nervosa and bulimia have become increasing problems for adolescent and college-aged females. Societal, psychological, and physiological causes of these disorders have been proposed.

Key Terms

Suggested Readings

Coleman, J. (Ed.), (1987). *Working with troubled adolescents.* Orlando, FL: Academic Press.
Includes chapters on adolescent individuation and family therapy, social skills training for adolescents, helping adolescents improve their identity, suicide, and eating disorders.

Erikson, E. H. (1968). *Identity: youth and crisis.* New York: Norton.
The book that stimulated the strong interest in the adolescent's quest for identity.

Johnston, L. L., O'Malley, P. M., & Bachman, J. G. (1987). *National trends in drug use and related factors among American high school students and young adults, 1975– 1986.* Ann Arbor, MI: Institute for Social Research, U. of Michigan.
A volume with many details about trends in adolescent drug use. The most comprehensive longitudinal study of adolescent drug use is described.

Journal of Youth and Adolescence
One of the premier research journals in the field of adolescence. Go to a library and leaf through the issues of the last few years to discover research interest in the area of family relations, peer relations, identity, and problems and disturbances.

Quay, H. C. (Ed.) (1987). *Handbook of Juvenile Delinquency.* New York: John Wiley.
State of the art information about delinquency by leading figures. Includes chapters on family processes, community-based interventions, and prevention.

SECTION
VII

Early Adulthood

How many roads must a man walk down/Before you call him a man? ▪

Bob Dylan

C H A P T E R

14

■

Physical and Cognitive Development

Robert is in his senior year of college and just had his twenty-first birthday last week. Looking to his future and pondering what life might be like over the next few years, he came up with the following tongue-in-cheek reasons not to take a job:

1. You have to work.
2. It's habit forming. Once you get a job, you'll want another, and then another . . . It's better not to start at all. Why do you think they call it work?
3. Once you stop being a student, you can never go back. Remember those pathetic people who came back to hang around your high school? You'll look even sillier showing up at mixers, pep rallies, and Sadie Hawkins dances after you have taken a position with some respectable accounting firm.
4. You will have to carpool with a sullen adolescent typist or a Hindu engineer/mathematician who loves "speaking my new language of English."
5. It's unbearably tedious. Not only that, but employees and their families are not eligible to win.
6. Taking a job means taking on new responsibilities. Before you know it, you will be married to an overweight hypochondriac with four sickly brats with crooked teeth and a house in the 'burbs. You will have to take out insurance policies on everything from health care to rodent invasions. Soon you will seriously be considering purchasing a condominium in Fort Lauderdale or Rio Rancho Retirement Village. All this can be avoided by the simple decision not to take a job.
7. People will start calling you "mister" and "sir." Hippies will resent you and call you a "capitalist roader." People with better jobs will shake their heads and say, "What a waste of human talent."
8. Fully employed people can never have sex.
9. You will have to say nice things about the boss's new "flame-thrower red" polyester golf pants, laugh at the boss's jokes about people who mismanage their finances, and carry on endless conversations with your boss about "pennant rallies," "the primaries," and "resort areas." You will have to nod your head with conviction when he refers to his employees as a "team" that works together to "bring home the bacon."
10. If you take a job, you will be an adult (*The Harvard Lampoon Big Book of College Life*).

In this chapter, we explore what it is like to take a job as the nature of careers and work in early adulthood is described. You also will read about changes in our cognitive development in early adulthood and the importance of sexuality in our lives as young adults. Information about early adulthood's physical changes is presented, too, but first we think about the transition from adolescence to adulthood.

The Transition from Adolescence to Adulthood

As Bob Dylan asked at the opening of section VII, "How many roads must a man walk down before you call him a man?" When does an adolescent become an adult? In chapter 12, we saw that it is not easy to tell when a boy or girl enters adolescence. Many developmentalists, though, believe the task of determining adolescence's beginning is easier than determining its end and adulthood's beginning. Although no consensus exists as to when adolescence is left behind and adulthood is entered, some criteria have been proposed.

Faced with a complex world of work, with highly specialized tasks, many post-teenagers spend an extended period of time in technical institutes, colleges, and postgraduate centers to acquire specialized skills, educational experiences, and professional training. For many, this creates an extended period of economic and personal temporariness. Earning levels are low and sporadic, and established residences may change frequently. Marriage and a family may be shunned. This period often lasts from two to eight years, although it is not unusual for it to last a decade or longer.

This transition in development is called **youth** by Kenneth Kenniston (1970). He argues that youth have not settled the questions whose answers once defined adulthood—questions about one's relationship to the existing society, about vocation, and about social roles and life-styles. Youth differs from adolescence because of youth's struggle between developing an autonomous self and becoming socially involved in contrast to adolescence's struggle for self-definition.

Two criteria that have been proposed as signalling the end of youth and the beginning of early adulthood are economic independence and independent decision making. Probably the most widely recognized marker of adulthood's entrance is the occasion when the individual takes a more-or-less permanent full-time job. This usually occurs when the individual finishes school—high school for some, college for others, and graduate school for still others. For those who finish high school, move away from home, and assume a career, the transition to adulthood seems to have taken place. But one out of every four individuals does not complete high school, and many individuals who finish college cannot find a job. Further, only a small percentage of graduates settle into jobs that remain permanent throughout their adult lives. Also, attaining economic independence from parents usually is a gradual process rather than an abrupt process. It is not unusual to find college graduates getting a job and continuing to live, or returning to live, with their parents, especially in today's economic climate.

The ability to make decisions is another characteristic that does not seem to be fully developed in youth. We refer broadly here to decision making about a career, about values, about family and relationships, and about life-style. As a youth, the individual may still be trying out many different roles, exploring alternative careers, thinking about a variety of life-styles, and considering the variety of relationships that are available. The individual who enters adulthood usually has made some of these decisions, especially in the areas of life-style and career.

While change characterizes the transition from adolescence to adulthood, keep in mind that considerable continuity still glues these periods together. Consider the data collected in a longitudinal study of more than 2,000

The process of entering into adulthood is more lengthy and complex than has usually been imagined. It begins around 17 and continues until 33. . . . A young man needs about 15 years to emerge from adolescence, find his place in adult society and commit himself to a more stable life.
Daniel J. Levinson, Seasons of A Man's Life, *1978*

Other than economic independence and independent decision making, can you come up with any other criteria that might be used to indicate the beginning of adult status?

I remember how quick I was on the tennis court when I was 21. By the age of 35, my reflexes were slower and I just couldn't adapt as quickly to fast shots. The Olympic gymnast shown here is 19 years old, at the peak of his physical strength and agility. In virtually every sport, especially those emphasizing quickness, speed, and strength, we reach our peak performance in our late teens or twenties, and then our performance begins to fall off. One exception is golf, a sport relying less on speed and quickness and more on experience.

males from the time they were in the tenth grade until five years after high school (Bachman, O'Malley, & Johnston, 1978). Some of the boys dropped out, others graduated from high school; some took jobs after graduating from high school, others went to college; some were employed, others were unemployed. The dominant picture of the boys as they went through this eight-year period was stability rather than change. For example, the tenth graders who had the highest self-esteem were virtually the same individuals who had the highest self-esteem five years after high school. A similar patterning was found for achievement orientation—those who were the most achievement-oriented in the tenth grade remained the most achievement-oriented eight years later. Some environmental changes produced differences in this transition period. For example, marriage reduced drug use, unemployment increased it. Success in college and career increased achievement orientation; less education and poor occupational performance diminished achievement orientation.

Physical Development

Physical status not only reaches its peak in early adulthood, it also begins to decline during this period. Eating behavior and obesity have become major concerns during early adulthood, as they have in other periods as well.

The Peak and Slowdown of Physical Performance

How many Olympic athletes have you seen over the age of 30? Carlos Lopes won the 1984 Olympic marathon at the age of 37, which was a rare feat. Of 137 Olympic athletes studied in one Olympics competition, only 21 were over the age of 30. All of the athletes who participated in events demanding extreme speed and agility, such as the 100-yard-dash and broad jump, were under 30 (Tanner, 1962). The peak of our physical performance usually occurs between 19 and 26 years of age.

We not only reach our peak performance during early adulthood, but during this time we are also our healthiest. More than nine out of ten individuals between the ages of 17 and 44 view their health as good or excellent (U.S. Department of Health, Education, & Welfare, 1976). Few young adults have chronic health problems, and young adults have fewer colds and respiratory ailments than they did during childhood.

But young adults rarely recognize that bad eating habits, heavy drinking, and smoking can impair their health status when they become older. Most college students know what it takes to prevent illness and promote health. In one study, college students' ranking of health-protective activities—nutrition, sleep, exercise, watching one's weight, and so on—virtually matched that of licensed nurses (Turk, Rudy, & Salovey, 1984). While most college students know what it takes to prevent illness and promote health, they don't fare very well when it comes to applying this information to themselves. In one investigation, college students reported that they probably would never have a heart attack or drinking problem, but that other college students would (Weinstein, 1984). The college students also said no relation exists between their risk of heart attack and how much they exercise, smoke, or eat meat or high cholesterol food such as eggs, even though they correctly recognized that factors such as family history influence risk. Many college students, it seems, have unrealistic, overly optimistic beliefs about their future health risks.

TABLE 14.1
Changes in usage rates for cigarettes, alcohol, marijuana, and other drugs

	Percentage of respondents reporting usage during the period		
	1968–69	**1969–70**	**1973–74**
Daily use of cigarettes	35	40	44
Weekly use of alcohol	31	44	58
Any use of marijuana	21	35	52
Any use of amphetamines, barbiturates, hallucinogens	12	18	24

From Jerald G. Bachman, Patrick M. O'Malley, and Jerome Johnston, Adolescence to Adulthood: Change and Stability in the Lives of Young Men *(Youth in Transition, Volume 6).* 1978, p. 187. Copyright © Institute for Social Research. Reprinted by permission.

As individuals move from adolescence to early adulthood, they often increase their use of drugs. For example, in the longitudinal study described earlier, as individuals moved from the tenth grade to five years after high school, they increased their cigarette smoking, drinking, marijuana smoking, and use of amphetamines, barbiturates, and hallucinogens (see table 14.1). Recent longitudinal data confirm that the period from late adolescence to the late twenties is the time of peak levels for many drugs; of special concern is the continuing epidemic of cocaine use among young adults. Approximately 20 percent of 27- and 28-year-olds use cocaine at least once a year and 8 percent of this age group uses it at least once every 30 days (Johnston, O'Malley, & Bachman, 1987). Daily drinking and daily smoking also occur more frequently among 27- and 28-year-olds than among high school seniors.

In early adulthood, few individuals stop to think about how their personal life-styles will affect their health later in their adult lives. As young adults, many of us develop a pattern of not eating breakfast, not eating regular meals, and relying on snacks as our main food source during the day, eating excessively to the point we exceed the normal weight for our age, smoking moderately or excessively, drinking moderately or excessively, failing to exercise, and getting by with only a few hours of sleep at night. These poor personal life-styles were associated with poor health in one investigation of 7,000 individuals from the ages of 20 to 70 (Belloc & Breslow, 1972). In the California Longitudinal Study—in which individuals were evaluated over a period of 40 years—physical health at age 30 predicted life satisfaction at age 70, more so for men than women (Mussen, Honzik, & Eichorn, 1982).

There are some hidden dangers in the peaks of performance and health in early adulthood. While young adults can draw on physical resources for a great deal of pleasure, often bouncing back easily from physical stress and abuse, this may lead them to push their bodies too far. The negative effects of abusing one's body may not show up in the first part of early adulthood, but they probably will surface later in early adulthood or in middle adulthood.

The tissue of life to be
We weave with colors all our own
And in the field of destiny
We reap as we have sown.
John Greenleaf Whittier, Raphael, *1842*

Muscle tone and strength usually begin to show signs of decline around the age of 30. And sagging chins and protruding abdomens may begin to appear (Marshall, 1973). The lessening of physical abilities is a common complaint among the just-turned-30s. Says one 30-year-old, "I played tennis last night. My knees are sore and my lower back aches. Last month, it was my elbow that hurt. Several years ago it wasn't that way. I could play all day and not be sore the next morning." Sensory systems show little change in early adulthood, but the lens of the eye does lose some of its elasticity and becomes less able to change shape and focus on near objects. Hearing peaks in adolescence, remains constant in the first part of early adulthood, and then begins to decline in the last part of early adulthood. And in the mid to late 20s, the body's fatty tissue increases. The motivation to be thin and to avoid obesity is a major obsession for many young adults, especially women.

Eating Behavior and Obesity

A tall, slender woman goes into the locker room of the fitness center, throws her towel across the bench, and looks squarely into the mirror and yells, "You fat pig. You are nothing but a fat pig." We are a nation obsessed with food, spending extraordinary amounts of time thinking about, eating, and avoiding food.

You may have inherited a tendency to be overweight. Only 10 percent of children who do not have obese parents become obese themselves; about 40 percent of children with one obese parent become obese; about 70 percent of children who have two obese parents become obese themselves. The extent to which this is due to experiences with parents or genes cannot be determined in studies with humans, but research with animals indicates that they can be bred with a propensity for fatness (Blundell, 1984).

The amount of stored fat in your body is an important factor in the set point of your body weight (it is not known how strongly genetic factors contribute to this). Fat is stored in adipose cells. When these cells are filled, you don't get hungry. When they are not full, you become hungry. When we gain weight, the number of fat cells increases, and we may not be able to get rid of them. An individual of normal weight has somewhere between 30 to 40 billion fat cells; obese individuals have as many as 80 to 120 billion fat cells. Interestingly, adults who were not obese as children but who become overweight as adults have larger fat cells than their normal weight counterparts, but they do not have more fat cells (VanItallie, 1984).

Metabolic rate also is important in understanding obesity. **Basal metabolism rate (BMR)** is the minimum amount of energy an individual uses in a resting state. As shown in figure 14.1, BMR varies with age and sex. Rates decline precipitously during adolescence and then more gradually during

Figure 14.1
The decline of basal metabolism rate through the life cycle. BMR varies with age and sex. Rates are usually higher for males and decline proportionally with age for both sexes.

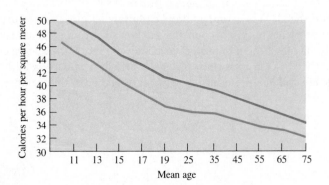

Early Adulthood

How important is exercise in an individual's effort to lose weight? Exercise not only burns up calories but it continues to raise the metabolic rate for several hours after the exercise. Exercise also can lower the body's set point for weight. When exercise is a component of weight-loss programs, individuals keep weight off longer than when calorie reduction alone is followed.

adulthood, and they are slightly higher for females than for males. Many individuals gradually increase their weight over a period of years. Figure 14.1 suggests that to some degree the weight gain is due to a declining basal metabolism rate. The declining BMR underscores that, to maintain weight in adulthood, we have to reduce our food intake.

Our gustatory system and taste preferences developed at a time when food was scarce. Few calories were easily accessible in the environment first encountered by *Homo sapiens*. A concentrated source of sugar (and thus calories) was ripe fruit. Early in the species' history a preference for sweet food and drinks probably developed because ripe fruit was so accessible. Today, food and drinks with high concentrations of sugar are readily available to most of us. But unlike the ripe fruit of our ancestors, which contained sugar *plus* vitamins and minerals, Gummi Bears and Cocoa Crispies fill us with empty calories.

Estimates indicate that about one-half of the adult population in the United States weighs over the upper limit of their normal weight range (Pfaffman, 1977). Further, the proportion of American children who are overweight increased more than 50 percent over the last two decades from the 1960s to the 1980s (Gortmaker, 1987). As individuals' weights have increased, the interest in losing weight has become a national obsession. Throughout history there have been dieters, but never before has there been a time when so many people spent so much time, energy, and money on their weight. Since its inception in 1963, Weight Watchers alone has enrolled more than 15 million members. Although men *and* women have gained weight and both sexes show strong concerns about losing weight, the obsession with dieting seems to be more intense among women (Chernin, 1981). A myriad of ways to lose weight exist. Which ones work? Does one work better than the rest? Do any of them work? To find the answers to these questions, turn to Focus on Life-Span Development 14.1.

FROM *THE LAST CHANCE FEEDING DIET* TO *SLIM CHANCE IN A FAT WORLD DIET*

Some individuals take drugs to lose weight. Amphetamines are widely used to decrease food consumption, although they may have adverse side effects—increased blood pressure and possible addiction, for example. Weight loss with amphetamines is usually short-lived. The ineffective drugs include over-the-counter drugs such as Dexatrim. No drug currently is available that has been proven successful in long-term weight reduction (Logue, 1986).

Exercise is a much more attractive alternative than weight-loss drugs such as amphetamines. Exercise not only burns up calories but it continues to raise the metabolic rate for several hours *after* the exercise. Exercise actually lowers your body's set point for weight, making it easier to maintain a lower weight (Bennett & Gurin, 1982). Nonetheless, it is difficult to get obese individuals to exercise. One problem is that moderate exercise does not reduce calorie consumption and in many cases individuals who exercise take in more calories than their sedentary counterparts (Stern, 1984). Still, exercise combined with conscious self-control of eating habits produces a viable weight-loss program. When exercise is a component of weight-loss programs, individuals keep weight off longer than when calorie reduction alone is followed.

What about the diets themselves? There is the Grapefruit Diet, the Drinking Man's Diet, the Beverly Hills Diet, and the Scarsdale Diet, just to name a few. It is difficult to pass a grocery store cashier counter without being assaulted by such diets etched on the covers of popular magazines. An analysis of 16 of these crash diets revealed that many of them do not provide adequate nutrients (Dwyer, 1980). Three of these diets—the Scarsdale Diet, the Last Chance Feeding Diet, and the Fasting Is a Way of Life Diet—were found to be dangerous because they cause dehydration. Many liquid protein diets are extremely low in important nutrients, and individuals have died from staying on them too long. Some diets—Slim Chance in a Fat World and Take It Off and Keep It Off, for example—do have well-balanced nutrition and contain appropriate information about the importance of self-control strategies in losing weight.

The diets of many competent programs follow the guidelines set forth by the American Dietetic Association. Their 1987 recommendations call for the following: a doubling of the average individual's intake of 10 to 15 grams of fiber per day (ten years ago fiber was not even on the list); lowering the percent of daily calories derived from fat to 30 percent; raising the percent of daily calories derived from complex carbohydrates (fruits, grains, and vegetables) to 50 to 60 percent. Weight Watchers is one diet program that adopts the guidelines of the American Dietetic Association.

Millions of individuals have joined groups such as Weight Watchers, NutriSystem, and TOPS (Take Off Pounds Sensibly). Reports of the success of these programs vary, although individuals who stay with programs do seem to lose some weight. But the dropout rates are astronomical, and those who stay with the programs usually do not reach their goal weights or maintain them for long. One of the reasons that long-term maintenance of weight loss is so difficult is the "yo-yo phenomenon." Severe calorie reduction invariably decreases

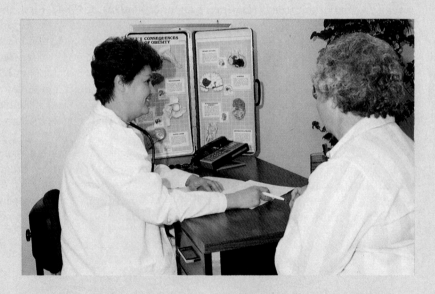

Diets come in many forms—some healthy, others unhealthy. Most crash diets do not provide adequate nutrients. These include the "Scarsdale Diet," "Last Chance Feeding Diet," and "Fasting Is a Way of Life Diet." The diets of many competent programs follow the guidelines of the American Dietetic Association.

metabolic rate. When an individual becomes discouraged, gives up on a diet, and increases calorie intake, weight gain occurs rapidly because metabolic rate is still reduced from the dieting experience. More pounds often are gained back than were taken off on the diet. A regular, *vigorous* exercise program seems to be the only practical way to counteract the tendency for calorie reduction to reduce metabolic rate.

No diet program is the panacea hoped for by millions of individuals who earnestly want to lose weight (Stunkard, in press). If one worked for everyone, we would not witness such high turnover rates. Some individuals may find success with a certain diet or weight-loss program, yet for others the same program fails miserably. The majority of overweight individuals shed very few pounds over the long-term. Despite

such dismal statistics, interest in the nature of obesity and its treatment shows no signs of slowing down. Perhaps we will discover ways to treat obesity more effectively, and possibly more moderate weights will become fashionable as well—weights that are medically acceptable and achieved by appropriate nutrition and exercise.

"Don't encourage him Sylvia."
From the Far Side Gallery *by Gary Larson.
Reprinted by permission of Chronicle
Features, San Francisco, California.*

Sexuality

The importance of sex in our adult lives was vividly captured by Woody Allen's observation, "Sex without love is an empty experience. Yes, but as empty experiences go, it is one of the best." Allen's comments suggest not only a motivation for sex, but also interpretation of its role in our lives. What are our sexual attitudes and behavior as young adults like?

Sexual Attitudes and Behavior

Four percent of the male elephant seals off the coast of California were responsible for 85 percent of the copulations in one recent breeding season. Television soap operas might lead us to conclude that humans are not very different from the elephant seal, mating and moving from partner to partner. However, humans do show more allegiance to one partner than most species. Our advanced brains enable us to ponder about the best strategy for us.

Heterosexual Attitudes and Behavior

Had you been a college student in 1940, you probably would have had a different attitude about sex than you do today, especially if you are a female. A review of college students' sexual practices and attitudes from 1900 to 1980 reveals two important trends (Darling, Kallen, & VanDusen, 1984). First, the percentage of young people reporting intercourse has drastically increased, and second, the proportion of females reporting intercourse has increased more rapidly than in the case of males, although males' initial base was greater (see figure 14.2). Prior to 1970, about twice as many college males as females reported having intercourse, but since 1970, the proportion of males and females is about equal. These changes suggest that major shifts away from a double standard in which it was more appropriate for males than females to have intercourse have occurred.

Two large surveys verify these trends. Morton Hunt's survey of more than 2,000 adults in the 1970s revealed more permissiveness toward sex than Alfred Kinsey's inquiries in the late 1940s (Hunt, 1974; Kinsey, Pomeroy, & Martin, 1948). Hunt's survey, though, may have overestimated sexual permissiveness because it was based on a sample of *Playboy* readers. Kinsey found

Figure 14.2
*Percentage of college youth reporting
having sexual intercourse at different
points in the twentieth century. Two lines
are drawn for males and two for females.
The lines represent the best two fits
through the data for males and the data
for females of the many studies surveyed.*

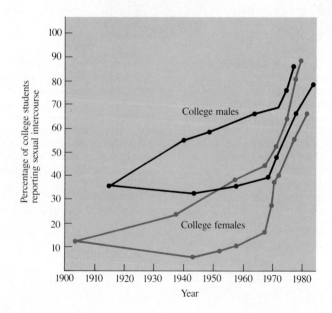

Early Adulthood

that foreplay consisted of a kiss or two in the 1940s, but Hunt discovered that foreplay had lengthened, now averaging fifteen minutes, in the 1970s. Hunt also found that individuals were using more varied techniques in their lovemaking in the 1970s. Oral-genital sex, virtually taboo at the time of Kinsey's survey, was more accepted in the 1970s.

Two more things about heterosexual attitudes and behavior are important to consider: the double standard we mentioned earlier and the nature of extramarital sex. While it has become more appropriate for females to engage in premarital sex, some vestiges of the double standard still exist. Matters are often left up to the female to set the limits on the male's overtures. And it is often thought that the female should not plan ahead to have sexual intercourse (by taking contraceptive precautions), but it is permissible for her to be swept up in the passion of the moment.

Why have we historically had a double standard in sexual relations?

The double standard is at work in extramarital relations, too, although not as extensively as in earlier years. In Kinsey's research, about half of the husbands and one-fourth of the wives had engaged in sexual intercourse with someone other than their spouse during their marriage. In Hunt's survey in the 1970s, the figure was still about the same for males, but had increased for females, especially younger females. The majority of us still disapprove of extramarital sex; but while we disapprove of it, we still engage in it, a clear instance of a gap between sexual attitudes and behavior.

Homosexual Attitudes and Behavior

Both the early and more recent surveys of sexuality indicate that about 4 percent of males and about 3 percent of females are exclusively homosexual. At least until several years ago, attitudes toward homosexuality were becoming increasingly permissive. But with the threat of AIDS, future surveys probably will indicate less acceptance of homosexuality.

How have sexual attitudes and behavior changed during the twentieth century? You probably can think of your own conversations and experiences with others to document these changes. Earlier generations had a more conservative orientation toward sexuality, especially females. However, the epidemic of AIDS and Herpes seems to have produced a more conservative sexual orientation in the last several years.

Why are some individuals homosexual whereas others are heterosexual? Speculation about this question has been extensive, but no firm answers are available (Savin-Williams, 1988). Homosexual and heterosexual males and females have similar physical responses during sexual arousal and seem to be aroused by the same types of tactile stimulation. Investigations suggest that in terms of a wide range of attitudes, behaviors, and adjustments, no differences between homosexuals and heterosexuals are present (Blumstein & Schwartz, 1983; Bell, Weinberg, & Mammersmith, 1981). Recognizing that homosexuality is not a form of mental illness, the American Psychiatric Association discontinued its classification of homosexuality as a disorder, except in those cases in which the individuals themselves consider their sexual orientation to be abnormal.

Heredity, hormonal imbalance, family processes, and chance learning are among the factors proposed as homosexuality's causes. Concerning family processes, it has been argued that a dominant mother and a weak father promote homosexuality; the evidence is far from consistent about this proposal, however. Concerning chance learning, someone may be seduced by an individual of the same sex and subsequently develop a homosexual preference. The most widely adopted view of experts on homosexuality today is that there are a number of ways to become a homosexual, including any of the aforementioned biological and environmental reasons (McWhirter & Reinisch, in press; Money, 1987).

Sexually Transmitted Diseases

Formally called venereal disease (or VD), sexually transmitted disease is primarily transmitted through sexual intercourse, although it can be transmitted orally. The most common sexually transmitted diseases that young adults are likely to get are chlamydia, gonorrhea, venereal warts, herpes, and AIDS. **Chlamydia** affects as many as 10 percent of all college students. The disease—which is named for the tiny bacteria that cause it—appears in both males and females. Males experience a burning sensation during urination and a mucoid discharge; females experience painful urination or a vaginal discharge. These signs often mimic gonorrhea; however, while penicillin is prescribed for the gonorrhea-like symptoms, the problem does not go away, as it would if gonorrhea were the culprit. If left untreated, the disease can infect the entire reproductive tract. This can lead to problems left by scar tissue that can prevent the female from becoming pregnant. Drugs have been developed to treat this common sexually transmitted disease and they are very effective.

Recently, an alarming increase has occurred in another sexually transmitted disease—herpes simplex virus II, also known as genital herpes. Estimates indicate that one in five sexually active adults has genital herpes (Oppenheimer, 1982). Its symptoms include irregular cycles of sores and blisters in the genital area. The herpes virus is potentially dangerous. If babies are exposed to the active virus during birth, they are vulnerable to brain damage or even death. And women with herpes are eight times more likely than uninfected women to develop cervical cancer (Harvard Medical School Newsletter, 1981). At present, herpes is incurable; the epidemic proportions of the disease may be curtailing the frequency of sexual activity among young adults.

At present another sexually transmitted disease—AIDS—is also incurable. The dramatic increase in **AIDS** (Acquired Immune Deficiency Syndrome) also has decreased sexual promiscuity. More about AIDS appears in Focus on Life-Span Development 14.2.

AIDS is caused by a virus that destroys the body's immune system. Consequently, many germs that would usually not harm someone with a normal immune system can produce devastating results and ultimately death.

In 1981, when AIDS was first recognized in the United States, there were fewer than 60 cases. By November, 1986, there were 27,000 cases of AIDS and 15,000 deaths from the disease. By March, 1987, there were more than 32,000 cases of AIDS and 20,000 deaths from the disease. Beginning in 1990, according to Dr. Frank Press, president of the National Academy of Sciences, "we will lose as many Americans each year to AIDS as we lost in the entire Vietnam War." Almost 60,000 Americans died in that war. According to federal health officials, 1–1.5 million Americans are now asymptomatic carriers of AIDS—those who are infected with the virus and presumably capable of infecting others but who show no clinical symptoms of AIDS.

A recent survey of 35,239 high school students in 11 states by the Centers for Disease Control in Atlanta revealed that many adolescents are misinformed about AIDS. Over 50 percent of the adolescents believed that an individual can get AIDS from a blood test; about the same percentage said that AIDS can be contracted from a public toliet. Experts say the disease can only be transmitted by sexual contact, sharing needles, or blood transfusions.

While 90 percent of AIDS cases continue to occur among homosexual males or intravenous drug users, a disproportionate increase among females who are heterosexual partners of bisexual males or of intravenous drug users has been noted from 1985–1988. This increase suggests that the risk of AIDS may be increasing among heterosexual individuals who have multiple sexual partners (Quinn & others, 1988).

Of special interest to parents and their children is the controversy surrounding individuals who have contracted the virus. For example, one 13-year-old hemophiliac contracted AIDS while receiving injections of a clotting agent. He was barred from resuming his seventh-grade classes. In another case in another school district, school officials and doctors met with more than 800 concerned parents to defend their decision to admit a 14-year-old AIDS patient to school. Some parents will not let their children attend schools where an identified AIDS patient is enrolled. Others believe children with the disease should not be society's outcasts based on our current knowledge of how the disease spreads.

AIDS is a lethal threat to individuals whose sexual activities put them at risk for contracting the disease—especially those who are sexually active with more than one partner and those who are intravenous drug users. Sexually active individuals—homosexual or heterosexual—can reduce the probability they will contract AIDS by following certain precautions (Nielson, 1987): First, sex with strangers or sex with individuals living in metropolitan locations where AIDS is most prevalent should be engaged in with extreme caution. Second, condoms may provide some protection against the virus, but data are inconclusive on this at this time. Third, a test is now available to determine if an individual has AIDS. Not everyone exposed to the AIDS virus contracts AIDS, but individuals who test positive for the AIDS virus should refrain from further sexual contacts until their physician informs them otherwise.

The Menstrual Cycle and Hormones

From early adolescence until some point in middle adulthood, a woman's body undergoes marked changes in hormone levels that are associated with the menstrual cycle. The latter part of the menstrual cycle, from about day 22 on, is associated with a greater incidence of depression, anxiety, and irritability than is the middle of the menstrual cycle, when ovulation is occurring. Women show higher levels of self-esteem and confidence during ovulation in comparison to other parts of the menstrual cycle (Bardwick, 1971). The weight of the evidence shows that mood swings definitely are associated with the middle of the menstrual cycle and the later premenstrual phase. However, it is not entirely clear whether the mood changes are due to a positive upswing of mood during the middle phase, a downward swing during the premenstrual phase, or a combination of both. Moreover, as many as 25 percent of all women report no mood shifts at all during these two phases (Hyde, 1985).

What causes the changes in mood that affect 75 percent of all women? Hormonal changes are clearly one factor. Female hormones reach their peak at about day 22 to day 24 of the menstrual cycle, just at the time when depression and irritability peak. By contrast, mood changes could affect hormone levels. If so, intense feelings of irritability and depression may feed back to the endocrine system and produce more estrogen.

At this point we have discussed a number of ideas about physical development and sexuality, as well as the transition from adolescence to adulthood. A summary of these ideas is presented in Concept Table 14.1. Now we examine the possibility that cognitive changes take place in early adulthood.

Cognitive Development

Do people continue to develop cognitively in adulthood or are they as smart as they ever will be by the end of adolescence? Do people continue to develop their creative skills in adulthood or are they as creative as they ever will be in childhood and adolescence?

Cognitive Stages

Piaget believed that an adolescent and an adult think in the same way. But some developmentalists believe it is not until adulthood that individuals consolidate their formal operational thinking. That is, they may begin to plan and hypothesize about problems as adolescents, but they become more systematic in approaching problems as adults. While some adults are more proficient at developing hypotheses and deducing solutions to problems than adolescents, many adults do not think in formal operational ways at all (Keating, 1980).

Other developmentalists believe that the absolute nature of adolescent logic and youth's buoyant optimism diminish in early adulthood. According to Gisela Labouvie-Vief (1982, 1986), a new integration of thought takes place in early adulthood. She thinks the adult years produce pragmatic constraints that require an adaptive strategy of less reliance on logical analysis in solving problems. Commitment, specialization, and channeling energy into finding one's niche in complex social and work systems replace the youth's fascination with idealized logic. If we assume that logical thought and buoyant optimism represent the criteria for cognitive maturity, we would have to admit that the cognitive activity of adults is too concrete and pragmatic. But from Labouvie-Vief's view, the adult's understanding of reality's constraints reflects cognitive maturity, not immaturity.

Other than an increase in pragmatic thinking, can you think of other ways that our cognitive development advances in early adulthood?

The Transition from Adolescence to Adulthood, Physical Development, and Sexuality

Concept	Processes/Related Ideas	Characteristics/Description
Transition from Adolescence to Adulthood	Youth	Transition proposed by Kenniston; period of economic and personal temporariness, and struggle between interest in self-autonomy and becoming socially involved. Averages 2–8 years but can be longer.
	Criteria for Adulthood	Two criteria are: economic independence and independent decision making. However, clear-cut criteria are yet to be established.
	Continuity and Change	There is both change and continuity in the transition from adolescence to adulthood.
Physical Development	The Peak and Slowdown in Physical Performance	Peak physical status is reached between 18–30, especially 19–26. Individuals' health also peaks in these years. There is a hidden hazard in these peaks of physical performance and health; bad health habits may be formed. Toward the latter part of early adulthood, a detectable slowdown and decline in physical status is apparent.
	Eating Behavior and Obesity	We have become a nation obsessed with eating, weight, and weight loss. Heredity and basal metabolism rate probably are involved in our weight. Estimates indicate that one-half of the adult population is overweight. Women show an especially intense interest in weight loss. Many weight-loss programs have been developed, but no program is the panacea dieters seek. Exercise seems to be the most beneficial component of weight-loss programs.
Sexuality	Heterosexual Attitudes and Behavior	Increased liberalization has occurred. Some dimensions of the double standard, however, still exist.
	Homosexual Attitudes and Behavior	Rates of homosexuality have remained constant in the twentieth century. Homosexuality is no longer classified as a disorder. No definitive conclusions about its cause have been reached.
	Sexually Transmitted Diseases	The most common sexually transmitted diseases are chlamydia, gonorrhea, venereal warts, herpes, and AIDS. The increase in herpes and AIDS probably has reduced sexual promiscuity.
	The Menstrual Cycle and Hormones	The relation between the menstrual cycle and personality fluctuations in females has been studied and there is a relation between mood swings and the middle and later premenstrual phase of the cycle.

Young adults are placed in circumstances that require them to use their intellect. K. Warner Schaie calls early adulthood the achieving stage of adulthood because it is at this point in our lives when we apply intelligence to instances that have strong consequences for achieving long-term goals.

What can be known? The
unknown.
My true self runs toward a hill
More! O more! Visible.

Theodore Roethek

Our cognitive abilities are very strong during early adulthood, and they do show adaptation to the pragmatic aspects of our lives. Less clear is whether our logical skills actually decline. Competence as a young adult probably requires doses of both logical thinking skills and pragmatic adaptation to reality. For example, as an architect designs a building, she logically analyzes and plans the structure but understands the cost constraints, environmental concerns, and time it will take to get the job done effectively.

Another perspective on adult cognitive changes is offered by K. Warner Schaie (1977). He believes that Piaget's cognitive changes describe increasing efficiency in the *acquisition* of new information. It is doubtful that adults go beyond the powerful methods of scientific thinking characteristic of formal operational thought in their quest for knowledge. However, says Schaie, adults do progress beyond adolescents in their *use* of intellect. For example, in early adulthood, we typically switch from acquiring knowledge to applying knowledge, using what we know to pursue careers and families. Schaie calls early adulthood the **achieving stage** because it is at this point in our lives when we apply intelligence to situations that have profound consequences for achieving long-term goals, such as those involving careers and knowledge. These solutions must be integrated into a life plan that extends far into the future.

Schaie believes that young adults who master the cognitive skills required for monitoring their own behavior, and therefore have acquired a considerable degree of independence, move into the next stage that involves social responsibility. The **responsibility stage** occurs when a family is established and attention is given to a spouse's and offspring's needs. Similar extensions of cognitive skills are needed as the individual's career develops and responsibility for others arises on the job and in the community. The responsibility stage often begins in early adulthood and extends into middle adulthood. In middle adulthood, another stage may develop—the **executive stage.** Many individuals' responsibilities become extremely complex. Individuals may become presidents of business firms, deans of academic institutions, officials of churches, or take other positions that require the individual to learn and understand how an organization works. Executives need to know who answers to whom, and for what purpose. They must monitor organizational activities over time (past, present, future) and up and down the organizational hierarchy. Attainment of the executive stage, of course, depends on exposure to opportunities that permit the development and practice of relevant skills.

In the later years of life, beyond the age of 60–65, the need to acquire knowledge declines even more. The need to monitor decisions also declines, because the future appears short and inconsequential. Executive monitoring also declines because often the individual has retired from the position that required this type of intellectual application. What, then, is the nature of older adult's intelligence, in Schaie's view? He says that there is a developmental transition from the childhood question ("What should I know?"), through the adult question ("How should I use what I know?"), to the later life question ("Why should I know?"). Schaie calls this final stage of adult cognitive development the **reintegrative stage,** a stage which closely corresponds to Erikson's final stage in the life cycle, ego integrity versus despair. Elderly people's acquisition and application of knowledge is—to a greater extent than earlier in life—related to their interests, attitudes, and values. The elderly are less likely to waste time on tasks that have no meaning for them. They are less likely to expend effort to solve a problem unless that problem is one they face

TABLE 14.2
The Cognitive Stages of Adulthood—Piaget, Labouvie-Vief, and Schaie

	Theorist		
	Piaget	Labouvie-Vief	Schaie
Period			
Adolescence	Formal Operations	Formal Operations	Formal Operations and Acquisitive Stage
Early Adulthood	Formal Operations	Pragmatic Stage	Achieving Stage
Middle Adulthood	Formal Operations	Pragmatic Stage	Responsibility Stage Executive Stage
Late Adulthood	Formal Operations	Pragmatic Stage	Reintegrative Stage

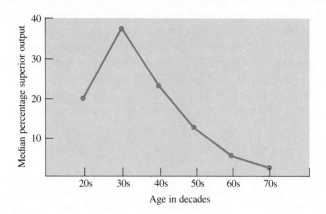

Figure 14.3
Percentage of superior output as a function of age. This generalized curve represents a combination of various fields of endeavor and various estimates of quality.

in their lives. For example, they tend to show little interest in abstract questions, such as "Which is better, communism or capitalism?" unless the questions relate to their motivation to make sense of their lives as a whole, such as, "What is the purpose of life?" or "What comes after death?" A summary of Schaie's adult cognitive stages, along with those proposed by Piaget and Labouvie-Vief, is presented in table 14.2.

Creativity
At the age of 30, Thomas Edison invented the phonograph, Hans Christian Anderson wrote his first volume of fairy tales, and Mozart composed *The Marriage of Figaro*. It hardly seems that these represent a decline in creativity during early adulthood. In several investigations, the quality of productivity of recognized adults was the highest in the decade of the thirties; approximately 80 percent of the most important creative contributions were completed by the age of fifty (Dennis, 1966; Lehman, 1960) (see figure 14.3). In another approach, the total productivity, not just the superior works, of creative individuals in the arts, sciences, and humanities who had lived long lives

The artist finds a greater pleasure in painting than in having completed the picture.
Seneca, Letters to Lucilius, *1st Century*

Figure 14.4
Percentage of total output as a function of age. The humanities, sciences, and arts are represented by the means of several specific disciplines.

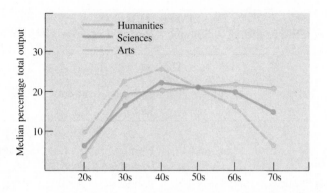

was investigated (Dennis, 1966). As shown in figure 14.4, the point in adult development at which creative production peaked varied from one discipline to another. In the humanities, the seventies was just as creative a decade as the forties. Artists and scientists, though, began to show a decline in creative productivity in their fifties. In all instances, the twenties was the least productive decade in terms of creativity. There are exceptions, of course. In the sciences, Benjamin Duggar discovered the antibiotic aureomycin when he was 72. The first major paper of Nobel laureates in science was published at the average age of 25. All laureates who were past 70, however, continued to publish scholarly papers in scientific journals. These data support the belief that individuals who are bright and productive during their early adult years maintain their creativity in their later years. It is inappropriate to conclude that there is a linear decrease in creativity during the adult years.

Careers and Work

At age 21, Thomas Smith graduated from college and accepted a job as a science teacher at a high school in Boston. At age 26, Sally Caruthers graduated from medical school and took a job as an intern at a hospital in Los Angeles. At age 20, Barbara Breck finished her training at a vocational school and went to work as a computer programmer for an engineering firm in Chicago. Earning a living, choosing an occupation, establishing a career, and developing in a career—these are important themes of early adulthood.

Exploration, Planning, and Decision Making
At some point toward the end of adolescence or the beginning of early adulthood, most individuals enter some type of occupation. Exploration of a number of career options is widely recommended by career counselors. Individuals often approach career exploration and decision making with ambiguity, uncertainty, and stress (Lock, 1988). In one investigation of individuals after they left high school, over half the position changes (such as student to student, student to job, job to job) made between leaving school and the age of 25 involved floundering and unplanned changes. The young adults were neither systematic nor intentional in their career exploration and planning (Super, Kowalski, & Gotkin, 1967).

How can we increase career exploration and planning among adolescents and young adults? In one investigation, a career education and guidance course was developed for disadvantaged inner-city high school students. A regular teacher, who was not especially motivated or competent, was the instructor and the research investigator was the consultant to the teacher (Hamdani,

Whatever you can do, or
dream you can, begin it.
Boldness has genius,
power and magic in it.
Johann Wolfgang von Goethe

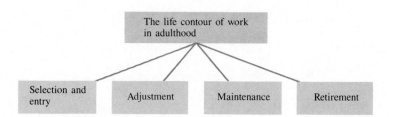

Figure 14.5
The life contour of work in adulthood.

1974). The semester-long course produced an increase in the disadvantaged students' career planning; they increased their use of resources for career planning and decision making in the process.

The Life Contour of Work in Adulthood

The occupational cycle has four main stages: selection and entry; adjustment; maintenance; and retirement (see figure 14.5). These stages are readily identifiable in careers that move in an orderly progression; they become more obscure in disorderly work patterns or work changes that require some form of readjustment. In chapter 16, we will discuss the stage of maintenance and career change in middle adulthood and in chapter 18, the stage of retirement and the work world of older adults are addressed. Here we focus on the two initial stages that take place primarily in early adulthood—selection and entry, and adjustment.

Entering an occupation signals the beginning of new roles and responsibilities for the individual. The career role is different from the roles the individual might have had as temporary or part-time worker during adolescence. Career role expectations for competence are high and the demands are real for the young adult. When an individual enters a job for the first time, she may be confronted by unanticipated problems and conditions. Transitions are required as the individual tries to adjust to the new role. Meeting the expectations of a career and adjusting to a new role are crucial for the individual at this time in adult development (Smither, 1988).

Adjustment is the key label in the second stage of life's work contour. This is the period Daniel Levinson (1978) calls "Age 30 Transition" in men. According to Levinson, once an individual enters an occupation, he must develop a distinct occupational identity and establish himself in the occupational world. Along the way, he may fail, drop out, or begin a new path. He may stay narrowly on a single track or try several new directions before settling firmly on one. This adjustment phase lasts several years. A professional may spend several years in academic study while an executive may spend his early years in lower- or middle-management jobs. Hourly workers usually need several years to explore the work world, become familiar with the industry and a labor union, and move beyond the apprentice status to a permanent occupational role.

The level of attainment reached by the individual in the early 30s varies (Landy, 1988). A professional may just be getting started or may have already become well established and widely known. One executive may be on the bottom rung of the corporate ladder; another may be near the top already. An hourly worker may be an unskilled laborer without job security or a highly skilled craftsman earning more than some executives or professionals. As suggested in Focus on Life-Span Development 14.3, however, some individuals face unemployment, a circumstance that produces stress whether the job loss is temporary, cyclical, or permanent.

The psychological meaning of job loss may depend on a number of factors, including the individual's personality, social status, and resources. This was the conclusion of an investigation by Terry Buss and F. Stevens Redburn (1983) that focused on how the shutdown of a steel plant in Youngstown, Ohio, affected workers. For example, a 50-year-old married worker with two adolescents, a limited education, no transferable job skills, and no pension would not react the same way as a 21-year-old apprentice electrician would.

It is well documented that both professional, semiskilled, and unskilled workers experience stress from losing their jobs, but is there any evidence that one set of workers suffers more than the others? In one investigation (Brenner, 1973), married men between the ages of 30 and 65 who were earning good salaries and were well educated were studied. White-collar workers were the most sensitive to the economic downturn and had the most to lose when income and self-image were considered.

In the Buss-Redburn study, managers and steelworkers were compared in 1978 and 1979. Managers were less affected one year after the plant closing. The steelworkers felt more helpless, victimized, and distrustful, tended to avoid social interaction, and were more aggressive. They were also more depressed and showed a greater degree of perceived immobility. Over time, the steelworkers were less trustful and continued to feel immobile, helpless, and stressed. Furthermore, they also reported more health problems and increased their intake of alcohol. In contrast, managers were coping much better than the steelworkers. Except for a lack of trust, their psychological profile either continued to improve or remained the same. However, in the second wave of interviews conducted in 1979, the managers began to report more family problems and a higher tendency to consume over-the-counter drugs. Nevertheless, the steelworkers were still more severely affected by the plant closing, indicating more aggressiveness, and feelings of victimization, distrust, and helplessness. Although unemployment has stressful effects on both laborers and managers, managers seem to handle it better.

Being unemployed in the 1980s may be as bad or in some cases worse than was true in the 1930s. The unemployed in the 1930s had a strong feeling that their jobs would return. Because many of today's workers are being replaced by technology, however, expectations that their jobs will reappear are less realistic.

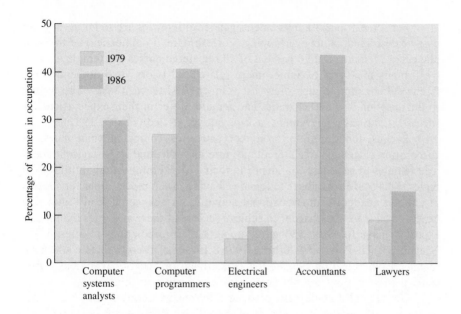

Figure 14.6
*Women in professions dominated by men:
1979 to 1986. Data from United States
Bureau of the Census.*

We have seen how the early years of adulthood mark the development and integration of cognitive capacities that enable individuals to attain purposeful, organized mastery of their personal lives and work. We have also seen the importance of work's role in our lives as young adults. Next, we consider one of the major changes in the work role.

Women's Changing Work Roles

There has been a significant increase in the number of females entering occupations previously thought to be appropriate only for males. Yet discrimination and inadequate opportunities for education are prominent issues affecting the achievement levels of females (Eccles, 1987). Women have diminished the gap between male and female earnings in the 1980s, but significant disparities still exist. The gap is smallest for workers in their 20s, presumably because women and men have had access to similar education and job opportunities in recent years. Overall, the average earnings for women who worked full time were 70 percent of those for men in 1986, up from 62 percent in 1979. More than half the remaining gap is explained by differences in such factors as education and work experience. Women are more than three times likely as men to have had interruptions in their work experience. Forty-seven percent of the women between 21 and 64 years of age had spent six months or more without a job since their twenty-first birthday; only 13 percent of the men had experienced this gap. Reasons for the interruptions included childbearing, child care, illness, disability, and unemployment.

How much progress have women made in moving into professions dominated by men? As shown in figure 14.6, they have made some progress in the 1980s, but fields such as computer systems analysis, computer programming, electrical engineering, accounting, and law are still male dominated.

One can live magnificently in this world,
if one knows how to work and how to love.
Count Leo Tolstoy, 1856

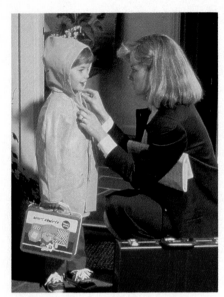

What issues do women face as they combine careers and family?

As women's work roles have changed, what adaptations has this forced men to make?

For some areas of achievement, gender differences are so large they can best be described as nonoverlapping. For example, no major league baseball players are female, and 96 percent of all registered nurses are female. In contrast, many measures of achievement-related behaviors yield no gender differences. For example, girls show just as much persistence at tasks. The answer to the question of whether males and females differ in their expectations for success at various achievement tasks is not yet settled (Eccles, 1987).

Because females are often stereotyped as less competent than males, incorporation of gender role stereotypes into an individual's self-concept could lead females to have less confidence in their general intellectual abilities than males. This could contribute to females' having lower expectations for success at difficult academic and vocational activities. It also could lead females to expect to have to work harder to achieve success at these activities than males expect to have to work. Evidence supports these predictions (Eccles, 1987; Nicholls, 1975; Parsons & others, 1976). Either of these beliefs could keep females from selecting demanding educational or vocational options, especially if these options are not perceived as important or interesting.

Gender roles could also produce different expectations of success depending on the gender stereotyping of the activity. Both educational programs and vocational options are gender stereotyped in our culture. Many high-level professions and both math-related and scientific technical courses and vocational fields are thought to be male activities. In contrast, teaching below the college level, working in clerical and related support jobs, and excelling in language-related courses are thought to be female activities by both children and adults (Eccles, 1987; Eccles & Hoffman, 1984; Huston, 1983). Incorporating these beliefs into self-concept could cause females to have lower expectations for success in male-typed activities and higher expectations for success in female-typed activities. This pattern could lead females to select female-typed activities over male-typed activities. Some support for this perspective has been found (Eccles, 1987). Some researchers, though, have found no gender differences in achievement expectations.

As greater numbers of women pursue careers, they are faced with issues involving career and family. Should they delay marriage and childbearing, and establish their career first? Or should they combine their career, marriage, and childbearing in their 20s? Some women in the last decade have embraced the domestic patterns of an earlier historical period. They have married, borne children, and committed themselves to full-time mothering. These "traditional" women have worked outside the home only intermittently, if at all, and have taken care to subordinate the work role to the family role.

Many other women, though, have veered from this time-honored path. They have postponed, and even forgone, motherhood. They have developed committed, permanent ties to the workplace that resemble the pattern once reserved for men alone. When they have had children, they have strived to combine a career and motherhood. While there have always been "career" women, today their numbers are growing at an unprecedented rate. More about the different paths taken by two young women appears in Focus on Life-Span Development 14.4. Recent research reveals that high-ability juniors and seniors in college show a strong interest in combining career *and* family in early adulthood (Fassinger, 1985).

THE LIFE AND CAREER PATHS OF JOANNE AND JOAN

The life paths of Joanne and Joan were very different (Gerson, 1986). Joanne grew up in a typical American family. While her father earned only a modest wage as a repairman, her mother stayed home to rear their four children because both parents believed that full-time mothering for the children was more important than additional income. However, they hoped that Joanne would educate herself for a better life. But Joanne was more interested in dating than in schoolwork or in her part-time job at a fast food restaurant. When she became pregnant at 17, she was happy to marry her boyfriend and to settle down in a role as a full-time mother. Two children, several brief and disenchanting sales jobs and 10 years later, Joanne still finds satisfaction in full-time mothering. At times she feels financial pressure to give up homemaking for paid work and resents being snubbed when she says her family is her career. But every time she searches the want ads, she vividly remembers how much she disliked her temporary jobs. Since her husband earns enough money to make ends meet, the urge to go to work quickly passes. Instead, Joanne is seriously thinking about having another child.

Joanne's life history reflects the traditional model of female development: An adult woman chooses a domestic life for which she was prepared emotionally and practically since childhood. Approximately 20 percent of women from a variety of social class and family backgrounds are believed to follow this life course (Gerson, 1986). These women are insulated from events that might steer them

away from their expected paths. They are neither pushed out of the home by economic necessity or marital instability nor pulled into the workplace by enticing opportunities. Instead, they remain committed to the domestic role that they assume is the woman's proper and natural place in society.

In contrast, consider Joan's path. Like Joanne, Joan assumed as a child that when she grew up she would become married, have children, and live happily ever after as a housewife. She harbored a vague wish to go to college, but her father thought women should not go to college, and as a low-paid laborer he could not afford to send her to college, anyway. Joan worked after high school as a filing clerk and married Frank, a salesman, two years later. Within six months of the ceremony, she was pregnant and planning to stay home with her young child. But things changed soon after her daughter was born. Unlike Joanne, she became bored and unhappy as a full-time mother. Taking care of the baby was not the ultimate fulfillment for Joan. Motherhood was a mixture of feelings for her—alternately rewarding and frustrating, joyful and depressive. Despite her reluctance to admit these feelings to anyone but herself, a growing sense of emptiness and the need for additional income spurred Joan to look for paid work. She took a job as a bank teller, perceiving it to be a temporary way to boost family income. But the right time to quit never came. Frank's income fell consistently short of their needs, and as his work frustrations mounted, their marriage began to falter. When Frank pressured Joan to have another child, she began to think more seriously about whether

she wanted to remain married to Frank. Just when the marriage seemed unbearable, Joan's boss gave her a chance to advance. She accepted the advance and decided to divorce Frank. Today, more than a decade later, Joan is dedicated to her career, aspires to upper-level management and does not plan to remarry or expand her family beyond one child. Joan's life represents an increasingly common pattern among women—one of rising work aspirations and ambivalence toward motherhood. Like their traditional counterparts, these women grew up wanting and preparing for a domestic role, only to find that events stimulated them to move in a different direction. About one-third of women today seem to follow this life pattern (Gerson, 1986). These women are more likely to experience unstable relationships with men, unanticipated opportunities for job advancement, economic squeezes at home and disappointment with mothering and full-time homemaking. As a consequence, heightened work ambitions replace their earlier home-centered orientation. Athough Joanne and Joan experienced similar childhood backgrounds and aspirations, their lives diverged increasingly as they were confronted with the opportunities and restrictions of early adulthood.

There are a number of other life trajectories that the career and family paths of women in early adulthood can take. More about the increasing dilemma of career and family roles in early adulthood appears in the next chapter as we discuss the nature of marriage, family, and adult life-styles.

CONCEPT TABLE

14.2

Cognitive Development and Careers and Work

Concept	Processes/Related Ideas	Characteristics/Description
Cognitive Development	Cognitive Stages	It is not until adulthood that many individuals consolidate their formal operational thinking, and many other adults do not think in formal operational ways at all. Labouvie-Vief argues that young adults enter a pragmatic stage of thought. Schaie proposed a sequence of cognitive stages: acquisitive, achieving, responsibility, executive, and reintegrative.
	Creativity	The highest productivity of superior works seems to be in the 30s, although when total productivity is considered, it depends on the discipline.
Careers and Work	Exploration, Planning, and Decision Making	Everything we know about career development suggests that young people should explore a variety of career options. Planning and decision making about careers is often disorganized and vaguely pursued.
	The Life Contour of Work	Work's life contour follows this course: Selection and entry, adjustment, maintenance, and retirement.
	Women's Changing Work Roles	There has been a tremendous influx of women into the labor force in recent years. Women have diminished the pay gap in the 80s, but a gap still exists. Women also have increased their presence in occupations previously dominated by men. As greater numbers of women pursue careers, they are faced with issues involving career and family. Special attention needs to be given to the career paths of the brightest and most gifted females, but not to the exclusion of promoting career exploration and options for all females.

Some of the brightest and most gifted females do not have achievement and career aspirations that match their talents. In one investigation, high-achieving females had much lower expectations for success than high-achieving males (Stipak & Hoffman, 1980). In the gifted research program at Johns Hopkins University, many mathematically precocious females did select scientific and medical careers, although only 46 percent aspired to a full-time career compared to 98 percent of the males (Fox, Brody, & Tobin, 1979).

To help talented females redirect their life paths, some high schools are using programs developed by college and universities. Project CHOICE (Creating Her Options In Career Education) was designed by Case Western University to detect barriers in reaching one's potential. Gifted eleventh-grade females received individualized counseling that included interviews with female role models, referral to appropriate occupational groups, and information about career workshops. A program at the University of Nebraska (Kerr, 1983) was successful in encouraging talented female high school students to pursue more prestigious careers. This was accomplished through individual counseling and participation in a "Perfect Future Day," in which girls shared their career fantasies and discussed barriers that might impede their fantasies. Internal and external constraints were evaluated, gender-role stereotypes were discouraged, and high aspirations were applauded. While these programs have short-term success in redirecting the career paths of high-ability females, in some instances the effects fade over time—six months or more, for example. It is important to be concerned about improving the career alternatives for all female youth, however, not just those of high ability.

At this point we have discussed a number of ideas about cognitive development and careers and work in early adulthood. A summary of these ideas is presented in Concept Table 14.2.

Summary

I. Transition from Adolescence to Adulthood
Kenniston proposed that the transition from adolescence to adulthood be called youth, a period of economic and personal temporariness, and struggle between interest in self-autonomy and becoming socially involved. This period averages from two to eight years but can be longer. Two criteria for adulthood are: economic independence and independent decision making. However, clear-cut criteria are yet to be established. There is both change and continuity in the transition from adolescence to adulthood.

II. Physical Development: The Peak and Slowdown
Peak physical status is reached between 18 and 30, especially 19 and 26. Individuals' health also peaks in these years. There is a hidden hazard in these peaks of physical performance and health; bad health habits can be formed. Toward the latter part of early adulthood, a detectable slowdown and decline in physical status is apparent.

III. Eating Behavior and Obesity
We have become a nation obsessed with eating, weight, and weight loss. Heredity and basal metabolism rate are involved in our weight. Estimates indicate that one-half of the adult population is overweight. Women show an especially intense interest in weight loss. Many weight-loss programs have been developed, but no program is the panacea dieters seek. Exercise seems to be the most beneficial component of weight-loss programs.

IV. Sexuality
Increased liberalization of heterosexual attitudes and behavior has occurred. Some dimensions of the double standard, however, still exist. Rates of homosexuality have remained constant in the twentieth century. Homosexuality is no longer classified as a disorder. No definitive conclusions about its cause have been reached. The most common sexually transmitted diseases are chlamydia, gonorrhea, venereal warts, herpes, and AIDS. The increase in herpes and AIDS probably has reduced sexual promiscuity. The relation between the menstrual cycle and personality fluctuations in females has been studied and there is a relation between mood swings and the middle and later premenstrual phase of the cycle.

V. Cognitive Stages
It is not until adulthood that many individuals consolidate their formal operational thinking, and many other adults do not think in formal operational ways at all. Labouvie-Vief argues that young adults enter a pragmatic stage of thought. Schaie proposed a sequence of cognitive stages: acquisitive, achieving, responsibility, executive, and reintegrative.

VI. Creativity
The highest productivity of superior works seems to be in the 30s, although when total productivity is considered, it depends on the discipline.

VII. Careers and Work
Everything we know about career development suggests that young people should explore a variety of career options. Planning and decision making about careers is often disorganized and vaguely pursued. Work's life contour follows this course: Selection and entry, adjustment, maintenance, and retirement.

VIII. Women's Changing Work Roles
There has been a tremendous influx of women into the labor force in recent years. Women have diminished the pay gap in the 80s, but a gap still exists. Women also have increased their presence in occupations previously dominated by men. As greater numbers of women pursue careers, they are faced with issues involving career and family. Special attention needs to be given to the career paths of the brightest and most gifted females, but not to the exclusion of promoting career exploration and options for all females.

Key Terms

Suggested Readings

Gerson, K. (1986). *Hard choices: How women decide about work, career, and motherhood.* Berkeley: U. of California Press.
This book addresses the increasing conflict between career and family faced by women. Includes many case studies of the life and career paths of women.

Hyde, J. S. (1986). *Understanding human sexuality* (3rd ed.). New York: McGraw-Hill.
This book covers many aspects of sexuality, including detailed discussion of heterosexual and homosexual attitudes and behavior, as well as the biological underpinnings of our sexuality.

Logue, A. W. (1986). *The psychology of eating and drinking.* New York: W. H. Freeman.
A well-written and authoritative coverage of what we know about eating behavior, obesity, and weight-loss programs.

Smelser, N. J., & Erikson, E. H. (1980). *Themes of work and love in adulthood.* Cambridge, MA: Harvard U. Press.
A volume of essays focused on the themes of work and love in adulthood, written by experts such as Erik Erikson, Roger Gould, and Daniel Levinson.

15

■

Social and Personality Development

Phil is a lovesick man. On two consecutive days he put expensive ads in New York City newspapers, urging, begging, pleading a woman named Edith to forgive him and continue their relationship.

The first ad read:

> Edith:
> I was torn two ways.
> Too full of child
> to relinquish the lesser.
> Older now,
> a balance struck,
> that a child forever behind me.
> Please forgive me,
> reconsider.
> Help make a new us;
> better now than before
> Phil

This ad was placed in the New York Post at a cost of $3,600. Another full-page ad appeared in the New York Times at a cost of $3,408. Phil's ads stirred up quite a bit of interest. Forty-two Ediths responded; Phil said he thought the whole process would be more private. As Phil would attest, relationships are very important to us. Some of us will go to almost any length and spend large sums of money to restore lost relationships (Worshel & Cooper, 1979).

Sherry is not searching for a particular man. She is at the point where she is, well, looking for Mr. Anybody. Sherry is actually more particular than she says, although she is frustrated by what she calls the great man shortage in this country. According to the 1980 U.S. census, for every 100 men over fifteen years of age who have never been married or are widowed or divorced, there are 123 women; for blacks, the ratio is 100 men for every 133 women.

William Novak, author of the *Great Man Shortage,* believes it is the quality of the gap that bothers most women. He says the quality problem exists because over the last fifteen years or so the combination of the feminist movement and women's tendency to seek therapy when their personal relationships do not work out has produced women who have outgrown men emotionally. Novak observes that the whole issue depresses many women because society has conditioned them to assume that their lack of a marriage partner is their own fault. He points out that women are saying to men, "You don't have to earn all the money anymore, and I don't want to do all the emotional work." One 37-year-old woman told Novak, "I'm no longer waiting for a man on a white horse. Now I'd settle for the horse" (Novak, 1981).

In reference to the shortage of available sensitive adult males, one woman commented, "I'm no longer waiting for a man on a white horse. Now I'd settle for the horse."

Our relationships bring us cherished and warm moments; they also can bring us moments we would rather forget, moments that are distasteful and harmful. Among the questions we ask and evaluate in this chapter are: What attracts us to others and what are love's faces? What is the nature of marriage and the family in early adulthood? What are the life styles of single adults and divorced adults like? How do we juggle our motivation for both intimacy and independence? How much continuity and discontinuity is there between the adult and childhood years?

Attraction and Close Relationships

Our social relationships involve more than mere interactions and acquaintances, although our close relationships begin as merely interactions and acquaintances. What attracts us to others and motivates us to spend more time with them? Another question needs to be asked, one that has intrigued philosophers, poets, and songwriters for centuries—What is love? Is it lustful and passionate as Shakespeare observed, "Sighing like a furnace, with a woeful ballad made to his mistress's eyebrow." Or should we be more cautious in our pursuit of love, as a Czech proverb advises, "Do not choose your wife at a dance, but in the field among the harvesters."

What Attracts Us to Each Other in the First Place?

Does just being around someone increase the likelihood a relationship will develop? Do birds of a feather flock together; that is, are we likely to associate with those who are similar to us? How important is the other person's attractiveness?

Physical proximity does not guarantee that we will develop a positive relationship with an individual. Familiarity can breed contempt, but familiarity is a condition that is necessary for close relationships to develop. For the most part, friends and lovers have been around each other for a long time; they have grown up together, gone to high school or college together, worked together, or gone to the same social events. Once we have been exposed to someone for a period of time, what is it about the individual that makes the relationship breed friendship and even love rather than contempt?

Birds of a feather do flock together. One of close relationships' most powerful lessons is that we like to associate with people who are similar to us. Our friends—and our lovers—are much more like us than unlike us. We share similar attitudes, behavior, and characteristics with those with whom we are closely involved: clothes, intelligence, personality, political attitudes, other friends, values, religious attitudes, life-style, physical attractiveness, and so on. In some limited cases and on some isolated characteristics, opposites may attract. An introvert may wish to be with an extravert, a blond may prefer a brunette, an individual from a low-income background may be attracted to someone with money, for example. But, overall, we are attracted to individuals with similar rather than opposite features (Berscheid, 1985; Hatfield & Sprecher, 1986).

We are motivated to form close relationships with those who are similar to us because similarity provides **consensual validation** of our own attitudes and behaviors. That is, if someone else has the same attitudes and behaviors as us, then this supports who we are. Also, because dissimilar others are unlike us and therefore more unknown, we may be able to gain more control over similar others, whose behavior and attitudes we can predict. And similarity implies that we will enjoy interacting with the other person in mutually satisfying activities, many of which require a partner with similarly disposed behavior and attitudes.

From the long list of characteristics on which partners in close relationships can be similar, one deserves special mention: physical attractiveness. How important is physical attractiveness in determining whether we like or love someone? In one experiment, college students assumed that a computer had determined their date on the basis of similar interests, but actually the dates were randomly assigned (Walster & others, 1966). The college students' social skills, physical appearance, intelligence, and personality were measured. Then a dance was set up for the matched partners. At intermission, the partners were asked in private to indicate the most positive aspects of their date that contributed to his or her attractivenss. The overwhelming reason was looks, not other factors such as personality or intelligence. Other research documents the importance of physical attraction in close relationships; it is associated with the number of dates female college students have in a year, how popular someone is with peers, attention given to an infant, positive encounters with teachers, and selection of a marital partner (Adams & Lavoie, 1974; Bar-Tal & Saxe, 1976; Dion & Berscheid, 1974; Langlois, 1974; Simpson, Campbell, & Berscheid, 1986). And as described in Focus on Life-Span Development 15.1, recent efforts have even been made to discover mathematical equations for calculating beauty.

Love comes in at the eye.
William Butler Yeats, A Drinking Song, *1909*

Early Adulthood

CALCULATING BEAUTY

C an we quantify beauty? In a series of experiments, 150 white, American, male college students were asked to rate the attractiveness of 50 women from pictures of their faces (Cunningham, 1986). The male college students were precise and consistent in what they saw as beauty in the female face.

What were the elements of the ideal female face? They included (see figure 15.A):

1. eye width three-tenths as wide as face at eye level
2. chin length one-fifth the height of face
3. distance from center of eye to bottom of eyebrow one-tenth the height of face
4. height of visible eyeball one-fourteenth the height of face
5. total area of nose less than one-twentieth the area of the face

These data describe an ideal face; they do not describe a real face. And they are images from a particular culture and a particular set of individuals in that culture (male college students from Louisville, Kentucky). On an individual basis, some of us may be drawn to particular features not in this assessment: freckles, or a strong, classical nose, for example.

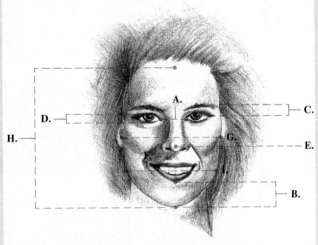

Ideal proportions

Based on subjective judgments of beauty contest participants, researchers derived formulas for facial features that predict the highest beauty ratings. Among the findings for facial features:

A. Eye separation: three-tenths the width of face at eye level (**G**)
B. Chin length: one-fifth the height of the face (**H**)
C. Distance from the center of the eye to the bottom of the eyebrow: one-tenth the height of face (**H**)
D. Height of the visible eyeball: one-fourteenth the height of face (**H**)
E. Total area of the nose: less than 5 percent of the area of the face.
F. Mouth width: 50 percent the width of face at mouth level (**I**).

Figure 15.A Ideal proportions.

But what is remarkable is the high level of agreement within a specific cultural sample of what constitutes physical beauty. There often is an advantage in the social world for those who are physically beautiful. We tend to equate physical beauty with goodness. We assume that beautiful women and handsome men are warm, sensitive, kind, interesting, and outgoing (Hatfield & Sprecher, 1986).

Is it any wonder that cosmetic facial surgery has been performed on such a widespread basis in recent years? Plastic surgeons report that individuals who undergo cosmetic facial surgery are seen by others as more self-assertive, intelligent, likeable, and able to succeed. Individuals who undergo cosmetic facial surgery are struck by how much their change of appearance changes the way others react to them, sometimes being disturbed by it.

Figure 15.1
Rocky Dennis, as portrayed by Eric Stoltz in the movie Mask. *Rocky faced ridicule throughout life from his peers because of his grotesque features. However, those who overcame their prejudices found Rocky to be a sensitive, caring friend.*

Why do we want to be associated with attractive individuals? Again, as with similarity, it is rewarding to be around physically attractive people. It provides us with consensual validation that we too are attractive. As part of the rewarding experience, our self-image is enhanced. It is also aesthetically pleasing to look at physically attractive individuals. We also assume that if individuals are physically attractive they will have other desirable traits that will interest us.

But we can't all have Linda Evans or Don Johnson as our friend or lover. How do we deal with this in our relationships? While beautiful women and handsome men seem to have an advantage, in the end we usually seek out someone at our own level of attractiveness. Most of us come away with a reasonably good chance of finding a "good match." Research indicates that this **matching hypothesis** holds up—that while we may prefer a more attractive individual in the abstract, in the real world we end up choosing someone who is close to our own level of attractiveness (Baron & Byrne, 1987).

Several additional points help to clarify the role of physical beauty and attraction in our close relationships. Much of the research has focused on initial encounters or short-term relationships; attraction over the course of months and years usually is not assessed. As relationships endure, physical attraction probably assumes less importance. Rocky Dennis, as portrayed in the movie *Mask,* is a case in point (see figure 15.1). His peers and even his mother initially wanted to avoid Rocky, whose face was severely distorted. But over the course of his childhood and adolescent years, the avoidance turned into attraction and love as people got to know him.

(a)

(b)

(c)

Changing standards of attractiveness. In the 1940s and 1950s, a Marilyn Monroe body build was ideal (a); by the 1970s, the more slender look of Twiggy was popular (b); today, a more curvacious, slenderized look like that of Christie Brinkley is considered ideal (c).

Our criteria for beauty may vary from one culture to another and from one point in history to another. So, while attempts are being made to quantify beauty and arrive at the ultimate criteria for such things as a beautiful female face, beauty is *relative*. In the 1940s and 1950s, a Marilyn Monroe body build (a well-rounded, Coke-bottle appearance) and face was the cultural ideal for women. By the 1970s, Twiggy and other virtually anorexic females were what women aspired to look like. And now, as we move toward the close of the 1980s, the desire for thinness has not ended, but what is beautiful is no longer pleasingly plump or anorexic but rather a tall stature with moderate curves.

Physical attraction is more important in close relationships than most individuals assumed. To ignore it and say it does not matter goes against an accumulating body of evidence. But as we already have witnessed, there is more to close relationships than physical attraction.

Ask a toad what is beauty . . . he will answer that it is a female with two great round eyes coming out of her little head, a large flat mouth, a yellow belly and a brown back.

Voltaire, Philosophical Dictionary, *1764*

The Faces of Love

Love refers to a vast territory of human behavior, behavior that usually includes an individual doing something positive toward another individual. In this vast territory are a number of paradoxes: people run away from those they claim they want to be near, possibly as a short-term strategy they hope will lead to long-term endearment; people injure others "for their own good," and so on (Berscheid, 1988). How can we classify and study such a complex phenomena as love? R. J. Sternberg (1986) says that love's social anatomy is made up of commitment, intimacy, and passion. C. S. Lewis (1960) and Ellen Berscheid (1988) believe love has four faces: altruism, friendship, romantic love, and affectionate love. Let's look at three of these four faces of love in the context of close relationships in early adulthood—friendship, romantic love, and affectionate love.

I flee who chases me,
And chase who flees me.
Ovid, The Loves, *A.D. 8*

Think about your life and the lives of other people you know. What are the common faces of love that appear in each of your lives?

Friendship

For many of us, finding a true friend is not an easy task. In the words of Henry Adams, "One friend in life is much, two are many, three hardly possible."
Friendship involves enjoyment (we like to spend time with our friends); acceptance (we take our friends as they are without trying to change them); trust

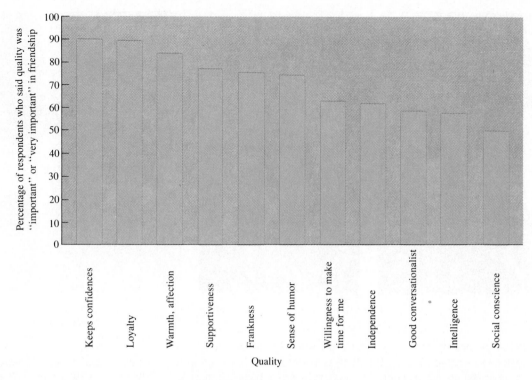

Figure 15.2
Characteristics people want in a friend.
REPRINTED FROM PSYCHOLOGY
TODAY MAGAZINE. Copyright © 1979
American Psychological Association.

(we assume our friends will act in our best interest); respect (we think our friends make good judgments); mutual assistance (we help and support our friends and they us); confiding (we share experiences and confidential matters with a friend); understanding (we feel that a friend knows us well and understands what we are like); and spontaneity (we feel free to be ourselves with a friend) (Davis, 1985). In an inquiry of more than 40,000 individuals, many of these characteristics surfaced when individuals were asked what a best friend should be like (Parlee, 1979) (see figure 15.2).

How is friendship different from love? The difference can be seen by looking at the scales of liking and loving developed by Zick Rubin (1970) (see table 15.1). Rubin says that liking involves our sense that someone else is similar to us; it includes positive evaluation of the individual. Loving, he believes, involves being close to someone; it includes dependency, a more selfless orientation to the individual, and qualities of absorption and exclusiveness.

But friends and lovers are similar in some ways. Keith Davis (1985) has found that friends and spouse/lovers share the characteristics of acceptance, trust, respect, confiding, understanding, spontaneity, mutual assistance, and happiness. However, he has found that relationships with our spouses or lovers are more likely to involve fascination and exclusiveness. Relationships with friends were perceived to be more stable, especially than those among unmarried lovers.

Romantic Love (Eros)
The fires of passion burn hot in **romantic love (Eros).** It is the type of love Juliet had in mind when she cried out, "O Romeo, Romeo, wherefore art thou Romeo?" It is the type of love portrayed in a new song that hits the charts virtually every week. It keeps "Dallas" and "Dynasty" at or near the top of television's most-watched nighttime series and "Days of Our Lives," "General

TABLE 15.1
Sample items from Rubin's loving and liking scales

Love scale

1. I feel that I can confide in_____about virtually everything.
2. If I could never be with_____, I would feel miserable.
3. One of my primary concerns is_____'s welfare.

Liking scale

1. I would highly recommend_____for a responsible job.
2. Most people would react favorably to_____after a brief acquaintance.
3. _____is the sort of person whom I myself would like to be.

Note: Subjects are asked to fill out the questionnaire in terms of their feelings for their boyfriend or girlfriend, and in terms of their feelings for a platonic friend of the opposite sex.

From Zick Rubin, "Measurement of Romantic Love" in Journal of Personality and Social Psychology, 16, *267, 1970. Copyright © 1970 by the American Psychological Association. Reprinted by permission of the author.*

Hospital," and "As the World Turns" at or near the top of television's most-watched daytime shows. It sells millions of books for writers like Danielle Steele. With such behavioral patterns as evidence, is it any wonder that well-known love researcher Ellen Berscheid (1988) says that it is romantic love we mean when we say that we are "in love" with someone? It is romantic love she believes we need to understand if we are to learn what love is all about.

Romantic love is the main reason we get married. In 1967, a well-known research study showed that men maintained that they would not get married if they were not "in love" with a woman, but that women were either undecided or said that they would get married even if they did not love the man (Kephart, 1967) (see figure 15.3). In the 1980s, women and men agree that they would not get married unless they were "in love" (Simpson, Campbell, & Berscheid, 1986) (see figure 15.4). And more than half of today's men and women say that not being "in love" is sufficient reason to dissolve a marriage.

Romantic love is especially important to college students. In one investigation, unattached college males and females were asked to identify their closest relationship. More than half named a romantic partner rather than a parent, sibling, or friend (Berscheid & Snyder, in preparation). It is about this romantic partner that an individual says, "I am *in love,*" not just "I *love.*"

Romantic love's importance appeared in a recent biography about Ingrid Bergman (Leamer, 1986). She once told a man she cared about him deeply, valued his friendship and affection, but simply was not in love with him. Upon hearing this, the man committed suicide. Romantic love possesses an awesome power; its fires are based on more than liking.

Romantic love is not an animal of a single emotion. It includes a complex intermingling of different emotions—fear, anger, sexual desire, joy, and jealousy, for example. Note that not all of these emotions are positive. In one investigation, romantic lovers were more likely to be the cause of depression than friends (Berscheid & Fei, 1977).

Berscheid (1983, 1988) believes that sexual desire has been vastly neglected in the study of romantic love. When pinned down to say what romantic love truly is, she concluded, "It is about 90 percent sexual desire." Berscheid

Figure 15.3
Percentage of respondents who would marry someone that they are not in love with in Kephart's 1967 study.

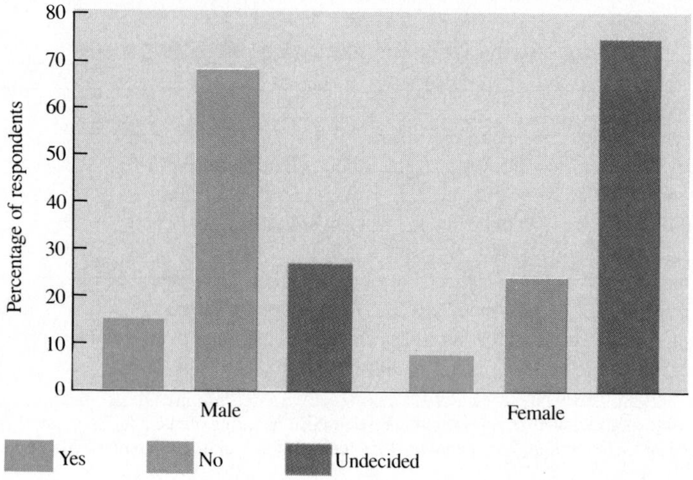

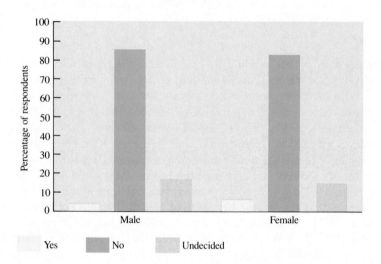

Figure 15.4
Percentage of respondents who would marry someone that they are not in love with in 1984.

When love ends, we seek to understand the causes the relationship did not work. What are some of the explanations we give as to why a relationship did not work? Are some of these explanations likely to be biased?

said that this still is an inadequate answer but "to discuss romantic love without also prominently mentioning the role sexual arousal and desire play in it is very much like printing a recipe for tiger soup that leaves out the main ingredient."

Affectionate Love

Love is more than just passion. That something more is usually called **affectionate love** (or companionate love); it also has been called attachment or emotional attachment. In affectionate love, we desire to have the other person near us and we have a deep affection for the other person. There is a growing belief that the early stages of love have more romantic ingredients, but as love lasts, passion tends to give way to affection. Philip Shaver (1986) described what this developmental course might be like. An initial phase of romantic love is fueled by mixtures of sexual attraction and gratification, a reduced sense of loneliness, uncertainty about the security of developing another attachment, and excitement aroused by exploring the novelty of another human being. With

Early Adulthood

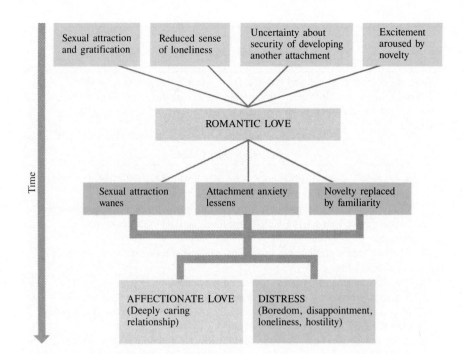

Figure 15.5
The developmental course of love.

time, sexual attraction wanes, attachment anxieties either lessen or produce conflict and withdrawal, novelty is replaced with familiarity, and lovers either find themselves securely attached in a deeply caring relationship or feeling distress—boredom, disappointment, loneliness, and hostility, for example. In the latter case, one or both partners may eventually seek another close relationship (see figure 15.5).

Marriage and the Family

Should I get married? If I wait any longer, will it be too late and will I get left out? Should we have children? How will children affect our marriage? These are some of the enduring and pressing questions young adults face.

Trends in Marriage

Until about 1930, the goal of a stable marriage was accepted as a legitimate endpoint of adult development. In the last 50 years, however, we have seen the emergence of personal fulfillment both inside and outside a marriage as a force that competes with marriage's stability as an adult developmental goal. The changing norm of male-female equality in marriage has produced marital relationships that are more fragile and intense than they were earlier in the twentieth century. More adults are remaining single longer in the 1980s and the average duration of a marriage in the United States is currently just over nine years. The divorce rate, which increased astronomically in the 1970s, has finally begun to slow down, although it still remains alarmingly high. Even with adults remaining single for longer and divorce a frequent occurrence, Americans still show a strong predilection for marriage—the proportion of women who never marry has remained at about 7 percent throughout the twentieth century, for example (Glick, 1979).

When two people are under the influence of the most violent, most insane, most delusive, and most transient of passions, they are required to swear that they will remain in that excited, abnormal, and exhausting condition continuously until death do them part.

George Bernard Shaw

TABLE 15.2
The Marriage Quiz

Take out a sheet of paper and number from 1 to 15. Answer each of the following items true or false. After completing the quiz, turn to page 457 for the correct answers. (This abbreviated quiz includes 15 of the original 20 items.)

Marriage Quiz Items

1. A husband's marital satisfaction is usually lower if his wife is employed full time than if she is a full-time homemaker.
2. Today most young, single, never-married people will eventually get married.
3. In most marriages having a child improves marital satisfaction for both spouses.
4. The best single predictor of overall marital satisfaction is the quality of a couple's sex life.
5. The divorce rate in America increased from 1960 to 1980.
6. A greater percentage of wives are in the work force today than in 1970.
7. Marital satisfaction for a wife is usually lower if she is employed full time than if she is a full-time homemaker.
8. If my spouse loves me, he/she should instinctively know what I want and need to be happy.
9. In a marriage in which the wife is employed full time, the husband usually assumes an equal share of the housekeeping.
10. For most couples marital satisfaction gradually increases from the first year of marriage through the childbearing years, the teen years, the empty nest period, and retirement.
11. No matter how I behave, my spouse should love me simply because he/she *is* my spouse.
12. One of the most frequent marital problems is poor communication.
13. Husbands usually make more life style adjustments in marriage than wives.
14. Couples who cohabitated before marriage usually report greater marital satisfaction than couples who did not.
15. I can change my spouse by pointing out his/her inadequacies, errors, etc.

Larson, J. (1988). The marriage quiz: College students' beliefs in selected myths about marriage. Family Relations, 37, *p. 4.*

Marital Expectations and Myths

Among the explanations of our nation's high divorce rate and high degree of dissatisfaction in many marriages is that we have such strong expectations of marriage. We expect our spouse to simultaneously be a lover, a friend, a confidant, a counselor, a career person, and a parent, for example. In one research investigation (Epstein & Eidelson, 1981), unhappily married couples expressed unrealistic expectations about marriage. Underlying unrealistic expectations about marriage are numerous myths about marriage (Crosby, 1985). A myth is a widely held belief unsupported by facts.

We are what we love.

Erik Erikson, 1968

To study college students' beliefs in the myths of marriage, Jeffry Larson (1988) constructed a marriage quiz to measure students' beliefs in myths about marriage and family relations. The college students responded incorrectly to almost half of the items on the marriage quiz. Female students missed fewer items than male students, and students with a less romantic perception of marriage missed fewer items than more romantically inclined students. See Table 15.2 (above) to take the marriage quiz.

Marital Satisfaction and Conflict

Beyond our unrealistic expectations, what else makes us satisfied with our marriage or so dissatisfied that we consider a divorce? Two views of marital satisfaction and conflict are: behavioral exchange and developmental construction. **Behavior exchange theory** emphasizes the hedonism and competence involved in marital relationships. Hedonism is reflected in the belief that each partner's reinforcement value for the other determines the degree of marital satisfaction; competency is reflected in the belief that the mastery of specific relationship skills determines the degree of marital satisfaction. In one investigation, the reward-punishment ratio of social exchanges was a good predictor of marital satisfaction; that is, the more rewards marital partners gave each other, the more satisfied they were with their marriage (Barnett & Nietzel, 1979). In another investigation, couples who were planning to marry were followed for two and a half years; the partner's rating of their positive communication was highly predictive of their marital satisfaction two and a half years later (Markman, 1979).

When two people marry, each individual brings to the marriage a long history of relationships with many people. The **developmental construction view** of marital satisfaction emphasizes the importance of this long history of relationships and the manner in which they are carried forward. Each of the partners has internalized a relationship with parents. The partners come from families that were divorced, widowed, or intact. Each of the partners may have had romantic relationships with individuals other than the spouse. Psychoanalytic theory has recognized the importance of carrying forward relationships but too often this has been tied to the first five years of life and to psychosexual development. The contemporary developmental construction view considers not only the early childhood years, but the continuing experiences of individuals later in childhood, adolescence, and adulthood. In addition, it is important to evaluate the nature of cohort effects. The immense change in the woman's career role and her increased assertiveness in male-female relationships undoubtedly has had a strong impact on how marital relationships are constructed. An example of how the developmental construction view can be used to understand the nature of marital relationships is presented in Focus on Life-Span Development 15.2.

As a couple stands at the threshold of marriage, their expectations are often extremely positive and extremely romantic. The challenges and adaptations of everyday living with each other usually bring stress that is unexpected. Positive communication prior to a marriage is one of the best predictors of marital satisfaction several years into a marriage.

After reading Focus 15.2 about Jack and Jane, think about other types of relationships two marital partners have had with their parents and how those relationships would predict marital satisfaction or dissatisfaction.

"You have no idea how nice it is to have someone to talk to."
Copyright © 1964 Don Orehek. Reprinted by permission.

Jane got married when she was 19. She and her husband, Jack, followed traditional gender roles at the time, both coming from traditional gender-role families. Jane's relationship with her mother was indulgent; her mother was highly involved in her life and was very permissive toward letting her do what she pleased. Jane's relationship with her father was warm and positive. She usually got what she wanted from her parents who rarely placed any restrictions on her negative behaviors, such as whining and crying. Jane's parents generally got along well and rarely engaged in conflict. Jack's relationship with his mother was cold, and so was his mother's relationship with Jack's father. Jack's father had high demands for his son's behavior and frequently communicated to him that he was just not working hard enough.

What did this history of relationships with parents bring to Jane and Jack's marriage? After several years of marriage, Jack was getting tired of Jane's immature behavior—she frequently whined about wanting things and showed little constraint in her spending

habits. Jane, being accustomed to considerable warmth from both her mother and father, was unhappy with the rather aloof attitude Jack had about their romantic relationship. During the first several years of their marriage, they had two children. While their marriage was an unhappy one, they had difficulty ending it. First, there were the children, then each had grown up in a small town and each had come from a family that had never encountered divorce. Gradually, Jane began to think about going back to school and pursuing a career. She developed intimate friendships with two women who had moved into her neighborhood. Both had careers and convinced Jane that she deserved to have her own identity outside of the marriage. It took her several years, but she finally confronted Jack with the idea that she wanted to return to school and pursue a career. He blew up at the mere mention of this change in their lives. Jack knew things had been bad in the marriage, but at least he had a wife who was living in line with the traditional gender-role orientation he had experienced in his family while he was growing up. He informed Jane

that if she took this step that he would seek a divorce. While it was a struggle for Jane, she decided that she could no longer live immersed in an unhappy marital relationship. Both marital partners agreed that divorce was the best solution.

In the course of portraying Jane and Jack's relationship histories, we see the role of coherence and continuity in relationships (relationships with parents were consistent over long periods of time and the marital relationship, bad from the start, was difficult to change), the internalization of relationships (the many thousands of hours spent with parents while growing up became part of the makeup of each of the marital partners and influenced the way they interacted with each other), carrying forward relationships to influence new relationships (longstanding relationships with parents were brought to the marital relationship and had a strong influence on marital dissatisfaction), and cohort effects (the development of the feminist movement and society's acceptance of a greater involvement of women in careers).

Families are undergoing significant changes. The number of one-child families is increasing. And men are apt to increase the amount of time they spend in fathering.

The Parental Role

For many adults, the parental role is well planned and coordinated with other roles in life and is developed with the individual's economic situation in mind. For others, the discovery that they are about to become parents is a startling surprise. In either event, the prospective parents may have mixed emotions and romantic illusions about having a child. Parenting consists of a number of interpersonal skills and emotional demands, yet there is little in the way of formal education for this task. Most parents learn parenting practices from their own parents—some they accept, some they discard. Husbands and wives may bring divergent viewpoints of parenting practices to the marriage. Unfortunately, when methods of parents are passed on from one generation to the next, both desirable and undesirable practices are perpetuated.

The needs and expectations of parents have stimulated many myths about parenting (Okun & Rappaport, 1980):

The birth of a child will save a failing marriage

As a possession or extension of the parent, the child will think, feel, and behave like the parents did in their childhood

Children will take care of parents in old age

Parents can expect respect and get obedience from their children

Having a child means that the parents will always have someone who loves them and is their best friend

Having a child gives the parents a "second chance" to achieve what they should have achieved

If parents learn the right techniques, they can mold their children into what they want

It's the parents fault when children fail

Mothers are naturally better parents than fathers

Parenting is an instinct and requires no training

In earlier times, women considered being a mother a full-time occupation. Currently, there is a tendency to have fewer children, and as birth control has become common practice, many individuals choose the time for children and how many children they will raise. The number of one-child families is increasing, for example. Giving birth to fewer children and reduced demands of child care free a significant portion of a woman's life span for other endeavors. Three accompanying changes are: (1) as a result of the increase in working women, there is less maternal investment in the child's development; (2) men are apt to invest a greater amount of time in fathering; and (3) parental care in the home is often supplemented by institutional care (day care, for example). As more women show an increased interest in developing a career, they are delaying the decision to have children to a later part of early adulthood than their cohorts did in earlier times. Such deliberate decision making about childbirth reflects an awareness of the role conflict and role overload that characterize many women's lives in the first part of young adulthood as they try to juggle roles of wife, mother, and career woman. It is during the early years of a child's life that parents report the greatest degree of dissatisfaction with marriage, possibly as a consequence of role conflict and role overload (Rollins & Feldman, 1970).

At this point, we have discussed a number of ideas about attraction and close relationships, and about marriage and the family in early adulthood. A summary of these ideas is presented in Concept Table 15.1. Next, we consider the diversity of life styles in adulthood.

The Diversity of Adult Life Styles

Today's adult life styles are diverse. We have single career families, dual career families, single parent families, including mother custody, father custody, and joint custody, the remarried or stepfamily, the kin family (made up of bilateral or intergenerationally linked members), or even the experimental family (individuals in multiadult households—communes—or cohabitating adults). And, of course, there are many single adults.

Single Adults

There is no rehearsal. One day you don't live alone, the next day you do. College ends. Your wife walks out. Your husband dies. Suddenly, you live in this increasingly modern condition, living alone. Maybe you like it, maybe you don't. Maybe you thrive on the solitude, maybe you ache as if in exile. Either way, chances are you are only half-prepared, if at all, to be sole proprietor of your bed, your toaster, and your time. Most of us were raised in the din and clutter of family life, jockeying for a place in the bathroom in the morning, fighting over a last piece of cake, and obliged to compromise on the simplest of choices—the volume of the stereo, the channel on the TV, for example. Few of us grew up thinking that home would be a way station in our life course (Schmich, 1987).

The number of individuals who live alone began to grow in the 1950s but it was in the 1970s that the pace skyrocketed. In the decade of the seventies, the number of men living by themselves increased 97 percent; the number of women, 55 percent. In the eighties, the growth has slowed considerably, but it continues and is expected to do so at least through the end of the century. In 1985, 20.6 million individuals lived alone in the United States, accounting for 11 percent of adults and 24 percent of all households. In some respects, the number of individuals living alone is a symptom of other changes: low birthrates, high divorce rates, long lives, and late marriages. But the group

CONCEPT TABLE

15.1

■

Attraction and Close Relationships, and Marriage and the Family		
Concept	**Processes/Related Ideas**	**Characteristics/Description**
Attraction and Close Relationships	Attraction	Familiarity precedes a close relationship. We like to associate with individuals who are similar to us. Physical attraction is an important ingredient of close relationships, especially at their beginning. Over time, this importance may wane. Physical attraction is relative, varying across cultures and historical time.
	The Faces of Love	Long and Berscheid believe that love has four faces: altruistic, friendship, romantic, and affectionate. Friends and lovers have similar and dissimilar characteristics. Romantic love is involved when we say we are "in love;" it includes passion and sexual attraction. Affectionate love, also called companionate love, is more important as relationships age.
Marriage and the Family	Trends in Marriage	Even though adults are remaining single longer and the divorce rate is high, we still show a strong predilection for marriage.
	Marital Expectations and Myths	Unrealistic expectations and myths about marriage contribute to marital dissatisfaction and divorce.
	Marital Satisfaction and Conflict	Two views are behavior exchange theory and the developmental construction view.
	The Parental Role	For some, the parental role is well planned and coordinated; for others, there is surprise and sometimes chaos. There are many myths about parenting, among them the myth that the birth of a child will save a failing marriage. Families are becoming smaller and many women are delaying childbirth until they have become well established in a career.

that grew the fastest in the 1970s was young adults, the majority of them young men. In that decade, the number of never-married people under 30 living by themselves more than tripled. For them, marriage was no longer the only way out of the house or the only route to sexual fulfillment.

A history of myths and stereotypes are associated with being single, ranging from "the swinging single" to "desperately lonely, suicidal single." Most singles, of course, are somewhere between these extremes. Single adults are often challenged by others to get married so they will no longer be termed selfish, irresponsible, impotent, frigid, and immature. Clearly, though, being a single adult has some advantages—time to make decisions about one's life course, time to develop personal resources to meet goals, freedom to make autonomous decisions and pursue one's own schedule and interests, opportunity to explore new places and try out new things, and availability of privacy.

Common problems of single adults focus on intimate relationships with other adults, confronting loneliness, and finding a niche in a society that is marriage oriented. Many single adults cite personal freedom as one of the major advantages of being a single adult. One woman who never married commented, "I enjoy knowing that I can satisfy my own whims without someone else's interferences. If I want to wash my hair at two o'clock in the morning, no one complains. I can eat when I'm hungry and watch my favorite television shows without contradictions from anyone. I enjoy these freedoms. I would feel very confined if I had to adjust to another person's schedule."

Some adults never marry. Initially, they are perceived as living glamorous, exciting lives. But once we reach the age of 30, there is increasing pressure on us to settle down and get married. If a woman wants to bear children, she may feel a sense of urgency when she reaches 30. This is when many single adults make a conscious decision to marry or to remain single. As one 30-year-old male recently commented, "It's real. You are supposed to get married by 30—that is a standard. It is part of getting on with your life that you are supposed to do. You have career and who-am-I concerns in your 20s. In your 30s, you have to get on with it, keep on track, make headway, financially and familywise." But getting married is less important than buying a house and some property to another 30 year old. A training manager for a computer company, Jane says, "I'm competent in making relationships and being committed, so I don't feel a big rush to get married. When it happens, it happens."

Divorced Adults

Divorce has become epidemic in our culture. Until recently, it was increasing annually by 10 percent, although its rate of increase has slowed as we approach the 1990s. While divorce has increased for all socioeconomic groups, those in disadvantaged groups have a higher incidence of divorce. Youthful marriage, low educational level, and low income are associated with increases in divorce. So too is premarital pregnancy. One investigation revealed that half of the women who were pregnant before marriage failed to live with the husband for more than five years (Sauber & Corrigan, 1970).

For those who do divorce, separation and divorce are complex and emotionally charged. In one investigation, six of the 48 divorced couples continued to have sexual intercourse during the first two years after separation (Hetherington, Cox, & Cox, 1978). Prior social scripts and patterns of interaction are difficult to break. Although divorce is a marker event in the relationship between spouses, it often does not signal the end of the relationship. Attachment to each other endures regardless of whether the former couple respects, likes, or is satisfied with the present relationship. Former spouses often alternate between feelings of seductiveness and hostility. They may also have thoughts of reconciliation. And while at times they may express love toward their former mate, the majority of feelings are negative and involve anger and hate.

Men and women seem to react differently to marital disruption. Divorced women report being more dissatisfied with their marriages than do divorced men, and more men than women wish that their marriages had not ended (Block & others, in press). Women seem better able than men to anticipate the reality of separation and divorce, but have high levels of stress and anxiety accompanying their anticipation (Chiraboga, Roberts, & Stein, 1978). By contrast, men seem to be more upset soon after the separation and divorce as the emptiness of the loss and the intensity of the stress is finally sensed (Berman & Turk, 1981). For instance, divorced men are more likely to be admitted to psychiatric hospitals than divorced women (Bloom, Asher, & White, 1978). For both men and women, those who are older or who have been married longer are more distraught, depressed, and angry after divorce than those who are younger or in marriages of shorter length (Chiraboga, 1982).

The stress of separation and divorce place both men and women at risk for psychological and physical dysfunction (Bloom, Asher, & White, 1982; Chase-Lansdale & Hetherington, in press). Separated and divorced women and men have higher rates of psychiatric disturbance, admission to psychiatric hospitals, clinical depression, alcoholism, and psychosomatic problems such as sleep disturbances than do married adults. There is increasing evidence that stressful events of many types—including marital separation—reduce the immune system's capabilities, rendering separated and divorced individuals vulnerable to disease and infection. In one recent investigation (Kiecolt-Glaser & Glaser, 1988), the most recently separated women (one year or less) were more likely to show impaired immunological functioning than women whose separations had occurred several years earlier (one to six years). Also in this investigation, unhappily married individuals had immune systems that were not functioning as effectively as those of happily married individuals.

Special problems surface for the divorced woman who is a displaced homemaker. She assumed that her work would probably always be in the home. Although her expertise in managing the home may be considerable, future employers do not recognize this experience as work experience. Donna is typical of a divorced displaced homemaker. She married young, and at age 18 had her first child. Her work experience consisted of a part-time job as a waitress in high school. Now 32 with three children—aged 14, 12, and 6—her husband recently divorced her and married someone else. The child support payments are barely enough for rent, clothing, and other necessities. Without any marketable skills, Donna is working as a salesclerk in a local department store. She cannot afford a housekeeper and worries about the children being unsupervised while she works. Creating a positive single identity is essential for divorced adults such as Donna, so they can come to grips with their loneliness, lack of autonomy, and financial hardship (Ahrons & Rodgers, 1987; Kaslow & Schwartz, 1987). Men, however, do not go through a divorce unscathed. They usually have fewer rights to their children, experience a decline in income (though not nearly as great as their ex-wives), and receive less emotional support. Divorce can also have a negative impact on a man's career. More about the lives of divorced adults is presented in Focus on Life-Span Development 15.3.

Separation and divorce are highly-charged emotional affairs. No one gets married to get divorced. Attachment in some form often continues after the separation and divorce. Prior social scripts and interactions are difficult patterns to break. Former spouses may vacillate between hostility and seduction.

Intimacy and Independence

As we go through our early adult years, most of us are motivated not only by intimacy but also by independence. What is the nature of intimacy's development? How do we juggle the motivation for intimacy and the motivation for independence?

Intimacy

Erik Erikson (1968) believes that intimacy should come after individuals are well on their way to establishing a stable and successful individual identity. Intimacy is another life crisis in Erikson's scheme—if intimacy is not developed in early adulthood, the individual may be left with what Erikson calls isolation. Intimacy versus isolation is the sixth stage in Erikson's eight-stage life-cycle perspective, corresponding roughly to the early adulthood years. Erikson refers to intimacy in both sexual relationships and friendships:

> As the young individual seeks at least tentative forms of playful intimacy in friendship and competition, in sex play and love, in argument and gossip, he is apt to experience a peculiar strain, as if such tentative engagement might turn

THE LIVES OF DIVORCED ADULTS—

FACIAL FLORA, WEIGHT CHANGES,

AND A NEED FOR INTIMACY

Imagine you are in your late 20s or early 30s and your marriage has just fractured. After several years in which the conflict between the two of you escalated, both of you decided that this marriage was not the best style of life for you and your two children. What is life as an adult going to be like in the next several years? Mavis Hetherington and her colleagues (1982) described in some detail the lives of adults in the two years following separation and subsequent divorce. One of the most marked changes in the year following the divorce was a decline in their feelings of competence. One might feel that he failed as a parent, another as a spouse; another individual expresses doubts about his ability to adjust well in a future marriage, yet another voices concern about her career ability. While there was often a flurry of social activity in the year after divorce, this usually represented an attempt to resolve some of the identity and loss of self-esteem problems experienced by divorced adults.

Even men who were fairly conservative showed some striking changes after the divorce. As Hetherington and her colleagues commented,

Facial flora began to sprout— beards, mustaches, and longer, more stylish haircuts were common. The former men in the grey flannel suits started to dress in a mod fashion. Jeans, leather jackets, boots, and shirts open to the waist with medallions on hairy chests appeared. We called this the Hip, Honda, and Hirsute Syndrome. To some extent, this was paralleled in a less marked way in women. Divorced women showed changes in appearance, with some women becoming neglectful of their appearance and others becoming extremely concerned with concomitant changes in hairstyles and color, makeup, and manner of dress. Weight losses and gains of over 15 pounds were common in our divorced women. One divorced man commented that he had followed a beautiful, slender woman down the street for several blocks before he recognized her as his ex-wife who had lost 40 pounds. "Why didn't she do this two years ago?" he complained. "Her overeating and obesity were a continuing conflict during our marriage." (p. 247)

One year after the divorce, the men were often involved in a frenzy of activities. While contacts with old friends had declined, dating and casual acquaintances at bars, clubs, parties, and social gatherings had increased. Many of the divorced women and men were participating in self-improvement programs one year after the divorce. However, by two years after the divorce, both social life for the divorced men and self-improvement programs for both divorced men and women had declined. While these activities kept the divorced adults busy and occupied after their divorce, the most important factor in their perception of themselves two years after the divorce was the establishment of a satisfying, intimate heterosexual relationship. By the end of the first year after the divorce, both males and females expressed a need for intimacy and a lack of satisfaction with casual sexual encounters. Women revealed intense feelings about casual sexual encounters, speaking about their feelings of desperation, overwhelming depression, and low self-esteem after such experiences.

into an interpersonal fusion amounting to a loss of identity and requiring, therefore, a tense inner reservation, a caution in commitment. Where a youth does not resolve such a commitment, he may isolate himself and enter, at best, only stereotyped and formalized interpersonal relations; or he may, in repeated hectic attempts and dismal failures, seek intimacy with the most improbable of partners. For where an assured sense of identity is missing, even friendships and affairs become desperate attempts at delineating the fuzzy outlines of identity by mutual narcissistic mirroring; to fall in love means to fall in love with one's mirror image, hurting oneself and damaging the mirror. (p. 167)

An inability to develop meaningful relationships with others in early adulthood can be harmful to an individual's personality. It may lead individuals to repudiate, ignore, or attack those who frustrate them. Such circumstances account for the shallow, almost pathetic attempts of youth to merge themselves with a leader. Many youths want to be apprentices or disciples of leaders and adults who will shelter them from the harm of an "outgroup" world. If this fails, and Erikson believes that it must, sooner or later the individuals will recoil into a self-search to discover where they went wrong. This introspection sometimes leads to painful depression and isolation and may contribute to mistrust of others and restrict the willingness to act on one's own initiative.

There are different styles of intimate interaction. One classification suggests five styles: intimate, preintimate, stereotyped, pseudointimate, and isolated (Orlofsky, Marcia, & Lesser, 1973). The **intimate style** forms and maintains one or more deep and long-lasting love relationships. The **preintimate style** has mixed emotions about commitment; this ambivalence is reflected in a strategy of offering love without obligations or long-lasting bonds. The **stereotyped style** consists of superficial relationships that tend to be dominated by friendship ties with same-sex rather than opposite-sex individuals. The **pseudointimate style** involves maintenance of a long-lasting heterosexual attachment with little or no depth or closeness. And, the **isolated style** encompasses withdrawal from social encounters and little or no intimate attachment to same- or opposite-sex individuals. Occasionally, the isolate shows signs of developing interpersonal relationships, but usually the interactions are stressful. In one investigation, intimate and preintimate individuals were more sensitive to their partner's needs and were more open in their friendships than individuals who were categorized according to the other three intimacy statuses (Orlofsky, 1976).

Intimacy and Independence

The early adult years are a time when individuals usually do develop an intimate relationship with another individual. An important aspect of this relationship is the commitment of the individuals to each other. At the same time, individuals show a strong interest in independence and freedom. Development in early adulthood often involves an intricate balance of intimacy and commitment on the one hand, and independence and freedom on the other (McAdams, 1988).

Recall that intimacy is the aspect of development that follows identity in Erikson's eight stages of development. A related aspect of developing an identity in adolescence and early adulthood is independence. At the same time individuals are trying to establish an identity, they face the difficulty of having

VERBENA. Copyright Perry Howze. Reprinted by permission.

to cope with increasing their independence from their parents, developing an intimate relationship with another individual, and increasing their friendship commitments, while also being able to think for themselves and do things without always relying on what others say or do.

The extent to which the young adult has begun to develop autonomy has important implications for early adulthood maturity. The young adult who has not sufficiently moved away from parental ties may have difficulty in both interpersonal relationships and a career. Consider the mother who overprotects her daughter, continues to support her financially, and does not want to let go of her. In early adulthood, the daughter may have difficulty developing mature intimate relationships and she may have career difficulties. When a promotion comes up that involves more responsibility and possibly more stress, she may turn it down. When things do not go well in her relationship with a young man, she may go crying to her mother.

The balance between intimacy and commitment on the one hand, and independence and freedom on the other, is delicate. Keep in mind that these important dimensions of adult development are not necessarily opposite ends of a continuum—some individuals are able to experience a healthy independence and freedom along with an intimate relationship. These dimensions may also fluctuate with social and historical change. As we have seen, changing gender roles have increased the extent to which many women exhibit a strong motivation for independence. Also keep in mind that intimacy and commitment, and independence and freedom, are not just concerns of early adulthood; they are important themes of development that are worked and reworked throughout the adult years.

Continuity and Discontinuity from Childhood to Adulthood

It is a common finding that the closer in time we measure personality characteristics the more similar an individual will look. Thus, if we measure an individual's self-concept at the age of 20 and then again at the age of 30 we probably will find more stability than if we measured the individual's self-concept at the age of 10 and then again at the age of 30. We no longer believe in the infant determinism of Freud's psychosexual theory, which argued that our personality as adults is virtually cast in stone by the time we are 5 years of age. But the first twenty years of life are not meaningless in predicting an adult's personality. And there is every reason to believe that later experiences in the early adult years are important in determining what the individual is like as a young adult. In trying to understand the young adult's personality, it would be misleading to look only at the adult's life in present tense, ignoring the developmental unfolding of personality. So, too, would it be far off target to only search through a 30-year-old's first five to ten years of life in trying to predict why he is having difficulty in a close relationship. The truth about adult personality development, then, lies somewhere between the infant determinism of Freud and a contextual approach that ignores the antecedents of the adult years altogether. The description of the paths of two lives from childhood to early adulthood in Focus on Life-Span Development 15.4 reveal both continuity and discontinuity in personality.

At this point we have discussed a number of ideas about the diversity of adult life styles, intimacy and independence, and continuity and discontinuity. A summary of these ideas is presented in Concept Table 15.2.

CARL AND DAVID—
THEIR LIFE PATHS FROM
CHILDHOOD TO EARLY ADULTHOOD

The following descriptions of two individuals, Carl and David, who were studied by Stella Chess and Alexander Thomas (1977) in their longitudinal investigation, reveal intriguing information about development from early childhood through early adulthood.

Carl. Carl requested a discussion with Dr. Chess toward the end of his first year in college because he felt depressed and was not coping very effectively with academic or social matters. He had few friends, and he said he had difficulty studying and remembering what he had read. Carl had been a good student in high school, where he had a number of friends and many interests. During his interview with Dr. Chess, he did not appear depressed, but rather expressed bewilderment at his situation, saying that it just wasn't like him to be doing so poorly socially and academically.

The longitudinal data indicated that during childhood Carl had been an extremely "difficult" child—he was intense, had negative reactions to new situations, and was slow to adapt to situations even after many exposures to them. This was true whether the new event was his first bath, his first day at elementary school, or his first shopping trip; each of these experiences produced stormy behavior in Carl. His parents realized that Carl's reactions to the world were not due to any failures in parenting but instead were part of

his temperament. They were patient with him and often gave him long periods of time and many chances to adapt to new situations that were frustrating to him. As a result, he did not become a behavior problem, even though "difficult" children have a higher tendency toward disturbed development (Thomas, Chess, and Birch, 1968).

Later in his elementary and secondary school years, Carl encountered few new situations and was able to develop a positive view of himself. But college brought a lot of changes into his life. He was now away from home in unfamiliar surroundings, with new teachers that placed more complex demands on him, with new peers that were harder to get to know, and with a girl he had started to live with. According to Chess and Thomas, the radically different college experiences reawakened the "difficult child" behavioral reactions and caused Carl to seek some assistance.

Only one session with Carl was necessary to help him get back on a more positive track. His temperamental pattern was discussed with him, including coping mechanisms he might employ to help him out in social and academic situations. By the end of the academic year, his grades had improved, he broke off the living arrangement with the girl, and he started forcing himself to get more involved in peer group activities.

David. Whereas Carl's temperamental pattern was still apparent in early adulthood, David's temperament showed a different pattern. In early childhood, David was one of the most active boys Chess and Thomas studied. He was always in motion, and usually appeared to be friendly and cheerful. Unfortunately, though, David's parents had some personality problems, including an intense need to compete. They continually bragged to others about what a superior child David was (although he did not have a superior IQ). Any problems David had in school were attributable, according to them, to poor teaching. As he progressed through the elementary and secondary school years, David's school performance and his interest in other activities went downhill. The parents totally blamed the school and its teachers for these problems. Picking up on his parents' cues that his failures were not his own fault, David never developed a critical, evaluative approach toward himself. When problems surfaced, he, like his parents, always put the blame on someone else. Apathy and lack of motivation began to dominate his daily life, preventing him from taking responsibility for his actions. Unfortunately, this attitude led to complete resistance to counseling sessions designed to help him get out of his dilemma.

The Diversity of Adult Life Styles, Intimacy and Independence, and Continuity and Discontinuity

Concept	Processes/Related Ideas	Characteristics/Description
The Diversity of Adult Life Styles	Single Adults	Being single has become an increasingly prominent life style. Myths and stereotypes about singles abound, ranging from "swinging single" to "desperately lonely, suicidal single." There are advantages and disadvantages to being single, autonomy being one of the advantages. Intimacy, loneliness, and a marriage-oriented society are concerns of single adults.
	Divorced Adults	Divorce has increased dramatically, although its rate of increase has begun to slow. Divorce is complex and emotional. In the first year following divorce, a disequilibrium in the divorced adult's behavior occurs, but by several years after the divorce, more stability has been achieved. The divorced displaced homemaker may encounter excessive stress. Men do not go through a divorce unscathed either.
Intimacy and Independence	Intimacy	Erikson argues that intimacy versus isolation, the sixth stage in his eight-stage theory of the life cycle, coincides with early adulthood. Five styles of intimate interaction are: intimate style, preintimate style, stereotyped style, pseudointimate style, and isolated style.
	Intimacy and Independence	There is a delicate balance between intimacy and commitment on the one hand, and independence and freedom on the other. These themes are germane to understanding early adulthood, but they are usually worked and reworked throughout the adult years.
Continuity and Discontinuity	Its Nature	The closer in time we measure personality, the more continuity we find. The first 20 years are important in predicting an adult's personality, but so, too, are continuing experiences in the adult years. The first five years are not as powerful as Freud believed in determining an adult's personality.

Summary

I. Attraction
Familiarity precedes a close relationship. We like to associate with individuals who are similar to us. Physical attraction is an important ingredient of close relationships, especially at their beginning. Over time, this importance may wane. Physical attraction is relative, varying across cultures and historical time.

II. The Faces of Love
Long and Berscheid believe that love has four faces: altruistic, friendship, romantic, and affectionate. Friends and lovers have similar and dissimilar characteristics. Romantic love is involved when we say we are "in love"; it includes passion and sexual attraction. Affectionate love, also called companionate love, is more important as relationships age.

III. Marriage
Even though adults are remaining single longer and the divorce rate is high, we still show a strong predilection for marriage. Unrealistic expectations and myths about marriage contribute to marital dissatisfaction and divorce. Two views of marital satisfaction and conflict are behavior exchange and developmental construction.

IV. **The Parental Role**
For some, the parental role is well planned and coordinated; for others, there is surprise and sometimes chaos. There are many myths about parenting, among them the myth that the birth of a child will save a failing marriage. Families are becoming smaller and many women are delaying childbirth until they have become well established in a career.

V. **Single Adults**
Being single has become an increasingly prominent life style. Myths and stereotypes about singles abound, ranging from "swinging single" to "desperately lonely, suicidal single." There are advantages and disadvantages to being single, one of the advantages being autonomy. Intimacy, loneliness, and a marriage-oriented society are concerns of single adults.

VI. **Divorced Adults**
Divorce has increased dramatically, but its rate has begun to slow. Divorce is complex and emotional. In the first year following divorce, a disequilibrium in the divorced adult's behavior occurs, but by several years after the divorce, more stability has been achieved. The divorced displaced homemaker may encounter excessive stress. Men do not go through a divorce unscathed.

VII. **Intimacy**
Erikson argues that intimacy versus isolation, the sixth stage in his eight-stage theory of the life cycle, coincides with early adulthood. Five styles of intimate interaction are: intimate style, preintimate style, stereotyped style, pseudointimate style, and isolated style.

VIII. **Intimacy and Independence**
There is a delicate balance between intimacy and commitment on the one hand, and independence and freedom on the other. These themes are germane to understanding early adulthood, but they usually are worked and reworked throughout the adulthood years.

IX. **Continuity and Discontinuity**
The closer in time we measure personality the more continuity we find. The first 20 years are important in predicting an adult's personality development, but so, too, are continuing experiences in the adult years. The first five years are not as powerful as Freud believed in determining an adult's personality.

Key Terms

consensual validation *436*
matching hypothesis *438*
friendship *439*
romantic love (Eros) *440*

affectionate love *442*
behavior exchange theory *445*
developmental construction view *445*
intimate style *453*

preintimate style *453*
stereotyped style *453*
pseudointimate style *453*
isolated style *453*

Answers to the Marriage Quiz
1. False
2. True
3. False
4. False
5. True
6. True
7. False
8. False
9. False
10. False
11. False
12. True
13. False
14. False
15. False

Suggested Readings

Ahrons, C. R., & Rodgers, R. H. (1987). *Divorced families.* New York: Norton.
A contemporary look at the nature of divorce and its effects on adult development and life styles.

Brehm, S. S. (1985). *Intimate relationships.* New York: Random House.
Describes the life cycle of relationships, from acquaintance to intimacy and sometimes to dissolution. Information about how to improve the intimacy of relationships is provided.

Gilmour, R., & Duck, S. (Eds.) (1986). *The emerging field of intimate relationships.* Hillsdale, NJ: Erlbaum.
Includes a number of models for understanding the nature of close relationships. Includes chapters on when the honeymoon's over, gender effects, the causes and consequences of jealousy, and loneliness.

Hatfield, E., & Sprecher, S. (1986). *Mirror, mirror . . . The importance of looks in everyday life.* Albany, NY: State University of New York Press.
Elaine Hatfield (formerly Elaine Walster) is a pioneer in the field of physical attractiveness and close relationships. This entertaining, insightful book details how looks affect sex, marriage, self-image, personality, and social skills.

S E C T I O N
VIII

Middle Adulthood

G enerations will depend on the ability of every procreating individual to face his children. ■

Erik Erikson

16

■

Physical and Cognitive Development

If I could save time in a bottle
the first thing that I'd like to do
is save every day till eternity passes away
just to spend them with you . . .

But there never seems to be enough time to do
the things you want to do once you find them.
Looked around enough to know that you're the one
I want to go through time with (Jim Croce, *Time in a Bottle*).

Our perception of time depends where we are in the life cycle. We are more concerned about time at some points in life than others. Jim Croce's *Time in a Bottle* reflects a time perspective that develops in the adult years. As young adults, love and intimacy assume prominent roles in our lives. We begin to look back at where we have been. As middle-aged adults, we look back even more and reflect on what we have done with the time we have had. We look toward the future more in terms of how much time remains to accomplish what we wish to do with our lives.

When we think about what happens to us when we become middle-aged, physical changes leap to the forefront of our thoughts—the lessening of physical powers, the arrival of sags, spreads, and lines, the appearance of menopause. Middle age also brings forth thoughts about whether our mind slows down at this point in the life cycle. We wonder, "Is my memory going to be worse when I become middle-aged?" for example. And we imagine where we will be in our careers in middle age. We think, "Will I be able to reach and maintain satisfaction in my career?" "Will I possibly change careers in midlife?" "Will I be able to find enough time for leisure and lead a balanced, happy life?" These are the themes of this chapter—physical, cognitive, and career development in middle adulthood.

Physical Development

I am 43 years of age at the time of this writing. When I was an adolescent and my father was 43 years old, I thought he was old; I could not conceive of myself ever being that old! But it happened, and now I've got a few gray hairs, I'm wearing reading glasses while I'm typing this sentence, and I can't run as fast as I could, although I still run 15–20 miles every week to keep my body from falling apart. At some point in our 40s, we become middle-aged. What physical changes accompany this change to middle adulthood? What is the health status of middle-aged adults? What kind of sexual changes occur?

Physical Changes
A host of physical changes characterize middle adulthood—some began to appear earlier in the individual's 30s, but at some point in the 40s, decline in physical development indicates that middle adulthood has arrived.

I wear them. They help me. But I
don't care for them . . .
My gaze feels aimed. It is as if
two manufactured beams had been lodged
in my sockets—hollow stiff and gray.
Like mailing tubes—and when
I pivot, vases topple down
from tabletops, and women frown.
John Updike

Seeing and hearing are two of the most troublesome and noticeable changes in middle adulthood. Accommodation of the eye—the ability to focus and maintain an image on the retina—experiences its sharpest decline between 40–59 years of age. In particular, middle-aged individuals begin to have difficulty viewing close objects (Kline & Schieber, 1985). The eye's blood supply also diminishes, although usually not until the 50s or 60s. The reduced blood supply may decrease the visual field's size and account for an increase in the eye's blind spot. And there is some evidence that the retina becomes less sensitive to low levels of illumination. In one investigation, the effects of illumination level on the work productivity of individuals in early and middle adulthood were studied (Hughes, 1978). The workers were asked to look for ten target numbers printed on sheets that had a total of 420 numbers printed on them. Each of the workers performed the task under three different levels of illumination. While increased levels of illumination increased performance for both age groups, the performance of middle-aged workers improved the most.

A host of physical changes accompany middle age, among them accommodation of the eye.

Hearing may also start to decline by the age of 40. Sensitivity to high pitches usually declines first; the ability to hear low pitched sounds does not seem to decline much in middle adulthood, though. And men usually lose their sensitivity to high pitched sounds sooner than women do. However, this sex difference might be due to the greater exposure of men to noise in occupations such as mining, automobile work, and so on (Olsho, Harkins, & Lenhardt, 1985).

Middle age is when your
age starts to show around your middle.
Bob Hope

As individuals go through their adult years, they get shorter—our bodies cannot hold off gravity forever! As muscles weaken, an adult's back weakens. As the disks between the bones of the spine deteriorate, the bones move closer to one another. For example, a man who is 5 feet 10 inches tall at age 30 will probably be 5 feet 9 ⅞ inches by age 50, and only 5 feet 9 ¼ inches by age 60.

Health Status

Health status becomes a major concern in middle adulthood. More time is spent worrying about health now than in early adulthood. Because middle adulthood is characterized by a general decline in physical fitness, some deterioration in health is to be expected. The main health nemeses of middle-aged adults are: cardiovascular disease, cancer, and weight. Cardiovascular disease is the number one killer in the United States, followed by cancer. Smoking-related cancer often surfaces for the first time in middle adulthood. And the Harvard Medical School Health Letter indicates that about 20 million Americans are on a serious diet at any particular moment. Being overweight is a critical health problem in middle adulthood. For individuals who are 30 percent or more overweight, the probability of dying in middle adulthood increases by about 40 percent. Obesity increases the probability that an individual will suffer a number of other ailments, among them hypertension and digestive disorders.

For most of us, some aspect of our health deteriorates in middle adulthood. Being overweight has become epidemic in our culture. For middle-aged individuals, the probability of dying increases by about 40 percent. Think about the middle-aged individuals you know. What percentage of them are overweight?

Since a youthful appearance is stressed in our culture, many individuals whose hair is graying, whose skin is wrinkling, whose body is sagging, and whose teeth are yellowing strive to make themselves look younger. Undergoing cosmetic surgery, dying hair, purchasing a wig, enrolling in a weight reduction program, participating in an exercise regimen, and taking heavy doses of vitamins are frequent occurrences in middle age. One investigation found that middle-aged women focus more attention on facial attractiveness than do older or younger women; in this same investigation middle-aged women were more

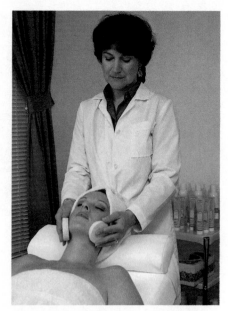

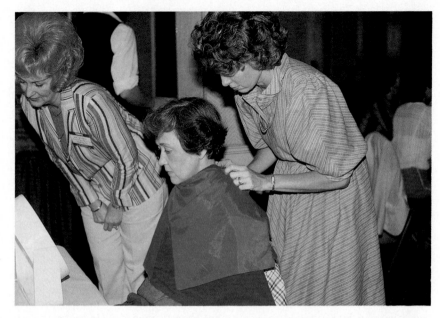

How do individuals deal with physical changes in middle age? A youthful appearance is stressed in our culture. Many individuals go to great lengths to make themselves look younger. Face lifts and tummy tucks have become much more common in the 1980s than in prior decades, especially in women. Why might women be more motivated to change their physical appearance in middle age than men in our culture?

When more time stretches before one, some assessments, however reluctantly and incompletely, begin to be made.

James Baldwin

likely to perceive the signs of aging as having a negative effect on their physical appearance (Nowak, 1977). In our culture, some aspects of aging in middle adulthood are taken as signs of attractiveness in men; similar signs may be perceived as disasters in women. Facial wrinkles and gray hair symbolize strength and maturity in men but may be perceived as unattractive in women.

How individuals deal with physical change and decline varies greatly from one individual to the next. One individual may be able to function well with severe physical problems or deteriorating health; another with the same problems may be hospitalized and bedridden. Some individuals call a doctor at the slightest hint of something being physically amiss; others ignore serious physical signs that might indicate the presence of a heart condition or cancer.

Emotional stability and personality are related to health in middle adulthood. In the California Longitudinal Study (Livson & Peskin, 1981; Peskin & Livson, 1981), as individuals aged from 34 to 50, those who were the most healthy were calm, self-controlled, and responsible. In the Chicago Stress Project, the personality style of **hardiness**—a sense of commitment (rather than alienation), control (rather than powerlessness), and a perception of problems as challenges (rather than threats)—was investigated to determine its role in health (Maddi, 1986). Business managers 32 to 65 years of age were studied over a five-year-period. During the five years, most of the managers experienced stressful events—divorce, job transfers, the death of a close friend, inferior performance evaluations at work, or working at a job with an unpleasant boss, for example. Managers who developed an illness (ranging from flu to heart attack) were compared to those who did not. The latter group was more likely to have a hardy personality (Kobasa, Maddi, & Kahn, 1982). And in an investigation of another group—in this case, business executives—hardiness along with exercise and social support were evaluated to determine whether they buffered stress and reduced illness (Kobasa & others, 1985). As shown in table 16.1, when all three factors were present in the executive's life, the level of illness dropped dramatically. This suggests the power of multiple

TABLE 16.1
Illness of High-Stress Business Executives: The Effects of Personal Hardiness, Exercise, and Support Systems

Resistance sources	Number of illnesses
All three high	357
Two high	2,049
One high	3,336
None high	6,474

Note: The measure of illness is based on the Seriousness of Illness Survey, a self-report checklist of 126 commonly recognized illnesses—severity weights were given to illnesses based on ratings by large numbers of physicians and lay persons.

From S. C. Kobasa, et al., "Relative effectiveness of hardiness, exercise, and social support as resources against illness" in Journal of Psychosomatic Research, 29, 525–553, *1985. Copyright © 1985 Pergamon Press, Inc. Reprinted by permission.*

buffers of stress, rather than a single buffer, in maintaining health. Developmentalists increasingly believe that life-style is an important determinant of health in middle adulthood. As we see next, special attention has been directed at discovering the role of life style in cardiovascular disease.

Cardiovascular Disease
The heart and coronary arteries change in middle adulthood. The heart of a 40-year-old pumps only 23 liters of blood per minute; the heart of a 20-year-old pumps 40 liters under comparable conditions. Just as the coronary arteries that supply blood to the heart narrow during middle adulthood, the level of cholesterol in the blood increases with age—at age 20, it is 180 milligrams; at 40, 220 mg; at age 60, 230 mg—and begins to accumulate on the artery walls, which are themselves thickening. The net result: arteries are more likely to become clogged, increasing the pressure on the arterial walls, which in turn pushes the heart to work harder to pump blood, thus making a stroke or heart attack more likely. Blood pressure, too, usually rises in the 40s and 50s. At menopause, a woman's blood pressure rises sharply and usually remains above that of a man through life's later years.

An extensive research effort has attempted to associate the incidence of cardiovascular disease in middle adulthood with life-style. Considerable attention has been focused on a life-style pattern called **Type-A behavior pattern.** A cluster of characteristics make up the Type-A behavioral pattern—excessively competitive, an accelerated pace of ordinary activities, impatience, doing several things at the same time, hostility, and an inability to hide the belief that time is a struggle in life. In the late 1950s, a secretary for two California cardiologists, Meyer Friedman and Ray Rosenman, observed that the chairs in their waiting room were tattered and torn, but only on the front edge. The cardiologists had noticed the impatience of their cardiac patients, often arriving exactly on time for their appointment and in a great hurry to leave. Subsequently they conducted a research investigation of 3,000 healthy men between the ages of 35 and 59 over a period of eight years (Friedman & Rosenman, 1974). During the eight years, the Type-A men had twice as many heart attacks or other forms of heart disease as anyone else. Autopsies of men who died revealed Type-A men had coronary arteries that were more obstructed than other men.

A sense of commitment, control, and a perception of problems predicted resistance to illness in middle-aged men. Can you think of other factors that might prevent illness in middle age?

All men should strive to learn before they die
What they are running from, and to, and why.
James Thurber, The Shore and the Sea, *1956*

"Could you walk a little faster, buddy? This is New York."
Drawing by M. Stevens; © *1987 The New Yorker Magazine, Inc.*

Since the original work of Freidman and Rosenman, an extensive effort examining the link between Type-A behavior and cardiovascular disease has cast some doubt on the strength of the association (Williams, 1988; Wright, 1987). Studies with large samples of Type-A subjects (on the order of one thousand or more) and carefully designed interviewing techniques still reveal an association between Type-A behavior and coronary risk, but the association is not as strong as once was believed. Today's strategy is to search for the specific ingredients of Type-A behavior—anger, time urgency, and chronic activation (a tendency to be keyed up, all day, every day), for example—to determine a more precise link between life-style and coronary risk. Debate still continues on just which of the ingredients of Type-A are responsible for coronary risk. Some researchers believe that individuals who are hostile or turn anger inward are more likely to develop heart disease (e.g., Williams, 1988); others argue that time urgency, chronic activation, and a tendency to do two things at one time are more at fault (e.g., Wright, 1987).

The dust has not completely settled in the debate about whether Type-A behavior in general should be abandoned in favor of its more precise components. Meyer Friedman still believes the cluster of anger, impatience, competitiveness, and irritation is related to heart disease, for example; His clinical staff reports success with counseling and behavior modification programs designed to reduce the intensity of the cluster in coronary risk patients. As one heart attack victim who went through counseling said, "I realized that there is more than one way of getting from point A to point B . . . If I had a problem before, I'd just drive forward and solve it at any cost. Now I know what I don't complete I'll finish tomorrow" (Fischman, 1987, p. 50). Thus, while empirical research studies chip away at the Type-A behavior pattern, trying to find which of its components are most strongly associated with coronary disease, the Type-A behavior pattern remains a strong contender in clinical analysis and treatment. Focus on Life-Span Development 16.1 reveals how one individual who suffered a heart attack modified his Type-A behavior.

Mort, age 52, has worked as an air-traffic controller for the last 15 years. An excitable individual, he compared the job to being in a mad cage. During peak air traffic, the tension was almost unbearable. In these frenzied moments, Mort's emotions were a mixture of rage, fear, and surprise. The tension spilled over into his family life. In his own words, "When I would get home, my nerves were hopping. I would take it out on the nearest person." Mort also said, "I never seem to have enough time to do what I want to do. Things always seem to be piled up and I'm always doing two or three things at the same time. Life is like a treadmill and I don't know how to get off." Sally, his wife, told Mort that if he could not calm his emotions and handle stress more effectively, she would leave him. She suggested he change to a less-upsetting job. He did not heed her advice. His intense emotional behavior continued, and she left him three years ago.

Two years ago, the roof fell in on Mort. He had a heart attack when the computer that monitors air traffic temporarily went down. Quadruple bypass surgery saved his life. His doctor talked with him about his Type-A behavior pattern and ways to change it. Mort agreed to participate in a therapy program designed to improve his patience, control of anger, and ability to relax. Mort was willing to adapt his behavior and

Air traffic controllers have described their job like "being in a pressure cooker about to go off." What is it about an air traffic controller's job that makes it so stressful? Think for a moment about the jobs you are considering when you complete your education. How would you rate the stress of these jobs you are thinking about taking?

follow the therapy guidelines. One reason Mort was a willing learner is that his father had a heart condition, one uncle died at young age of a cardiac infarction, and a second had undergone bypass surgery twice. He knew that, with his family history, at his age, and with his intense pressures, that he had become a high-risk case.

Once back at work, his boss agreed to keep his work week at a maximum of 40 hours per week and

to refrain from assigning him to peak air traffic periods. He began to watch his diet and to run 15 miles a week. On weekends he began to play golf. Last week his doctor informed him that his physical condition is better than it has been for years. Mort knows that he has to continue monitoring his life-style, but he feels a number of productive years are ahead of him now that he has modified his life-style.

Illness, Cancer, and the Immune System

Psychologists once were hesitant to associate psychological states with illness because they could not imagine a physiological connection (Maier & Laudenslager, 1985). Evidence for this connection has increased and researchers in this field, known by the imposing name of **psychoneuroimmunology,** are beginning to explain how psychological factors influence physical health. The new field of psychoneuroimmunology explores connections between psychological factors, such as emotions and attitudes, the nervous system, and the immune system.

The immune system keeps us healthy by recognizing foreign materials such as bacteria, viruses, and tumors, and then by destroying them. Its machinery consists of billions of white blood cells in the lymph system. Researchers have shown that when certain types of lymph cells—called natural killer (NK) cells—are highly active, cancer is less likely to develop. The NK cells seem to be part of an early immune surveillance system that keeps tumors from growing and spreading. Just how they do this important task is still not clear.

Exploratory efforts are beginning to uncover some connections between psychological factors and the immune system. Sandra Levy (1984, 1985) investigated NK-cell activity when cancer spread to the lymph nodes of women treated for breast cancer. Women who accepted the disease and adjusted to their condition had less NK-cell activity than women who became angry and agitated about their disease. Levy believes acceptance of the disease reflects a belief of helplessness; in contrast, anger and agitation suggest that something might be done to alter the disease. In this way, beliefs about control may affect NK-cell activity.

AIDS is another disease that may be affected by psychoneuroimmunological factors. When an individual is told that he has been exposed to the AIDS virus, he often goes into a deep depression. Since depression is thought to adversely affect the immune system, the AIDS patient ends up with an even greater suppression of the immune system.

Much of what we know about psychoneuroimmunology needs further clarification, verification, and explanation (Baum & others, in press). The next several decades should witness increased growth in this field: it is hoped that more precise links between psychological factors, the brain, and the immune system will be revealed. The outcome of this research could provide more successful treatments of our most baffling diseases, cancer and AIDS among them (Corless & Pittman-Lindeman, 1987).

Sexuality

What kind of sexual changes take place during middle adulthood? What are the biological factors involved? What are our sexual attitudes and behavior like as we go through middle adulthood?

Biological Changes

Most of us know something about menopause. But is what we know accurate? Stop for a moment and think about your knowledge of menopause. What is menopause? When does it occur? Can it be treated? Most of us share some assumptions about menopause—we may think that it is a deficiency disease, that it involves numerous complaints, that women who are undergoing menopause deeply regret losing their reproductive capacity, their sexuality, and their femininity, and that they become deeply depressed. Are these assumptions accurate?

In their 40s, women's ovaries begin to produce less estrogen; in their late 40s and early 50s, menstruation stops, and, not much later, the production of ova also stop. This is **menopause,** a marker that signals the cessation of childbearing capability. The entire process of declining reproductive ability is referred to as the **climacteric.** Ovaries cease to produce the hormones estrogen and progesterone, although some estrogen continues to be produced by the adrenal glands. Estrogen's dramatic decline produces some uncomfortable physical symptoms in some menopausal women—"hot flashes," nausea, fatigue, and rapid heart beat, for example. Some menopausal women report depression and irritability, but in some instances, these feelings may be related to other circumstances in the woman's life, such as becoming divorced, losing a job, caring for a sick parent, and so on (Strickland, 1987).

The comments of the following two women reveal the extensive variation menopause may bring. One woman commented, "I had hot flashes several times a week for almost six months. I didn't get as embarrassed as some of my friends who also had hot flashes, but I found the 'heat wave' sensation uncomfortable." Another woman commented, "I am constantly amazed and delighted to discover new things about my body, something menstruation did not allow me to do. I have new responses, desires, sensations, freed and apart from the distraction of menses (periods)."

Recent research investigations reveal that menopause does not produce psychological problems or physical problems for the majority of women. For example, in a large survey of more than 8,000 randomly selected women, the majority judged menopause to be a positive experience—feeling relief that they no longer had to worry about becoming pregnant or having periods—or a neutral experience—with no particular feelings at all about it (McKinlay & McKinlay, 1984). Only three percent said they regretted reaching menopause. Except for some temporary bothersome symptoms, such as hot flashes, sweating, and menstrual irregularity, most women simply said that menopause was not nearly the big deal that a lot of people make it out to be.

Why, then, do so many individuals have the idea that menopause is such a big deal? Why do we have so many erroneous assumptions—that menopausal women will lose their sexuality and femininity, that they will become deeply depressed, and that they will experience extensive physical pain? Much of the research on menopause is based on small, selective samples of women who go to physicians or therapists because they are having problems associated with menopause. These women are unrepresentative of the large population of women in the United States; because, until recently, most research was conducted with atypical women, in too many instances, menopause was described as a psychological crisis.

For the minority of menopausal women whose experiences are physically painful and psychologically difficult, **estrogen replacement therapy** may be beneficial. The painful symptoms appear to be related either to low estrogen levels or to hormonal imbalance. Estrogen replacement therapy has been successful in relieving low-estrogen menopausal symptoms like hot flashes and sweating. Medical experts increasingly recommend that, prior to menopause, women have their level of estrogen monitored. In this way, once menopause occurs and estrogen level declines, the physician knows just how much estrogen to replace to maintain a woman's normal level.

Our portrayal of menopause has been much more positive than was usually painted in the past. While menopause overall is not the negative experience for most women it once was thought to be, the loss of fertility is an important marker in one sense for women—it means that they have to make final decisions about having children. Women in their 30s who have never had children sometimes speak about being up against the biological clock, because they cannot postpone questions about having children much longer (Blechman & Brownell, 1987).

Do men go through anything like the menopause that women experience? That is, is there a male menopause? During middle adulthood, most men do not lose their capacity to father children, although there usually is a modest decline in their sexual potency at this time. Men do experience hormonal changes in their 50s and 60s, but nothing like the dramatic drop in estrogen that women experience. Testosterone production begins to decline about 1 percent a year during middle adulthood, and sperm count usually shows a slow decline, but men do not lose their fertility in middle age. What has been referred to as male menopause, then, probably has less to do with hormonal change than with the psychological adjustment men must make when they are faced with declining physical energy and family and work pressures. Testosterone therapy has not been found to relieve such symptoms, suggesting that they are not induced by hormonal change.

Sexual Attitudes and Behavior

Although a man's or a woman's ability to function sexually shows little biological decline in middle adulthood, sexual activity usually occurs on a less frequent basis than in early adulthood. Career interest, family matters, energy level, and routine may contribute to this decline. But a large percentage of individuals in middle adulthood continue to engage in sexual activity on a reasonably frequent basis. For example, in one national survey of 502 men and women between 46 and 71 years of age, approximately 68 percent of the 51- to 55-year-old respondents said that they had a moderate or strong interest in sex and approximately 52 percent said that they had sexual intercourse once a week or more (Pfeiffer, Verwoerdt, & Davis, 1974).

Sexual attitudes and behavior are domains of development where cohort effects can be dramatic. What are the current social factors that might influence the sexuality of the next generation of middle-aged women, for example? For the answer to this question, turn to Focus on Life-Span Development 16.2.

At this point we have discussed a number of ideas about physical development in middle adulthood. A summary of these ideas is presented in Concept Table 16.1. Next, we study the possibility of cognitive change in middle adulthood.

What is sex in the next generation of middle-aged men probably going to be like?

SEX IN THE NEXT
GENERATION OF
MIDDLE-AGED WOMEN

Three main factors should create change in the sexuality of the next generation of middle-aged women: greater acceptance of women as sexual beings throughout life; the growing absence of stable male sexual partners for many women, due to high divorce rates and the shorter life expectancy of males than females; and women's changing role in the paid work force (Luria & Meade, 1984).

The middle-aged woman probably will be seen as asexual far less often than she is today. Increased health and longer life spans should convince older people that sexuality is a life-span process, not something that ends at 40. But middle age, with its skewed sex ratio, means that more women than men will be without stable sex partners. Current data on young women indicate that the relational aspects of sex will become more salient than the genital aspects of sex.

As the base rate for early female masturbation goes up, as it has, a safe prediction is that tomorrow's divorced, widowed, or never-married middle-aged woman will enjoy solitary sex more frequently than did her older sister or mother in similar circumstances. It is unlikely to be a simple substitute for social sex. Short- or long-term sexual relationships outside of legal marriage are already increasing—a trend that probably will continue. Extramarital sex will frequently occur in the transition out of marriage and into new sexual and marital arrangements. Among

At different points in our journey through life's human cycle, we have seen the importance of considering cohort effects. One area in which cohort effects are prominent is sexual attitudes and behavior. How are cohort effects likely to be present in the next generation of middle-aged women?

middle-aged women of the recent past, an extramarital affair was predicted by marital unhappiness. This is not as true for women now beginning to push middle age; they are somewhat more likely to be seeking variety. These women will have had more premarital sexual experience than middle-aged women of the past. Their experience, sexual values, and knowledge of scripts for sexual solicitation may be higher.

How will being in the paid labor force affect the middle-aged woman's sexual life? Women who marry late, who have entered the labor force well

before marriage, and who know that they will remain in the labor force throughout marriage, probably will be more equal partners in marriage than their mothers and grandmothers. In the past, males have set the pace and rate of sexual activity more than females; perhaps in the future we will see sexual rate-setting to be more of an equal decision on the part of males and females, just as probably will be the case in the social, affectional aspects of marriage. More women of the future will probably spend part of their adult life without spouses. Divorce will be even more frequent than today. The fatigue and lack of time produced by full-time work, especially in the case of single mothers, may place even more constraints on the sex lives of postmarried women than on those of their married counterparts. For a woman with no live-in, stable sexual partner, sex requires more negotiation, time, and effort, as well as social skills and economic resouces. Some women will consider the effort worthwhile; others will join the take-it-or-leave-it group. However, exposure to the paid work world may promote social skills that are useful in the sexual marketplace when women reenter it after marriage. And the shared work world of men and women provides more women independent access to a pool of potentially available sexual and marriage partners. Above all else, the range of their sexual choices will be greater than for their mothers and grandmothers.

Physical Development in Middle Adulthood		
Concept	**Processes/Related Ideas**	**Characteristics/Description**
Physical Changes	Their Nature	A host of physical changes occur—at some point in the 40s, decline in physical development usually indicates that middle adulthood has arrived. Seeing and hearing decline, and individuals actually become shorter.
Health Status	Its Nature	Health status becomes a major concern in middle adulthood. Some deterioration in health is to be expected. The main health nemeses of middle-aged adults are: cardiovascular disease, cancer, and weight. How individuals deal with physical decline varies greatly from one individual to another. Emotional stability and personality—especially hardiness—are related to health in middle adulthood.
	Cardiovascular Disease	The heart and coronary arteries become less efficient in middle age, and cardiovascular disease is the number one cause of death. Considerable interest has focused on the role of life-style—especially the Type-A behavior pattern—in cardiovascular disease. Today, researchers are searching for the key dimensions of Type-A behavior that predict cardiovascular disease—anger is one viable candidate. Others believe the global category of Type-A behavior merits retention, especially in clinical circles.
	Illness, Cancer, and the Immune System	The field of psychoneuroimmunology is beginning to explain how psychological factors affect health. Research on cancer suggests that an unwillingness to accept the disease may affect the immune system and help it to fight cancer cells.
Sexuality	Biological Changes	Menopause is a marker that signals the cessation of childbearing capability, arriving usually in the late 40s and early 50s. The vast majority of women do not have substantial problems with menopause, although the public perception of menopause has often been negative. Estrogen replacement therapy is effective in reducing the physical pain of menopause. Men do not experience an inability to father children, although their testosterone level gradually drops off; clearly, a male menopause, like the dramatic decline in estrogen in women, does not occur.
Sexual Attitudes and Behavior	Their Nature	Sexual behavior usually occurs on a less frequent basis in middle adulthood than in early adulthood. Nonetheless, a majority of middle-aged adults show a moderate or strong interest in sex. Changing women's roles and other societal changes probably mean that future generations of middle-aged women will experience sexuality differently than their counterparts of today and the past.

Cognitive Development

We have seen that the decline in some physical characteristics during middle adulthood is not just imagined. The middle-aged adult may not see as well, run as fast, or be as healthy as in the 20s and 30s. But what about cognitive characteristics? In chapter 14, we saw that our cognitive abilities are very strong during early adulthood. Do they decline as we enter and move through middle adulthood?

The aspect of cognition that has been investigated more than any other in this regard is memory. Putting the pieces of this research together, we find that memory decline in middle adulthood is more likely to occur when long-term rather than short-term memory is involved (Craik, 1977). For example, a middle-aged man can remember a phone number he heard twenty seconds ago, but he probably won't remember it as efficiently the next day. Memory is also more likely to decline when organization and imagery are not used (Hultsch, 1971; Smith, 1977). By using memory strategies such as organizing lists of phone numbers into different categories or imagining that the phone numbers represent different objects around the house, memory in middle adulthood can be improved. Memory also tends to decline when the information to be recalled is recently acquired information or when the information is not used often (Riege & Inman, 1981). For example, a middle-aged adult may easily remember chess moves, baseball rules, or television schedules if she has used this information extensively in the past. And finally, memory tends to decline if recall rather than recognition is required (Mandler, 1980). If the middle-aged man is shown a list of phone numbers and asked to select the numbers he heard yesterday (recognition), this can be done more efficiently than recalling the number without the list. To see how the recall-recognition distinction works with remembering the names and faces of high school classmates, turn to Focus on Life-Span Development 16.3. Memory in middle adulthood will also decline if health is poor and attitudes are negative (Poon, 1985). More about the nature of cognitive change in adulthood appears in chapter 18, where we discuss general changes in intelligence, problem-solving skills, and further ideas about memory.

Developmentalists recently have shown a keen interest in the nature and extent of memory changes in middle age. How might this middle-aged man's memory be different than when he was a young adult?

Drawing by Lorenz; © 1988 The New Yorker Magazine, Inc.

"Hey, good buddy! How you doin'?"

"Can't kick, big fella. What's shakin'?"

REMEMBERING THE NAMES AND
FACES OF HIGH SCHOOL CLASSMATES

I have now been to three high school reunions. I can't think of any other circumstance I have been placed in that jogged my memory more than those reunions. You look across the room and see a face and say to yourself, "Now who is that? I know who it is but I just can't remember her name." If and when you go to a high school reunion, what factors might be at work in determining your memory of your classmates? Might there be some strategies you could call on that would improve your memory of them?

How many names and faces of your high school classmates do you remember? If you are a young adult, do you think this will become more difficult when you become middle-aged? Do you think it would depend on the way we assessed your memory—that is, whether your memory for high school classmates was evaluated by free recall or by recognition?

One investigation sought the answers to these questions (Bahrick, Bahrick, & Wittlinger, 1975). Face recognition, name recognition, and name-face matching were assessed. Free recall of names and cued recall of names in response to faces also were assessed. The individuals ranged from 3 months since high school graduation to 47 years since graduation. As indicated in figure 16.A, recognition of names and faces, and matching names with faces, remained virtually constant (and nearly perfect) up to a retention interval of 34 years. This means that adults who were over 50 years of age were performing just as well as 18-year-olds. In contrast, the recall measures—especially free recall—showed clear evidence of age-related decline. Note especially the steady drop in free recall from the three-year interval (adults about 21 years old) to the 47-year interval (adults about 65 years old). This decline could be due to forgetting, or it could be due to age-related changes in recall memory's efficiency, or both.

One of the saddest things is that the only thing a man can do for eight hours a day, day after day, is work. You can't eat eight hours a day nor drink for eight hours a day nor make love for eight hours.
William Faulkner, Writers at Work, *1958.*

Are middle-aged workers as satisfied with their jobs as young adult workers? What is the career ladder in middle adulthood like? How extensive is mid-life career change? What are some different pathways for men and women in the workplace? What is leisure at mid-life like? These are among the most important questions to answer about careers, work, and leisure in middle adulthood—we consider each of them in turn.

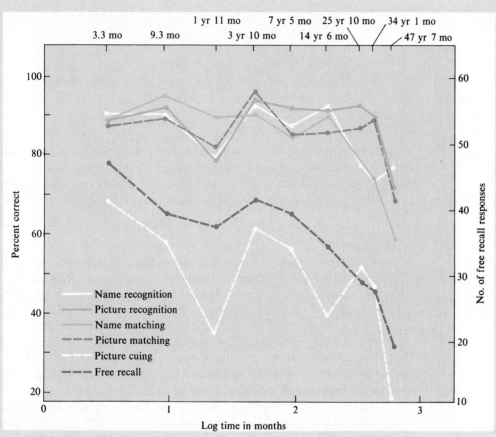

Figure 16.A *Recognition and recall of names and faces of high school colleagues. From Bahrick, Bahrick, and Wittinger, "Recognition and recall of names and faces of high school colleagues" in* Journal of Experimental Psychology, *104, 54–75, 1975. Copyright © 1975 by the American Psychological Association. Reprinted by permission of author.*

Job Satisfaction

Work satisfaction increases steadily throughout the work life—from age 20 to at least age 60, for both college-educated and noncollege-educated adults (Rhodes, 1983; Tamir, 1982) (see figure 16.1). This same pattern has been found for both women and men. Satisfaction probably increases because as we get older we get paid more, we are in higher positions, and we have more job security. There also is a greater commitment to the job as we get older—we take our jobs more seriously, have lower rates of avoidable absenteeism,

Figure 16.1
Increasing job satisfaction during the adult years.

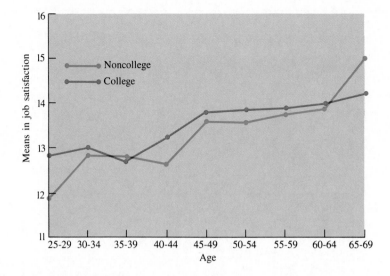

What might be the most important ingredients of job satisfaction in middle adulthood? That is, what is it about jobs in middle age that cause people to enjoy them?

and are more involved with our work in middle adulthood than in early adulthood. Younger adults are still experimenting with their work, still searching for the right occupation, so they may be inclined to seek out what is wrong with their current job rather than focusing on what is right about it (Rhodes, 1983).

Career Ladders

Many of us think of our adult work life as a series of discrete steps, much like the rungs on a ladder. In a factory, an individual might move from laborer, to foreman, to superintendent, to production manager, and so on up the ladder. In a business, an individual might move from salesperson, to sales manager, to regional sales manager, to national sales manager, to vice-president of the company, and then even possibly to president of the company, for example. Not all occupations have such clearly defined steps, but most jobs involve a hierarchy in which low-level workers and high-level workers are clearly distinguished. How can an individual move up the career ladder?

Having a college education helps a great deal; a college degree is associated with earlier career advancement and greater career advancement (Bray & Howard, 1983; Golan, 1986). And individuals who are promoted early go further up the career ladder than those who are promoted late. Most career advancement occurs early in our adult lives. By the ages of 40 to 45, most of us have gone as far as we will up the career ladder. In one investigation of a large corporation, this occurred regardless of whether the positions involved were nonmanagement, lower management, or foreman (Rosenbaum, 1984).

Mid-Life Career Change

Only about 10 percent of Americans change jobs in mid-life—as we saw earlier, job satisfaction usually increases in mid-life. But for those 10 percent who do change jobs in mid-life, what are some of the psychological reasons behind this dramatic life change? Of course, some of them get fired but others may do so because of their own motivation. The mid-life career experience has been described as a turning point in adulthood by Daniel Levinson (1978). One aspect of the mid-life period involves adjusting idealistic hope to realistic possibilities in light of how much time is left in an occupation. Middle-aged adults may focus on how much time they have left before retirement and the speed with which they are reaching their occupational goals (Pines & Aronson, 1988). If individuals perceive that they are behind schedule, or if their goals are now perceived as unrealistic, reassessment and readjustment may take place. Levinson (1978) believes this may result in a sadness over unfulfilled dreams. He found that many middle-aged men feel constrained by their bosses, their wives, and their children. Such feelings, he says, may produce rebellion, which can assume several forms—extramarital affairs, divorce, alcoholism, suicide, or career change.

Work Pathways of Men and Women

Most men begin work in early adulthood and work more or less continuously until they retire, unless they return to school or become unemployed. Unstable patterns of work are much more common among low-income workers than among middle-income workers, although a continuous pattern of work is still the norm among low-income workers.

The most common path for both working- and middle-class women is to work for awhile after finishing high school or even college; to marry and have children; then, when children are a little older, to go back to part-time work to supplement the husband's income. As the children begin to leave home, she goes back to school for some updating of earlier skills or for a retraining program so she can assume a full-time paid job in her 40s and 50s, when she is relatively free of responsibilities.

For the professional or career woman, the picture is somewhat different, since she has more invested in keeping up her professional skills. Four career patterns among professional women have been identified (Golan, 1986; Paloma, Pendelton, & Garland, 1982): 1) *regular,* the woman who pursued her professional training immediately after graduation, who began to work and continued to do so without interruption or with minimal interruption throughout the years; 2) *interrupted career,* the woman who began as in the regular pattern but interrupted her career for several years—usually for childrearing—and then went back to work full-time; 3) *second career,* the woman who started her professional training near or after the time the children left home or after a divorce; and 4) *modified second career,* the woman who started her professional training while the children were still at home but old enough not to need full-time mothering, then started to work, possibly part-time, until the last child left home or became independent when she shifted to a full-time career.

Many of the careers we adopt involve a series of discrete steps, much like the rungs on a ladder. Even if the steps are not discrete, most careers involve a hierarchy of low-level and high-level workers that can be distinguished. Think about the careers you want to follow when you complete your education. What are the career ladders like in these occupations? What factors will aid your effort to move up in the hierarchy of the careers?

Why do women go back to work during middle adulthood? What stands out is that reasons are rarely as simple as earning money, although in those families where the husband has become ill or disabled, or, for other reasons, has not been able to keep up his breadwinner role, income is undoubtedly the main motive. Many middle-aged women enter the labor force when they are confronted with the need to support themselves and their family, but boredom, loneliness, and the desire for new interests probably are involved, too. Today's 50-year-old women are taking courses in computer programming, enrolling in schools of social work and studying for a real estate salesperson's license in far greater numbers than their mothers or grandmothers did in similar circumstances. The trend toward dual career couples, so prevalent in their children's generation, is also now penetrating middle adulthood. Both positive and negative reasons may be behind a middle-aged woman entering the labor force, as exemplified in the situation discussed in Focus on Life-Span Development 16.4.

Martha, dressed in a tailored gray suit, had signed up for an adult education course, "Real Estate Sales." At the coffee break, another student in the course asked Martha why she was taking the course. Martha said that she had worked since she was an adolescent. Back in Omaha, where she was raised, her father was an alcohlic. He used to beat up her mother and sometimes he took out his frustrations on Martha and her eight brothers and sisters. She decided to get out as soon as she could. While still in high school, she worked part-time as a cashier. She went back to the restaurant to work full-time when she graduated. There she met her first husband, Bobby, a jazz drummer. Once they moved to Chicago, she immediately found a new job, this time as a waitress. She held on to it through the birth of her two sons because Bobby traveled most of the time and stopped over only when the band was in town.

Then one day she found a note saying that the band was moving east and he would not be back. She packed the kids in the car and moved to Los Angeles, where she found a job as a telephone operator, working nights. Once the boys were in school for the full day, she took a secretarial course and eventually started to work in the typing pool at an aircraft company. She moved up the secretarial ranks until she became a private secretary for a sales executive. Eventually she married her boss. They bought a nice house in Pasadena and settled down. She had to give up her job because it was against company policy for executives' wives to work for the company.

For the next thirteen years, Martha was a company wife, entertaining the right people, showing up with her husband at the right places, organizing and running the household. She worked hard to keep the kids in line and eventually they made it through college. Once the kids were gone, she and Roy socialized a lot and sometimes she would travel with him when he was on company business. Then, suddenly, three years ago, the roof fell in. The aircraft industry was experiencing a recession and her husband's company was being taken over by another company. Without warning, Roy, her husband, was fired. Martha tried to help him as much as she could. She worked up his job resume and sent out dozens of letters to other companies for him. Unfortunately, employment opportunities for a man of Roy's status and age were drying up. Besides, Roy took his firing hard and began to drink heavily. Martha would come home from shopping and find him sitting in the den with a drink in his hand instead of pursuing employment leads.

By now, Martha felt that she was a survivor, that she could take care of herself. After two more years of pampering Roy, she realized that he seemed to have lost his motivation and probably would never get a decent job again. She decided it was up to her, so she compiled a quick inventory of what she had to offer and decided that she probably would do best by going into sales herself. That was when she noticed the ad for this course and decided to enroll. What are Martha's plans? She already passed her realtor's exam and has started to sell property. She is thinking of moving away from Los Angeles, possibly up the coast to Santa Barbara. She does not have much to tie her down since she and Roy are on the verge of obtaining a divorce (Golan, 1986).

Leisure

As adults, we must not only learn how to work well, but we also need to learn how to relax and enjoy leisure. Henry Ford was known as a man who emphasized that our salvation rests in our work. Few people were aware of Ford's frequent trips to his mansion in Dearborn, Michigan, where he relaxed and participated extensively in leisure activities. Similarly, President Ronald Reagan seems to have found a better balance between work and leisure than many of us. With the kind of work ethic on which our country is based, it is not surprising to find that many adults view leisure as boring and unnecessary. But even Aristotle recognized leisure's importance in life, stressing that we should not only work well but use leisure well. He even described leisure as better because it was the end of work. How can we define leisure? **Leisure** refers to the pleasant times after work when individuals are free to pursue activities and interests of their own choosing—hobbies, sports, or reading, for example.

Ninety years ago, the average work week was 72 hours. Only in the last three to four decades has it averaged 40 hours. What do most of us do now that we have more free time than cohorts at the beginning of this century? One of the basic themes of research on leisure is the increasing reliance on television over other forms of mass media as a form of entertainment. Sports are also an integral part of the nation's leisure activities, either through direct participation or as a spectator. The diversity of sports allows many individuals to escape the rigors and pressures of everyday life, even if only for a few hours a week.

What is leisure in middle adulthood like? When Mark became 40 years old, he decided that he needed to develop some leisure activities and interests. He bought a personal computer and joined a computer club. Now Mark looks forward to coming home from work and "playing" with his "toy." At the age of 43, Barbara sent her last child off to college and told her husband that she was going to spend the next several years reading the many books she had bought but had never found time to read. Mark and Barbara chose different leisure activities, but their actions suggest that middle adulthood is a time when leisure activities assume added importance. For example, some developmentalists believe that middle adulthood is a time of questioning how time should be spent and of reassessing priorities (Gould, 1978).

Sigmund Freud once commented that the two things adults need to do well to adapt to society's demands are to work and to love. To his list of two we add "to play." In our fast-paced society, it is all too easy to get caught up in the frenzied, hectic pace of our achievement-oriented work world and ignore leisure and play. Imagine your life as a middle-aged adult. What would be the ideal mix of work and leisure? What leisure activities do you want to enjoy as a middle-aged adult?

Leisure may be an especially important aspect of middle adulthood because of the changes many individuals experience at this point in the adult life cycle. The changes include physical changes, relationship changes with spouse and children, and career changes. By middle adulthood, more money is available to many individuals, and there may be more free time and paid vacations. These mid-life changes may produce expanded opportunities for leisure. For many individuals, middle adulthood is the first time in their lives when they have the opportunity to diversify their interests.

Adults at mid-life need to begin preparing both financially and psychologically for retirement. Constructive and fulfilling leisure activities in middle adulthood are an important part of this preparation. If an adult develops leisure activities that can be continued into retirement, the transition from work to retirement may be softened.

We have discussed a number of ideas about cognitive development and about careers, work, and leisure. A summary of these ideas is presented in Concept Table 16.2.

There is only one cure for birth and death save to enjoy the interval.

George Santayana

CONCEPT TABLE

16.2

Cognitive Development and Careers, Work, and Leisure

Concept	Processes/Related Ideas	Characteristics/Description
Cognitive Development	Its Nature	Some decline in memory occurs during middle adulthood, although strategies can be used to reduce the decline. Deficits are greater in long-term than in short-term memory. Processes such as organization and imagery can be used to reduce deficits in memory. Deficits are greater when the information is recently acquired or not used often, and when recall rather than recognition is assessed. Poor health and negative attitudes are related to memory decline.
Careers, Work, and Leisure	Job Satisfaction	Work satisfaction increases steadily throughout life—from age 20 to at least age 60, for both college-educated and noncollege-educated adults.
	Career Ladders	Many of us think of our adult work life as series of discrete steps, much like the rungs of a ladder. Having a college education helps us move up the ladder. Most career advancement occurs early in our adult lives, at least by 40–45, and individuals who are promoted early go further.
	Mid-Life Career Change	Only about 10 percent of Americans change jobs in mid-life, some because they are fired, others because of their own motivation. In mid-life, we often evaluate our possibilities in terms of how much time we have left in an occupation.
	Work Pathways of Men and Women	A continuous pattern of work is more common among men than among women, although low-income men have more unstable work patterns than middle-income men. It is not unusual for women to go back to work for reasons other than money.
	Leisure	We not only need to learn to work well but we also need to learn to enjoy leisure. Mid-life may be an especially important time for leisure because of the physical changes that occur and because of preparation for an active retirement.

Summary

I. **Physical Changes**
A host of physical changes occur. At some point in the 40s, decline in physical development usually indicates that middle adulthood has arrived. Seeing and hearing decline, and individuals actually become shorter.

II. **Health Status**
Health status becomes a major concern in middle adulthood.

Some deterioration in health is to be expected. The main health nemeses of middle adulthood are: cardiovascular disease, cancer, and weight. How individuals deal with physical decline varies greatly from one individual to the next. Emotional stability and personality—especially hardiness—are related to health in middle adulthood.

III. **Cardiovascular Disease and Illness, Cancer, and the Immune System**
The heart and coronary arteries become less efficient in middle age, and cardiovascular disease is the number one cause of death. Considerable interest has focused on the role of life-style—especially the Type-A behavior pattern—in cardiovascular

disease. Today, researchers are searching for the key dimensions of Type-A behavior that predict cardiovascular disease; anger is one viable candidate. Others believe the global concept of Type-A behavior merits retention, especially in clinical circles. The field of psychoneuroimmunology is beginning to explain how psychological factors affect health. Research on cancer suggests that an unwillingness to accept the disease may affect the immune system and help it to fight cancer cells.

IV. Biological Changes in Sexuality

Menopause is a marker that signals the cessation of childbearing capability, usually arriving in the late 40s and early 50s. The vast majority of women do not have substantial problems with menopause, although the public perception of menopause has often been negative. Estrogen replacement therapy is effective in reducing the physical pain of menopause. Men do not experience an inability to father children, although their testosterone level gradually drops off; clearly, a male menopause, like the dramatic decline in women's estrogen, does not occur.

V. Sexual Attitudes and Behavior

Sexual behavior usually occurs on a less frequent basis in middle adulthood than in early adulthood. Nonetheless, a majority of middle-aged adults show a moderate or strong interest in sex. Changing women's roles and other societal changes probably mean future generations of middle-aged women will experience sexuality differently than their counterparts of today and the past.

VI. Cognitive Development

Some decline in memory occurs during middle adulthood, although strategies such as organization and imagery can be used to reduce the decline. Deficits are greater in long-term than in short-term memory, when information is recently acquired or not used often, when recall rather than recognition is assessed, and when health is poor and attitudes are negative.

VII. Job Satisfaction and Career Ladders

Work satisfaction increases steadily throughout life—from age 20 to at least age 60, for both college-educated and noncollege-educated adults. Many of us think of our adult work life as a series of discrete steps, much like the rungs of a ladder. Having a college education helps us move up the ladder. Most career advancement occurs early in our adult lives, at least by 40–45, and individuals who are promoted early go further.

VIII. Mid-Life Career Change and Work Pathways of Men and Women

Only about 10 percent of Americans change jobs in mid-life, some because they are fired, others because of self-motivation. In mid-life, we often evaluate our possibilities in terms of how much time we have left in an occupation. A continuous pattern of work is more common among men than among women, although low-income men have more unstable work patterns than middle-income men. It is not unusual for women to go back to work for reasons other than money.

IX. Leisure

We not only need to learn how to work well but we also need to learn how to enjoy leisure. Mid-life may be an especially important time for leisure because of the physical changes that occur and because of preparation for an active retirement.

Key Terms

Suggested Readings

Baruch, G., & Brooks-Gunn, J. (Eds.) (1985). *Women in midlife.* New York: Plenum
An authoritative, up-to-date overview of many aspects of women's development in middle adulthood. Includes chapters on sexuality, health care, and reproductive issues, including menopause.

Carroll, C., & Miller, D. (1986). *Health: The Science of Human Adaptation.* Dubuque, IA: Wm. C. Brown.
A college-level introduction to health. Includes valuable information on health in middle adulthood.

Golan, N. (1986). *The perilous bridge.* New York: The Free Press.
An easy-to-read book on helping individuals through mid-life transitions. Includes a number of case studies.

Okun, B. F. (1984). *Working with adults: Individual, family, and career development.* Monterey, CA: Brooks/Cole.
Includes valuable information on counseling individuals about career decisions at mid-life.

Tamir, L. M. (1982). *Men in their forties.* New York: Springer.
An excellent research report on the mid-life concerns of men, including valuable information about their work orientation.

17

■

Social and Personality Development

The generations of living
things pass in a short
time, and like runners hand
on the torch of life. ■

Lucretius

Forty-five-year-old Sarah feels tired, depressed, and angry. She became pregnant when she was 17 and married Ben. They stayed together for three years and then he left her for another woman. Sarah went to work as a sales clerk to help make ends meet. She remarried eight years later to Alan who had two children of his own from a previous marriage. Sarah stopped working for several years, but then Alan started going out on her. She found out about it from a friend. Sarah stayed with Alan for another year, but finally he was gone so much that she could not take it anymore and she decided to divorce him. Sarah went back to work again as a sales clerk; she has been in the same position for 16 years now. During those 16 years, she has dated a number of men but the relationships never seem to work out. Her son never finished high school and has drug problems. Her father just died last year and Sarah is trying to help her mother financially, although she can barely pay her own bills. Sarah looks in the mirror and does not like what she sees—she sees her past as a shambles and the future does not look rosy, either.

Forty-five-year-old Wanda feels energetic, happy, and satisfied. She graduated from college and worked for three years as a high school math teacher. She married Andy, who had just finished law school. One year later, they had their first child, Josh. Wanda stayed home with Josh for two years, then returned to her job as a math teacher. Even during her pregnancy, Wanda stayed active and exercised regularly, playing tennis almost every day. After her pregnancy, she kept up her exercise habits. Wanda and Andy had another child, Wendy, and now as they move into their middle-aged years, Josh and Wendy are both off to college, and Wanda and Andy are enjoying spending more time with each other. Last weekend they visited Josh at his college and the weekend before they visited Wendy at her college. Wanda continued working as a high school math teacher until six years ago. She had developed considerable computer skills as part of her job and taken some computer courses at a nearby college, doubling up during the summer months. She resigned her math teaching job and took a job with a computer company, where she has already worked her way into management. Wanda looks in the mirror and likes what she sees—she sees her past as enjoyable, although not without hills and valleys, and she looks to the future with zest and enthusiasm.

The life paths of Sarah and Wanda have been very different. They represent the individual variation, the divergence of what mid-life is like. For some, mid-life is the worst time period of life; for others, it is the best. In this chapter we explore some of the common themes of mid-life—the nature of relationships, the chances that we will experience a mid-life crisis or not, the personality characteristics that take on greater meaning in mid-life, and the degree we change or stay the same as we go through the years of middle adulthood.

"Thus ends another evening of dancing on the edge of the volcano."
Drawing by Lorenz; © 1987 The New Yorker Magazine, Inc.

Relationships

Attachment and love are important to our well-being throughout our lives. What are marital relationships like in middle adulthood? Do our friendships change? What is the nature of sibling relationships in middle adulthood? How do intergenerational relationships contribute to our development? These are among the important questions about relationships in middle adulthood that we address.

Love and Marriage at Mid-Life

Remember from chapter 15 that two major forms of love are romantic love and affectionate love. The fires of romantic love are strong in early adulthood. Affectionate or companionate love increases during middle adulthood. That is, physical attraction, romance, and passion are more important in new relationships, especially in early adulthood, whereas security, loyalty, and mutual emotional interest become more important as relationships mature, especially in middle adulthood. Some developmentalists believe mutuality plays a key role in maturity of relationships, occurring when partners share knowledge with each other, assume responsibility for each other's satisfaction, and share private information that governs their relationship (Berscheid, 1985; Levinger, 1974). For example, as indicated in figure 17.1, we begin a relationship with someone at a zero point of contact and then gradually move from a surface relationship into more intense, mutual interaction, sharing ourselves more and more with the other individual as the relationship deepens. At the final stage, a major intersection, we probably are experiencing affectionate or companionate love.

To explore the nature of age and sex differences in satisfying love relationships, in one investigation 102 happily married couples in early adulthood (average age 28), middle adulthood (average age 45), and late adulthood

Figure 17.1
The development of relationships.

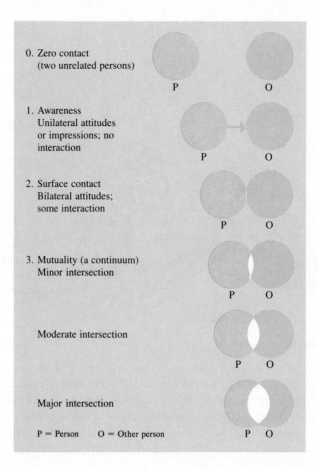

(average age 65) were interviewed (Reedy, Birren, & Schaie, 1981). As indicated in figure 17.2, passion and sexual intimacy were more important in early adulthood, and tender feelings of affection and loyalty were more important in later-life love relationships. Young adult lovers also rated communication as more characteristic of their love than their older counterparts. Aside from the age differences, however, there were some striking similarities in the nature of satisfying love relationships. At all ages, emotional security was ranked as the most important factor in love, followed by respect, communication, help and play behaviors, sexual intimacy, and loyalty. Clearly, there is more to satisfying love relationships than sex. The findings in this research also suggested that women believe emotional security is more important in love than men do.

Even some marriages that were difficult and rocky during early adulthood turn out to be better adjusted during middle adulthood. Although the partners may have lived through a great deal of turmoil, they eventually discover a deep and solid foundation on which to anchor their relationship. In middle adulthood, the partners may have fewer financial worries, less housework and chores, and more time with each other. Partners who engage in mutual activities usually view their marriage as more positive at this time.

An important event in a family is the launching of a child into adult life, to a career or family independent of the family of origin. Parents face new adjustments as disequilibrium is created by the child's absence (Bassoff, 1988). In the 1950s and 1960s, social scientists believed that as more time was spent in the post-childrearing years, marital satisfaction would go down. This was called the **empty nest syndrome.** This view assumes that parents experience a

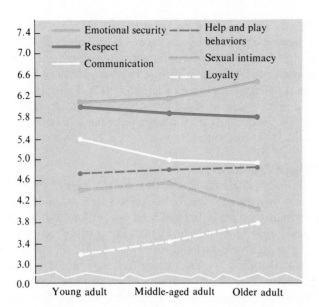

great deal of satisfaction from their children and that, when they leave home, marital satisfaction drops because a sense of emptiness is felt. While this may hold true for some parents who live vicariously through their children, the empty nest usually does not lower marital satisfaction. Instead, just the opposite often happens—marital satisfaction increases in the post-childrearing years (Glenn, 1975; Sherman, 1987). Now with their children gone, marital partners have more time to pursue career interests and more time for each other.

As marital partners grow older, many of their earlier incompatibilities brought about by differences in religion, race, social class, levels of education, family backgrounds, and personality patterns have either been worked out and adjusted to or have contributed to the breakup of the marriage (Golan, 1986). Divorce in middle adulthood may be more positive in some ways, more negative in others, than divorce in early adulthood. For mature individuals, the perils of divorce may be fewer and less intense than for younger individuals. They have more resources, and they can use this time as an opportunity to simplify their lives by disposing of possessions, such as a large home, which they no longer need. Their children are adults and may be able to cope with their parents' divorce more effectively. Each partner may have attained a better understanding of himself or herself and may be searching for changes that could include the end to a poor marriage.

In contrast, the emotional and time commitment to marriage that has existed for so many years may not be lightly given up. Many mid-life individuals perceive this as failing in the best years of their lives. The divorcer may see the situation as an escape from an untenable relationship; the divorced partner, however, usually sees it as betrayal, the ending of a relationship that had been built up over many years and that involved a great deal of commitment and trust.

Friendships and Sibling Relationships

Friendships continue to be important in middle adulthood just as they are in early adulthood. It takes time to develop intimate friendships, so it seems likely that friendships that have endured over the adult years will be deeper than those that have just been formed in early adulthood.

I remember vividly the day two years ago we returned to our house after taking our youngest daughter to college. The silence was deafening. The house was quieter after our first daughter left for college four years ago, but this time the quiet was even more noticeable. Even two decades ago it was believed that marital satisfaction decreased when children left home to attend college or pursue an occupation. In today's world, the evidence indicates the opposite—an upswing in marital satisfaction as the nest empties. Why do you think this cohort effect has taken place?

Sibling relationships also persist over the entire life cycle for most adults. Eighty-five percent of today's adults have at least one living sibling. Sibling relationships in adulthood may be extremely close, apathetic, or highly rivalrous. The majority of sibling relationships in adulthood have been found to be close in several investigations (e.g., Cicirelli, 1982; Scott, 1983). Those siblings who are psychologically close to each other in adulthood tended to be that way in childhood; it is rare for sibling closeness to develop for the first time in adulthood (Dunn, 1984).

Intergenerational Relationships

In Samuel Butler's (1902) novel, *The Way of All Flesh,* Theobold Pontifex had been raised by a harsh father but believed that he would be more lenient toward his own son than his father had been toward him. But he also believed, as had his father, that he must be on guard against being too indulgent. Theobold was not able to break the mold cast by his father. In one incident in the novel, Theobold thrashed his son, Ernest, for mispronouncing a word. With each new generation, personality characteristics, attitudes, and values are replicated or changed. As older family members die, their emotional, intellectual, personal, and genetic legacies are carried on in the next generation. Their children become the oldest generation and their grandchildren the second generation (Datan, Greene, & Reese, 1986).

For the most part, family members maintain considerable contact across generations. As we continue to maintain contact with our parents and our children as we age, both similarity and dissimilarity across generations is found. For example, parent-child similarity is most noticeable in religious and political areas, least in gender roles, life-style, and work orientation. An example of how relationships are transmitted across generations appears in the California Longitudinal Study (Elder, Caspi, & Downey, 1986). Children whose parents had a high degree of marital conflict and who were unaffectionate subsequently had tension in their own marriages and were ineffective in disciplining their own children (now the third generation).

Sex differences also characterize intergenerational relationships. Daughters have more involved relationships, especially with their mothers, in the adult years, than sons do (Troll & Bengston, 1982). And same-sex ties are stronger overall than opposite-sex ties—in an investigation of three generations in Chicago, same-sex ties were stronger across generations than opposite-sex ties (Wilen, 1979).

Middle-aged individuals play an important role in intergenerational relationships. Often individuals are parents to adolescent offspring while their own parents are about to enter late adulthood. While individuals in middle adulthood may be guiding and financially supporting their adolescent children, they may have to deal with parents who no longer have a secure base in times of emotional difficulties or financial problems. Instead, the older parents may need affection and financial support from their middle-aged children (Lowy, 1981). These simultaneous pressures from adolescents and aging parents may contribute to stress in middle adulthood.

At this point we have discussed a number of ideas about relationships in middle adulthood. A summary of these ideas is presented in Concept Table 17.1. Now we turn our attention to theories of personality that address the nature of personality in mid-life.

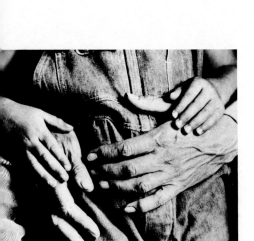

There is generally continuing contact across generations within families. Greater continuity takes place in some areas more than in others. The middle-aged generation plays a special role in linking generations.

In case you're worried about what's going to become of the younger generation, it's going to grow up and start worrying about the younger generation.

Roger Allen

Are we likely to see more or less contact across generations in future decades? Explain your answer.

Middle Adulthood

Relationships		
Concept	**Processes/Related Ideas**	**Characteristics/Description**
Love and Marriage	Love	Affectionate or companionate love increases in middle adulthood, especially in marriages that have endured for many years.
	Empty Nest	Marital satisfaction usually increases in the post-childrearing years, that is when children leave home to go to college or to work.
	Divorce	Divorce in middle adulthood may be more positive or more negative than divorce in early adulthood.
Friendships and Sibling Relationships	Their Nature	Friendships continue to be important in middle adulthood; longstanding friendships are more intimate. Sibling relationships continue throughout life; many are close in adulthood, if they were close in childhood, although some are apathetic or highly conflicted.
Intergenerational Relationships	Contact	There generally is continuing contact across generations in families. Greater continuity occurs in political and religious attitudes, lesser continuity occurs in gender roles, life-style and work orientation. Females are closer across generations than males.
	Middle Age	The middle-aged generation plays a special role in linking generations. However, financial and caregiving obligations to youth and to aging parents may create stress for middle-aged adults.

Personality Theories and Middle Age

How should we conceptualize personality in middle age? Is mid-life a stage that is beset with crisis? How important are life events, like divorce and death, in understanding personality at mid-life? To what extent do social and historical circumstances modify how personality develops in middle adulthood? How much individual variation characterizes middle adulthood?

The Adult Stage Theories

Adult stage theories have been plentiful and they have contributed to the view that mid-life is a crisis in development. Three prominent adult stage theories are Erik Erikson's life-cycle view, Roger Gould's transformations, and Daniel Levinson's seasons of a man's life. George Vaillant's view represents an important expansion of Erikson's theory. We consider each of these perspectives in turn.

Erikson's Stage of Generativity Versus Stagnation

In middle adulthood, Erikson believes that individuals need to assist the younger generation in developing and leading useful lives. Generativity versus stagnation is the seventh stage in Erikson's eight stage view of the human life cycle, corresponding roughly with the middle adulthood years. The successful

TABLE 17.1
Gould's transformations in adult development

Stage	Approximate age	Development(s)
1	16 to 18	Desire to escape parental control.
2	18 to 22	Leaving the family: peer group orientation.
3	22 to 28	Developing independence: commitment to a career and to children.
4	29 to 34	Questioning self: role confusion; marriage and career vulnerable to dissatisfaction.
5	35 to 43	Period of urgency to attain life's goals: awareness of time limitation. Realignment of life's goals.
6	43 to 53	Settling down: acceptance of one's life.
7	53 to 60	More tolerance: acceptance of past; less negativisim; general mellowing.

From Roger L. Gould, M.D., Transformations. Copyright © 1978 Roger Gould, M.D. Reprinted by permission of Simon & Schuster, Inc.

rearing of children is especially important in developing generativity. Childless adults need to find substitute young children through adoption, guardianship, a close relationship with children of relatives, or a positive relationship with children through teaching or community work. The positive side of this stage—generativity—suggests a feeling of being able to positively shape the next generation. By contrast, stagnation (sometimes called self-absorption), or the feeling of having done nothing for the next generation, is the unhealthy outcome.

Research conducted by Carol Ryff (1987), who has directly compared the views of men and women from different age groups, has found that, indeed, generativity is a major concern of middle-aged adults. She concluded that individuals who have achieved generativity see themselves as leaders and decision makers who are interested in helping and guiding younger people.

Gould's Transformations
Psychiatrist Roger Gould (1975, 1978, 1980) links stage and crisis in his view of developmental transformations. He emphasizes that mid-life is every bit as turbulent as adolescence, with the exception that during middle adulthood striving to handle crisis probably will produce a happier, healthier life. Gould studied 524 men and women, whom he described as going through seven stages of adult life (see table 17.1). He believes that in our twenties we assume new roles; in our 30s we begin to feel stuck with our responsibilities; and in our 40s we begin to feel a sense of urgency that our lives are speeding by. Handling the mid-life crisis and realizing that a sense of urgency is a natural reaction to this stage helps to keep us on the path of adult maturity, Gould says. His study has been criticized—it probably contains middle-class bias, no reliability of clinical judgments was conducted, and no statistical analysis was performed.

[handwritten in left margin: Integrity VS Despair / Life's review / good result → feeling / of gaining the virtue / of wisdom]

Whoever, in middle age, attempts to realize the wishes and hopes of his early youth, invariably deceives himself.
Goethe, Elective Affinities, *1809*

Figure 17.3
Levinson's seasons of a man's life.

Late adulthood

65

Late adult transition

60

Culmination of
middle
adulthood

55

Age fifty
transition

50

Entering
middle
adulthood

Middle
adulthood

45

Mid-life transition

40

Settling down

33

Age thirty
transition

28

Entering the
adult world

Early
adulthood

22

Early adult transition

17

Childhood and
adolescence

Levinson's Seasons of a Man's Life

In *Seasons of a Man's Life,* clinical psychologist Daniel Levinson (1978, 1980) and his colleagues at Yale University reported the results of their extensive interviews with forty middle-aged men. His interviews were conducted with hourly workers, business executives, academic biologists, and novelists. He bolstered his conclusions with information from the biographies of famous men and the development of memorable characters in literature. Although Levinson's major interest focused on mid-life change, he described a number of stages and transitions in the life cycle, ranging in age from 17 to 65 years of age—these are shown in figure 17.3.

Like Robert Havighurst (1952), Levinson emphasizes that developmental tasks must be mastered at each of these stages. In early adulthood, the two major tasks to be mastered are exploring the possibilities for adult living and developing a stable life structure. Levinson sees the 20s as a *novice*

Daniel Levinson believes we live our lives in seasons. In the 20s, the season is a novice phase of development, a time of transition from dependence to independence. The transition of the 20s is marked by a dream of the type of life the individual wants to have. If you are in this period of life's human cycle now, how accurately does Levinson's description fit your life? If you are older, look back to your 20s—did your life fit Levinson's scheme?

Middle age is such a foggy place.
                    Roger Rosenblatt, 1987

Levinson argues that his adult stages are basically the same for women as for men. Can you think of some types of women for whom the stages might not be as workable?

phase of adult development. At the end of one's teens, a transition from dependence to independence should occur. This transition is marked by the formation of a dream—an image of the kind of life the youth wants to have, especially in terms of a career and marriage. The novice phase is a time of reasonably free experimentation and of testing the dream in the real world.

From about the ages of 28 to 33, the individual goes through a transition period in which he must face the more serious question of determining his goals. During the thirties, the individual usually focuses on family and career development. In the later years of this period, the individual enters a phase of Becoming One's Own Man (or BOOM, as Levinson calls it). By age 40, the individual has reached a stable location in his career, has outgrown his earlier, more tenuous attempts at learning to become an adult, and now must look forward to the kind of life he will lead as a middle-aged adult.

According to Levinson, the change to middle adulthood lasts about five years and requires the adult to come to grips with four major conflicts that have existed in his life since adolescence: 1) being young versus being old (more about this polarity in mid-life is presented in Focus on Life-Span Development 17.1); 2) being destructive versus being constructive; 3) being masculine versus being feminine; and 4) being attached to others versus being separated from them. Seventy to eighty percent of the men Levinson interviewed found the mid-life transition (ages 40 to 45) tumultuous and psychologically painful, as many aspects of their lives came into question. According to Levinson, the success of the mid-life transition rests on how effectively the individual reduces the polarities and accepts each of them as an integral part of his being.

Because Levinson interviewed middle-aged males, we can consider the data about middle adulthood more valid than the data about early adulthood. When individuals are asked to remember information about earlier parts of their lives, they may distort and forget things. The original Levinson data included no females, although recently Levinson (1987) reported that his stages, transitions, and the crisis of middle age hold for females as well as males. Like Gould's report, Levinson's work included no statistical analysis. However, the quality and quantity of the Levinson biographies are outstanding in the clinical tradition.

Vaillant's Expansion of Erikson's Stages

George Vaillant (1977) believes that two additional stages should be added to Erikson's adult stages. The stage of **career consolidation** occurs from approximately 23 to 35 years of age. The stage of **keeping the meaning versus rigidity** occurs from 45 to 55 years of age. This is a time of relaxation for many adults, who have met goals, or, if they have not, accept the fact. At this time, adults show concern about extracting some meaning from their lives and fight against falling into a rigid orientation.

THE SENSE OF MORTALITY
AND THE WISH FOR IMMORTALITY

For Daniel Levinson (1978), in the mid-life transition the young versus the old polarity is experienced with a special force. As early adulthood comes to a close, the individual is faced with new fears of the loss of youth. He feels that the young—represented by the child, the adolescent, and the young adult—is dying. The image of old age hangs over him like a pall.

The individual's physical decline is normally very moderate and allows for competent functioning. But the physical decline may be experienced catastrophically. He fears that he will soon lose all the youthful qualities that made life worthwhile. Reminders of mortality occur in more frequent illness, death, and loss of others. In the late 30s and early 40s, the probability of such losses go up considerably. There are more heart attacks, more depressions, alcoholism, job failures, troubles with children or parents, stress of all kinds, says Levinson.

Why should the recognition of mortality be so painful? Levinson believes the answer lies in our wish for immortality. At mid-life, the growing recognition of mortality collides with the powerful wish for immortality. Beyond the concern with personal survival, there is a concern with meaning. It is not unusual for the 40-year-old to feel that his life has been wasted, that it just has not had any meaning. Levinson describes

Daniel J. Levinson, Yale psychologist, believes that the mid-life transition involves a confrontation with feeling young versus feeling old. New fears of losing one's youth spring forth. The young—represented by the child, the adolescent, and the young adult—is dying. The image of old age occupies the middle-age adult's mind. Is the middle-age adult's preoccupation with the young-old polarity as pervasive as Levinson argues? Is there more individual variation than his view suggests?

billionaire Howard Hughes as a dramatic example of decline in mid-life. He converted a small fortune into a fantastic empire. But in the end, with all his power, he died of starvation, disease, and emotional isolation. He could invest his money for great profit, but he could not invest his self in successful

interpersonal relations or obtain any psychological benefits from it. He finally suffocated within the cocoon he had built around himself.

During and after the mid-life transition, the individual tries to transform the young-old polarity and create a middle-aged self, wiser and more mature than before yet still connected to the youthful sources of energy, imagination, and daring. He comes to grasp more clearly the flow of generations and the continuity of the human species. His personal immortality, whatever its form, lies within the larger human continuity. He feels more responsible for the generations that will follow his own. Acquiring a greater individuality, a firmer sense of who he is and what matters most to him, he also understands more deeply that he is merely a speck of sand in the vast history of humankind. Slowly the omnipotent young hero recedes; in his place emerges a middle-aged man with more knowledge of his limitations as well as a greater real power and authority.

In a poem written when he was about 50, the American poet Theodore Roethke portrays his own experience of mortality:

. . . he dares to live
Who stops being a bird, yet beats
his wings
Against the immense immeasurable
emptiness of things.

Figure 17.4
*A comparison of the stage theories of
Levinson, Gould, and Erikson-Vaillant.*

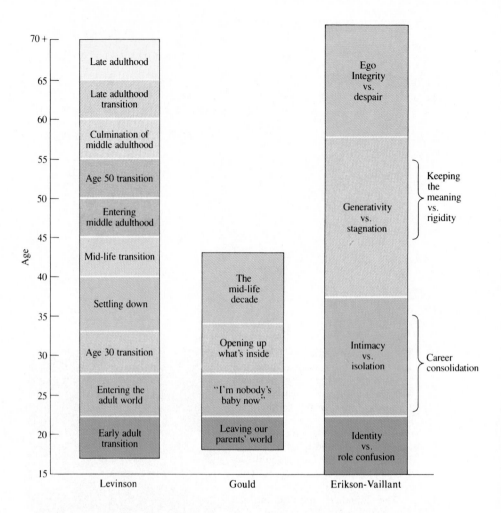

Conclusions about the Adult Stage Theories

When Vaillant's stages are added to Erikson's stages there is at least reasonable agreement among Gould, Levinson, and Vaillant about adult stages. All
would concur with a general outline of adult development that begins with the
change from identity to intimacy, then from career consolidation to generativity, and finally from searching for meaning to some final integration. Thus,
although the labels are different, the underlying themes of these adult developmental stage theories are remarkably similar (see figure 17.4).

The adult developmental perspectives of Erikson, Gould, Levinson, and
Vaillant emphasize the importance of developmental stages in the life cycle.
Though information about stages can be helpful in pinpointing dominant
themes that characterize many individuals at particular points in development, there are several important ideas to keep in mind when considering these
perspectives as viable models of adult development. First, the research on which
they are based has not been very scientific. Second, there has been a tendency
to focus on the stages as crises in development, especially the mid-life crisis.
Third, there is an alternative perspective that emphasizes the importance of
life events rather than stages in development. Fourth, there often is considerable individual variation in the way people experience the stages. In Focus
on Life-Span Development 17.2, further critical evaluation of the popular stage-
crisis theories suggests why some scientists are skeptical about their claims.

You come to a place in your life when
what you've been is going to form what
you will be. If you've wasted what you
have in you, it's too late to do much about
it. If you've invested yourself in life,
you're pretty certain to get a return. If
you are inwardly a serious person, in the
middle years it will pay off.

Lillian Hellman

How culture bound do you think the stage
perspectives of Erikson, Gould, Levinson,
and Vaillant are? Are there some
primitive island cultures and possibly
some non-Western societies to which the
stages would not apply?

WHY GAIL SHEEHY'S *PASSAGES*
IS NOT ACCEPTED BY SCIENTISTS

In 1976, Gail Sheehy's book, *Passages,* was so popular that it topped the *New York Times* best-seller list for 27 weeks. Sheehy's goal in *Passages* was to describe adult development. She cited discussions about Daniel Levinson and Roger Gould and information from interviews with 115 men and women as her main sources.

Sheehy argues that we all go through developmental stages roughly bound by chronological age. Each stage contains problems we must solve before we can progress to the next stage. The periods between the stages are called *passages.* Sheehy uses catch phrases to describe each stage: the "trying twenties," "catch-thirty," the "deadline decade" (between thirty-five and forty-five), and the "age forty crucible." Sheehy's advice never wavers: adults in transition may feel miserable, but those who face up to agonizing self-evaluation, who appraise their weaknesses as well as their strengths, who set goals for the future, and who try to be as independent as possible will be

Gail Sheehy's book, Passages, *was a dramatic success. Why did developmentalists show much less appreciation of Sheehy's book than the public?*

happier than those who do not fully experience these trials.

Sheehy believes these passages earn us an *authentic identity.* This identity is not based on the authority of one's parents or on cultural prescriptions. Intead, it is constructed through one's own strenuous efforts. Sheehy says that adults who allow themselves to fully experience life's issues and examine their lives are the individuals who find their identity and thrive.

Unfortunately, Sheehy does not disclose such elementary information as the sex and racial composition of her sample of 115 adults, how the sample was selected, what questions were asked in the interviews and by whom, and the length of the interviews. The data may be biased toward individuals experiencing a great deal of stress because a disproportionate number of divorced adults were in the sample. The author described the cases only to buttress a point about adult development; no mention was made of how representative the cases were. In addition, Sheehy conducted no statistical analyses.

The popular conception of adolescence has been one of storm and stress. So it also has become with midlife. The popular press has promoted a conception of middle age as a turbulent time filled with upheaval and stress. Recently, the sexual indiscretions of such well-known evangelists like Jim Bakker and Jimmy Swaggart have only fueled this popular conception. But few amongst us middle-aged adults drive off into the sunset in a 911 Porsche with a 25-year-old striptease dancer draped over our body. As with adolescent turmoil, midlife crises are much rarer than the popular press's stories would lead us to believe.

"Goodbye, Alice. I've got to get this California thing out of my system."
Drawing by Leo Cullum; © 1984 The New Yorker Magazine, Inc.

Crisis and Cohort

Daniel Levinson (1978, 1987) views mid-life as a crisis, believing that the middle-aged adult is suspended between the past and the future, trying to cope with this gap that threatens life's continuity. George Vaillant (1977) concludes that just as adolescence is a time for detecting parental flaws and discovering the truth about childhood, the 40s is a decade of reassessing and recording the truth about the adolescent and adulthood years. However, while Levinson sees mid-life as a crisis, Vaillant believes that only a minority of adults experience a mid-life crisis:

> Just as pop psychologists have reveled in the not-so-common high drama of adolescent turmoil, just so the popular press, sensing good copy, had made all too much of the mid-life crisis. The term *mid-life crisis* brings to mind some variation of the renegade minister who leaves behind four children and the congregation that loved him in order to drive off in a magenta Porsche with a twenty-five-year-old striptease artiste. . . .As with adolescent turmoil, mid-life crises are much rarer in community samples (pp. 222–23).

Vaillant's study—called the Grant Study—involved a follow-up of Harvard University men in their early 30s and in their late 40s, who initially had been interviewed as undergraduates. In Vaillant's words, "The high drama in Gail Sheehy's best-selling *Passages* was rarely observed in the lives of the Grant Study men," p. 223.

Some developmentalists believe that changing times and different social expectations influence how different cohorts—remember that these are groups of individuals born in the same year or time period—move through the life cycle. Bernice Neugarten (1964) has been emphasizing the power of age-group or cohort since the 1960s. Our values, attitudes, expectations, and behaviors are influenced by the period in which we live. For example, individuals born during the difficult times of the Depression may have a different outlook on life than those born during the optimistic 1950s, says Neugarten.

Neugarten (1986) believes that the social environment of a particular age group can alter its social clock—the timetable according to which individuals are expected to accomplish life's tasks, such as getting married, having

children, or establishing themselves in a career. Social clocks provide guides for our lives; individuals whose lives are not synchronized with these social clocks find life to be more stressful than those who are on schedule, says Neugarten.

Neugarten first began examining adults' social clocks for significant life events in the late 1950s. In the late 1970s, she examined their social clocks once again. As shown in table 17.2, there has been a dramatic decline in middle-class, middle-aged individuals' conceptions about the right age for major life events and achievements.

Trying to tease out universal truths and patterns about adult development from one birth cohort is complicated because the findings may not apply to another birth cohort. Most of the individuals studied by Levinson, Gould,

TABLE 17.2

Middle-Class, Middle-Aged Individuals' Conceptions of the Right Age for Major Life Events and Achievements: Late 1950s and Late 1970s

Activity/Event	Appropriate Age Range	Late '50s Study % Who Agree		Late '70s Study % Who Agree	
		Men	Women	Men	Women
Best age for a man to marry	20–25	80%	90%	42%	42%
Best age for a woman to marry	19–24	85	90	44	36
When most people should become grandparents	45–50	84	79	64	57
Best age for most people to finish school and go to work	20–22	86	82	36	38
When most men should be settled on a career	24–26	74	64	24	26
When most men hold their top jobs	45–50	71	58	38	31
When most people should be ready to retire	60–65	83	86	66	41
When a man has the most responsibilities	35–50	79	75	49	50
When a man accomplishes most	40–50	82	71	46	41
The prime of life for a man	35–50	86	80	59	66
When a woman has the most responsibilities	25–40	93	91	59	53
When a woman accomplishes most	30–45	94	92	57	48

From P. M. Passuth, D. R. Maines, and B. L. Neugarten, 1984. "Age Norms and Age Constraints Twenty Years Later" Paper presented at the annual meeting of the Midwest Sociological Society, Chicago. Reprinted by permission.

and Vaillant, for example, were born before and during the Depression. What was true for these individuals may not be true for today's 40-year-olds, born in the optimistic aftermath of World War II, or the post baby-boom generation just approaching adulthood. The profile of mid-life men in Levinson's, Gould's, and Vaillant's studies may have been burned out at a premature age rather than reflecting a normal developmental pattern that all men go through so early in life (Rossi, in press).

The Life-Events Approach

An alternative to the stage approach to adult development is the life-events approach. In the early version of the life-events approach, life events were viewed as taxing circumstances for individuals, forcing them to change their personality (Holmes & Rahe, 1967). Such events as the death of a spouse, divorce, marriage, and so on were believed to involve varying degrees of stress, and therefore, likely to influence the individual's development.

Today's **life-events approach** is more sophisticated (Brim & Ryff, 1980; Hultsch & Plemons, 1979), emphasizing the factors that mediate the influence of life events on adult development—physical health, intelligence, personality, family supports, and income, for example. We also need to know how the individual appraises the life event's threat and how she copes with stress involved. One individual may perceive a life event as highly stressful, another individual may perceive the same life event as a challenge. We need to consider the life stage of the individual and the sociocultural circumstances that are present. For example, divorce may be more stressful after many years of marriage when individuals are in their 50s than when they have only been married several years and are in their 20s (Chiriboga, 1982). Individuals may be able to cope more effectively with divorce in 1990 than in 1950 because divorce has become more commonplace and accepted in today's society. Figure 17.5 portrays how these factors could produce change in adult development.

Though the life-events approach is a valuable situation to understanding adult development, like other approaches to adult development, it has its drawbacks (Dohrenwend & Dohrenwend, 1978; Lazarus & DeLongis, 1983; Maddi, 1986). One of the most significant drawbacks is that the life-events approach places too much emphasis on change, not adequately recognizing the stability that, at least to some degree, characterizes adult development. Another drawback is that it may not be life's major events that are the primary sources of stress, but our daily experiences. Enduring a boring but tense job or marriage and living in poverty do not show up on scales of major life events. Yet the everyday pounding we take from these living conditions can add up to a highly stressful life and eventually illness. Some psychologists (e.g., Lazarus & Folkman, 1984) believe we can gain greater insight into the source of life's stresses by focusing more on daily hassles and daily uplifts. To learn more about daily hassles and daily uplifts, especially those most common among college students and middle-aged adults, turn to Focus on Life-Span Development 17.3. Critics of the daily hassles approach argue that some of the same problems involved with life events scales occur when assessing daily

What is the right age to experience major life events and achievements? Be sure to consider cohort effects in answering this question.

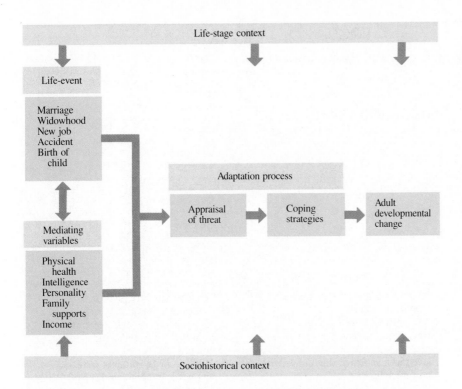

Figure 17.5
A life-events framework for understanding adult developmental change.

hassles (Dohrenwend & Shrout, 1985). For example, knowing about an individual's daily hassles tells us nothing about physical changes, how the individual copes with hassles, and how individuals perceive hassles.

Individual Variation

One way to look at personality development is to focus on similarities; another way is to focus on differences. The stage theories of Erikson, Gould, Levinson, and Vaillant all attempt to describe the universals—not the individual variation—in adult development. In an extensive investigation of a random sample of 500 men at mid-life, Michael Farrell and Stanley Rosenberg (1981) concluded that extensive individual variation characterized the men. They emphasize the individual as an active agent who interprets, shapes, alters, and gives meaning to his life.

The ability to set aside unproductive worries and preoccupations is believed to be an important factor in functioning under stress. In Vaillant's (1977) Grant Study, pervasive personal preoccupations were maladaptive in both the work and marriage of college students over a thirty-year-period after leaving college. Some individuals in the Grant Study had personal preoccupations, others did not. While collectively we are geese, each of us, individually, walks with the tread of a fox. In the words of Simon Weil, "Every person cries out to be read differently."

At this point we have discussed a number of ideas about personality theories and middle age. A summary of these ideas is presented in Concept Table 17.2. Now we turn to information about longitudinal studies of personality development in middle adulthood.

If a man does not keep pace with his companions, perhaps it is because he hears a different drummer. Let him step to the music he hears, however measured or far away.

Henry David Thoreau, 1854

FOCUS

■

DAILY HASSLES AND UPLIFTS

These thoughts reflect the belief that daily hassles might be better predictors of stress in our lives than major life events. Support for this view comes from a study of 210 police officers in Florida (Spielberger & Grier, 1983). The day-to-day friction associated with an inefficient judicial system and distorted press accounts of police work were far more stressful than responding to a felony in progress or making arrests.

It's not the large things that send a man to the madhouse . . . no, it's the continuing series of small tragedies that send a man to the madhouse . . . not the death of his love but a shoelace that snaps with no time left.

—Charles Bukowski

How about your own life? What are the biggest hassles in your life? In one investigation, the most frequent daily hassles of college students were wasting time, concerns about meeting high standards, and being lonely (Kanner & others,

1981). The most frequent uplifts of the college students were having fun, laughing, entertainment, getting along well with friends, and completing a task.

While college students were coping with academic and social problems in this investigation, middle-aged adults more often reported economic concerns—rising prices and taxes, for example. Table 17.A provides information about the ten most frequent daily hassles and uplifts experienced by the middle-aged adults.

TABLE 17.A
Ten Most Frequent Daily Hassles and Uplifts of Middle-Aged Adults Over a Nine-Month Period

Item	% of times checked[a]	Item	% of times checked
Hassles		Uplifts	
1. Concerns about weight	52.4	1. Relating well with your spouse or lover	76.3
2. Health of a family member	48.1	2. Relating well with friends	74.4
3. Rising prices of common goods	43.7	3. Completing a task	73.3
4. Home maintenance	42.8	4. Feeling healthy	72.7
5. Too many things to do	38.6	5. Getting enough sleep	69.7
6. Misplacing or losing things	38.1	6. Eating out	68.4
7. Yard work or outside home maintenance	38.1	7. Meeting your responsibilities	68.1
8. Property, investment, or taxes	37.6	8. Visiting, phoning, or writing someone	67.7
9. Crime	37.1	9. Spending time with family	66.7
10. Physical appearance	35.9	10. Home (inside) pleasing to you	65.5

a. The "% of times checked" figures represent the mean percentage of people checking the item each month averaged over the nine monthly administrations.

From A. D. Kanner, et al., "Comparison of two modes of stress management: Daily hassles and uplifts versus major life events" in Journal of Behavioral Medicine, 4, *1981. Copyright © 1981 Plenum Publishing Corporation. Reprinted by permission.*

Personality Theories and Middle Age		
Concept	**Processes/Related Ideas**	**Characteristics/Description**
Adult Stage Theories	Generativity versus Stagnation	In middle adulthood, individuals need to assist the next generation in developing and leading useful lives.
	Gould's Transformations	Mid-life is as turbulent as adolescence except that during mid-life striving to handle a crisis produces a healthy, happier life. In our 40s we begin to feel a sense of urgency as we see our lives speeding by.
	Levinson's Seasons of a Man's Life	Developmental tasks should be mastered at different points in development. Changes in middle adulthood focus on four conflicts: being young vs. being old; being destructive vs. being constructive; being masculine vs. being feminine; being attached to others vs. being separated from them.
	Vaillant's Expansion of Erikson's Stages	Career consolidation occurs from 23 to 35 years of age; keeping the meaning vs. rigidity occurs from 45 to 55 years of age.
	Conclusions	Adult development begins with a change from identity to intimacy, then from career consolidation to generativity, and finally from searching for meaning to some final integration. Criticisms of the stage theories have been made.
Crisis and Cohort	Crisis	A majority of individuals do not experience a mid-life crisis.
	Cohort	Changing times and different social expectations influence how different cohorts move through the life cycle.
The Life-Events Approach	The Early Version	Life events produce taxing circumstances and can be studied for their stressful impact.
	Today's Version	More sophisticated, it includes sociohistorical circumstances, factors that mediate life events, appraisal of the life events, and how the individual copes with the events.
	Criticisms	Too much emphasis on change and inadequate attention to life's daily hassles and uplifts.
Individual Variation	Its Nature	One approach to adult personality development is to emphasize similarities, another is to emphasize differences. Individual variation in adult development is substantial.

Longitudinal Studies of Personality Development in Adulthood

A number of longitudinal studies have assessed the personality development of adults. These studies are especially helpful in charting the most important dimensions of personality at different points in adult development and in evaluating the degree personality changes or stays the same.

One of the earliest longitudinal studies of adult personality development was conducted by Bernice Neugarten (1964)—it is known as the Kansas City study and involved the investigation of individuals 40 to 80 years of age over

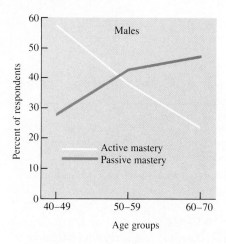

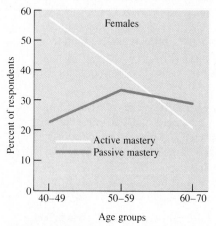

Figure 17.6
Active and passive mastery through the adult years.

a 10-year period. The adults were given personality tests, they filled out questionnaires, and they were interviewed. Neugarten concluded that both continuity and age-changes in personality were present. Adaptive characteristics showed the most stability—these included styles of coping, attaining life satisfaction, and strength of goal-directed behavior. Some consistent age differences occurred in the individual's inner versus outer orientation and active versus passive mastery. For example, 40-year-olds felt that they had control over their environment and risk taking did not bother them much. However, 60-year-olds were more likely to perceive the environment as threatening and sometimes dangerous and they had a more passive view of the self. This personality change in adulthood was described by Neugarten as going from active to passive mastery—as shown in figure 17.6, this change occurred for both males and females.

Another major longitudinal study of adult personality development has been conducted by Paul Costa and R. R. McRae at the Veterans Administration Outpatient Clinic in Boston. It involves approximately 2,000 men in their 20s through their 80s. Measures include assessments of personality, attitudes, and values (Costa, 1986, 1988; Costa & McRae, 1982; Costa & others, 1987). Costa and McRae believe that personality can be best understood in terms of three dimensions: neuroticism, extraversion, and openness to experience. Neuroticism includes how anxious, stable, depressed, self-conscious, impulsive, and vulnerable the individual is, extraversion includes the individual's attachment, gregariousness, assertiveness, activity, excitement seeking, and positive emotions; and openness to experience includes the individual's openness to fantasy, feelings, ideas, and values. Costa and McRae conclude that considerable stability in these three dimensions of personality—neuroticism, extraversion, and openness to experience—characterizes adult development.

By far the longest longitudinal study is the California Longitudinal Study. Initially, more than 500 children and their parents were studied in the late 1920s and early 1930s. In *Present and Past in Middle Life* (Eichorn & others, 1981), the profile of these individuals' lives was described as they became middle aged. The results from early adolescence to mid-life did not support either extreme in the debate over whether personality is characterized by stability or change. Some characteristics were more stable than others, however. Dimensions more directly concerned with self (cognitively invested, self confident, and open or closed self) were more consistent than dimensions more directly concerned with interpersonal relationships (nurturant or hostile and undercontrolled or overcontrolled).

Another recent longitudinal investigation of adult personality development has been conducted by Ravenna Helson and her colleagues (Helson, Mitchell, & Moane, 1984; Helson & Moane, 1987; Helson & Wink, 1987). They initially studied 132 women who were seniors at Mills College in California in the late 1950s; in 1981, at which time they were 42 to 45 years old, they were studied again. They distinguished three main groups among the Mills women: family-oriented, career-oriented (whether or not they also wanted famlies); and those who followed neither path (women with no children who pursued only low-level work). Despite their different college profiles and their diverging life paths, the women in all three groups experienced some similar psychological changes over their adult years, although the women in the third group changed less than those committed to career or family. Between the ages of 27 and the early 40s, there was a shift toward less traditionally feminine attitudes, including greater dominance, greater interest in events outside the family, and more emotional stability.

(a)

(b)

How much does our personality change and how much does it stay the same through adulthood? In the early 1970s, Jerry Rubin was a Yippie demonstrator (a), but in the 1980s, Rubin became a Wall Street businessman (b). Rubin says that his transformation underscores continuity in personality: whether Yippie or Wall Street Yuppie, he approached life with curiosity and enthusiasm.

During their early 40s, many of the women shared the concerns that stage theorists such as Levinson and Gould found in men: concern for young and old, introspectiveness, interest in roots, and awareness of limitation and death. However, the researchers in the Mills College study concluded that rather than being a mid-life crisis, what was being experienced was mid-life consciousness. They also indicated that commitment to the tasks of early adulthood—whether to a career or family (or both)—helped women learn to control their impulses, develop interpersonal skills, become independent, and work hard to achieve goals. Women who did not commit themselves to one of these life-style patterns faced fewer challenges and did not develop as fully as the other women (Rosenfeld & Stark, 1987).

What can we conclude from the series of longitudinal studies about constancy and change in personality during the adult years? Richard Alpert was an achievement-oriented, hardworking college professor in the 1960s. In the 1970s, Richard Alpert became Ram Dass, a free-spirited guru in search of an expanded state of consciousness. Most individuals would look at Alpert and Ram Dass and see two very different people. But Harvard psychologist David McClelland, who has known Alpert and Ram Dass well, says that Dass is the same old Richard, still charming, still concerned with inner experience, and still power hungry.

Jerry Rubin views his own transformation from yippie to Wall Street businessman in a way that underscores continuity in personality. Rubin says that discovering his identity was accomplished in a typical Jerry Rubin fashion—trying out anything and everything, jumping around wild-eyed and crazy. Whether yippie or Wall Street businessman, Rubin approached life with enthusiasm and curiosity (Rubin, 1981).

William James (1890) said that our basic personality is set like plaster by the time we are 30 and never softens again. Like Jerry Rubin and David McClelland, James believed that our bodies and attitudes may change through the adult years, but not the basic core of our personality. Paul Costa's (1986, 1987) research clearly supports this stability. He believes that whether we are extraverted or introverted, how adjusted we are, and how open we are to new experience do not change much during our adult lives. Look at an individual at age 25 who is shy and quiet and then observe the individual again at age 50, says Costa, and you will find the same shy and quiet individual.

We are adaptive human beings, resilient throughout our adult lives, but we do not become entirely new personalities. In a way we change but remain the same— amidst change is an underlying coherence and stability. Think about adults you know or have known. How well does their adult development fit our description of both stability and change in their lives?

Yet many adult developmentalists are enthusiastic about our capacity for change as adults, arguing that too much importance has been attached to personality change in childhood and not enough importance has been placed on change in adulthood. A more moderate view on the stability-change view comes from the California Longitudinal Study (Eichorn & others, 1981; Mussen, Honzik, & Eichorn, 1982). They believe some stability exists over the long course of adult development, but that adults are more capable of change than Costa thinks. For example, the shy, introverted individual at age 25 may not be completely extraverted at age 50, but he may be less introverted than he was when he was 25. Perhaps he married someone who encouraged him to be more outgoing and supported his social ventures; perhaps he changed jobs at age 30 and became a salesperson, placing him in a circumstance where he was required to develop his social skills.

Humans are adaptive beings; we are resilient throughout our adult lives. But we do not become entirely new personalities either. In a sense we become different but we still are the same—amidst change is some underlying coherence and stability.

The more things change, the more they remain the same.
Alphonse Karr, Les Guêpes, *1849*

Summary

I. **Love and Marriage**
Affectionate or companionate love increases in middle adulthood, especially in marriages that have endured many years. Marital satisfaction usually increases in the post-childrearing years, that is, when children leave home to go to college or to work. Divorce in middle adulthood may be more positive or negative than divorce in early adulthood.

II. **Friendships and Sibling Relationships**
Friendships continue to be important in middle adulthood; longstanding friendships are more intimate. Sibling relationships continue throughout life; many are close in adulthood, if they were close in childhood, although some are apathetic or highly conflicted.

III. **Intergenerational Relationships**
Generally, there is continuing contact across generations in families. Greater continuity occurs in political and religious attitudes, lesser continuity occurs in gender roles, life-styles, and work orientation. Females are closer across generations than males. The middle-aged generation plays a special role in linking generations. However, financial and caregiving obligations to youth and to aging parents may create stress for middle-aged adults.

Middle Adulthood

IV. **Adult Stage Theories**

In Erikson's life-cycle theory, generativity versus stagnation is the seventh stage, corresponding roughly with middle adulthood; it is a time when adults need to assist the next generation in developing and leading useful lives. In Gould's transformations, mid-life is as turbulent as adolescence except that during mid-life striving to handle a crisis produces a healthy, happier life. For Gould, our 40s represent a time when we begin to feel a sense of urgency as we see our lives speeding by. In Levinson's seasons of a man's life, developmental tasks should be mastered at different points in development. Changes in middle adulthood focus on four conflicts: being young vs. being old, being destructive vs. being constructive, being masculine vs. being feminine, and being attached to others vs. being separated from them. In Vaillant's expansion of Erikson's stages, career consolidation occurs from 23 to 35 years of age; keeping the meaning vs. rigidity occurs from 45 to 55 years of age. In conclusion, the adult stage theories suggest that adult development begins with a change from identity to intimacy, then from career consolidation to generativity, and finally from searching for meaning to some final integration. Criticisms of the stage theories have been made.

V. **Crisis and Cohort**

A majority of individuals do not experience a mid-life crisis. Changing times and social expectations influence how different cohorts move through the life cycle.

VI. **The Life-Events Approach**

In the early version, life events were perceived as taxing circumstances and were studied for their stressful impact. In today's more sophisticated version, sociohistorical circumstances, factors that mediate life events, appraisal of the life events, and how the individual copes with the events are considered. Too much emphasis on change and inadequate attention to life's daily hassles and uplifts are criticisms of the life-events approach.

VII. **Individual Variation**

One approach to adult personality development emphasizes similarities, another emphasizes differences. The adult stage theories emphasize similarity; however, there is substantial individual variation in adult development.

VIII. **Longitudinal Studies of Personality Development in Adulthood**

In Neugarten's study, the most consistent characteristics were adaptive characteristics—styles of coping, attaining life satisfaction, and strength of goal-directed behavior. Two significant changes as individuals went through middle age were an increase in passive mastery and interiority. Costa and McRae report extensive stability in adult personality development, especially in neuroticism, extraversion, and openness to experience. In the California Longitudinal Study, the extremes in the stablity-change argument were not supported. Characteristics associated with the self were more stable than those associated with interpersonal relationships. In the Mills College Study of adult women, there was a shift toward less traditionally feminine characteristics from age 27 to the early 40s. In their early 40s, these women experienced many of the concerns stage theorists such as Gould and Levinson found in men. However, it was concluded that rather than a mid-life crisis, this represented mid-life consciousness. In summary, the longitudinal studies portray individuals as becoming different but still remaining the same—amidst change there is some underlying coherence and stability.

Key Terms

empty nest syndrome   487
career consolidation   492
keeping the meaning versus rigidity   492
life-events approach   498

Suggested Readings

Eichorn, D. H., Clausen, J. A., Haan, N., Honzik, M. P., & Mussen, P. H. (1981). *Present and past in middle life.* New York: Academic Press.
Includes details about the California Longitudinal Study, that spans from childhood through middle age.

Levinson, D. (1978). *Seasons of a man's life.* New York: Ballantine Books.
Levinson's well-known book provides extensive biographical material about 40 men and their adult development as well as commentary about the adult development of famous individuals.

Scholossberg, N. K. (1984). *Counseling adults in transition.* New York: Springer.
A helping skills model is developed for counseling individuals in middle adulthood.

Sherman, E. (1987). *Meaning in mid-life transitions.* Albany: State University of New York Press.
Extensive case studies of individuals as they make the transition through mid-life. Separate chapters on generativity and mortality.

Troll, L. E., & Bengston, V. L. (1982). Intergenerational relations throughout the lifespan. In B. B. Wolman (Ed.), *Handbook of developmental psychology.* Englewood Cliffs, NJ: Prentice-Hall.
An excellent overview of the complexity of intergenerational relations, with special attention given to cohort effects.

S E C T I O N

IX

Late Adulthood

E ach of us stands alone at the heart of the earth pierced through by a ray of sunlight: And suddenly it is evening. ■

Salvatore Quasimodo

CHAPTER

18

■

Physical and Cognitive Development

"No wise man ever wished to be younger," said Jonathan Swift. Without doubt, a 70-year-old body does not work as well as it once did. It is also true that an individual's fear of aging often is greater than it needs to be. As more individuals live to a ripe *and* active old age, our image of aging and how we react to aging is changing. While on the average, a 75-year-old's joints should be stiffening, individuals can practice not to be average. For example, a 70-year-old man may *choose* to train for and run a marathon; an 80-year-old woman whose capacity for work is undiminished may *choose* to continue making and selling children's toys.

Both George Gallup, the pollster, and I. F. Stone, the author, believe that intellectual curiosity keeps one alive in old age. Gallup, in his late 80s, says that intellectual curiosity is especially important. He says, "A lot of people die just from boredom. I have a whole program that will keep me going until age 100 at least." Stone, in his mid-80s, says, "There are great joys in one's later years—as many as there are in one's youth. One of them is learning and studying. The things you study have much more significance; you understand them more fully. I'm studying ancient Greek language and civilization. It's difficult work, but very rewarding. My advice is to persist. The mind is like a muscle—you must exercise it." (Conniff, 1981).

We ask some exciting and provocative questions in this chapter: How long can we live? What are your chances of living to be 100? Why do we age? What are the nature of physical changes in late adulthood? Can physical decline be slowed down? Can exercise make us healthier in our old age? Do older people have sex? Do our cognitive abilities decline in old age? If so, can the decline be slowed down? What is the nature of work and retirement in old age?

Physical Development

Linus Pauling, now in his 80s, believes that Vitamin C diminishes the aging process. Aging researcher Roy Walford fasts two days a week because he believes undernutrition (not malnutrition) also diminishes the aging process. In animals, underfeeding has been shown to not only delay death but to forestall the decay of the immune system. In humans, though, we do not have evidence that underfeeding or Vitamin C prolongs life. What do we know about longevity?

Longevity

We are no longer a youthful society. Remember from chapter 1 that, as more individuals live to older ages, the proportion of individuals at different ages has become increasingly similar. Indeed, the concept of a period called late adulthood is a recent one—until the twentieth century most individuals died before they were 65. In the 1980 census, the number of individuals 65 and older climbed by 28 percent over figures for 1970; now there are more than 25 million people in the 65 and over category.

Nonetheless, while a much greater percentage of individuals are living to an older age, the life span has remained virtually unchanged since the beginning of recorded history. **Life span** is the upper boundary of life. What has changed is **life expectancy**—the number of individuals expected to reach what seems to be an unbudging endpoint. Even though improvements in medicine, nutrition, exercise, and life-style have given us an additional 22 years of life since 1900, few of us will live to be 100. To learn more about what life at 100 or even older is like, read Focus on Life-Span Development 18.1.

What about you? What chance do you have of living to be 100? By taking the test in table 18.1, you can obtain a rough estimate of your chance and discover some of the most important contributors to longevity. According to the questionnaire, heredity and family health (weight, diet, smoking, and exercise), education, personality, and life-style are factors in longevity.

Just as actuaries predict longevity for the purpose of insurance risks on the basis of age, sex, and race, developmentalists have also evaluated the factors that predict longevity. In the most comprehensive investigation of longevity, known as the Duke Longitudinal Study (Palmore, 1980, 1982; Palmore & Jeffers, 1971), older adults have been assessed over a 25 year period. A total of 270 volunteers were examined for the first time in 1959 with a series of physical, mental, social, and laboratory tasks. At that time, the adults ranged in age from 60 to 94 with a mean age of 70. What were the factors that predicted their longevity 25 years later? Not surprisingly, health was the best predictor. Nonsmoking, intelligence, education, work satisfaction, usefulness, and happiness in 1959 also predicted whether these individuals would still be alive in 1981. Also, finances predicted longevity for men; activity level predicted longevity for women.

Beginning at the age of 25, females begin to outnumber males, a gap that widens during the remainder of the adult years. By the time individuals are 75 years of age, more than 61 percent of the population is female; for those 85 and over, the figure is almost 70 percent female. Why might this be so? Social factors such as health attitudes, habits, life-styles, and occupation probably are important. For example, among such leading causes of death in the United States as cancer of the respiratory system, motor vehicle accidents, suicide, cirrhosis of the liver, emphysema, and coronary heart disease, men are more likely to die from such factors than are women. These causes of death are associated with life-style. For example, the sex difference in deaths due to lung cancer and emphysema is probably associated with men being heavier smokers than women.

However, if life expectancy is influenced extensively by the stress of work, the sex difference in longevity should be narrowing, since so many more women have entered the labor force. Yet in the last 40 years, just the opposite has occurred. Apparently, self-esteem and work satisfaction outweigh the stress of work when longevity is at issue.

The sex difference in longevity also is influenced by biological factors. In virtually all species, females outlive males. Women have more resistance to infections and degenerative diseases. For example, the female's estrogen production helps to protect her from arteriosclerosis (hardening of the arteries). And the X chromosome women carry may be associated with the production of more antibodies to fight off disease.

To me old age is always fifteen years older than I am.

Bernard Baruch

'Tis very certain that the desire for life prolongs it.

Byron, Don Juan, *1819*

What factors do you believe will be the most important in increasing longevity 50 years from now, in approximately the year 2040? Will they be any different than those that are the most critical today? Will some factors assume more importance, less importance?

CHARLIE SMITH, THE ABKHASIANS,

AND 1,200 CENTENARIANS

This Abkhasian is reportedly 118 years old. Controversy, though, has swirled about the authenticity of the Abkhasians' longevity. What is the nature of this controversy?

I magine that you are 120 years old. Would you still be able to write your name? Could you think clearly? What would your body look like? Would you be able to walk? To run? Could you still have sex? Would you have an interest in sex? Would your eyes and ears still function? Could you work?

Has anyone ever lived to be 120 years old? Supposedly, one American, Charlie Smith (?1842–1979), lived to be 137 years old. In three areas of the world, not just a single person but many people have reportedly lived more than 130 years. These areas are the Republic of Georgia in Russia, the Vilcabamba valley in Ecuador, and the province of Hunza in Kashmir. Three people over 100 years old (centenarians) per 100,000 people is considered normal. But in the Russian region where the Abkhasian people live, approximately 400 centenarians per 100,000 people have been reported. Some of the Abkhasians are said to be 120 to 170 years old (Benet, 1976).

However, there is reason to believe that some of these claims are false (Medvedev, 1974). Indeed, we really do not have sound documentation of anyone living more than 115 to 120 years. In the case of the Abkhasians, birth registrations, as well as other documents such as marriage certificates and military registrations, are not available. In most instances, the ages of the Abkhasians have been based on the individuals' recall of important historical events and interviews with other members of the village (Benet, 1976). In the Russian villages where people have been reported to live a long life, the elderly experience unparalleled esteem and honor. Centenarians are often given special positions in the community, such as the leader of social celebrations. Thus there is a strong motivation to give one's age as older than one really is. One individual who claimed to be 130 years of age was found to have used his father's birth certificate during World War I to escape army duty. Later it was discovered that he was only 78 years old (Hayflick, 1975).

What about Charlie Smith? Was he 137 years old when he died? Charlie was very, very old, but it cannot be documented that he was actually 137. In 1956, officials of the Social Security Administration began to collect information about American centenarians who were receiving benefits. Charlie Smith was visited in 1961. He gave his birthdate as July 4, 1842, and his place of birth as Liberia. On one occasion, he said he had been bought at a slave auction in New Orleans in 1854. Charlie Smith of Galveston, Texas, bought him and gave the young boy his own name. Charlie was 21 years of age in 1863 when he supposedly was freed under the Emancipation Proclamation, but he decided to stay with the Smiths. By the end of the nineteenth century, Charlie had settled in Florida. He worked in turpentine camps, and at one point owned a turpentine farm in Homeland, Florida. Smith's records at the Social Security Administration do not provide evidence of his birthdate, but they do mention that he began to earn benefits based on

This older adult is from the Vilcabamba region of Ecuador where individuals also are reported to live to very old ages. Accurate documentation of longevity in the Vilcabamba region also has not been available. At this point in history, most scientists believe there is a limit on how many years individuals can live.

Social Security credits by picking oranges at the age of 113 (Freeman, 1982).

Charlie Smith lived to be very old—exactly how old we will never know. He seems to have lived a very active life even after the age of 100. Many other Americans have lived to be 100 as well. In a recent book,

Living to Be 100: 1200 Who Did and How They Did It (Segerberg, 1982). Social Security Administration interviews of 1,127 individuals from 1963 to 1972 were searched for physical, psychological, and social information. Seventy-three other individuals were interviewed. Especially entertaining are the bizarre reasons several of the centenarians gave as to why they were able to live to be 100: "because I slept with my head to the north," "because of eating a lot of fatty pork and salt," and "because I don't believe in germs." While the impressions are those of a journalist, not a scientist, the following conclusions based on what it takes to live a long life seem to make sense. Organized purposeful behavior, discipline and hard work, freedom and independence, balanced diet, family orientation, good peer and friendship relations, and low ambition were among the most important factors related to high self-esteem and low levels of stress, both of which are associated with longevity.

The following test gives you a rough guide for predicting your longevity. The basic life expectancy for males is age 67, and for females age 75. Write down your basic life expectancy. If you are in your 50s or 60s, you should add 10 years to the basic figure because you have already proved yourself to be a durable individual. If you are over age 60 and active, you can even add another 2 years.

Basic life expectancy

Decide how each item below applies to you and add or substract the appropriate number of years from your basic life expectancy.

1. Family history
   Add 5 years if two or more of your grandparents lived to eighty or beyond.   _____
   Subtract 4 years if any parent, grandparent, sister, or brother died of heart attack or stroke before 50.   _____
   Subtract 2 years if anyone died from these diseases before 60.   _____
   Subtract 3 years for each case of diabetes, thyroid disorder, breast cancer, cancer of the digestive
   system, asthma, or chronic bronchitis among parents or grandparents.   _____

2. Marital status
   If you are married, add 4 years.   _____
   If you are over 25 and not married, subtract 1 year for every unwedded decade.   _____

3. Economic status
   Add 2 years if your family income is over $40,000 per year.   _____
   Subtract 3 years if you have been poor for the greater part of your life.   _____

4. Physique
   Subtract 1 year for every 10 pounds you are overweight.   _____
   For each inch your girth measurement exceeds your chest measurement deduct 2 years.   _____
   Add 3 years if you are over 40 and not overweight.   _____

5. Exercise
   Regular and moderate (jogging three times a week), add 3 years.   _____
   Regular and vigorous (long-distance running three times a week), add 5 years.   _____
   Subtract 3 years if your job is sedentary.   _____
   Add 3 years if it is active.   _____

6. Alcohol
   Add 2 years if you are a light drinker (one to three drinks a day).   _____
   Subtract 5 to 10 years if you are a heavy drinker (more than four drinks per day).   _____
   Subtract 1 year if you are a teetotaler.   _____

Biological Theories of Aging

Even if we keep a remarkably healthy profile through our adult lives, we begin to age at some point. What are the biological explanations of aging? A theory that looks within the body's cells to explain aging is a **microbiological theory** of aging; one that looks at a more macro level to explain aging is called a **macrobiological theory** of aging. The label *micro* is used because a cell is a very small unit of analysis; the label *macro* refers to a larger, more global level of analysis. Some microbiological and macrobiological theories attribute aging to wear and tear on the body, others to a biological clock within the body.

Microbiological Theories

As cells age, they have a more difficult time disposing of their wastes. Eventually this "garbage" takes up as much as 20 percent of a cell's space. Imagine the cell's working molecules as waiters in a nightclub trying to move across a dance floor that becomes increasingly crowded. Service would become slower

7. Smoking
Two or more packs of cigarettes per day, subtract 8 years. _____
One to two packs per day, subtract 2 years. _____
Less than one pack, subtract 2 years. _____
Subtract 2 years if you regularly smoke a pipe or cigars. _____

8. Disposition
Add 2 years if you are a reasoned, practical person. _____
Subtract 2 years if you are aggressive, intense, and competitive. _____
Add 1 to 5 years if you are basically happy and content with life. _____
Subtract 1 to 5 years if you are often unhappy, worried, and often feel guilty. _____

9. Education
Less than high school, subtract 2 years. _____
Four years of school beyond high school, add 1 year. _____
Five or more years beyond high school, add 3 years. _____

10. Environment
If you have lived most of your life in a rural environment, add 4 years. _____
Subtract 2 years if you have lived most of your life in an urban environment. _____

11. Sleep
More than 9 hours a day, subtract 5 years. _____

12. Temperature
Add 2 years if your home's thermostat is set at no more than 68° F. _____

13. Health care
Regular medical checkups and regular dental care, add 3 years. _____
Frequently ill, subtract 2 years. _____

Your life expectancy total _____

and slower until eventually it might come to a complete standstill. Most scientists view this phenomenon as a result, rather than a cause, of aging, though.

As cells age, their molecules can become linked or attached to each other in ways that stop vital biochemical cycles and create other forms of havoc as they disrupt cell functioning. The cross-linkage view, like the garbage-accumulation view, is now thought to be a consequence rather than a cause of aging.

Might there also be a biological clock within our cells that causes us to age? Leonard Hayflick (1977, 1987) thinks so. He has demonstrated that the body's cells can only divide a limited number of times. Cells from human embryonic tissue can divide only about 50 times, for example. Cells extracted from older individuals still have dividing capability, however, so we rarely live to the end of our life-span potential. Based on the way human cells divide, scientists place the upper limit of the human life span at 110 to 120 years.

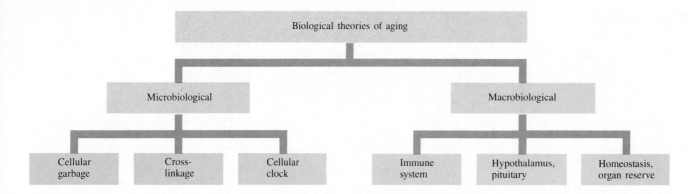

Figure 18.1
Biological theories of aging.

Macrobiological Theories

Aging also may be influenced by the immune system, the brain, and homeostasis. Regarding the immune system, in early adulthood, the thymus (a gland in the upper chest whose hormones stimulate the white blood cells needed to fight infection and cancer) has already begun to shrink. As life continues, the immune system loses some of its ability to recognize and attack bacteria and other invaders, as well as cancer cells. The immune cells also may start to attack the body's own healthy cells, possibly producing autoimmune diseases such as rheumatoid arthritis and some kidney ailments (Walford, 1969).

Other scientists argue that the aging timer is located in the brain, more specifically the hypothalamus and pituitary gland, which are involved in the release of hormones. In this view, beginning at puberty, the pituitary gland releases a hormone, or a family of hormones, that causes the body to decline at a programmed rate. This "aging" hormone—which has not yet been isolated or proven to exist—hinders the cell's ability to take in thyroxine, the hormone secreted by the thyroid gland. Thyroxine controls the metabolic rate in the body's key cardiovascular and immune systems, whose failure often is involved in many diseases that kill older individuals (Rosenfeld, 1985).

Aging might also be related to the decline in the body's organ reserve. At the level of the organism, life may be defined as internal homeostasis. The body's internal world is balanced and regulated within strict limits. Neural and endocrine systems monitor heart, lungs, liver, kidneys, and other organs to maintain this balance. In young adulthood, biologists estimate that we have an organ reserve that is 10 times that required to sustain life. This organ reserve allows a stressed individual to restore homeostasis, or balance, when the body is damaged by something external. But beginning at about 30 years of age, our organ reserve begins a gradual drop that continues through the remainder of our life. Eventually our organ reserve capacity reaches zero, and we die even if a disease is not present. After the age of 30, an individual's mortality rate doubles every eight years because of this decline in organ reserve (Upton, 1977).

While no one knows for sure why we age, scientists today believe we have a biological clock that ultimately will be identified. Some scientists argue that the clock resides in the cells of the body, others argue that it lies in the brain or certain glands, and yet others argue that it lies in the homestatic balance of the body and organ reserve in general. A summary of the theories of aging we have described is shown in figure 18.1.

The Course of Physical Decline in Late Adulthood

What are some of the common ravages that hit us sooner or later in old age? At 30, we were not bad specimens—a little slower, a little plumper probably, but already our body had passed its peak. At 50, we probably were not the specimens we were when we were 30. We had become shorter, our reflexes diminished, we were not as strong, we had gained even more weight, we did not have as much stamina, and our cardiovascular system was less efficient. By 70, the human specimen shows further decline.

The diminished efficiency of the circulatory system is a special concern. There is less elastin, the molecules that dictate the heart's elasticity, and there is more collagen, the stiff protein that makes up about one third of the body's protein. An individual's heart rate does not rise as predictably in response to stress as was the case during middle adulthood. The heart muscle cannot contract and relax as fast. The arteries are more resistant to blood flow. Heart output—about 5 quarts a minute at age 50—subsequently drops about one percent a year. With the heart muscle less efficient and the vessels more resistant, heart rate and blood pressure both rise—and both are related to heart disease. Even for the healthy older individual, blood pressure that was 100/75 at age 25 probably will be 160/90 at age 70. The blood also carries less oxygen to the brain and lungs. If elderly individuals rise too quickly from a chair, they may get dizzy; if they climb a set of stairs too speedily, they may get out of breath.

In late adulthood, the decline in vision that, for most of us, began in early or middle adulthood becomes more pronounced. Night driving becomes especially difficult, to some extent because tolerance for glare diminishes. Dark adaptation is slower, meaning that older individuals take longer to recover their vision when going from well-lighted rooms to semidarkness. The area of the visual field becomes smaller, suggesting that a stimulus's intensity in the peripheral area of the visual field needs to be increased if the stimulus is to be seen. Events taking place away from the center of the visual field may not be detected (Kline & Schieber, 1985; Whitbourne, 1985).

This visual decline can usually be traced to reduction in the quality or intensity of light reaching the retina. In extreme old age, these changes may be accompanied by degenerative changes in the retina, causing severe difficulty in seeing. Large print books and magnifers may be needed in such cases. Legal blindness is defined as corrected distance vision of 20/200 in the better eye or a visual field restricted to 20 degrees as large as the diameter. Legal blindness occurs in less than 100 out of every 100,000 individuals under the age of 21; it increases to 1400 out of every 100,000 individuals at the age of 69, still indicating that the vast majority of older adults can see quite well with glasses.

Although hearing impairment may begin in middle adulthood, it usually does not become much of an impediment until late adulthood. Even then, some but not all hearing problems may be corrected by hearing aids. Only 19 percent of individuals from 45 to 54 experience some type of hearing problem, but from 75 to 79 the figure has reached 75 percent (Harris, 1975). It has been estimated that 15 percent of the population over the age of 65 is legally deaf, usually due to the degeneration of the cochlea, the primary neural receptor for hearing in the inner ear (Olsho, Harkins, & Lenhardt, 1985). Wearing two hearing aids that are balanced to correct each ear separately can sometimes help hearing-impaired adults.

How many of us older persons have really been prepared for the second half of life, for old age, and eternity?
Carl Jung, Modern Man in Search of a Soul, *1933.*

Not only do we experience declines in vision and hearing as we age, but we may also become less sensitive to taste and smell. Sensitivity to bitter and sour tastes persists longer than sensitivity to sweet and salty tastes. However, in healthy older adults, there is less decline in sensitivity to taste and smell than in those who are not healthy (Engen, 1977). One loss of sensory sensitivity as we age may be advantageous, though. Older adults are less sensitive to pain and suffer from it less than younger adults (Kenshalo, 1977). Of course, although decreased sensitivity to pain may help the elderly cope with disease and injury, it can be harmful if it masks injury and illness that need to be treated.

Illness and Impairment

As we age, the probability we will have some disease or illness increases. For example, a majority of individuals who are still alive at the age of 80 are likely to have some impairment. Many of the chronic diseases of the elderly—cancer and heart disease, for example—lead to long-term illness and impairment. Other chronic conditions—arthritis and hypertension, for example—do not directly cause death but usually leave the afflicted individual with some type of physical impairment such as lameness or blindness. Almost two of every five individuals between the ages of 65 and 75 have some impairment of physical functioning. After age 75, the rate rises to three of five (Riley & Foner, 1968). The four most prevalent chronic conditons that impair the health of the elderly are arthritis (38 percent), hearing impairment (20 percent), visual impairment (20 percent), and heart condition (20 percent). Sex differences indicate that elderly women have higher incidences of arthritis and hypertension, are more likely to have visual problems, but less likely to have hearing problems than elderly men do.

Although adults over the age of 65 often have a physical impairment, many of them can still carry on their everyday activities or work. Chronic conditions associated with the greatest limitation on work are heart condition (52 percent), diabetes (34 percent), asthma (27 percent), and arthritis (27 percent) (Harris, 1978). Low income also is strongly related to health problems in late adulthood. Approximately three times as many poor as nonpoor individuals report that their activities are limited by chronic diseases (Wilson & White, 1977).

The Brain and Nervous System

The brain is of considerable interest to scientists who study the course of physical decline in late adulthood. As we age we lose a number of neurons, the basic cellular unit of the nervous system. Some researchers estimate that the loss may be as high as 50 percent over the adult years, although others believe the loss is substantially less and that an accurate assessment of neuron loss has not been made in human brains (Bondareff, 1985). Perhaps a more reasonable estimate is that 5 to 10 percent of our neurons atrophy until we reach the 70s. After that, neuron loss may accelerate (Leaf, 1973).

A significant aspect of the aging process may be that neurons do not replace themselves (Moushegian, 1988). Nonetheless, generally it is believed that the brain has remarkable recovery and repair capability, losing only a small portion of its ability to function in the late adulthood years (Labouvie-Vief, 1985). The adaptive nature of the brain was demonstrated in a recent investigation (Coleman, 1986). From the 40s through the 70s, the growth of dendrites increased. Dendrites are the receiving part of the neuron or nerve

All we know about older adults indicates that they are healthier and happier the more active they are. Several decades ago, it was believed that older adults should be more passive and inactive to be well adjusted and satisfied with life. In today's world, we believe that, while older adults may be in the evening of life's human cycle, they were not meant to passively live out their remaining years.

cell; they are thought to be especially important because they make up approximately 95 percent of the neuron's surface. But in very old people, those in their 90s, dendritic growth was no longer taking place. Through the 70s, then, dendritic growth may compensate for neuron loss, but not when individuals reach their 90s.

Exercise

While we may be in the evening of our lives in late adulthood, we are not meant to passively live out our remaining years. Everything we know about older adults suggests they are healthier and happier the more active they are. The possibility that regular exercise can lead to a healthier late adulthood, and possibly extend life, has been raised. Recently, an investigation over an eight-year period of more than 17,000 men and women at the Aerobics Institute in Dallas, Texas, found that sedentary participants were more than twice as likely to die during that period than those who were moderately fit (Blair, 1988; Blair & Kohl, 1988). Examples of the exercise programs included running two miles in 20 minutes twice a week or walking three miles in 45 minutes twice a week.

Exercise is an excellent way to maintain health. Being fit means being able to do the things you want to do, whether you are young or old. While there usually is a need for a decrease in exercise intensity as the older adult ages, individuals vary extensively in the degree to which such reduction is necessary. The body's capacity for exercise in late adulthood is influenced by the extent the body has been kept in shape at earlier points in the life cycle. It is not uncommon to discover individuals in late adulthood who participate in the Senior Olympics—athletic competition for senior citizens—to have a greater capacity for exercise than some young adults (Wiswell, 1980). More about exercise's role in maintaining a healthier and happier life as an older adult is presented in Focus on Life-Span Development 18.2.

Active older people are more satisfied with their lives than inactive older people. Older people should be encouraged to take trips, exercise, attend meetings, and get out in the world rather than merely sit at home.

What can we do as a society to get older people to exercise more? Should the government be involved? If so, how?

A 72-YEAR-OLD COMPETITIVE RUNNER

AND JOGGING HOGS

Figure 18.A *The experimental setting for jogging hogs.*

I magine you are 72 years old. You have just awakened from 10 hours of restful sleep. You fix yourself a yogurt shake for breakfast and then put on your Nike running shoes and shorts. You drive to the location where the race is to begin. The New York Marathon will start in 30 minutes. You see some friendly competitors, most of whom are much younger than you, but you also see some others who look to be about your age. You chat with them for a few minutes about the race conditions. John Pianfetti, age 72, and Madge Sharples, age 65, recently completed the New York Marathon. Older adults do not have to run marathons to be healthy and happy, but even moderate exercise can benefit their health. By getting men and women aged 50 to 87 to do calisthenics, walk, run, stretch, and swim for 42 weeks, researchers found dramatic changes in the oxygen transport systems of the participants' bodies (Adams & deVries, 1973; deVries, 1970). The improvements

occurred regardless of age or prior exercise history.

Jogging hogs have shown the dramatic effects of exercise on health. In one investigation (Bloor & White, 1983), a group of hogs were trained to run approximately 100 miles per week (see figure 18.A).

Then, the researchers narrowed the arteries that supplied blood to the hogs' hearts. The hearts of the jogging hogs developed extensive alternate pathways for blood supply and 42 percent of the threatened heart tissue was salvaged compared to only 17 percent in a control group of nonjogging hogs.

Many older adults simply feel that they do not need to exercise, yet most aging experts emphasize that the single most effective way to accelerate the aging process is to do nothing. In some instances, the news media have promoted barriers to exercise in older adults by dramatizing the occasional cardiac problem that occurs during exercise. In practical terms, though, we can expect an exercise class of 50 individuals meeting three times a week to have only one cardiac fatality in every 6.5 years. Deciding to exercise is a crucial step for the older adult. Current health should be carefully reviewed and realistic goals for improvement should be set.

Sexuality

Aging does induce some changes in human sexual performance, moreso in the male than in the female. Orgasm becomes less frequent in males, occurring in every second to third act of intercourse rather than every time. More direct stimulation usually is needed to produce an erection. In the absence of two circumstances—actual disease and the belief that old people are or should be asexual—sexuality can be lifelong. Even when actual intercourse is impaired by infirmity, other relationship needs persist, among them closeness, sensuality, and being valued as a man or a woman.

Such a view, of course, is contrary to folklore, to the beliefs of many individuals in society, and even to many physicians and health-care personnel. Fortunately, many elderly individuals went on having sex without talking about it, unabashed by the accepted and destructive social image of the dirty old man and the asexual, undesirable older woman. Bear in mind that many individuals who are now in their 80s were reared when there was a Victorian attitude toward sex. In early surveys of sexual attitudes, older individuals were not asked about their sexuality, possibly because everyone thought they did not have sex or because the investigators believed it would be embarrassing to ask them about sex (Comfort, 1976; Pfeiffer & Davis, 1974).

Various therapies for elderly individuals who report sexual difficulties have been effective. In one investigation, sex education—which consisted largely of simply giving sexual information—led to increased sexual interest, knowledge, and activity in the elderly (White & Catania, 1981).

At this point we have described many ideas about physical development in late adulthood. A summary of these ideas is presented in Concept Table 18.1. Now we turn to the nature of cognitive development in late adulthood.

Cognitive Development

At the age of 70, Dr. John Rock introduced the birth-control pill. At age 89, Arthur Rubinstein gave one of his best performances at New York's Carnegie Hall. From 85 to 90 years of age, Pablo Picasso completed three sets of drawings. And at age 76, Anna Mary Robertson Moses took up painting—as Grandma Moses, she became internationally famous and staged 15 one-woman shows throughout Europe. Figure 18.2 shows her painting of a New York winter when she was 84 years old. Are these feats rare exceptions?

Physical Development		
Concept	Processes/Related Ideas	Characteristics/Description
Longevity	Its Nature	Life expectancy is increasing but the life span is not. Among the most important factors in longevity are heredity and family, health, personality characteristics, and life-style. Beginning at age 25, females outnumber males, a gap that widens as individuals age; this sex difference probably is due to social and biological factors.
Biological Theories of Aging	Microbiological Theories	Microbiological theories look within the body's cells for the clues to aging; among the most popular microbiological theories are cellular garbage, cross-linkage, and cellular clock.
	Macrobiological Theories	Macrobiological theories look for more global causes of aging than the cellular, microbiological theories; three popular macrobiological theories involve the immune system, the hypothalamus and pituitary gland, and organ reserve and homeostasis.
The Course of Physical Decline	Its Nature	The circulatory system becomes less efficient, as do vision and hearing. The vast majority of individuals in late adulthood can have their vision corrected so they can continue to work or function in their world, and hearing aids also can diminish the problem of hearing loss. Decline in taste and smell may occur, although the decline is barely noticeable in healthy older people.
Illness and Impairment	Its Nature	As we age, the probability that we will have some disease increases. It is rare to find anyone over the age of 80 who is free from disease or illness. Many of the chronic diseases of the elderly, such as heart disease and cancer, produce long-term illness and impairment. Other chronic conditions, such as arthritis and hypertension, usually require reduced activity but are not as life-threatening. Low income is related to health problems in late adulthood.
Exercise	Its Nature	While there may be some need for a reduction in exercise in late adulthood, the physical benefits of exercise have been demonstrated.
Sexuality	Its Nature	Aging in late adulthood does include changes in sexual performance, moreso for males than females. Nonetheless, there are no known age limits to sexual activity.

Late Adulthood

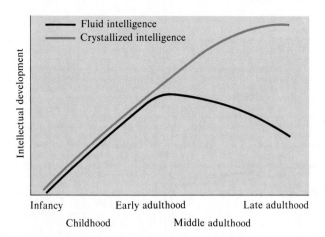

Figure 18.3
Fluid and crystallized intellectual development across the life span.

The graph shows two curves labeled "Fluid intelligence" and "Crystallized intelligence" plotted against "Intellectual development" (y-axis) and life stages (x-axis): Infancy, Childhood, Early adulthood, Middle adulthood, Late adulthood.

Intelligence

The issue of intellectual decline through the adult years is a provocative one. David Wechsler (1972) concluded that the decline in intelligence is simply part of the general aging process we all go through. But the issue is more complex. John Horn thinks some abilities decline while others do not (Horn & Donaldson, 1980). As shown in figure 18.3, Horn argues that **crystallized intelligence** (based on cumulative learning experiences) increases throughout the life span, while **fluid intelligence** (the ability to perceive and manipulate information) steadily declines from middle adulthood.

Some serious criticisms of Horn's hypothesis have come from Paul Baltes and K. Warner Schaie (Baltes, 1987; Baltes & Kliegl, 1986; Schaie, 1984). They believe many of the data on intelligence and aging, such as Horn's, are flawed because they were collected in a cross-sectional manner. Recall from chapter 1 that in a cross-sectional study, individuals of different ages are tested at the same time. For example, a cross-sectional study might assess the intelligence of different groups of 40- and 70-year-old individuals in a single evaluation, say in 1986. The average 40-year-old individual and the average 70-year-old individual tested in 1986 were born and reared in different eras, which produced different opportunities. For instance, as the 70-year-old individuals grew up, they had fewer educational opportunities, which probably influenced their scores on intelligence tests; so, if we find differences in intelligence levels of 40- and 70-year-old individuals when we assess them in a cross-sectional manner, the differences may be due to something like educational opportunities instead of age.

By contrast, a longitudinal study might evaluate the intelligence of the same individuals at age 40 and then again at age 70. Remember from chapter 1 that in a longitudinal study, the same individuals are retested after a period of years. The longitudinal data collected by Schaie (1984) and others do not reveal an intellectual decline in adulthood.

In thinking about how to study intelligence in late adulthood, we need to consider what components should be investigated and how they should be measured (Kaufman, 1988). Horn, Baltes, and Schaie, for the most part, have studied general intelligence and several of its subfactors, such as fluid and crystallized intelligence, through psychometric testing (standardized intelligence tests). Are we likely to find a decline in intelligence if we focus on important intellectual processes such as speed of processing, memory, and problem solving and observe them in different contexts?

"I was grinding out barnyards and farmhouses and cows in the meadow. And then, suddenly, I figured to hell with it."
Drawing by Stevenson; © 1971 The New Yorker Magazine, Inc.

Speed of Processing, Memory, and Problem Solving

While our speed of processing information seems to slow down in late adulthood, there is considerable individual variation in this ability. And when the slowdown occurs, it is not clear that this affects our lives in any substantial way. For example, in one experiment, researchers tested the reaction time and typing skills of typists of all ages (Salthouse & Somberg, 1982). They found that while the reactions of the older typists were usually slower, they actually typed just as fast as the younger typists. Possibly the older typists were faster when they were younger and had slowed down, but the results in another condition lead the researchers to think that something else was involved. When they limited the number of characters that the typists could look ahead, the older typists slowed substantially; the younger typists were affected much less by this restriction. The researchers believe the older typists had learned to look farther ahead, allowing them to type as fast as their younger counterparts.

A similar substitution of experience for speed may explain how older individuals maintain their skills in many other cognitive domains, among them memory and problem solving (Meer, 1986; Poon, 1985). Because of this, many researchers now realize that measuring performance in the laboratory may only give a rough estimate of an individual's ability in the real world. Possibly if we observed memory and problem solving in the real world, less decline in late adulthood would be discovered. Nancy Denney (1986) points out that most tests of memory and problem-solving abilities measure how older adults perform abstract or trivial activities, not unlike those found on school exams.

In her research, Denney assessed cognition among older adults by observing how they handled a landlord who would not fix their stove and what they would do if a Social Security check did not arrive on time. Denney revealed that the ability to solve such practical problems actually increased through the 40s and 50s as individuals got practical experience. She also found that individuals in their 70s were no worse at this type of practical problem solving than their counterparts in their 20s, who were quite good at solving practical problems.

Training Cognitive Skills

If cognitive skills are atrophying in late adulthood, can they be retrained? An increasing number of developmentalists believe that they can (Baltes, 1987; Baltes & Baltes, in press; Denney, 1982; Lachman, 1988; Perlmutter, in press; Schaie & Willis, 1986). For example, in the investigation conducted by K. Warner Schaie and Sherry Willis (1986), more than 4,000 individuals, most of whom were older adults, were studied. Using individualized training, the researchers improved the spatial orientation and reasoning skills for two-thirds of the individuals. Nearly 40 percent of those whose abilities had declined returned to a level they had reached 14 years earlier.

It is always in season for the old to learn.
Aeschylus, 525–456 B.C.

Mnemonics can be used also to improve the cognitive skills of older adults. **Mnemonics** are simply techniques for improving memory. In the fifth century B.C., the Greek poet Simonides attended a banquet. After he left, the building collapsed, crushing the guests and maiming their bodies beyond recognition. Simonides was able to identify the bodies by using a memory technique. He generated vivid images of each individual and mentally pictured where they had sat at the banquet table. The technique used by Simonides is called the **method of loci.** Recently, ten elderly subjects in Berlin, Germany, were systematically trained in the use of the method of loci (Kliegl & Baltes, 1987). The training involved practice with the technique using a map with 40 Berlin landmarks. The older adults also were trained to use chunking in their memory of the landmarks. **Chunking** involves organizing items into meaningful or manageable units. Telephone numbers, social security numbers, and license plate numbers are common examples of how chunking can help us and elderly individuals remember large amounts of information in our everyday lives. Using the method of loci and chunking, the elderly adults could recall more than 32 of the 40 Berlin landmarks, provided their study time for each word was self-paced. Later they were able to apply what they had learned in their method of loci and chunking training to recall long lists of digits. One 69-year-old woman correctly recalled 120 digits presented in intervals of 8s. Such results suggest substantial memory capacity in healthy, mentally fit older adults.

Older adults may not be as quick with their thoughts as younger adults, but when it comes to something we might call wisdom, that is an entirely different matter. Wisdom, like good wine, improves with age.

Older people need the opportunity to put their wisdom in action.

always practical solve things differently solutions always unselfish

With the ancient is wisdom;
and in the lengths of days understanding.
Job 12:12

Do you agree with the components of wisdom we have outlined? What would you add or subtract from the list?

Wisdom

Wisdom, like a good wine, gets better with age. What is this thing we call wisdom? **Wisdom** is an interpretive knowledge that combines depth and breadth; it involves understanding the limits and conditions of life and living—mortality, health, physical capacity, emotional range, social constraints, and personal talents; and it involves the accumulation of lifelong expertise in dealing with one's own life tasks and watching others deal with theirs (Baltes & others, 1988; Erikson, 1980; Smith, Dixon, & Baltes, in press). One tangible sign of wisdom is sound or good judgment regarding the conduct of one's life. Thus, wisdom, moreso than standard conceptions of intelligence, focuses more on life's pragmatic concerns and human conditions. This practical knowledge system takes many years to acquire, accumulating both through incidental experiences and through intentional, planned experiences. Wisdom probably involves a superior understanding of maxims and proverbs, such as "you can't win them all"; "when things are at their worst, they are bound to get better"; "it takes time to get things right"; "money isn't everything"; "appearances are deceiving"; and "experience is the best teacher." But wisdom is more than just knowing these maxims and proverbs; it is understanding them through experience.

What does this mean to the basic issue of intellectual decline in adulthood? Remember that we do not have just one intelligence but many intelligences. Older adults are not as intelligent as younger adults when it comes to speed of processing information and this probably harms their performance on many traditional school-related tasks and standardized intelligence tests. But when we consider general knowledge and something we call wisdom, that is an entirely different matter (Charness, 1988; Salthouse, 1988).

Work and Retirement

How productive are older workers? Are there different stages we go through when we retire? Who seems to adjust better to retirement than others? What is the changing pattern of retirement in the United States and around the world?

Work

Retirement is the rule rather than the exception in the United States, but some individuals do maintain their productivity throughout their life. Some older adults who have worked hard throughout their life may continue to do so until their death. Remember the comment earlier in the chapter by George Gallup, who indicated that he had a work agenda that would keep him busy until he is 100 years old. Some elderly individuals follow a work schedule that exhausts the young worker; some older adults demonstrate highly creative skills, sometimes outperforming their younger counterparts (Landy, 1989; Smither, 1988). In business and industry, there is a positive relation between age and productivity that favors the older worker. Older workers have a 20 percent better attendance record than younger workers, for example. Somewhat surprisingly, they also have fewer disabling injuries and their frequency of accidents is lower than for young adults (Comfort, 1976). Recent changes in the federal law that allows individuals over the age of 65 to continue working then sounds like a wise and humane decision.

One national survey focused on the characteristics of older workers in the United States (Flanagan, 1981). The individuals ranged in age from 68 to 73. Each of the 500 men and 500 women participated in an extensive four to five hour interview about their education, family, employment, and quality of life. Only 4 percent of the men were working full-time, while an additional 12 percent were working part-time. The same percentage of women were working full-time but only 8 percent were working part-time. Most of the men were in jobs that did not require professional training. About 41 percent were in general labor and service-type jobs requiring no special skills. Nearly 14 percent more were in mechanical, technical, or construction trades, while 33 percent were in sales or clerical positions. Only about 12 percent were in jobs requiring college training. However, more women (29 percent) were in occupations requiring college training, with teachers accounting for the bulk of these jobs. Unskilled labor jobs accounted for about 31 percent of the women who worked, while sales and clerical jobs represented 39 percent of women who worked either full- or part-time. The older adults expressed a great deal of pride and life satisfaction in their ability to continue their work into late adulthood.

Wisdom consists of many components. One of those components is the accumulation of lifelong expertise in dealing with one's own life tasks. The older woman shown here has many years of experience playing musical instruments and over the years has developed a sense for how to entertain audiences.

The night hath not yet come: We are not quite cut off from labor by the falling light; some work remains for us to do and dare.

*Henry Wadsworth Longfellow,
Morituri Salutamous, 1875*

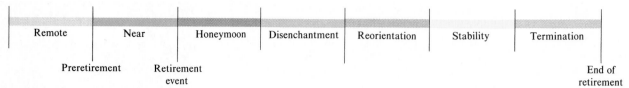

| Remote | Near | Honeymoon | Disenchantment | Reorientation | Stability | Termination |

Preretirement   Retirement event   End of retirement

Figure 18.4
Seven stages of retirement.

Even for those who do not move, retirement is a moving experience.
Richard Armour

Retirement comes in many forms. Regardless of its form, individuals can adapt more efficiently to retirement if they familiarize themselves with the benefits and pensions they can expect to receive long before retirement begins. The 1980s has witnessed a surge in preretirement planning.

Stages of Retirement

Developmentalists have described stages of retirement that they believe we go through. One view suggests seven stages of retirement—remote, near, honeymoon, disenchantment, reorientation, stability, and termination (see figure 18.4) (Atchley, 1976).

Most of us go to work with the vague belief that we will not die on the job and that we will enjoy the fruits of our labor at some point in the distant future. In this **remote stage** of retirement, most individuals do nothing to prepare themselves for retirement. As they age toward possible retirement, they may deny that eventually it will happen. Only when the **near stage** is reached does the worker usually participate in a preretirement program. These programs usually help individuals to decide when and how they should retire by familiarizing them with the benefits and pensions they can expect to receive or involve discussion of more comprehensive issues, such as physical and mental health. As individuals have become more aware of the importance of financial planning, the 1980s has witnessed a surge of participation in preretirement planning (Stagner, 1985).

After retirement, five stages remain to be experienced. Just after retirement, it is not unusual for individuals to feel euphoric. They may be able to do all of the things they never had time to do before and they may enjoy leisure activities more. Individuals who are forced to retire, or who retire because they are angry about their job, however, are less likely to experience the positive aspects of this early stage of retirement, called the **honeymoon stage.** This stage eventually gives way to a routine. If the routine is satisfying, adjustment to retirement usually is successful. Individuals whose life-styles did not entirely revolve around their jobs before retirement are more likely to make the retirement adjustment and develop a satisfying routine than those who did not develop leisure activities during their working years. Even individuals who initially experience retirement as a honeymoon usually later feel some form of letdown, or in some cases, even depression. Preretirement fantasies about retirement may be unrealistic, resulting in the **disenchantment stage** of retirement.

At some point, though, individuals who are disenchanted with retirement come to grips with themselves, *reorient* themselves to retirement's reality and discover ways to successfully cope with it. The major purpose of this **reorientation stage** is to explore, evaluate, and make some decisions about the type of life-style that probably will produce life satisfaction in retirement. The **stability stage** of retirement is reached when individuals have decided upon a set of criteria for evaluating choices in retirement and how they will perform once they have made these choices. For some individuals, this stage may occur after the honeymoon stage, but for others the transition is slower and more difficult. At some point the retirement role loses its significance and relevance in the eyes of the older adult. Some of these individuals go to work again, often

accepting a job that is totally unrelated to what they had done before retirement. Full-time leisure may become boring to them or they may need money to support themselves. Also, sickness or disability may alter retirement—this may cause the autonomy and self-sufficiency of the stable stage to give way to dependency on others, both physically and financially. This final stage of retirement is called the **termination stage.**

Because individuals retire at different ages and for different reasons, there is no particular timing or sequencing to the seven stages. Nonetheless, the seven stages help us to think about the different ways we can experience retirement and the adjustments that are involved.

Those Who Adjust Best to Retirement

Who adjusts best to retirement? Older adults who adjust best to retirement are healthy, have adequate income, are active, are better educated, have an extended social network including both friends and family, and usually were more satisfied with their lives before they retired (Palmore & others, 1985). Older adults with inadequate income, poor health, and who must adjust to other stress that occurs at the same time as retirement, such as the death of a spouse, have the most difficult time adjusting to retirement (Stull & Hatch, 1984).

Issues in Work and Retirement

For individuals who retire today, two special problems greet them. First, the individual who retires is automatically pushed into a more leisurely pace of life, whether such a life is desired or not. At the same time, the individual may be deprived of financial resources. Second, the retired individual has to live in a work-oriented world in which retired individuals may be perceived as outsiders. These circumstances may contribute to feelings of helplessness, low self-esteem, isolation, and feeling unwanted. Many individuals, though, cope effectively with retirement, even in the face of a society that devalues the retired individual (Heckhausen, 1986).

At some point in our lives, we face the issue of how to handle retirement in a work-oriented world. Health and money are special concerns of the retiring individual. Senator Claude Pepper believes that older adults should be allowed to continue work if they desire. Most experts recommend more flexibility than our current system permits. Some individuals, such as those shown here, may have looked forward most of their lives to retirement and greatly enjoyed its more relaxed freedom. Others may not know what to do with themselves when they retire—their life satisfaction might be improved if they continue working.

Issues of work and retirement will affect each of us in coming decades. Where do you stand on the issue of forced retirement at a specific age, such as 65? Explain your stand.

Increased national interest focuses on issues of work and retirement. At a 1981 White House Conference on Aging and in a 1980 colloquium at the Andrus Gerontology Center at the University of Southern California, the nature of the debate surfaced. Among the resolutions adopted at the White House Conference on Aging were: no reduction in Social Security Benefits or Medicare and Medicaid spending; and the creation of a national health insurance program that would cover home health services for the elderly. From these recommendations, it can be seen that health and money are pervasive concerns of the elderly. At the University of Southern California colloquium, Claude Pepper, himself in his 80s and chairman of the House of Representatives Committee on Aging, described why older Americans should be allowed to continue to work. According to Pepper, mandatory retirement wastes human talent, places a burden on the public and private pension system, and devalues the older adult's dignity.

What are some of the alternative work patterns that could be adopted for older adults? They include: alterations in time spent on the job (phased retirement, part-time work, job sharing, for example); alterations in the design of the job itself (a slower pace, for example); and alteration of roles within the organization (lateral transfers, for example) (Gonda, 1981).

While the United States has extended the retirement age upward, early retirement continues to be followed in large numbers. In many European countries—both capitalist and Communist-bloc—officials have experimented with various financial inducements designed to reduce or control unemployment by encouraging the retirement of older workers. West Germany, Sweden, Great Britain, Italy, France, Czechosolvakia, Hungary, and the Soviet Union are among the nations that are moving toward earlier retirement.

The United States seems to be trapped between two important concerns. On the one hand, we are increasingly conscious of the aging of the population and the illogic and injustice of current retirement policies. On the other hand, we worry about the possible effects of changing present retirement systems, especially the impact on the employment possibilities of younger workers. Through all of the debate, retirement's many faces need to be considered. And the realization that many older adults may have a lot of time ahead of them to weigh the advantages and disadvantages of having nothing really meaningful to do also needs to be addressed (Forman, 1984; Morris & Bass, 1988).

At this point we have discussed many different aspects of cognitive development and work and retirement in late adulthood. A summary of these ideas is presented in Concept Table 18.2.

Late Adulthood

Cognitive Development and Work and Retirement		
Concept	**Processes/Related Ideas**	**Characteristics/Description**
Cognitive Development	Intelligence	There is extensive debate over the issue of whether intelligence declines in late adulthood. Horn argues that fluid intelligence declines but that crystallized intelligence increases throughout the life span. Schaie and Baltes argue that longitudinal data reveal little or no decline in intelligence while cross-sectional data do because of cohort effects.
	Speed of Processing, Memory, and Problem Solving	Speed of processing information declines in late adulthood but strategies can be used to reduce the impact of this decline. Recent naturalistic research on memory and problem solving suggest the decline in these congitive processes may have been exaggerated.
	Training Cognitive Skills	Increasing evidence suggests that the elderly's cognitive skills can be trained through techniques such as mnemonics.
	Wisdom	Wisdom, moreso than standard conceptions of intelligence, focuses on life's pragmatic concerns and human conditions. Many developmentalists believe that wisdom increases in late adulthood.
Work and Retirement	Work	By age 70, only a small portion of men and women are in the labor force, although some individuals continue a life of strong productivity throughout late adulthood.
	Retirement Stages	One theory of retirement emphasizes seven stages: remote, near, honeymoon, disenchantment, reorientation, stability, and termination. Many individuals do not experience the stages in this order, although the stages help us to think about the different ways we can experience retirement.
	Those Who Adjust Best to Retirement	Individuals who are healthy, have adequate income, are active, are better educated, have an extended social network of friends and family, and usually were more satisfied with their lives before they retired.
	Issues in Work and Retirement in the United States and around the World	An individual who retires is automatically forced into a more leisurely life-style, and the retired individual faces living in a work-oriented society. Issues of work and retirement focus on alterations in time spent on the job, alterations in the job itself, and alterations of roles within organizations. While the United States has moved toward increasing the age for retirement, many European countries have lowered the age of retirement.

Summary

I. **Longevity**

Life expectancy is increasing but the life span is not. Among the most important factors in longevity are heredity and family, health, personality characteristics, and life-style. Beginning at age 25, females outnumber males, a gap that widens as individuals age; this sex difference is probably due to social and biologial factors.

II. **Biological Theories of Aging**

Microbiological theories of aging look within the body's cells for the clues to aging; among the most popular microbiological views are cellular garbage, cross-linkage, and cellular clock. Macrobiological theories look for more global causes of aging than the cellular, microbiological theories; three popular macrobiological views involve the immune system, the hypothalamus and pituitary gland, and organ reserve and homeostasis.

III. **The Course of Physical Decline and Illness and Impairment**

The circulatory system becomes less efficient, as do vision and hearing. The vast majority of individuals in late adulthood can have their vision corrected so they can continue to work and function in their world, and hearing aids also can diminish the problem of hearing loss. Decline in taste and smell may occur, although the decline is barely noticeable in healthy older people. As we age, the probability that we will have some disease increases. It is rare to find anyone over the age of 80 who is free from disease or illness. Many of the chronic diseases of the elderly—such as heart disease and cancer—produce long-term illness and impairment. Other chronic conditions—such as arthritis and hypertension— usually require reduced activity but are not as life-threatening. Low income is related to health problems in late adulthood.

IV. **Exercise**

While there may be some need for a reduction in exercise in late adulthood, the physical benefits of exercise have been demonstrated. What has not been demonstrated yet is whether exercise extends life.

V. **Sexuality**

Aging in late adulthood includes changes in sexual performance, moreso for men than for women. Nonetheless, there are no known limits to sexual activity.

VI. **Intelligence and Speed of Processing, Memory, and Problem Solving**

There is extensive debate over the stimulating issue of whether intelligence declines in late adulthood. Horn argues that a decline in fluid intelligence occurs, but that crystallized intelligence increases throughout the life span. Schaie and Baltes argue that longitudinal data reveal little or no decline in intelligence, while cross-sectional data do because of cohort effects. Speed of processing information declines in late adulthood but strategies can reduce the impact of this decline. Recent naturalistic studies on memory and problem solving suggest the decline in these cognitive processes may have been exaggerated.

VII. **Training Cognitive Skills and Wisdom**

Increasing evidence suggests that the elderly's cognitive skills can be trained through techniques such as mnemonics. Wisdom, moreso than standard conceptions of intelligence, focuses on life's pragmatic concerns and human conditions. Many developmentalists believe that wisdom increases in late adulthood.

VIII. **Work and Retirement Stages**

By age 70, only a small portion of men and women are in the labor force, although some individuals continue a life of strong productivity throughout late adulthood. One theory of retirement emphasizes seven stages: remote, near, honeymoon, disenchantment, reorientation, stability, and termination. Many individuals do not experience the stages in this order, but the stages help us to think about the different ways we can experience retirement.

IX. **Those Who Adjust Best to Retirement, and Issues in Work and Retirement**

Individuals who are healthy, have adequate income, are active, are better educated, have an extended social network of family and friends, and usually were more satisfied with their lives before they retired adjust to retirement the best. An individual who retires is automatically forced into a more leisurely life-style and the retired individual faces living in a work-oriented society. Issues of work and retirement focus on alterations in time spent on the job, alterations in the job itself, and alterations of roles within organizations. While the United States has moved toward increasing the age for retirement, many European countries have lowered the age of retirement.

Key Terms

life span *511*

life expectancy *511*

microbiological theory *514*

macrobiological theory *514*

crystallized intelligence *523*

fluid intelligence *523*

mnemonics *525*

method of loci *525*

chunking *525*

wisdom *526*

remote stage *528*

near stage *528*

honeymoon stage *528*

disenchantment stage *528*

reorientation stage *528*

stability stage *528*

termination stage *529*

Suggested Readings

Ostrow, A. C. (1984). *Physical activity and the older adult: Psychological Perspectives.* Princeton, NJ: Princeton Book Co.
Covers a wide range of changes in physical development brought about by aging and discusses the effects of exercise on these changes.

Palmore, E. B., Burchett, B. M., Fillenbaum, G. G., George, L. K., & Wallman, L. M. (1985). *Retirement: Causes and Consequences.* New York: Springer.
Why we retire and what happens to us after we retire are described.

Rybash, J. M., Hoyer, W. J., & Roodin, P. A. (1986). *Adult cognition and aging.* New York: Pergamon.
The issues surrounding aging and intelligence are explored in some detail.

Schooler, C., & Schaie, K. W. (Eds.) (1987). *Cognitive functioning and social structure over the life course.* Norwood, NJ: Ablex.
A number of articles about cognitive change in adulthood with special attention given to the issue of cognitive decline and cognitive training in older adults.

Woodruff, D. E. (1977). *Can you live to be 100?* New York: Chatham Square Press.
Description of factors that influence longevity and considerable information that allows you to estimate your chances of living to be 100.

C H A P T E R

19

■

Social and Personality Development

> row old along with me!
> The best is yet to be,
> The last of life,
> for which the first was
> made. ■
>
> *Browning*

As individuals survey their life history in late adulthood, one common theme for grandparents is the satisfaction derived from their grandchildren. Imagine yourself as an older adult. If you were engaging in a life review of your history when you become an older adult, expand your imaginative powers and speculate about what your life review might be like. If you already are an older adult, you probably will have engaged in this practice on a number of occasions.

Edna is a 75-year-old woman who has spent more time reflecting on what her life has been like since she entered late adulthood. Recently, she thought to herself:

> I think about my life a lot—it is in the back of my mind on many occasions. Thoughts of the past come into my mind when I look at my children and their children. When I walk down the street I think back to when I was a young girl . . . to the enjoyable moments with my friends and my parents. I think about my husband, our wedding . . . the times we struggled but made ends meet. He is gone now, but I have so many good memories of him.

On another occasion, Edna passed by a mirror and looked at herself:

> I see all these wrinkles and this little old lady whose body is slumping. I said to myself how old I looked. It made me think of death. It made me think of my past—what I had done wrong, what I had done right.

Several years ago after her husband had died, Edna was hospitalized for two months. She thought to herself:

> I feel so unhappy, so depressed. My husband is gone forever. I'm mad. I hate all of this. Why does it have to be this way? I'm mad at myself. When I look myself over, I think, "You could have done things a lot better. Maybe if you had done things differently you wouldn't feel like this."

On yet another occasion, some six months after she left the hospital, Edna's reflections revealed some of the adaptive and constructive outcomes a life review can provide:

> I am a lot more optimistic about my life now than I was six months ago. I have six marvelous grandchildren and two great daughters. I decided to get a tape recorder and talk about my positive feelings I had been having lately about my life. I wanted to tell my life story so my grandchildren could listen to it when they grow up. I acted like I was telling the story directly to them. I hope they will listen to it after I am gone.

Late adulthood is a time when we review our lives—later in the chapter we will explore this pervasive characteristic of older adults more fully and describe other aspects of the older adult's personality development. Among the other topics we evaluate are: the cultural and social world of the elderly; marital, family, and social relationships in old age; and the mental health of older adults.

Cultural and Social Worlds in Old Age

Could social experiences partly explain why we age? Do we stereotype old people in the United States? What is aging like in other cultures? How devastating is poverty to the elderly? What support systems benefit the elderly? We consider each of these questions in turn.

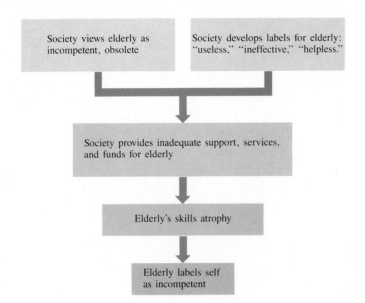

Figure 19.1
Social breakdown syndrome.

Social Theories of Aging

For too many years, it was believed that the best way to age was to be disengaged. **Disengagement theory** argues that as older adults slow down they gradually withdraw from society (Cumming & Henry, 1961). Disengagement is a mutual activity in which the older adult not only disengages from society, but society disengages from the older adult. According to the theory, the older adult develops an increasing self-preoccupation, lessens emotional ties with others, and shows a decreasing interest in society's affairs. Reduction of social interaction and increased self-preoccupation was thought to increase life satisfaction among older adults.

Disengagement theory predicted that low morale would accompany high activity, that disengagement is inevitable, and that disengagement is sought out by the elderly. Disengagement theory was in error. A series of investigations failed to support these contentions (Maddox, 1968; Neugarten, Havighurst, & Tobin, 1968; Reichard, Levson, & Peterson, 1962). When individuals continue to live active, energetic, and productive lives as older adults, their life satisfaction does not go down; sometimes it even goes up.

According to **activity theory,** the more active and involved older adults are, the less likely they will age and the more likely they will be satisfied with their lives. Activity theory suggests that individuals should continue their middle adulthood roles through late adulthood; if these roles are taken away from them (such as forced retirement, for example), it is important for them to find substitute roles that keep them active and involved in society's activities.

A third social theory of aging is **social breakdown-reconstruction theory** (Kuypers & Bengston, 1973). This theory argues that aging is promoted through negative psychological functioning, which consists of a poor self-concept, negative feedback from others and from society, and a lack of skills to deal with the world. As suggested in figure 19.1, social breakdown occurs in a sequence that begins with negative social views and treatment of older adults and ends with identifying and labeling one's self as incompetent. To prevent social breakdown from developing, we need to reorganize our social system so that older adults will be treated with more respect and so that they

Even the oldest tree some fruit may bear;
And as the evening twilight fades away
The sky is filled with stars, invisible by day.

Henry Wadsworth Longfellow,
Morituri Salutamus, 1875

Figure 19.2
Social reconstruction syndrome.

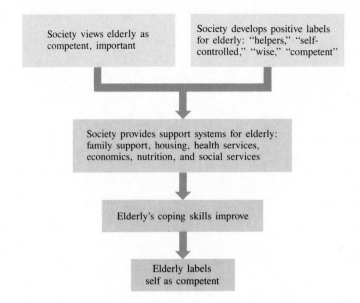

will develop better self-images and feel more competent about their roles in society. Figure 19.2 shows how social reconstruction could reverse social breakdown. Both activity theory and social breakdown-reconstruction theory argue that older adults' capabilities and competence are far greater than society has acknowledged in the past. Encouragement of their active participation in society should increase their life satisfaction and positive feelings about themselves. Focus on Life-Span Development 19.1 describes a program that provides a meaningful activity for older adults.

Aging in the United States and in Other Cultures

Ageism has become a new word in our vocabulary. Like sexism, it is one of society's uglier words. It refers to prejudice against older adults. Many older adults, unfortunately, face painful discrimination and they may be too polite and timid to attack it. Older adults may not be hired for new jobs or may be eased out of old ones because they are perceived as too rigid or feebleminded. They may be shunned socially, possibly because they are perceived as senile or boring. At other times, they may be perceived as children, described with adjectives like "cute" and "adorable." The elderly may be edged out of their family life by children who see them as sick, ugly, and parasitic. In sum, the elderly may be perceived as incapable of thinking clearly, learning new things, enjoying sex, contributing to the community, and holding responsible jobs—inhumane perceptions to be sure, but often painfully real (Butler, 1987; Gatz, 1989; Gatz & Pearson, 1988; Kimmel, 1988; Schaie, 1988).

For many generations, the elderly in China and Japan experienced higher status than the elderly in the United States (Palmore, 1975; Palmore & Maeda, 1985). In Japan, the elderly are more integrated into their families than the elderly in most industrialized countries. More than 75 percent live with their children; few single older adults live alone. Respect for the elderly surfaces in many circumstances: the best seats may be reserved for the elderly; cooking caters to the tastes of the elderly; and individuals bow to the elderly.

However, the image of the elderly Japanese who is spared the heartbreak associated with aging in the United States by the respect and devotion he receives from children, grandchildren, and society probably is idealized and overexaggerated (Tobin, 1987). Americans' images of the elderly in other cul-

Can you think of programs in addition to the foster grandparent program described in the box that improve the active participation of the elderly in society? Describe one or more of these programs.

"I used to be old, too, but it wasn't my cup of tea."
Drawing by Weber; © 1977 The New Yorker Magazine, Inc.

THREE GENERATIONS OF LOVE

T he Foster Grandparent Program in Wayne County, Michigan, serves the needs of two increasing populations—elderly adults who need some meaningful activity and teenage parents who need understanding and guidance in raising their children (Walls, 1987). The Teenage Parent Alternative School Program includes a Child Care Center where, each weekday morning, the blue Foster Grandparent Program van pulls up in front of the school and nine older women step out in their bright red smocks, ready to begin their 4-hour-day. They play with the infants, feed them, take them for walks, and give them a great deal of warmth and attention.

When the teenage parents are in the room, the foster grandparents talk with them, listen to their problems, and give them support. One foster grandparent commented that several of the teenage girls enjoyed talking about their boyfriends or problems they might be having. She said that this was part of her responsibility—to listen to their problems and hope that she can help them. Most of the teenage girls do not have extended families; the foster grandparent program allows them to see another generation's view of life—a generation with which they would otherwise have little association. In some cases, foster grandmothers take the place of the grandmother the adolescent girl does

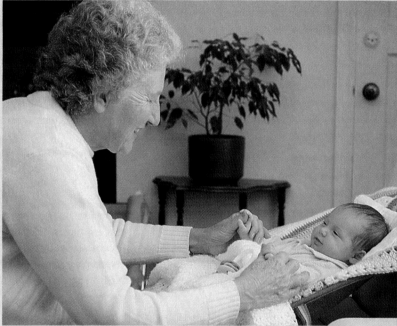

This foster grandmother has gained tremendous satisfaction by volunteering her services. Working with foster grandchildren has given her life renewed energy and reduced her loneliness.

not have or rarely sees. The grandmothers take great pride in their "grandchildren," giving glowing reports of what "their" grandchild learned to do that day.

The work is important to the older women. Not only are they keeping themselves busy and useful by volunteering, but they also form new friendships and sometimes create new "families." For some of the grandparents, working at the school is their main social outlet. They have

little contact with their families, so the program fills a void in their lives. One foster grandmother said, "I'm reborn! It takes me out of my apartment for four hours. I was a very lonely, lonely person before I joined" (Walls, 1987, p. 4). She recalls with pleasure her return to the school after several days vacation. When she came into the room, three of the children ran to her excitedly and exclaimed, "Grandma's back!"

tures may be idealized, too—we imagine elderly Eskimos adrift on blocks of ice, and 120-year-old Russian yogurt eaters, in addition to the honored elders of Japan. For example, as Japan has become more urbanized and Westernized, fewer elderly live with their children and more elderly adults return to work, usually in a lower-status job, with lower pay, with a loss of fringe benefits, and with a loss of union membership. The Japanese culture has acted as a powerful brake in slowing the decline in the respect for the elderly—today respect for the elderly in Japan is greater than in the United States, but not as strong as the idealized images we sometimes have.

Social Class and Ethnicity

Individuals may experience a substantial decline in income in late adulthood. The elderly have a higher poverty rate than any other age category. In 1985, almost 12 percent of individuals age 65 and over fell below the poverty line; this compares with 0 percent in Sweden and 3 percent in Canada. However, 23 percent of the elderly live in poverty in Great Britain (Smeeding, Torrey, & Rein, 1986). Of special concern are the elderly in minority groups, especially blacks and Hispanics, who are overrepresented in the elderly poor (Atchley, in press; Jackson, 1988; Markides, 1987). Consider Harry, a 72-year-old black, who lives in a run-down hotel in Los Angeles. He suffers from arthritis and uses a walker. He has had several serious falls and broken both of his arms. He has not been able to work for years, and government payments are rarely enough to meet his needs.

Support Systems for the Elderly

The United States has given attention to caring for the elderly but most *gerontologists*—those who study aging and the elderly—believe enough has not been done. A reasonable breadth of services in all states has developed, funded through such programs as the Older Americans Act, the Mental Health Act, and the Social Security System (Gelfand, 1988). The family plays an important role in providing support for the elderly. In many countries, families provide most of the assistance required by the elderly, allowing the elderly to remain in the community. At the same time, the care of an elderly family member can place stress on a family that may need support services itself to augment its caregiving role. However, the strong preference among aging parents is to maintain separate households apart from their children (Berman, 1987).

The MASH program in San Antonio, Texas, provided social support for older Hispanics. Able-bodied elders were trained to give family-care services to their peers. The recipients of MASH services were the frail and handicapped. The MASH volunteers, who were taught how to fill out the many government forms, provided a valuable service to their elderly peers, helping them get the services to which they were entitled. Many other support systems for the elderly have been developed.

Families and Social Relationships

What is the nature of marital relationships in older adults? Do older adults date? What is the nature of their friendships and social networks? What is the grandparent's role? These are some of the important questions to ask about the families and social relationships of older adults.

Do you have any ideas about how we can intervene to make the lives of low income and ethnic minority older adults healthier and happier? Describe at least one strategy that could be implemented.

So closely interwoven have been our lives, our purposes, and experiences that, separated, we have a feeling of incompleteness—united, such strengths of self-assertion that no ordinary obstacles, differences, or dangers ever appear to us insurmountable.

Elizabeth Cady Stanton,
Eighty Years and More

Retirement alters a couple's life-style. In many instances, husbands move toward more expressive roles, especially in becoming a helper around the house.

The Aging Couple, Life-Styles, and Dating

The time from retirement until death sometimes is referred to as the final stage in the marriage process. Retirement alters a couple's life-style, requiring adaptation. The greatest changes occur in the traditional family, in which the husband works and the wife is a homemaker. The husband may not know what to do with his time, and the wife may feel uneasy having him around the house all of the time. In traditional families, both partners may need to move toward more expressive roles. The husband must adjust from being the good provider to being a helper around the house; the wife must change from being only a good homemaker to being even more loving and understanding. Marital happiness as an older adult is also affected by each partner's ability to deal with personal conflicts, including aging, illness, and eventual death (Duvall & Miller, 1985).

Individuals who are married in late adulthood usually are happier than those who are single (Lee, 1978). Marital satisfaction is greater for women than for men, possibly because women place more emphasis on attaining satisfaction through marriage than men do. However, as more women develop careers, we would anticipate that this sex difference may not continue.

Not all older adults are married. At least 8 percent of all individuals who reach the age of 65 have never been married. Contrary to the popular stereotype, older adults who have never been married seem to have the least difficulty coping with loneliness in old age. Many of them discovered long ago how to live autonomously and how to become self-reliant (Gubrium, 1975).

Few of us imagine older couples taking an interest in the opposite sex other than for companionship, perhaps being interested in a game of bridge or conversation on the porch, but not much else. In fact, there are a number of older adults who date. The increased health and longevity of older adults has resulted in a much larger pool of active older adults. And the increased divorce rate has added many more older adults to this pool. More about the dating world of older adults is presented in Focus on Life-Span Development 19.2.

The richest love is that which submits to the arbitration of time.
Lawrence Durrell, Clea, *1960*

I could be handy, mending a fuse
when your lights are gone.
You can knit a sweater by the fireside,
Sunday morning go for a ride.
Doing the garden, digging the weeds,
who could ask for more?
Will you still need me, will you still feed me, when I'm sixty-four?
John Lennon and Paul McCartney

K ris Bulcroft and Margaret
O'Conner-Roden (1986)
observed singles' dances for older
adults at a senior center. They
noticed a sense of anticipation, festive
dress, and flirtatious behavior that
were not dissimilar from what we
perceive in young adults. They
subsequently interviewed 45 older
adults between the ages of 60 and 92
(average age=68) who were
widowed or divorced and who had
been actively dating during the last
year. Most of the older adults were
from middle-class backgrounds and
they were asked questions about how
they met, what they did on a date,
how important sexuality is in their
relationship, and the nature of family
and friends' reactions to their dating.

Most of the elderly daters did not
approach dating with a casual
attitude of "playing the field." They
saw dating as distinct from
friendship, although companionship
was a key ingredient of over-60
dating. One of the main findings was
the similarity between how older and

*We usually don't think of older adults as
being dating partners. In recent years,
developmentalists have become aware
that dating is more frequent among older
adults than they previously believed.
What is the nature of dating among older
adults?*

younger daters feel when they fall in
love—perspiring hands, a feeling of
awkwardness, an inability to
concentrate, anxiety when away from
the loved one, and heart palpitations.
One 65-year-old man said, "Love is
when you look across the room at
someone and your heart goes pitty-
pat." One 72-year-old widow
commented, "You know when you
are in love when the one you love is
away and you feel empty." And one
68-year-old divorcee remarked,
"When you fall in love at my age
there's initially a kind of 'oh, gee!'
feeling . . . and it's just a little
scary."

Older adults were just as likely as
younger adults to desire romantic
displays like candlelight dinners, long
walks in the park, and gifts of candy
or flowers. In addition to traditional
dates of going out for pizza and to
dances, older couples also went
camping, enjoyed the opera, and flew
to Hawaii for the weekend. The pace
of dating seemed to be accelerated in

later life. Older adults said they simply did not have time to play the field, favoring a more direct, no-game-playing approach to building a relationship with the opposite sex. Sexuality was an important aspect of the dating relationship for most of the older adults. Sexuality included intercourse, but the stronger emphasis was on hugging, kissing, and touching. This physical closeness helped to fulfill the intimacy needs of the older adults. Recall from our discussion in chapter 15 that passionate love is especially intense among young adults. For older daters, it is different. They have learned from experience that passionate love cannot be maintained with the same early level of intensity. But since most of them have been in marriages that lasted for decades, most of them know companionate love's value.

Older couples also felt the need to hide the intimate aspects of their dating because they feared social

Sexuality is an important consideration in the dating relationship of older adults. Sexuality includes intercourse, but stronger emphasis is placed on hugging, kissing, and touching.

disapproval. As one 63-year-old retiree commented, "Yeah, my girlfriend (age 64) lives just down the hall from me . . . when she spends the night she usually brings her cordless phone . . . just in case her daughter calls." Another 61-year-old woman said that her 68-year-old boyfriend had been spending three or four nights a week at her house for the past year, but she has not been able to tell her family, and she hides his shoes when her grandchildren visit. However, most family and friends supported the dating of the older adults, including them in family and social gatherings.

What is the age of love? The star-crossed lovers Romeo and Juliet were adolescents; Anthony and Cleopatra's intense love affair took place in the prime of their health and beauty; Lady Di was barely 20 when she married Prince Charles. But as we have seen, old is never too old for blushing cheeks, sparkling eyes, and affectionate touches.

The importance of friendship as a support system virtually knows no age boundaries. In late adulthood, friendships with unrelated adults may help to replace the warmth, companionship, and attachment previously experienced in one's family.

I am the family face;
Flesh perishes, I live on,
Projecting trait and trace
Through time to times anon,
And leaping from place to place
Over oblivion.

Thomas Hardy, 1917

At some point in our middle adulthood or late adulthood years, the majority of us will become a grandparent. What are the different meanings attached to the grandparent role? What do you think you will be like as a grandparent? Would you treat your grandchildren any differently than your grandparents treated you?

Regardless of their age, individuals also seem to place a high value on time spent with friends, at times higher than time spent with relatives. Life events may influence our friendships. In divorce or death, friendship usually provides an important support system; these events may intensify our friendships. Friendships among the elderly may become especially important in the years to come. Because individuals are having fewer children, families are becoming smaller. As individuals age, they will have fewer individuals to depend on for emotional and financial support. The mobility of our society also increases the distance between older and younger adults. Friendships with unrelated adults may help to replace the warmth, companionship, and nurturance traditionally supplied by families.

Grandparenting

Think for a moment about your images of grandparents. We generally think of grandparents as old people, but there are many middle-aged grandparents too. About three of every four adults over the age of 65 has at least one living grandchild, and most grandparents have some regular contact with their grandchildren. What is the meaning of the grandparent role? How do grandparents interact with their grandchildren? As more individuals live to an older age and as more families live in a greater variety of family structures, the grandparent's role may undergo change (Cherlin & Furstenberg, 1988).

Three prominent meanings are attached to the grandparent role (Neugarten & Weinstein, 1964). For some older adults, being a grandparent is a source of biological reward and continuity. In such cases, feelings of renewal (youth) or extensions of the self and family into the future emerge. For others, being a grandparent is a source of emotional self-fulfillment, generating feelings of companionship and satisfaction that may have been missing in earlier adult-child relationships. And for yet others, being a grandparent is not as important as it is for some individuals, experienced as a remote role.

The grandparent role may have different functions in different families, in different ethnic groups and cultures, and in different situations. For example, in one investigation of white, black, and Mexican-American grandparents and grandchildren, the Mexican-American grandparents saw their grandchildren more frequently, provided more support for the grandchildren and their parents, and had more satisfying relationships with their grandchildren (Bengston, 1985). And, in an investigation of three generations of families in Chicago, grandmothers had closer relationships with their children and grandchildren and gave more personal advice than grandfathers did (Hagestad, 1985).

The diversity of grandparenting also was apparent in an early investigation of how grandparents interacted with their grandchildren (Neugarten & Weinstein, 1964). Three styles were dominant—formal, funseeking, and distant figure. In the formal style, the grandparent performed what was considered to be a proper and prescribed role. These grandparents showed a strong interest in their grandchildren, but left parenting to the parents and were careful not to give childrearing advice. In the funseeking style, the grandparent was informal and playful. Grandchildren were a source of leisure activity; mutual satisfaction was emphasized. A substantial portion of grandparents were distant figures. In the distant figure style, the grandparent

	Social and Cultural Worlds and Families and Social Relationships	
Concept	**Processes/Related Ideas**	**Characteristics/Description**
Social and Cultural Worlds	Social Theories of Aging	Three prominent theories are disengagement theory, activity theory, and social breakdown-reconstruction theory. No support has been found for disengagement theory.
	Aging in the United States and in Other Cultures	Ageism is prejudice against older people; too many stereotypes still exist about older people. For many generations, the elderly in China and Japan have experienced higher status than the elderly in the United States. Today, respect for the elderly in Japan has diminished to some degree, but still remains above that accorded the elderly in the United States.
	Social Class and Ethnicity	Late adulthood often is a time of declining income; the elderly's poverty rate is 12 percent. Of special concern is the elderly in minority groups, who are overrepresented in the elderly poor.
	Support Systems for the Elderly	While a breadth of services has been developed to help the elderly, there is still considerable burden placed on many families. Most older adults prefer to maintain separate households from their children.
Families and Social Relationships	The Aging Couple, Life-Styles, and Dating	The time from retirement until death is sometimes referred to as the final stage in the marriage process. Retirement alters a couple's life-style, requiring adaptation. Married adults in old age are usually happier than singles, although singles may adjust easier to loneliness. Dating has become increasingly common in older adults, in some cases being similar to dating in younger adults, in other cases being dissimilar. Regardless of age, friendships are an important dimension of social relationships; they may become more intense in times of loss.
	Grandparenting	The grandparent role has at least three meanings—biological, emotional, and remote, and at least three styles of interaction—formal, funseeking, and distant. The grandparent role may be diverse and have different functions in different families, ethnic groups, cultures, and situations.

was benevolent but interaction occurred on an infrequent basis. Grandparents who were over the age of 65 were more likely to display a formal style of interaction; those under 65 were more likely to display a funseeking style.

At this point we have discussed a number of ideas about cultural and social worlds in old age and about families and social relationships. A summary of these ideas is presented in Concept Table 19.1. Now we turn to information about the nature of personality in late adulthood.

How do you think the grandparent's role will change in the future? Consider such factors as the increased mobility of our society, the increased number of people growing up in divorced and stepparent families, the increased longevity of our population, and changing gender roles.

Personality

What is our personality like in late adulthood? How extensively do we review our life when we become an older adult? What contributes to our life satisfaction as an older adult? Do our gender roles change when we become old? We consider each of these questions in turn.

Personality Development

Psychoanalytic theorists Sigmund Freud and Carl Jung saw old age as similar to childhood. For example, Freud believed that, in old age, we return to the narcissistic interests of early childhood. Jung said that, in old age, thought is deeply submerged in the unconscious mind; little contact with reality in old age was possible, he thought. More recently, developmentalists have crafted a view of old age that is more constructive and adaptive (Erikson, Erikson, & Kivnick, 1986).

Erik Erikson (1968) believes that late adulthood is characterized by the last of eight life cycle stages, *integrity versus despair.* In Erikson's view, the later years of life are a time for looking back at what we have done with our lives. Through many different routes, the older adult may have developed a positive outlook in each of the preceding periods. If so, retrospective glances and reminiscence will reveal a picture of a life well spent and the older adult will be satisfied (integrity). But if the older adult resolved one or more of the earlier stages in a negative way (being isolated in early adulthood or stagnated in middle adulthood, for example), retrospective glances may reveal doubt, gloom, and despair over the total worth of one's life. Erikson's own words capture the richness of his thought about the crisis of integrity versus despair in older adults:

> A meaningful old age, then . . . serves the need for that integrated heritage which gives indispensable perspective to the life cycle. Strength here takes the form of that detached yet active concern with life bounded by death, which we call *wisdom* in its many connotations from ripened "wits" to accumulated knowledge, mature judgment, and inclusive understanding. Not that each man can evolve wisdom for himself. For most, a living *tradition* provides the essence of it. But the end of the life cycle also evokes "ultimate concerns" for what change may have to transcend the limitations of his identity. . . .
>
> To whatever abyss ultimate concerns may lead individual men, man as a psychosocial creature will face, toward the end of his life, a new edition of the identity crisis which we may state in the words, "I am what survives of me." (1968, pp. 140–41.)

Robert Peck (1968) reworked Erikson's eighth stage of integrity versus despair by proposing three challenges that older adults must face: First, in *differentiation versus work role preoccupation,* it is important for older adults to establish a varied set of valued activities so that time spent in an occupation and with children can be filled. Second, in *body transcendence versus body preoccupation,* although most older adults experience illnesses, some seem to be able to enjoy life through creative activities and human interactions that allow them to go beyond their aging body. And, third, in *ego transcendence versus preoccupation,* although death is inevitable and probably not too far away, many older adults feel at ease with themselves by realizing that they have contributed to the future through competent rearing of their children or through their vocation and ideas.

In the end, the power behind development is life.

Erik Erikson, 1980

Robert Peck believes this older adult faces three challenges—establishing a varied set of valued activities, enjoying life through creative activities that go beyond his aging body, and feeling at ease with himself by realizing that he has contributed to future generations.

Most developmentalists agree that late adulthood is a time of **life review,** a process that is set in motion by looking forward to death (Butler, 1975). Sometimes the life review proceeds quietly; at other times, it may be intense, requiring considerable work to achieve some sense of personality integration. The life review may be observed initially in stray and insignificant thoughts about oneself and one's life history. These thoughts may continue to emerge in brief intermittent spurts or become essentially continuous. One 76-year-old man commented, "My life is in the back of my mind. It can't be any other way. Thoughts of the past play on me. Sometimes I play with them, encouraging and savoring them; at other times I dismiss them."

As the past marches in review, the older adult surveys it, observes it, and reflects on it. Reconsideration of previous experiences and their meaning occurs, often with revision or expanded understanding taking place. This reorganization of the past may provide a more valid picture for the individual, providing new and significant meaning to one's life. It may also help prepare the individual for death, in the process reducing fear. Remember our description of the 75-year-old woman at the beginning of the chapter, who decided to get a tape recorder and describe her life so her grandchildren would have something to remember her by when she is gone.

As the life review proceeds, the older adult may reveal to a spouse, children, or other close associates, unknown characteristics and experiences that previously had been undisclosed. In return, they may reveal previously unknown or undisclosed truths. Hidden themes of great meaning to the individual may emerge, changing the nature of the older adult's sense of self.

Virtually every older adult engages in a life review process. As the past marches in review, the older adult surveys it, observes it, and reflects on it. You might want to talk with several older adults and ask them to tell you about their lives to get a sense for how older adults review their life histories.

Life Satisfaction

Life satisfaction is the satisfaction with life in general or life as a whole. Developmentalists have been interested in the factors that contribute to life satisfaction, especially among older adults. Older adults with adequate income and good health are more likely to be satisfied with their lives than their low income counterparts who are in poor health (Markides & Martin, 1979). The more active an individual is as an older adult also is associated with life satisfaction—older adults who go to church, go to meetings, go on trips, play golf, go to dances, and exercise regularly are more satisfied with their lives than those who stay home and wrap themselves in a cocoon. Whether an older adult is retired or still in the labor force is not a good predictor of life satisfaction. Older adults who have an extended social network of friends and family also are more satisfied with their lives than more isolated older adults (Palmore & others, 1985). Some researchers, however, believe that a close attachment to one or more individuals is more important than support networks as a whole (Levitt, in press; Levitt & others, in press). More about how to achieve life satisfaction as an older adult appears in Focus on Life-Span Development 19.3.

In a well-known study of gifted adults, the older adult males attached more significance to family relations than to an occupation or work (Sears, 1977). In the same study, gifted older women were more satisfied with their lives if they had been in the labor force (Sears & Barbee, 1977). Nonworking older gifted women were less satisfied with their family lives than their working counterparts; many of these nonworking gifted older women would not opt for a career if they could relive their lives.

As this older adult reflects on his life history, he may reconsider previous experiences and reinterpret their meaning. Hidden themes may emerge that provide an understanding for the older adult, helping him put together the pieces of life's puzzle.

Royal Rousell is 83 years old and he is very satisfied with his life (Rousell, 1985). He has been a resident of a retirement community for 7 years. He serves as the coeditor of Community Newsletter with his wife Dorothy.

Rousell says that he has been old for a long time but that aging is a wonderful experience, a priceless gift. He sees aging as a natural development, not as an affliction. He describes aging as the only way he and his loved ones can enjoy a long life. Rousell describes four important characteristics of aging successfully.

First, it is important to keep a good balance between physical and mental capacities. Both types of activities should be stimulating, not stressful. Second, we should disengage or abandon some activities and interests from our younger years and replace them with new ones more commensurate with our advanced age. Third, we need to be satisfied with our lives, which can be enhanced by carefully evaluating ourselves and setting goals that we can attain. Fourth, we should maximize our use of time. No one who is not old can possibly

understand how precious time is. What a blessing another day of life is to an older adult, says Rousell. Enjoy every minute as an older adult.

Independence is at the top of Rousell's list of goals. The stereotype of old age is that the older we become the more dependent we will become. It does not always have to be this way. Rousell says that he feels more independent at the age of 83 than he did at the age of 63. Why?

Because he has learned how to be old *and* happy.

Gender Roles

Do our gender roles change when we become older adults? Some developmentalists believe there is decreasing femininity in women and decreasing masculinity in men when they reach the late adulthood years (Gutmann, 1975). The evidence suggests that older men do become more feminine—nurturant, sensitive, and so on—but it appears that older women do not necessarily become more masculine—assertive, dominant, and so on (Turner, 1982). Keep in mind that cohort effects are especially important to consider in areas like gender roles. As sociohistorical changes take place and are assessed more frequently in life-span investigations, what were once perceived to be age effects may turn out to be cohort effects.

Problems and Disturbances and Mental Health in Late Adulthood

What is the nature of mental health among older adults? What are the most common mental health problems of the elderly? What are the most effective mental health interventions with older adults?

The Mental Health of Older Adults

While a substantial portion of the population can now look forward to a longer life, the life may unfortunately be hampered by a mental disability in old age. This prospect is both troubling to the individual and costly to society. Mental disturbance makes an individual increasingly dependent on the help and care of others; the cost of mental health disturbance in older adults is estimated at more than 40 billion dollars per year in the United States. More important than the loss in dollars, though, is the loss of human potential and the suffering (Kety, 1980; Neugarten, 1989; Siegler, 1989).

Mental health not only embraces the absence of mental illness, difficulties, and frustrations but also reflects one's ability to deal with life's issues in effective and satisfying ways. Because older adults are more likely to have some type of physical illness, the interweaving of physical and mental problems is more common in later adulthood than in early adulthood (Birren & Sloane, 1980).

How common is mental disturbance in older adults? At least 10 percent of individuals over 65 have mental health problems severe enough to warrant professional attention (La Rue, Dessonville, & Jarvik, 1985). Two disorders that are especially prevalent among older adults are depression and Alzheimer's disease.

Depression

The individual classified as having **major depression** is sad, demoralized, bored, and self-derogatory; she does not feel well, loses stamina easily, has a poor appetite, and seems listless and unmotivated. Depression is so widespread it has been called the "common cold" of mental disorders. Estimates of depression's frequency among older adults vary; depressions severe enough to warrant intervention are generally estimated to affect as many as 10 percent of elderly adults (Gaylord & Zung, 1987). Professors, corporate executives, laborers, retired individuals—no one is immune to depression, not even Ernest Hemingway, famous author who experienced major depression. Major depression may not only envelop the individual in sadness, but suicidal tendencies may also surface. To learn more about Hemingway's major depression and suicide, turn to Focus on Life-Span Development 19.4.

Alzheimer's Disease

Mary's family thought she was having vision problems when at age 65 she could not remember how to do the crossword puzzles she loved so much. Soon her family detected other symptoms pointing to a more serious condition. Mary no longer recognized her husband and even ran away from him in terror several times. She thought he was a stranger who was going to attack her, although he was an extremely kind and gentle man. Mary's family finally took her to a hospital, where she was diagnosed as having **Alzheimer's disease,** a progressive, degenerative disorder that involves deterioration of the brain's cells.

HEMINGWAY

S uicide was a recurrent theme in Ernest Hemingway's (1899–1961) life. Even before his father's suicide, Hemingway seemed obsessed by the theme of self-destruction. As a young boy, he enjoyed reading Stevenson's "The Suicide Club." At one point in his adult life, Hemingway said he would rather go out in a blaze of light than have his body worn out and old and his illusions shattered.

Hemingway's suicidal thoughts sometimes coincided with his marital crisis. Just before marrying Hadley, Hemingway became apprehensive about his new responsibilities and alarmed her by the mention of suicide. Five years later, during a crisis with Pauline, he calmly told her he would have committed suicide if their love affair had not been resolved happily. Hemingway was strangely comforted by the morbid thoughts of death. When feeling low, he would think about death and ways of dying; the best way he thought, unless he could arrange to die in his sleep, would be to go off an ocean liner at night.

Hemingway committed suicide in his sixties. His suicide raised the question of why a man with good

Hemingway as a healthy, productive adult.

A depressed Hemingway shortly before his suicide.

looks, sporting skills, friends, women, wealth, fame, genius, and a Nobel Prize would kill himself. Hemingway developed a combination of physical and mental disturbances. He had neglected his health for many years, suffering from weight loss, skin disease, alcoholism, diabetes, hypertension, and impotence. His body was in a shambles. He dreaded

becoming an invalid and the slow death this would bring. At this point, the severely depressed Hemingway was losing his memory and no longer could write. One month before his suicide, Hemingway said, "Staying healthy. Working good. Eating and drinking with his friends. Enjoying himself in bed. I haven't any of them." (Meyers, 1985, p. 559)

Her condition progressed to the point where her personality changed, she had trouble sleeping, she had difficulty controlling her body functions, she showed a loss of appetite, and she became depressed.

Alzheimer's disease was discovered in 1906, and researchers have still not found the causes or cure for it. Approximately 2.5 million individuals over the age of 65 in the United States have Alzheimer's disease. As increasing numbers of individuals live to older ages, it has been predicted that Alzheimer's disease could triple in the next fifty years. Because of the increasing prevalence of Alzheimer's disease, researchers have stepped up their efforts to understand the causes of the disease and to discover more effective ways to treat it (Jarvik & Winograd, 1988).

For roughly one in ten Alzheimer's victims, the disease is clearly inherited. On the average, Alzheimer's will strike 50 percent of the offspring of someone with this hereditary form of the disease. Families with an incidence of Alzheimer's disease are three times as likely to have a case of Down's syndrome, a severe form of mental retardation, in their family as well. Scientists have yet to isolate the gene or genetic combination responsible, but they are getting closer—it is on chromosome twenty-one (Barnes, 1987). The brains of Alzheimer's patients are filled with plaque, formed from pieces of nerve cells and a protein called amyloid. The plaque accumulates at sites of nerve cell connections and chokes off communication between nerve cells. But it is not known whether the plaque causes Alzheimer's or is a secondary effect caused by other factors. Researchers currently are investigating the genes that control amyloid production for possible clues about the cause of Alzheimer's disease.

Something also goes wrong with the neurotransmitter acetylcholine in Alzheimer's patients; this chemical is especially important in memory and the motor control of muscles. It may be that the problems in acetylcholine production are due to a defective gene. One strategy for treating Alzheimer's patients involves the use of drugs to block the pathway that leads to acetylcholine breakdown. In one investigation, a drug by the name of THA improved the memory and coping skills of 16 of 17 Alzheimer's patients by increasing acetylcholine production (Summers, 1986). But most scientists believe that increasing acetylcholine production does not attack the cause of Alzheimer's disease. Eventually, the acetylcholine-producing cells in Alzheimer's patients die and THA only works as long as there is at least some acetylcholine around.

With more knowledge about the genetic basis of Alzheimer's disease, though, scientists are optimistic that the cause of Alzheimer's disease will be discovered and the expression of the disorder curtailed. Even if the gene defect is discovered, it is clear that more than just a gene defect is involved. Some trigger must set off the disease. What that trigger (or triggers) might be is still not known, although Alzheimer's disease is associated with diet, smoking, stress, head injury, and thyroid problems.

Whether or not special living conditions can improve the motor skills of Alzheimer's patients is being studied, too. Color codes and bright lights may help the daily functioning of the Alzheimer's patient. Dance and exercise may improve motor abilities. The family's role as a support system for Alzheimer's patients also is being evaluated. Psychologists believe the family can help improve the mental outlook of the Alzheimer's patient.

Mental Health Treatment

Older adults receive disproportionately few mental health services. One estimate is that only 2.7 percent of all clinical services provided by psychologists go to older adults, although individuals aged 65 and over make up more than 11 percent of the population. The proportion of community mental health services rendered to older adults has remained relatively stable—at or about 4 percent in the 1970s and 1980s (Lebowitz, 1987; VandeBos, Stapp, & Kolburg, 1981).

Psychotherapy can be expensive. Although reduced fees and sometimes no fee can be arranged in public hospitals for older adults from low income backgrounds, many older adults who need psychotherapy do not get it. It has been said that psychotherapists like to work with young, attractive, verbal, intelligent, and successful clients (called YAVISes) rather than those who are quiet, ugly, old, institutionalized, and different (called QUOIDs). While mental health professionals have become increasingly sensitive to such problems, surveys indicate that 70 percent of psychotherapists report never seeing older clients (VandeBos, Stapp, & Kolburg, 1981). Psychotherapists have been accused of failing to see older adults because they perceive that older adults have a poor prognosis for therapy success, they do not feel they have adequate training to treat older adults, who may have special problems requiring special treatment, and they may have stereotypes that label older adults as low status and unworthy recipients of treatment.

There are many different types of mental health treatment available to older adults. Some common mechanisms of change that improve the mental health of older adults are (Gatz & others, 1985): (1) fostering a sense of control, self-efficacy, and hope; (2) establishing a relationship with a helper; (3) providing or elucidating a sense of meaning; and (4) educative activities and the development of skills (Gallagher & Thompson, 1986; Rodin, 1986; Steuer & Hammen, 1986).

How can we better meet the mental health needs of the elderly? First, psychologists must be encouraged to include more older adults in their client lists, and the elderly must be convinced that they can benefit from therapy. Second, we must make mental health care affordable—Medicare currently pays lower percentages for mental health care than for physical health care, for example (Roybal, 1988).

At this point we have discussed a number of ideas about personality and mental health in older adults. A summary of these ideas is presented in Concept Table 19.2.

Personality and Mental Health		
Concept	**Processes/Related Ideas**	**Characteristics/Description**
Personality	Personality Development	Erikson proposed that late adulthood is characterized by the stage of integrity versus despair, a time when we look back and evaluate what we have done with our lives. Peck reworked Erikson's final stage. Most older adults engage in a life review process.
	Life Satisfaction	The satisfaction with life in general; income, health, activity level, close relationships, and social networks are associated with life satisfaction in late adulthood.
	Gender Roles	There is stronger evidence that men become more "feminine"—nurturant, sensitive—as older adults than there is that women become more "masculine"—assertive, dominant—as older adults.
Problems and Disturbances and Mental Health	The Mental Health of Older Adults	At least 10 percent of older adults have mental health problems sufficient to need professional help.
	Depression	The "common cold" of mental disorders; depression severe enough to warrant professional attention appears in as many as 1 out of 10 older adults.
	Alzheimer's Disease	Approximately 2.5 million older adults have this progressive, degenerative disorder that involves deterioration of the brain's cells. Special attention is being given to Alzheimer's genetic basis.
	Mental Health Treatment	A number of barriers to mental health treatment in older adults exist; older adults receive disproportionately less mental health treatment. There are many different ways to treat the mental health problems of the elderly.

Summary

I. **Social Theories of Aging**
Three prominent theories are disengagement theory, activity theory, and social breakdown-reconstruction theory. No support has been found for disengagement theory.

II. **Aging in the United States, Other Cultures, Social Class, and Ethnicity**
Ageism is a prejudice against older people; too many stereotypes still exist about older people. For many generations, the elderly in China and Japan have experienced higher status than the elderly in the United States.

Today, respect for the elderly in Japan has diminished to some degree, but still remains above that accorded the elderly in the United States. Late adulthood often is a time of declining income; the elderly's poverty rate is 12 percent. Of special concern are the elderly in minority groups, who are overrepresented in the elderly poor.

III. **Support Systems for the Elderly**
While a breadth of services has been developed to help the elderly, there is still considerable burden placed on many families. Most older adults prefer to maintain separate households from their children.

IV. **The Aging Couple, Life-Styles, and Dating**
The time from retirement until death is sometimes referred to as the final stage of the marital process. Retirement alters a couple's life-style, requiring adaptation. Married couples in old age are usually happier than singles, although singles may adjust more easily to loneliness. Dating has become increasingly common in older adults, in some cases being similar to dating in younger adults, in other cases dissimilar. Regardless of age, friendships are an important dimension of social relationships; they may intensify in times of loss.

V. Grandparenting

The grandparent role has at least three meanings—biological, emotional, and remote, and at least three styles of interaction—formal, funseeking, and distant. The grandparent role may be diverse and have different functions in different families, ethnic groups, cultures, and situations.

VI. Personality Development

Erikson proposed that late adulthood is characterized by the stage of integrity versus despair, a time when we look back and evaluate what we have done with our lives. Peck reworked Erikson's final stage. Most older adults engage in a life review process.

VII. Life Satisfaction and Gender Roles

Life satisfaction is the satisfaction with life in general. Income, health, activity level, close relationships, and social networks are associated with life satisfaction in late adulthood. There is stronger evidence that men become more "feminine"—nurturant, sensitive—as older adults than there is that women become more "masculine,"—assertive, dominant—as older adults.

VIII. Problems and Disturbances and Mental Health

At least 10 percent of older adults have mental health problems sufficient to warrant professional help. Depression is the "common cold" of mental disorders; it is severe enough in older adults to warrant professional attention in as many as 1 out of 10 older adults. Approximately 2.5 million older adults in the United States have Alzheimer's disease, a progressive, degenerative disorder that involves deterioration of the brain's cells. Special attention is being given to Alzheimer's genetic basis. A number of barriers to mental health treatment in older adults exist. Older adults receive disproportionately less mental health treatment than younger adults. There are many different ways to treat the mental health problems of older adults.

Key Terms

disengagement theory *537*
activity theory *537*
social breakdown-reconstruction

theory *537*
ageism *538*
life review *547*

life satisfaction *547*
major depression *549*
Alzheimer's disease *549*

Suggested Readings

Carstensen, L. L. & Edelstein, B. A. (Eds.) (1987). *Handbook of clinical gerontology*. New York: Pergamon. *Includes extensive, up-to-date treatment of Alzheimer's disease, depression, treatment strategies, and the prevention of mental health problems.*

Gatz, M., Popkin, S. J., Pino, C. D., & VandenBos, G. R. (1985). Psychological interventions with older adults. In J. E. Birren & K. W. Schaie (Eds.), *Handbook of the psychology of aging* (2nd ed.) New York: Van Nostrand Reinhold. *Discussion of the mental health therapy needs of the elderly; summarizes a number of different treatment strategies with older adults.*

The Gerontologist
This journal includes many articles on the social and personality development of older adults. Extensive discussion of the mental health of older adults is usually covered. Go to your library and leaf through the issues of the last several years to discover researchers' interests in these areas.

Maddox, G. (Ed.) (1987). *The encyclopedia of aging*. New York: Springer.
Covers a number of topics pertaining to social, personality, and mental health needs of the elderly; contemporary information on the cultural and social worlds of older adults is provided.

Whitbourne, S. (1987). Personality development in adulthood and old age. In K. W. Schaie (Ed.), *Annual review of gerontology and geriatrics* (Vol. 7). New York: Springer. *Coverage of personality change in old age is included; the roles of coping, adaption, and context are emphasized.*

SECTION
X

■

Death and Dying

D o not go gentle into that
good night
Old age should burn and rave at
close of day;
Rage, rage against the dying of
the light. ■

Dylan Thomas

Death and Dying

> **M**an is the only animal that finds his own existence a problem which he has to solve and from which he cannot escape. In the same sense man is the only animal who knows he must die. ■
>
> *Erich Fromm*

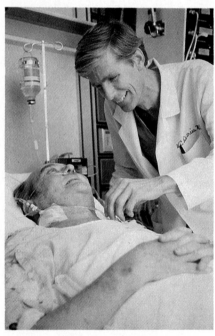

Barney Clark, the first recipient of an artificial heart, is shown with his doctor. What ethical issues were raised by giving Barney Clark a key that he could use to turn off the compressor if at any time he wanted to stop living?

On December 2, 1982, Barney Clark became the first human to be given a permanent artificial heart. The retired Seattle dentist seemed ideally suited for the new technique. He was dying of a heart disease that did not respond to other treatments, and at age 65, Barney was considered too old for a conventional transplant. Otherwise he was in good physical condition. Psychologically, Barney also seemed to be a good candidate: He had a strong will to live, an intelligent, thorough understanding of his disease and his options, and a loving, supportive family.

Barney Clark's options—no doubt preferable to death—were not without their drawbacks. Unlike a transplant, the artificial heart would not let him be completely mobile. For the remainder of his life, Barney would be connected to a bulky compressor by two six-foot hoses. Everyone involved was uncertain what the quality of Barney's life would be like with the artificial heart. Barney chose to have the implantation and the event received an enormous amount of publicity, virtually all of it ecstatic over the new technology. One small item, though, was often overlooked in the publicity surrounding the artificial heart operation. Barney Clark had been given a key that he could use to turn off the compressor if at any time he wanted to cease living. Barney Clark never used the key. Fifteen weeks after the history-making operation, Barney Clark died. Although he never used the key, the fact that he was given the key raises some important ethical issues about voluntary death (Rachels, 1986).

Giving Barney Clark the key acknowledged that, in his case, suicide was permissible. This is unusual because in our society we rarely have acknowledged the permission to commit suicide. Giving him the key symbolized the social acceptance of the act. Would it have been acceptable for Barney Clark to solicit the help of others to end his life? Should he also have been given the right to have his wife or his best friend turn the key for him? These are difficult questions and we explore them further in this chapter. Among other intriguing questions we evaluate are: How do we define death? How is death viewed in different cultures? How is death viewed at different points in the life cycle? How do we face our own death? How should we communicate with a dying person? What are the contexts in which people die? And, how do we cope with the death of someone else?

Death, Sociohistorical Contexts, and the Life Cycle

Epicurus thought of death as annihilation, the absolute end of one's existence. Yet he believed there was nothing bad about it. In a letter to one of his followers, he wrote:

> Become accustomed to the belief that death is nothing new to us. For all good and evil consists in sensation, but death is deprivation of sensation. . . . So long as we exist death is not with us; but when death comes, then we do not exist.

Is there one point in the process of dying which is *the* point at which death takes place, or should death be viewed as a more gradual process? Should we painlessly put to death people who are suffering extensively? Is death more painful in some cultures than Epicurus seemed to believe? Do we view death differently when we become older than when we are younger?

Defining Death

Twenty years ago, an individual was considered dead when breathing stopped and no heartbeat could be heard. Rigor mortis, dilation of pupils, and a relaxation of the sphincter muscle were markers of death. In the 1980s, though, determining death has become more complex. Modern medicine has contributed a neurological definition of death—**brain death**—in which all electrical activity of the brain has ceased for a specified period of time as determined by an electroencephalogram (EEG). A flat recording by an EEG marks brain death, regardless of how vital other organs may seem under resuscitation. When an individual is dying, the cells of the brain's higher areas become deprived of oxygen and die within five to ten minutes. The lower brain centers—such as those that monitor heartbeat and respiration—die next. When the individual's heart stops beating but is restored by resuscitation, an individual who technically has died may be revived. Unfortunately, if the higher brain centers have been deprived of oxygen, the individual probably will not recover mental and motor capabilities, or if recovered, impairment probably will be severe (Weir, 1986).

The ability of modern medicine to resuscitate a dying individual complicates the definition of death. A heart that has stopped can be massaged or stimulated electrically and can continue pumping indefinitely even though the brain remains irreparably damaged. Numerous individuals with irreversible brain damage have been kept alive for years by intravenous feeding and artificial breathing devices. Such cases illustrate some of the ethical and legal questions posed as a result of our ability to resuscitate and prolong life. Some of the most common issues are: Is the individual dead when the brain dies but the heart is stimulated and continues pumping blood? Should individuals who are unconscious and have no chance for recovery be permitted to die—that is, should their treatment be terminated? Does the individual have the right to die? Who should be making such decisions?

Considering our discussion of factors involved in defining death, how would *you* define death?

Euthanasia

Euthanasia is the act of painlessly putting to death individuals who are suffering from an incurable disease or severe disability; sometimes it is referred to as mercy killing. Distinctions are made between *active euthanasia*—death induced by some positive action, such as the injection of a lethal dose of a drug—and *passive euthanasia*—death induced by the withdrawal of some life-sustaining therapeutic device, such as when a respirator or heart-lung machine is turned off. Some medical ethicists argue that passive euthanasia is not a form of euthanasia at all, but simply the process of letting nature take its course. Today, active euthanasia is illegal in all countries of the world, except in several specific cases in the Netherlands (Levinson, 1987).

Technological advances in life-support devices raise the issue of quality of life. Should individuals be kept alive in undignified and hopeless states? The trend seems to be toward acceptance of passive euthanasia in the case of terminally ill patients. The inflammatory argument that once equated this

On October 11, 1983, an infant known to the public only as "Baby Jane Doe," was born in New York. She suffered from multiple defects including spina bifida (a broken and protruding spine), hydrocephaly (excess fluid on the brain), and microencephaly (an abnormally small brain). A CAT scan indicated that part of her cerebral cortex was missing completely. The parents were told that without surgery, the infant would die in two years; with surgery, she would have a 50–50 chance of surviving into her 20s, but even then she would be severely mentally retarded and physically impaired, paralysed, epileptic, unable to leave her bed, and there would be a continuous risk of such diseases as meningitis. In the face of all of these devastating problems, the parents chose not to authorize the surgery.

A lawyer representing a conservative right-to-life group petitioned the New York State Supreme Court to order that the surgery be performed on Baby Jane Doe. However, higher courts in New York quickly overturned the order, calling the order "offensive." He then asked the Supreme Court to order the surgery; the Court declined to hear the case.

Then the executive branch of the federal government entered the case. The Department of Justice filed suit demanding to see hospital records for Baby Jane Doe; the Department argued that she was being discriminated against. However, the suit was dismissed in federal court, with the judge concluding that:

The papers submitted to the court demonstrate conclusively that the decision of the parents to refuse consent to the surgical procedures was a reasonable one based on due consideration of the medical options available and on a genuine concern for the best interests of the child.

In May, 1984, though, Congress passed *new* "Baby Jane Doe" legislation, requiring states receiving federal child-abuse prevention grants to adopt rules covering "medical neglect." The American Medical Association promised to fight the legislation in court.

The debate over the Baby Jane Doe case focuses primarily on the question of parental autonomy— whether parents have the right to decide if life-saving surgery should be performed on a child that will have an extremely subnormal life— and the question of the value of an infant's life. Again, the point is made that these are questions with no easy answers and questions that involve issues about which each of us may have deeply held convictions (Rachels, 1986).

practice with suicide rarely is heard today. However, experts do not yet entirely agree on the precise boundaries or the exact mechanisms by which treatment decisions should be implemented. Can a comatose patient's life support systems be disconnected when the patient has left no written instructions to that effect? Does the family of a comatose patient have the right to overrule the attending physician's decision to continue life support systems? These are searching questions with no simple or universally agreed upon answers. A provocative case involving an innocent infant named "Baby Jane Doe" is presented in Focus on Life-Span Development 20.1, where issues pertaining to parents' rights and the value of a human life are raised.

Death and Sociohistorical Contexts

When, where, and how people die have changed historically. Two hundred years ago, almost one out of every two children died before the age of 10, and one parent died before children had grown up. Today, death occurs most often among the elderly. Life expectancy has increased from 47 years for an individual born in 1900 to 75 years for someone born today. As our population has aged and become more mobile, more older adults die apart from their

(a)

(b)

(c)

(d)

families. In the United States, more than 80 percent of all deaths occur in institutions or hospitals, for example. The care of a dying older person has shifted away from the family and minimized our exposure to death and its painful surroundings.

The ancient Greeks faced death as they faced life—openly and directly. To live a full life and die with glory was the prevailing attitude of the Greeks. Individuals are more conscious of death in times of war, famine, and plague. While Americans are conditioned from early in life to live as though they were immortal, in much of the world this fiction cannot be maintained. Death crowds the streets of Calcutta in daily overdisplay, as it does the scrubby villages of Africa's Sahel. Children live with the ultimate toll of malnutrition and disease, mothers lose as many babies as survive into adulthood, and it is rare that a family remains intact for many years. Even in peasant areas where life is better, and health and maturity may be reasonable expectations, the presence of dying people in the house, the large attendance at funerals, and the daily contact with aging adults prepare the young for death and provide them with guidelines of how to die. By contrast, in the United States, it is not uncommon to reach adulthood without having seen someone die.

Most societies throughout history have had philosophical or religious beliefs about death. And most societies have some form of ritual that deals with death (see figure 20.1). For example, elderly Eskimos in Greenland who can

Figure 20.1
(a) Most societies have some form of ritual associated with death. Shown here is a Chinese burial service in Singapore. (b) Family memorial day at the National Cemetery in Seoul, Korea. (c) A cremation in Katmando, Nepal. (d) The deceased person's belongings are left on a mountainside in Tibet.

Figure 20.2
A death ritual in the Tanala culture of Madagascar, where death is dealt with in a peaceful manner.

How many different rituals for death can you think of that take place in the United States? Describe them, and explain their role in death and life.

no longer contribute to their society may walk off alone never to be seen again, or they may be given a departure ceremony at which they are honored, then ritually killed. In some tribes, an old man wants his oldest son or favorite daughter to put a string around his neck and hoist him to his death. This may be performed at the height of a party where there is good food, gaiety, and dancing (Freuchen, 1961).

In most societies, death is not viewed as the end of existence—though the biological body has died, the spiritual body is believed to live on. This religious perspective is favored by Americans as well. However, cultures may differ in their perceptions of death and their reactions to death. In the Gond culture of India, death is believed to be caused by magic and demons. The members of the Gond culture show an angry reaction to death. In the Tanala culture of Madagascar, death is believed to be caused by natural forces. The members of the Tanala culture show a much more peaceful reaction to death than their counterparts in the Gond culture (see figure 20.2). Other cultural variations in attitudes toward death include beliefs about reincarnation, which is an important aspect of the Hindu and Buddist religions (see figure 20.3).

Perceptions of death vary and reflect diverse values and philosophies. Death may be seen as a punishment for one's sins, an act of atonement, or a judgment of a just God. For some, death means loneliness; for others, death is a quest for happiness. For still others, death represents redemption, a relief from the trials and tribulations of the earthly world. Some embrace death and welcome it; others abhor and fear it. For those who welcome it, death may be seen as the fitting end to a fulfilled life. From this perspective, how we depart from earth is influenced by how we have lived. In the words of Leonardo da Vinci, death should come to an individual after a full life just as sleep comes after a hard day's work.

In many ways, we are death avoiders and death deniers in the United States. This denial can take many forms:

The tendency of the funeral industry to gloss over death and fashion greater lifelike qualities in the dead

The adoption of euphemistic language for death—exiting, passing on, never say die, and good for life, which implies forever, for example

The persistent search for a fountain of youth

The rejection and isolation of the aged who may remind us of death

The adoption of the concept of a pleasant and rewarding afterlife, suggesting that we are immortal

Emphasis of the medical community on the prolongation of biological life rather than an emphasis on diminishing human suffering

But even though we are death avoiders and death deniers, ultimately we face death—others' and our own.

Attitudes about Death across the Life Cycle
Each of us lives in relationship to death at every point in the life span, and our attitudes toward death change as we develop and age (Kastenbaum, 1985). Children who are two or three years of age rarely get upset by the sight of a

(a)

(b)

Figure 20.3
(a) *In the Hindu religion, beliefs in reincarnation are strong, as indicated in this painting,* Kāliya Damana.
(b) *Buddhists also believe in reincarnation. Shown here is a Buddhist painting of reincarnation.*
Source: (a) Asian Art Museum of San Francisco. The Avery Brundage Collection. Gift of Mr. and Mrs. George Hopper Fitch.

dead animal or by being told that a person has died. Children at this age generally have no idea of what death really means. They may confuse death with sleep, or ask in a puzzled way, "Why doesn't it move?"

Though children vary somewhat in the age at which they begin to understand death, the limitations of preoperational thought make it difficult for a child to comprehend the meaning of death before the age of 7 or 8. Young children unfortunately may blame themselves for the death of someone they know well, illogically reasoning that the event may have happened because they disobeyed the person who died. Children under the age of 6 rarely perceive that death is universal, inevitable, and final. Instead, young children usually think that only people who want to die, or who are bad or careless, actually do die. Young children believe that the dead can be brought back to life. Sometime between the ages of 5 and 7 these ideas give way to more realistic perceptions of death. In one early investigation of children's perception of death, children 3 to 5 years of age denied the existence of death, children 6 to 9 years of age believed that death exists but only happens to some people, and children 9 years or older recognized death's finality and universality (Nagy, 1948).

Most psychologists believe that honesty is the best strategy in discussing death with children. Treating the concept as unmentionable is thought to be an inappropriate strategy. Yet most of us have grown up in a society in which death is rarely discussed. In one investigation, the attitudes of 30,000 young adults toward death were evaluated (Shneidman, 1973). More than 30 percent said they could not recall any discussion of death during their childhood; an equal number said that while death was discussed, the discussion took place in an uncomfortable atmosphere. Almost one of every two respondents said that the death of a grandparent was their first personal encounter with death.

In adolescence, the prospect of death, like the prospect of aging, is often regarded as a notion that is so remote that it does not have much relevance. The subject of death may be avoided, glossed over, kidded about, neutralized, and controlled by a cool, spectator-like orientation. This perspective is typical of the adolescent's self-conscious thought. Some adolescents do show a concern for death, both in trying to fathom its meaning and in confronting the actual prospect of their own demise.

Our discussion of middle adulthood indicated that mid-life is a time when individuals begin to think more intensely about how much time is left in their lives. Surveys indicate that middle-aged adults fear death more than young adults or older adults (Kalish & Reynolds, 1976; Riley, 1970). Older adults, though, think about death more and talk about it more in conversations with others than do middle-aged and young adults. In old age, one's own death may take on an appropriateness it lacked in earlier years. And some of the increased thinking and conversing about death, as well as achieving a sense of integrity, may help the older person accept death. Also, in the later years of life, more peers become ill and die, so the surviving elderly are forced to examine the meanings of life and death more than in their earlier years. The elderly are also less likely to have unfinished business. They probably do not have children who need to be guided to maturity; their spouses are more likely to be dead; they are less likely to have work-related projects that require completion. Lacking such anticipations, death may seem less emotionally painful to them. But even among old people, attitudes toward death sometimes are as individual as the people who hold them. One 82-year-old woman declared that she had lived her life and was now ready to see it come to an end; another 82-year-old woman declared that death would be a regrettable interruption of her participation in activities and relationships (Kastenbaum, 1969; Kalish, 1987).

At this point we have discussed a number of ideas about death, sociohistorical circumstances, and the life cycle. A summary of these ideas is presented in Concept Table 20.1. Next, we focus on the provocative topic of how we will face our own death.

Facing One's Own Death

This chapter opened with a quote from Erich Fromm (1955) about man being the only animal who knows he must die. Knowledge of death's inevitability permits us to establish priorities and structure our time accordingly. As we age, these priorities and structurings change, undoubtedly in recognition of diminishing future time. Values concerning the most important uses of time also change. For example, when asked how they would spend six remaining months of life, younger adults described activities such as traveling and accomplishing things they previously had not done; older adults described more inner-focused activities—contemplation and meditation, for example (Kalish & Reynolds, 1976).

Most dying individuals want an opportunity to make some decisions regarding their own life and death. Some individuals want to complete unfinished business; they want time to resolve problems and conflicts and to put their affairs in order. Might there be a sequence of stages we go through as we face death?

Kübler-Ross's Stages of Dying

Elisabeth Kübler-Ross (1969) divided the behavior of dying individuals into five stages: denial and isolation, anger, bargaining, depression, and acceptance. In the first stage, **denial and isolation,** the individual denies that death really is going to take place; she may say, "No, it can't be me. It's not possible." This is a common reaction to terminal illness. However, denial is usually only a temporary defense and is eventually replaced with increased acceptance when the individual is confronted with such matters as financial considerations, unfinished business, and worry about surviving family members.

Sustained and soothed
By an unfaltering trust, approach thy grave,
Like one who wraps the drapery of his couch
About him, and lies down to pleasant dreams.

William Cullen Bryant,
Thanatopsis, *1811*

Years following years steal something every day:
At last they steal us from ourselves away.

Alexander Pope

Death and Dying

CONCEPT TABLE

20.1

Death, Sociohistorical Circumstances, and the Life Cycle		
Concept	**Processes/Related Ideas**	**Characteristics/Description**
Defining Death	Brain Death	A neurological definition, in which all electrical activity has ceased for a specified time—measured by EEG.
	Modern Medicine Complications	The ability of modern medicine to resuscitate a dying person and keep individuals alive through feeding and breathing devices has complicated the definition of death.
Euthanasia	Its Nature	Refers to the act of painlessly putting to death individuals who are suffering from an incurable disease or severe disability. It raises controversial ethical issues.
Death and Sociohistorical Circumstances	Its Nature	When, where, and why people die have changed historically. Most societies throughout history have had philosophical or religious beliefs about death; and most societies have some form of ritual that deals with death. Most societies do not view death as the end of existence—spiritual life is thought to continue. The United States is a death-denying and death-avoiding culture.
Attitudes about Death across the Life Cycle	Childhood	Children at 2 to 3 years of age usually show no upset at the sight of a dead person or animal. They confuse death with sleep. In the preoperational stage, children believe death is reversible and do not perceive it to be universal. Most children 9 years or older perceive death's finality and universality.
	Adolescence	Death may be glossed over; self-conscious thought may lead to a detached orientation toward death. Some adolescents, though, do show a concern for death.
	Adulthood	Middle age is a time when individuals show a heightened concern about and fear of death. The older adult thinks about and converses about death more, but often accepts it more. Individual variation in attitudes toward death is prominent.

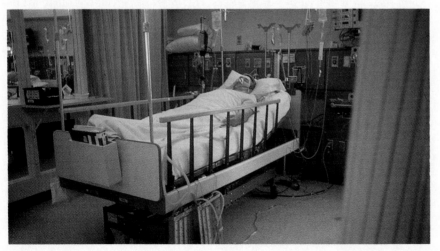

We can cope with our impending death in a number of different ways. Kübler-Ross describes five different ways individuals cope with dying. Describe the five ways and give an example of each.

Figure 20.4
Kübler-Ross's stages of dying.

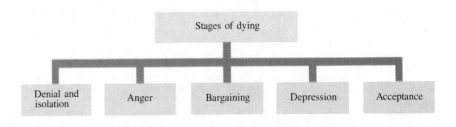

```
                    Stages of dying
    ┌──────────┬─────────┬──────────┬────────────┬────────────┐
 Denial and    Anger    Bargaining  Depression   Acceptance
 isolation
```

According to Elisabeth Kübler-Ross, we go through five different stages of dying: denial and isolation, anger, bargaining, depression, and acceptance. Today's interpretation of Kübler-Ross's stages suggests that adaptation does not require us to go through the stages in order.

The art of living well and
the art of dying well are one.
        Epicurus, 3rd Century B.C.

In the second stage, **anger,** the dying individual recognizes that denial can no longer be maintained; denial often gives way to anger, resentment, rage, and envy. Now the individual's question becomes, "Why me?" At this point, the individual becomes increasingly difficult to care for as anger may become displaced and projected onto physicians, nurses, family members, and even God. The realization of loss is great, and those who symbolize life, energy, and competent functioning are especially salient targets of the dying individual's resentment and jealousy.

In the third stage, **bargaining,** the individual develops the hope that death somehow can be postponed or delayed. Some individuals enter into a brief period of bargaining or negotiation—often with God—as they try to delay their death. Psychologically, the individual is saying, "Yes, me, but . . ." In exchange for a few more days, weeks, or months of life, the individual promises to lead a reformed life dedicated to God or to the service of others.

In the fourth stage, **depression,** as the dying individual comes to accept death's certainty, a period of depression or preparatory grief may appear. The dying individual may become very silent, refuse visitors, and spend much of the time crying or grieving. This behavior should be perceived as normal in this circumstance and is actually an effort to disconnect the self from all love objects. Attempts to cheer up the dying individual at this stage should be discouraged, says Kübler-Ross, because the dying individual has a real need to contemplate impending death.

In the fifth stage, **acceptance,** the individual develops a sense of peace, a unique acceptance of one's fate, and in many cases, a desire to be left alone. This stage may be devoid of feelings; physical pain and discomfort are often absent. Kübler-Ross describes this stage as the end of the struggle, the final resting stage before death. A summary of Kübler-Ross's stages of dying are shown in figure 20.4.

No one has been able to confirm that people indeed go through the stages in the order described by Kübler-Ross. Kübler-Ross herself feels that she has been misread, saying that she never intended the stages to be an invariant sequence of steps toward death. Even though Kübler-Ross (1974) recognizes the importance of individual variation in how we face death, she still believes that the optimal way to face death is in the sequence she has proposed.

Some individuals, though, struggle until the very end, desperately trying to hang onto their lives. Acceptance of death never comes for them. Some psychologists believe that the harder individuals fight to avoid the inevitable death they face and the more they deny it, the more difficulty they will have in dying peacefully and in a dignified way; other psychologists argue that not confronting death until the very end may be adaptive for some individuals (Kalish, 1981, 1987; Lifton, 1977; Shneidman, 1973). At any one moment, a number of emotions may wax and wane. Hope, disbelief, bewilderment, anger, and acceptance may come and go as individuals try to make sense out of what is happening to them.

Perceived Control and Denial

Perceived control and denial may work together as an adaptive strategy for some older adults who face death. When individuals are led to believe they can influence and control events—such as prolonging their lives—they may become more alert and cheerful. Perceived control may even prolong life. In one investigation, a group of institutionalized elderly adults were given the opportunity to make decisions actively and to be personally responsible for something outside of themselves—a plant (Rodin & Langer, 1977). The elderly adults soon began to act more alert and to feel better than those who were left in the usual passive institutional routine in which all decisions were made for them by the staff. Eighteen months later a follow-up revealed that only half as many of the elderly had died in the perceived control group as in the passive group. Perceived control over one's environment, then, may literally be a matter of life or death (Rodin, 1986).

Denial also may be a fruitful way for some individuals to approach death. It is not unusual for dying individuals to deny death right up until the time they die. Life without hope represents learned helplessness in its most extreme form. Denial can protect us from the tortuous feeling that we are going to die. Denial may come in different forms (Weisman, 1972). First, we can deny the facts. For example, a woman who has been told by her physician that a scheduled operation is for cancer may believe that the operation is for a benign tumor. Second, we can deny the implications of a disease or life-threatening situation. For example, a man may accept the fact that he has a disease but may deny that it leads to death. Third, we can deny that we will be extinguished even if we die biologically; we can have faith in our spiritual immortality.

Denial can be adaptive or maladaptive. Denial can be used to avoid the destructive impact of shock by delaying the necessity of dealing with one's death. Denial can insulate the individual from having to cope with intense feelings of anger and hurt. But if denial keeps us from having a life-saving operation, it clearly is maladaptive. Denial is neither good, nor bad; an evaluation of its adaptive qualities needs to be made on an individual basis (Kalish, 1981).

The Contexts in Which People Die

For dying individuals, the context in which they die can be an important consideration. Most deaths in the United States occur in a hospital; a smaller number occur in other institutions such as nursing homes and board-and-care centers. Hospitals offer several important advantages to the dying individual—professional staff members are readily available and the medical technology present may prolong life, for example. Yet a hospital may not be the best place for many people to die. Most individuals say they would rather die at home (Kalish & Reynolds, 1976). But many feel that they will be a burden at home, that there is limited space there, and that dying at home may alter prior relationships, such as being cared for by one's children. Individuals who are facing death also worry about the competency and availability of emergency medical treatment if they remain at home.

A third context for dying—in addition to hospital and home—that has received increased attention in recent years is the **hospice,** a humanized institution committed to making the end of life as free from pain, anxiety, and depression as possible. The hospice's goals contrast with those of a hospital—curing illness and prolonging life. The hospice movement began toward the end of the 1960s in London when a new kind of medical institution, St. Christopher's Hospice, opened. Little effort is made to prolong life at St. Christopher's—there are no heart-lung machines and there is no intensive care unit, for example. A primary goal is to bring pain under control and to help the dying patient face death in a psychologically healthy way. The hospice also makes every effort to include the dying individual's family; it is believed that this strategy not only benefits the dying individual but family members as well, probably diminishing their guilt after the family member's death.

The hospice movement has grown rapidly in the United States. By 1987, there were close to 200 hospices (Kitch, 1987). The hospice advocates continue to underscore that it is possible to control pain for almost any dying individual and that it is possible to create an environment for the patient that is superior to that found in most hospitals.

Coping with the Death of Someone Else

Loss can come in many forms in our lives—divorce, a pet's death, loss of a job—but no loss is greater than the loss that comes through the death of someone we love and care for—a parent, a sibling, a spouse, a relative, or a friend. In the ratings of life's stresses that require the most adjustment, death of a spouse is given the highest number. How should we communicate with a dying individual? How do we cope with the death of someone we love?

Communicating with a Dying Person

Most psychologists believe that it is best for dying individuals to know that they are dying and that significant others know they are dying so they can interact and communicate with each other on the basis of this mutual knowledge. What are some of the advantages of this open awareness context for the dying individual? Four such advantages are (Kalish, 1981): the dying individual can close his life in accord with his own ideas about proper dying; the dying individual may be able to complete some plans and projects, can make arrangements for survivors, and can participate in decisions about a funeral and burial; the dying individual has the opportunity to reminisce, to converse with others who have been important individuals in her life, and to end life conscious of what life has been like; and the dying individual has more understanding of what is happening within her body and what the medical staff is doing to her.

It may be easier to die when people we love and like can converse freely with us about what is happening to us, even if it involves considerable sadness. Focus on Life-Span Development 20.2 describes an open communication with a dying 81-year-old woman.

In addition to an open communication system, what are some other suggestions for conversing with a dying individual? Some experts believe that conversation should not focus on mental pathology or preparation for death, but should focus on strengths of the individual and preparation for the remainder of life (LeShan, 1966). And since external accomplishments are not possible, communication should be directed more at internal growth. Keep in mind also that caring does not have to come from a mental health professional only; a concerned nurse, an attentive physician, a sensitive spouse, an intimate friend can provide an important support system for the dying individual.

Consider the close relationships with the people in your life. How would you communicate with them if they were dying? Would their developmental status affect how you talked to them? If so, how?

Richard Kalish (1981) described a circumstance where he used an open communication system to interact with his 81-year-old aunt, who was extremely ill and had been so for two years. Doctors predicted that she would probably not live for many more weeks. Kalish's home was 800 miles away, but he was able to visit her and his uncle for several days. It bothered him to see her hooked into a machine that held her life. The ugly wig she had worn for the past several years had been discarded, and there were only a few wisps of her hair left. Her teeth had been placed in the drawer beside her bed since she could not take solid food. At this point, she was not concerned with how she looked.

Kalish and his uncle were in her room talking with her as she moved in and out of awareness. He was standing at the foot of the bed and Kalish was sitting next to her, holding her hand. The uncle began talking about her coming to see Kalish as soon as she could be up and around again, probably next summer, he said. She tuned the comments out. Then, Kalish found a situation to get the uncle out of the room.

When Kalish was alone with his aunt, he stood up and kissed her. He told her he loved her, realizing he had never said that to her before, hadn't even thought about it. Then Kalish said, "Bea I have to leave now. I may never see you again, and I want you to know how much I love you." Her eyes were closed and she was breathing strangely, but she winced at the words. Kalish became frightened that he had said too much, so he hesitated and said, "Well, I hope I will see you again, but I might not." He then left.

She died before he could visit again, and he has always wondered about whether he should have said what he did. But it seemed important to say it. Even though it pained her to hear him, she knew that it was true, and she had not shrunk from painful circumstances in the past. Kalish said that it had been easy for him to write and talk about death and dying over many years, but that it was very difficult to be in the situation where someone that he loved was dying. Kalish said that he did what he tells other people to do. When he heard three weeks later that Bea had died, he considered himself fortunate to have had the opportunity to be with her before she died and to have been both caring and honest.

Stages and Dimensions of Grief

Grief is the emotional numbness, disbelief, separation anxiety, despair, sadness, and loneliness that accompany the loss of someone we love. One view indicates that we go through three stages of grief after we lose someone we love: shock, despair, and recovery (Averill, 1968). Another perspective indicates that we go through four stages: numbness, pining, depression, and recovery (Parkes, 1972).

In the first view of grief, at stage one the survivor feels shock, disbelief, and numbness, often weeping or becoming easily agitated. This stage occurs just after death and usually lasts for one to three days. It is not unlike the denial and anger stages Kübler-Ross proposed for the dying individual. At stage two, there is painful longing for the dead, memories and visual images of the deceased, sadness, insomnia, irritability, and restlessness. Beginning not long after the death, this stage often peaks in the second to fourth weeks following the death and may subside after several months although it can persist for one to two years. Elements of bargaining for the return of the deceased person may appear, again corresponding to one of Kübler-Ross's stages. Stage three usually appears within a year after the death. Analogous to Kübler-Ross's acceptance stage, this grief resolution stage is marked by a resumption of ordinary activities, a greater probability of recalling pleasant memories about the deceased, and establishment of new relationships with others.

However, just as we found that Kübler-Ross's stages of dying are not invariant and that individuals do not have to go through them in the order she suggested to adapt effectively, the same can be said for grief's stages (Klass, 1988; Rando, 1988). Rather than talking about grief's stages, perhaps it is more accurate to talk about grief's dimensions (Middleton & Raphael, 1987). One recent description emphasized that grief is not a simple, decrescendoing emotional state, but rather a complex, evolving process with multiple dimensions (Jacobs & others, 1987). In this view, pining for the lost person is one important dimension. Pining or yearning reflects an intermittent, and recurrent wish or need to recover the lost person. Another important dimension of grief is separation anxiety, which includes not only pining and preoccupation with thoughts of the deceased person, but also focuses on places and things associated with the deceased, as well as crying or sighing as a type of suppressed cry. Another dimension of grief is the typical immediate reaction to a loss discussed earlier—emotional blunting, numbness, disbelief, and outbursts of panic or extreme tearfulness. Yet another dimension of grief involves despair and sadness, which include a sense of hopelessness and defeat, depressive symptoms, apathy, loss of meaning for activities that used to involve the person who is gone, and growing desolation. This dimension does not represent a clear-cut stage but rather occurs repeatedly in one context or another starting shortly after a loss. Nonetheless, as time passes, pining and protest over the loss tend to diminish, episodes of depression and apathy may remain or increase.

While the sense of separation anxiety and loss may continue to the end of one's life, most of us emerge from grief's tears, turning our attention once again to productive tasks and regaining a more positive view of life (Rando, 1988).

Making Sense Out of the World

One beneficial aspect of grieving is that it stimulates many individuals to try to make sense out of their world. A common occurrence is to go over again and again all of the events that led up to the death. In the days and weeks after the death, the closest family members share experiences with each other, sometimes reminiscing over family experiences (Kalish, 1981).

Each individual may offer a piece of death's puzzle. "When I saw him last Saturday, he looked as though he were rallying," says one family member. "Do you think it might have had something to do with his sister's illness?" remarks another. "I doubt it, but I heard from an aide that he fell going to the bathroom that morning," comments yet another. "That explains the bruise

It is sweet to mingle tears with tears; griefs; where they wound in solitude, wound more deeply.

Senaca

Death and Dying

on his elbow," says the first individual. "No wonder he told me that he was angry because he could not seem to do anything right," chimes in a fourth family member. And so it goes in the attempt to understand why someone who was rallying on Saturday was dead on Wednesday.

When a death is caused by an accident or a disaster, the effort to make sense of it is pursued more vigorously. As added pieces of news come trickling in, they are integrated into the puzzle. The bereaved want to put the death into a perspective that they can understand—divine intervention, a curse from a neighboring tribe, a logical sequence of cause and effect, or whatever it may be.

In some instances, when famous individuals die, solving the puzzle of the death may become a national obsession and can drag on for years. Such was the case in the assassination of President John F. Kennedy. Some individuals are still trying to make sense of the entire event. That the death was the act of one unstable man working alone strikes many individuals as improbable. How can such an absurd set of circumstances destroy such a powerful man? ask some individuals.

Eventually, each of us finds an adequate "story" of the dying and death—of John F. Kennedy, of our father, or of our friend. Versions of the death may differ—whether the physician did all she could to save the patient, whether Aunt Bertha showed up frequently at the hospital or not, whether the operation succeeded or not, whether the individual was ready to die or not. Each individual's version satisfies him, and that version, with slight modifications, becomes the official version for the teller.

Widowhood
Usually the most difficult loss is the death of a spouse. There are more than 12 million widowed people in the United States; widows outnumber widowers above five-fold (Campbell & Silverman, 1987). The death of a spouse is usually unpreventable, may involve the shattering of a long-term attachment bond, may require the pursuit of new roles and statuses, may lead to financial hardship, and may leave the survivor without a major support system (Osterweis, Solomon, & Green, 1984). Thus, it is not surprising that a spouse's death is associated with depression, increases in physician consultations, hospitalization, increase in health-compromising behaviors such as smoking and drinking, and mortality rates over and above the expected norm (Kaprio, Kosenvuo, & Rita, 1987; Zisook, 1987; Zisook, Schuchter, & Lyons, 1987).

Widowhood may be experienced differently depending on sociohistorical circumstances (Lopata, 1987a). Modernization of societies has resulted in many widows living independently, free from the control of the patriarchal family and able to maintain themselves economically through paid employment or the Social Security System, in the case of the United States. Although there are isolated widows—unable to reengage in social relations and social roles after a past tie is broken through death—many widows have support systems and eventually reimmerse themselves in their families, their neighborhood, friendship networks, or occupations and organizations.

Keep in mind that widowhood may be experienced in many different ways (Lopata, 1987b). Some widows are passive, accepting changes produced by the death of a husband. Others acquire personal abilities and may even bloom in widowhood. Some stay in pockets of high tradition, surrounded by,

(a)

(b)

Figure 20.5
(a) *A New Orleans street funeral. (b) The cremation of this 98 year-old woman in Bali, Indonesia, is a festive occasion. Strangers and townspeople alike are invited to share a feast with music and dancing.*

but almost oblivious to, changes around them. Others eagerly seek new resources and social roles. Sometimes the initiative to cope with widowhood comes from within; at other times it comes from support systems.

Forms of Mourning and the Funeral

The **suttee** is the now outlawed Hindu practice of burning a dead man's widow to increase his family's prestige and firmly establish an image of her in his memory. In some cultures, a ceremonial meal is held. In others a black armband is worn for one year following a death (see figure 20.5). From these examples, it is obvious that cultures vary in how they practice mourning.

The funeral is an important aspect of mourning in many cultures. One consideration involves what to do with the body. In the United States, most bodies are placed in caskets under the earth or in mausoleums. About 9 percent are cremated. Most individuals who are cremated have their ashes spread in the crematorium's garden; others wish their ashes to be taken to specific locations. A viewing of the body occurs after about 75 percent of the deaths in the United States.

The funeral industry has been the source of controversy in recent years. Funeral directors and their supporters argue that the funeral provides a form of closure to the relationship with the deceased, especially when there is an open casket. Their dissenters, however, stress that funeral directors are just trying to make money; they further argue that the art of embalming is grotesque.

One way to avoid the exploitation that may occur because bereavement may make us vulnerable to more expensive funeral arrangements is to purchase them in advance. However, most of us do not follow this procedure. In one survey, only 24 percent of individuals 60 and over had made any funeral arrangements (Kalish & Reynolds, 1976).

We have discussed a number of ideas about facing one's own death and coping with the death of someone else. A summary of these ideas is presented in Concept Table 20.2. We have come to the end of life's journey. My hope is that you now have a better understanding of the journey and that the wisdom this understanding might bring can help you in your own journey through life's remaining years.

Summary

I. **Defining Death**
Brain death is a neurological definition, in which all electrical activity has ceased for a specified time—it is measured by the EEG. Modern medicine has complicated the definition of death. Dying individuals can be resuscitated and be kept alive through feeding and breathing devices.

II. **Euthanasia**
Euthanasia is the act of painlessly putting to death individuals who are suffering from an incurable disease or severe disability. It raises controversial ethical issues.

III. **Death and Sociohistorical Circumstances**
When, where, and why people die have changed historically. Most societies through history have had philosophical or religious beliefs about death; and most societies have some form of ritual that deals with death. Most societies do not view death as the end of existence—spiritual life is thought to continue. The United States is a death-denying and death-avoiding culture.

IV. **Attitudes about Death across the Life Cycle**
Children at 2 to 3 years of age usually show no upset at the sight of a dead person or animal. They confuse death with sleep. In the preoperational stage, children believe death is reversible and do not perceive it to be universal. Most children 9 years or older perceive death's finality and universality. In adolescence, death may be glossed over; self-conscious thought may lead to a detached orientation toward death. Some adolescents, though,

Facing One's Own Death and Coping with the Death of Someone Else		
Concept	**Processes/Related Ideas**	**Characteristics/Description**
Facing One's Own Death	Kübler-Ross's Stages of Dying	She proposed five stages: denial and isolation, anger, bargaining, depression, and acceptance. Not all individuals go through the same sequence. Some individuals may struggle to the end.
	Perceived Control and Denial	Perceived control and denial may work together as an adaptive orientation for the dying individual. Denial can be adaptive or maladaptive, depending on the circumstance.
	The Contexts in which People Die	Most deaths in the United States occur in hospitals; this has advantages and disadvantages. Most individuals say they would rather die at home, but they worry that they will be a burden and they worry about the lack of medical care. The hospice is a humanized environment with a commitment to making the end of life as free from pain and depression as possible; the hospice movement has grown rapidly.
Coping with the Death of Someone Else	Communicating with a Dying Person	Most psychologists recommend an open communication system; this system should not dwell on pathology or preparation for death, but emphasize the dying person's strengths.
	Stages and Dimensions of Grief	Grief is the emotional numbness, disbelief, separation, anxiety, despair, sadness, and loneliness that accompany the loss of someone we love. One view suggests we go through three stages of grief: shock, despair, and recovery. Another indicates that we go through four stages: numbness, pining, depression, and recovery. We do not necessarily go through the stages in order; many developmentalists believe we should describe grief's dimensions rather than grief's stages. In some cases, grieving may last for years.
	Making Sense out of the World	The grieving process may stimulate individuals to strive to make sense out of their world; each individual may contribute a piece to death's puzzle.
	Widowhood	Usually the most difficult loss is the death of a spouse. A spouse's death is associated with depression, health-compromising behavior, and increased mortality rates. Widowhood is experienced differently depending on sociohistorical circumstances.
	Forms of Mourning and the Funeral	They vary from culture to culture. The most important aspect of mourning in most cultures is the funeral. In recent years, the funeral industry has been the focus of controversy.

show a concern for death. Middle age is a time when individuals show a heightened concern about and fear of death. The older adult thinks about and converses about death more, but often accepts it more. Individual variation in attitudes toward death is prominent.

V. **Kübler-Ross's Stages of Dying**
She proposed five stages: denial and isolation, anger, bargaining, depression, and acceptance. Not all individuals go through the same sequence. Some individuals may struggle to the end.

VI. **Perceived Control and Denial**
Perceived control and denial may work together as an adaptive orientation for the dying individual. Denial can be adaptive or maladaptive, depending on the circumstance.

VII. **The Contexts in Which People Die**
Most deaths in the United States occur in hospitals; this has advantages and disadvantages.

Most individuals say they would rather die at home, but they worry that they will be a burden and they worry about the lack of medical care. The hospice is a humanized environment with a commitment to making the end of life as free of pain and depression as possible; the hospice movement has grown rapidly.

VIII. **Communicating with a Dying Person**
Most psychologists recommend an open communication system; this system should not dwell on pathology or preparation for death, but emphasize the dying person's strengths.

IX. **Stages and Dimensions of Grief**
Grief is the emotional numbness, disbelief, separation anxiety, despair, sadness, and loneliness that accompany the loss of someone we love. One view suggests that we go through three stages of grief—shock, despair, and recovery; another view suggests four stages—numbness,

pining, depression, and recovery. We do not necessarily go through the stages in order; many developmentalists believe we should describe grief's dimensions rather than grief's stages. In some cases, grieving may last for years. The grieving process may stimulate individuals to strive to make sense out of their world; each individual may contribute a piece of death's puzzle. Usually the most difficult loss is a spouse's death, which is associated with depression, health-compromising behavior, and increased mortality rates. Widowhood is experienced differently, depending on sociohistorical circumstances.

X. **Forms of Mourning and the Funeral**
Mourning varies from culture to culture. The most important aspect of mourning in most cultures is the funeral. In recent years, the funeral industry has been enveloped in controversy.

Key Terms

Suggested Readings

Campbell, S., & Silverman, P. R. (1987). *Widower.* New York: Prentice Hall Press.
A book about what happens to men when their wives die. Includes many detailed case studies of widowers.

Kalish, R. A. (1981). *Death, grief, and caring relationships.* Monterey, CA: Brooks/Cole.
An excellent overview of death's many faces; includes considerable information about communicating with the dying individual.

Kastenbaum, R. (1985). Dying and death: A life-span approach. In J. E. Birren & K. W. Schaie (Eds.),

Handbook of the psychology of aging (2nd ed.). New York: Van Nostrand Reinhold.
Focuses on the experience of death and attitudes toward death at different points in the human life cycle.

Lopata, H. Z. (Ed.)(1987). *Widows.* Durham, NC: Duke U. Press.
Information about widows in different cultures, with special attention given to the Middle East, Asia, and the Pacific; emphasis is placed on support systems for widows.

Psychiatric Clinics of North America, Vol. 10, September, 1987. Grief and Bereavement.
The entire issue of this journal is devoted to understanding and treating grief; contributions by leading mental health specialists on grief therapy.

Weir, R. F. (Ed.)(1986). *Ethical issues in death and dying.* New York: Columbia U. Press.
Includes chapters on guidelines for determining death, handicapped infants, treatment abatement of critically ill patients, euthanasia, and suicide.

G L O S S A R Y

acceptance   The dying individual develops a sense of peace and acceptance of one's fate. The final stage of the five stages of dying by Elizabeth Kübler-Ross.   *568*

accommodation   In Piaget's theory of cognitive development, the act of modifying a current mode or structure of thought to deal with new features of the environment.   *46*

achieving stage   A point in early adulthood when we apply intelligence to situations that have profound consequences for achieving long-term goals, such as those involving careers and knowledge.   *420*

activity theory   According to this theory, the more active and involved older adults are, the less likely they will age and the more likely they will be satisifed with their lives.   *537*

adolescence   The period of transition from childhood to early adulthood, entered at approximately 11 to 13 years of age and ending at age 18 to 21. This period is characterized by the onset of physical, cognitive, and social changes.   *15*

adolescent egocentrism   In adolescence, two types of thinking represent the emergence of egocentrism—the imaginary audience and the personal fable. Adolescents' egocentrism involves the belief that others are as interested in them as much as they are, personal uniqueness, and a sense of indestructibility.   *363*

adoption study   A strategy of research used to assess the role of heredity in behavior by comparing an adopted child's similarity to his or her biological parents and to his or her adopted parents.   *85*

affectionate love   A desire to have the other person near us and a deep affection for the other person.   *442*

afterbirth   The third birth stage; involves the detachment and expelling of the placenta, fetal membranes, and umbilical cord after delivery.   *114*

ageism   Prejudice against older adults.   *538*

AIDS   Acquired immune deficiency syndrome. Failure of the body's immune system that leaves afflicted individuals vulnerable to a variety of diseases.   *416*

altruism   An unselfish interest in helping someone.   *278*

Alzheimer's disease   A progressive, degenerative disorder that involves deterioration of the brain's cells.   *549*

amniocentesis   A procedure by which cells of the fetus are removed from the amniotic sac to test for the presence of certain chromosomal and metabolic disorders.   *83*

amnion   A sort of bag or envelope that contains clear fluid in which the developing embryo floats.   *102*

anal stage   Freud's second psychosexual stage, lasting from about 18 months of age to 3 years, during which the child seeks pleasure through exercising the anus and eliminating waste.   *39*

androgen   Hormone that matures mainly in males and is produced by the sex glands.   *270*

androgyny   A gender-role orientation consisting of a combination of both masculine and feminine characteristics in the same individual.   *336*

anger   The dying individual recognizes that denial can no longer be maintained; denial often gives way to anger. The second stage of the five stages of dying by Elisabeth Kübler-Ross.   *568*

animism   The belief that inanimate objects have "lifelike" qualities and are capable of action. Piaget described this as characteristic of preoperational thought.   *228*

anorexia nervosa   An eating disorder that leads to self-starvation; primarily found in females.   *396*

anoxia   Lack of sufficient oxygen to the brain, causing neurological damage or death.   *114*

Apgar scale   Method used to assess the health of newborns one and five minutes after birth; evaluates heart rate, respiratory effort, muscle tone, body color, and reflex irritability.   *118*

aptitude-treatment interaction (ATI)   A field of educational research that determines the best learning conditions for a particular student by considering the interaction between the student's abilities and various teaching methods.   *329*

assimilation   In Piaget's theory of cognitive development, the act of incorporating a feature of the environment into an existing mode or structure of thought.   *46*

associative learning   Involves short-term memory, rote learning, attention, and simple reasoning skills.   *88*

associative play   A type of play in which there is social interaction with little or no organization. Children engage in play activities similar to those of other children; however, they appear to be more interested in being associated with one another than in the tasks they are involved with.   *262*

attachment   A relationship between an infant and one or more adult caregivers during the developmental period of birth to 2 years; characterized by a unique bonding between the two social figures involved.   *190*

authoritarian parenting   A style of parenting that has a restrictive, punitive orientation and places limits and controls on the child with little verbal give-and-take between the child and the parent. This form of parenting is linked with the following social behaviors of the child; an anxiety about social comparison, failure to initiate activity, and ineffective social interaction.   *249*

authoritative parenting   A style of parenting that encourages the child to be independent, but still places limits, demands, and controls on his or her actions. There is extensive verbal give-and-take, and parents demonstrate a high degree of warmth and nurturance toward the child. This form of parenting is associated with social competency of the child, particularly self-reliance and social responsibility.   *249*

autism   A severe mental illness of early childhood; characterized by absorption in fantasy, isolation, and extremely defective thinking and language abilities.   *208*

autonomous morality   The second stage of moral development in Piaget's theory. The child becomes aware that rules and laws are created by people relative to social systems and that, in judging an action, one should consider the actor's intentions as well as the act's consequences.   *276*

autonomy versus shame and doubt   The second stage in Erikson's eight-stage theory of development, during which the child may develop either the healthy attitude that he or she is capable of independent control of actions or an unhealthy attitude that he or she is capable of independent control of actions or an unhealthy attitude of shame or doubt in that he or she is incapable of such control.   *43*

baby-talk register   A way of speaking to babies, characterized by high pitch, exaggerated intonation, and simple sentences.   *174*

bargaining   The dying individual develops the hope that death can somehow be postponed or delayed. The third stage of the five stages of dying by Elisabeth Kübler-Ross.   *568*

basal metabolism rate (BMR)   The minimum amount of energy a person uses in a state of rest.   *410*

Bayley Scales of Infant Development   Developmental scales developed by Nancy Bayley with three components—a Mental scale, a Motor scale, and an Infants Behavior profile.   *164*

behavior exchange theory   Emphasizes the hedonism and competence involved in marital relationships. Hedonism is reflected in the belief that each partner's reinforcement value for the other determines the degree of marital satisfaction; competency is reflected in the belief that the mastery of specific relationship skills determine the degree of marital satisfaction.   *445*

behavior genetics   The discipline concerned with the degree and nature of the hereditary basis of behavior.   *85*

bimodal perception   The ability to relate and integrate information about two sensory modalities, such as vision and hearing.   *147*

biological processes   The influences of evolution, genetics, neurological development, and physical growth on development. These factors contribute to the stability and continuity of the individual.   *14*

blastocyst   The inner layer of the blastula that later develops into the embryo.   *101*

blastula   An early embryo form typically having the form of a hollow, fluid-filled, rounded cavity bounded by a single layer of cells.   *100*

bonding   The forming of a close personal relationship (as between a mother and child) especially through frequent or constant association.   *120*

brain death   A neurological definition of death in which all electrical activity of the brain has ceased for a specified period of time as determined by an electroencephalogram (EEG).   *561*

Brazelton Neonatal Behavioral Assessment Scale   A test that detects an infant's neurological integrity; includes an evaluation of the infant's reaction to people along with assessment of 20 reflexes and the infant's reaction to various circumstances.   *118*

Brazelton training   Involves using the Brazelton scale to show parents how their newborn responds to people. Parents are shown how the neonate can respond positively to people and how such responses can be stimulated. Brazelton training has been shown to improve infants' social skills.   *120*

breech position   The baby's position in the uterus that would cause the buttocks to be the first part to emerge from the vagina.   *114*

bulimia   A binge-and-purge syndrome that is marked by periods of very heavy eating followed by self-induced vomiting; occurs primarily in females.   *397*

canalization   The narrow path or developmental course that certain characteristics take, apparently as preservative forces help to protect or buffer an individual from environmental extremes.   *84*

care perspective   An approach to moral development proposed by Gilligan in which people are viewed in terms of their connectedness with other people and the focus is on their communication with others.   *342*

career consolidation   A stage that George Vaillant believes should be added to Erikson's adult stages. Occurs from approximately 23 to 35 years of age.   *492*

case study   An in-depth look at an individual which provides information that will help the psychologist understand life-span development.   *24*

centration   The focusing, or centering, of attention on one characteristic to the exclusion of all others. Piagetian term, characteristic of preoperational thought.   *229*

cephalocaudal pattern   A general pattern of physical growth that suggests that the greatest growth in anatomical differentiation occurs first in the region of the head and later in lower regions.   *135*

child-centered   A form of education with an emphasis on the individual child, wide-ranging experiences, exploration, and enjoyment.   *241*

chlamydia   A sexually transmitted disease which affects as many as 10 percent of all college students.   *416*

chorionic villus test   A procedure by which a small sample of the placenta is removed during the first trimester, between the ninth and tenth weeks, with the diagnostic results usually requiring two to three weeks.   *83*

chromosomes   Threadlike structures in each human cell that come in structurally similar pairs (23 pairs in humans).   *76*

chunking   A memory technique that involves organizing items into meaningful or manageable units.   *525*

class inclusion reasoning   Comparing the relative number of objects in a subset with the number of objects in the larger set.   *237*

climacteric   The entire process of declining reproductive ability.   *469*

cliques Peer groups that are smaller in size than a crowd, involve greater member intimacy, and have more group cohesion. Members of a clique are attracted to one another on the basis of similar interests and social ideas. *381*

cognitive learning Involves abstract thinking, symbolic thought, conceptual learning, and the use of language in problem solving. *88*

cognitive processes Mental activities, such as thought, perception, attention, problem solving, and language, that influence development. *14*

cognitive social learning theory Theory associated with Bandura and Mischel stressing that environment-behavior relations are mediated by cognitive factors. *55*

cohort effects Effects that are due to a subject's time of birth or generation, but not actually to his or her age. *30*

commitment The extent to which the adolescent shows a personal investment in what she is going to do. *388*

community rights versus individual rights Kohlberg's fifth stage. The individual understands that values and laws are relative and that standards may vary from one individual to another. *341*

concrete operational stage In Piagetian theory, the stage of thought that follows preoperational thought, lasting from about 7 to 11 years of age and marked primarily by a need to anchor thought to concrete objects and events. This stage reveals conservation skills and is characterized by decentered and reversible thought. *47*

conditional positive regard Love and praise are given only if the individual conforms to parental or social standards. Rogers' concept. *57*

connectedness Reflected in mutuality and permeability. Mutuality refers to the adolescent's sensitivity to and respect for the views of others. Permeability indexes openness and responsiveness to the views of others. *389*

conscience The inner voice of self-observation, self-guidance, and self-punishment. *268*

consensual validation Another individual with similar attitudes and behaviors as us, supports who we are. *436*

conservation The idea that amount stays the same or is conserved regardless of how shape changes. *229*

constructivist view The belief that what one experiences is a construction based on sensory input plus information retrieved from memory—a kind of representation of the world one builds up in one's mind. *140*

continuity of development A gradual, cumulative change from conception to death. *19*

control group The group in psychological experiments that is exposed to all experimental conditions except the independent variable; the comparison or baseline group. *27*

control processes Learning and memory strategies that draw heavily on information processing capacities and are under the learner's conscious control. *289*

conventional reasoning The second level in Kohlberg's theory of moral development in which the child's internalization of moral values is intermediate. He or she abides by certain standards of other people, such as parents (stage 3) or the rules of society (stage 4). *340*

convergent thinking A type of thinking wherein attention is directed toward finding a single solution to a problem; contrasts with divergent thinking. Guilford's term. *308*

cooperative play Play that is the prototype for the games of middle childhood in which a sense of group identity is present and activity is organized. *262*

coordination of secondary reactions During the substage of sensorimotor development, the infant readily combines and recombines previously learned schemes in a coordinated fashion. Piagetian term. *157*

coregulation A gradual transfer of control from parent to child; a transition period between the strong parental control of the preschool years and the increased relinquishment of general supervision that occurs during adolescence. *332*

correlational strategy A research strategy in which the investigator observes if and how two factors are associated with one another, but does not systematically change characteristics in the child's environment. From research using a correlational strategy one cannot infer causal relationships. *25*

creativity The term used to describe an act or contribution to society that is unique or original. *309*

crisis A period during which the adolescent is choosing among meaningful alternatives. *388*

critical period Certain time frames in development that are optimal for the emergence of certain behaviors. Specific forms of stimulation are required during these periods for normal development to proceed. *60*

cross-sectional approach A method used to study a large number of representative persons or variables at a given period in time; frequently employed in the establishment of normative data. *28*

crowd The largest and least personal of peer group relationships. Crowd members meet because of their mutual interest in activities, not because of mutual attraction to each other. *381*

crystallized intelligence Intelligence based on cumulative learning experiences. *523*

cultural-familial retardation Type of retardation in which there is a family pattern of below-average intellectual capabilities and a family history extending across more than one generation, with others in the family having the same profile. *306*

culture fair tests Intelligence tests developed in an attempt to eliminate cultural bias. *302*

deep structure Concerns the syntactic relations among words in a sentence; employs syntactic categories, such as noun phrase, verb phrase, noun, verb, and article. *168*

defense mechanisms Unconscious processes of the ego that keep disturbing and unacceptable impulses from being expressed directly. *38*

denial and isolation The dying individual denies that death really is going to take place. Stage one of the five stages of dying by Elisabeth Kübler-Ross. *566*

Denver Developmental Screening Test Devised to diagnose developmental delay in children from birth through 6 years of age. The test includes an evaluation of language and personal-social ability in addition to separate assessments of gross and fine motor skills. *220*

dependent variable The variable that is measured or recorded by the experimenter for changes that are presumed to be under the control of the independent or manipulated variable. *27*

depression The fourth stage of the five stages of dying by Elisabeth Kübler-Ross. *568*

designer drugs Drugs made by chemically reengineering an existing controlled substance to create a drug that is currently legal. *391*

development Refers to a pattern of change or movement that begins at conception and continues throughout the entire life span. *14*

developmental construction view Considers the continuing experiences of individuals in childhood, adolescence, and adulthood, and the effects of these experiences on the construction of present relationships. *445*

developmental quotient (DQ) An infant's test scores in four categories of behavior—motor, language, adaptive, and personal-social—combined into one overall developmental score. *164*

discontinuity of development Stresses distinct stages in the life-span. Emphasizes change. *20*

disenchantment stage (of retirement) When preretirement fantasies about retirement do not live up to the reality. No longer a viable view. *528*

disengagement theory The theory that as older adults slow down they gradually withdraw from society. *537*

dishabituation Renewed interest shown by an infant when a new stimulus is presented and distinguished from the old stimulus after habituation has occurred. *159*

displacement The characteristic of language whereby an individual can communicate information about another time and place. Guilford's term. *167*

divergent thinking A type of thinking that produces many different answers to a single question. *308*

DNA (deoxyribonucleic acid) A complex molecule running along the length of each chromosome; forms the bases for genetic structure in humans. *76*

dominant-recessive genes In the process of genetic transmission, a dominant gene is one that exerts its full characteristic effect regardless of its gene partner; a recessive gene is one whose code is masked by a dominant gene and is only expressed when paired with another recessive gene. *80*

Down's syndrome A disorder characterized by physical and mental retardation and a rather typical appearance, and attributable to either translocation or nondisjunction of chromosome 21. In the most common cases, individuals have 47 instead of 46 chromosomes, with 3 rather than 2 chromosomes in the twenty-first set. *76*

dyzygotic A term that refers to fraternal twins who come from two different eggs and are therefore genetically more different than identical twins. *85*

early adulthood Begins in the late teens or early 20s and lasts through the 30s. This is a time for developing personal and economic independence. *15*

early childhood Also called the preschool years; extends from the end of infancy to about 5 or 6 years of age, roughly corresponding to the period when the child prepares for formal schooling. *15*

echoing Repetition of what the child says to you, especially if it is an incomplete phrase or sentence. *175*

ecological view A view that sees complex information being perceived "directly" by picking up the invariants rather than engaging in any complex constructive mental activity. *140*

ectoderm The outer layer of the blastocyst; eventually becomes the child's hair, skin, nails, and nervous system. *101*

ectomorphic Characterized by a thin body shape. *286*

ego Freud's structure of personality that tests reality and mediates between the demands of the id and the superego. *37*

egocentrism The inability to distinguish between one's own perspective and the perspective of someone else. *228*

embryonic period A period lasting from about two to eight weeks after conception during which the ectoderm, mesoderm, and endoderm develop, and primitive human form takes shape. *101*

empathy The ability to participate in the feelings or ideas of another person. *278*

empty nest syndrome This view assumes that parents experience a great deal of satisfaction from their children and that, when they leave home, marital satisfaction drops because a sense of emptiness is felt. Recently has not been supported. *485*

endoderm The inner layer of the blastocyst; develops into the digestive system, lungs, pancreas, and liver. *101*

endomorphic A rounded somewhat "chubby" body build. *286*

epigenetic principle States that anything that grows has a ground plan, and out of this ground plan the parts arise, each one having its special time of ascendancy. Erikson's term. *42*

erogenous zones Body parts which are sensitive to pleasure. *39*

estradiol Hormone responsible for pubertal development in females; one of the hormones in a complex hormonal system associated with the physical changes of puberty in females. *354*

estrogen replacement therapy The addition of estrogen, by the physician, to maintain a woman's normal level once menopause occurs. *469*

estrogen Hormones that mature mainly in females and are produced by the sex glands. *270*

ethology The view that behavior is biologically determined; emphasizes critical or sensitive periods of development. Developed by European zoologists such as Lorenz. *60*

euthanasia The act of painlessly putting to death individuals who are suffering from an incurable disease or severe disability; sometimes referred to as mercy killing. *561*

executive stage A stage that may occur in middle adulthood where many individuals' responsibilities become extremely complex. *420*

exosystem Refers to settings in which the child does not participate, although important decisions that affect the individual's life are made in these settings. In Bronfenbrenner's ecological model. *186*

expanding Restating what the child has said in a more linguistically sophisticated form. *175*

experimental group The group of subjects in an experiment that is exposed to the independent variable. *27*

experimental strategy A research strategy in which the experimenter introduces a change into the child's environment and then measures the effects of that change on the child's subsequent behavior. The experimental strategy allows for the inference of causal relationships. *26*

expressive orientation Feminine dimension of gender roles; emphasizes interpersonal, affective quality of relationships. *337*

extrinsic motivation Behavior that is influenced by external rewards. *312*

father absence tradition Children from father absent and father present families were compared, and differences in their development were attributed to the absence of the father. *254*

fetal alcohol syndrome (FAS) A cluster of characteristics identified in children born to mothers who are heavy drinkers. Children may show abnormal behavior, such as hyperactivity or seizures, and the majority of FAS children score below average on intelligence, with a number of them in the mentally retarded range. *109*

fetal period The period of prenatal development that begins eight weeks after conception and lasts, on the average, for seven months. *102*

fine motor skills Skills involving more fine-grained movements, such as finger dexterity. *136*

first habits and primary circular reactions Develops between one to four months of age, the infant learns to coordinate sensation and types of schemes or structures. Piagetian concept. *156*

fixation An obsessive or unhealthy preoccupation or attachment. *39*

fluid intelligence The ability to perceive and manipulate information. *523*

formal operational stage The final stage of thought in Piaget's model of cognitive development; appears between 11 and 15 years of age, when the individual is believed to achieve the most advanced form of thought possible. The most important feature characterizing this stage is the development of abstract thought. *47*

friendship The attachment to another individual by affection or esteem. *439*

gametes The sex cells; the means by which genes are transmitted from parents to offspring. *76*

gender roles Social expectations of how we should act and think as males and females. *270*

gender schema A cognitive structure that organizes the world in terms of male and female. *271*

generativity versus stagnation The seventh stage of Erikson's eight-stage theory of development; is positively resolved if an adult assists the younger generation in developing and leading useful lives. *43*

genes Segments of chromosomes; comprised of DNA. *76*

genital stage Freud's last psychosexual stage, lasting from the beginning of puberty through the rest of the life cycle, during which sexual energy is focused on others, and work and love become important themes. *40*

genotype The unique combination of genes that forms the genetic structure of each individual. *84*

germinal period The period from conception until about 12 to 14 days later. *100*

gifted Describes an individual with well-above-average intellectual capacity (an IQ of 120 or more, for example) or an individual with a superior talent for something. *307*

grammar The formal description of syntactic rules. *168*

grief The emotional numbness, disbelief, separation anxiety, despair, sadness, and loneliness that accompany the loss of someone we love. *571*

gross motor skills Skills involving large muscle activities, like moving one's arms or walking. *136*

habituation Technique used to study infants' perceptual world. Repeated presentation of the same stimulus causes a drop in the infant's interest. *159*

hardiness A sense of commitment (rather than alienation), control (rather than powerlessness), and a perception of problems as challenges (rather than threats). Related to reduced stress. *464*

heteronomous morality The first stage of moral development in Piaget's theory. Justice and rules are conceived of as unchangeable properties of the world, removed from the control of people. *276*

heritability A mathematical estimate of the degree to which a particular characteristic is genetically determined. *85*

hermaphrodites Individuals whose hormone level is imbalanced (as in a developing male with insufficient androgen, or a female exposed to excess androgen). The genitals are intermediate between male and female. *270*

hierarchy of motives Maslow's idea that we need to satisfy our basic physiological needs before we can go on to realize higher needs. *58*

holophrase hypotheses A single word is used to imply a complete sentence. *176*

honeymoon stage (of retirement) Just after retirement, the individual may feel euphoric about being able to do all of the things he never had time to do before, and he may enjoy leisure activities more. *528*

hospice A humanized institution committed to making the end of life as free from pain, anxiety, and depression as possible. *569*

humanistic approach Psychological tradition that places a strong emphasis on the role of the self and self-concept as central to understanding development. Also emphasizes ability of individual to reach his or her potential. *56*

hypotheses Assumptions that can be tested to determine their accuracy. *21*

hypothetical deductive reasoning Ability to entertain many possibilities and to test many solutions in a planful way when faced with having to solve a problem; an important aspect of logical thought in the formal operational stage. *361*

id Freudian part of the personality governed by the pleasure principle; contains all drives present at birth, including sexual and aggressive instincts. *37*

identity achievement Adolescents who have undergone a crisis and made a commitment. To reach the identity-achieved status, it is necessary for the adolescent to first experience a crisis and then make an enduring commitment. Marcia's term. *388*

identity diffusion Adolescents who have not experienced any crisis (explored any meaningful alternatives) or made any commitments. Marcia's term. *388*

identity foreclosure Adolescents who have made a commitment but not experienced a crisis. Marcia's term. *388*

identity moratorium Adolescents in the midst of a crisis, but their commitments are either absent or only vaguely defined. Marcia's term. *388*

identity versus identity confusion The fifth stage in Erikson's eight-stage theory of development during which the adolescent may become confident and purposeful or may develop an ill-defined identity. *43*

imaginary audience The egocentric belief that others are as preoccupied with the adolescent's behavior as he or she is with himself or herself. *363*

immanent justice If a rule is broken, punishment will be meted out immediately. Piagetian concept. *276*

implantation The firm attachment of the zygote to the uterine wall that occurs about 10 days after conception. *101*

imprinting The process of establishing an attachment on first exposure to an object. Ethological term. *60*

in vitro **fertilization** A procedure in which the mother's ovum is removed surgically and fertilized in a laboratory medium with live sperm cells obtained from the father or male donor. Then the fertilized egg is stored in a laboratory solution that substitutes for the uterine environment and is finally implanted in the mother's uterus. *78*

independent variable The factor in an experiment that is manipulated or controlled by the experimenter to determine its impact on the subject's behavior. *27*

individualism and purpose Kohlberg's second stage. Moral thinking is based on rewards and self-interest. *340*

individuation The formation of the individual's personal identity, which includes the development of one's sense of self and the forging of a special place for oneself within the social order. Adolescents develop a more distinct view of themselves as unique persons and more readily differentiate themselves from others than they did as children. *389*

industry versus inferiority The fourth stage of Erikson's eight-stage theory of development during which the school-aged child may develop a capacity for work and task-directedness or may view himself or herself as inadequate. *43*

infancy Begins at birth and extends through the 18th to 24th month. A time of extensive dependency on adults and development of abilities such as thought and language. *15*

infantile amnesia Phenomenon that, as children and adults, humans have little or no memory for events experienced before 3 years of age. *162*

infinite generativity Characteristic of language that allows a finite set of rules to generate an infinite number of sentences through sequencing. *167*

information processing approach Theory of cognition that is concerned with the processing of information; involves such processes as attention, perception, memory, thinking, and problem solving. *50*

initiative versus guilt The third stage in Erikson's eight-stage theory of development, occurring during the preschool years, during which the child may develop a desire for achievement or he or she may be held back by self-criticism. *43, 268*

innate goodness view Eighteenth-century belief that children are basically and inherently good and should be permitted to grow naturally with little parental monitoring or constraints. *8*

instrumental orientation Used to describe the masculine dimension of gender roles. *337*

integration The feminine dimension of gender roles, emphasizing interpersonal relationships. *337*

integrity versus despair The eighth stage of Erikson's eight stages of development where in the later years of life the individual looks back and sees either a life well spent, or if not having resolved the previous stages successfully may feel doubt or despair. *43*

intelligence quotient (IQ) Calculated by using the concept of mental age and comparing it with the child's chronological age. *295*

intelligence Verbal ability, problem-solving skills, and the ability to learn from and adapt to the experiences of everyday life. *294*

intentionality The separation of means and goals in accomplishing simple feats. *157*

internalization of schemes A substage of Piaget's sensorimotor development in which the 18- to 24-month-old infant develops the ability to use primitive symbols. *157*

interpersonal norms Kohlberg's third stage. The individual values caring, trusting, and loyalty to others as the basis of moral judgments. *340*

interviews A method of study in which the researcher asks questions of a person and records that person's responses. *23*

intimacy Intimate self-disclosure and the sharing of private thoughts; private and personal knowledge about another. *328*

intimacy versus isolation The sixth stage of Erikson's eight-stage theory of development during which the young adult may achieve a capacity for honesty and close relationships or may be unable to form these ties, resulting in a feeling of isolation. *43*

intimate style Interaction style that forms and maintains one or more deep and long-lasting love relationships. *453*

intrinsic motivation Behavior that is motivated by an underlying need for competence and self-determination; also referred to as mastery and competence motivation. *311*

intuitive thought substage A substage of the preoperational stage, during which the child begins to reason about various matters and wants to know the answers to all sorts of questions. *229*

isolated style Withdrawal from social encounters and little or no intimate attachment to same or opposite sex individuals. *453*

jigsaw classroom A classroom where the emphasis is on cooperation among equals instead of unequal competition. *331*

justice perspective An approach to moral development proposed by Gilligan in which people are differentiated and seen as standing alone. The focus is on the rights of the individual (that is, on justice). *342*

juvenile delinquent The label applied to an adolescent who breaks the law or engages in behavior that is considered illegal. *394*

keeping the meaning versus rigidity A stage that George Vaillant believes should be added to Erikson's adult stages. At this time, adults show concern about extracting some meaning from their lives and fight against falling into a rigid orientation. *492*

Klinefelter's syndrome Males have an extra X chromosome (making them XXY instead of just XY). *80*

labeling The identification of words associated with objects. *175*

laboratory A controlled setting in which much of the real world with its complex factors has been removed. *23*

Lamaze method A form of prepared or natural childbirth that involves a way for the pregnant mother to cope with the pain of childbirth in an active way to avoid or reduce medication. *112*

language The words, their pronunciation, and the methods of combining them used and understood by a considerable community. *167*

language acquisition device (LAD) David McNeil's proposition that the child comes into the world wired to detect certain language categories—phonology, syntax, and semantics, for example. *169*

late adulthood Lasts from approximately 60 to 70 years of age until death. It is a time of adjustment to decreasing strength and health, reduced income, and for reviewing one's life. *15*

latency stage Freud's fourth psychosexual stage, lasting from about age 6 to age 12 (the elementary school years), during which the child concentrates on such activities as school and getting along in society. Stressful problems of the previous phallic stage are repressed. *40*

Leboyer method A birth procedure developed to make the birth experience less stressful for the infant; "birth without violence." *112*

leisure The pleasant times after work when individuals are free to pursue activities and interests of their own choosing. *479*

life expectancy The expected duration of life. The percentage of people who live to a certain age. *511*

life review The older adult surveys, observes and reflects upon his past. *547*

life span The duration of existence of an individual. The limit on how long people can live. *511*

life-cycle perspective A perspective which emphasizes that changes occur during adulthood, while still recognizing the importance of infancy and childhood as building blocks for the adult years. *11*

life-events approach An approach which emphasizes the factors that mediate the influence of life events on adult development—physical health, intelligence, personality, family supports, and income, for example. Also, how the individual appraises the life event's threat and copes with the stress are involved. *498*

long-term memory Information we retain indefinitely that can be used over and over again. *289*

longitudinal approach A method of study in which the same subject or group of subjects is repeatedly tested over a significant period of time. *29*

low-birth-weight infants Infants born after a regular gestation period of 38 to 42 weeks, but who weigh less than 5½ pounds. *115*

macrobiological theory A theory that looks at a more macro level to explain aging. *514*

macrosystem The most abstract level in Bronfenbrenner's portrayal of culture; refers to the attitudes and ideologies of the culture. *186*

major depression Causes the individual to feel sad, demoralized, bored and self-derogatory; individual has low energy and poor appetite, and experiences listlessness and lack of motivation. *549*

matching hypothesis The hypothesis that says we choose someone who is close to our own level of attractiveness even if we prefer a more attractive individual in the abstract. *438*

maturation The orderly sequence of changes dictated by the genetic blueprint we each have. *18*

MDMA A designer drug also known by the names of Ecstasy, Adam, and XTC. Has stimulant and mildly hallucinogenic qualities. *390*

mean length of utterance (MLU) A measure developed by Roger Brown to chart a child's language development. Morphemes are used as the unit of analysis. *177*

meiosis The process by which gametes reproduce, which allows for mixing genetic material. *76*

memory The retention of information over time. *160*

menarche The first menstruation in pubertal females. *352*

menopause Signals the end of childbearing capability. *469*

mental age (MA) Concept developed by Binet that describes the general level of a child's intellectual functioning. *295*

mental retardation Significantly subaverage general intellectual functioning existing concurrently with deficits in adaptive behavior and manifested during the developmental period. *305*

mesosystem Refers to linkages between microsystems or connections between contexts; for example, the relation of family experiences to school experiences. Bronfenbrenner's term. *186*

mesoderm The middle layer of cells in the embryo; becomes the circulatory system, bones, muscle, excretory system, and reproductive system. *101*

mesomorphic Athletic, muscular body build. *286*

metamemory Knowledge of one's own memory, including knowledge that learning information is different from simply perceiving information, diagnostic knowledge of the various factors contributing to performance of different memory tasks, and knowledge of how to monitor memory during the course of learning. *290*

metaphor An implied comparison between two ideas that is conveyed by the abstract meaning contained in the words used to make the comparison. *361*

method of loci A memory technique where the individual gets a mental picture of an event she has experienced and looks for detail. *525*

microbiological theory A theory that looks within the body's cells to explain aging. *514*

microsystem Refers to contexts in which the child has face-to-face interactions with others who are influential in his or her life. Bronfenbrenner's term. *184*

middle adulthood Lasts from approximately 40 to 65. It is a time of expanding personal and social involvement and responsibility. *15*

middle and late childhood Extends from about 6 to 11 years of age and is sometimes called the elementary school years. A time when a sense of industry is developed. *15*

mnemonics Techniques for improving memory. *525*

monozygotic A term that refers to identical twins, meaning that they come from the same egg. *85*

Montessori approach A philosophy of education, a psychology of the child, and a group of practical educational exercises that can be used to teach children. Children are permitted considerable freedom and spontaneity, and are encouraged to work independently. *218*

moral development The acquisition of rules and conventions about what people should do in their interactions with others. *275*

Moro reflex An infantile startle response that is common to all neonates but that disappears by about three to four months of age. When startled, the neonate arches its back and throws its head back, flinging out its arms and legs. The neonate then rapidly closes its arms and legs to the center of the body. *129*

morpheme The smallest unit of language that carries meaning. *168*

morphology The rules for combining morphemes. *168*

***n* achievement** Refers to the need and motivation to achieve and the individual's internal striving for success; viewed as a general property of the individual, remaining consistent across different domains and time. McClelland's term. *309*

natural selection A principle that provides an explanation of the evolutionary process; the belief that human and other organisms whose characteristics are the most adaptive to the environment are more likely to survive; thus, the more favorable characteristics are perpetuated through reproduction. *73*

naturalistic observation (field studies) Research conducted in real-world or natural settings; for example, observing a child at home, in school, on the playground, etc. *23*

nature-nurture controversy The "nature" proponents claim that biological and genetic factors are the most important determinants of development; the "nurture" proponents claim that environment and experience are more important. *18*

near stage (of retirement) When retirement is close. *528*

neglected children Children who are not necessarily disliked by their peers but who often do not have many friends. *325*

nonnutritive sucking Sucking behavior by the child that is unrelated to the child's feeding. *131*

normal distribution Frequency distribution that is very symmetrical, with a majority of the cases falling in the middle of the possible range of scores and fewer scores appearing toward the ends of the range. *295*

object permanence Significant sensorimotor accomplishment in which the infant grasps that objects and events continue to exist even though the child is not in direct perceptual contact with them. Piagetian concept. *158*

observation An act of recognizing or noting a fact or occurrence. *22*

Oedipus complex A Freudian conflict beginning in early childhood in which the boy exhibits sexual desire for the mother and hostility and fear of the father. *39*

onlooker play A type of play characterized by the child watching other children playing, but not joining in the activities. *261*

operant conditioning (instrumental conditioning) A type of learning described by Skinner in which the individual operates or acts on his or her environment, and what happens to the individual, in turn, controls his or her behavior. That is, the individual's behavior is determined by the consequences of that behavior. Behavior followed by a positive stimulus is likely to recur, while behavior followed by a negative stimulus is not as likely to recur. *54*

operations Internalized sets of actions that allow the child to do mentally what before was done physically. Operations are highly organized and conform to certain rules and principles of logic. In Piaget's theory, operations are mental actions of representations that are reversible. *47, 225*

oral stage The first psychosexual stage in Freud's theory of development, lasting from birth to around one year. This stage centers on the child's pleasure from stimulation of the oral area—mouth, lips, tongue, and gums. *39*

organic retardation Retardation caused by a genetic disorder or brain damage. *306*

organogenesis The first two months of prenatal development when the organ systems are being formed; may be adversely influenced by environmental events. *102*

original sin view Middle Ages, Catholic, and Puritan concept of children, reflecting the philosophical perspective that children are basically evil. *8*

overextensions The tendency of children to misuse words by extending one word's meaning to include a whole set of objects that are not related to or are inappropriate for the word's meaning. *176*

overgeneralizations The practice of a child to take a language rule and applying it where it is not appropriate; "foots" instead of "feet." *239*

oxytocin A hormone that stimulates uterine contractions and is widely used to speed up delivery. *115*

parallel play Parten's term. A type of play in which the child plays separately from the others, but with toys like those the others are using or in a manner that mimics their play. *262*

peers Refers to children or adolescents who are about the same age or at the same behavioral level. *257*

Perceived Competence Scale for Children Harter's measure emphasizing the assessment of the child's sense of competence across different domains rather than viewing perceived competence as a unitary concept. *334*

perception The interpretation of what is sensed. *140*

permissive indifferent parenting A style of parenting in which parents are uninvolved. Associated with poor self-control in children. *250*

permissive indulgent parenting A style of parenting in which the parents are highly involved in their children's lives, giving them considerable freedom to regulate their own behavior and taking a nonpunitive stance. These parents are rejecting as well as undemanding, and the result is usually a lack of self-control on the part of the child. *249*

personal fable Type of adolescent egocentrism that refers to the adolescent's sense of personal uniqueness and indestructibility. *363*

phallic stage Freud's third psychosexual stage, lasting from about the third to the sixth year, during which the child focuses on the genital area. *39*

phenomenological approach A theoretical view that places greater emphasis on understanding the individual's perception of an event than on the behavioral account of the event. *56*

phenotypes The observed and measurable characteristics of individuals, including physical characteristics, such as height, weight, eye color, and skin pigmentation, and psychological characteristics, such as intelligence, creativity, personality, and social tendencies. *84*

phonology The study of language's sound system. *167*

PKU syndrome (phenylketonuria) A disorder, caused by a recessive gene, that leads to the absence of an enzyme necessary to convert phenylalanine into tyrosine. This leads to an accumulation of phenylpyruvic acid, which has a damaging effect on the developing nervous system of a child. *76*

placenta A disk-shaped group of tissues in which small blood vessels from the mother and the offspring intertwine but do not join. *101*

play therapy Therapy that allows the child to work off his or her frustrations and serves as a medium through which the therapist can analyze many of the child's conflicts and methods of coping with them. *260*

pleasure principle Principle governing the id to constantly seek pleasure and avoid pain, regardless of what impact pleasure seeking and pain avoiding will have in the real world. *37*

polygenic inheritance A complex form of genetic transmission involving the interaction of many different genes to produce certain traits. *83*

postconventional moral reasoning The highest level of morality in Kohlberg's theory of moral development, in which moral values are completely internalized and not based on the standards of others. The moral code that is adopted may be among the principles generally accepted by the community (stage 5), or it may be more individualized (stage 6). *340*

pragmatics Rules that pertain to the social context of language and how people use language in conversation. *168*

precipitate A delivery that takes the baby less than 10 minutes to be squeezed through the birth canal. The rapidity of this delivery may disturb the normal flow of blood in the infant, and the pressure on the head may lead to hemorrhaging. *114*

preconventional reasoning The first and lowest level in Kohlberg's theory of moral development. No internalization of morality occurs here. Moral thought follows the belief that morality is determined by the external environment, particularly rewarding and punishing circumstances. *340*

preintimate style Interaction style that is characterized by mixed emotions about commitment. *453*

prenatal period Extends from conception to birth. *14*

preoperational stage The second stage of Piaget's cognitive theory of development that lasts from about 2 to 7 years of age. Although logical thought is present, there are several "flaws" such as egocentrism, that limit the individual. *47*

pretend play A type of play in which the child transforms the physical environment into a symbol by engaging in make-believe activities and playing out different roles. *262*

preterm infant Refers to baby born before 38 weeks in the womb. *115*

primary circular reactions A scheme based upon the 1- to 4-month-old infant's attempt to reproduce an interesting or pleasurable event that initially occurred by chance. Piagetian concept. *156*

Project Follow-Through A program instituted in 1967 as an adjunct to Project Head Start. Under this program, different kinds of educational programs were devised to see whether specific programs were effective. *241*

Project Head Start Compensatory education program designed to provide the children from low-income families with an opportunity to experience an enriched early environment and to acquire the skills and experiences considered prerequisite for success in school. *241*

proximodistal pattern A general pattern of physical growth and development that suggests that the pattern of growth starts at the center of the body and moves toward the extremities. *135*

pseudointimate style Maintenance of a long-lasting heterosexual attachment with little or no depth or closeness. *453*

psychoneuroimmunology The study of how psychological factors influence physical health, especially the brain and immune system. *468*

puberty The point in development at which the individual becomes capable of reproduction; usually linked with the onset of adolescence; a period of rapid change to maturation. *353*

punishment Refers to the situation in which a response is followed by an event that reduces the likelihood that the response will occur again. *54*

punishment and obedience orientation Kohlberg's first stage. Moral thinking is based on punishments. Children obey because parents tell them to obey. *340*

questionnaire Similar to a highly structured interview except that the respondent reads the question and marks his or her answer on the paper rather than verbally responding to the interviewer. *24*

reaction formation Freudian defense mechanism that wards off an unacceptable impulse by overemphasizing its opposite in thought and behavior. *38*

reaction range A range of one's potential phenotypical outcomes, given one's genotype and the influences of environmental conditions. The reaction range limits how much environmental change can modify an individual's behavioral characteristics. *84*

reality principle A principle of the ego that finds ways to satisfy the wants and needs of the id within the boundaries of reality. *37*

recasting Responding to a child's utterance by expressing the same or a similar meaning in a different way, perhaps by turning it into a question. *174*

reciprocal socialization A view of the socialization process as a mutual interaction between parents and the child. The child socializes the parent just as the parent socializes the child. *188*

reflexive smile A smile that does not occur in response to external stimuli. *132*

regression Freudian defense mechanism that occurs when the individual reverts to an earlier stage of development. *38*

rehearsal The extended processing of to-be-remembered material after it has been presented; a control process used to facilitate long-term memory. *289*

reinforcement Stimulation following a response that increases the probability that the same response will occur again in the same situation. *54*

reintegrative stage Closely corresponds to Erikson's final stage in the life cycle, ego integrity versus despair. Elderly people's acquisition and application of knowledge is, to a greater extent than earlier in life, related to their interests, attitudes, and values. *420*

rejected children Children who are overtly disliked by their peers and who often have more long-term maladjustment than neglected children. *325*

REM sleep Rapid eye movement sleep. *133*

remote stage When an individual feels that retirement is at some distant point in the future. *528*

reorientation stage (of retirement) When the retiree comes to grips with the reality of retirement and discovers ways to successfully cope with it. *528*

repression Freudian defense mechanism in which an anxiety-arousing memory or impulse is prevented from becoming conscious. *38*

reproduction A process that involves the fertilization of a female gamete (ovum) by a male gamete (sperm) to create a single-celled zygote. *76*

responsibility stage This stage occurs when a family is established and attention is given to a spouse's and offspring's needs. *420*

rhythmic motor behavior Rapid, repetitious movements of the limbs, torso, and head during the first year of life. These motor behaviors occur frequently and appear to be a source of pleasure for the infant. *136*

romantic love (Eros) A sensual love that focuses upon beauty and physical attractiveness. Also called passionate love. *440*

satire A literary work in which irony, derision, or wit in any form is used to expose folly or wickedness. *361*

scaffolding Mothers provide a framework around which they and their infants interact. An example involves turn-taking as in the game of peek-a-boo. *188*

schemata Active organizations of past experiences that provide a structure from which new information can be judged; a frame of reference for recording events or data. *290*

scheme The basic unit for an organized pattern of sensorimotor functioning in Piaget's theory. *155*

scientific method A series of steps used to obtain accurate information: identify and analyze the problem, collect data, draw conclusions, and revise theories. *22*

scripts Schemata for events. *290*

secondary circular reactions Schemes based upon the 4- to 8-month old infant becoming more object oriented, or focused on the world, and moving beyond preoccupation with the self in sense-action interactions. Piagetian term. *157*

secure attachment When the infant uses the caregiver, usually the mother, as a secure base from which to explore the environment. *191*

self-actualization The last stage of Maslow's hierarchy of needs is becoming everything you are capable of becoming. *59*

self-assertion Term used to attain greater specificity of gender role. It describes the masculine dimension of gender roles and includes such characteristics as leadership, dominance, independence, competitiveness, and individualism. *337*

semantics Language rules that pertain to the meaning of words and sentences. *168*

sensation The detection of the environment through stimulation of receptors in the sense organs. *140*

sensitive period Less rigid interpretation of the critical period that implies that a given effect can be produced more readily during one period than earlier or later. *61*

sensorimotor stage The earliest stage of Piaget's model of cognitive development, lasting from birth to about 2 years of age. This stage extends from simple reflexes through the use of primitive symbols as the means of coordinating sensation and action. *47*

sequential approach Research approach that combines the features of cross-sectional and longitudinal designs in a search for more effective ways to study development. This approach allows researchers to see whether the same pattern of development is produced by each of the research strategies. *29*

short-term memory A level of memory storage where stimuli are stored and retrieved for up to 30 seconds, assuming that there is no rehearsal. *236*

simple reflexes Reflexive behaviors that the infant has at birth such as rooting and sucking. Piagetian concept. *155*

social breakdown-reconstruction theory This theory argues that aging is promoted through negative psychological functioning, which consists of a poor self-concept, negative feedback from others and from society, and a lack of skills to deal with the world. *537*

social learning theory View that behavior is learned through social interaction. In recent years, cognitive factors have been emphasized as mediators of environment-behavior relations. Associated with behaviorism. *55*

social processes A person's interaction with other individuals in the environment and these interactions' effect on development. *14*

social smile Smile that occurs in response to a face. *132*

social system morality Kohlberg's fourth stage. Moral judgments are based on understanding the social order of law, justice, and duty. *340*

solitary play A type of play in which the child plays alone and independently of those around him or her, with little or no concern for anything else that is going on. *261*

stability stage (of retirement) When individuals have decided upon a set of criteria for evaluating choices in retirement and how they will perform once they have made these choices. *528*

stability-change issue Addresses the degree we become older renditions of our early existence or whether we can develop into someone different than we were at an earlier point in development. *20*

standardized tests Questionnaires, structured interviews, or behavioral tests that are developed to identify an individual's characteristics or abilities, relative to those of a large group of similar individuals. *24*

stereotyped style Characterized by superficial relationships that tend to be dominated by friendship ties with same-sex rather than opposite-sex individuals. *453*

storm and stress view View of adolescence proposed by Hall that sees adolescence as a turbulent time charged with conflict and characterized by contradiction and wide swings in mood and emotion. *9*

structure-process dilemma Whether your greater processing capacity as an adult is a consequence that as a child might be what allows you to learn more or whether your greater processing capacity as an adult is a consequence of your greater knowledge, which allows you to process information more effectively. *303*

sublimation The Freudian defense mechanism of replacing a distasteful course of action for a socially acceptable one. *38*

superego Freudian part of the personality that serves as the internal representative of the values of one's parents and society; the moral branch of the personality. *38*

surface structure The actual order of words in a spoken sentence. *168*

suttee The now outlawed Hindu practice of burning a dead man's widow to increase his family's prestige and firmly establish an image of her in his memory. *574*

symbolic function substage Substage of preoperational thought that exists roughly between the ages of 2 to 4 years. The child begins to use symbols (mental representations) to represent objects that are not present. *225*

syntax A set of language rules that involves the combining of words into acceptable phrases and sentences. *168*

***tabula rasa* view** Locke's view that children are not innately evil, but instead are like a blank tablet, becoming a particular kind of child or adult because of his or her particular life experiences. *8*

telegraphic speech Speech that includes content words, such as nouns and verbs, but omits the extra words that only serve a grammatical function, such as prepositions and articles. *176*

teratology The field of study that investigates the causes of congenital (birth) defects. *104*

termination stage (of retirement) The point where retirement loses its significance and relevance in the eyes of the older adult. *529*

tertiary circular reactions Schemes in which the 12- to 18-month-old infant purposefully explores new possibilities with objects, continuously changing what is done to them and exploring the results. Piagetian concept. *157*

tertiary circular reactions, novelty, and curiosity Develops between 12 to 18 months of age, the infant becomes intrigued by the variety of properties that objects possess and by the multiplicity of things she can make happen to objects. Piagetian concept. *157*

testis determining factor (TDF) Genes carried on the twenty-third chromosome pair believed to determine an individual's sex. *83*

testosterone A male sex hormone important in the development of sexual characteristics and behavior. *353*

theories Are general beliefs that help us to explain the data or facts we have observed and make predictions. *21*

top-dog phenomenon Moving from the top position (in elementary school, as the oldest, biggest, and most powerful students in the school) to the lowest position (in middle or junior high school, as the youngest, smallest, and least powerful group of students). *368*

triarchic theory of intelligence R. J. Sternberg's model of intelligence that recognizes the importance of both process and knowledge. Sternberg believes that each of us has three types of intelligence—componential intelligence, experiential intelligence and contextual intelligence. *304*

trophoblast The outer layer of the blastula that provides nutrition and support for the embryo. *101*

trust versus mistrust The first stage in Erikson's eight stage theory of development, during which infants develop either the comfortable feeling that those around them care for their needs or the worry that their needs will not be taken care of. *42*

Turner's syndrome Women are minus an X chromosome making them XO instead of XX. *80*

twin study A strategy of research that focuses on the genetic relationship between identical twins (monozygotic) and fraternal twins (dizygotic). *85*

two-factor theory A theory of intelligence stressing that intelligence consists of *g* for general intelligence and *s* for specific intelligence. *296*

Type A babies or anxious-avoident attachment Exhibits insecurity by avoiding the mother, for example, ignoring her, averting her gaze, and failing to seek proximity. *192*

Type A behavior pattern Excessivily competitive, an accelerated pace of ordinary activities, impatience, hostility, and the feeling that there are not enough hours in a day. *465*

Type B babies or secure attachment A positive bond that develops between the infant and the caregiver; promotes the healthy exploration of the world because the caregiver provides a secure base to which the infant can return if stressors are encountered. *192*

Type C babies or anxious-resistant Exhibit insecurity by resisting the mother, for example, clinging to her but at the same time fighting against the closeness perhaps by kicking and pushing away. *192*

ultrasound sonography High-frequency sound waves directed into a pregnant woman's abdomen. The echo from the sounds is transformed into a visual representation of the fetus' inner structures. *83*

umbilical cord Contains two arteries and one vein and connects the baby to the placenta. *101*

unconditional positive regard When an individual is valued regardless of negative or socially unacceptable behavior. Rogers' concept. *58*

underextension A tendency of children to misuse words by not extending one word's meaning to other appropriate contexts for the word. *176*

undifferentiated Refers to individuals who perceive themselves as neither masculine nor feminine in gender-role orientation. *336*

universal ethical principles Kohlberg's sixth and highest stage. Moral standards based on universal human rights. *341*

unoccupied play A type of play in which the child is not engaged in activities that are normally regarded as play. The child may stand in one spot, look around the room, or perform random movements that seem to have no goal. *261*

Wechsler Scales Widely used individual intelligence test developed by David Wechsler. *296*

wisdom The ability to discern inner qualities by accumulated philosophic or scientific knowledge. *526*

XYY syndrome An extra Y chromosome in the male. *80*

youth The period of development entered as early as 17 to 18 years of age or as late as 21 to 24 years of age: a time of extended sense of economic and personal "temporariness." *407*

zygote A single-celled fertilized ovum (egg) created in the reproductive process. *76/ 100*

REFERENCES

Abramovitch, R., Corter, C., Pepler, D. J., & Stanhope, L. (1986). Sibling and peer interaction: A final follow-up and comparison. *Child Development, 47,* 217–229.

Achenbach, T. M., & Edelbrock, C. S. (1981). Behavioral problems and competencies reported by parents of normal and disturbed children aged four through sixteen. *Monographs of the Society for Research in Child Development, 46 (1, Serial No. 188).*

Acredelo, L. P., & Hake, J. L. (1982). Infant perception. In B. B. Wolman (Ed.), *Handbook of developmental psychology.* Englewood Cliffs, NJ: Prentice Hall.

Adams, G. M., & deVries, H. A. (1973). Physiological effects of an exercise training regimen among women aged 52 to 79. *Journal of Gerontology, 28,* 50–55.

Adams, G. R., & Lavoie, J. C. (1974). The effect of sex of child, conduct, and facial attractiveness on teacher expectancy. *Education, 95,* 76–83.

Agnew, N. McK., & Pyke, S. W. (1987). *The science game* (4th ed.). Englewood Cliffs, NJ: Prentice Hall.

Ahrons, C. R., & Rodgers, R. H. (1987). *Divorced families.* New York: Norton.

Ainsworth, M. D. S. (1967). *Infancy in Uganda: Infant care and the growth of love.* Baltimore, MD: Johns Hopkins U. Press.

Ainsworth, M. D. S. (1979). Infant-mother attachment. *American Psychologist, 34,* 932–937.

Ainsworth, M. D. S. (1988, August). *Attachments beyond infancy.* Paper presented at the meeting of the American Psychological Association, Atlanta.

Ainsworth, M. D. S., Blehar, M. C., Waters, E., & Wall, S. (1978). *Patterns of attachment: A psychological study of the strange situation.* Hillsdale, NJ: Erlbaum.

Alan Guttmacher Institute (1981). *Teenage pregnancy: The problem that has not gone away.* New York: Author.

Alexander, D. (1987, April). *High interest areas in child development for the NICHD in the NIH centennial year.* Paper presented at the biennial meeting of the Society for Research in Child Development, Baltimore.

Als, H. (1988, November). *Intensive care unit stress for the high-risk preterm infant: Neurofunctional and emotional sequelae.* Paper presented at the Developmental Intervention in Neonatal Care Conference, San Diego, CA.

Amsterdam, B. K. (1968). *Mirror behavior in children under two years of age.* Unpublished doctoral dissertation, U. of North Carolina, Chapel Hill.

Anastasi, A. (1988). *Psychological testing* (6th ed.). New York: Macmillan.

Anders, T. F., & Chalemian, R. J. (1974). The effect of circumcision on sleep-wake states in human neonates. *Psychosomatic Medicine, 36,* 174–179.

Anderson, D. R., Lorch, E. P., Field, D. E., Collins, P. A., & Nathan, J. G. (1985, April). *Television viewing at home: Age trends in visual attention and time with TV.* Paper presented at the biennial meeting of the Society for Research in Child Development, Toronto.

Aries, P. (1962). *Centuries of childhood* (R. Baldrick, Trans.). New York: Knopf.

Aronson, E. (1986, August). *Teaching students things they think they already know about: The case of prejudice and desegregation.* Paper presented at the meeting of the American Psychological Association, Washington, DC.

Asarnow, J. R., & Callan, J. W. (1985). Boys with peer adjustment problems: Social cognitive processes. *Journal of Consulting and Clinical Psychology, 53,* 80–87.

Asher, J., & Garcia, R. (1969). The optimal age to learn a foreign language. *Modern Language Journal, 53,* 334–341.

Asher, J. (1987). Born to be shy? *Psychology Today,* April, 56–64.

Asher, S. R., & Dodge, K. A. (1986). Identifying children who are rejected by their peers. *Developmental Psychology, 22,* 444–449.

Ashmead, D. H., & Perlmutter, M. (1979, August). *Infant memory in everyday life.* Paper presented at the meeting of the American Psychological Association, New York City.

Aslin, R. N. (1987). Visual and auditory development in infancy. In J. D. Osofsky (Ed.), *Handbook of infant development* (2nd ed.). New York: Wiley.

Atchley, R. C. (1976). *The sociology of retirement.* Cambridge, MA: Schenkman.

Atchley, R. C. (in press). Demographic factors and adult psychological development. In K. W. Schaie & C. Schooler (Eds.), *Social structure and aging.* Hillsdale, NJ: Erlbaum.

Atkinson, J. W., & Raynor, I. O. (1974). *Motivation and achievement.* New York: Wiley.

Auerback, K. (1987, April). *Breastfeeding and attachment in employed mothers.* Paper presented at the biennial meeting of the Society for Research in Child Development, Baltimore.

Averill, J. R. (1968). Grief: Its nature and significance. *Psychological Bulletin, 70,* 721–748.

Bachman, J., O'Malley, P., & Johnston, L. (1978). *Youth in transition, Vol. VI. Adolescence to adulthood—change and stability of the lives of young men.* Ann Arbor: Institute of Social Research, U. of Michigan.

Bachman, J. G. (1982, June). *The American high school student: A profile based on national survey data.* Paper presented at conference on "The American High School Today and Tomorrow," Berkeley, CA.

Bahrick, H. P., Bahrick, P. O., & Wittlinger, R. P. (1975). Fifty years of memory for names and faces: A cross-sectional approach. *Journal of Experimental Psychology: General, 104,* 54–75.

Bahrick, L. E. (1988). Intermodal learning in infancy: Learning on the basis of two kinds of invariant relations in audible and visible events. *Child Development, 59,* 197–209.

Bakeman, R., & Brown, J. V. (1980). Early interaction: Consequences for social and mental development at three years. *Child Development, 51,* 437–447.

Baltes, P. B. (1973). Prototypical paradigms and questions in life-span research on development and aging. *The Gerontologist, 113,* 458–467.

Baltes, P. B. (1987). Theoretical propositions of life-span developmental psychology: On the dynamics between growth and decline. *Developmental Psychology, 23,* 611–626.

Baltes, P. B., & Baltes, M. M. (Eds.). (in press). *Successful aging.* New York: Cambridge U. Press.

Baltes, P. B., & Kliegl, R. (1986). On the dynamics between growth and decline in the aging of intelligence and memory. In K. Poeck, H. J. Freund, & H. Ganshirt (Eds.), *Neurology.* Heidelberg, WG: Springer-Verlag.

Baltes, P. B., Reese, H. W., & Lipsett, L. P. (1980). Life-span developmental psychology. *Annual Review of Psychology, 31,* 65–110.

Baltes, P. B., Smith, J., Staudinger, V. M., & Sowarka, D. (1988). Wisdom: One facet of successful aging? In M. Perlmutter (Ed.), *Late-life potential.* Washington, DC: Gerontological Society of America.

Bandura, A. (1965). Influence of models' reinforcement contingencies on the acquisition of imitative responses. *Journal of Personality and Social Psychology, 1,* 589–595.

Bandura, A. (1977). *Social learning theory.* Englewood Cliffs, NJ: Prentice Hall.

Bandura, A. (1986). *Social foundations of thought and action: A social cognitive theory.* Englewood Cliffs, NJ: Prentice Hall.

Bane, M. J. (1978). *HEW policy toward children, youth, and families.* Office of the Assistant Secretary for Planning and Evaluation, Cambridge, MA.

Banks, M. S., & Salapatek, P. (1983). Infant visual perception. In P. H. Mussen (Ed.), *Handbook of child psychology* (4th ed.), Vol. 2. New York: Wiley.

Bar-Tal, D. (1976). Perceptions of similarly and dissimilarly attractive couples and individuals. *Journal of Personality and Social Psychology, 33,* 772–781.

Barcus, F. E. (1978). *Commercial children's television on weekends and weekday afternoons.* Newtonville, MA: Action for Children's Television.

Bardwick, J. (1971). *The psychology of women: A study of biocultural conflicts.* New York: Harper & Row.

Barenboim, C. (1981). The development of person perception in childhood and adolescence: From behavioral comparisons to psychological constructs to psychological comparisons. *Child Development, 52,* 129–144.

589

Barenboim, C. (1985, April). *Person perception and interpersonal behavior.* Paper presented at the biennial meeting of the Society for Research in Child Development, Toronto.

Barker, R., & Wright, H. F. (1951). *One boy's day.* New York: Harper & Row.

Barnes, D. M. (1987). Defect in Alzheimer's is on Chromosome 21. *Science, 235,* 846–847.

Barnes, G. M. (1984). Adolescent alcohol abuse and other problem behaviors: Their relationships and common parental influences. *Journal of Youth and Adolescence, 13,* 329–348.

Barnes, K. E. (1971). Preschool play norms: A replication. *Developmental Psychology, 4,* 99–103.

Barnett, L. R., & Netzel, M. T. (1979). Relationship of instrumental and affection behaviors and self-esteem to marital satisfaction in distressed and nondistressed couples. *Journal of Consulting and Clinical Psychology, 47,* 946–954.

Baron, J. B., & Sternberg, R. J. (Eds.). (1987). *Teaching thinking skills.* New York: W. H. Freeman.

Baron, R. A., & Byrne, D. (1987). *Social psychology* (5th ed.). Boston: Allyn & Bacon.

Barrett, K. C., & Campos, J. J. (1987). A functionalist approach to emotions. In J. D. Osofsky (Ed.), *Handbook of infant development.* New York: Wiley.

Bar-Tal, D., & Saxe, L. (1976). Perceptions of similarly and dissimilarly attractive couples and individuals. *Journal of Personality and Social Psychology, 33,* 772–781.

Baskett, L. M., & Johnston, S. M. (1982). The young child's interaction with parents versus siblings. *Child Development, 53,* 643–650.

Bassoff, E. (1988). *Mothers and daughters: Loving and letting go.* New York: New American Library.

Bates, E., O'Connell, B., & Shore, C. (1987). Language and communication in infancy. In J. D. Osofsky (Ed.), *Handbook of infant development.* New York: Wiley.

Batson, C. D. (in press). Prosocial motivation: Is it ever truly altruistic? In L. Berkowitz (Ed.), *Advances in experimental social psychology.* New York: Academic Press.

Baum, A., Davidson, L. M., Singer, J. E., & Street, S. W. (in press). Stress is a psychophysiological process. In A. Baum & J. Singer (Eds.), *Stress.* Hillsdale, NJ: Erlbaum.

Baumeiser, A. A. (1987). Mental retardation: Some conceptions and dilemmas. *American Psychologist, 42,* 796–800.

Baumrind, D. (1971). Current patterns of parental authority. *Developmental Psychology Monographs, 4* (1, Pt. 2).

Bayley, N. (1969). *Manual for the Bayley scales of infant development.* New York: The Psychological Corporation.

Beck, J., & Morgan, P. A. (1986). Designer drug confusion: A focus on MDMA. *Journal of Drug Education, 16,* 287–302.

Bell, A. P., Weinberg, M. S., & Mannersmith, S. K. (1981). *Sexual preference: Its development in men and women.* New York: Simon & Schuster.

Bell, S. M., & Ainsworth, M. D. S. (1972). Infant crying and maternal responsiveness. *Child Development, 43,* 1171–1190.

Belloc, N. B., & Breslow, L. (1972). Relationships of physical health status and health practices. *Preventive Medicine, 1,* 409–421.

Belsky, J. (1981). Early human experience: A family perspective. *Developmental Psychology, 17,* 3–23.

Belsky, J. (1987, April). *Science, social policy, and day care: A personal odyssey.* Paper presented at the Society for Research in Child Development, Baltimore.

Belsky, J. (in press). Nonmaternal care in the first year of life and infant-parent attachment security. *Child Development.*

Belson, W. (1979). *Television violence and the adolescent boy.* London: Saxon House.

Bem, S. L. (1977). On the utility of alternative procedures for assessing psychological androgyny. *Journal of Consulting and Clinical Psychology, 45,* 196–205.

Bem, S. L. (1985). Androgyny and gender schema theory: Conceptual and empirical integration. In T. B. Sonderegger (Ed.), *Nebraska Symposium on Motivation.* Lincoln, NE: U. of Nebraska Press.

Benet, S. (1976). *How to live to be 100.* New York: The Dial Press.

Bengston, V. L. (1985). Diversity and symbolism in grandparent roles. In V. L. Bengston & J. F. Robertson (Eds.). *Grandparenthood.* Beverly Hills, CA: Sage.

Bennett, W. I., & Gurin, J. (1982). *The dieter's dilemma: Eating less and weighing more.* New York: Basic Books.

Berg, W. K., & Berg, K. M. (1987). Psychophysiological development in infancy: State, startle, and attention. In J. D. Osofsky (Ed.), *Handbook of infant development* (2nd ed.). New York: Wiley.

Berko, J. (1958). The child's learning of English morphology. *Word, 14,* 150–177.

Berlyne, D. E. (1960). *Conflict, arousal, and curiosity.* New York: McGraw-Hill.

Berman, H. J. (1987). Adult children and their parents: Irredeemable obligation and irreplaceable loss. *Journal of Gerontological Social Work, 10,* 21–30.

Berman, W. H., & Turk, D. C. (1981). Adaptation to divorce: Problems and coping strategies. *Journal of Marriage and the Family, 43,* 179–189.

Berndt, T. J. (1979). Developmental changes in conformity to peers and parents. *Developmental Psychology, 15,* 608–616.

Berndt, T. J. (1982). The features and effects of friendships in early adolescence. *Child Development, 53,* 1447–1460.

Berscheid, E. (1983). Emotion. In H. H. Kelley, E. Berscheid, A. Cristensen, J. Harvey, T. L. Juston, G. Levinger, E. McClintock, A. Peplau, & D. R. Peterson (Eds.), *Close relationships.* San Francisco, CA: W. H. Freeman.

Berscheid, E. (1985). Interpersonal attraction. In G. Lindzey & E. Aronson (Eds.), *Handbook of social psychology* (3rd ed.), Vol. 2. New York: Random House.

Berscheid, E. (1988). Some comments on love's anatomy: Or, whatever happened to old-fashioned lust? In R. J. Sternberg & M. L. Barnes (Eds.), *Anatomy of love.* New Haven: Yale University Press.

Berscheid, E., and Fei, J. (1977). Sexual jealousy and romantic love. In G. Clinton & G. Smith (Eds.), *Sexual jealousy.* Englewood Cliffs, NJ: Prentice Hall.

Berscheid, E., & Snyder, M. (in press). *The measurement of relationship closeness.* Minneapolis, MN: U. of Minnesota.

Binder, A. (1987). A historical and theoretical introduction. In H. C. Quay (Ed.), *Handbook of juvenile delinquency.* New York: Wiley.

Birren, J. E., & Sloane, R. B. (Eds.). (1980). *Handbook of mental health and aging.* Englewood Cliffs, NJ: Prentice Hall.

Blair, S. N. (1988, June). *Personal communication.* Dallas, TX: The Aerobics Institute.

Blair, S. N., & Kohl, H. W. (1988). Physical activity: Which is more important for health? *Medicine and Science and Sports and Exercise,* Vol. 20, 2, Supplement, pp. 5–7.

Blasi, A. (1988). Identity and the development of the self. In D. Lapsley & F. C. Power (Eds.). *Self, ego, and identity: Integrative approaches.* New York: Springer.

Blechman, E. A., & Brownell, K. D. (Eds.). *Handbook of behavioral medicine for women.* Elsmford, NY: Pergamon.

Block, J. (1976). Issues, problems, and pitfalls in assessing sex differences: A critical review of the psychology of sex differences. *Merrill-Palmer Quarterly, 22,* 283–308.

Block, J., & Block, J. H. (1988). Longitudinally foretelling drug usage in adolescence: Early childhood personality and environmental precursors. *Child Development, 59,* 336–355.

Block, J. H., Block, J., & Gjerde, P. F. (1986). The personality of children prior to divorce. *Child Development, 57,* 827–840.

Block, J. H., Block, J., & Gjerde, P. F. (in press). Parental functioning and the home environment in families of divorce: Prospective and concurrent analysis. *Journal of the American Academy of Child Psychiatry.*

Bloom, B. L., Asher, S. J., & White, S. W. (1978). Marital disruption as a stressor: A review and analysis. *Psychological Bulletin, 85,* 867–894.

Bloom, B. S. (1983, April). *The development of exceptional talent.* Paper presented at the biennial meeting of the Society for Research in Child Development, Detroit.

Bloor, C., & White, F. (1983). Unpublished manuscript. University of California at San Diego, LaJolla, CA.

Blum, R. W., & Goldhagen, J. (1981). Teenage pregnancy in perspective. *Clinical Pediatrics, 20,* 335–340.

Blumberg, M. L. (1974). Psychopathology of the abusing parent. *American Journal of Psychotherapy, 28,* 1121–1129.

Blumenfeld, P. C., Pintrich, P. R., Wessels, K., & Meece, J. (1981, April). *Age, and sex differences in the impact of classroom experiences on self perceptions.* Paper presented at the biennial meeting of the Society for Research in Child Development, Boston.

Blumenthal, S. J., & Kupfer, D. J. (1988). Overview of early detection and treatment strategies for suicidal behavior in young people. *Journal of Youth and Adolescence, 17,* 1–14.

Blumstein, P., & Schwartz, P. (1983). *American couples: Money, work, sex.* New York: Morrow.

Blundell, J. E. (1984). Systems and interactions: An approach to the pharmacology of feeding. In A. J. Stunkard & E. Stellar (Eds.), *Eating and its disorders.* New York: Raven Press.

Blyth, D. A., Bulcroft, R., & Simmons, R. G. (1981, August). *The impact of puberty on adolescents: A longitudinal study.* Paper presented at the meeting of the American Psychological Association, Los Angeles.

Blyth, D. A., Durant, D., & Moosbrugger, L. (1985, April). *Perceived intimacy in the social relationships of drug- and nondrug-using adolescents.* Paper presented at the biennial meeting of the Society for Research in Child Development, Toronto.

Bolter, J. D. (1984). *Turing's man.* Chapel Hill, NC: U. of North Carolina Press.

Bondareff, W. (1985). The neural basis of aging. In J. E. Birren & K. W. Schaie (Eds.), *Handbook of the psychology of aging* (2nd ed.). New York: Van Nostrand Reinhold.

Bornstein, M. H. (1988). Perceptual development across the life cycle. In M. H. Bornstein & M. E. Lamb (Eds.), *Developmental psychology* (2nd ed.), Hillsdale, NJ: Erlbaum.

Bornstein, M. H. (Ed.) (1987). *Sensitive periods in development.* Hillsdale, NJ: Erlbaum.

Bornstein, M. H., & Sigman, M. D. (1986). Continuity in mental development from infancy. *Child Development, 57,* 251–274.

Borovsky, D., Hill, W., & Rovee-Collier, C. (1987, April). *Developmental changes in infant long-term memory.* Paper presented at the biennial meeting of the Society for Research in Child Development, Baltimore.

Borstelmann, L. J. (1983). Children before psychology: Ideas about children from antiquity to the late 1800s. In P. H. Mussen (Ed.), *Handbook of Child Psychology* (4th ed.), Vol. 1. New York: Wiley.

Boston Women's Health Book Collective, Inc. (1978). Ourselves and our children: A book by & for parents. New York: Random House.

Bouchard, T. J., Heston, L., Eckert, E., Keyes, M., & Resnick, S. (1981). The Minnesota study of twins reared apart: Project description and sample results in the developmental domain. *Twin Research, 3,* 227–233.

Bower, T. G. R. (1982). *Development in infancy* (2nd ed.). San Francisco: W. H. Freeman.

Bowlby, J. (1969). *Attachment and loss,* Vol. 1. London: Hogarth.

Bowlby, J. (1973). *Attachment and loss,* Vol. 2. London: Hogarth.

Bowlby, J. (1980). *Attachment and loss,* Vol. 3. London: Hogarth.

Brackbill, Y. (1979). Obstetric medication and infant behavior. In J. D. Osofsky (Ed.), *Handbook of infant development.* New York: Wiley.

Brand, E., Clingempeel, W. E., & Bowen-Woodward, K. (in press). Family relationships and children's psychological adjustment in stepmother and stepfather families: Findings and conclusions from the Philadelphia Stepfamily Research Project. In E. M. Hetherington & J. D. Arasteh (Eds.), *Impact of divorce, single-parenting, and stepparenting on children.* Hillsdale, NJ: Erlbaum.

Bray, D. W., & Howard, A. (1983). The AT&T longitudinal studies of managers. In K. W. Schaie (Ed.), *Longitudinal studies of adult psychological development.* New York: Guilford Press.

Bray, J. H. (in press). The effects of early remarriage on children's development: Preliminary analyses of the developmental issues in stepfamily research project. In E. M. Hetherington & J. D. Arasteh (Eds.), *Impact of divorce, single-parenting, and stepparenting on children.* Hillsdale, NJ: Erlbaum.

Brazelton, T. B. (1956). Sucking in infancy. *Pediatrics, 17,* 400–404.

Brazelton, T. B. (1973). *Neonatal behavioral assessment scale.* London: Heinemann Medical Books.

Brazelton, T. B. (1979). Behavioral competence in the newborn infant. *Seminars in Perinatology, 3,* 35–44.

Brazelton, T. B. (1984). *Neonatal behavioral assessment scale* (2nd ed.). Philadelphia: Lippincott.

Brazelton, T. B. (1987, August). *Opportunities for intervention with infants at risk.* Paper presented at the meeting of the American Psychological Association, New York City.

Brazelton, T. B., Nugent, J. K., & Lester, B. M. (1987). Neonatal behavioral assessment scale. In J. D. Osofsky (Ed.), *Handbook of infant development* (2nd ed.). New York: Wiley.

Brazelton, T. B. (1988, November). *Family stresses and emotional issues of parents during NICU hospitalization.* Paper presented at Developmental Interventions in Neonatal Care Conference, San Diego, CA.

Brenner, M. H., (1973). *Mental illness and the economy.* Cambridge, MA: Harvard U. Press.

Bretherton, I. (1987). New perspectives on attachment relations: Security, communication, and internal working models. In J. D. Osofsky (Ed.), *Handbook of infant development.* New York: Wiley.

Bretherton, I., Fritz, J., Zahn-Waxley, C., & Ridgeway, D. (1986). Learning to talk about emotions. *Child Development, 57,* 529–548.

Brim, O. G., & Riff, C. D. (1980). On the properties of life events. In P. B. Baltes & O. G. Brim (Eds.), *Life-span development and behavior.* New York: Academic Press.

Broman, S. H., Bien, E., & Shaughnessy, P. (in press). *Retardation in young children.* Hillsdale, NJ: Erlbaum.

Bronfenbrenner, U. (1979). Contexts of child rearing: Problems and prospects. *American Psychologist, 34,* 844–850.

Bronfenbrenner, U. (1987, August). *Recent advances in theory and design.* Paper presented at the meeting of the American Psychological Association, New York City.

Bronstein, P. (1988). Marital and parenting roles in transition. In P. Bronstein & C. P. Cowen (Eds.), *Contemporary Fatherhood.* New York: Wiley.

Brooks-Gunn, J. (1987). Pubertal processes and girls' psychological adaptation. In R. M. Lerner & T. T. Foch (Eds.), *Biological and psychological interactions in early adolescence.* Hillsdale, NJ: Erlbaum.

Brooks-Gunn, J. (1988). Antecedents and consequences of variations in girls' maturational timing. In M. D. Levine & E. R. McAnarney (Eds.), *Early adolescent transitions.* Lexington, MA: Lexington Books.

Brooks-Gunn, J., & Warren, M. P. (in press). The psychological significance of secondary sexual characteristics in 9- to 11-year old girls. *Child Development.*

Brown, A. L., Bransford, J. D., Ferrara, R. A., & Campione, J. C. (1983). Learning, remembering and understanding. In P. H. Mussen (Ed.), *Handbook of child psychology* (4th ed.), Vol. 3. New York: Wiley.

Brown, A. L., & Smiley, S. S. (1977). Rating the importance of structural units of prose passages: A problem of metacognitive development. *Child Development, 48,* 1–8.

Brown, B. B., & Lohr, M. J. (in press). Peer group affiliation and adolescent self-esteem: An integration of ego identity and symbolic interaction theories. *Journal of Personality and Social Psychology.*

Brown, F. (1973). *The reform of secondary education: Report of the national commission on the reform of secondary education.* New York: McGraw-Hill.

Brown, J. L. (1964). States in newborn infants. *Merrill-Palmer Quarterly, 10,* 313–327.

Brown, R. (1973). *A first language: The early stages.* Cambridge, MA: Harvard U. Press.

Brown, R. (1985). *Social psychology* (2nd ed.). New York: Free Press.

Brown, R., Cazden, C. B., & Bellugi-Klima, U. (1969). The child's grammar from I to III. In J. P. Hill (Ed.), *Minnesota Symposia on Child Psychology,* Vol. 2. Minneapolis: University of Minnesota Press.

Bruner, J., & Sherwood, V. (1976). Peek-a-boo and the learning of rule structures. In J. Bruner, A. Jolly, & K. Silva (Eds.), *Play: Its role in evolution and development.* Harmondsworth: Penguin.

Bryant, B. (1985). The neighborhood walk: Sources for support in middle childhood. *Monographs of the Society for Research in Child Development, 50* (3, Serial No. 210).

Buhrmester, D., & Furman, W. (1987). The development of companionship and intimacy. *Child Development, 58,* 1100–1113.

Bukowski, W. M., Newcomb, A. F., & Hoza, B. (1987). Friendship conceptions among early adolescents: A longitudinal study of stability and change. *Journal of Early Adolescence, 7,* 143–152.

Bulcroft, K., & O'Conner-Roden, M. (1986, June). Never too late. *Psychology Today,* pp. 66–69.

Bullock, M. (1985). Animism in childhood thinking: A new look at an old question. *Developmental Psychology, 21,* 217–225.

Burkett, C. L. (1985, April). *Childrearing behaviors and the self-esteem of preschool-age children.* Paper presented at the biennial meeting of the Society for Research in Child Development, Toronto.

Buss, A. H., & Plomin, R. (1984). *A temperament theory of personality development.* New York: Wiley-Interscience.

Buss, A. H., & Plomin, R. (1987). Commentary. In Goldsmith, H. H., Buss, A. H., Plomin, R., Rothbart, M. K., Thomas, A., Chess, A., Hinde, R. R., & McCall, R. B. Roundtable: What is temperament? Four approaches. *Child Development, 58,* 505–529.

Buss, T., & Redburn, F. S. (1983). Unpublished manuscript, Center for Urban Studies, Youngstown State University, Youngstown, OH.

Butler, R. N. (1975). *Why survive? Being old in America.* New York: Harper & Row.

Butler, R. N. (1987). Ageism. In G. L. Maddox (Ed.), *The encyclopedia of aging.* New York: Springer.

Butler, S. (1902). The way of all flesh. In Shrewsbury, (Ed.), *The works of Samuel Butler* (Vol. 17). New York: AMS Press.

Calhoun, J. A. (1988, March). *Gang violence.* Testimony to the House Select Committee on Children, Youth, and Families, Washington, DC.

Camara, K. A., & Resnick, G. (in press). Interparental conflict and cooperation: Factors moderating children's post-divorce adjustment. In E. M. Hetherington & J. D. Arasteh (Eds.), *Impact of divorce, single-parenting, and stepparenting on children.* Hillsdale, NJ: Erlbaum.

Campbell, B. (1985). *Human evolution,* 3rd ed. Hawthorne, NY: Aldine.

Campbell, S., & Silverman, P. R. (1987). *Widower.* New York: Prentice Hall.

Campos, J. J., Barrett, K. C., Lamb, M. E., Goldsmith, H. H., & Stenberg, C. (1983). Socioemotional development. In P. H. Mussen (Ed.), *Handbook of child psychology* (4th ed.), Vol. 2. New York: Wiley.

Campos, J. J., Langer, A., & Krowitz, A. (1970). Cardiac responses on the visual cliff in prelocomotor human infants. *Science, 170,* 196–197.

Carey, S. (1977). The child as word learner. In M. Halle, J. Bresman, & G. A. Miller (Eds.), *Linguistic theory and psychological reality.* Cambridge, MA: MIT Press.

Carper, L. (1978, April). Sex roles in the nursery. *Harper's.*

Case, R. (1988, August). *The mind's staircase: Stages in the development of human intelligence.* Paper presented at the meeting of the American Psychological Association, Atlanta, GA.

Case, R., Kurland, D. M., & Goldberg, J. (1982). Operational efficiency and the growth of short-term memory span. *Journal of Experimental Child Psychology, 33,* 386–404.

Cavett, D. (1974). *Cavett.* San Diego: Harcourt Brace Jovanovich.

Charness, N. (1988). The role of theories of cognitive aging: Comment on Salthouse. *Psychology and Aging, 3,* 17–21.

Chase-Lansdale, P. L., & Hetherington, E. M. (in press). The impact of divorce on life-span development: Short and long-term effects. In P. B. Baltes, D. L. Featherman, & R. M. Lerner (Eds.), *Life-span development and behavior.* Hillsdale, NJ: Erlbaum.

Chasnoff, I. J., Burns, K. A., & Burns, W. J. (1987, April). *Cocaine and pregnancy.* Paper presented at the Society for Research in Child Development, Baltimore.

Cherlin, A. J., & Furstenberg, F. F. (1988). *The new American grandparent.* New York: Basic Books.

Chernin, K. (1981). *The obsession: Reflections on the tyranny of slenderness.* New York: Harper & Row.

Chess, S., & Thomas, A. (1977). Temperamental individuality from childhood to adolescence. *Journal of Child Psychiatry, 16,* 218–226.

Chess, S., & Thomas, A. (1986). *Temperament in clinical practice.* New York: Guilford.

Chi, M. T. (1978). Knowledge structures and memory development. In R. S. Siegler (Ed.), *Children's thinking: What develops?* Hillsdale, NJ: Erlbaum.

Chiraboga, D. A., Roberts, J., & Stein, J. A. (1978). Psychological well-being during marital separation. *Journal of Divorce, 2,* 21036.

Chiraboga, D. A. (1982). Adaptation to marital separation in later and earlier life. *Journal of Gerontology, 37,* 109–114.

Chiraboga, D. A. (1982). An examination of life events as possible antecedents of life change. *Journal of Gerontology, 36,* 604–624.

Chomsky, N. (1957). *Syntactic structures.* The Hague: Mouton.

Cicirelli, V. (1977). Family structure and interaction: Sibling effects on socialization. In M. McMillan & M. Sergio (Eds.), *Child psychiatry: Treatment and research.* New York: Brunner/Mazel.

Cicirelli, V. G. (1982). Sibling influence throughout the life span. In M. E. Lamb & B. Sutton-Smith (Eds.), *Sibling relationships.* Hillsdale, NJ: Erlbaum.

Clark, E. V. (1983). Meanings and concepts. In P. H. Mussen (Ed.), *Handbook of child psychology* (4th ed.), Vol. 4. New York: Wiley.

Clark, H. H., & Clark, E. V. (1977). *Psychology and language.* New York: Harcourt Brace Jovanovich.

Clark, M. S., Powell, M. C., Ovellette, R., & Milberg, S. (1987). Recipient's mood, relationship type, and helping. *Journal of Personality and Social Psychology, 53,* 94–103.

Clark, S. D., Zabin, L. S., & Hardy, J. B. (1984). Sex, contraception, and parenthood: Experience and attitudes among urban black young men. *Family Planning Perspectives, 16,* 77–82.

Clarke-Stewart, K. (1988). Infant day care: Maligned or malignant? *American Psychologist*

Clarke-Stewart, K. A., & Fein, G. G. (1983). Early childhood programs. In P. H. Mussen (Ed.), *Handbook of child psychology* (4th ed.), Vol. 2. New York: Wiley.

Cohen, A. K. (1964). Foreward. In P. Musgrove (Ed.), *Youth and social order.* Bloomington, IN: Indiana U. Press.

Cohn, J. F., & Tronick, E. Z. (1987). Mother-infant face-to-face interaction: The sequence of dyadic states at 3, 6, and 9 months. *Developmental Psychology, 23,* 68–77.

Cohn, J. F., & Tronick, E. Z. (1988). Mother-infant face-to-face interaction: Influence is bidirectional and unrelated to periodic cycles in either partners' behavior. *Developmental Psychology, 24,* 386–392.

Coie, J. D., & Kupersmidt, J. (1983). A behavioral analysis of emerging social status in boys' groups. *Child Development, 54,* 1400–1416.

Colby, A., & Kohlberg, L. (1987). *The measurement of moral judgment:* Volumes I and II. Cambridge, England: Cambridge U. Press.

Colby, A., Kohlberg, L., Gibbs, J., & Lieberman, M. (1983). A longitudinal study of moral judgment. *Monographs of the Society for Research in Child Development* (Serial No. 201).

Cole, S. (1981). *Working kids on working.* New York: Lothrop, Lee & Shepard.

Coleman, J., Bremner, R., Clark, B., Davis, J., Eichorn, D., Grilliches, Z., Kett, J., Ryder, N., Doering, Z., & Mays, J. (1974). *Youth, transition to adulthood.* Chicago: U. of Chicago Press.

Coleman, J. S. (1961). *The adolescent society.* New York: Free Press.

Coletta, N. D. (1978). *Divorced mothers at two income levels: Stress, support, and child rearing practices.* Unpublished thesis, Cornell University.

Collins, A. W. (1985, April). *Cognition, affect, and development in parent-child relationships.* Paper presented at the biennial meeting of the Society for Research in Child Development, Toronto.

Collins, W. A. (1987). *Research on the transition to adolescence.* Unpublished manuscript, U. of Minnesota.

Colman, P. D. (1986, August). *Regulation of dendritic extent: Human aging brain and Alzheimer's disease.* Paper presented at the meeting of the American Psychological Association, Washington, DC.

Comfort, A. (1976). *A good age.* New York: Crown.

Conger, J. J. (1988). Hostages to the future: Youth, values, and the public interest. *American Psychologist, 43,* 291–300.

Conniff, R. (1981, May/June). Living longer. *Next.*

Coons, S., & Guilleminault, C. (1982). Development of sleep-wake patterns and non-rapid eye movement sleep stages during the first six months of life in normal infants. *Pediatrics, 69,* 793–798.

Coons, S., & Guilleminault, C. (1984). Development of consolidated sleep and wakeful periods in relation to the day/night cycle in infancy. *Developmental Medicine and Child Neurology, 26,* 169–176.

Cooper, C. R., & Ayers-Lopez, S. (1985). Family and peer systems in early adolescence: New models of the role of relationships in development. *Journal of Early Adolescence, 5,* 9–22.

Cooper, C. R., Grotevant, H. D., Moore, M. S., & Condon, S. M. (1982, August). *Family support and conflict: Both foster adolescent identity and role taking.* Paper presented at the meeting of the American Psychological Association, Washington, DC.

Coopersmith, S. (1967). *The antecedents of self-esteem.* New York: W. H. Freeman.

Corboy, L. (1987, April). *Interventions for increasing breastfeeding rates among low-income women.* Paper presented at the biennial meeting of the Society for Research on Child Development, Baltimore.

Corless, I. B., & Pittman-Lindeman, M. (1987). *AIDS.* New York: Hemisphere.

Corrigan, R. (1981). The effects of task and practice on search for invisibly displaced objects. *Developmental Review, 1,* 1–17.

Costa, P. T. (1986, August). *The scope of individuality.* Paper presented at the meeting of the American Psychological Association, Washington, DC.

Costa, P. T. (1988, August). *Personality, continuity and the changes of adult life.* Paper presented at the American Psychological Association, Atlanta.

Costa, P. T., & McRae, R. R. (1980). Still stable after all these years: Personality as a key to some issues in aging. In P. B. Baltes & O. G. Brim (Eds.), *Life-span development and behavior.* New York: Academic Press.

Costa, P. T., Zonderman, A. B., McCrae, R. R., Cornon-Huntely, J., Locke, B. Z., & Barbano, H. E. (1987). Longitudinal analyses of psychological well-being in a national sample: Stability and mean levels. *Journal of Gerontology, 42,* 50–55.

Cowan, C. P., & Cowan, P. A. (1987). Men's involvement in parenthood. In P. Berman & F. Pedersen (Eds.), *Men's transitions to parenthood.* Hillsdale, NJ: Erlbaum.

Cowan, P. A. (1988). Becoming a father: A time of change, an opportunity for development. In P. Bronstein & C. P. Cowan (Eds.), *Fatherhood today.* New York: Wiley.

Craik, F. I. M. (1977). Age differences in human memory. In J. E. Birren & K. W. Schaie (Eds.), *Handbook of the psychology of aging.* New York: Van Nostrand Reinhold.

Crist, S. & Meyer, G. (1978). *The Harvard Lampoon big book of college life.* New York: Doubleday.

Cronbach, L. J., & Snow, R. E. (1977). *Aptitudes and instructional methods.* New York: Irvington Books.

Crosby, J. (1985). *Illusion and disillusion: The self in love and marriage.* Belmont, CA: Wadsworth.

Cross, K. P. (1984, November). The rising tide of school reform reports. *Phi Delta Kappan,* pp. 167–172.

Culp, R. E., & Osofsky, J. D. (1987, April). *Transition to parenthood in the early postpartum period.* Paper presented at the biennial meeting of the Society for Research in Child Development, Baltimore.

Cumming, E., & Henry, W. (1961). *Growing old.* New York: Basic Books.

Cunningham, M. R. (1986). Measuring the physical in physical attractiveness: Quasiexperiment on the sociobiology of female facial beauty. *Journal of Personality and Social Psychology, 50,* 925–935.

Curtiss, S. (1977). *Genie.* New York: Academic Press.

Damon, W. (1988). *The moral child.* New York: Macmillan.

Darling, C. A., Kallen, D. J., & VanDusen, J. E. (1984). Sex in transition, 1900–1984. *Journal of Youth and Adolescence, 13,* 385–399.

Darwin, C. (1859). *On the origin of species.* London: John Murray.

Datan, N., Greene, A. L., & Reese, H. W. (1986). *Life-span developmental psychology.* Hillsdale, NJ: Erlbaum.

Datan, N., Rodeheaver, D., & Hughes, F. (1987). Adult development and aging. *Annual Review of Psychology, 38,* 153–180.

Davis, K. E. (1985, February). Near and dear: Friendship and love compared. *Psychology Today,* pp. 22–29.

Deci, E. L. (1975). *Intrinsic motivation.* New York: Plenum.

DeFries, J. C., Plomin, R., Vandenberg, S. G., & Kuse, A. R. (1981). Parent-offspring resemblance in cognitive abilities in the Colorado adoption project: Biological, adoption, and control parents and one-year-old children. *Intelligence, 5,* 245–277.

DeLoache, J. S., Cassidy, D. J., & Carpenter, C. J. (1987). The Three Bears are all boys: Mother's gender labeling of neutral picture book characters. *Sex Roles, 17,* 163–178.

Demorest, A., Meyer, C., Phelps, E., Gardner, H., & Winner, E. (1984). Words speak louder than actions: Understanding deliberately false remarks. *Child Development, 55,* 1527–1534.

Dempster, F. N. (1981). Memory span: Sources of individual and developmental differences. *Psychological Bulletin, 80,* 63–100.

Denham, S. A. (1986). Social cognition, prosocial behavior, and emotion in preschoolers: Contextual validation. *Child Development, 57,* 194–201.

Denney, N. (1982). Aging and cognitive changes. In B. B. Wolman (Ed.), *Handbook of developmental psychology.* Englewood Cliffs, NJ: Prentice Hall.

Denney, N. (1986, August). *Practical problem solving.* Paper presented at the meeting of the American Psychological Association, Washington, DC.

Dennis, W. (1966). Creative productivity between the ages of 20 and 80 years. *Journal of Gerontology, 21,* 1–18.

Deutsch, C., Deutsch, M., Jordan, T., & Grallo, R. (1981, August). *Long-term effects of Project Head Start.* Paper presented at the meeting of the American Psychological Association, Los Angeles.

de Villiers, J. G., & de Villiers, P. A. (1978). *Language acquisition.* Cambridge, MA: Harvard U. Press.

deVries, H. A. (1970). Physiological effects of an exercise training regimen upon men aged 52 to 88. *Journal of Gerontology, 25,* 325–336.

Dickinson, G. E. (1975). Dating behavior of black and white adolescents before and after desegregation. *Journal of Marriage and the Family, 37,* 602–608.

Dillon, R. S. (1980). *Diagnosis and management of endocrine and metabolic disorders* (2nd ed.). Philadelphia: Lea & Febiger.

Dion, K., & Berscheid, E. (1974). Physical attractiveness and peer perception among children. *Sociometry, 37,* 1–12.

Dodge, K. A. (1983). Behavioral antecedents of peer social status. *Child Development, 54,* 1386–1399.

Dodge, K. A., Petit, G. S., McClaskey, C. L., & Brown, M. M. (1986). Social competence in children. *Monographs of the Society for Research in Child Development, 51* (2, Serial No. 213).

Dohrenwend, B. S., & Dohrenwend, B. P. (1978). Some issues in research on stressful life events. *Journal of Nervous and Mental Disease, 166,* 7–15.

Dohrenwend, B. S., & Shrout, P. E. (1985). "Hassles" in the conceptualization and measurement of life stress variables. *American Psychologist, 40,* 780–785.

Dolgin, K. G., & Behrend, D. A. (1984). Children's knowledge about animates and inanimates. *Child Development, 55,* 1646–1650.

Doll, G. (1988, Spring). Daycare. *Vanderbilt Magazine*, p. 29.

Douvan, E., & Adelson, J. (1966). *The adolescent experience.* New York: Wiley.

Downs, A. C., & Langlois, J. H. (1988). Sex typing: Construct and measurement issues. *Sex Roles, 18,* 87–100.

Dreyer, P. H. (1982). Sexuality during adolescence. In B. B. Wolman (Ed.), *Handbook of developmental psychology.* Englewood Cliffs, NJ: Prentice-Hall.

Duck, S. W. (1975). Personality similarity and friendship choices by adolescents. *European Journal of Social Psychology, 5,* 351–365.

Dugdale, S., & Kibbey, D. (1980). *Fractions curriculum of the PLATO elementary mathematical project.* Urbana-Champaign, IL: Computer-based Education Research Laboratory.

Dunn, J. (1984). Sibling studies and the developmental impact of critical incidents. In P. B. Baltes & O. G. Brim (Eds.), *Life-span development and behavior* (Vol. 6). Orlando, FL: Academic Press.

Dunn, J., & Kendrick, C. (1982). *Siblings.* Cambridge, MA: Harvard U. Press.

Dunphy, D. C. (1963). The social structure of urban adolescent peer groups. *Society, 26,* 230–246.

Durden-Smith, J., & Desimone, D. (1983). *Sex and the brain,* New York: Arbor House.

Duvall, E. M., & Miller, B. C. (1985). *Marriage and family development* (6th ed.). New York: Harper & Row.

Dwyer, J. (1980). Sixteen popular diets: Brief nutritional analyses. In A. J. Stunkard (Ed.), *Obesity.* Philadelphia: W. B. Saunders.

Earley, L. A., Griesler, P. C., & Rovee-Collier, C. (1985, April). *Ontogenetic changes in retention in early infancy.* Paper presented at the biennial meeting of the Society for Research in Child Development, Toronto.

East, P. L., Hess, L. E., & Lerner, R. M. (1987). Peer social support and adjustment of early adolescent peer groups. *Journal of Early Adolescence, 7,* 153–163.

Eccles, J. S. (1987, August). *Understanding motivation: Achievement beliefs, gender roles, and changing educational environments.* Paper presented at the meeting of the American Psychological Association, New York City.

Eccles, J. S. (1987). Gender roles and achievement patterns: An expectancy value perspective. In J. M. Reinisch, L. A. Rosenblum, & S. A. Sanders (Eds.), *Masculinity/Femininity.* New York: Oxford U. Press.

Eccles, J. S., & Hoffman, L. W. (1984). Sex roles, socialization, and occupational behavior. In H. W. Stevenson & A. E. Siegel (Eds.), *Research in child development and public policy* (Vol. 1). Chicago: U. of Chicago Press.

Edleman, M. W. (1987). *Families in peril: An agenda for social change.* New York: Alan Guttmacher Institute.

Egeland, B., Jacobvitz, D., & Papatola, K. (in press). Intergenerational continuity of parental abuse. In J. Lancaster & R. Gelles (Eds.), *Biosocial aspects of child abuse.* New York: Jossey-Bass.

Egeland, B., Jacobvitz, D., & Sroufe, L. A. (1987). *Breaking the cycle of abuse: Relationship predictors.* Minneapolis: U. of Minnesota.

Eichorn, D. H., Clausen, J. A., Haan, N., Honzik, M. P., & Mussen, P. H. (Eds.). (1981). *Present and past in middle life.* New York: Academic Press.

Eisenberg, N. (1987). The relation of altruism and other moral behaviors to moral cognition: Methodological and conceptual issues. In N. Eisenberg (Ed.), *Contemporary topics in developmental psychology.* New York: Wiley.

Eitzen, D. S. (1975). Athletics in the status system of male adolescents. A replication of Coleman's *The Adolescent Society. Adolescence, 10,* 267–276.

Elder, G. H., Caspi, A., & Burton, L. M. (1988). Adolescent transition in developmental perspective: Sociological and historical insights. In M. R. Gunnar & W. A. Collins (Eds.), *Development during the transition to adolescence.* Hillsdale, NJ: Erlbaum.

Elder, G. H., Caspi, A., & Downey, G. (1986). Problem behavior and family relationships: A multigenerational analysis. In A. Sorensen, F. Weinert, & L. Sherrod (Eds.), *Human development and the life course.* Hillsdale, NJ: Erlbaum.

Elkind, D. (1970, April 5). Erik Erikson's eight ages of man. *New York Times Magazine.*

Elkind, D. (1976). *Child development and education: A Piagetian perspective.* New York: Oxford U. Press.

Elkind, D. (1981). *The hurried child.* Reading, MA: Addison-Wesley.

Elkind, D. (1986). Egocentrism redux. *Developmental Review, 5,* 218–226.

Emde, R. N., Gaensbauer, T. G., & Harmon, R. J. (1976). Emotional expression in infancy: A biobehavioral study. *Psychological Issues,* Monograph Series, 10 (37).

Engen, T. (1977). Taste and smell. In J. E. Birren & K. W. Schaie (Eds.), *Handbook of the psychology of aging.* New York: Van Nostrand.

Entwisle, D. R., Alexander, K. L., Pallas, A. M., & Cadigan, D. (1987). The emergent academic self-image of first graders: Its response to social structures. *Child Development, 58,* 1190–1206.

Epstein, N., & Eidelson, R. J. (1981). Unrealistic beliefs of clinical couples: Their relationship to expectations, goals, and satisfaction. *American Journal of Family Therapy, 9,* 13–21.

Erik, E. H., Erikson, J. M., & Kivnick, H. Q. (1986). *Vital involvement in old age.* New York: Norton.

Erikson, E. H. (1950). *Childhood and society.* New York: Norton.

Erikson, E. H. (1962). *Young man Luther.* New York: Norton.

Erikson, E. H. (1968). *Identity: Youth and crisis.* New York: Norton.

Erikson, E. H. (1969). *Gandhi's truth.* New York: Norton.

Erikson, E. H. (1980). *Identity and the life cycle.* New York: Norton.

Eron, L. D. (1987). The development of aggression from the perspective of a developing behaviorism. *American Psychologist, 42,* 435–442.

Escalona, S. (1988). Cognition in its relationship to total development in the first year. In B. Inhelder, D. DeCaprona, & A. Cornu-Wells (Eds.), *Piaget today.* Hillsdale, NJ: Erlbaum.

Eschel, Y., & Klein, Z. (1981). Development of academic self-concept of lower-class and middle-class primary school children. *Journal of Educational Psychology, 73,* 287–293.

Etzel, R. (1988, October). *Children of smokers.* Paper presented at the American Academy of Pediatrics meeting, New Orleans.

Fagot, B. (1975, April). *Teacher reinforcement of feminine-preferred behavior revisited.* Paper presented at the biennial meeting of the Society for Research in Child Development, Denver.

Falbo, T., & Polit, D. F. (1986). A quantitative review of the only-child literature: Research evidence and theory development. *Psychological Bulletin, 100,* 176–189.

Fantz, R. L. (1958). Pattern vision in young infants. *Psychological Record, 8,* 43–49.

Fantz, R. L. (1961). The origin of form perception. *Scientific American, 204,* 66–72.

Fassinger, R. E. (1985). A causal model of college women's career choice. *Journal of Vocational Behavior, 27,* 123–153.

Fein, G. G. (1986). Pretend play. In D. Görlitz & J. F. Wohlwill (Eds.), *Curiosity, imagination, and play.* Hillsdale, NJ: Erlbaum.

Feingold, A. (1988). Cognitive gender differences are disappearing. *American Psychologist, 43,* 95–103.

Feiring, C., & Lewis, M. (1978). The child as a member of the family system. *Behavioral Science, 23,* 225–233.

Feldstein, M., & Ellwood, D. (1982). Teenage unemployment: What is the problem? In R. Freeman & D. Wise (Eds.), *The youth labor market problem.* Chicago: U. of Chicago Press.

Field, T. M. (1979). Visual and cardiac responses to animate and inanimate faces by young term and preterm infants. *Child Development, 50,* 188–194.

Field, T. M., Woodson, R., Greenberg, R., & Cohen, D. (1982). Discrimination and imitation of facial expressions by neonates. *Science, 218,* 179–181.

Fincher, J. (1982). Before their time. *Science 82,*

Finney, J. W., & Moos, R. H. (1979). Treatment and outcome for empirical subtypes of alcoholic patients. *Journal of Consulting and Clinical Psychology, 47,* 25–38.

Fischer, K. W., & Lazerson, A. (1984). *Human development.* San Francisco: W. H. Freeman.

Fischman, J. (1987, February). Type A on trial. *Psychology Today,* pp. 42–50.

Flanagan, J. (1981, August). *Some characteristics of 70-year-old workers.* Paper presented at the meeting of the American Psychological Association, Los Angeles.

Flavell, J. H. (1979). Metacognition and cognitive monitoring: A new area of psychological inquiry. *American Psychologist, 34,* 906–911.

Flavell, J. H. (1985). *Cognitive development* (2nd ed.). Englewood Cliffs, NJ: Prentice Hall.

Flavell, J. H., & Wellman, H. M. (1977). Metamemory. In R. V. Kail & J. W. Hagen (Eds.), *Perspectives on the development of memory and cognition.* Hillsdale, NJ: Erlbaum.

Flavell, J. H., Beach, D. R., & Chinsky, J. M. (1966). Spontaneous verbal rehearsal in a memory task as a function of age. *Child Development, 37,* 283–299.

Flavell, J. H., Shipstead, S. G., & Croft, K. (1978). *What young children think you see when their eyes are closed.* Unpublished manuscript, Stanford U., Palo Alto, CA.

Fogel, A. (1988). Cyclicity and stability in mother-infant face-to-face interaction: A comment on Cohn and Tronick (1988). *Developmental Psychology, 24,* 393–395.

Fogel, A., & Melson, G. F. (Eds.) (1987). *Origins of nurturance.* Hillsdale, NJ: Erlbaum.

Ford, M. E. (1986). *Androgyny as self-assertion and integration: Implications for psychological and social competence.* Unpublished manuscript, Stanford University School of Education, Stanford, CA.

Forman, B. I. (1984, June). Reconsidering retirement: Understanding emerging trends. *The Futurist.*

Foulkes, D. (1982). *Children's dreams: Longitudinal studies.* New York: Wiley.

Fox, L. H., Brody, L., & Tobin, D. (1979). *Women and mathematics.* Baltimore: Intellectually Gifted Study Group, Johns Hopkins U. Press.

Fox, N., Kagan, J., & Weiskopf, F. (1979). The growth of memory during infancy. *Genetic Psychology Monographs, 99,* 91–130.

Fraiberg, S. (1977). *Insights from the blind: Comparative studies of blind and sighted infants.* New York: Basic Books.

Freedman, J. L. (1984). Effects of television violence on aggressiveness. *Psychological Bulletin, 96,* 227–246.

Freeman, J. (1982). The old, old, very old Charlie Smith. *The Gerontologist, 22,* 532.

Freuchen, P. (1961). *Book of the Eskimos.* Cleveland: World Press.

Freud, A., & Dann, S. (1951). Instinctual anxiety during puberty. In A. Freud, *The ego and its mechanisms of defense.* New York: International Universities Press.

Freud, S. (1917). *A general introduction to psychoanalysis.* New York: Washington Square Press.

Friederich, L. K., & Stein, A. H. (1973). Aggressive and prosocial TV programs and the natural behavior of preschool children. *Monographs of the Society for Research in Child Development, 38* (4, Serial No. 151).

Friedman, M., & Rosenman, R. (1974). *Type A behavior and your heart.* New York: Knopf.

Frith, C. H. (1986, May). *Toxicity studies in animals.* Paper presented at the MDMA multidisciplinary conference, San Francisco, CA.

Fromm, E. (1955). *The sane society.* New York: Fawcett Books.

Frommer, E., & O'Shea, C. (1973). Antenatal identification of women liable to have problems in managing their infants. *British Journal of Psychiatry, 123,* 149–156.

Furstenberg, F. F. (in press). Child care after divorce and remarriage. In E. M. Hetherington & J. Arasteh (Eds.), *Impact of divorce, single-parenting, and stepparenting on children.* Hillsdale, NJ: Erlbaum.

Furstenberg, J. J., Brooks-Gunn, J., & Morgan, S. P. (1987). *Adolescent mothers in later life.* New York: Cambridge U. Press.

Furth, H. G., & Wachs, H. (1975). *Thinking goes to school.* New York: Oxford University Press.

Gage, N. L. (1965). Desirable behaviors of teachers. *Urban Education, 1,* 85–96.

Gagne, E. D. (1985). *The cognitive psychology of school learning.* Boston: Little, Brown.

Gagne, E. D., Weidemann, C., Bell, M. S., & Ander, T. D. (in press). Training thirteen-year-olds to elaborate while studying text. *Journal of Human Learning.*

Gallagher, D., & Thompson, L. W. (1986). Cognitive therapy for depression in the elderly: A promising model for treatment and research. In L. Breslau & M. Haug (Eds.), *Depression in the elderly.* New York: Springer.

Gallagher, J., & Bidell, T. (1988, June). *Piaget's concept of a procedural system: Applications to contemporary education.* Paper presented at the Annual Symposium of the Jean Piaget Society, Philadelphia.

Galst, J. P. (1980). Television food commercials and pronutritional public service announcements as determinants of young children's snack choices. *Child Development, 51,* 935–938.

Garbarino, J. (1976). The ecological correlates of child abuse: The impact of socioeconomic stress on mothers. *Child Development, 47,* 178–185.

Gardner, B. T., & Gardner, R. A. (1971). Two-way communication with an infant chimpanzee. In A. Schrier & F. Stollnitz (Eds.), *Behavior of nonhuman primates.* Vol. 4. New York: Academic Press.

Gardner, B. T. & Gardner, R. A. (1986). Discovering the meaning of private signals. *British Journal for the Philosophy of Science, 27,* 477–495.

Gardner, H. (1983). *Frames of mind.* New York: Basic Books.

Garelik, G. (1985, October). Are the progeny prodigies? *Discover Magazine, 6,* 45–47, 78–84.

Garfinkel, P. E., & Garner, D. M. (1982). *Anorexia nervosa.* New York: Brunner/Mazel.

Gatz, M. (1989). Clinical psychology and aging. *The Psychology of Aging.* Washington, DC. American Psychological Association.

Gatz, M., & Pearson, C. G. (1988). Ageism and the provision of psychological services. *American Psychologist, 43,* 184–188.

Gatz, M., Popkin, S. J., Pino, C. D., & VandenBos, G. R. (1985). Psychological interventions with older adults. In J. E. Birren & K. W. Schaie (Eds.), *Handbook of the psychology of aging* (2nd ed.). New York: Van Nostrand Reinhold.

Gaylord, S., & Zung, W. K. (1987). Affective disorders among the aged. In L. L. Carstensen & B. A. Edelstein (Eds.), *Handbook of clinical gerontology.* New York: Pergamon.

Geis, G., & Monahan, J. (1976). The social ecology of violence. In T. Lickona (Ed.), *Moral development and behavior.* New York: Holt, Rinehart & Winston.

Gelfand, D. (1988). *The aging network* (3rd ed.). New York: Springer.

Gelman, R., & Baillargeon, R. (1983). A review of some Piagetian concepts. In P. H. Mussen (Ed.), *Handbook of child psychology* (4th ed.), Vol. 3. New York: Wiley.

Gelman, R. (1969). Conservation acquisition: A problem of learning to attend to relevant attributes. *Journal of Experimental Child Psychology, 7,* 67–87.

Gelman, R. (1979). Preschool thought. *American Psychologist, 34,* 900–905.

Gerson, K. (1986). *Hard choices: How women decide about work, career, and motherhood.* Berkeley, CA: U. of California Press.

Gesell, A. (1934). *An atlas of infant behavior.* New Haven, CT: Yale University Press.

Gesell, A. (1954). The ontogenesis of infant behavior. In L. Carmichael (Ed.), *Manual of child psychology.* New York: Wiley.

Gesell, A. L. (1928). *Infancy and human growth.* New York: Macmillan.

Gewirtz, J. (1977). Maternal responding and the conditioning of infant crying: Directions of influence within the attachment-acquisition process. In B. C. Etzel, J. M. LeBlanc, & D. M. Baer (Eds.), *New developments in behavioral research.* Hillsdale, NJ: Erlbaum.

Gibson, E. J. (1969). *The principles of perceptual learning and development.* New York: Appleton-Century-Crofts.

Gibson, E. J. (1986, October). *The concept of affordance in development.* Paper presented at the Symposium on Human Development and Communication Sciences, U. of Texas at Dallas, Richardson, TX.

Gibson, E. J. (in press). Exploratory behavior in the development of perceiving, acting, and acquiring of knowledge. *Annual Review of Psychology.*

Gibson, E. J., & Spelke, E. S. (1983). The development of perception. In P. H. Mussen (Ed.), *Handbook of child psychology* (4th ed.), Vol. 3. New York: Wiley.

Gibson, E. J., & Walk, R. D. (1960). The "visual cliff." *Scientific American, 202,* 64–71.

Gibson, J. J. (1979). *The ecological approach to visual perception.* Boston: Houghton Mifflin.

Gill, S., Stockard, J., Johnson, M., & Williams, S. (1987). Measuring gender differences: The expressive dimension and critique of the androgyny scales. *Sex Roles, 17,* 375–400.

Gilligan, C. (1982). *In a different voice.* Cambridge, MA: Harvard U. Press.

Gilligan, C. (1985, April). *Response to critics.* Paper presented at the biennial meeting of the Society for Research in Child Development, Toronto.

Ginsburg, H., & Opper, S. (1988). Piaget's theory of intellectual development (2nd ed.). Englewood Cliffs, NJ: Prentice Hall.

Gjerde, P. (1985, April). *Adolescent depression and parental socialization patterns: A prospective study.* Paper presented at the biennial meeting of the Society for Research in Child Development, Toronto.

Gleason, J. B. (1988). Language and socialization. In F. Kessel (Ed.), *The development of language and language researchers.* Hillsdale, NJ: Erlbaum.

Glenn, N. (1975). Psychological well-being in the post-parental stage: Some evidence from national surveys. *Journal of Marriage and the Family, 39,* 5–13.

Glick, P. C. (1979). Future American families. *The Washington COFO MEMO 2* (Summer/Fall).

Golan, N. (1986). *The perilous bridge.* New York: The Free Press.

Gold, M. (1987). Social ecology. In H. C. Quay (Ed.). *Handbook of juvenile delinquency.* New York: Wiley.

Gold, M., & Yanof, D. S. (1985). Mothers, daughters, and girlfriends. *Journal of Personality and Social Psychology, 49,* 654–659.

Goldman, J. A., Fujimura, J. B., Contois, J. H., & Lerman, R. H. (1987, April). *Interactions among preschool children following the ingestion of sucrose.* Paper presented at the biennial meeting of the Society for Research in Child Development, Baltimore.

Goldman, J. A., Lerman, R. H., Contois, J. H., & Udall, J. N. (1986). Behavioral effects of sucrose on preschool children. *Journal of Abnormal Child Psychology, 14,* 565–577.

Goldsmith, H. H. (1988, August). *Does early temperament predict later development?* Paper presented at the meeting of the American Psychological Association, Atlanta.

Goldsmith, H. H., Buss, A. H., Plomin, R., Rothbart, R., Thomas, A., Chess, S., Hinde, R. A., & McCall, R. B. (1987). Roundtable: What is temperament? Four approaches. *Child Development, 58,* 505–529.

Goldsmith, H. H., & Gottesman, I. I. (1981). Origins of variation in behavioral style: A longitudinal study of temperament in young twins. *Child Development, 52,* 91–103.

Golman-Rakic, P. S., Isseroff, A., Schwartz, M. L., & Bugbee, N. M. (1983). The neurobiology of cognitive development. In P. H. Mussen (Ed.), *Handbook of child psychology* (4th ed.), Vol. 2. New York: Wiley.

Gonda, J. (1981). Convocation on work, aging, and retirement: A review. *Human Development, 24,* 286–292.

Goodlad, J. I. (1983). *A place called school.* New York: McGraw-Hill.

Görlitz, D., & Wohlwill, J. F. (Eds.) (1987). *Curiosity, imagination, and play.* Hillsdale, NJ: Erlbaum.

Gorski, P. A. (1988, November). *Iatrogenic stressors: Progress, plight, and promise.* Paper presented at Developmental Interventions in Neonatal Care Conference, San Diego, CA.

Gortmaker, S. L. (1987). *American Journal of Diseases of Children,*

Gottlieb, D. (1966). Teaching and students: The views of Negro and white teachers. *Sociology of Education, 37,* 345–353.

Gottman, J. M., & Parker, J. G. (Eds.). (1987). *Conversations of friends.* New York: Cambridge U. Press.

Gould, R. L. (1975). Adult life stages: Growth toward self-tolerance. *Psychology Today, 8,* 74–78.

Gould, R. L. (1978). *Transformations: Growth and change in adult life.* New York: Simon & Schuster.

Gould, R. L. (1980). Transformations during early and middle adult years. In N. J. Smelser & E. H. Erikson (Eds.), *Themes of work and love in adulthood.* Cambridge, MA: Harvard U. Press.

Graham, D. (1981). The obstetric and neonatal consequences of adolescent pregnancy. In E. R. McAnarney & G. Stickle (Eds.). *Pregnancy and childbearing during adolescence: Research priorities for the 1980s.* New York: Alan R. Liss.

Graham, S. (1984). Communicating sympathy and anger to black and white students: The cognitive (attributional) antecedents of affective cues. *Journal of Personality and Social Psychology, 47,* 40–54.

Graham, S. (1986, August). *Can attribution theory tell us something about motivation in blacks?* Paper presented at the meeting of the American Psychological Association, Washington, DC.

Graham, S. (1987, August). *Developing relations between attributions, affect, and intended social behavior.* Paper presented at the meeting of the American Psychological Association, New York City.

Greenberger, E. (1987, August). *Teenagers who work: Research goes to congress and meets the media.* Paper presented at the meeting of the American Psychological Association, New York City.

Greenberger, E., & Steinberg, L. (1981). Sex differences in early work experience: Harbinger of things to come? *Social Forces, 62,* 467–482.

Greene, B. (1988, May) The children's hour. *Esquire,* 47–49.

Grieser, D. L., & Kuhl, P. K. (1988). Maternal speech to infants in tonal language: Support for universal prosodic features in motherese. *Developmental Psychology, 24,* 14–20.

Grossman, F. K., Pollack, W. S., & Golding, E. (1988). Fathers and children: Predicting the quality and quantity of fathering. *Developmental Psychology, 24,* 82–91.

Grotevant, H. D. (1984, February). *Exploration and negotiation of differences within families during adolescence.* Paper presented at the biennial conference on adolescence, Tuscon, AR.

Grotevant, H. D., & Cooper, C. R. (1985). Patterns of interaction in family relationships and the development of identity exploration in adolescence. *Child Development, 56,* 415–428.

Gubrium, J. F. (1975). *Living and dying at Murray Manor.* New York: St. Martin's Press.

Guilford, J. P. (1967). *The structure of intellect.* New York: McGraw-Hill.

Gunnar, M. R., Malone, S., & Fisch, R. O. (1987). The psychobiology of stress and coping in the human neonate: Studies of the adrenocortical activity in response to stress in the first week of life. In T. Field, P. McCabe, & N. Schneiderman (Eds.), *Stress and coping.* Hillsdale, NJ: Erlbaum.

Gutmann, D. L. (1975). Parenthood: A key to the comparative study of the life cycle. In N. Datan & L. Ginsberg (Eds.), *Life-span developmental psychology: Normative life crises.* New York: Academic Press.

Hagestad, G. O. (1985). Continuity and connectedness. In V. L. Bengston (Ed.), *Grandparenthood.* Beverly Hills, CA: Sage.

Hall, G. S. (1904). *Adolescence* (Vols. I and II). Englewood Cliffs, NJ: Prentice Hall.

Hamburg, B. (1974). Early adolescence: A specific and stressful stage of the life cycle. In G. Coelho, D. A. Hamburg, & J. E. Adams (Eds.), *Coping and adaptation.* New York: Basic Books.

Hamburg, B. (1986). Subsets of adolescent mothers: Developmental, biomedical and psychosocial issues. In J. Lancaster & B. Hamburg (Eds.), *Schoolage pregnancy and parenthood: Biosocial dimensions.* New York: Aldine DeGruyter.

Hamdani, R. J. (1974). *Exploratory behavior and vocational development among disadvantaged inner-city adolescents.* Unpublished doctoral dissertation, Columbia University.

Harlow, H. F., & Zimmerman, R. R. (1959). Affectional responses in the infant monkey. *Science, 130,* 421–432.

Harris, C. S. (1978). *Fact book on aging: A profile of America's older population.* Washington, DC: National Council on Aging.

Harris, F. R., Wolf, M. M., & Baer, D. M. (1964). Effects of adult social reinforcement on child behavior. *Young Children, 20,* 8–17.

Harris, L. (1975). *The myth and reality of aging in America*. Washington, DC: National Council on Aging.

Harter, S. (1981). A new self-report scale of intrinsic versus extrinsic motivation in the classroom: Motivational and informational components. *Developmental Psychology, 17*, 300–312.

Harter, S. (1982). The Perceived Competence Scale for Children. *Child Development, 53*, 87–97.

Harter, S. (1983). Developmental perspectives on the self system. In P. H. Mussen (Ed.), *Handbook of child psychology* (4th ed.), Vol. 4. New York: Wiley.

Hartley, R. E., Frank, L. K. & Goldenson, R. M. (1952). *Understanding children's play*. New York: Columbia U. Press.

Hartshorne, H., & May, M. A. (1928–30). *Studies in the nature of character*. New York: MacMillan.

Hartup, W. W. (1983). Peer relations. In P. H. Mussen (Ed.), *Handbook of child psychology* (4th ed.), Vol. 4. New York: Wiley.

Harvard Medical School Newsletter (1981, April). Cambridge, MA: Department of Continuing Education, Harvard Medical School.

Hatfield, E., & Sprecher, S. (1986). *Mirror, mirror . . . The importance of looks in everyday life*. Albany: State University of New York Press.

Havighurst, R. J. (1972). *Developmental tasks and education* (3rd ed.). New York: McKay.

Hawkins, J., Pea, R. D., Glick, J., & Scribner, S. (1984). "Merds that laugh don't like mushrooms": Evidence for deductive reasoning by preschoolers. *Developmental Psychology, 20*, 584–594.

Hawkins, J. A., & Berndt, T. J. (1985, April). *Adjustment following the transition to junior high school*. Paper presented at the biennial meeting of the Society for Research in Child Development, Toronto.

Hay, A. (1987). *Learning to control a conversation*. Paper presented at biennial meeting of the Society for Research in Child Development, Baltimore.

Hayden-Thomson, L., Rubin, K. H., & Hymel, S. (1987). Sex preferences in sociometric choices. *Developmental Psychology, 23*, 558–562.

Hayes, D. (Ed.). (1987). *Risking the future: Adolescent sexuality, pregnancy, and childbearing* (Vol. 1). Washington, DC: National Academy Press.

Hayes, K. J., & Hayes, C. (1951). Picture perception in a home-raised chimpanzee. *Journal of Comparative and Physiological Psychology, 46*, 470–474.

Hayflick, L. (1975, September). Why grow old? *Stanford Magazine*, 36–43.

Hayflick, L. (1977). The cellular basis for biological aging. In C. E. Finch & L. Hayflick (Eds.), *Handbook of the biology of aging*. New York: Van Nostrand.

Hayflick, L. (1987). The cell biology and theoretical basis of aging. In L. Carstensen & B. A. Edelstein (Eds.), *Handbook of clinical gerontology*. New York: Pergamon.

Hazen, N. L., Lockman, J. J., & Pick, H. L. (1978). The development of children's representations of large-scale environments. *Child Development, 49*, 623–636.

Heckhausen, H. (1986). Achievement and motivation through the life span. In A. B. Sorensen, F. E. Weinert, & L. R. Sherrod (Eds.), *Human development and the life course*. Hillsdale, NJ: Erlbaum.

Helson, R., & Moane, G. (1987). Personality change in women from college to midlife. *Journal of Personality and Social Psychology, 53*, 176–186.

Helson, R., Mitchell, V., & Moane, G. (1984). Personality change in women from college to midlife. *Journal of Personality and Social Psychology, 53*, 176–186.

Helson, R., & Wink, P. (1987). Two conceptions of maturity examined in the findings of a longitudinal study. *Journal of Personality and Social Psychology, 53*, 531–541.

Henderson, N. (1982). Human behavior genetics. *Annual Review of Psychology, 33*, 403–440.

Hetherington, E. M. (1972). Effects of father-absence on personality development in adolescent daughters. *Developmental Psychology, 7*, 313–326.

Hetherington, E. M. (1977, November). *My heart belongs to Daddy: A study of the marriages of daughters of divorcees and widows*. Paper presented at the meeting of the National Association for the Education of Young Children, Washington, DC.

Hetherington, E. M. (1987, April). *The effects of divorce on children*. Presidential address at the biennial meeting of the Society for Research in Child Development, Baltimore.

Hetherington, E. M. (in press). Coping with family transitions: Winners, losers, and survivors. *Child Development*.

Hetherington, E. M., & Baltes, P. B. (1988). Child psychology and life-span development. In E. M. Hetherington, R. M. Lerner, & M. Perlmutter (Eds.), *Child development in a life-span perspective*. Hillsdale, NJ: Erlbaum.

Hetherington, E. M., Cox, M., & Cox, R. (1978). The aftermath of divorce. In J. H. Stevens & M. Mathews (Eds.), *Mother-child/ father-child relations*. Washington, DC: NAEYC.

Hetherington, E. M., Cox, M., & Cox, R. (1982). Effects of divorce on children and parents. In M. E. Lamb (Ed.), *Nontraditional families*. Hillsdale, NJ: Erlbaum.

Hetherington, E. M., Hagan, M. S., & Anderson, E. R. (1988). Family transitions: A child's perspective. *American Psychologist*.

Hewlitt, B. S. (1987). Intimate fathers: Patterns of paternal holding among Aka pygmies. In M. E. Lamb (Ed.), *The father's role: Cross-cultural perspectives*. Hillsdale, NJ: Erlbaum.

Hill, C. R., & Stafford, F. P. (1980). Parental care of children: Time diary estimate of quantity, predictability, and variety. *Journal of Human Resources, 15*, 219–239.

Hill, J. P. (1980). The early adolescent and the family. In *The seventy-ninth yearbook of the National Society for the Study of Education*. Chicago: U. of Chicago Press.

Hill, J. P., & Holmbeck, G. N. (in press). Attachment and autonomy during adolescence. *Annals of Child Development*.

Hill, J. P., Holmbeck, G. N., Marlow, L., Green, T. M., & Lynch, M. E. (1985). Pubertal status and parent-child relations in families of seventh-grade boys. *Journal of Early Adolescence, 5*, 31–44.

Hinde, R. (1983). Ethology and child development. In P. H. Mussen (Ed.), *Handbook of child psychology* (4th ed.), Vol. 2. New York: Wiley.

Hinde, R., & Stevenson-Hinde, J. (Eds.). (1987). *Towards understanding families*. London: Cambridge U. Press.

Ho, D. Y. F. (1987). Fatherhood in Chinese culture. In M. E. Lamb (Ed.), *The father's role: Cross-cultural perspectives*. Hillsdale, NJ: Erlbaum.

Hodapp, R. M., Goldfield, E. C., & Boyatzis, C. J. (1984). The use and effectiveness of maternal scaffolding in mother-infant games. *Child Development, 55*, 772–781.

Hoffman, L. W. (1979). Maternal employment: 1979. *American Psychologist, 34*, 859–865.

Holmes, T. H., & Rahe, R. H. (1967). The social readjustment rating scale. *Journal of Psychosomatic Research, 11*, 213–218.

Horn, J. L., & Donaldson, G. (1980). Cognitive development II: Adulthood development of human abilities. In O. G. Brim & J. Kagan (Eds.) *Constancy and change in human development*. Cambridge, MA: Harvard U. Press.

Howard, J. (1988, November). *Developmental and behavioral concerns of drug dependent mothers*. Paper presented at the Developmental Intervention in Neonatal Care Conference, San Diego, CA.

Howard, M. (1983, March). Postponing sexual involvement: A new approach. *Siecus Report*, pp. 5–6, 8.

Howes, C. (1988, April). *Can the age of entry and the quality of infant child care predict behaviors in kindergarten?* Paper presented at the International Conference on Infant Studies, Washington, DC.

Huesmann, L. R., Eron, L. D., Dubow, E. F., & Seebauer, E. (in press). Television viewing habits in childhood and adult aggression. *Child Development*.

Hughes, P. C. Reported in Fozard, J. L., & Popkin, S. J. (1978). Optimizing adult development. *American Psychologist, 33*, 975–989.

Hultsch, D. F., & Plemons, J. K. (1979). Life events and life-span development. In P. B. Baltes & O. G. Brim (Eds.), *Life-span development and behavior.* New York: Academic Press.

Hultsch, D. F. (1971). Adult age differences in free classification and free recall. *Developmental Psychology, 4,* 338–342.

Humphreys, L. G. (1985). A conceptualization of intellectual giftedness. In F. D. Horowitz & M. O'Brien (Eds.), *The gifted and the talented.* Washington, DC: American Psychological Association.

Hunt, M. (1974). *Sexual behavior in the 1970s.* Chicago: Playboy Press.

Hurley, L. S. (1980). *Developmental nutrition.* Englewood Cliffs, NJ: Prentice Hall.

Huston, A. C. (1983). Sex-typing. In P. H. Mussen (Ed.), *Handbook of child psychology* (4th ed.), Vol. 4. New York: Wiley.

Huston, A. C., Siegle, J., & Bremer, M. (1983, April). *Family environment and television use by preschool children.* Paper presented at the biennial meeting of the Society for Research in Child Development, Detroit.

Huston-Stein, A., & Higgens-Trenk, A. (1978). Development of females from childhood through adulthood: Career and feminine role orientations. In P. Baltes (Ed.), *Life-span development and behavior* (Vol. 1). New York: Academic Press.

Hutchings, D. E., & Fifer, W. P. (1986). Neurobehavioral effects in human and animal offspring following prenatal exposure to methadone. In E. P. Riley & C. V. Vorhees (Eds.), *Handbook of behavioral teratology.* New York: Plenum.

Hwang, P. (1987). The changing role of Swedish fathers. In M. E. Lamb (Ed.), *The father's role: Cross-cultural perspectives.* Hillsdale, NJ: Erlbaum.

Hyde, J. S. (1984). Children's understanding of sexist language. *Developmental Psychology, 14,* 119–124.

Hyde, J. S. (1985). *Half the human experience* (3rd ed.). Lexington, MA: D. C. Heath.

Hyde, J. S., & Linn, M. C. (Eds.). (1986). *The psychology of gender: Advances through meta-analysis.* Baltimore, MD: Johns Hopkins U. Press.

Inhelder, B., DeCapron, D., & Cornu-Wells, A. (Eds.) (in press). *Piaget today.* Hillsdale, NJ: Erlbaum.

Irvine, M. J., Johnston, D. W., Jenner, D. A., & Marie, G. V. (1986). Relaxation and stress management in the treatment of essential hypertension. *Journal of Psychosomatic Research, 30,* 437–450.

Izard, C. E. (1982). *Measuring emotions in infants and young children.* New York: Cambridge U. Press.

Izard, C. E., & Malatesta, C. Z. (1987). Differential emotions theory of early emotional development. In J. D. Osofsky (Ed.), *Handbook of infant development.* New York: Wiley.

Jackson, J. S. (Ed.). (1988). *The Black American elderly.* New York: Springer.

Jacobs, S. C., Dosten, T. R., Kasl, S. V., Ostfeld, A. M., Berkman, L., & Charpentier, M. P. H. (1987). Attachment theory and multiple dimensions of grief. *Omega, 18,* 41–52.

James, W. (1950/1890). *The principles of psychology.* New York: Dover.

Janos, P. M., & Robinson, N. M. (1985). Psychosocial development in intellectually gifted children. In F. D. Horowitz & M. O'Brien (Eds.), *The gifted and the talented.* Washington, DC: American Psychological Association.

Jarvik, L. F., & Winograd, C. H. (1988). *Treatments for the Alzheimer patient.* New York: Springer.

Jeans, P. C., Smith, M. B., & Stearns, G. (1955). Incidence of prematurity in relation to maternal nutrition. *Journal of the American Dietary Association, 31,* 576–581.

Jensen, A. R. (1969). How much can we boost IQ and scholastic achievement? *Harvard Educational Review, 39,* 1–123.

Jensen, A. R. (1985). The nature of black-white differences in psychometric tests. *Behavior and Brain Sciences, 8,* 193–263.

Johnston, L. D., Bachman, J. G., & O'Malley, P. M. (1988, January). *Illicit drug use by American high school seniors, college students, and young adults.* Institute for Social Research, U. of Michigan, Ann Arbor.

Johnston, L. D., O'Malley, P. M., & Bachman, J. G. (1987). *National trends in drug use and related factors among American high school students and young adults, 1975–1986.* Institute of Social Research, U. of Michigan, Ann Arbor.

Jones, E. (1953). *The life and work of Sigmund Freud* (Vol. 1). New York: Basic Books.

Jones, M. C. (1965). Psychological correlates of somatic development. *Child Development, 36,* 899–911.

Jose, P. E. (1985, April). *Development of the immanent justice judgment in moral evaluation.* Paper presented at the biennial meeting of the Society for Research in Child Development, Toronto.

Juster, F. T. (in press). A note on recent changes in time use. In F. T. Juster & F. Stafford (Eds.). *Studies in the measurement of time allocation.* Ann Arbor, MI: Institute for Social Research.

Kagan, J. (1984). *The nature of the child.* New York: Basic Books.

Kagan, J. (1987a). Perspectives on infancy. In J. Osofsky (Ed.), *Handbook of infant development* (2nd ed.). New York: Wiley.

Kagan, J. (1987, April,b). *Temperamental bases for reactions to uncertainty.* Paper presented at the biennial meeting of the Society for Research in Child Development, Baltimore.

Kagan, J., Kearsley, R. B., & Zelazo, P. R. (1978). *Infancy.* Cambridge, MA: Harvard U. Press.

Kail, R., & Pellegrino, J. W. (1985). *Human intelligence.* New York: W. H. Freeman.

Kaitz, M., Meschulach-Sarfaty, O., Auerbach, J., & Eidelman, A. (1988). A reexamination of newborns' ability to imitate facial expressions. *Developmental Psychology, 24,* 3–7.

Kalish, R. A. (1981). *Death, grief, and caring relationships.* Monterey, CA: Brooks/Cole.

Kalish, R. A. (1987). Death. In G. L. Maddox (Ed.), *Encyclopedia of aging.* New York: Springer.

Kalish, R. A., & Reynolds, D. K. (1976). *An overview of death and ethnicity.* Farmingdale, NY: Baywood.

Kaprio, J., Koskenvuo, M., & Rita, H. (1987). Mortality after bereavement: A prospective study of 95,647 widowed persons. *American Journal of Public Health, 77,* 283.

Kaslow, F. W., & Schwartz, L. L. (1987). *The dynamics of divorce: A life cycle perspective.* New York: Brunner/Mazel.

Kastenbaum, R. (1969). Death and bereavement in later life. In A. H. Kutscher (Ed.), *Death and bereavement.* Springfield, IL: Charles C. Thomas.

Kastenbaum, R. (1985). Dying and death: A life-span approach. In J. E. Birren & K. W. Schaie (Eds.), *Handbook of the psychology of aging* (2nd ed.). New York: Van Nostrand Reinhold.

Katz, P. A. (1987, August). *Children and social issues.* Paper presented at the meeting of the American Psychological Association, New York City.

Kaufman, A. S. (1988, August). *Has anybody really measured adult intelligence?* Paper presented at the meeting of the American Psychological Association, Atlanta.

Keating, D. (1980). Thinking processes in adolescence. In J. Adelson (Ed.), *Handbook of adolescent psychology.* New York: Wiley.

Keil, F. C. (1984). Mechanisms in cognitive development and the structure of knowledge. In R. J. Sternberg (Ed.), *Mechanisms of cognitive development.* New York: W. H. Freeman.

Kellogg, W. N., & Kellogg, C. A. (1933). *The ape and the child.* New York: McGraw-Hill.

Kelly, J. B. (1987, August). *Children of divorce: Long-term effects and clinical implications.* Paper presented at the meeting of the American Psychological Association, New York City.

Kenniston, K. (1970). Youth: A "new" stage of life. *The American Scholar, 39,* 631–654.

Kenshalo, D. R. (1977). Age changes in touch, vibration, temperature, kinesthesis, and pain sensitivity. In J. E. Birren & K. W. Schaie (Eds.), *Handbook of the psychology of aging.* New York: Van Nostrand Reinhold.

Kephart, W. M. (1967). Some correlates of romantic love. *Journal of Marriage and the Family, 29,* 470–474.

Kerr, B. A. (1983). Raising the career aspirations of gifted girls. *Vocational Guidance Quarterly, 32,* 37–43.

Kessen, W., Haith, M. M., & Salapatek, P. (1970). Human infancy. In P. H. Mussen (Ed.), *Manual of child psychology* (3rd ed.), Vol.1. New York: Wiley.

Kety, S. (1980). Foreword. In J. E. Birren & R. B. Sloane (Eds.), *Handbook of mental health and aging.* Englewood Cliffs, NJ: Prentice Hall.

Kiecolt-Glaser, J. K., & Glaser, R. (1988). Behavioral influences on immune function. In T. Field, P. McCabe, & N. Schneiderman (Eds.), *Stress and coping across development.* Hillsdale, NJ: Erlbaum.

Kimmel, D. C. (1988). Ageism, psychology, and public policy. *American Psychologist, 43,* 175–178.

King, H. E. (1961). Psychological effects of excitation of the limbic system. In D. E. Sheer (Ed.), *Electrical stimulation of the brain.* Austin, TX: U. of Texas Press.

Kinsey, A. C., Pomeroy, W. B., & Martin, E. E. (1948). *Sexual behavior in the human male.* Philadelphia: W. B. Saunders.

Kitch, D. L. (1987). Hospice. In R. J. Corsini (Ed.), *Concise encyclopedia of psychology.* New York: Wiley.

Klass, D. (1988). *Parental grief.* New York: Springer.

Klaus, M. H. (1988, November). *Recognizing and managing stress in the caregiver.* Paper presented at Developmental Interventions in Neonatal Care Conference, San Diego, CA.

Klaus, M. M., & Kennell, H. H. (1976). *Maternal-infant bonding.* St. Louis: Mosby.

Kliegl, R., & Baltes, P. B. (1987). Theory-guided analysis of mechanisms of development and aging through testing-the-limits and research on expertise. In C. Schooler & K. W. Schaie (Eds.), *Cognitive functioning and social structure over the life course.* Norwood, NJ: Ablex.

Kline, D. W., & Schieber, F. (1985). Vision and aging. In J. E. Birren & K. W. Schaie (Eds.), *Handbook of the psychology of aging* (2nd ed.). New York: Van Nostrand Reinhold.

Kobak, R. R., & Sceery, A. (1988). Attachment in late adolescence: Working models, affect regulations and representations of self and others. *Child Development, 59,* 135–146.

Kobasa, S. C., Maddi, S., & Kahn, S. (1982). Hardiness and health: A prospective study. *Journal of Personality and Social Psychology, 42,* 168–177.

Kobasa, S. C., Maddi, S., Puccetti, M. C., & Zola, M. (1985). Relative effectiveness of hardiness, exercise, and social support as resources against illness. *Journal of Psychosomatic Research, 29,* 525–533.

Kohlberg, L. (1958). *The development of modes of moral thinking and choice in the years 10 to 16.* Unpublished doctoral dissertation, U. of Chicago, Chicago, IL.

Kohlberg, L. (1966). A cognitive-developmental analysis of children's role concepts and attitudes. In E. E. Maccoby (Ed.), *The development of sex differences.* Palo Alto, CA: Stanford U. Press.

Kohlberg, L. (1969). Stage and sequence: The cognitive-developmental approach to socialization. In D. A. Goslin (Ed.), *Handbook of socialization theory and research.* Chicago: Rand McNally.

Kohlberg, L. (1976). Moral stages and moralization: The cognitive-developmental approach. In T. Lickona (Ed.), *Moral development and behavior.* New York: Holt, Rinehart, & Winston.

Kohlberg, L. (1986). A current statement on some theoretical issues. In S. Modgil & C. Modgil (Eds.), *Lawrence Kohlberg.* Philadelphia: Falmer Press.

Kohlberg, L., & Higgins, A. (1987). School democracy and social interaction. In W. M. Kurtines & J. L. Gewirtz (Eds.), *Moral development through social interaction.* New York: Wiley.

Kohn, A. (1987). *No contest: The case against competition.* Boston: Houghton Mifflin.

Kohut, H. (1977). *The restoration of the self.* New York: Norton.

Kopp, C. B. (1983). Risk factors in development. In P. H. Mussen (Ed.), *Handbook of child psychology* (4th ed.), Vol. 2. New York: Wiley.

Kopp, C. B. (1987). Developmental risk: Historical reflections. In J. D. Osofsky (Ed.), *Handbook of infant development* (2nd ed.). New York: Wiley.

Kopp, C. B., & Parmalee, A. H. (1979). Prenatal and perinatal influences on behavior. In J. D. Osofsky (Ed.), *Handbook of infant development.* New York: Wiley.

Korner, A. F., Hutchinson, C. A., Koperski, J. A., Kraemer, H. C., & Schneider, P. A. (1981). Stability of individual differences of neonatal motor and crying responses. *Child Development, 40,* 137–141.

Krogman, W. M. (1970). Growth of head, face, trunk, and limbs in Philadelphia white and Negro children of elementary and high school age. *Monographs of the Society for Research in Child Development, 35* (3, Serial No. 136).

Kübler-Ross, E. (1969). *On death and dying.* New York: Macmillan.

Kübler-Ross, E. (1974). *Questions and answers on death and dying.* New York: Macmillan.

Kuhn, D. (1984). Cognitive development. In M. H. Bornstein & M. E. Lamb (Eds.), *Developmental psychology: An advanced textbook.* Hillsdale, NJ: Erlbaum.

Kuypers, J. A., & Bengston, V. L. (1973). Social breakdown and competence. A model of normal aging. *Human Development, 16,* 181–201.

La Barbera, J. D., Izard, C. E., Vietze, P., & Parisi, S. A. (1976). Four- and six-month-old infants' visual responses to joy, anger, and neutral expressions. *Child Development, 47,* 535–538.

La Rue, A., Dessonville, C., & Jarvik, L. F. (1985). Aging and mental disorders. In J. E. Birren & K. W. Schaie (Eds.), *Handbook of the psychology of aging* (2nd ed.). New York: Van Nostrand Reinhold.

Labouvie-Vief, G. (1982). Dynamic development and mature autonomy: A theoretical prologue. *Human Development, 25,* 161–191.

Labouvie-Vief, G. (1985). Intelligence and cognition. In J. E. Birren & K. W. Schaie (Eds.). *Handbook on the psychology of aging* (2nd ed.). New York: Van Nostrand Reinhold.

Labouvie-Vief, G. (1986, August). *Modes of knowing and life-span cognition.* Paper presented at the meeting of the American Psychological Association, Washington, DC.

Lachman, M. E. (1988, August). *Personal control in later life: Implications for cognitive aging.* Paper presented at the meeting of the American Psychological Association, Atlanta.

Lagerspetz, K. (1979). Modification of aggressiveness in mice. In S. Feshbach & A. Fraczek (Eds.), *Aggression and behavior change: Biological and social processes.* New York: Praeger.

Lamb, M. E. (1977). The development of mother-infant and father-infant attachments in the second year of life. *Developmental Psychology, 13,* 637–648.

Lamb, M. E. (1986). *The father's role: Applied perspectives.* New York: Wiley.

Lamb, M. E. (1987). *The father's role: Cross-cultural perspectives.* Hillsdale, NJ: Erlbaum.

Lamb, M. E. (1988). Social and emotional development in infancy. In M. H. Bornstein & M. E. Lamb (Eds.), *Developmental psychology: An advanced textbook.* Hillsdale, NJ: Erlbaum.

Lamb, M. E., Frodi, A. M., Hwang, C. P., Frodi, M., & Steinberg, J. (1982). Mother- and father-infant interaction involving play and holding in traditional and nontraditional Swedish families. *Developmental Psychology, 18,* 215–221.

Lamb, M. E., Thompson, R. A., Gardner, W. R., Charnov, E. L., & Estes, D. P. (1984). Security of infantile attachment as assessed in the "strange situation": Its study and biological interpretation. *The Behavioral and Brain Sciences, 7,* 121–171.

Landesman-Dwyer, S., & Sackett, G. P. (1983, April). *Prenatal nicotine exposure and sleep-wake patterns in infancy.* Paper presented at the biennial meeting of Society for Research in Child Development, Detroit.

Landy, F. J. (1989). *Psychology of work behavior* (4th ed.). Chicago: Dorsey Press.

Lane, H. (1976). *The wild boy of Aveyron.* Cambridge, MA: Harvard U. Press.

Langlois, J. (1981). *From the eye of the beholder to behavioral reality.* Paper presented at the Ontario Symposium, "Physical appearance, stigma, and social behavior." Toronto, Canada.

Lapsley, D. K., Enright, R. D., & Serlin, R. C. (1985). Toward a theoretical perspective on the legislation of adolescence. *Journal of Early Adolescence, 5,* 441–466.

Lapsley, D. K., & Murphy, M. N. (1985). Another look at the theoretical assumptions of adolescent egocentrism. *Developmental Review, 5,* 201–217.

Lapsley, D. K., & Power, F. C. (Eds.). (1988). *Self, ego, and identity: Integrative approaches.* New York: Springer.

Lapsley, D. K., & Quintana, S. M. (1985). Integrative themes in social and developmental theories of self. In J. B. Pryor & J. Day (Eds.), *Social and developmental perspectives of social cognition.* New York: Springer-Verlag.

Larson, J. H. (1988). The Marriage Quiz: College students' beliefs in selected myths about marriage. *Family Relations, 37,* 3–11.

La Rue, A., Dessonville, C., & Jarvik, L. F. (1985). Aging and mental disorders. In J. E. Birren & K. W. Schaie (Eds.), *Handbook of the psychology of aging* (2nd ed.). New York: Van Nostrand Reinhold.

Lazar, I., Darlington, R., & Collaborators. (1982). Lasting effects of early childhood education: A report from the consortium for longitudinal studies. *Monographs of the Society for Research in Child Development, 47,* Nos. 2–3 (Whole No. 195).

Lazarus, R. S., & DeLongis, A. (1983). Psychological stress and coping in aging. *American Psychologist, 38,* 245–254.

Lazarus, R. S., & Folkman, S. (1984). *Stress, appraisal, and coping.* New York: Springer.

Leaf, A. (1973, September). Getting old. *Scientific American,* pp. 44–53.

Leamer, L. (1986). *As time goes by.* New York: Harper & Row.

Lebowitz, B. D. (1987). Mental health services. In G. L. Maddox (Ed.), *The encyclopedia of aging.* New York: Springer.

Leboyer, F. (1975). *Birth without violence.* New York: Knopf.

Lee, G. R. (1978). Marriage and morale in late life. *Journal of Marriage and the Family, 40,* 131–139.

Lee, V. E., Brooks-Gunn, J., & Schnur, E. (1988). Does Head Start Work? A 1-year follow-up comparison of disadvantaged children attending Head Start, no preschool, and other preschool programs. *Developmental Psychology, 24,* 210–222.

Lefkowitz, M. M., Eron, L. D., Walder, L. O., & Huesmann, L. R. (1972). Television violence and children's aggression: A follow-up study. In G. A. Comstock & E. A. Rubenstein (Eds.), *Television and social behavior* (Vol. 3). Washington, DC: U.S. Government Printing Office.

Lehman, H. C. (1960). The age decrement in outstanding scientific creativity. *American Psychologist, 15,* 128–134.

Leiffer, A. D. (1973). *Television and the development of social behavior.* Paper presented at the meeting of the International Society for the Study of Behavioral Development, Ann Arbor, MI.

Leiffer, A. D., Gordon, N. J., & Graves, S. B. (1974). Children's television: More than entertainment. *Harvard Educational Review, 44,* 213–245.

Lenneberg, E. H., Rebelsky, F. G., & Nichols, I. A. (1965). The vocalization of infants born to deaf and hearing parents. *Human Development, 8,* 23–37.

Lenneberg, E. H. (1962). *Biological foundations of language.* New York: Wiley.

Lepper, M., Greene, D., & Nisbett, R. R. (1973). Undermining children's instrinsic interest with extrinsic rewards. *Journal of Personality and Social Psychology, 28,* 129–137.

Lepper, M. R. (1985). Microcomputers in education: Motivational and social issues. *American Psychologist, 40,* 1–19.

Lerner, J. V., Hertzog, C., Hooker, K. A., Hassibi, M., & Thomas, A. (1988). A longitudinal study of negative emotional states and adjustment from early childhood through adolescence. *Child Development, 59,* 356–366.

Lerner, M. J. (1982). The justice motive in human relations and the economic model of man: A radical analysis of facts and fictions. In V. J. Derlega & J. Grzelak (Eds.), *Cooperation and helping behavior: Theories and research.* New York: Academic Press.

Lerner, R. M. (1987). A life-span perspective for early adolescence. In R. M. Lerner & T. T. Foch (Eds.), *Biological-psychosocial interactions in early adolescence.* Hillsdale, NJ: Erlbaum.

Lerner, R. M. (1988). Early adolescent transitions: The lore and the laws of adolescence. In M. D. Levine & E. R. McAnarney (Eds.), *Early adolescent transitions.* Lexington, MA: Lexington Books.

LeShan, L. L. (1966). An emotional life-history pattern associated with neoplastic disease. *Annals of the New York Academy of Sciences, 125,* 780–793.

Leverant, R. (1986). MDMA reconsidered. *Journal of Psychoactive Drugs, 18,* 373–379.

Levin, J. R. (1980). *The mnemonic '80s: Keywords in the classroom.* Theoretical paper No. 86, Wisconsin Research and Development Center for Individualizing Schooling, Madison, WI.

Levinger, G. (1974). A three-level approach to attraction: Toward an understanding of pair relatedness. In T. Huston (Ed.), *Foundations of interpersonal attraction.* New York: Academic Press.

Levinson, D. J. (1978). *The seasons of a man's life.* New York: Knopf.

Levinson, D. J. (1980). Toward a conception of the adult life course. In N. J. Smelser & E. H. Erikson (Eds.), *Themes of work and love in adulthood.* Cambridge, MA: Harvard U. Press.

Levinson, D. J. (1987, August). *The seasons of a woman's life.* Paper presented at the meeting of the American Psychological Association, New York City.

Levinson, R. J. (1987). Euthanasia. In G. L. Maddox (Ed.). *The encyclopedia of aging.* New York: Springer.

Levitt, M. J. (in press). Attachment and close relationships: A life span perspective. In J. L. Gewirtz & W. F. Kurtines (Eds.), *Intersections with attachment.* Hillsdale, NJ: Erlbaum.

Levitt, M. J., Clark, M. C., Rotton, J., & Finley, G. E. (in press). Social support, perceived control, and well-being: A study of an environmentally distressed population. *International Journal of Aging and Human Development.*

Levy, S. (1984). The process and outcome of "adjustment" in the cancer patient: A reply to Taylor. *American Psychologist, 39,* 1327.

Levy, S. (1985). *Behavior and cancer.* San Francisco: Jossey Bass.

Lewin, T. (1987, August 16). The new debate over life, death. *Dallas Morning News,* pp. 1A,19A.

Lewinsohn, P. M., Antonuccio, D. O., Steinmetz, J., & Teri, L. (1984). *The coping with depression course: A psychoeducational intervention for unipolar depression.* Eugene, OR: Castalia Pub.

Lewis, C. S. (1960). *The four loves.* New York: Harcourt Brace & World.

Lewis, M. (1987). Social development in infancy and childhood. In J. D. Osofsky (Ed.), *Handbook of infant development* (2nd ed.). New York: Wiley.

Lewis, M., & Brooks-Gunn, J. (1979). *Social cognition and the acquisition of the self.* New York: Plenum.

Lewkowicz, D. J. (1988). Sensory dominance in infants: 1. Six-month-old infants' response to auditory-visual compounds. *Developmental Psychology, 24,* 155–171.

Liben, L. S., Downs, D., & Daggs, D. (1988, June). *Geographic education: The value of a Piagetian perspective.* Paper presented at the Annual Symposium of the Jean Piaget Society, Philadelphia.

Liebert, R. M., & Spratkin, J. N. (1988). *The early window: Effects of television on children and youth* (3rd ed.). Elmsford, NY: Pergamon.

Lifshitz, F., Pugliese, M. T., Moses, N., & Weyman-Daum, M. (1987). Parental health beliefs as a cause of non-organic failure to thrive. *Pediatrics, 80,* 175–182.

Lifton, R. J. (1977). The sense of immortality: On death and the continuity of life. In H. Feifel (Ed.), *New meanings of death.* New York: McGraw-Hill.

Lipsitt, L. P., Engen, T., & Kaye, H. (1963). Developmental changes in the olfactory threshold of the neonate. *Child Development, 34,* 371–376.

Lipsitt, L. P., Reilly, B. M., Butcher, M. J., & Greenwood, M. M. (1976). The stability and interrelationships of newborn sucking and heart rate. *Developmental Psychology, 9,* 305–310.

Lipsitz, J. (1980, March). *Sexual development in young adolescents.* Invited speech given at the American Association of Sex Educators, Counselors, and Therapists.

Lipsitz, J. (1983, October). *Making it the hard way: Adolescents in the 1980s.* Testimony prepared for the Crisis Intervention Task Force, House Select Committee on Children, Youth, and Families, Washington, DC.

Lipsitz, J. (1984). *Successful schools for young adolescents.* New Brunswick, NJ: Transaction Books.

Livson, N., & Peskin, H. (1981). Psychological health at age 40. Prediction from adolescent personality. In D. M. Eichorn, J. Clausen, N. Haan, M. Honzik, & P. Mussen (Eds.), *Present and past in middle life*. New York: Academic Press.

Lock, R. D. (1988). *Job search and taking care of your career direction*. Pacific Grove, CA: Brooks/Cole.

Lockheed, M. E. (1985). Women, girls, and computers: A first look at the evidence. *Sex Roles, 13*, 115–122.

Loehlin, J. C., & Nichols, R. C. (1976). *Heredity, environment, and personality: A study of 850 sets of twins*. Austin: U. of Texas Press.

Logue, A. W. (1986). *Eating and drinking*. New York: W. H. Freeman.

Long, T., & Long, L. (1983). *Latchkey children*. New York: Penguin.

Lopata, H. Z. (1987a). Widowhood. In G. L. Maddox (Ed.), *Encyclopedia of aging*. New York: Springer.

Lopata, H. Z. (Ed.). (1987b). *Widows: The Middle East, Asia, and the Pacific*. Durham, NC: Duke U. Press.

Lorden, R. B., & Falkenberg, S. D. (1988, August). *Applications of cognitive research to improvement of classroom teaching and learning*. Paper presented at the meeting of the American Psychological Association, Atlanta.

Lorenz, K. Z. (1965). *Evolution and the modification of behavior*. Chicago: U. of Chicago Press.

Lowy, L. (1981, August). *The older generation: What is due, what is owed?* Paper presented at the meeting of the American Psychological Association, Los Angeles.

Luria, A., & Herzog, E. (1985, April). *Gender segregation across and within settings*. Paper presented at the biennial meeting of the Society for Research in Child Development, Toronto.

Luria, Z., & Meade, R. G. (1984). Sexuality and the middle-aged woman. In G. K. Baruch & J. Brooks-Gunn (Eds.), *Women in midlife*. New York: Plenum.

Lykken, D. T. (1982). Research with twins: The concept of emergenesis. *Psychophysiology, 19*, 361–373.

Lyle, J., & Hoffman, H. R. (1972). Children's use of television and other media. In E. A. Rubenstein, G. A. Comstock, & J. P. Murray (Eds.), *Television and social behavior*, Vol. 4. Washington, D.C.: U.S. Government Printing Office.

Maccoby, E. E. (1980). *Social development*. San Diego: Harcourt Brace Jovanovich.

Maccoby, E. E. (1984). Middle childhood in the context of the family. In *Development during middle childhood*. Washington, DC: National Academy Press.

Maccoby, E. E. (1987, November). Interview with Elizabeth Hall: All in the family. *Psychology Today*, pp. 54–60.

Maccoby, E. E. (1987). The varied meanings of "masculine" and "feminine." In J. M. Reinisch, L. A. Rosenblum, & S. A. Sanders (Eds.), *Masculinity/femininity*. New York: Oxford U. Press.

Maccoby, E. E., & Jacklin, C. N. (1974). *The psychology of sex differences*. Palo Alto, CA: Stanford U. Press.

Maccoby, E. E., & Jacklin, C. N. (in press). Gender segregation in childhood. In H. Reese (Ed.), *Advances in child development and behavior*, Vol. 20. New York: Academic Press.

Maccoby, E. E., & Martin, J. A. (1983). Socialization in the context of the family: Parent-child interaction. In P. H. Mussen (Ed.), *Handbook of child psychology* (4th ed.), Vol. 4. New York: Wiley.

MacFarlane, J. A. (1975). Olfaction in the development of social preferences in the human neonate. In *Parent-infant interaction, Ciba Foundation Symposium, 33*. Amsterdam: Elsevier.

Maddi, S. (1986, August). *The great stress-illness controversy*. Paper presented at the meeting of the American Psychological Association, Washington, DC.

Maddox, G. L. (1968). Disengagement theory: A critical evaluation. *The Gerontologist, 4*, 80–83.

Maddux, J. E., Roberts, M. C., Sledden, E. A., & Wright, L. (1986). Developmental issues in child health psychology. *American Psychologist, 41*, 24–34.

Mahler, M. (1979). *Separation-individuation*, (Vol. 2). London: Jason Aronson.

Maier, S. F., & Laudenslager, M. (1985, August). Stress and health: Exploring the links. *Psychology Today*, pp. 44–49.

Main, M., & Cassidy, J. (1988). Categories of response in reunion with the parent at age 6: Predictable from infant attachment classifications and stable over a 1-month period. *Developmental Psychology, 24*, 415–426.

Main, M., Kaplan, N., & Cassidy, J. (1985). Security in infancy, childhood, and adulthood: A move to the level of representation. *Monographs of the Society for Research in Child Development, 50* (Serial No. 209).

Mandler, G. (1980). Recognizing the judgment of previous occurrence. *Psychology Review, 87*, 252–271.

Mandler, J. M. (1983). Representation. In P. H. Mussen (Ed.), *Handbook of child psychology* (4th ed.), Vol. 3. New York: Wiley.

Maratsos, M. (1983). Some current issues in the study of the acquisition of grammar. In P. H. Mussen (Ed.), *Handbook of child psychology* (4th ed.), Vol. 3. New York: Wiley.

Marcia, J. (1966). Identity six years after: A follow-up study. *Journal of Youth and Adolescence, 5*, 145–160.

Marcia, J. (1980). Ego identity development. In J. Adelson (Ed.), *Handbook of adolescent psychology*. New York: Wiley.

Marcia, J. (1987). The identity status approach to the study of ego identity development. In T. Honess & K. Yardley (Eds.), *Self and identity: Perspectives across the lifespan*. London: Routledge and Kegan Paul.

Markman, H. J. (1979). Application of a behavioral model of marriage in predicting relationship satisfaction of couples planning marriage. *Journal of Consulting and Clinical Psychology, 47*, 743–749.

Markides, K., & Martin, H. (1979). A causal model of life satisfaction among the elderly. *Journal of Gerontology, 34*, 86–93.

Markides, K. S. (1987). Minorities and aging. In G. L. Maddox (Ed.), *The encyclopedia of aging*. New York: Springer.

Marshall, W. A. (1973). The body. In R. R. Sears & S. S. Feldman (Eds.), *The seven ages of man*. Los Altos, CA: William Kaufmann.

Martin, J. (1976). *The education of adolescents*. Washington, DC: U.S. Office of Education.

Maslow, A. H. (1954). *Motivation and personality*. New York: Harper & Row.

Maslow, A. H. (1971). *The farther reaches of human nature*. New York: Viking.

Massey, C. M., & Gelman, R. (1988). Preschoolers' ability to decide whether a photographed object can move itself. *Developmental Psychology, 24*, 307–317.

Masten, A. S. (1988). Toward a developmental psychopathology of early adolescence. In M. D. Levine & E. R. McAnarney (Eds.), *Early adolescent transitions*. Lexington, MA: Lexington Books.

Matas, L., Arend, R. A., & Sroufe, L. A. (1978). Continuity in adaptation: Quality of attachment and later competence. *Child Development, 49*, 547–556.

Matheny, A. P., Dolan, R. S., & Wilson, R. S. (1976). Relation between twins' similarity: Testing an assumption. *Behavior Genetics, 6*, 343–351.

McAdams, D. P. (1988). *Power, intimacy, and the life story*. New York: Guilford.

McAdoo, H. P., & McAdoo, J. L. (Eds.). (1985). *Black children: Social, educational, and parental environments*. Beverly Hills, CA: Sage.

McCall, R. B., Eichorn, D. H., & Hogarty, P. S. (1977). Transitions in early mental development. *Monographs of the Society for Research in Child Development, 41* (3, Serial No. 171).

McCandless, B. R. (1973). *Male caregivers in day care: Demonstration project*. Atlanta, GA: Emory University.

McCartney, K., & Phillips, D. (in press). Motherhood and child care. In B. Birns & D. Daye (Eds.), *The different faces of motherhood*. New York: Plenum.

McClelland, D. C. (1955). Some social consequences of achievement motivation. In M. R. Jones (Ed.), *The Nebraska Symposium on Motivation*. Lincoln, NE: U. of Nebraska Press.

McClelland, D. C., Atkinson, J. W., Clark, R. W., & Lowell, E. L. (1953). *The achievement motive.* New York: Appleton-Century-Crofts.

McDaniel, M. A., & Pressley, M. (1987). *Imagery and related mnemonic processes.* New York: Springer-Verlag.

McKinlay, S. M., & McKinlay, J. B. (1984). *Health status and health care utilization by menopausal women.* Unpublished manuscript, Cambridge Research Center, American Institutes for Research, Cambridge, MA.

McLaughlin L., & Chassin, L. (1985, April). *Adolescents at risk for future alcohol abuse.* Paper presented at the biennial meeting of the Society for Research in Child Development, Toronto.

McNeil, D. (1970). *The acquisition of language.* New York: Harper & Row.

McQuire, W. J. (1986). The myth of mass media effectiveness. In G. Comstock (Ed.), *Public communication and behavior* (Vol. 1). New York: Academic Press.

McWhirter, D. P., & Reinisch, J. M. (Eds.). (in press) *Homosexuality/heterosexuality: Concepts of sexual orientation.* New York: Oxford U. Press.

Medrich, E. A., Rosen, J., Rubin, V., & Buckley, S. (1982). *The serious business of growing up.* Berkeley, CA: U. of California Press.

Medvedev, Z. A. (1974). The nucleic acids in the development of aging. In B. L. Strehler (Ed.), *Advances in gerontological research* (Vol.1). New York: Academic Press.

Meer, J. (1986, June). The reason of age. *Psychology Today,* pp. 60–64.

Meltzoff, A. N. (1987, April). *Imitation by nine-month olds in immediate and deferred tests.* Paper presented at the biennial meeting of the Society for Research in Child Development, Baltimore.

Meltzoff, A. N. (1988). Infant imitation and memory: Nine-month-olds in immediate and deferred tests. *Child Development, 59,* 217–225.

Meltzoff, A. N., & Moore, M. K. (1977). Interpreting "imitative" responses in early infancy. *Science, 205,* 217–219.

Meredith, H. V. (1978). Research between 1960 and 1970 on the standing height of young children in different parts of the world. In H. W. Reese & L. P. Lipsitt (Eds.), *Advances in Child Development and Behavior,* Vol.12. New York: Academic Press.

Meyerhoff, M. K., & White, B. L. (1986). Making the grade as parents. *Psychology Today,* September, 38–45.

Meyers, J. (1985). *Hemingway.* New York: Harper & Row.

Middleton, W., & Raphael, B. (1987). Bereavement: State of the art and state of the science. *Psychiatric Clinics of North America, 10,* 329–343.

Milham, J., Widmayer, S., Bauer, C. R., & Peterson, L. (1983, April). *Predictory cognitive deficits for pre-term, low birthweight infants.* Paper presented at the biennial meeting of the Society for Research in Child Development, Detroit.

Miller, G. (1981). *Language and speech.* New York: W. H. Freeman.

Minnett, A. M., Vandell, D. L., & Santrock, J. W. (1983). The effects of sibling status on sibling interaction: Influence of birth order, age spacing, sex of the child, and sex of the sibling. *Child Development, 54,* 1064–1072.

Minuchin, P. P., & Shapiro, E. K. (1983). The school as a context for social development. In P. H. Mussen (Ed.), *Handbook of child psychology* (4th ed.), Vol. 4. New York: Wiley.

Mischel, W. (1973). Toward a cognitive social learning reconceptualization of personality. *Psychological Review, 80,* 252–283.

Mischel, W. (1984). Convergences and challenges in the search for consistency. *American Psychologist, 39,* 351–364.

Mischel, W., & Patterson, C. J. (1976). Substantive and structural elements of effective plans for self-control. *Journal of Personality and Social Psychology, 34,* 942–950.

Moely, B. E., Olson, F. A., Halwes, T. G., & Flavell, J. H. (1969). Production deficiency in young children's clustered recall. *Developmental Psychology, 1,* 26–34.

Money, J. (1987). Propaedeutics of Diecious G-I/R: Theoretical foundations for understanding dimorphic gender-identity role. In J. M. Reinisch, L. A. Rosenblum, & S. A. Sanders (Eds.), *Masculinity/femininity.* New York: Oxford U. Press.

Money, J. (1987). Sin, sickness, or status? Homosexual gender identity and psychoneuroendocrinology. *American Psychologist, 42,* 384–399.

Money, J., & Ehrhardt, A. A. (1972). *Man and woman, boy and girl.* Baltimore: Johns Hopkins Press.

Monroe, R. (1988). *Creative brainstorms.* New York: Irvington.

Montemayor, R., & Hanson, E. (1985). A naturalistic view of conflict between adolescents and their parents and siblings. *Journal of Early Adolescence, 5,* 23–30.

Morris, D. S. W., & Bass, S. (Eds.). (1988). *Retirement reconsidered.* New York: Springer.

Morse, W. C. (1964). Self-concept in the school setting. *Childhood Education, 41,* 195–198.

Moushegian, G. (1988, January). Personal Communication. Program in Psychology and Human Development, U. of Texas at Dallas, Richardson, TX.

Murphy, S. (1986). Unpublished ethnographic data. Reported in Beck, J., & Morgan, P. A. (1986). Designer drug confusion: A focus on MDMA. *Journal of Drug Education, 16,* 297.

Murray, F. B. (1978, August). *Generation of educational practice from developmental theory.* Paper presented at the meeting of the American Psychological Association, Toronto.

Mussen, P. H., Honzik, M., & Eichorn, D. (1982). Early adult antecedents of life satisfaction at age 70. *Journal of Gerontology, 37,* 316–322.

Nagy, M. (1948). The child's theories concerning death. *Journal of Genetic Psychology, 73,* 3–27.

Neimark, E. D. (1982). Adolescent thought: Transition to formal operations. In B. B. Wolman (Ed.), *Handbook of developmental psychology.* Englewood Cliffs, NJ: Prentice Hall.

Nelson, K. E. (1978). How children represent knowledge of their world in and out of language. In R. S. Siegler (Ed.), *Children's thinking: What develops?* Hillsdale, NJ: Erlbaum.

Neugarten, B. L. (1964). *Personality in middle and late life.* New York: Atherton Press.

Neugarten, B. L. (1980). Must everything be a mid-life crisis? Annual editions, *Human Development 80/81,* Guilford, CT: Dushkin, pp. 289–290.

Neugarten, B. L. (1986). The aging society. In A. Pifer & L. Bronte (Eds.), *Our aging society: Paradox and promise.* New York: Norton.

Neugarten, B. L. (1988, August). *Policy issues for an aging society.* Paper presented at the meeting of the American Psychological Association, Atlanta.

Neugarten, B. L. (1989). Policy issues for an aging society. *The Psychology of Aging.* Washington, DC. American Psychological Association.

Neugarten, B. L., Havighurst, R. J., & Tobin, S. S. (1968). Personality and patterns of aging. In B. L. Neugarten (Ed.), *Middle age and aging.* Chicago: U. of Chicago Press.

Neugarten, B. L., & Weinstein, K. K. (1964). The changing American grandparent. *Journal of Marriage and the Family, 26,* 199–204.

Newcomb, M. D., & Bentler, P. M. (1988). Impact of adolescent drug use and social support on problems of young adults: A longitudinal study. *Journal of Abnormal Psychology, 97,* 64–75.

Nicholls, J. G. (1975). Causal attributions and other achievement-related cognitions: Effects of task outcomes, attainment value, and sex. *Journal of Personality and Social Psychology, 31,* 379–389.

Nicholls, J. G. (1984). Conceptions of ability and achievement motivation. In R. E. Ames & C. Ames (Eds.), *Motivation in education.* New York: Academic Press.

Nielson, L. (1987). *Adolescent psychology.* New York: Holt, Rinehart & Winston.

Nielson Television Index (1981). *Child and teenage television viewing* (Special Release). New York: NTI.

Nottelman, E. D., Susman, E. J., Blue, J. H., Inoff-Germain, G., Dorn, L. D., Loriaux, D. L., Cutler, G. B., & Chrousos, G. P. (1987). Gonadal and adrenal hormone correlates of adjustment in early adolescence. In R. M. Lerner & T. T. Foch (Eds.), *Biological-psychological interactions in early adolescence.* Hillsdale, NJ: Erlbaum.

Novak, W. (1981). *The great American man shortage.* New York: Basic Books.

Nowak, C. A. (1977). Does youthfulness equal attractiveness. In L. E. Troll, J. Israel, & K. Israel (Eds.), *Looking ahead: A woman's guide to the problems and joys of growing older.* Englewood Cliffs, NJ: Prentice Hall.

Offord, D. R., & Boyle, M. H. (1988). The epidemiology of antisocial behavior in early adolescents. In M. D. Levine & E. R. McAnarney (Eds.), *Early adolescent transitions.* Lexington, MA: Lexington Books.

Okun, B. F., & Rappaport, L. J. (1980). *Working with families: An introduction to family therapy.* North Scituate, MA: Duxbury Press.

Olsho, L. W., Harkins, S. W., & Lenhardt, M. L. (1985). Aging and the auditory system. In J. E. Birren & K. W. Schaie (Eds.), *Handbook of the psychology of aging* (2nd ed.). New York: Van Nostrand Reinhold.

Olson, G. M., & Stauss, M. S. (1984). The development of infant memory. In M. Moscovitch (Ed.), *Infant memory.* New York: Plenum.

Olweus, D. (1980). Bullying among schoolboys. In R. Barnen (Ed.), *Children and violence.* Stockholm: Adaemic Litteratur.

Oppenheimer, M. (1982, October). What you should know about herpes. *Seventeen Magazine,* pp. 154–155, 170.

Orlofsky, J. (1976). Intimacy status: Relationship to interpersonal perception. *Journal of Youth and Adolescence, 5,* 73–88.

Orlofsky, J., Marcia, J., & Lesser, I. (1973). Ego identity status and the intimacy vs. isolation crisis of young adulthood. *Journal of Personality and Social Psychology, 27,* 211–219.

Osofsky, H. J., Osofsky, J. D., Culp, R., Krantz, K., & Tobiasen, J. (1985). Transition to parenthood: Risk factors for parents and infants. *Journal of Psychosomatic Obstetrics & Gynecology, 4,* 303–315.

Osterweis, M., Solomon, F., & Green, M. (1984). *Bereavement reactions, consequences, and care.* Washington, DC: National Academy of Sciences.

Ottinger, D. R., & Simmons, J. E. (1964). Behavior of human neonates and prenatal maternal anxiety. *Psychological Reports, 14,* 391–394.

Oyama, S. (1973). *A sensitive period for the acquisition of a second language.* Unpublished doctoral dissertation, Harvard University.

Palmore, E. B. (1975). *The honorable elders: A cross-cultural analysis of aging in Japan.* Durham, NC: Duke U. Press.

Palmore, E. B. (1980). Predictors of longevity. In S. Haynes & M. Feinleib (Eds.), *Epidemiology of aging.* Washington, DC: U.S. Government Printing Office.

Palmore, E. B. (1982). Predictors of the longevity difference: A 25-year follow-up. *The Gerontologist, 22,* 513–518.

Palmore, E. B., Burchett, B. M., Fillenbaum, C. G., George, L. K., & Wallman, L. M. (1985). *Retirement: Causes and consequences.* New York: Springer.

Palmore, E. B., & Jeffers, F. C. (1971). *Prediction of the life span.* Lexington, MA: Heath.

Palmore, E. B., & Maeda, D. (1985). *The honorable elders revisited.* Durham, NC: Duke U. Press.

Paloma, M., Pendleton, B. F., & Garland, T. N. (1982). Reconsidering the dual career marriage: A longitudinal approach. In J. Aldous (Ed.), *Two paychecks: Life in dual-earner families.* Beverly Hills, CA: Sage.

Parcel, G. S., Tiernan, K., Nadar, P. R., & Gottlob, D. (1979). Health education and kindergarten children. *Journal of School Health, 49,* 129–131.

Paris, S. C., & Lindauer, B. K. (1982). The development of cognitive skills during childhood. In B. B. Wolman (Ed.), *Handbook of developmental psychology.* Englewood Cliffs, NJ: Prentice Hall.

Parke, R. D. (1976, September). *Child abuse: An overview.* Paper presented at the meeting of the American Psychological Association, Washington, D.C.

Parke, R. D., & Lewis, N. G. (1980). The family in context: A multilevel interactional analysis of child abuse. In R. W. Henderson (Ed.), *Parent-child interaction.* New York: Academic Press.

Parke R. D., & Sawin, D. B. (1980). The family in early infancy. In F. Pedersen (Ed.), *The father-infant relationship: Observational studies in a family context.* New York: Praeger.

Parke, R. D., & Suomi, S. (1981). Adult male-infant relationships: Human and non-human primate evidence. In K. Immelmann, G. W. Barlow, L. Petrinovich, & M. Main (Eds.), *Behavioral development: The Bielefeld Interdisciplinary Project.* New York: Cambridge U. Press.

Parkes, C. M. (1972). *Bereavement: Studies of grief in adult life.* New York: International Universities Press.

Parlee, M. B. (1979, April). The friendship bond: PT's survey report on friendship in America. *Psychology Today,* pp. 43–54, 113.

Parmalee, A., Wenner, W., & Schultz, H. (1964). Infant sleep patterns from birth to 16 weeks of age. *Journal of Pediatrics, 65,* 576–572.

Parmalee, A. H. (1986). Children's illnesses: Their beneficial effects on behavioral development. *Child Development, 57,* 1–10.

Parsons, J. E., Ruble, D. N., Hodges, K. L., & Small, A. W. (1976). Cognitive-developmental factors in emerging sex differences in achievement-related expectancies. *Journal of Social Issues, 32,* 47–61.

Parten, M. (1932). Social play among preschool children. *Journal of Abnormal and Social Psychology, 27,* 243–269.

Pasley, K., & Ihinger-Tallman, M. (Eds.). (1987). *Remarriage and stepparenting.* New York: Guilford.

Patterson, G. R., & Stouthamer-Loeber, M. (1984). The correlation of family management practices and delinquency. *Child Development, 55,* 1299–1307.

Pawson, M., & Morris, N. (1972). The role of the father in pregnancy and labor. In N. Morris (Ed.), *Psychological medicine in obstetrics and gynecology.* Basel: Karger.

Peck, R. C. (1968). Psychological developments in the second half of life. In B. L. Neugarten (Ed.), *Middle age and aging.* Chicago: U. of Chicago Press.

Pedersen, A. C. (1987, September). Those gangly years. *Psychology Today,* pp. 28–34.

Pedersen, F. A., Anderson, B. J., & Cain, R. L. (1980). Parent-infant and husband-wife interactions observed at age five months. In F. A. Pedersen (Ed.), *The father-infant relationship: Observational studies in the family setting.* New York: Praeger.

Penner, S. G. (1987). Parental responses to grammatical and ungrammatical child utterances. *Child Development, 58,* 376–384.

Pepler, D. J. (1988, June). *Peer relations of aggressive children: What's going wrong?* Paper presented at the meeting of the Canadian Psychological Association, Montreal.

Perlmutter, M. (Ed.). (in press). *Late-life potential.* Washington, DC: Gerontological Association of America.

Peskin, H. (1967). Pubertal onset and ego functioning. *Journal of Abnormal Psychology, 72,* 1–15.

Peskin, H., & Livson, N. (1981). Uses of the past in adult psychological health. In D. M. Eichorn, J. Clausen, N. Haan, M. Honzik, & P. Mussen (Eds.), *Present and past in middle life.* New York: Academic Press.

Petersen, A. C. (1979, January). Can puberty come any faster? *Psychology Today,* pp. 45–56.

Petersen, A. C. (1987). The nature of biological-psychosocial interactions: The sample case of early adolescence. In R. M. Lerner & T. T. Foch (Eds.), *Biological-psychosocial interactions in early adolescence.* Hillsdale, NJ: Erlbaum.

Petersen, A. C., Crouter, A. C., & Wilson, J. (1988). Heterosexual behavior and sexuality among normal adolescents. In M. D. Levine & E. R. McAnarney (Eds.), *Early adolescent transitions.* Lexington, MA: Lexington Books.

Peterson, P. L. (1977). Interactive effects of student anxiety, achievement orientation, and teacher behavior on student achievement and attitude. *Journal of Educational Psychology, 69,* 779–792.

Pettit, G. S., Dodge, K. A., & Brown, M. M. (1988). Early family experience, social problem solving patterns, and children's social competence. *Child Development, 59,* 107–120.

Pfaffman, C. (1977). Biological and behavioral substrates of the sweet tooth. In J. M. Weijfenbach (Ed.), *Taste and development.* Bethesda, MD: U.S. Department of Health, Education, and Welfare.

Pfeiffer, E., & Davis, G. (1974). Determinants of sexual behavior in middle and old age. In E. Palmore (Ed.). *Normal aging II*. Durham, NC: Duke U. Press.

Pfeiffer, E., Verwoerdt, A., & Davis, G. C. (1974). Sexual behavior in middle life. In E. Palmore (Ed.), *Normal aging II: Reports from the Duke longitudinal studies, 1970–1973*. Durham, NC: Duke U. Press.

Phares, E. J. (1984). *Introduction to personality*. Glenview, IL: Scott, Foresman.

Phares, E. J. (1984). *Personality*. Columbus, OH: Charles E. Merrill.

Piaget, J. (1932). *The moral judgment of the child*. New York: Harcourt Brace Jovanovich.

Piaget, J. (1952). *The origins of intelligence in children*. New York: International Universities Press.

Piaget, J. (1954). *The construction of reality in the child*. New York: Basic Books.

Piaget, J. (1962). *Play, dreams, and imitation in childhood*. New York: Norton.

Piaget, J. (1967). *The child's construction of the world*. Totowa, NJ: Littlefield, Adams & Co.

Piaget, J., & Inhelder, B. (1969). *The child's conception of space*. (F. J. Langdon & J. L. Lunzer, Trans.). New York: Norton (originally published 1948).

Pierce, C., & VandDeVeer, D. (1988). *AIDS*. Belmont, CA: Wadsworth.

Pines, A., & Aronson, E. (1988). *Career burnout*. New York: The Free Press.

Pines, M. (1987). Mirroring and child development. In T. Honess & K. Yardley (Eds.), *Self and identity: Perspectives across the lifespan*. London: Routledge and Kegan Paul.

Pinker, S. (1984). *Language learnability and language development*. Cambridge, MA: Harvard U. Press.

Pipes, P. (1988). Nutrition in childhood. In S. R. Williams & B. S. Worthington-Roberts (Eds.), *Nutrition throughout the life cycle*. St. Louis: Times Mirror/Mosby.

Pipp, S., Fischer, K. W., & Jennings, S. (1987). Acquisition of self- and mother knowledge in infancy. *Developmental Psychology, 23*, 86–96.

Pittman, T. S., & Heller, J. S. (1987). Social motivation. *Annual Review of Psychology, 38*, 461–489.

Pleck, J. H. (1984). *Working wives and family well-being*. Beverly Hills, CA: Sage.

Plomin, R. (1987a). Developmental behavioral genetics and infancy. In J. D. Osofsky (Ed.), *Handbook of Infant Development*. New York: Wiley.

Plomin, R. (1987, April,b). *Adoption studies: Nurture as well as nature*. Paper presented at the biennial meeting of the Society for Research in Child Development, Baltimore.

Plomin, R., & Thompson, L. (1987). Life-span developmental behavioral genetics. In P. B. Baltes, D. L. Featherman, & R. M. Lerner (Eds.), *Life-span development and behavior*, Vol. 7. Hillsdale, NJ: Erlbaum.

Polivy, J., & Thomsen, L. (1987). Eating, dieting, and body image. In E. A. Blechman & K. D. Brownell (Eds.), *Handbook of behavioral medicine for women*. Elmsford, NY: Pergamon.

Poon, L. W. (1985). Differences in human memory with aging: Nature causes, and clinical implications. In J. E. Birren & K. W. Schaie (Eds.), *Handbook of the psychology of aging* (2nd ed.). New York: Van Nostrand Reinhold.

Porter, F. L., Porges, S. W., & Marshall, R. E. (1988). Newborn pain cries and vasal tone: Parallel changes in response to circumcision. *Child Development, 59*, 495–515.

Prechtl, H. F. R. (1965). Problems of behavioral studies in the newborn infant. In D. S. Lehrman, R. A. Hinde, & E. Shaw (Eds.), *Advances in the study of behavior*. New York: Academic Press.

Premack, A. J., & Premack, D. (1972). Teaching language to an ape. *Scientific American, 227*, 92–98.

Price, J., & Feshbach, S. (1982, August). *Emotional adjustment correlates of television viewing in children*. Paper presented at the meeting of the American Psychological Association, Washington, DC.

Quinn, T. C., Glasser, D., Cannon, R. O., & Others (1988). Human immunodeficiency virus infection among patients attending clinics for sexually transmitted diseases. *The New England Journal of Medicine, 318*, 197–202.

Rachels, J. (1986). *The end of life*. New York: Oxford U. Press.

Rando, T. A. (1988). *Grieving: How to go on living when someone you love dies*. Lexington, MA: Lexington Books.

Ratner, N., & Bruner, J. S. (1978). Games, social exchange, and the acquisition of language. *Journal of Child Language, 5*, 1–15.

Reedy, M. N., Birren, J. E., & Schaie, K. W. (1981). Age and sex differences in satisfying relationships across the adult life span. *Human Development, 24*, 52–66.

Reichard, S., Levson, F., & Peterson, P. (1962). *Aging and personality: A study of 87 older men*. New York: Wiley.

Revitch, E., & Schlesinger, L. B. (1978). Murder: Evaluation, classification, and prediction. In I. L. Kutash, S. B. Kutash, & L. B. Schlesinger (Eds.), *Violence*. San Francisco: Jossey-Bass.

Rhodes, S. R. (1983). Age-related differences in work attitudes and behavior: A review and conceptual analysis. *Psychological Bulletin, 93*, 329–367.

Rich, C. L., Young, D., & Fowler, R. C. (1986). San Diego suicide study. *Archives of General Psychiatry, 43*, 577–582.

Riddle, D. B., & Prinz, R. (1984, August). *Sugar consumption in young children*. Paper presented at the Meeting of The American Psychological Association, Toronto.

Riege, W. H., & Inman, V. (1981). Age differences in nonverbal memory tasks. *Journal of Gerontology, 36*, 51–58.

Riegel, K. (1977). The dialectics of time. In N. Datan & H. W. Reese (Eds.), *Life-span developmental psychology: Dialectical perspective on experimental research*. New York: Academic Press.

Riley, M. W., & Foner, A. (1968). *Aging and society* (Vol. 1). New York: Russell Sage.

Riley, M. W. (1970). What people think about death. In O. G. Brim, H. E. Freeman, S. Levine, & N. A. Scotch (Eds.), *The dying patient*. New York: Sage.

Roberts, D. E., & Maccoby, N. (1985). Effects of mass media effectiveness. In G. Lindzey & E. Aronson (Eds.), *Handbook of social psychology* (3rd ed.). Vol. 2. New York: Random House.

Robinson, H. F. (1977). *Exploring teaching in early childhood education*. Boston: Allyn & Bacon.

Robinson, N. M. (1987). Psychology and mental retardation. *American Psychologist, 42*, 791.

Rode, S. S., Chang, P., Fisch, R. O., & Sroufe, L. A. (1981). Attachment patterns of infants separated at birth. *Developmental Psychology, 17*, 188–191.

Rodin, J. (1986). Health, control, and aging. In M. M. Baltes & P. B. Baltes (Eds.), *The psychology of control and aging*. Hillsdale, NJ: Erlbaum.

Rodin, J., & Langer, E. J. (1977). Long-term effects of a control-relevant intervention with the institutionalized aged. *Journal of Personality and Social Psychology, 35*, 397–402.

Rodman, H., Pratto, D. J., & Nelson, R. S. (1988). Toward a definition of self-care children: A commentary on Steinberg (1986). *Developmental Psychology, 24*, 292–294.

Rogers, C. R. (1961). *On becoming a person*. Boston: Houghton Mifflin.

Rogers, C. R. (1963). The actualizing tendency in relation to "motives" and consciousness. In M. R. Jones (Ed.), *Nebraska Symposium on Motivation*. Lincoln, NE: U. of Nebraska Press.

Rogers, C. R. (1967). Carl R. Rogers. In E. G. Boring & G. Lindzey (Eds.), *A history of psychology in autobiography*. New York: Macmillan.

Rogers, C. R. (1974). In retrospect: Forty-six years. *American Psychologist, 29*, 115–123.

Rogers, C. R. (1980). *A way of being*. Boston: Houghton Mifflin.

Rogers, T., Kuiper, N., & Kirker, W. (1977). Self-reference and the encoding of personal information. *Journal of Personality and Social Psychology, 35*, 677–688.

Rollins, B. C., & Feldman, H. (1970). Marital satisfaction over the family life cycle. *Journal of Marriage and the Family, 32*, 20–28.

Rose, S. A., & Ruff, H. A. (1987). Cross-modal abilities in human infants. In J. D. Osofsky (Ed.), *Handbook of infant development* (2nd ed.). New York: Wiley.

Rosenbaum, A. (1983). *The young people's Yellow Pages: A national sourcebook for youth.* New York: Putnam.

Rosenbaum, J. E. (1984). *Career mobility in a corporate hierarchy.* New York: Academic Press.

Rosenblith, J. F., & Sims-Knight, J. E. (1985). *In the beginning: Development in the first two years.* Monterey, CA: Brooks/Cole.

Rosenfeld, A., & Stark, E. (1987, May). The prime of our lives. *Psychology Today,* pp. 62–72.

Rosenfeld, A. (1985, New Year's). Stretching the span. *The Wilson Quarterly.*

Rosenthal, R., & Jacobsen, L. (1968). *Pygmalian in the classroom.* New York: Holt, Rinehart & Winston.

Rossi, A. (in press). A life course approach to gender, aging, and intergenerational relations. In K. W. Schaie & C. Schooler (Eds.), *Social structures and aging.* Hillsdale, NJ: Erlbaum.

Rothbart, M. K. (in press). Temperament and the development of inhibited approach. *Child Development.*

Rothbart, M. L. K. (1971). Birth order and mother-child interaction. *Dissertation Abstracts, 27,* 45–57.

Rousell, R. H. (1985). Aging upward: How to win while growing old. *Aging,* No. 349.

Rovee-Collier, C. (1987). Learning and memory in children. In J. D. Osofsky (Ed.), *Handbook of infant development* (2nd ed.). New York: Wiley.

Roybal, E. R. (1988). Mental health and aging: The need for an expanded federal response. *American Psychologist, 43,* 189–194.

Rubin, K. H. (1978). Role-taking in childhood: Some methodological considerations. *Child Development, 49,* 428–433.

Rubin, Z. (1970). Measurement and romantic love. *Journal of Personality and Social Psychology, 16,* 265–273.

Rubin, Z. (1981, May). Does personality really change after 20? *Psychology Today.*

Rubin, Z., & Mitchell, C. (1976). Couples research as couples counseling. *American Psychologist, 31,* 17–25.

Ruble, D. N. (1987). The acquisition of self-knowledge: A self-socialization perspective. In N. Eisenberg (Ed.), *Contemporary topics in developmental psychology.* New York: Wiley.

Rutter, D. R., & Durkin, K. (1987). Turn-taking in mother-infant interaction: An examination of vocalization and gaze. *Developmental Psychology, 23,* 54–61.

Rutter, M. (1983, April). *Influences from family and school.* Paper presented at the meeting of the Society for Research in Child Development, Detroit.

Rutter, M., & Schopher, E. (1987). Autism and persuasive developmental disorders: Concepts and diagnostic issues. *Journal of Autism and Developmental Disorders, 17,* 159–186.

Sagan, C. (1980). *Cosmos.* New York: Random House.

Salthouse, T. A. (1988). Initiating the formalization of theories of cognitive aging. *Psychology and Aging, 3,* 3–16.

Salthouse, T. A., & Somberg, B. L. (1982). Skilled performance: Effects of adult age and experience on elementary processes. *Journal of Experimental Psychology: General, III,* 176–207.

Santrock, J. W. (1987). *Adolescence* (3rd ed.). Dubuque, IA: Wm. C. Brown.

Santrock, J. W., & Bartlett, J. C. (1986). *Developmental psychology.* Dubuque, IA: Wm. C. Brown.

Santrock, J. W., & Sitterle, K. A. (1987). Parent-child relationships in stepmother families. In K. Pasley & M. Ihinger-Tallman (Eds.), *Remarriage and stepparenting.* New York: Guilford.

Santrock, J. W., Sitterle, K. A., & Warshak, R. A. (1988). Parent-child relationships in stepfather families. In P. Bronstein & C. Cowan (Eds.), *The father's role today: Men's changing roles in the family.* New York: Wiley.

Santrock, J. W., Sitterle, K. A., & Warshak, R. A. (1988). Parent-child relationships in stepfather families. In P. Bronstein & C. P. Cowan (Eds.), *Fatherhood today.* New York: Wiley.

Santrock, J. W., Smith, P. C., & Bourbeau, P. (1976). Effects of group social comparison upon aggressive and regressive behavior in children. *Child Development, 47,* 831–837.

Santrock, J. W., & Warshak, R. A. (1979). Father custody and social development in boys and girls. *Journal of Social Issues, 35,* 112–125.

Santrock, J. W., & Warshak, R. A. (1986) Development, relationships, and legal/clinical considerations in father custody families. In M. E. Lamb (Ed.), *The father's role: Applied perspectives.* New York: Wiley.

Sauber, M., & Corrigan, E. M. (1970). *The six year experience of unwed mothers as parents.* New York: Community Council of Greater New York.

Savin-Williams, R. C. (1988). Theoretical perspectives accounting for adolescent homosexuality. *Journal of Adolescent Health Care, 9,* 95–104.

Scardamalia, M., Bereiter, C., & Goelman, H. (1982). The role of production factors in writing ability. In M. Nystrand (Ed.), *What writers know: The language, process, and structure of written discourse.* New York: Academic Press.

Scarr, S. (1984). *Mother care/Other care.* New York: Basic Books.

Scarr, S. (1984, May). Interview. *Psychology Today,* pp. 59–63.

Scarr, S., & Kidd, K. K. (1983). Developmental behavior genetics. In P. H. Mussen (Ed.), *Handbook of child psychology* (4th ed., Vol. 2). New York: Wiley.

Scarr, S., & Weinberg, R. A. (1976). IQ test performance of black children adopted by white families. *American Psychologist, 31,* 726–739.

Scarr, S., & Weinberg, R. A. (1979). Nature and nurture strike (out) again. *Intelligence, 3,* 31–39.

Scarr, S., & Weinberg, R. A. (1980). Calling all camps! The war is over. *American Sociological Review, 45,* 859–865.

Schacter, D. L., & Moscovitch, M. (1984). Infants, amnesiacs, and dissociable memory systems. In M. Moscovitch (Ed.), Infant memory. New York: Plenum Press.

Schaffer, H. R. (1977). *Mothering.* Cambridge, MA: Harvard U. Press.

Schaffer, H. R., & Emerson, P. E. (1964). The development of social attachments in infancy. *Monographs of the Society for Research in Child Development, 29* (3, Serial No. 94).

Schaie, K. W. (1977). Toward a stage theory of adult cognitive development. *Aging and Human Development, 8,* 129–138.

Schaie, K. W. (1984). The Seattle Longitudinal Study: A 21-year exploration of psychometric intelligence in adulthood. In K. W. Schaie (Ed.), *Longitudinal studies of adult psychological development.* New York: Guilford Press.

Schaie, K. W. (1988). Ageism in psychological research. *American Psychologist, 43,* 179–183.

Schaie, K. W., & Willis, S. L. (1986). Can adult intellectual decline be reversed? *Developmental Psychology, 22,* 223–232.

Schank, R., & Abelson, R. (1977). *Scripts, plans, goals, and understanding.* Hillsdale, NJ: Erlbaum.

Schmich, M. T. (1987, July 29). *Living alone.* Dallas Morning News, Section C, pp. 1,4.

Schorr, L. B. (in press). *Within our reach: Breaking the cycle of disadvantage and despair.* New York: Doubleday/Anchor.

Schunk, D. H. (1983). Developing children's self-efficacy and skills: The roles of social comparative information and goal-setting. *Contemporary Educational Psychology, 8,* 76–86.

Schuster, C. (1986, May 1). *Statement to congressional subcommittee on bills relating to designer drugs.* Washington, DC.

Schwartz, D., & Mayaux, M. J. (1982). Female fecundity as a function of age: Results of artificial insemination in nulliparous women with azoospermic husbands. *New England Journal of Medicine, 306,* 404–406.

Schwartzberg, A. Z. (1988). Adolescent substance abuse. *Adolescent psychiatry* (Vol. 15.). Chicago: U. of Chicago Press.

Scott, J. P. (1983). Siblings and other kin. In T. Brubaker (Ed.), *Family relationships in later life.* Beverly Hills, CA: Sage.

Sears, P. S., & Barbee, A. H. (1977). Care and life satisfactions among Terman's gifted women. In J. C. Stanley, W. C. George, & C. H. Solano (Eds.), *The gifted and the creative: A 50-year perspective.* Baltimore: Johns Hopkins Press.

Sears, R. R., & Feldman, S. S. (Eds.). (1973). *The seven ages of man.* Los Altos, CA: William Kaufmann.

Sears, R. R. (1977). Sources of life satisfaction of the Terman gifted men. *American Psychologist, 32,* 119–128.

Segerberg, O. (1982). *Living to be 100: 1200 who did and how they did it.* New York: Charles Scribner's Sons.

Selman, R. L. (1980). *The growth of interpersonal understanding.* New York: Academic Press.

Serbin, L. A., Tonick, I. J., & Sternglanz, S. (1977). Shaping cooperative cross-sex play. *Child Development, 48,* 924–929.

Sexton, M., & Hebel, J. R. (1984). A clinical trial of change in maternal smoking and its effects on birth weight. *Journal of the American Medical Association, 251,* 911–915.

Seymour, R. B., Wesson, D. R., & Smith, D. E. (1986). Editor's introduction. *Journal of Psychoactive Drugs, 18,* 287–289.

Shantz, C. O. (1988). Conflicts between children. *Child Development, 58,* 283–305.

Shantz, C. U. (1983). Social cognition. In P. H. Mussen (Ed.), *Handbook of child psychology* (4th ed.), Vol. 3. New York: Wiley.

Shatz, M., & Gelman, R. (1973). The development of communication skills: Modifications in the speech of young children as a function of the listener. *Monographs of the Society for Research in Child Development, 38* (Serial No. 152).

Shaver, P. (1986, August). *Being lonely, falling in love: Perspectives from attachment theory.* Paper presented at the meeting of the American Psychological Association, Washington, DC.

Sheehy, G. (1976). *Passages.* New York: Dutton.

Sheingold, K., & Tenney, Y. J. (1982). Memory for a salient childhood event. In U. Neisser (Ed.), *Memory observed.* San Francisco: W. H. Freeman.

Sherman, E. (1987). *Meaning in mid-life transitions.* Albany: State University of New York Press.

Shirley, M. M. (1933). *The first two years.* Minneapolis: U. of Minnesota Press.

Shneidman, E. S. (1971). Suicide among the gifted. *Suicide and Life-Threatening Behavior, 1,* 23–45.

Shneidman, E. S. (1973). *Deaths of man.* New York: Quadrangle/New York Times.

Siegel, R. (1985). Treatment of cocaine abuse: Historical and contemporary perspectives. *Journal of Psychoactive Drugs, 17,* 1–9.

Siegler, I. C. (1989). Developmental health psychology. *The Psychology of Aging.* Washington, DC. American Psychological Association.

Simmons, R. G., & Blyth, D. A. (1987). *Moving into adolescence.* Hawthorne, NY: Aldine.

Simmons, R. G., Burgeson, R., Carton-Ford, S., & Blyth, D. A. (1987). The impact of cumulative change in early adolescence. *Child Development, 58,* 1235–1243.

Simpson, J. A., Campbell, B., & Berscheid, E. (1986). The association between love and marriage: Kephart (1967) twice revisited. *Personality and Social Psychology Bulletin, 12,* 363–372.

Singer, D. (1972, June). Piglet, Pooh, and Piaget. *Psychology Today,* pp. 70–74.

Singer, D. G., & Singer, J. L. (1987). Practical suggestions for controlling television. *Journal of Early Adolescence, 7,* 365–369.

Singer, J. L. (1984). *The human personality.* San Diego: Harcourt Brace Jovanovich.

Sizer, T. R. (1984). *Horace's compromise: The dilemma of the American high school today.* Boston: Houghton Mifflin.

Skinner, B. F. (1938). *The behavior of organisms: An experimental analysis.* New York: Appleton-Century-Crofts.

Skinner, B. F. (1948). *Walden two.* New York: Macmillan.

Skinner, B. F. (1957). *Verbal behavior.* New York: Appleton-Century-Crofts.

Slavin, R. E. (1983). When does cooperative learning increase student achievement? *Psychological Bulletin, 94,* 429–445.

Slavin, R. E. (1987). Developmental and motivational perspectives on cooperative learning: A reconciliation. *Child Development, 58,* 1161–1167.

Slobin, D. (1972, July). Children and language: They learn the same all around the world, *Psychology Today,* pp. 71–76.

Smeeding, T. M., Torrey, B. B., & Rein, M. (1986, May). *The economic status of the young and the old in six countries.* Paper presented at the meeting of the American Association for the Advancement of Science, Philadelphia.

Smith, A. D. (1977). Adult age differences in cued recall. *Developmental Psychology, 13,* 326–331.

Smith, J., Dixon, R. A., & Baltes, P. B. (in press). Expertise in life planning: A new research approach to investigating aspects of wisdom. In M. L. Commons, J. D. Sinnott, F. A. Richards, & C. Armon (Eds.) *Beyond formal operations II: Comparisons and applications of adolescent and adult models.* New York: Praeger.

Smither, R. D. (1988). *The psychology of work and human performance.* New York: Harper & Row.

Snarey, J. (1987, June). A question of morality. *Psychology Today,* pp. 6–8.

Snyder, J., & Patterson, G. R. (1987). Family interaction and delinquent behavior. In H. C. Quay (Ed.), *Handbook of juvenile delinquency.* New York: Wiley.

Soreson, R. C. (1973). *Adolescent sexuality in contemporary America.* New York: World.

Spearman, C. E. (1927). *The abilities of man.* New York: Macmillan.

Spelke, E. S. (1979). Perceiving bimodally specified events in infancy. *Developmental Psychology, 15,* 626–636.

Spence, J. T., & Helmreich, R. L. (1978). *Masculinity and femininity: Their psychological dimensions.* Austin, TX: U. of Texas Press.

Spence, M., & DeCasper, A. J. (1982). *Human fetuses perceive human speech.* Paper presented at the International Conference on Infant Studies, Austin, TX.

Spielberger, C. D., & Grier, K. (1983). Unpublished manuscript, University of South Florida, Tampa.

Sroufe, L. A. (1985). Attachment classification from the perspective of infant-caregiver relationships and infant temperament. *Child Development, 56,* 1–14.

Sroufe, L. A. (1987). *The role of infant-caregiver attachment in development.* Unpublished manuscript. Institute of Child Development, U. of Minnesota.

Sroufe, L. A. (in press). The role of infant-caregiver attachment in development. In J. Belsky & T. M. Nezworski (Eds.), *Clinical implications of attachment.* Hillsdale, NJ: Erlbaum.

Sroufe, L. A., & Waters, E. (1976). The ontogenesis of smiling and laughter: A perspective on the organization of development in infancy. *Psychological Review, 83,* 173–189.

Stagner, R. (1985). Aging in industry. In J. E. Birren & K. W. Schaie (Eds.), *Handbook of the psychology of aging* (2nd ed.). New York: Van Nostrand Reinhold.

Stallings, J. (1975). Implementation and child effects of teaching practices in Follow Through classrooms. *Monographs of the Society for Research in Child Psychology, 40* (Serial No. 163).

Steinberg, L. (1981). Transformations in family relations at puberty. *Developmental Psychology, 17,* 833–840.

Steinberg, L. (1986). Latchkey children and susceptibility to peer pressure: An ecological analysis. *Developmental Psychology, 22,* 433–439.

Steinberg, L. (1987). Impact of puberty on family relations: Effects of pubertal status and pubertal timing. *Developmental Psychology, 23,* 451–460.

Steinberg, L. (1988). Reciprocal relation between parent-child distance and pubertal maturation. *Developmental Psychology, 24,* 122–128.

Steinberg, L. (1988). Simple solutions to a complex problem: A response to Rodman, Pratto, and Nelson (1988). *Developmental Psychology, 24,* 295–296.

Steiner, J. E. (1979). Human facial expressions in response to taste and smell stimulation. In H. Reese and L. Lipsitt (Eds.). *Advances in child development and behavior,* Vol. 13. New York: Academic Press.

Stern, D. N., Beebe, B., Jaffe, J., & Bennett, S. L. (1977). The infant's stimulus world during social interaction: A study of caregiver behaviors with particular reference to repetition and timing. In H. R. Schaffer (Ed.), *Studies in mother-infant interaction.* London: Academic Press.

Stern, J. S. (1984). Is obesity a disease of inactivity? In A. J. Stunkard & E. Stellar (Eds.), *Eating and its disorders.* New York: Raven Press.

Sternberg, R. J. (1985). *Beyond IQ*. New York: Cambridge U. Press.

Sternberg, R. J. (1986). *Intelligence Applied*. San Diego: Harcourt Brace Jovanovich.

Sternberg, R. J. (1986). A triangular theory of love. *Psychological Review, 93,* 119–135.

Sternberg, R. J. (1987, August a). *The future of intelligence testing.* Paper presented at the meeting of the American Psychological Association, New York City.

Sternberg, R. J. (1987b). Intelligence. In R. J. Sternberg, & E. E. Smith (Eds.), *The psychology of human thought.* New York: Cambridge U. Press.

Sternberg, R. J., & Lubart, T. (1988, August). *A model of creativity and its development.* Paper presented at the meeting of the American Psychological Association, Atlanta, GA.

Steuer, J. L., & Hammen, C. L. (1986). Cognitive-behavioral group therapy for the depressed elderly: Issues and adaptations. *Cognitive Therapy and Research.*

Stevenson, H. W. (1974). Reflections on the China visit. *Society for Research in Child Development Newsletter,* Fall, 3.

Stevenson, H. W., Stigler, J. W., & Lee, S. (1986). Achievement in mathematics. In H. W. Stevenson, H. Azuma, & K. Hakuta (Eds.), *Child development and education in Japan.* San Francisco: W. H. Freeman.

Stipak, J. D., & Hoffman, J. M. (1980). Children's achievement-related expectancies as a function of academic performance histories and sex. *Journal of Educational Psychology, 72,* 861–865.

Streissguth, A. P., Martin, D. C., Sandman, B. M., Kirchner, G. L., & Darby, B. L. (1984). Intra-uterine alcohol and nicotine exposure: Attention and reaction time in four-year-old children. *Developmental Psychology, 20,* 533–541.

Strickland, B. R. (1987). Menopause. In E. A. Blechaman & K. D. Brownell (Eds.), *Handbook of behavioral medicine for women.* Elmsford, NY: Pergamon.

Stull, D. E., & Hatch, L. R. (1984). Unravelling the effects of multiple life changes. *Research on Aging, 6,* 560–571.

Stunkard, A. J. (in press). The regulation of body weight and the treatment of obesity. In H. Weiner & A. Baum (Eds.), *Eating regulations and discontrol.* Hillsdale, NJ: Erlbaum.

Sullivan, H. S. (1953). *The interpersonal theory of psychiatry.* New York: Norton.

Sullivan, K., & Sullivan, A. (1980). Adolescent-parent separation. *Developmental Psychology, 16,* 93–99.

Summers, W. K. (1986). *The New England Journal of Medicine.*

Suomi, S. J. (1987, April). *Individual differences in rhesus monkey behavioral and adrenocortical responses to social challenge: Correlations with measures of heart rate variability.* Paper presented at the biennial meeting of the Society for Research in Child Development, Baltimore.

Suomi, S. J., Harlow, H. F., & Domek, C. J. (1970). Effect of repetitive infant-infant separations of young monkeys. *Journal of Abnormal Psychology, 76,* 161–172.

Super, D. E., Kowalski, R., & Gotkin, E. (1967). *Floundering and trial after high school.* Unpublished manuscript, Columbia University.

Susman, E. J., Inoff-Germain, G., Nottelmann, E. D., Loriaux, D. L., Cutler, G. B., & Chrousos, G. P. (1987). Hormones, emotional dispositions, and aggressive attributes in young adolescents. *Child Development, 58,* 1114–1134.

Sutton-Smith, B. (1973). *Child psychology.* New York: Appleton-Century-Crofts.

Sutton-Smith, B. (1985, October). The child at play. *Psychology Today,* pp. 64–65.

Tamir, L. M. (1982). *Men in their forties.* New York: Springer.

Tangney, J. P. (in press). Aspects of the family and children's television viewing content preferences. *Child Development.*

Tanner, J. M. (1962). *Growth in adolescence.* Oxford: Blackwell.

Tellegen, A., Lykken, D. T., Bouchard, T. J., Wilcox, K. J., Segal, N. L., & Rich, S. (in press). *Journal of Personality and Social Psychology.*

Terman, L. (1925). *Genetic studies of genius: Vol. 1. Mental and physical traits of a thousand gifted children.* Stanford, CA: Stanford U. Press.

Terrace, H. (1979). *Nim.* New York: Knopf.

Thelen, E. (1981). Rhythmical behavior in infancy: An ethological perspective. *Developmental Psychology, 17,* 237–257.

Thelen, E. (1987, October). *Order, adaptation, and change: A synergetic approach to development.* Paper presented at the 22nd Annual Minnesota Symposium on Child Psychology, Minneapolis.

Thomas, A., & Chess, S. (1987). Commentary. In Goldsmith, H. H., Buss, A. H., Plomin, R., Rothbart, M. K., Thomas, A., Chess, A., Hinde, R. R., & McCall, R. B. Roundtable: What is temperament? Four approaches. *Child Development, 58,* 505–529.

Thomas, A., Chess, S., & Birch, H. G. (1968). *Temperament and behavior disorders in children.* New York: New York University Press.

Thomas, A., Chess, S., & Birch, H. G. (1970). The origin of personality. *Scientific American, 233,* 102–109.

Thornburg, H. D. (1981). Sources of sex education among early adolescents. *Journal of Early Adolescence, 1,* 171–184.

Thorndike, R. L., Hagen, E. P., & Sattler, J. M. (1985). *Stanford-Binet* (4th ed.). Chicago: Riverside Publishing.

Timberlake, B., Fox, R. A., Baisch, M. J., & Goldberg, B. D. (1987). Prenatal education for pregnant adolescents. *Journal of School Health, 57,* 105–108.

Tobin, J. J. (1987). The American idealization of old age in Japan. *The Gerontologist, 27,* 53–58.

Tomlinson-Keasy, C., Warren, L. W., & Elliott, J. E. (1986). Suicide among gifted women: A prospective study. *Journal of Abnormal Psychology, 95,* 123–130.

Troll, L. E., & Bengston, V. L. (1982). Intergenerational relations through the life span. In B. B. Wolman (Ed.), *Developmental psychology.* Englewood Cliffs, NJ: Prentice Hall.

Trotter, R. J. (1987, December). Project Day-Care. *Psychology Today,* pp. 32–38.

Trudel, M., & Jacques, M. (1987, April). *A cross-lag analysis of associations between temperament and attachment in the first year.* Paper presented at the biennial meeting of the society for Research in Child Development, Baltimore.

Tuchmann-Duplessis, H. (1975). Drug effects on the fetus. *Monographs on Drugs,* Vol. 2. Sydney: ADIS Press.

Tulkin, S. R., & Kagan, J. (1971). Mother-child interaction in the first year of life. *Child Development, 43,* 31–41.

Turk, D. C., Rudy, T. E., & Salovey, P. (1984). Health protection: Attitudes and behaviors of LPN's, teachers, and college students. *Health Psychology, 3,* 189–210.

Turkle, S. (1984). *The second self.* Cambridge, MA: Harvard U. Press.

Turner, B. F. (1982). Sex-related differences in aging. In B. B. Wolman (Ed.), *Handbook of developmental psychology.* Englewood, Cliffs, NJ: Prentice Hall.

Tyack, D. (1976). Ways of seeing: An essay on the history of compulsory schooling. *Harvard Educational Review, 46,* 355–389.

U.S. Department of Health, Education, and Welfare (1976). *The condition of education in the United States.* Washington, DC: U.S. Government Printing Office.

Upton, A. C. (1977). Pathology. In L. E. Finch & L. Hayflick (Eds.). *Handbook of the biology of aging.* New York: Van Nostrand.

Vaillant, G. E. (1977). *Adaptation to life.* Boston: Little, Brown.

VandenBos, G. R., Stapp, J., and Kolburg, R. R. (1981). Health service providers in psychology: Results of the 1978 APA Human Resources Survey. *American Psychologist, 36,* 1395–1418.

Vandell, D. L. (1987). Baby sister/Baby brother: Reactions to the birth of a sibling and patterns of early sibling relations. In F. F. Schachter & R. K. Stone (Eds.), *Practical concerns about siblings.* New York: The Haworth Press.

Vandell, D. L., & Corasaniti, M. A. (1988). Variations in early child care: Do they predict subsequent social, emotional, and cognitive differences?

Vandell, D. L., & Corasaniti, M. A. (in press). The relation between third graders' after school care and social, academic, and emotional functioning.

Vandell, D. L., Minnett, A., & Santrock, J. W. (in press). Age differences in sibling relationships during middle childhood. *Applied Developmental Psychology.*

Vandell, D. L., & Wilson, K. S. (1988). Infants' interactions with mother, sibling, and peer: Contrasts and relations between interaction systems. *Child Development, 48,* 176–186.

VanItallie, T. B. (1984). The enduring storage capacity of fat: Implications for the treatment of obesity. In A. J. Stunkard & E. Stellar (Eds.), *Eating and its disorders.* New York: Raven Press.

Visher, E., & Visher, J. (1978). Common problems of stepparents and their spouses. *American Journal of Orthopsychiatry, 48,* 252–262.

Vorhees, C. V., & Mollnow, E. (1987). Behavioral teratogenesis: Long-term influences in behavior from early exposure to environmental agents. In J. D. Osofsky (Ed.), *Handbook of infant development.* New York: Wiley.

Vuchinich, S., Emery, R. E., & Cassidy, J. (in press). Family members as third parties in dyadic family conflict: Strategies, alliances, and outcomes. *Child Development.*

Waddington, C. H. (1957). *The strategy of the genes.* London: Allen & Son.

Wagennar, A. C. (1983). *Alcohol, young drivers, and traffic accidents.* Lexington, MA: D. C. Heath.

Walford, R. L. (1969). *The immunologic theory of aging.* Baltimore: Williams & Wilkins.

Wallach, M. A. (1985). Creative testing and giftedness. In F. D. Horowitz & M. O'Brien (Eds.), *The gifted and the talented.* Washington, DC: American Psychological Association.

Wallach, M. A., & Kogan, N. (1965). *Modes of thinking in young children.* New York: Holt, Rinehart & Winston.

Wallerstein, J., Corbin, S. B., & Lewis, J. M. (in press). *Children of divorce: A ten-year study.*

Wallerstein, J. S. (1982, July). *Children of divorce: Preliminary report of a 10-year follow-up.* Paper presented at the 10th International Congress of the International Association for Child and Adolescent Psychiatry and Allied Professions, Dublin, Ireland.

Wallerstein, J. S., & Kelly, J. B. (1980). *Surviving the breakup: How children actually cope with divorce.* New York: Basic Books.

Walls, N. (1987, Spring). Three generations of love. *Aging International,* pp. 2–5.

Walster, E., Aronson, E., Abrahams, D., & Rottman, L. (1966). Importance of physical attractiveness in dating behavior. *Journal of Personality and Social Psychology, 4,* 508–516.

Warren, J. V. (1975). Medical and toxicological issues. In *Sweetners: Issues and Uncertainties,* National Academy of Science Forum, Fourth of a Series (pp. 36–40). Washington, DC: National Academy of Sciences.

Waters, E., & Sroufe, L. A. (1983). Social competence as a developmental construct. *Developmental Review, 3,* 79–97.

Watson, J. B. (1928). *Psychological care of infant and child.* New York: Norton.

Webb, W. B. (1975). *Sleep: The gentle tyrant.* Englewood Cliffs, NJ: Prentice Hall.

Wechsler, D. (1949). *Wechsler Intelligence Scale for Children.* New York: The Psychological Corporation.

Wechsler, D. (1955). *Wechsler Adult Intelligence Scale.* New York: The Psychological Corporation.

Wechsler, D. (1967). *Wechsler Preschool and Primary Scale for Intelligence.* New York: The Psychological Corporation.

Wechsler, D. (1972). "Hold" and "Don't Hold" test. In S. M. Chown (Ed.), *Human aging.* New York: Penguin.

Wechsler, D. (1974). *Wechsler Intelligence Scale for Children-Revised.* New York: The Psychological Corporation.

Wechsler, D. (1981). *Wechsler Adult Intelligence Scale-Revised.* New York: The Psychological Corporation.

Weinberg, R. A. (1987, April). *The ten-year follow-up study of transracially adopted children and biological offspring of the adoptive families.* Paper presented at biennial meeting of the Society for Research in Child Development, Baltimore.

Weiner, I. B. (1980). Psychopathology in adolescence. In J. Adleson (Ed.), *Handbook of adolescent psychology.* New York: Wiley.

Weinert, F., & Perlmutter, M. (Eds.). (1988). *Memory development.* Hillsdale, NJ: Erlbaum.

Weinstein, N. D. (1984). Reducing unrealistic optimism about illness susceptibility. *Health Psychology, 3,* 431–457.

Weir, R. F. (Ed.). (1986). *Ethical issues in death and dying.* New York: Columbia U. Press.

Weisman, A. D. (1972). *On dying and denying.* New York: Behavioral Publications.

Wellman, W. H. (1988). The early development of memory strategies. In F. Weinert & M. Perlmutter (Eds.), *Memory development.* Hillsdale, NJ: Erlbaum.

Wender, P. H., Kety, S. S., Rosenthal, D., Schulsinger, F., Ortmann, J., & Lunde, I. (1986). Psychiatric disorders in the biological and adoptive families of adopted individuals with affective disorders. *Archives of General Psychiatry, 43,* 923–929.

Werner, E. E. (1979). *Cross-cultural child development: A view from planet earth.* Monterey, CA: Brooks/Cole.

Werner, E. E., & Smith, R. S. (1982). *Vulnerable but invincible: A longitudinal study of resilient children and youth.* New York: McGraw-Hill.

Whitbourne, S. K. (1985). *The aging body.* New York: Springer-Verlag.

White, B. L. (1988). *Educating the infant and toddler.* Lexington, MA: Lexington Books.

White, C. B., & Catania, J. (1981). Psychoeducational intervention for sexuality with aged, family members of the aged, and people who work with the aged. *International Journal of Aging and Human Development.*

White, M. A. (Ed.). (In press). *What curriculum for the information age?* Hillsdale, NJ: Erlbaum.

White, R. W. (1959). Motivation reconsidered: The concept of competence. *Psychological Review, 66,* 297–333.

White, S. H. (1985, April). *Risings and fallings of developmental psychology.* Paper presented at the biennial meeting of the Society for Research in Child Development, Toronto.

Whitehurst, G. J. (1985, April). *The role of imitation in language learning by children with language delay.* Paper presented at the biennial meeting of Society for Research in Child Development, Toronto.

Whitehurst, G. J., & Valdez-Menchaca, M. C. (1988). What is the role of reinforcement in early language acquisition? *Child Development, 59,* 430–440.

Widmayer, S., & Field, T. (1980). Effects of Brazelton demonstrations on early patterns of preterm infants and their teenage mothers. *Infant Behavior and Development, 3,* 79–89.

Wilen, J. (1979, November). *Changing relationships among grandparents, parents, and their young adult children.* Paper presented at the annual meeting of the Gerontological Association, Washington, DC.

Williams, R. B. (1988). Is there life after type A? In T. Field, P. McCabe, & N. Schneiderman (Eds.), *Stress and coping across development.* Hillsdale, NJ: Erlbaum.

Wilson, R. W., & White, E. L. (1977). Changes in morbidity, disability, and utilization differentials between the poor and the nonpoor, data from the Health Interview Survey, 1964 and 1973. *Medical Care, 15,* 636–646.

Windle, W. F. (1940). *Physiology of the human fetus.* Philadelphia: Saunders.

Wing, J. W. (1977). *Early childhood autism.* Elmsford, NY: Pergamon Press.

Winner, E. (1986, August). Where pelicans kiss seals. *Psychology Today,* pp. 24–35.

Winner, E., & Gardner, H. (1988). Creating a world with words. In F. Kessel (Ed.), *The development of language and language researchers.* Hillsdale, NJ: Erlbaum.

Wiswell, R. A. (1980). Relaxation, exercise, and aging. In J. E. Birren & R. B. Sloane (Eds.), *Handbook of mental health and aging.* Englewood Cliffs, NJ: Prentice Hall.

Witkin, H. A., Mednick, S. A., Schulsinger, R., Bakkestrom, E., Christiansen, K. O., Goodenbough, D. R., Hirchhorn, K., Lunsteen, C., Owen, D. R., Philip, J., Ruben, D. B., & Stocking, M. (1976). Criminality in XYY and XXY men. *Science, 193,* 547–55.

Wodarski, J. S., & Hoffman, S. D. (1984). Alcohol education for adolescents. *Social Work in Education, 6,* 69–92.

Wolff, P. H. (1966). The causes, controls, and organization of behavior in the neonate. *Psychological Issues, 5* (1, Whole No. 7).

Wolff, P. H. (1987). *The development of behavioral states and the expression of emotions in early infancy.* Chicago: U. of Chicago Press.

Worobey, J., & Belsky, J. (1982). Employing the Brazelton Scale to influence mothering: An experimental comparison of three strategies. *Developmental Psychology, 18,* 736–743.

Worschel, S., & Cooper, J. (1979). *Understanding social psychology.* Homewood, IL: Dorsey Press.

Worthington, B. S. (1988). Maternal nutrition and the course and outcome of pregnancy. In S. R. Williams & B. S. Worthington (Eds.), *Nutrition throughout the life cycle.* St. Louis: Times Mirror/Mosby.

Wright, L. (1987, August). *Type A behavior and coronary artery disease: Quest for the active ingredient and the illusive mechanism.* Paper presented at the meeting of the American Psychological Association, New York City.

Wylie, R. C. (1979) *The self-concept,* Vol. 2. Lincoln, NE: U. of Nebraska Press.

Zahn-Waxler, C., Radke-Yarrow, M., & King, R. M. (1979). Child rearing and children's prosocial initiations toward victims of distress. *Child Development, 50,* 319–330.

Zeiss, A. M., & Lewinsohn, P. M. (1986, Fall). Adapting behavioral treatment of depression to meet the needs of the elderly. *Clinical Psychologist, 98–100.*

Zelnick, M., & Kantner, J. F. (1977). Sexual and contraceptive experiences of young unmarried women in the United States, 1976 and 1971. *Family Planning Perspectives, 9,* 55–71.

Zelnick, M., & Kantner, J. F. (1980). Sexual activity, contraceptive use and pregnancy among women aged fifteen to nineteen in 1976. *Family Planning Perspectives, 12,* 135–142.

Zembar, M. J., & Naus, M. J. (1985, April). *The combined effect of knowledge base and mnemonic strategies on children's memory.* Paper presented at the biennial meeting of the Society for Research in Child Development.

Zeskind, P. S. (1987). Adult heart rate responses to infant cry sounds. *British Journal of Developmental Psychology, 5,* 73–79.

Zeskind, P. S., & Marshall, T. R. (1988). The relation between variations in pitch and maternal perceptions of infant crying. *Child Development, 59,* 193–196.

Zigler, E. F., & Farber, E. A. (1985). Commonalities between the intellectual extremes: Giftedness and mental retardation. In F. D. Horowitz & M. O'Brien (Eds.), *The gifted and the talented.* Washington, DC: American Psychological Association.

Zigler, E. F. (1987, April). *Child care for parents who work outside the home: Problems and solutions.* Paper presented at the biennial meeting of the Society for Research in Child Development, Baltimore.

Zigler, E. F. (1987, August). *Issues in mental retardation research.* Paper presented at the meeting of the American Psychological Association, New York City.

Zill, N. (in press). Behavior, achievement, and health problems among children in stepfamilies: Findings from a national survey of child health. In E. M. Hetherington & J. D. Arasteh (Eds.), *Impact of divorce, single-parenting, and stepparenting on children.* Hillsdale, NJ: Erlbaum.

Zisook, S. (1987). Adjustment to widowhood. In S. Zisook (Ed.), *Biopsychosocial aspects of grief and bereavement.* Washington, DC: American Psychiatric Press.

Zisook, S., Shuchter, S. R., & Lyons, L. E. (1987). Predictors of psychological reactions during the early stages of widowhood. *Psychiatric Clinics of North America, 10,* 355–368.

611

Psychology: The Science of Mind and Behavior, 2d ed. Copyright © 1988 Wm. C. Brown Publishers, Dubuque, Iowa. All Rights Reserved. Reprinted by permission. **Fig. 10.10** From Mark R. Lepper, "Microcomputers in Education" in *American Psychologist, 40,* 1–9, 1985. Copyright © 1985 American Psychological Association. Reprinted by permission of the author. **Fig. 10.11** From Mark R. Lepper, D. Greene, and R. E. Nisbett, "Undermining Children's Intrinsic Interest with Extrinsic Rewards" in *Journal of Personality and Social Psychology, 28,* 129–137, 1973. Copyright © 1973 American Psychological Association. Reprinted by permission of the author.

Chapter 11

Fig. 11.3 From John W. Santrock, *Children.* Copyright © 1988 Wm. C. Brown Publishers, Dubuque, Iowa. All Rights Reserved. Reprinted by permission. **Fig. 11.5** From A. Colby, et al., "A longitudinal study of moral judgement" in *Monographs of The Society for Research in Child Development,* 1982. Copyright © 1982 by The Society for Research in Child Development. Reprinted by permission. **Fig. 11.6** From T. Achenbach and C. S. Edelbrock, "Behavioral problems and competencies reported by parents of normal and disturbed children aged four through sixteen" in *Monographs of the Society for Research in Child Development,* Ser. No. 188, Vol. 46, No. 1. Copyright © 1981 by the Society for Research in Child Development. Reprinted by permission. **Table 11.1** From John W. Santrock, *Psychology: The Science of Mind and Behavior,* 2d ed. Copyright © 1988 Wm. C. Brown Publishers, Dubuque, Iowa. All Rights Reserved. Reprinted by permission. **Page 333 Marginal Quotation** From *Now We are Six* by A. A. Milne. Copyright 1927 by E. P. Dutton, renewed 1955 by A. A. Milne. Reprinted by permission of the publisher, E. P. Dutton, a division of NAL Penguin, Inc., and the Canadian Publishers, McClelland and Stewart, Toronto.

Chapter 12

Fig. 12.1 From A. F. Roche, "Secular trends in stature, weight, and maturation" in *Monographs of The Society for Research in Child Development,* Ser. No. 179, Vol. 44. Copyright © 1977 The Society for Research in Child Development. Reprinted by permission. **Fig. 12.2** From J. M. Tanner, R. H. Whitehouse, and M. Takaishi, "Standards from birth to maturity for height, weight, height velocity, and weight velocity: British children 1965" in *Archives of Diseases in Childhood, 41,* 1966. Reprinted by permission of the British Medical Society, London. **Fig. 12.5** From D. A. Blythe, R. Bulcroft, and R. G. Simmons, "The impact of puberty on adolescence: A longitudinal study" in *Girls at Puberty* by Jeanne Brooks-Gunn. Copyright © 1981 Plenum Publishing Corporation. Reprinted by permission. **Fig. 12.6** From E. J. Jones, et al., "Teenage Pregnancy in Developed Countries" in *Family Planning Perspectives,* vol. 17, no. 2, March/April 1985. Copyright © 1985 The Alan Guttmacher Institute.

Reprinted by permission. **Page 359 Focus on Life-Span Development 12.1** From John W. Santrock, *Adolescence,* 3d ed. Copyright © 1987 Wm. C. Brown Publishers, Dubuque, Iowa. All Rights Reserved. Reprinted by permission. **Page 367 Focus on Life-Span Development 12.3** Published by permission of Transaction Publishers, from *Successful Schools for Young Adolescents,* by Joan Lipsitz. Copyright © 1983 by Transaction Publishers.

Chapter 13

Fig. 13.1 From Dexter C. Dunphy, "The Social Structure of Peer Groups" in *SOCIOMETRY,* Vol. 26, 1963, figure 1, p. 263. Copyright © 1963 American Sociological Association, Washington, D.C. Reprinted by permission. **Fig. 13.2** From Dexter D. Dunphy, "The Social Structure of Urban Adolescent Peer Groups" in *Sociometry,* Vol. 26, 236, 1963. Copyright © 1963 American Sociological Association. Reprinted by permission. **Table 13.2** From John W. Santrock, *Children.* Copyright © 1988 Wm. C. Brown Publishers, Dubuque, Iowa. All Rights Reserved. Reprinted by permission. **Page 386 Focus on Life-Span Development 13.1** Excerpted from Erik Erikson, *Childhood and Society,* 1950; Erik Erikson, *Young Man Luther,* 1962; Erik Erikson, *Identity, Youth, and Crisis,* 1968; and Erik Erikson, *Ghandi,* 1969. All published by W. W. Norton Company, New York.

Chapter 14

Excerpt, page 406 (msp 778–779) From "10 Reasons Not to Get a Job" by S. Christ and G. Meyer in *The Harvard Lampoon Big Book of College Life.* Copyright © Harvard Lampoon, Inc. **Fig. 14.1** From L. L. Langley, *Physiology of Man.* Copyright © 1971 Van Nostrand Reinhold Company. Reprinted by permission of the author. **Fig. 14.2** From C. A. Darling, D. J. Kallen, and J. E. VanDeusen, "Sex in Transition: 1900–1984" in *Journal of Youth and Adolescence, 13,* 1984. Copyright © 1984 Plenum Publishing Corporation. Reprinted by permission. **Figs. 14.3 and 14.4** From Jack Botwinick, *Cognitive Processes in Maturity and Old Age.* Copyright © 1967 Springer Publishing Company. Reprinted by permission of the author. **Page 417 Focus on Life-Span Development 14.3** From John W. Santrock, *Adult Development and Aging.* Copyright © 1985 Wm. C. Brown Publishers, Dubuque, Iowa. All Rights Reserved. Reprinted by permission.

Chapter 15

Table 15.2 From J. Larson, "The Marriage Quiz: College Students' Beliefs in Selected Myths About Marriage" in *Family Relations, 37,* 3–11, 1988. Copyright © 1988 National Council on Family Relations, 1910 W. County Rd. B, Suite 147, St. Paul, MN. **Fig. 15.3** From W. M. Kepart, "Some correlates of romantic love" in *Journal of Marriage and the Family, 29,* 1967. Copyrighted 1967 by National Council of Family Relations, 1910 W.

County Road B, Suite 147, St. Paul, MN. Reprinted by permission. **Page 437 (Fig. 15.A)** From John W. Santrock, *Psychology: The Science of Mind and Behavior,* 2d ed. Copyright © 1988 Wm. C. Brown Publishers, Dubuque, Iowa. All Rights Reserved. Reprinted by permission. **Page 455 Focus on Life-Span Development 15.4** From T. Chess and A. Thomas, "Temperamental individuality from childhood to adolescence" in *Journal of Child Psychiatry, 16,* 1977. Copyright © 1977 Pergamon Press Ltd., Oxford, England. Reprinted by permission.

Chapter 16

Page 462 Chapter Opener "TIME IN A BOTTLE" by Jim Croce. © 1971, 1972 Denjac Music Co. & MCA Music, Inc. (ASCAP). All Worldwide Rights Administered by Denjac Music Corp. Used by permission. All Rights Reserved. **Fig. 16.1** Data from Lois M. Tamir, *Men in Their Forties: The Transition to Middle Age* (Book No. 363). Copyright © 1982 Springer Publishing Company. Reprinted by permission.

Chapter 17

Fig. 17.1 From George Levinger and Diedrick Snoek, *Attraction in Relationship: A New Look at Interpersonal Attraction.* Copyright © 1971 General Learning Press. Reprinted by permission of the author. **Fig. 17.2** From M. N. Reedy, J. E. Birren, and K. W. Schaie, "Age and sex differences in the life span" in *Human Development, 24,* 52–66. Copyright © 1981 S. Karger, Basel, Switzerland. Reprinted by permission. **Fig. 17.3** From D. J. Levinson, "Toward a conception of the adult life course" in N. J. Smelzer and E. H. Erikson, (Eds.), *Themes of Work and Love in Adulthood.* Copyright © 1980 Harvard University Press. Reprinted by permission. **Fig. 17.4** From John W. Santrock, *Adult Development and Aging.* Copyright © 1985 Wm. C. Brown Publishers, Dubuque, Iowa. All Rights Reserved. Reprinted by permission. **Fig. 17.5** From D. F. Hultsch and J. K. Plemons, "Life events and life span development" in *Life Span Development and Behavior,* Vol. 2, by P. B. Baltes and O. G. Brun. Copyright © 1979 Academic Press, Inc. Reprinted by permission. **Fig. 17.6** From D. Hultsch and F. Deutsch, *Adult Development and Aging.* Copyright © 1980 McGraw-Hill Book Company, New York. Reprinted by permission. **Page 493 Focus on Life-Span Development 17.2** From John W. Santrock, *Psychology: The Science of Mind and Behavior,* 2d ed. Copyright © 1988 Wm. C. Brown Publishers, Dubuque, Iowa. All Rights Reserved. Reprinted by permission.

Chapter 18

Fig. 18.4 From *The Social Forces in Later Life* by Robert C. Atchley. © 1977 by Wadsworth Publishing Company, Inc. Reprinted by permission of Wadsworth, Inc., Belmont, CA. **Page 512 Focus on Life-Span Development 18.1** From John W. Santrock, *Psychology: The Science of Mind and Behavior,* 2d ed. Copyright © 1988 Wm. C. Brown Publishers, Dubuque, Iowa. All Rights Reserved. Reprinted by permission.

Chapter 19

Section X Opener Dylan Thomas, "Do Not Go Gentle Into That Good Night" from *The Poems of Dylan Thomas.* Reprinted by permission of New Directions Publishing Corporation, New York and David Higham Associates, London. **Page 541** **Marginal Quotation** "WHEN I'M SIXTY-FOUR" by John Lennon and Paul McCartney. © 1967 NORTHERN SONGS LIMITED. All Rights for the U.S., Canada, and Mexico Controlled and Administered by SBK BLACKWOOD MUSIC INC. Under license from ATV MUSIC (MACLEN). All Rights Reserved. International Copyright Secured. Used by permission.

Photos

Section Openers

Section I: © Robert Frerck/Odyssey Productions; **Section II:** © Lennart Nilsson, from A CHILD IS BORN, Dell Publishing Co., New York; **Section III:** © Joel Gordon; **Section IV:** © Elizabeth Crews/The Image Works; **Section V:** © Jean Pierre Horlin/The Image Bank; **Section VI:** © Alan Carey/The Image Works; **Section VII:** © R. Michael Stuckey/Comstock; **Section VIII:** © Alan Carey/The Image Works; **Section IX:** © Dick Durrance II/Woodfin Camp; **Section X:** © John Griffin/The Image Works

Chapter 1

Chapter opener: © Peter M. Miller/The Image Bank; **p. 10:** © National Library of Medicine; **p. 17:** © Mike Mazzaschi/Stock Boston; **Fig. 1.9:** © Herb Gehr/Life Magazine © Time, Inc. 1947; **p. 20a:** © NASA; **p. 20b:** © Frank Keillor/Jeroboam; **Fig. 1.10a:** © Cary Wolinsky/Stock Boston; **Fig. 1.10b:** © Carl Glassman/The Image Works; **p. 27:** © Cleo; **Fig. 1.7a:** © Dr. Landrum Shettles; **Fig. 1.7b:** © Helena Frost/Frost Publishing Group, Ltd.; **Fig. 1.7c:** © Jean-Claude Lejeune; **Fig. 1.7d,e:** © James L. Shaffer; **Fig. 1.7f:** © Nancy Anne Dawe; **Fig. 1.7g:** © Steve Elmore/Tom Stack & Associates; **Fig. 1.7h:** © Tom Lippert/Instock

Chapter 2

Chapter opener: © Joe Munroe/Photo Researchers; **p. 40a:** © Julie O'Neil; **p. 40b:** © Michael Siluk; **p. 40c:** © IPA/The Image Works; **p. 40d:** © Patsy Davidson/The Image Works; **p. 40e:** © Jeffrey W. Myers/Stock Boston; **p. 42:** © UPI/Bettmann Newsphotos; **p. 44a:** © Mark Antman/The Image Works; **p. 44b:** © John Eastcott/Yva Momatiuk/The Image Works; **p. 44c:** © Miro Vintoniv/Stock Boston; **p. 44d:** © Stacy Pick/Stock Boston; **p. 44e:** © Michael Siluk; **p. 44f:** © Bob Daemmrich/The Image Works; **p. 44g:** © Jeff Persons/Stock Boston; **p. 44h:** © Tom Stack/Tom Stack & Associates; **p. 46:** © Yves DeBraine/Black Star; **p. 47a:** © Julie O'Neil; **p. 47b:** © Gale Zucker/Stock Boston; **p. 47c:** © Liane Enkelis/Stock Boston; **p. 47d:** Mary L. Baer/Tom Stack & Associates; **p. 54:** © Christopher S. Johnson/Stock Boston; **p. 55:** © Albert Bandura; **p. 57:** Courtesy, National Library of Medicine; **p. 58:** © Bettmann Archives; **Fig. 2.9:** Photo by Nina Leen/LIFE Magazine © Time, Inc.; **p. 61:** Courtesy Robert Hinde

Chapter 3

Chapter opener: © James G. White; **p. 72:** © John Carter/Photo Researchers; **p. 73:** © J. A. Bishop and L. M. Cook; **Fig. 3.2a:** (left) © NASA/Photo Researchers, (right) © Patricia Caulfield/Photo Researchers; **Fig. 3.2b:** (left) © Edith Haun/Stock Boston, (right) © Miguel Castro/Photo Researchers; **Fig. 3.2c:** (left) © Cleo, (right) © Photog, The National Audubon Society Collection/Photo Researchers; **p. 75a:** © Ed Robinson/Tom Stack & Associates; **p. 75b:** © Jeff Albertson/Stock Boston; **p. 75c:** © Chris Crowley/Tom Stack & Associates; **p. 75d:** © A. Franklin; **Fig. 3.4:** © Regents of the University of California; **Fig. 3.6:** © Lennart Nilsson, BEHOLD MAN, Little, Brown and Co.; **Fig. 3.A:** © AP/Wide World Photos; **Fig. 3.C:** © Eric Kroll/Taurus Photos; **Fig. 3.D and E:** © Enrico Ferorelli/DOT, Inc.; **Fig. 3.F:** © Nancy Anne Dawe; **Fig. 3.G:** © Adrienne T. Gibson/Tom Stack & Associates

Chapter 4

Chapter opener: © Tom Grill/Comstock; **Fig. 4.1 and Fig. 4.3:** © Lennart Nilsson, BEHOLD MAN, Little, Brown and Company; **p. 109:** © Dr. Ann Pytkowicz Streissguth, University of Washington, SCIENCE 209 (18 July 1980) 353–361 © 1980 by the AAAS; **p. 112:** © Erika Stone; **p. 113:** © David R. Austen/Stock Boston; **p. 116:** © C & W Shields, Inc.; **p. 117:** © Charles Gupton/Stock Boston; **p. 121:** © Jeffrey W. Myers/Stock Boston

Chapter 5

Chapter opener: © Niki Mareschal/The Image Bank; **p. 127:** © Taeke Henstra, Petit Format/Photo Researchers; **Fig. 5.1:** Dreamstage Scientific catalog. J. Allen Hobson, Hoffman-LaRoche, Inc.; **p. 134:** © Will McIntyre/Photo Researchers; **p. 136:** (top) © Julie O'Neill, (bottom) © John Coletti/Stock Boston; **Fig. 5.7:** © David Linton; **Fig. 5.9:** © William Vandivert and SCIENTIFIC AMERICAN; **p. 145:** © Michael Siluk

Chapter 6

Chapter opener: © Jim Tuten/Black Star; **p. 156a:** © Cleo; **p. 156b:** © C & W Shields, Inc.; **p. 156c:** © Gabor Demjen/Stock Boston; **p. 156d:** © Elizabeth Crew/The Image Works; **p. 156e:** © William Hopkins; **p. 156f:** © Patricia Agre/Photo Researchers; **p. 158:** © James L. Shaffer; **p. 160:** © Cleo; **Fig. 6.1:** © Dr. Carolyn K. Rovee-Collier, Rutgers University; **p. 161:** © Suzanne Arms/Jeroboam; **p. 163:** Fig. 2 from "Discrimination and Imitation of Facial Expressions" by T. M. Field, et al. SCIENCE 218 (8 Oct. 1982) © by the AAAS; **Fig. 6.5:** © Dr. James Bartlett; **Fig. 6.7:** © The Bettmann Archives; **Fig. 6.A:** © Robert and Beatrix Gardner; **Fig. 6.B:** © Susan Kuklin; **p. 174:** © Mark Antman/The Image Works

Chapter 7

Chapter opener: © Suzanne Szasz/Photo Researchers; **Fig. 7.1a:** © Leonard Lee Rue III/Photo Researchers; **Fig. 7.1b:** © Mitch Reardon/Photo Researchers; **Fig. 7.3a:** © Anthony Bannister/Earth Scenes; **Fig. 7.3b:** © Chagnon/Anthro Photo; **p. 190:** © University of Wisconsin, Harlow Primate Laboratory; **p. 195:** © William Hopkins; **Fig. 7.A:** © Kathy Tarantola; **Fig. 7.B:** © Dr. Barry Hewlitt; **Fig. 7.8 a, b, d, e, g and h:** © Erika Stone; **Fig. 7.8 c and f:** © Nancy Anne Dawe

Chapter 8

Chapter opener: © Suzanne Szasz/Photo Researchers; **p. 219:** © Owen Franken/Stock Boston; **p. 220 and p. 224:** © James L. Shaffer; **p. 232:** © Mark M. Walker; **p. 238:** © Cleo; **p. 241:** © Elizabeth Crews/The Image Works

Chapter 9

Chapter opener: © Robert Frerck/Odyssey Productions; **p. 249:** © Nancy Anne Dawe; **p. 253:** © John Coletti/Stock Boston; **p. 257:** © James L. Shaffer; **p. 258:** © Erik Anderson/Stock Boston; **p. 266:** © Tom Lippert/Instock, Inc.; **p. 269:** © Robert Torres; **p. 273:** © Alan Carey/The Image Works; **p. 278:** © Ulli Seer/The Image Bank

Chapter 10

Chapter opener: © W. Lane/The Image Bank; **p. 287:** © Bob Daemmrich/Stock Boston; **p. 291:** © Nancy Anne Dawe; **p. 293:** © Jordan Information Bureau/Frost Publishing Group; **p. 301:** (left) © UPI/Bettmann Newsphotos, (right) © Historical Pictures Service Chicago; **p. 304:** © Julie O'Neil; **p. 306:** © Jill Cannefax/EKM-Nepenthe; **p. 307:** © Mark Antman/The Image Works; **p. 313:** © Cleo

Chapter 11

Chapter opener: © Alvin Upitis/The Image Bank; **p. 321:** © Jeff Persons/Stock Boston; **p. 325:** © Mark Antman/The Image Works; **p. 328:** © Cary Wolinsky/Stock Boston; **p. 333:** © Michael Siluk; **p. 335:** © Robert Frerck/Odyssey Productions; **p. 345:** © Bob Coyle

Chapter 12

Chapter opener: © Ellis Herwig/Stock Boston; **p. 353:** © Yokhi R. Okamoto/Photo Researchers; **p. 357:** © Abigail Heyman/Archive Pictures, Inc.; **p. 363:** © Marla Murphy/Amwest; **p. 364:** © William Hopkins; **p. 368:** © Mark M. Walker; **Fig. 12.7:** © Michael Siluk

Chapter 13

Chapter opener: © Craig Aurness/Woodfin Camp; **p. 377:** © Cleo; **p. 381:** © James L. Shaffer; **p. 382:** © William E. Frost/Frost Publishing Group, Ltd.; **pp. 383 and 384:** © James L. Shaffer; **p. 387:** (left) © The Bettmann Archives, (right) © Historical Pictures Service Chicago; **p. 393:** © Alan Carey/The Image Works; **p. 396:** © Susan Rosenberg/Photo Researchers

Chapter 14

Chapter opener: © John P. Kelley/The Image Bank; **p. 408:** © Tom Stack/Tom Stack & Associates; **p. 411:** © Jon Feingersh/Tom Stack & Associates; **p. 413:** © James L. Shaffer; **p. 415:** © Tom Grill/Comstock; **p. 420:** © Gerard Fritz/Amwest; **p. 426:** © Elyse Lewin/The Image Bank

Chapter 15

Chapter opener: © Larry Dale Gordon/The Image Bank; **p. 435:** © Michael Salas/The Image Bank; **Fig. 15.1 and p. 439a:** © Courtesy of The Academy of Motion Picture Arts and Sciences; **p. 439b:** © AP/Wide World Photos, Inc.; **p. 439c:** © MOVIE STAR NEWS; **p. 445:** © Cary Wolinski/Stock Boston; **p. 447:** © James L. Shaffer; **p. 451:** © David Schaefer

Chapter 16

Chapter opener: © Mieke Maas/The Image Bank; **p. 463:** (top) © Michael Melford/The Image Bank, (bottom) © Larry Mangino/The Image Works; **p. 464a:** © Nancy Anne Dawe; **p. 464b:** © Gale Zucker/Stock Boston; **p. 467:** © Bill Gallery/Stock Boston; **p. 471:** © Michael Grecco/Stock Boston; **p. 473:** © Joe Sohm/The Image Works; **p. 474:** © Marla Shelton/Amwest; **p. 477:** © Nancy Anne Dawe; **p. 479:** (top) © Alan Carey/The Image Works, (bottom) © Marla Murphy/Amwest

Chapter 17

Chapter opener: © Walter Bibikow/The Image Bank; **p. 487:** © Nancy Anne Dawe; **p. 492:** © George Gardner/The Image Works; **p. 493:** © Steven R. Krous/Stock Boston; **p. 495:** © David Schaefer; **pp. 496 and 498:** © Nancy Anne Dawe; **p. 503a:** © Owen Franken/Stock Boston; **p. 503b:** © UPI/Bettmann Newsphotos; **p. 504:** © M & C Werner/Comstock

Chapter 18

Chapter opener: © Harald Sund/The Image Bank; **p. 512:** © Sovfoto/Eastfoto; **p. 513:** © Nick Sapieha/Stock Boston; **p. 519:** (left) © Marla Murphy/Amwest; **p. 519:** (right) © Bruce Kliewe/Jeroboam, Inc.; **p. 520:** Courtesy School of Medicine, University of California, San Diego; **p. 521:** © AP/Wide World Photos; **p. 525:** © John Isaac/The Frost Publishing Group; **p. 526:** © Blair Seitz/Photo Researchers; **p. 527:** © James L. Shaffer; **p. 528:** © William E. Frost/The Frost Publishing Group; **p. 530:** © Y. A. Momatiuk/Amwest

Chapter 19

Chapter opener: © Elyse Lewin/The Image Bank; **p. 536:** © Mike Mazzaschi/Stock Boston; **p. 539:** © Art Walker/Amwest; **p. 541:** © James L. Shaffer; **p. 542 and p. 543:** © Michael Siluk; **p. 544:** (top) © Edith G. Haun/Stock Boston, (bottom) © Cleo; **p. 546:** © Barbara Alper/Stock Boston; **p. 547:** (top) © Steve Hansen/Stock Boston, (bottom) © Anthony Nicholls/Amwest; **p. 550:** (left and right) © UPI/Bettmann Newsphotos

Chapter 20

Chapter opener: © David Burnett/Stock Boston; **p. 560:** © AP/Wide World Photos; **Fig. 20.1a:** © Patrick Ward/Stock Boston; **Fig. 20.1b:** © David Burnett/Stock Boston; **Fig. 20.1c:** © Owen Franken/Stock Boston; **Fig. 20.1d:** © Spencer Swanger/Tom Stack and Associates; **Fig. 20.2:** © Frans Lanting; **Fig. 20.3b:** © Chris Nicholson; **p. 567:** © Herb Snitzer/Stock Boston; **p. 568:** © Eastcott/Momatiuk/The Image Works; **Fig. 20.5a:** © Carl Purcell; **Fig. 20.5b:** © Jackson Hill/Southern Lights Photography, Inc.